Collectibles
PRICE GUIDE 2007

Collectibles
PRICE GUIDE 2007

Judith Miller
and Mark Hill

DK PUBLISHING

LONDON, NEW YORK,
MELBOURNE, MUNICH AND DELHI

A joint production from DORLING KINDERSLEY
and THE PRICE GUIDE COMPANY

THE PRICE GUIDE COMPANY LIMITED

Publisher Judith Miller

Collectibles Specialist Mark Hill

Publishing Manager Julie Brooke

Assistant Editor Sara Sturgess

Digital Image Co-ordinator Ellen Sinclair

Sub-editors Jessica Bishop, Dan Dunlavey, Karen Morden, Carolyn Malarkey

Design and DTP Tim & Ali Scrivens, TJ Graphics

Photographers Graham Rae, Bruce Boyajian, John McKenzie, Byron Slater, Steve Tanner, Heike Löwenstein, Andy Johnson, Adam Gault

Indexer Hilary Bird

Workflow Consultant Bob Bousfield

Business Advisor Nick Croydon

DORLING KINDERSLEY LIMITED

Publishing Director Jackie Douglas

Managing Art Editor Christine Keilty

Managing Editor Julie Oughton

DTP Designer Adam Walker

Production Rita Sinha

Production Manager Sarah Coltman

While every care has been taken in the compilation of this guide, neither the authors nor the publishers accept any liability for any financial or other loss incurred by reliance placed on the information contained in *Collectibles Price Guide 2007*

First American Edition, 2006
06 07 08 09 10 10 9 8 7 6 5 4 3 2 1

Published in the United States by
DK Publishing
375 Hudson Street
New York, New York 10014

The Price Guide Company Ltd
info@thepriceguidecompany.com

DK Books are available at special discounts for bulk purchases for sales, promotions, premiums, fund-raising, or educational use. For details contact DK Publishing Special Markets, 375 Hudson Street, New York, New York 10014 or SpecialSales@dk.com.

A CIP catalog record for this book is available from the Library of Congress.

ISBN-13: 978-0-7566-2297-8
ISBN-10: 0-7566-2297-2

Printed and bound in Germany by GGP Media GmbH, Pößneck

Discover more at

www.dk.com

CONTENTS

CONTENTS

LIST OF CONSULTANTS

Beads

Stefany Tomalin
Author & Collector

Ceramics

Robert Culicover
Hi & Lo Modern, NJ

Judith Keefer
Flo Blue Shoppe, MI

Judith Miller
The Price Guide Company (UK) Ltd

Susan Tillipman
These Old Jugs, MD

Canadiana

June O'Neil
R.A. O'Neil, Toronto

Duncan McLean
Waddingtons, Toronto

Chocolate Molds

The Hanes Family
Dad's Follies

Dolls

Sharon Wendrow
Memory Lane Collectibles, NY

Eyewear

Barbara Blau
South Street Antiques Market, PA

Esther Harris
Vintage Eyewear of New York

Glass

Mark Block
Block Glass Ltd, Conneticut

Mark Hill
The Price Guide Company (UK) Ltd

Marbles

Robert Block
AuctionBlocks

Plastics & Bakelite

Gill Friedman
Mod Girl, PA

Posters

Robert Chisholm & Lars Larsson
Chisholm Larsson Gallery, NY

Nicholas Lowry
Swann's, NY

Sixties & Seventies

Sasha Keen & Stacey LoAlbo
Neet O Rama, NJ

Teddies & Soft Toys

Dottie Ayers
The Calico Teddy, MD

Barbara Lauver
Harper General Store, MD

Toys

Richard & Jeanne Bertoia
Bertoia Auctions, NJ

Watches

Mark Laino
Mark of Time, Pennsylvania

We are very grateful to our friends and experts who gave us so much help – Greg Belhorn of Belhorn Auction Services, Rick & Sharon Corley of Toy Road Antiques, Joe & Sharon Happle of Sign of the Tymes, David Rago of David Rago Auctions.

WHAT'S HOT

The world of collectibles has continued to change dramatically over the past year. New areas have been revealed, knowledge about existing areas has deepened through extensive research, and the vogue for 'retro' style has continued. The phenomenon of online trading has continued to be the single most important factor to change the way collectibles are bought and sold. A few quick clicks of a mouse are now enough to start anyone on the road to amassing a collection of...well, absolutely anything that takes their fancy. The world, in short, has become our oyster.

GLITTERING TREASURES

Since the publication of my first Collectors' Guide on Costume Jewelry in 2004, I have watched what was already a growing market go from strength to strength. Signed pieces by those such as Trifari, Kenneth Jay Lane and Coro have remained highly sought after. Prices for some of their most characteristic designs have even shown notable price rises over the past year. Within those names, prices for some pieces or the work of certain designers, such as Alfred Philippe at Trifari, have really rocketed. For example, a Trifari 'Crane' pin designed by Philippe sold for over $8,000 at Indianapolis earlier in the year proving that costume jewelry is now big business and can command even higher prices than comparable items of precious jewelry. However, well designed and well made unsigned pieces, and those from the 1960s and '70s, can still offer excellent value for money – but now may be the best time to buy as prices are creeping upwards.

Look out for novelty forms and designs that are typical of their era, as these tend to be the most desirable.

I've also seen what can only be described as a 'globalisation' of the market. Boundaries that once stopped a collector in one market from learning about, and collecting, the hot trends that gripped other nations have fallen away. With access to dealers' stores and auctions through the internet, collectors are no longer limited by what they find in local flea markets, yard sales and antiques and collectibles fairs. As costume jewelry, like many collectibles, is small and light in weight, it can be packed easily and sent anywhere in the world.

Of course, as well as making even more collectibles available, it has also meant that prices for items from overseas have levelled off. Whereas before, these pieces might fetch a much higher price due to their scarcity abroad, this has now changed as collectors globally are able to bid on equal terms.

A 1980s Kenneth Jay Lane umbrella pin. Worth $70-100. JJ

PLASTIC FANTASTIC

The interest in costume jewelry is not just limited to 'all that glitters'. The bright colors and stylish, modern forms of Bakelite and plastic jewelry that was produced during the 1920s and '30s look just as good when worn today. Those in cherry reds, hot oranges and bright greens are fetching the highest

An American Jeff Oestereich contemporary studio pottery bowl, with impressed maker's mark. **Worth $80-120 TOJ**

But its not just vintage pieces that are attracting increasing levels of interest. Work produced by today's potters and ceramic designers is often undervalued when it comes up for sale again on the 'secondary' market. Once again a knowledge of the marks and styles used by today's masters, this time combined with an awareness of their current work and career, could mean a future, modern masterpiece lands on your lap. It's generally wrong to look at this market from a purely investment point of view, so always ask yourself if you will still love the piece after it has been staring at you from the shelf for ten years.

prices, particularly if they are chunky and deeply carved.

MAD ABOUT POTS

One area that my collectibles specialist Mark Hill and I both think is just about to boom is postwar and contemporary studio ceramics. Although top names such as Peter Voulkos and the Natzlers are well known to specialist collectors, with people often paying tens of thousands of dollars to own examples of their work, there were other potters working at the same period who have been largely ignored. This is often due to a lack of knowledge or understanding, particularly over the marks they used to sign their works or how they fit into the history of 20th century ceramic design. Research can uncover where they studied, or who they were taught by, with the quality of the design of a piece being the first clue that it may be an undiscovered treasure. Wise collectors are investing in books showing the marks used by these potters, and are learning how to recognise their styles. Unrecognised pieces can be sold for sums as low as a few dollars, so our advice is to never quickly pass over the $10 bargain table at a show or yard sale!

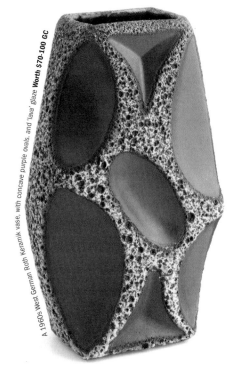

A 1960s West German Roth Keramik vase, with concave purple ovals, and 'lava' glaze **Worth $70-100 GC**

MAKING A STATEMENT

It's usually the 'look' of a piece that initially catches your eye and leads to you taking it home. You may not know much about it, but it just 'speaks' to you on some level. As more and more people come to the world of collectibles looking for 'statement' pieces to add character to their homes, the style and eye appeal of a piece are becoming increasingly important factors to desirability and value. Nowhere is this more apparent than in the recent developments regarding West German and Italian ceramics of the 1960s and '70s. Exported all over the world and highly fashionable in their day, until recently they were laughed at and put in attics, or even thrown away, as new styles and fashions were introduced. Those that survived the experience sat, forgotten, in thrift stores, often fetching no more than a couple of dollars. However, their

immense decorative appeal, combined with research that has revealed their importance to 20th century ceramic design, has meant that a new group of fans has begun to collect them. As a result, prices have begun to rise, and look set to carry on doing so.

STREAMLINED STYLING

It's not all about new markets however, and the Art Deco style of the 1920s and '30s still fetches high prices. Classics such as Roseville's 'Futura' range continue to attract an ever-increasing number of buyers, particularly for those pieces that combine typical colors and patterns with forms that are characteristic of the style.

Produced slightly more recently, the eccentric forms and bright colours used during the late 1970s and 1980s by the so-called 'Postmodern' designers are becoming more popular once again. As these pieces are still thought

A 1930s Art Deco Roseville 'Futura' Blue Triangle vase. **Worth $300-400 BEL**

A Postmodern Peter Shire handpainted ceramic teapot. **Worth $600-900 GM** to be too garish by many people, we think that it may take a little more time for collectors to adjust to a style that many of us still consider to be 'yesterday's' fashion. Nevertheless, the world of collecting is full of examples of areas that were highly fashionable once, were then forgotten, only to be re-discovered soon after and become popular once again.

CLASSIC GLASS

Twentieth century glass continues to excite many collectors. One of the main hot beds of glass design lay in West Virginia at the Blenko factory and its output is undoubtedly one of the most innovative – and collectible – today. Characterized by bright, vibrant colors, the company employed a number of talented designers who devised many of the outlandish forms that make the company's vintage production so sought after today. Indeed this is the key to desirability and value for much Blenko glass: the more unusual and striking the shape, the better. Size is also important, with floor standing pieces generally being the most valuable. Beware though, as many companies in the State imitated Blenko to try to share in its success. Although no less beautiful, these pieces are often less valuable, although they can make a more affordable starting point to collecting glass design from this period. To avoid making what could be an expensive mistake, the best

advice is to familiarize yourself with the shapes and colors that the company produced. This makes a fully illustrated, full color guide like this all the more useful.

Increased trade over the internet in this area – and many others – has also led to more and more information being posted on message boards, websites. While this generally serves as a benefit to the market, increasing awareness and helping people to make the right decisions when buying and selling, it is important to remember that not everyone is an expert. Anyone can contribute to this global community of collectors, but they may not always be right and the importance of a trusted book must never be under-estimated.

INDIVIDUAL STYLE

One area that nobody can dictate to you is your personal style. The recent 'retro' trend followed by models all over the world and an increased desire to stand out from the crowd has had a major effect on this. As a result the market for vintage clothing has boomed, particularly for those pieces that sum up the style of the era they were made in.

A Blenko Turquoise decanter, designed by Wayne Husted. **Worth $500-600 HLM**

A pair of 1950s triple-laminated Raybert 'Baccara' frames, with hand-cut 'flame' rims. **Worth $250-300 VE**

One increasingly popular area is eyewear, from the sunglasses we save for vacations to the glasses we wear every day. After all, when people meet you, what is it they look at the most? Your face! We change our clothes every day, but rarely our glasses. This is gradually changing. Many of today's designers are either being inspired by, or adopting, the styles of the past. This has made original designs hotly sought after, particularly if they sum up the period in their shape and coloring. Of course, some frames do not fit neatly into the look of any style or decade and yet are enormously appealing, having what can only be described as 'specs appeal'!

A 1950s Dunhill 'Aquarium' lighter, showing a duck. **Worth $3,500-4,500 WW**

CHANGING HABITS

Smoking was once seen as both a fashionable and a healthy activity, incredible as this sounds to us today. From the 1920s to the 1950s many stylish, and eccentric, accessories were produced and are being hunted by collectors today. Typical examples are Dunhill lighters. Whilst those in precious metals, often with ingenious features such as inset watches, now fetch large sums of money, nobody could have predicted the rise of the plastic 'Aquarium' lighter. The couple of hundred dollars that these fetched only a few short years ago seemed high, but the thousands of dollars that they sell for now make them well worth tracking down. Of course, many were sold or thrown away, which has added to their rarity. The same is true of much advertising memorabilia. Pieces that advertise well known brands are the most popular, particularly if they show the characters or logos associated with that brand. Tobacco and food advertising have become among the most sought after, mainly as so many people can identify with them.

Having worked with so many different collectibles over the years, I realise that a personal connection is one of the key aspects of starting a collection and helps to explain why the collectibles field is so broad. It is that variety – and the chance I might find a piece I've been searching for or that reminds me of a special time in my life – that makes every collectibles fair a potential treasure trove.

Judith Miller.

A 1920s Cracker Jack card shop display. **Worth $700-1,000 LDE**

HOW TO USE THIS BOOK

Subcategory Heading
Indicates the subcategory of the main category heading and describes the general contents of the page.

Category Heading
Indicates the general category as listed in the table of contents on pp.5–6.

A Closer Look at...
Here, we highlight particularly interesting items or show identifying features, pointing out rare or desirable qualities.

The Source Code
The image is credited to its source with a code. See the "Key to Illustrations" on pp.576-580 for a full listing of dealers and auction houses.

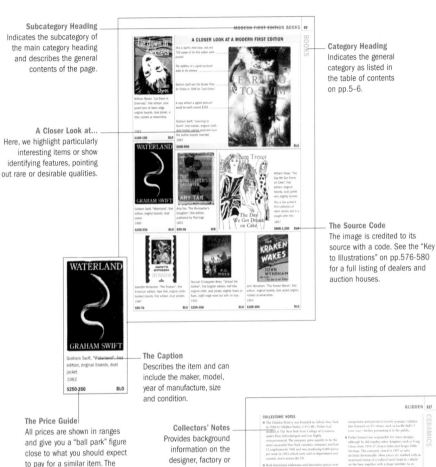

The Caption
Describes the item and can include the maker, model, year of manufacture, size and condition.

The Price Guide
All prices are shown in ranges and give you a "ball park" figure close to what you should expect to pay for a similar item. The great joy of collectibles is that there is not a recommended retail price. The price given is not necessarily that which a dealer will pay you. As a general rule, expect to receive approximately 30 per cent less. When selling, pay attention to the dealer or auction house specialist to understand why this may be, and consider that they have to run a business as well as make a living. When buying, listen again. Condition, market forces and location of the place of sale will all affect a price. If no price is available, the letters NPA will be used.

Collectors' Notes
Provides background information on the designer, factory or make of the piece or style in question.

The Object
All collectibles are shown in full colour, which is a vital aid to identification and valuation.

Find out more...
To help you seek further information, these boxes list websites, books, and museums where you can find out more.

COLLECTORS' NOTES

■ Coca-Cola has international appeal, and is the best-selling drink in most countries in the world. This, combined with an instantly recognisable logo and early, aggressive marketing campaign, makes it one of the most widely collected brands in the world.

■ The formula for the 'pick-me-up' drink was developed by Dr John Pemberton in 1886 and was originally sold as 'Pemberton's French Wine Coca'. Asa Griggs Candler took control of the company in 1887 and it was Candler who started the trend for aggressive advertising leading to the company's vast array of advertising merchandise and its market position today.

■ As there is a seemingly endless variety of memorabilia, collectors tend to focus on one area, such as trays, postcards or bottles, or artwork by artists such as Haddon Sundblom and Hamilton King.

■ Pre-1900s advertising is extremely rare and is often the most desirable. As a result, fakes are found so it is advisable to familiarise yourself with the company's changing logos and designs, which will help to date and authenticate pieces.

A Coca-Cola advertising pocket mirror, marked "From the painting, copyright 1906, by Wolf & Co., Phila., Bastian Bros. Co., Roch., N.Y., Duplicate Mirrors 5¢ Postage, Coca-Cola Company, Atlanta, Ga.".

This is an early, collectible piece of advertising memorabilia. This image can also be seen on a 1907 serving tray and calendar, both of which are even more desirable.

1907   2.75in (7cm) high

$400-600   **SOTT**

A 'The Prize Winning Coca-Cola – Drink Coca-Cola Delicious & Refreshing 5¢' watch fob, in mint condition.

Reproductions of these are being made, so buy from a reputable dealer.

1.75in (4.5cm) wide

$450-550   **LDE**

A Coca-Cola green glass seltzer soda siphon, reading "Coca-Cola Bottling Co. Sharon PA, 28oz Capacity" and "Lynbrook Cold Beer".

12.25in (31cm) high

$350-450   **PWE**

A Coca-Cola diecast toy truck, retaining original decals on either side and on the tailgate, all over surface rust and scratches.

20in (51cm) long

$250-350   **JDJ**

A 1940s Coca-Cola sign, by Kay Displays Inc.

Kay Displays Inc. worked with Coca-Cola from 1934 and designed some of Coca-Cola's most sought-after signs. Their patriotic signs produced during US participation in WWII are the most desirable. The company closed in 1951.

27.25in (69cm) long

$200-300   **SOTT**

A 1941 Tournament of Roses souvenir programme, sponsored by Coca-Cola, with information about pandas inside.

1941   6in (15cm) high

$100-150   **LDE**

A Coca-Cola 'Hi-Fi Club' membership card.

The Hi-Fi Club was a 1960s dance club for teenagers sponsored and promoted by Coca-Cola. Although membership was free, a membership card was required to gain entrance to the dances, which were held in schools and similar venues. Each dance held a competition, the prizes from which are very popular with collectors today.

4in (10cm) wide

$80-120   **LDE**

A 1980s Coca-Cola sweatshirt, size large.

$30-40   **BR**

COLLECTORS' NOTES

- Vintage advertising is one of the liveliest markets open to collectors, with plenty of variety to base a collection around. Much of it is driven by nostalgia, with familiar brands and characters being sought-after. Advertising figurines is a relatively new area that is gaining ground rapidly.

- There are a number of factors to consider as regards value. Top brands will often be more expensive as they will attract a larger band of often well established collectors who will vie to own the best pieces. Eye appeal is important, with the presence of superb, complex artwork or popular characters adding to value. Artwork in the dominant style of the period, such as Art Deco of the 1930s, will also be popular.

- Subject matter also counts. Tobacco advertising is currently highly sought-after, particularly if early.

Some subjects cross collecting areas, such as railway advertising, meaning that more collectors will be interested, often leading to higher prices. Size and rarity of a particular item are also important factors.

- Original packaging, both as a form of advertising and for the objects themselves (such as figurines) can be rare as most of it was thrown away after the contents had been used. Point of sale items, such as those used in general stores attract great attention, again as most of it was used and often damaged.

- Condition is particularly important, with collectors always trying to add those in the best condition to their collections. The presence of original contents does not affect the value, unless the object has not been opened and still has intact seals, such as the tax seals on tobacco packets.

An American 'Big Boy' Restaurant printed vinyl advertising figure.

In 1936, Californian diner owner Bob Wian developed a huge double-decker cheeseburger. A customer then sketched a well-fed young customer with a curl in his hair on his napkin, and "ohhhh boy", the company's logo was born.

$20-30　　　　　**MTS**

An American Kellogg's 'Pop!' rubber advertising figure, in original box.

2006 is the 100th anniversary of Kellogg's. Pop! and his older brothers Snap! and Crackle! first appeared on boxes in 1932, becoming characters in 1933 and appearing on TV first in the 1960s.

8.5in (21.5cm) high

$40-50　　　　　**BH**

A 1960s Carltonware 'Flowers Brewmaster' beer advertising figure, with gilt highlights and on inscribed black bases.

9.25in (23.5cm) high

$80-120　　　　　**SAS**

A 1930s American Baudis Metalcraft Co. 'Worcester Salt' bronze painted metal advertising elephant money bank.

4.25in (11cm) high

$100-150　　　　**SOTT**

A late 1960s Japanese Sony Corp. soft vinyl 'Sony Boy' advertising figure, with moving head.

Sony Boy first appeared c1962, with his wholesome all-American looks aiming to persuade American customers that Sony products were not cheap and disposable. This is the middle of three sizes, the largest can be worth up to $1,000.

8in (20cm) high

A Robertson's 'Golden Shred' marmalade small hard plastic advertising eggcup.

2.25in (6cm) high

$35-45　　　　　**PA**

A Japanese Sony Corp. 'Sony Boy' small advertising figurine.

3.75in (9.5cm) high

$100-150　　　　　**PA**

$200-250　　　　　**PA**

An American Hotpoint Appliances 'General Electric Radio' hand-painted composition advertising figure, by the Cameo Doll Co. and designed by Joseph Kallus, with wooden jointed arms and legs and parade hat reading "General Electric Radio".

c1930   18in (45.50cm) high

$800-1,200   **JDJ**

A CLOSER LOOK AT AN ADVERTISING FIGURE

The Cameo Doll Company was founded in 1913 and was known for producing very fine quality composition, bisque, celluloid and plastic dolls until the 1970s, with their most famous product being Kewpie dolls.

The founder was Joseph Kallus, who also designed dolls for other companies including Ideal and Effanbee.

He wears a sash reading 'Radiotrons', which was a valve manufactured by RCA, and his hat is modelled as a radio valve.

Kallus was also known for his dolls that were used as advertising figurines but were meant to emulate traditional jointed wooden toys.

An American Cameo Doll Co. 'RCA Radio' hand-painted composition advertising figure, with wood jointed arms and legs and 'Radiotrons' sash.

c1930   16in (40.50cm) high

$600-700   **JDJ**

An American Old King Cole of Canton, Ohio 'Nipper' papier-mâché dog figure, with studded collar and maker's label, repainted.

Nipper was a real dog, born in 1884. After his first owner died, he was adopted by artist Francis Barraud who painted a picture of him listening to his gramophone which he entitled 'His Master's Voice'. Barraud then sold the painting to The Gramophone Company who used it throughout their incarnations as a company logo until the 1960s. In 1978 the logo was revived and is still in use today. Handle as many papier-mâché originals, made from c1915, as possible to learn how to spot the many reproductions on the market today.

c1930   36in (91.5cm) high

$700-900   **EG**

A 1970s Thomson Publishing Company 'Thomcat' painted ceramic advertising money bank.

11in (28cm) high

$70-90   **PA**

A Royal Doulton 'Penguin Books' hand-painted ceramic advertising figurine.

1987   4.75in (12cm) high

$70-90   **PA**

A German T-Mobile 'Telekarte' plastic advertising figurine, the base reading "Limiteierte Cobit 94 Hannover 16-23.03.1994 EDITION".

1994   6in (15cm) high

$70-90   **PA**

A 1930s/40s American Hanes 'Merrichild Sleepers' sleepwear painted plaster advertising figurine.

5.75in (14.5cm) wide

$120-180   **PA**

An American 1930s-40s 'Diaprex Belle Moss' painted plaster advertising ashtray.

4.25in (11cm) high

$200-250   **PA**

A 1960s American Wolverine Brand 'Hush Puppies Shoes' painted foam flat-back shop display dog figurine.

Hush Puppies were launched in 1959 and got their name from a treat used by Southerners to placate and calm barking dogs.

16.25in (41cm) high

$50-70   **SOTT**

A Japanese 'Red Goose Shoes' painted plaster advertising nodder.

These are extremely delicate as the nodding body is very heavy and easily damaged. This example is in mint condition.

6in (15.5cm) high

$300-350   **PA**

A 1960s-70s American 'Buddy Lee' molded hard plastic advertising doll, dressed in stripey Lee denim dungarees.

Buddy Lee was first used as a promotional character in 1921.

13in (33cm) high

$200-300   **PA**

A 1960s American Knox Hats Santa Claus plastic money bank, from a Christmas advertising campaign.

5.75in (14.5cm) high

$35-45   **PA**

An American Continental Radial tire ceramic advertising money bank.

Fewer of these figurines would have been made than for other collecting areas, such as foods. Automobilia is also a highly collectible subject area.

5in (13cm) high

$300-350   **PA**

A 1930s American 'Eaton Manufacturing Company Reliance Division' of Massillon, Ohio ceramic advertising ashtray, possibly for nuts and bolts.

7in (18cm) high

$350-400   **PA**

An American GTA Seeds 'Ernie Pig' cast plaster advertising money bank.

7.5in (19cm) high

$80-120   **PA**

A rare Japanese 'Staggs Built Homes', Phoenix, Arizona 'Happy Homer' advertising nodder.

These nodders are rare, especially in mint condition, like this example. It will also appeal to nodder collectors as the form and subject is highly unusual. A pair of similar promotional salt and peppers were made in an edition of 1,000 and given to people who had homes built - they can fetch up to $300.

c1953   6in (15cm) high

$400-500   **PA**

A 1990s MGM Grand Hotel lion ceramic advertising figurine.

5.25in (13.5cm) high

$10-15   **PA**

An American Spohn's Udder-Aid tin, the balm listed as being "For Minor Irritations of The Udder".

Many veterinary or farm-related tins are often very rare as they were typically thrown away when the contents had been used. When they were kept, they were usually stored in poor conditions or re-used roughly. As such, condition plays a major factor in value. Those in excellent condition fetch considerably higher sums. Bright, appealing artwork typical of the period will also add value. This collecting area is becoming more popular.

1.25in (8cm) high

$70-90 PKA

An American Dairy Association Co. Inc of Lydonville VT antiseptic 'Bag Balm' tin.

2.75in (7cm) high

$40-50 PKA

An early 20thC American 'Corona Wool Fat Compound' tin.

c1910 *3.25in (8cm) high*

$60-80 PKA

An early 20thC American Dr LeGear's Medicine Co. of St Louis, Missouri 'Antiseptic Udder Ointment' tin.

2.75in (7cm) high

$50-70 PKA

A late 19thC Dr David Roberts Calf Medicine tin, with printed paper label.

3.75in (9.5cm) high

$22-28 PKA

An American International Stock Food Co. of Minneapolis, Minnesota 'International Gall Heal' round yellow tin, which 'Heals While Horses Rest'.

1906 *3.25in (8cm) high*

$80-120 PKA

An American Dr A.C. Daniels' 'Gall Salve' circular tin.

As well as being scarce and early, this tin is in excellent, bright condition.

c1910 *3in (7.5cm) diam*

$80-120 PKA

An early 20thC Kennel Supply Co. of Jacksonville Tennessee 'Headstart Dog Food' tin, with printed label.

The appearance of a Scottie dog boosts the value of this tin.

c1920 *4.5in (11.5cm) high*

$50-60 SOTT

An American Polk Miller Products Corp. Sergeant's 'Condition Pills for Dogs & Puppies' card box.

c1939 *2.75in (7cm) high*

$50-70 PKA

An American Hartz Mountain Products 'E-Z Kleen' flea powder tin.

As with the example on the previous page – spot the Scottie!

3.5in (9cm) high

$30-40   **PKA**

A rare 1960s promotional Beacon 'FlavAroma Dog Feed' plastic wall thermometer.

Made for display in stores, comparatively few would have been produced due to the expense of making and shipping such a delicate item. Even fewer would have survived. The bright colours, and cute and appealing artwork further adds to the value.

13.5in (34cm) diam

$280-320   **SOTT**

A Spratt's Patent Limited of Newark, New Jersey 'Spratt's Flea & Insect' powder tin.

4.25in (11cm) high

$70-90   **SOTT**

A 1930s American Solarine Company of Baltimore, MD 'Matador' insect spray tin, with image of a matador killing insects with a cloud of the spray.

4.5in (11.5cm) high

$50-70   **PKA**

A Bonide Chemical Co. of Utica, New York 'Crow-Fez' bird and rodent repellent tin.

1930   5.25in (13cm) high

$60-80   **PKA**

A 1950s Pennsylvania Salt Mfg Co. of Philadelphia 'Kryocide Natural Cryolite' home and garden insecticide tin, with paper label and original contents.

6in (15.5cm) high

$35-45   **PKA**

A 1930s American Nip Co. of Rochester, New York 'Rat Nip' rat killer card box.

6.75in (17cm) high

$45-55   **PKA**

An American McGill 'Can't Miss Four Way' wood and sprung iron wire rat trap.

McGill's also marketed a smaller trap for mice, which is usually worth around 30-50 per cent less.

7in (18cm) long

$45-55   **PKA**

A very large American Jno. J. Bagley & Co. of Detroit, Mich. 'Game Fine Tobacco' store tin, for 48 five cents packages.

As well as being a more impressive size, larger tins such as this are much rarer than smaller portable tins as less were made. The bright, multi-coloured and complex printed artwork is also visually appealing. Early tobacco tins and advertising are a popular collecting area.

11.5in (29.5cm) wide

$400-600   SOTT

An American Scotten Dillon Co., Detroit 'Dan Patch Cut Plug' tobacco plug tin.

6in (15.5cm) long

$120-180   SOTT

An American Penn Tobacco Co. 'Honeymoon' tobacco pocket tin.

5in (11.5cm) high

$150-200   SOTT

A very rare American Christian Peper Tobacco Co. of St Louis Missouri 'English Walnut' tobacco pocket tin.

'Pocket' tins, with their rounded edges, pocket size and shape have seen price rises in recent years. The condition and eye-appeal of the artwork is important to value, with patriotic tins being particularly sought-after. Examples with the paper tax labels intact will be worth more.

4.5in (11.5cm) high

$700-1000   SOTT

A Valley Farm Brand 'Pure Cocoa' tin, lacks lid, packed for A.H. Phillips Inc Springfield, Massachusetts.

6in (15cm) high

$25-35   PKA

An early 20thC 'Fairway Cocoa' tin, with paper label.

Although it is damaged, the colorful artwork of children is appealing.

$120-180   TRA

An American Jonathan Levi Company Inc of Schenectady, New York 'WGY Brand Coffee' tin.

1923   6in (15.5cm) high

$60-80   SOTT

A Reid Murdoch of Chicago Illinois 'Monarch Green Tea' tin.

5.75in (14.5cm) high

$50-70   PKA

An E.M. Chase Tea Co. of Manchester, New Hampshire 'Chase's Tea' general store counter-top dipsensing tin, with French and English language.

9in (23cm) high

$300-400 PKA

Three Canadian Gorman, Eckert & Co. of London, Ontario printed tin general store storage bins, with roll-up lids, for 'Nutmegs', 'Cocoanut' and 'Whole Cloves'.

10in (25.5cm) high

$300-500 WAD

An American Lutted Candy Co. 'Uncle Sam's' painted tin peanut warmer, with original hinged glass lid and extensive painted decoration around the body panels.

These would have been used at events such as baseball and other sporting games.

c1900-10 23in (58.5cm) high

$700-900 HA

An American W.M. Schield Mfg Co. of St Louis, Missouri 'Red Devil Cleanser' tin, with paper label.

4.75in (12cm) high

$70-90 SOTT

Three Canadian Harry Horne Co. Ltd of Toronto Circus Club Marshmallow tins, with printed cat, pig and elephant decoration.

7in (18cm) high

$600-800 WAD

A rare American Aluminum Cleaner Corp, of New York City 'Clown Cleaner' tin, with paper label.

8in (20.5cm) high

$35-45 SOTT

A British June Talcum powder tin, with fine and complex printed decoration, in near mint condition.

5.25in (13.5cm) high

$280-320 TRA

A 1950s FlameGlo of Yorkville, Connecticut magic color crystals tin.

As well as helping to start a home fire, these crystals made the fire glow in different colors.

6in (15cm) high

$30-40 PKA

A 1930s American Johnson & Johnson 'Girl Scouts Official First Aid Kit' tin.

6in (15cm) high

$30-50 BH

An American Tea & Coffee Co. Inc of Nashville, Tennessee 'American Ace Tea' printed card tea box, with biplane image.

The biplane image on the box makes is sought-after.

c1925   3.25in (8.5cm) high

$60-80   **SOTT**

A late 1920s Arm & Hammer 'Church & Co's Soda' baking soda card box.

1926   4in (10cm) high

$15-20   **SOTT**

A Valley Farm's 'Bing Crosby Ice Cream' Sales Inc one-pint ice cream card box, with 'The Cream Of The Stars' wording.

Celebrity endorsed packaging is highly collectable, as it crosses a number of collecting areas. The typically Fifties colors, fame of the celebrity and condition make this a sought-after piece.

1953   4.25in (10.5cm) wide

$30-40   **PKA**

A Fralingers of Atlantic City, New Jersey card box for one-pound of Salt Water Taffy.

Salt Water Taffy was reputedly named in the 1880s after a high wave washed over Joseph Fralinger's beachside candy stand. The term stuck and by 1889 had become a household name for this pre-eminent souvenir of Atlantic City. The one-pound box remains the most popular quantity today.

1926   9in (22.5cm) long

$25-35   **PKA**

A Canadian stoneware bottle for W.H Donovan of Halifax, Nova Scotia.

8.25in (21cm) high

$50-60   **ING**

A 1950s Hollywood Shoe Polish Inc. 'Sani-Boot n Saddle' cream card box and bottle.

The cowboy iconograhy, combined with the glamor of Hollywood and an endorsement by LIFE magazine, was a hard to beat act!

Box 6.5in (16.5cm) high

$50-70   **PKA**

An American Bauer & Black of Chicago Pep Extra Large Athletic Supporter card box.

6.75in (17cm) long

$18-22   **PKA**

A 1950s American Machin-Bier Co. Inc of New York small-sized 'Nu-Kumfort Athletic Support' for the 'Relief of Fatigue & Strain'.

6.75in (17cm) long

$25-35   **PKA**

A 1950s American box of three unused Arcross deodorant soaps.

Box 10in (25.5cm) wide

$30-40   **PKA**

An American Burdick Enamel Sign Co. and
Ingram-Richardson Mfg. Co. 'Tom Keene Cigar'
enameled and curved tin advertising sign.

15in (38cm) high

$300-400 JDJ

A large American Anheuser-Busch 'Budweiser'
embossed enameled tin advertising sign,
mounted on original wood frame hanger.

72in (183cm) long

$550-650 JDJ

A CLOSER LOOK AT A METAL SIGN

The company that made this, American Art
Works of Coshocton, Ohio, later made tip trays
for Coca-Cola, and are renowned for their fine
quality complexly printed metal items.

The inclusion of a black lady makes it
desirable to collectors of black memorabilia,
interestingly, she is not the stereotypical fat
'mama', but a slim, kindly looking lady.

The goose with outstretched
wings sitting on the window ledge was the product's
logo and also hints at the company's name as
Phoenixes are often depicted with outstretched wings.

This product was made in Memphis,
Tennessee, and advertising pieces from
the South are often hard to find as few
were made, particularly of this quality.

A very rare late 19thC Phoenix Cotton Oil Co.'s 'Gander Brand Cooking & Salad Oil'
printed tin advertising sign.

The high value is also due to the superb condition of this rare piece.

19in (48.5cm) wide

$2,000-3,000 PKA

An American Shonk Works AmerCan Co. of Maywood Illinois
'American-Maid Bread' printed tin sign, for Ivan B. Nordheim.

1919   29.5in (75cm) long

$180-220 SOTT

An American 'Drugs' sidewalk double-sided sign, with galvanised
sheet metal body and inserted milk glass letters.

68in (172.50cm) wide

$280-320 JDJ

A rare 1880s American The Meek & Beach
Co. Coshocton, Ohio 'Susquehanna'
whiskey embossed and printed tin sign.

22in (56cm) wide

$700-1,000 PKA

An American 'Buster Brown Shoes' plaster
relief advertising sign, showing a winking
Buster Brown and Tige.

18in (45.50cm) high

$180-220 JDJ

An American Mayo's tobacco printed
canvas advertising banner.

c1910   47in (119.5cm) long

$220-280 HA

A 'Fresh up with 7-UP' double-sided printed and die-cut card advertising fan pull.

c1937   9in (23cm) high

$60-80   **SOTT**

A CLOSER LOOK AT A CARD SIGN

Sailor Jack and Bingo the Dog were used from 1918 on boxes and advertising and were registered as the company's logos in 1919.

Apart from a few creases, he is in excellent condition, with vibrant colors.

Shaped, die-cut cards such as this are more desirable to collectors, particularly when finely printed and from a major brand, as with this example.

This is an early example, from shortly after the characters were introduced and its survival is very rare.

A rare American Cracker Jack popcorn die-cut wall hanging shop display, with Bingo the dog.

c1925

$800-1,000   **LDE**

A 1930s American 7-UP printed card store counter display standee.

The colors on this rare and fun piece are still unusually vibrant.

20in (50.5cm) high

$250-300   **SOTT**

An American ADS 'Pure Norwegian Cod Liver Oil' color lithographed advertising card sign.

Note the mis-spelling of the word 'Develops'.

23.5in (59.5cm) high

$250-300   **PKA**

A 1930s Art Deco Parke-Davis 'Medicated Throat Discs for Singers', printed by Litho Rusling Wood Inc., New York.

20.5in (52cm) high

$150-200   **PKA**

A rare Gene Sarazen die-cut cardboard golf ball advertising display, picturing Gene Sarazen and "Hol-Hi" golf balls.

16in (40.5cm) high

$500-600   **HA**

An American 'Itch-Me-Not' counter top printed card standee.

7in (18cm) wide

$15-25   **PKA**

A late 19thC color lithographic advertising broadside for Lambertville Rubber Co. of Lambertville, New Jersey 'Snag-Proof' boots and shoes, printed by Ketterlinus of Philadelphia.

Broadsides were early printed advertising posters or leaflets that mainly used words instead of images. This example is unusually finely printed and has appealing artwork.

24in (35.5cm) high

$1,000-1,500   **AAC**

ADVERTISING

A 1930s 'Campbell's 5 cents' tomato juice clerk's button.

Popular brand names or characters can fetch higher prices as there is often a wider, established group of collectors.

2.5in (6.5cm) diam

$120-180   LDE

A Frishmuth's Tobacco advertising button, by F.F. Pulver Co. of Rochester, NY.

1in (2.5cm) diam

$60-80   TRA

A Chew Flagum 'No.15 Holland' advertising pin back.

0.75in (2cm) diam

$50-70   TRA

A 1950s Orange Crush advertising celluloid button plaque.

9in (23cm) wide

$70-100   SOTT

A Bozo the Clown 'Bozo Bread' punched tin lapel pin, with fold-over bar and catch.

2in (5cm) diam

$50-70   LDE

A Litchfield Mfg. Co., Waterloo, Iowa "Bull Dog" Cylinder advertising pin-back.

0.75in (2cm) diam

$50-70   TRA

A New Chevrolet Six, Queen of The Shows advertising button.

1in (2.5cm) diam

$35-45   TRA

A Sharples Co., Chicago, ILL, 'The Tubular Cream Separator' advertising button.

1.25in (3cm) diam

$80-120   TRA

A Globe Feed 'Makes 'Em Lay' chicken food advertising button.

0.75in (2cm) diam

$15-25   TRA

An early 20thC American color lithographed pocket mirror, with two angels.

2.25in (5.5cm) diam

$100-150 LDE

An American 'Firestone Tires' advertising mirror.

2.25in (5.5cm) diam

$120-180 LDE

An American 'Van Camp's Pork and Beans' advertising mirror.

2.25in (5.5cm) diam

$100-150 LDE

An American 'Red Seal Cigar' advertising mirror.

1.75in (4.5cm) diam

$40-50 LDE

An American 'Mennen's Flesh Tint Talcum' advertising mirror.

2.75in (7cm) high

$60-80 LDE

An American 'Angelus Marshmallows' celluloid-cased advertising tape measure.

1.5in (4cm) diam

$80-120 TRA

An American 'Prest-O-Lite' car batteries celluloid advertising tape measure.

1.5in (4cm) diam

$60-80 TRA

An American Goodyear Tires advertising tape measure.

1.5in (4cm) diam

$60-80 TRA

A rare 'Leslie's Baking Powder' printed Bakelite tape measure.

This is made from a different type of early plastic than the majority, which is unusual. The fine lines like those found in ivory perhaps indicate that it is 'Ivorine'.

1.5in (4cm) diam

$280-320 TRA

An American Heckers Buckwheat 'The Sunny Days of Childhood' advertising nursery rhyme song sheet booklet, printed by W.F. Shaw.

1879   *11.5in (29cm) high*

$35-45   **AAC**

An American 'Babbitt's Cleanser' die-cut advertising booklet, with a figure on the front cover.

1910   *6.5in (16.5cm) high*

$22-28   **SOTT**

An American Beech-Nut Brand peanut butter recipe book, filled with delicious recipes involving peanut butter, published by Beech-Nut Packing Co. of Canajoharie, New York.

1914   *6.75in (17cm) high*

$30-40   **SOTT**

An American 'Care of The Teeth' Metropolitan Life Insurance advertising booklet, by Thaddeus P. Hyatt, DFS.

$40-50   **SOTT**

A 1950s American Marshmallow Fluff 'The New Yummy Book' advertising recipe booklet, with wording stating that it was 'Approved by Good Housekeeping Magazine Bureau'.

                    6.75in (17cm) high

$4-6   **SOTT**

An American Fruit Despatch Co. of New York 'Serve Bananas' advertising recipe card.

1940   *6.25in (16cm) high*

$3-5   **SOTT**

An American 'Dr Miles Medical Co.' color lithographed calendar, compliments of F.P. Clark, Druggist, North Baltimore, Ohio.

1901   *9.75in (24.5cm) high*

$100-150   **TRA**

An American 'Sperry Mills Flour Co'. silk embroidered flour sack, decorated with a native American with head dress.

The material, decoration and Native American logo make this a desirable piece. Few would have survived, especially in this condition.

31.5in (80cm) high

$350-450   **SWO**

An American 'Dr Ransom's Hive Syrup and Tolu Used for over 40 years by Physicians and Families' color lithographed trade card.

Tradecards were primarily produced in the late 19thC and are highly collectible. Those with charming or amusing period imagery, complex and well-printed designs and, as here, die-cut shapes are usually the most valuable. They fell out of favor after other forms of advertising, such as posters and newspapers, became more viable and less costly.

c1900   *8.25in (21cm) high*

$100-150   **TRA**

An American 'Old Judson' printed tinplate advertising hanging match-safe, with striker to bottom of match holder.

These would have been hung in stores or bars so that a customer with cravings could light up straight after buying his tobacco. The printing on this example is very fine and the condition is excellent for such a functional piece.

5in (13cm) high

$250-300   DCOL

A Morris & Yeoman's 'Lady Tablet' printed card hatpin packet.

4in (10cm) long

$50-70   TRA

An American Dover Mfg Co. of Canal Dover, Ohio 'Safety Always Best Automatic Electric Iron' advertising tip tray, from the Pan-Pacific World Expo, San Francisco, with the Palace of Fine Arts in the background.

1915   *4.25in (10.5cm) diam*

$250-300   DCOL

An American 'Drink Smile' thermometer, with printed card scale.

7in (18cm) diam

$220-280   SOTT

An American J.P. Palley's Hambone 5¢ Cigars embossed and lithographed double-sided card cigar pull.

7in (18cm) diam

$60-80   SOTT

A 1970s American 'Jack In The Box' advertising clicker.

2.25in (6cm) high

$70-100   LDE

An American 'Compliments of Wisconsin Central RY' advertising pocket ball game.

The railway connection and fact that this is a game make this as valuable as it is. This particular railway ran between Chicago & Minneapolis.

1.75in (4.5cm) diam

$100-150   LDE

An American Crest Professional Services painted plaster advertising tooth counter top display, with wording 'Help Prevent Decay'.

7.75in (19.5cm) high

$200-250   PKA

An American W.K. Kellogg 'Old Time Jigsaw Puzzle', by APC.

c1976   *5.5in (14cm) high*

$10-15   BH

FIND OUT MORE...

Antique Advertising Association of America, *PO Box 1121, Morton Grove, IL, 60053, USA, tel: 001 708 446 0904, www.pastimes.org.*

An oval pressed brass and brown agate pillbox.

A small rectangular double-opening box, made from clear, green- and white-veined agate and silver-plated metal, with ball clips.

This could have been used for pills, snuff or tobacco.

A small lidded pillbox, made from green-, white- and brown-veined agate and silver-plated metal.

3.25in (8cm) wide

3.25in (8.5cm) wide

1.5in (3.5cm) wide

$120-180   **AB**

$80-120   **AB**

$40-60   **AB**

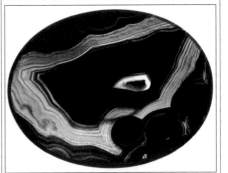

A carved agate and brass bow-fronted box, with beveled interior panels and engraved brass fittings, on agate ball feet.

Agate was popular during the 19thC due to its durability, variety of colors and suitability for carving or setting into mounts. Agate jewelry is hotly sought-after. Shaped agate-walled boxes, particularly with bow walls, are very rare due to the wastage generated by creating the curve and the time taken to achieve it.

An oval one-piece agate bowl, with small foot.

3.75in (9.5cm) widest

9.25in (23.5cm) wide

$1,000-1,500   **AB**

$380-420   **AB**

A silver-plated melon or cheese scoop, with a carved tapering agate handle and slightly curved blade.

A display piece of four joined agate spheres, carved from four separate pieces.

7in (18cm) long

2.25in (5.5cm) high

$60-80   **AB**

$120-180   **AB**

COLLECTORS' NOTES

■ The New York World's Fairs, held in 1939 and again from 1964-65, championed technology, the future and humankind in the 'world of tomorrow'. At the first fair, this message was particularly poignant after the Great Depression of the 1930s. Similarly, the message of second fair was also pertinent after WWII and the subsequent recovery and boom of the 1950s.

■ Much memorabilia is based around the buildings that were custom built for each exhibition, primarily the 1939 Trylon and Perisphere and the 1964 Unisphere. Typical memorabilia colors are blue and orange, matching the schemes of the fairs. Whilst 1939 memorabilia is hotly sought-after and generally more valuable, particularly if it is in the Art Deco style of the day, the value and desirability of memorabilia from the 1964-65 fair is growing as so many collectors nostalgically remember visiting the fair themselves.

■ Values cross a wide spectrum, and items such as souvenir pins can be found for a couple of dollars. Look for well-made pieces that typify the fair and also those that were made in small quantities, such as for single events or small groups, as these can be more valuable. Condition is important and mint condition examples will fetch higher prices.

A rare 1939 New York World's Fair chrome-plated greyhound figurine, with commemorative plaque to his back showing the Trylon and Perisphere, the base stamped "3333 JB".

Both the chrome-plating and the elegant greyhound were typical features of the Art Deco period.

c1939   5in (13cm) long

$180-220   **LDE**

A 1939 New York World's Fair souvenir ribbon on its original card, by the Silk Label Mfg Co.

Although not hard to find in itself, this example is rare due to its excellent, unstained and unfaded condition and the presence of its original card.

c1939   8.75in (22cm) high

$70-100   **LDE**

A pair of 1964 New York World's Fair novelty plastic spectacles, by Foster Grant, the frames modelled as the Unisphere, mounted on their rare original card.

c1964   6.25in (16cm) wide

$50-60   **SOTT**

A 1939 New York World's Fair yellow and black Catalin pencil sharpener, with transfer wording to front.

4in (10cm) high

$200-250   **MG**

A 1939 New York World's Fair Ballantine Inn advertising beer mat/coaster.

4.25in (10.5cm) diam

$22-28   **SOTT**

A 1964 New York World's Fair printed tinplate souvenir 'Daily Dime Bank', by United States Steel, showing the Unisphere, mounted on its original card.

5in (13cm) high

$50-70   **LDE**

A pair of 1934 Chicago World's Fair printed glass salt and pepper shakers, with plastic lids.

3.5in (9cm) high

$80-120   **MA**

AMERICANA

A late 19thC 'The Statue – Bedloes Island' Statue of Liberty souvenir card, with a print of Lady Liberty, dated 1887.

The subject and age of this card and the delicate nature of the still almost complete die-cut and impressed reverse make this a rare and appealing piece of Americana.

1887   *4.25in (11cm) high*

$70-90   **LDE**

A mid-to late 19thC General Zachary Taylor porcelain mug, printed in black with a named portrait on a profusely gilded white ground.

Taylor was born in 1784 in Virginia and entered the army in 1809. He was ordered to Florida in 1836 and Texas in 1845 where he won a major victory against the Mexican force in 1847. Emerging a hero, he was awarded the Whig presidential nomination, becoming the 12th US President in 1849. He died in 1850.

3.25in (8cm) high

$1,200-1,800   **SAS**

A late 19thC General Zachary Taylor small earthenware commemorative nursery plate, the border moulded with fruiting foliage and decorated in colors, the centre printed in green with a named and inscribed portrait.

4.75in (12cm) diam

$1,000-1,500   **SAS**

A Royal Doulton 'President Wilson' blue-glazed stoneware barrel-shaped commemorative jug, moulded with a portrait of Wilson and inscribed and dated for 'peace and victory'.

1919   7.25in (18.5cm) high

$700-1,000   **SAS**

A Franklin D. 'Teddy' Roosevelt photographic 'watch fob' campaign pin, with plastic back and a leather band with buckle.

c1932   5in (12.5cm) high

$100-150   **LDE**

A Photo Jewelry MFg Co. of Chicago 'Roosevelt The American' photographic campaign pin.

c1932   1in (2.5cm) diam

$60-80   **LDE**

A 1950s American card fire cracker candy container.

7in (18cm) high

$12-18   **SOTT**

A patriotic 'The Day We Celebrate' postcard of a girl draped in the Stars & Stripes, the reverse with handwritten message and stamp post-dated 1974.

The fact this is postmarked two years before the Bicentennial shows the high level of merchandise produced to celebrate this historic event.

5.5in (14cm) high

$12-18   **SOTT**

A pair of 1940s American Fiedler & Fiedler Mold & Die Works plastic 'Uncle Moses' and 'Aunt Jemima' small salt and pepper shakers.

3.5in (9cm) high

$40-50   **SOTT**

"The Day we celebrate"

1776

COLLECTORS' NOTES

- Cutting away the fussiness and ornament of the prevailing Art Nouveau style with its clean lines and extreme modernity, Art Deco revolutionised and dominated Western style, affecting nearly all levels of society, from the mid-1920s until WWII. There is consequently a wide array of items available for today's collector.

- Art Deco style is suited to today's homes. Look for clean lines and minimal surface decoration. Where decoration appears, it is often geometric or stylised, breaking away from the traditional representations of patterns found in the 19th and early 20th century.

- Colors vary from dramatic monochrome black, white and silvers to bold reds, oranges and greens. Consider material as well as form and color. As new technologies developed, materials such as plastics were used. Aluminum, chrome and enamel are also typical.

- Themes range from architecture, inspired by the new skyscrapers, to speeding cars and trains and desired luxury. Lamps and figurines - often dancing or sporty ladies - are popular areas. Consider marks, decoration and materials, and look for signs of age, wear and construction, as reproductions are very common.

An Art Deco patinated spelter figure of a lady, dancing on the face of the moon, mounted on a cream onyx socle.

11in (28cm) high

$500-700 GHOU

An Art Deco patinated spelter figure of a female dancer, modelled holding an onyx ball mounted on an onyx socle.

12.5in (31.5cm) high

$600-800 GHOU

An Art Deco patinated spelter figure of a female dancer, with her leg raised, mounted on an onyx socle.

12in (30.5cm) high

$600-800 GHOU

An Art Deco patinated spelter (zinc alloy) figure-match striker, after Josef Lorenzl, modelled as a scarf dancer upon a marble socle.

Spelter figurines were made in imitation of more expensive bronze and ivory figurines designed by notable names such as Ferdinand Preiss, Demetre Chiparus and Josef Lorenzl. Spelter figurines tend to be less well detailed and formed, hence their greater affordability, then and now.

11in (28cm) high

$300-500 GHOU

An Art Deco patinated spelter figure of a lady, with her leg, mounted on an onyx socle.

13in (33cm) high

$300-500 GHOU

An Art Deco patinated spelter figure of a female dancer, in period dress and hat, mounted on an onyx socle.

10.5in (26.5cm) high

$300-400 GHOU

An Art Deco style cold-painted plaster figure of a maiden with hound.

Although painted plaster figures were produced during the Art Deco period itself, they were also produced afterwards. Such reproductions fetch considerably less.

19.25in (49cm) long

$60-80 DN

An American Manning-Bowman bird's-eye maple mantel clock.

The light, finely grained appearance and luxurious appeal of bird's eye maple made it a highly popular wood used during the Art Deco period.

11.25in (28.5cm) wide

$650-850   **DETC**

An American Revere Clock Co. electric clock of truncated pyramid form, with am/pm indicator and half hour strike, mechanism by Telechron.

Telechron are noted for their movements, see the example on p362 for more information.

c1925   13.5in (34.5cm) wide

$450-650   **DETC**

A CLOSER LOOK AT AN ART DECO FIGURINE

Goldscheider was founded in Vienna, Austria in 1885 and closed in 1953. Their finely hand-painted Art Deco figurines, made mainly from 1922-35, are highly sought-after.

The delicate arms on this example have been restored, had this not been the case it could have fetched up to double the value.

They are noted for their elegant and complex forms, such as outstretched arms and flowing dresses, made up of many molded pieces joined together skilfully and invisibly.

Goldscheider's figurines also display fashions of the day, such as long, elegant dresses and bobbed, short haircuts typical of the 'flapper' girl.

An Art Deco Goldscheider ceramic figurine, impressed marks, restored arms.

British company Myott also made some superb figurines for Goldscheider in the 1940s and a limited number were also produced after WWII. Always examine an example closely for mold lines and other production 'shortcuts', which can indicate a piece made after WWII.

8.75in (22.5cm) high

$500-800   **WW**

An American desk or mantel clock on a stand, with an illuminated pressed glass fish, the movement by Sessions.

c1935   11.5in (29cm) wide

$300-500   **DETC**

An opaque green glass wall clock, depicting a couple pursuing different activities at 12, 3, 6 and 9 o'clock.

c1930   14in (35.5cm) wide

$650-750   **DETC**

An early 20thC Winterhalder and Hofmeier clockwork calendar, the chromed case with octagonal bezel, the silvered dial with an outer ring of weekdays in black and Sundays in red, on a wood stand.

6in (15cm) high

$300-400   **CHEF**

An American Art Deco original artwork for the book cover for 'The Baccarat Club' by Jesse Louisa Rickard, the artwork by Wenck.

1929   7.5in (19cm) high

$80-120   **DD**

A 1930s American Art Deco theatrical advertisement for 'The Bijou Theater' in New York, designed by Chappell.

This advertisement plays on the ritzy glamour and skyscraper-filled modernity of the Big City.

8in (20cm) high

$35-45   **DD**

An Art Deco stamp, with geometric design.

Images of speeding vehicles are typical of Art Deco designs. With the brightly colored geometric design, the paintings of Robert Delauney are suggested.

c1928   1.5in (4cm) high

$30-40   **DD**

A 1920s American Art Deco stationery box graphic.

1.5in (29cm) high

$50-70   **DD**

An American Art Deco geometric picture frame, black glass and mirror, containing a photo of Joan Crawford.

c1930   11.5in (29cm) high

$500-700   **DD**

A pair of Art Deco chrome and bakelite candelabra-style boudoir lamps.

c1935   16.5in (42cm) high

$650-750   **DETC**

A 1930s Art Deco polished chrome Chase bud vase.

The Chase Brass & Copper Company was founded in Waterbury, Connecticut in 1876 and produced metalwares for the home from the 1930s. The strong Art Deco styling, most often in chrome, was hugely popular. Production of homewares ceased at the outbreak of WWII.

9in (23cm) high

$70-100   **DD**

A pair of 1930s Art Deco Chase Corp. copper bookends, designed by Walter von Nessen.

5in (12.5cm) high

$300-500   **DETC**

A 1930s English Art Deco 'Bunting' designer radiant heater, in the form of a yacht, the two chrome tin sails acting as heat reflectors, the mast as heating rod.

29in (73.5cm) high

$300-400   **GORL**

An Art Deco silver-plated tea set, consisting of teapot, water jug, sugar bowl and milk jug, each of cubist form with bakelite handles and finials, maker's and registration marks to underside.

$300-500   **ROS**

COLLECTORS' NOTES

- Notaphily, the collecting of paper money, first became popular in the 1960s and grew in the 1970s when it became a separate collecting area from coins.

- Notes are often decorated with vignettes and detailed scenes that are not only decorative but are designed to foil counterfeiters. These vignettes often form the basis of a collection with themes including famous people, wildlife, battles or other historical events. Other collecting themes include special or significant serial numbers, wartime currency or notes from a specific country or period.

- As banknotes are produced in limited editions, they tend to accrue in value steadily, so collectors can often see a return on their investment quite quickly compared with many other collecting areas.

- Condition has a huge effect on value, and notes in mint condition are highly sought-after. Store banknotes flat in plastic wallets and take care when handling them.

A scarce Hong Kong & Shanghai Banking Corporation 500 dollars note, dated 1st February 1965, light wear to edges.

1965

$550-650   **BLO**

An Italian Regie Finanze-Torino 100 lire note, unissued, printed in black on one-side with arms at left center, in extremely fine condition.

1746

$180-220   **BLO**

A Maltese Banco Anglo Maltese 50 pounds note, dated "18--", unissued, printed in black on one side with St. George slaying dragon at upper left, worn down left edge of counterfoil otherwise in extremely fine condition.

$650-750   **BLO**

A Spanish Aramburu Hermanos 500 reales de vellón, dated "18--", unissued, printed in black on one side with brown and green panel across center and arms at upper center, in about uncirculated condition.

$50-70   **BLO**

A rare Government of Tonga Treasury four shillings note, dated 16th January 1933, with a couple of short edge tears and three small holes in body, otherwise in fine condition.

$150-200   **BLO**

An English Treasury one pound note, with John Bradbury printed signature, in very fine condition.

1914-16

$220-280   BLO

An English Treasury one pound note, with Sir Norman Fenwick Warren Fisher printed signature, in very fine condition.

1919-22

$70-100   BLO

A Bank of England five pounds note, dated 2 June 1950, with Percival S. Beale printed signature, with light pencil marks top right and short tear bottom edge.

$70-100   BLO

A CLOSER LOOK AT A BANKNOTE

A Central Bank of Ireland 100 pounds note, dated 19.7.1947, with Joseph Brennan and J.J. McElligott signatures, inked letters right side, pinholes, few edge nicks plus short tear bottom edge, good early date.

1947

$350-450   BLO

Prior to 1900 there were approximately 100 banks in Ireland that produced their own banknotes.

By the 1960s, this number had been reduced to just six.

This is an early example, issued in Dublin.

It has been hand-signed by William James Alexander, one of the directors of the bank.

A rare Irish Alexanders Bank, Dublin two pounds note, dated 7 September 1819, issued for partnership, good to very fine condition.

1819

$1,000-1,500   BLO

An Irish Central Bank of Ireland, fifty pound notes, dated 01.11.1982, in fine condition.

1982

$150-200   BLO

A Scottish Royal Bank of Scotland plc., five pounds note, new issue with Jack Nicklaus on back, uncirculated.

2006

$7-9   BLO

COLLECTORS' NOTES

- Beads were one of the first forms of personal decoration. The earliest examples found used materials taken from nature, such as shells, stones, seeds and feathers. Beads and jewelery often held great social and cultural importance and a study of the object often leads to a greater understanding of the people producing and wearing them.

- Bead collecting tends to falls between jewelery and tribal art, and as a result is often overlooked as a collecting area in its own right. Given their wide range

of materials, ages and countries of origin they make an ideal collecting field to suit a wide range of budgets and tastes. Examples here are mainly African trade beads.

- Although glass is a common material, almost none was made in Africa. It was either produced from recycled bottles or older beads, or was produced in Europe, particularly Venice, and then exported to Africa.

- Many types are copied today, so make sure you know if you are buying an antique or modern example.

A strand of 1920s-30s Bohemian glass 'wedding' beads, for the African market.

21.5in (54.5cm) long

$100-150   **VC**

A strand of 1930s-50s Venetian millefiori glass beads.

15in (38cm) long

$70-100   **VC**

A necklace of fused recycled 'powderglass' 'king' beads, by the Krobo people of Ghana, African or Venetian for the African market, with polychrome decoration, strung with a Moroccon silver clasp.

Necklace 15in (38cm) long

Beads $7-9 (each)   **VC**

A strand of Neolithic African beads, including agate and cornelian, excavated in Djenné, southern Mali.

Strand 21in (53.5cm) long

$50-70   **VC**

Three turned agate beads.

The agate was probably mined in Africa, shipped to India for shaping and then exported back to Africa for sale.

Largest 4in (10cm) long

$10-15 (each)   **VC**

Two 20thC Ethiopian silver-plated brass pendants, decorated with Coptic symbols.

These pendants are worn by the Jewish Falasha people of the Gondar region of Ethiopia. They often combine Jewish and Christian symbols such as the Star of David and a cross.

Largest 2.5in (6.5cm) high

$70-100 (each)   **VC**

Six 20thC Ethiopian silver telsum charms.

0.75in (2cm) wide

$7-10 (each)   **VC**

A large seven-layer chevron glass bead, Venetian for the African market.

c1600s   *1in (2.5cm) wide*

$70-100   **VC**

A CLOSER LOOK AT KIFFA BEADS

Traditionally there is very little glass-making in Africa, so these beads are produced using an inventive method.

As this process is very time consuming, they were not made in great quantities. The beads are still made today, but do not show the complex and clearly delineated patterns of older examples.

Clear glass is crushed to a fine powder between stones and then mixed with saliva to form a core for the bead. Colored glass power is added over this core with a needle in complex patterns. The beads are then fired in a tin can or on a pottery sherd over hot coals.

The triangular beads were used as forehead pendants, and are the result of a T-shaped frame used to support the bead during production.

A collection of late 20thC African 'kiffa' glass beads.

Kiffa beads, also known as murakad, are named after the city of Kiffa in Mauretania, where they were first discovered by a Westerner.

Largest 0.75in (2cm) long

$22-28 (each)   **VC**

Five Venetian glass 'Rosetta' beads, with five layers of polychrome glass.

These beads can be found with varying numbers of layers. With beveled edges they are known as chevron beads.

0.5in (1.5cm) wide

$7-9 (each)   **VC**

Three 18thC Venetian miniature chevron glass beads, each with seven layers.

The process of producing these chevron beads was invented in Venice about 500 years ago. These tiny glass beads demonstrate the level of skill found in 18thC Venetian glass makers. The sides have been beveled to show the various layers when the beads are strung on a necklace.

Largest 0.25in (0.5cm) wide

$22-28 (each)   **VC**

Five late 19th/early 20thC millefiori glass beads, Venetian for the African market.

Largest 1.5in (4cm) long

$12-18   **VC**

Four late 19th/early 20thC millefiori glass 'elbow' beads, Venetian for the African market.

These beads are named for their bent shape.

2in (5cm) long

$35-45 (each)   **VC**

A late 19th/early 20thC millefiore glass 'elbow' bead, Venetian for the African market, with West African gold pendant mount.

2.5in (6.5cm) long

$80-120   **VC**

FIND OUT MORE...

The Bead Society of Great Britain, *www.beadsociety.freeserve.co.uk.*

The Bead Study Trust, *www.beadstudytrust.org.uk.*

http://bead-database.org, *online interactive bead database.*

http://beadcollector.net/openforum/index.html, *US online discussion forum.*

COLLECTORS' NOTES

■ The black cat has been a powerful, often negative, symbol for centuries and features in traditional folklore, usually connected to witchcraft and evil.

■ Although predominately considered a sign of bad luck, some countries see them as favourable symbols. In the UK, a black cat crossing your path is considered a sign of good things to come. However the opposite is believed in other countries, such as the US.

■ This negative association probably began in ancient Babylonian and Hebrew mythologies which equated cats curled in hearths with serpents.

■ Black cats as familiars are also associated with witches; their dark coloring making them perfect for remaining unseen at night and in the 1930s the Wiccan religion adopted the black cat as an official symbol. This connection means that black cats are commonly featured in Halloween memorabilia.

■ Despite its negative connotations, the black cat has been used in product advertising and as company logos, such as the Eveready Battery.

A 1930s German black cat painted composition candy container, with "GERMANY" printed on base.

4.75in (12cm) high

$280-320   **SOTT**

A 1960s Japanese black cat ceramic figure, marked "JAPAN".

5in (12.5cm) high

$35-45   **PKA**

A homemade Felix-style black cat wood doorstop.

10.5in (27cm) high

$30-50   **PKA**

One of a pair of small black cat ceramic bud vases.

3.25in (8cm) high

$30-40   **PKA**

A one of a pair of small black cat ceramic bud vases.

3.25in (8cm) high

$30-40   **PKA**

A 1930s black cat hand-made wooden trump indicator, for a game of cards.

3.5in (9cm) high

$100-150   **PKA**

A Japanese black cat small hand-painted ceramic posy or trinket holder, marked "JAPAN".

3in (7.5cm) wide

$30-40   **PKA**

A set of three black cat numbered game pencils, with carved and turned wooden bases.

4.75in (12cm) high

$80-120   **PKA**

An English Channel Tubular Railway Preliminary Co. Ltd. certificate for five founders shares, with vignettes of English and French coasts and train in tube on seabed, text in English and French, in very fine condition.

1892

$180-220   **BLO**

An English Great North of England Railway Co. certificate for one share, with a chain link at left with names of towns on the proposed route, in very fine condition.

1836

$280-320   **BLO**

A scarce English Middlesbrough & Guisbrough Railway Co. certificate for one share, with a large vignette of locomotive pulling coal wagons passing mine, cut-cancelled at bottom right corner, not effecting print, in very fine condition.

1857

$700-900   **BLO**

An English Wharfdale Railway Co. certificate for one share, with a vignette of the famous 'Craven Heffer', large red seal, in very fine condition.

The Craven Heffer was an extremely large cow, which made vast profits for its owner by being exhibited around the UK.

1846

$120-180   **BLO**

An English Whitehead Aircraft (1917) Ltd., certificate for cumulative participating ordinary shares, with a vignette of airfield with biplanes either side, large underprint of biplane, in very fine condition.

1918

$220-280   **BLO**

A Chinese Kiangsu Province Water Conservancy Construction Loan bond for 10 yuan, with a large vignette of a river scene, mountains and Sun Yat Sen, with coupons six to 26, folded, otherwise in very fine condition.

1934

$220-280   **BLO**

An Irish Waterford, Wexford, Wicklow & Dublin Railway Co. certificate for one share, ornate design with coat of arms at top, green seal, in very fine condition.

1847

$180-220   **BLO**

A scarce Great East Asia War Special Loan of the Imperial Government of Japan treasury bond for 1,000 yen, vignette of building at right, equestrian statue at left, with coupons two to 18, two punch holes in top margin.

1943

$400-500   **BLO**

COLLECTORS' NOTES

■ True first editions, as far as collectors are concerned, are from the first printing, or impression, of the first edition. To identify one, look for the number '1' in the series of numbers on the copyright page.

■ Some publishers state clearly that a book is a first edition, or use letters. Check that the publishing date and copyright date match, and learn about different publishing styles indicating first editions.

■ 'First' numbers are limited – values usually rise as desirability increases. Very famous, iconic titles will always be prized, but a classic title published at the height of an author's career will often be worth less than an early and less well-received work as these are usually produced in much smaller numbers.

■ Condition is another key indicator of value. Dust jackets are very important – values of modern titles can fall by 50 per cent or more without them.

■ Authors' signatures are a bonus, while dedications are slightly less desirable unless the person is famous or connected with the author. A good tip is to buy (preferably) signed copies of up-and-coming authors nominated for major prizes, like the Booker, before the winner is announced.

■ There are many perennially popular authors such as Iris Murdoch, Agatha Christie and Ian Fleming, but fashion does play a significant role. Books made into successful, popular films usually increase in value as interest surges.

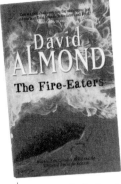

David Almond, "The Fire-Eaters", first edition, published by Hodder, signed by the author.

2003

$30-60   **BIB**

Martin Amis, "Dead Babies", first edition, presentation copy from the author, original boards, dust jacket.

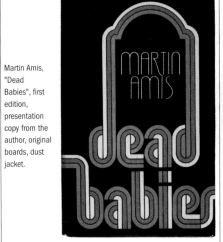

1975

$800-1,000   **BLO**

John Banville, "Nightspawn", first edition, original boards, dust jacket, tanned at upper edge and spine.

1971

$350-450   **BLO**

Pat Barker, "The Eye in the Door", first edition, original boards, dust jacket.

1993

$120-180   **BLO**

Julian Barnes, "The Lemon Table", first edition, published by Jonathan Cape, signed by the author.

2004

$30-40   **BIB**

Saul Bellow, "The Victim", first English edition, original boards, spine faded, tanned and rubbed.

This was the author's second book.

1948

$200-300   **BLO**

Tim Bowler, "Starseeker", first edition, published by Oxford Press.

2002

$12-18   **BIB**

William Boyd, "A Good Man in Africa", first edition, original boards, dust jacket a little creased at spine ends.

1981

$400-500   **BLO**

Michael Bracewell, "Perfect Tense", first edition, published by Jonathan Cape.

$15-20   **BIB**

Ray Bradbury, "Fahrenheit 451", first English edition, original boards, dust jacket.

1954

$700-900   **BLO**

Ray Bradbury, "Dark Carnival", first English edition, some isolated foxing, original cloth covers and dust jacket.

Even though the dust jackets of this work were supposed to have been price clipped by the publisher before circulation, this copy seems to have escaped that fate, remaining unclipped.

1948

$800-1,000   **BLO**

Bruce Chatwin, "In Patagonia", first edition, original boards, dust jacket.

1977

$500-600   **BLO**

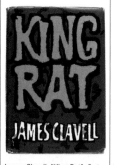

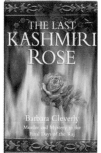

Tracy Chevalier, "The Virgin Blue", first edition, published by Penguin.

1997

$30-60   **BIB**

Lee Child, "Echo Burning", first edition, published by Bantam Press.

2001

$12-18   **BIB**

James Clavell, "King Rat", first English edition, peripheral foxing near beginning, original boards, dust jacket slightly bumped in one corner.

$80-120   **BLO**

Barbara Cleverly, "The Last Kashmiri Rose", first edition, original cloth, dust jacket.

2001

$150-250   **BLO**

Jim Crace, "Six", first edition, published by Viking, signed by the author.

2003

$300-400 BIB

The Lucky Ones

Rachel Cusk, "The Lucky Ones", first edition, published by Fourth Estate.

2003

$25-35 BIB

Linda Davies, "Into the Fire", first edition, published by Harper Collins.

1999

$20-30 BIB

Jill Dawson, "Wild Boy", first edition, published by Sceptre, signed by the author.

2003

$20-30 BIB

Louis De Bernières, "Red Dog", first edition, published by Secker & Warburg.

2001

$12-18 BIB

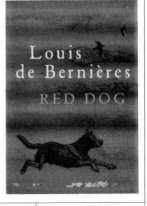

Len Deighton, "The Ipcress File", first edition, original boards, dust jacket.

1962

$500-600 BLO

Sebastian Faulks, "A Trick of the Light", first edition, faint water-staining to edges of front endpapers, original boards, dust jacket, a little creased at edges.

1984

$300-400 BLO

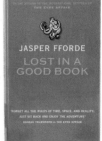

Jasper Fforde, "Lost in a Good Book", first edition, published by Hodder & Stoughton, signed by the author.

The signature is in upper case, which is rare for this author.

2002

$50-90 BIB

Louise Doughty, "Dance with Me", first edition, published by Touch Stone.

1996

$10-15 BIB

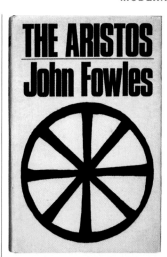

John Fowles, "The Aristos", first edition, original boards, price clipped dust jacket, slightly tanned at spine.

Price clipping refers to the price found on the bottom corner of the dust jacket being cut off. This was normally done by the buyer, and very rarely by a publisher if the price changed between printing and releasing a book. Unclipped examples are more desirable.

Frederick Forsyth, "The Day of the Jackal", first edition, ink ownership signature on title page, original boards, dust jacket very slightly rubbed at edges and with a couple of small tears, price clipped.

1971

$150-200   **BLO**

1965

$600-900   **BLO**

John Fowles, "The Collector", first edition, original brick red boards, dust jacket, a little tanned at spine and edges.

1963

$600-900   **BLO**

Michael Frayn, "Spies", first edition, published by Faber & Faber, signed by the author.

2002

$25-35   **BIB**

Nicci French, "Land of the Living", first edition, published by Michael Joseph, signed by both authors.

2002

$30-40   **BIB**

Terry Pratchett & Neil Gaiman, "Good Omens", first edition, published by Gollancz, signed by Terry Pratchett.

1990

$50-80   **BIB**

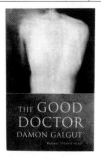

Damon Galgut, "The Good Doctor", first edition, published by Atlantic, Booker prize listed.

Works by literary award winning authors are often more sought-after.

2003

$20-30   **BIB**

Alex Garland, "The Coma", first edition, published by Faber & Faber, signed by the author.

2004

$25-35   **BIB**

William Golding, "Lord of the Flies", first edition, second impression, small ink ownership inscription on front endpaper, original cloth, dust jacket, very small chips to head of spine.

1954

$300-400   **BLO**

Sue Grafton, "'B' is for Burglar", first edition, original boards, dust jacket.

1985

$450-650 BLO

Caroline Graham, "The Killings at Badger's Drift", first edition, margins a little browned, original boards, dust jacket.

1987

$120-180 BLO

James Graham (Jack Higgins), "A Game for Heroes", first edition, original boards, dust jacket.

1970

$300-400 BLO

Caroline Graham, "The Envy of the Stranger", first edition, signed on title page.

1984

$100-150 BLO

Henry Green, "Nothing", first edition, published by Hogarth Press, London, spine slightly faded and bumped, in like dust jacket, spine a trifle darkened, back panel dusty, top edge and corners slightly rubbed.

1950

$70-90 PB

Abdulrazak Gurnah, "Paradise", first edition, published by Hamish Hamilton, Booker prize listed.

1994

$30-40 BIB

Shirley Hazzard, "The Great Fire", first edition, published by Virago, signed by author.

2003

$30-60 BIB

Zoë Heller, "Notes on a Scandal", first edition, published by Viking, signed by the author.

2003

$120-180 BIB

Jack Higgins, "In the Hour Before Midnight", first edition, original boards, gilt spine, dust jacket a little tanned and a little creased at upper edge.

1969

$200-300 BLO

Tobias Hill, "The Cryptographer", first edition, published by Faber & Faber, signed by the author.

2003

$20-30   **BIB**

Robin Hobb, "The Farseer I: Assassin's Apprentice", first edition, original boards, dust jacket.

1995

$120-180   **BLO**

Robin Hobb, "The Tawny Man III: Fool's Fate", first edition, published by Voyager, signed by the author.

2003

$20-40   **BIB**

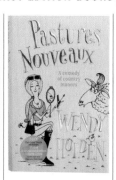

Wendy Holden, "Pastures Nouveaux", first edition, published by Headline, signed by the author.

2001

$20-30   **BIB**

John Irving, "The Water-Method Man", first US edition, published by Random House, New York.

1972

$500-700   **BRB**

Howard Jacobson, "Who's Sorry Now", first edition, published by Jonathan Cape, signed by the author.

2002

$30-60   **BIB**

P.D. James, "The Black Tower", first edition, original boards, dust jacket, designed by Errol Le Cain.

Kazuo Ishiguro, "The Remains of the Day", first edition, original boards, dust jacket.

Books that have been made into successful films, such as this one, tend to be more sought-after.

1989

$200-300   **BLO**

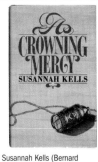

Susannah Kells (Bernard Cornwall), "A Crowning Mercy", small ink name on front pastedown, first edition, original boards, dust jacket.

1983

$150-250   **BLO**

$150-200   **BLO**

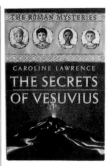

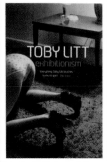

Caroline Lawrence, "The Secrets of the Vesuvius", first edition, published by Orion, signed by the author.

2001

$20-30 BIB

Andrea Levy, "Small Island", first edition, published by Review, signed by the author.

2004

$30-60 BIB

Toby Litt, "Exhibitionism", first edition, published by Hamish Hamilton, signed by the author.

2002

$20-40 BIB

Gabriel García Márquez, "No One Writes to the Colonel", ink ownership signature on title, original boards, dust jacket, small clean tear to one corner.

1971

$200-300 BLO

Alistair MacLean, "H.M.S. Ulysses", first edition, signed by the author, original boards, dust jacket, slightly rubbed and browned at extremities.

Gabriel García Márquez, "One Hundred Years of Solitude", first American edition, later state with row of numbers on p.424, original cloth, dust jacket, second state without exclamation mark at end of second paragraph on front flap.

1955

$700-900 BLO

1970

$200-300 BLO

Cormac McCarthy, "Blood Meridian or The Evening Redness in the West", first English edition, original cloth, dust jacket.

1989

$200-300 BLO

Cormac McCarthy, "Outer Dark", first English edition, original cloth, dust jacket slightly edge-worn at spine.

1970

$300-400 BLO

George McDonald Fraser, "Black Ajax", first edition, published by Harper Collins, signed by the author.

1997

$20-30 BIB

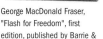

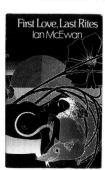

Patrick O'Brian, "The Mauritius Command", first edition, original boards, dust jacket.

1977

$700-900   BLO

George MacDonald Fraser, "Flash for Freedom", first edition, published by Barrie & Jenkins.

1971

$120-180   BIB

Ian McEwan, "First Love, Last Rites", first edition, original boards, dust jacket.

1975

$600-800   BLO

Magnus Mills, "The Restraint of Beasts", first edition, published by Flamingo.

1998

$20-40   BIB

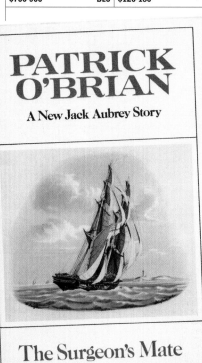

V.S. Naipaul, "Half a Life", first edition, published by Picador, signed by the author.

2001

$40-60   BIB

Maggie O'Farrell, "My Lover's Lover", first edition, published by Review.

2002

$20-30   BIB

Patrick O'Brian, "The Nutmeg of Consolation", first edition, original cloth, dust jacket.

1991

$250-350   BLO

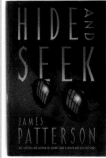

James Patterson, "Hide and Seek", first edition, published by Harper Collins.

1996

$30-40   BIB

Patrick O'Brian, "The Surgeon's Mate", first edition, original boards, dust jacket.

This is the scarcest Jack Aubrey title. The success of the 2003 film 'Master and Commander' has increased interest in the series.

1980

$1,200-1,800   BLO

Ellis Peters, "Dead Man's Ransom", first edition, original cloth, dust jacket, slightly faded at spine.

1984

$120-180   **BLO**

Ellis Peters, " A Nice Derangement of Epitaphs", first edition, original cloth, dust jacket, torn and repaired internally but with no loss, slight edge creasing.

1965

$120-180   **BLO**

DBC Pierre, "Vernon God Little", first edition, published by Faber & Faber.

2003

$100-150   **BIB**

Ian Rankin, "Knots & Crosses", first edition, ex-library copy, with stamps on title and rear pastedown, some creases.

1987

$450-550   **BLO**

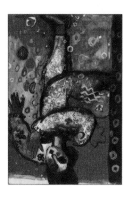

Ian Rankin, "Hide & Seek", first edition, original boards, dust jacket, slightly rubbed.

1991

$350-450   **BLO**

Ian Rankin, "The Flood", first edition, Edinburgh, original boards, dust jacket.

1986

$1,000-1,500   **BLO**

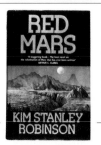

Kim Stanley Robinson. "Red Mars", first edition, original boards, dust jacket, a little creased at upper edges.

1992

$250-350   **BLO**

Arundhati Roy, "The God of Small Things", first edition, published by Flamingo.

1997

$40-60   **BIB**

Salman Rushdie, "Midnight's Children", first American edition, original cloth-backed boards, dust jacket, very slight edge creasing near spine head, uncut.

1981

$200-300   **BLO**

William Styron, "Lie Down in Darkness", first edition, dust jacket torn at lower edge, original boards, dust jacket, a little rubbed at extremities.

1952

$100-150   BLO

A CLOSER LOOK AT A MODERN FIRST EDITION

This is Swift's third book, and only 750 copies of the first edition were printed.

The addition of a signed postcard adds to the interest.

Graham Swift won the Booker Prize for Fiction in 1996 for 'Last Orders'.

A copy without a signed postcard would be worth around $350.

Graham Swift, "Learning to Swim", first edition, original cloth, dust jacket, signed postcard from the author loosely inserted.

1982

$600-800

BLO

Graham Swift, "Waterland", first edition, original boards, dust jacket.

1983

$250-350   BLO

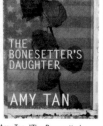

Amy Tan, "The Bonesetter's Daughter", first edition, published by Flamingo.

2001

$20-30   BIB

William Trevor, "The Day We Got Drunk on Cake", first edition, original boards, dust jacket, very slightly tanned.

This is the author's first collection of short stories and is a sought-after title.

1967

$800-1,200   BLO

Jeanette Winterson, "The Passion", first American edition, New York, original cloth-backed boards, first edition, dust jackets.

1987

$50-70   BLO

Percival Christopher Wren, "Sinbad the Soldier", first English edition, half-title, original cloth, dust jacket, slightly foxed on flaps, slight edge ware but with no loss.

1935

$250-350   BLO

John Wyndham, "The Kraken Wakes", first edition, original boards, dust jacket slightly rubbed at extremities.

1953

$200-300   BLO

COLLECTORS' NOTES

■ Early paperbacks were inspired by the popular fiction found in magazines from the 1920s and 30s onwards. Intended as 'throwaway' reads, the name 'pulp' fiction derives from the cheap pulped paper or newsprint used in the manufacture of the original magazines.

■ The golden years for paperback books stretch from the years following WWII to the 1960s. During this period thousands of 'pulp' titles, aimed at the mass market, were produced for adults. Typical genres include crime, science fiction and addiction and many collectors limit their collections to such specific areas.

■ It is the colorful or kitsch designs on the covers, particularly on books printed from the late 1940s, that catch the attention of many of today's collectors.

Many feature graphics in the distinctive style of an era, or scantily clad ravished dames. During the 1950s, some titles were outlawed and destroyed due to their obscene content or cover. Surviving examples can attract a cult following.

■ Condition is key in determining value and the cover in particular should be free of damage such as tears, stains and fading. Mint examples are worth more.

■ Some titles and editions are rarer than others, the earliest examples are usually more collectible. A well known pulp fiction author – such as Hank Janson or Ben Sarto – can add appeal, but the value more typically lies in the cover artwork. Look for notable artists such as Reginald Heade or F. W Perle.

Fredric Brown, "Murder Can Be Fun", published by Boardman Books.

1952

$50-70   **PCC**

John Eagle, "The Hoodlums", published by Avon, New York.
1953

$12-18   **PCC**

Carol Carnac, "Murder As A Fine Art", published by the Crime Club.

$7-9   **ZDB**

Ashley Carter, "Against All Odds", A Star Book, the paperback division of W.H. Allen & Co Ltd.

1982

$7-9   **PCC**

Philip Chambers, "Bullets to Baghdad", published by Sexton Blake Library, Fleetway Publications Ltd, cover artwork by Jacoby.

1960

$7-9   **ZDB**

James Hadley Chase, "The Dead Stay Dumb", published by Corgi Books, first published in 1947.

1980

$7-9   **ZDB**

David Dodge, "A Drug On The Market", published by Corgi Books, first published 1949.

1953

$12-14   **PCC**

Harlan Ellison, "Gentleman Junkie",
Pyramid Books, New York.

1975

$15-20   **MBO**

Hal Ellson, "Stairway To
Nowhere", published by
Pedigree books.

*Titles involving
delinquency, particularly
amongst the young, can
be sought after. This is
especially true if the image
is dramatic and illustrates
the style of rebels of the
period, typified by James
Dean, as this cover does.*

1959

$70-100   **PCC**

Arthur Farmer, "Sin Ship",
Private Edition Books, North
Hollywood.

$20-30   **MBO**

Henry Gregor Felsen, "Hot Rod",
published by Bantam Books.

1951

$12-18   **MBO**

Jack Finney, "The Body
Snatchers".

1957

$20-30   **PCC**

Steve Fisher, "Hot Spot",
published by Pedigree Books.

1959

$28-32   **PCC**

Pierre Flammeche, "When
Passion Rules", published by
Archer Press, with cover by
Reginald Heade.

$50-70   **PCC**

Erie Stanley Gardener, "Perry
Mason Solves The Case Of The
Golddiggers Purse", published
by Pocket Books, first
paperback edition, first
published in 1949.

1952

$12-14   **PCC**

Darcy Glinto, "Snow Vogue", published by Robin Hood Press.

$50-70   **PCC**

Harry Grey, "The Hoods", Signet Books, The New American Library, 7th print, with quote from Mickey Spillane on the cover.

This book formed the basis for the Sergio Leone's 1984 film "Once Upon a Time in America".

1959

$30-40   **MBO**

Evan Hunter, "The Blackboard Jungle", published by Panther Books.

In 1955, the book was made into a film starring Sidney Poitier, Glenn Ford and Anne Francis. It was nominated for 3 Oscars.

1960

$12-14   **PCC**

Hank Janson, "The Unseen Assassin", published by Alexander Moring Ltd.

1955

$50-70   **PCC**

John D. MacDonald, "Deadly Welcome", published by Pan Books Ltd.

1964

$7-9   **ZDB**

A CLOSER LOOK AT A PAPERBACK BOOK

Richard Matheson (b.1926), is an American author and screenwriter, best known for his science fiction, fantasy and horror novels.

This is Matheson's first novel. First titles are often printed in smaller quantities than later works, making this example harder to find and more sought-after.

Many of Matheson's books have reached the silver screen, this title was filmed in 1974 and starred Alain Delon.

Matheson's second novel 'Fury on Sunday' is also sought-after.

Richard Matheson, "Someone Is Bleeding", published by Banner Books, L.Miller & Sons Ltd.

1953

$220-280   **PCC**

Spike Morelli, "You'll Never Get Me", published by Archer, Reginald Heade cover.

1952

$70-90   **PCC**

Peter O'Donnell, "Modesty Blaise: The Night of Morning Star", published by Pan Books.

1984

$12-14   **ZDB**

Geoffrey Pardoe, "Traffic In Souls", published by E. Halle Ltd.

1959

$20-30   **PCC**

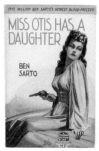

Ben Sarto, "Miss Otis Has A Daughter", published by Modern Fiction.

1948

$50-70   PCC

Robert Selman, "Once Upon a Crime", a Sundown Book, published by W. Foulsham Ltd.

1950

$20-30   PCC

Georges Simenon, "The Witnesses", published by Four Square Books.

1958

$7-9   ZDB

Mickey Spillane, "The Long Wait", published by Dragon Books, No.29 by Arthur Barker Ltd, first published in 1951.

Spillane (b.1918) has been one of the most popular writers in the US despite being criticized for the then high levels of violence and sex included in his novels. His most famous creation was the hard-boiled detective Mike Hammer.

1958

$12-14   PCC

Mickey Spillane, "The Big Kill", published by Corgi Books.

1962

$7-9   ZDB

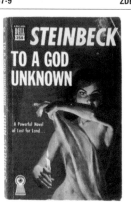

John Steinbeck, "To A God Unknown", published by Dell Publishing Company, first published 1933.

1933

$12-18   MBO

Michael Storme, "Dame In My Bed", published by Archer Press, with Reginald Heade cover.

1951

$70-90   PCC

Jim Thompson, "A Hell Of A Woman", published by Banner Books.

1954

$220-280 PCC

Edgar Wallace, "When The Gangs Came To London", published by Arrow Books.

1957

$7-9   ZDB

Piers Anthony, "Var The Stick", Corgi Sci Fi, published by Corgi Books.

1975

$7-9   ZDB

Robert Bassett, "Witchfinder General", published by Pan Books.

1968

$12-14   ZDB

Ray Buckland, "Ancient & Modern Witchcraft", HC Publishers Inc, New York.

Both the colorful and lurid cover art and the topic make this a desirable title.

1970

$20-30   MBO

Randall Conway, "Out Of This World", published by John Spencer & Co. Ltd.

$28-32   ZDB

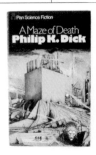

Reed De Rouen, "Split Image", a Digit Book.

1963

$7-9   ZDB

Philip K. Dick, "A Maze of Death", Pan Science Fiction, published by Pan Books Ltd.

1973

$7-9   ZDB

John Falkner, "Overlords of Andromeda", published by Panther Books.

1955

$15-20   ZDB

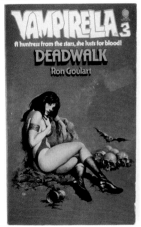

Hank Janson, "One Against Time", published by Alexander Moring Ltd., with cover artwork by Reginald Heade.

The Reginald Heade cover, the combination of a science fiction theme and a busty female, and the popularity of author Hank Janson make this more valuable.

Ron Goulart, "Vampirella 3: Deadwalk", published by Sphere Books.

1977

$12-14   PCC

$50-70   PCC

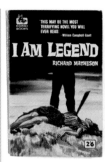

Richard Matheson, "I Am Legend", published by Corgi Books.
1960
$20-30   **PCC**

Frederik Pohl & C. M. Kornbluth, "The Space Merchants", A Digit Book.
$7-9   **ZDB**

John Rankine, "Space 1999: Astral Quest", An Orbit Book, published by Futura Publications Ltd.
1975
$7-9   **ZDB**

Clifford D. Simak, "Time and Again", Magnum Books, published by Methuen Paperbacks Ltd.
1977
$7-9   **ZDB**

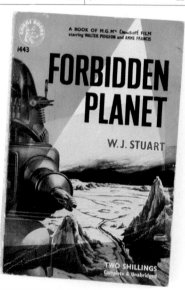

Guy N. Smith, "The Slime Beast", published by New English Library.
1976
$12-14   **ZDB**

W.J. Stuart, "Forbidden Planet", first UK edition.

This is the novelisation of the 1956 film, whose characters and setting were inspired by Shakespeare's The Tempest. The presence of Robbie the robot on the cover adds desirability.

1956
$30-50   **PCC**

E.C. Tubb, "The Terra Data", published by Arrow Books.
1985
$7-9   **ZDB**

Jules Verne, "Journey To The Centre of the Earth", published by Digit Books.
1959
$7-9   **ZDB**

"Worlds of Fantasy No.8", includes "Martian Terror" by Ray Mason, by John Spencer & Co Ltd.
$22-28   **ZDB**

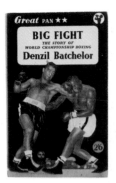

Denzil Batchelor, "Big Fight", published by Pan Books Ltd.

1956

$7-9   ZDB

Justin Cartwright, "The New Avengers: Fighting Men", published by Futura Publications Ltd.

1977

$7-9   ZDB

Leslie Charteris, "The Saint In New York", published by Hodder & Stoughton.

1964

$7-9   ZDB

L.P. Easton, "Target..Rome", published by Badger Books.

$7-9   ZDB

Ian Fleming, "The Diamond Smugglers", published by Pan Books.

This was one of Fleming's few non-fiction books.

1965

$22-28   ZDB

John Gardner, "James Bond: For Special Services", Coronet Books, published by Hodder & Stoughton.

1995

$7-9   ZDB

Marco Garon, "Silent River", published by Curtis Books.

Mark Garon was one of the pseudonyms of Dennis Hughes. Silent River is from a series of books featuring the character Rex Brandon, who bears similarities to Tarzan.

1951

$70-100   PCC

Marco Garon, "Leopard God", published by Curtis Books.

1952

$70-100   PCC

George G. Gilman, "Edge No. 48: School for Slaughter", published by New English Library.

1985

$7-9   ZDB

Billie Holiday with William Dufty, "Lady Sings The Blues", published by Ace Books.

1960

$12-14 ZDB

William Hope Hodgson, "The Night Land: Volume II", published by Pan/Ballantine.

1973

$12-14 ZDB

Wilhelm Johnen, "Duel Under The Stars", published by Kimber Pocket Editions.

1958

$7-9 ZDB

Robert K. Lander, "With Flame And Sabre", published by Badger Books.

1957

$7-9 PCC

Wilfred McNeilly, "Danger Man: No Way Out", published by Consul Books.

1966

$7-9 ZDB

Alistair Revie, "That Kind Of Girl", a Digit Book.

1963

$12-14 ZDB

Edgar Rice Burroughs, "Tarzan's Quest", published by Four Square Books Ltd.

1960

$12-14 ZDB

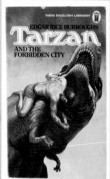

Edgar Rice Burroughs, "Tarzan And The Forbidden City", published by New English Library.

1976.

$7-9 ZDB

Kenneth Robson, "Doc Savage 1: The Man Of Bronze", published by Corgi Books.

1975

$12-14 ZDB

Richard Sapir & Warren Murphy, "The Destroyer 34: Chain Reaction", published by Corgi Books.

1980

$7-9 ZDB

Russell Thorndike, "Doctor Syn", published by Arrow Books, first published by Rich & Cowan in 1915.

1966

$22-28 ZDB

Russell Thorndike, "The Courageous Exploits of Dr Syn", published by An Arrow Adventure, first published by Rich & Cowan in 1939.

1959

$22-28 ZDB

Russell Thorndike, "The Further Adventures of Doctor Syn", published by Arrow Books, story first published in 1936.

1966

$22-28 ZDB

Russell Thorndike, "Doctor Syn Returns", published by Arrow Books.

1959

$22-28 ZDB

Edgar Wallace, "Penelope Of Polyantha", published by Hodder & Stoughton.

Wallace was one of the scriptwriters on the original King Kong film from 1933.

$22-28 ZDB

F. van Wyck Mason, "The Barbarians", published by Panther Books.

1958

$7-9 ZDB

"Affinity", published by the British Reader's Digest, June 1947.

$50-70 PCC

FIND OUT MORE...

The Mushroom Jungle – A History of Postwar Paperback Publishing, by Steve Holland, published by Zeon Books, 1997.

Huxford's Paperback Value Guide, by Sharon & Bob Huxford, published by Corgi Books, 2003.

Michael Bond, "More About Paddington", first edition, original cloth and dust jacket, chipping at head and foot of spine.

This is the second book featuring children's favourite Paddington Bear, the first was published the previous year.

1959

$450-550 BLO

Eoin Colfer, "Artemis Fowl", first edition, published by Viking, signed by the author and with a signed compliment slip.

2001

$220-280 BIB

Richmal Crompton, "William And The Monster", published by Armada Paperbacks.

1965

$7-9 ZDB

Cornelia Funke, "The Thief Lord", first English edition, published by Chicken House, signed by the author.

2002

$80-120 BIB

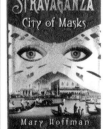

Jamila Gavin, "The Blood Stone", first edition, published by Egmont.

2003

$22-28 BIB

Roald Dahl, "Matilda", first edition, published by Jonathan Cape, London, signed by the author in the year of publication.

Signed copies of Dahl's books are scarce and the fact it was signed in the year of publication makes it more desirable.

1988

$3,500-4,500 BRB

Debi Gliori, "Deep Trouble", first edition, first printing, published by Doubleday, signed by the author.

2004

$25-35 BIB

Mary Hoffman, "Stravaganza - City of Masks", first edition, published by Bloomsbury.

2002

$22-28 BIB

BOOKS

Brian Jacques, "Redwall", first edition, double page map, with "Tales of Redwall" bookmark loosely inserted, original boards, dust jacket, a mint copy.

1986

$350-450 BLO

Brian Jacques, "Salamandastron", first edition, published by Hutchinson, London.

1992

$700-800 BIB

Capt. W.E. Johns, "Biggles and the Lost Sovereigns", first edition, published by the Brockhampton Press.

1964

$180-220 BIB

Roy McKie and P.D. Eastman, "Snow", first edition review copy, published by Random House, New York.

1962

$400-500 BRB

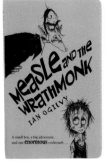

Ian Ogilvy, "Measle and the Wrathmonk", first edition, published by the Oxford Press, signed by the author.

2004

$22-28 BIB

Terry Pratchett, "The Amazing Maurice and His Educated Rodents", first edition, published by Doubleday, signed by the author.

2001

$25-35 BIB

A CLOSER LOOK AT A CHILDREN'S BOOK

This UK first edition would have been published in much smaller numbers than his later, better known titles such as the 'His Dark Materials' trilogy.

Count Karlstein is one of Pullman's earliest novels and his first children's novel.

Although not as well known as J.K. Rowling, Pullman's children's books also tend to be very popular with adults and his more recent works has won a number of awards.

A film of the first book from the 'His Dark Materials' trilogy in planned. Its release will increase the author's profile and should raise interest in collecting his books.

Philip Pullman, "The Broken Bridge", first edition, published by Macmillian, original pictorial wrappers, unattached sticker signed by the author loosely inserted.

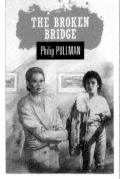

1990

$650-750 BLO

Philip Pullman, "Count Karlstein", first edition, original cloth, dust jacket, slight edge wear to upper margin with small tear at front, no loss or disruption to image.

1982

$1,200-1,800 BLO

Philip Pullman, "I Was a Rat! ... or The Scarlet Slippers", first edition, illustrations by Peter Bailey, original pictorial boards.
1999

$220-280 BLO

Philip Reeve, "Predator's Gold", first edition, published by Scholastic, signed by the author.
2003

$25-35 BIB

J.K. Rowling, "Harri Potter a Maen yr Athronydd", first Welsh edition of The Sorcerer's Stone, published by Bloomsbury, signed by the author.

A UK first edition copy of the English language version can be worth over $18,000.

2003

$35-45 BIB

Malcolm Saville, "Spring Comes To Nettleford", paperback published by Armada.
1971

$7-9 ZDB

Margery Sharp, "The Rescuers", first edition, published by Collins, London.
1959

$400-500 BRB

Paul Stewart and Chris Riddell, "Stormchaser", first edition, original boards, dust jacket.

This is the particularly scarce second book in the seven book series.

2000

$700-900 BLO

G.P. Taylor, "Shadowmancer", first special edition, published by Faber & Faber.

This special edition contains a previously unpublished final chapter.

2003

$28-32 BIB

E.B. White, "Charlotte's Web, first edition, published by Harper & Brothers, New York.
1952

$2,000-2,500 BRB

A Canadian redware waisted crock, from Ontario.

c1870   *8.5in (21.5cm) high*

$80-120   **RAON**

A Canadian redware three-litre crock, stamped "3L", from Ontario.

c1870   *7.75in (19.5cm) high*

$40-60   **RAON**

A rare Canadian Brantford Pottery flower pot, with attached tray, plain finish and glazed upper area, cracked.

As so much redware was utilitarian, it was either damaged, or broken and discarded. Flowerpots are not commonly seen. The production of redware began to decline from the 1880s as storage habits changed and other materials took over.

c1870   *4.75in (12cm) high*

$30-40   **RAON**

A Canadian Bennington Brantford Pottery bowl, with moulded exterior and brown and yellow speckled glaze, some rim chips.

The Brantford Pottery was founded in 1849 by American stoneware potter Justin Morton and grew to be one of the largest potteries in Canada. It produced slip-molded wares, such as this, from the 1850s.

c1895   *10.25in (26cm) diam*

$70-100   **RAON**

A Canadian Medalta stoneware three imperial gallon salt-glazed stoneware crock, stamped and "Medalta Potteries Ltd Medicine Hat, Alberta".

Crocks stamped with maker's names are usually more sought-after.

c1890   *12.25in (31cm) high*

$70-90   **RAON**

A Canadian Brantford Pottery earthenware pitcher, with molded foliate pattern and graduated glaze, impressed "BRANTFORD" on the base.

A very similar pitcher, in green, is shown on p247 of 'The Book of Canadian Antiques', Donald Blake Webster, 1974.

c1895   *6.75in (17cm) high*

$120-180   **ING**

A Wood & Sons 'Alpine White' Ironstone plate, transfer-printed to commemorate the centenary of the Confederation of Canada.

1967   *9.75in (25cm) diam*

$30-40   **RAON**

A 1930s ceramic plate, with a brown transfer print of the Town Hall, Port Perry, Ontario, and with 22ct gold highlights.

The Town Hall was built in 1873 and was recognized by Canada's Historic Sites and Monuments Board as an important historic building in 1996.

8.75in (22cm) diam

$30-40   **RAON**

A rare T. & R. Boote Sydenham Shape ironstone advertising plate, with transfer print reading "W.M. CHURCH McNab Street HAMILTON C.W.", with registered design mark for 1853.

'CW' stands for Canada West (later known as Ontario), which was created by the merger of Upper Canada and Lower Canada in 1840. This union paved the way for the later Confederation in 1867.

c1853   *8.5in (21.5cm) diam*

$70-90   **RAON**

A CLOSER LOOK AT A DEICHMANN BOWL

The form and glaze are simple with only minimal decoration and recall Scandinavian designs – both Erica and Kjell Deichmann were trained in ceramics in Denmark before moving to New Brunswick, Canada.

Kjell modeled the pieces, and Erica was responsible for glazes. The pottery had a reputation for its glazes; over 5,000 types were developed.

Considered pioneers in Canadian crafts, the Deichmanns were among Canada's first studio potters, operating a studio from 1935-63.

Pieces are usually marked on the base, typically with a stylised 'D'. Their work is becoming increasingly sought-after.

A Deichmann tapering bowl with semi-lustrous grey/cream glaze, inscribed on the base.

8.25in (21cm) diam

$250-350   **TCF**

An octagonal ceramic plate, transfer-printed in black with a named portrait of Edward Blake, minor chip to rim.

Dominick Edward Blake (1833-1912) was Premier of Ontario from 1871 to 1872 and leader of the Liberal Party of Canada from 1880 to 1887. He is the only federal Liberal leader never to have become Prime Minister of Canada.

$150-200   **SAS**

A 1940s/50s Royal Winton 'View Ware' souvenir plate for Newfoundland, with a transfer print of a seal.

This is part of a large number of ceramic souvenir wares produced by British maker Royal Winton and imported into Canada. Although images of major sights are found, so are many local views. This was due to the fact that the company would decorate as few as 12 dozen assorted pieces for a client who supplied a photograph of a view for the company to copy.

6in (15.5cm) wide

$20-30   **TFR**

A Wedgwood hand-painted commemorative plate for the town of Orillia, Ontario, showing the town's coat of arms.

Orillia's coat of arms was designed by the Scot W.S. Frost, Mayor of Orillia from 1911-12.

10in (25.5cm) diam

$70-100   **TFR**

A 1930s Shelley jug, with transfer print of an Royal Canadian Airforce plane, with "RCAF Trenton Canada" wording and "Designed exclusively for Blakeley's" printed on the base.

3.25in (8.5cm) high

$220-280   **TCF**

A pair of Beauce Pottery vases, marked "cb Canada 4003".

Beauceware (1943-89) was made in Quebec and is becoming increasingly sought-after. For more detail see 'Beauce Pottery' by Cogne, Dubé and Trepannier, published by Les Editions CIP.

7in (18cm) high

$40-60   **ING**

A Quebec Artcraft leaf-shaped dish, impressed "QuebecArtcraft 203/3".

Quebec Artcraft (c1947-c1950) was founded by Rudolph Elsterman in Sainte-Agathe-Des-Monts and produced pieces similar in style to Beauce.

15in (38cm) long

$30-40   **ING**

A Canadian 'Pattern' hooked rug, with scrolling and rose motifs, from Quebec.

A Canadian 'Freehand' hooked rug, using a stocking-type material, from Quebec.

The use of stocking-type material helps to date this rug to an earlier period.

Hooked rugs were made in Canada from the mid-19thC, with the earliest surviving example being from New Brunswick and dating to c1860. Broadly, there are two types, 'Pattern' rugs where the design was hooked through a printed pattern which could be followed, and 'Freehand' where the pattern was developed solely by the maker. As well as the type, the complexity of the design, colors, motifs, condition and age have a bearing on value.

A Canadian 'Freehand' hooked rug, using a stocking type material, from Quebec.

c1930-c1940 37in (94cm) long

$120-180   RAON

c1950   59in (150cm) long

$220-280   RAON

c1930-c1940 37in (94cm) long

$70-90   RAON

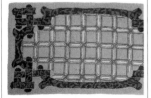

A Canadian 'Pattern' hooked rug from Eastern Ontario.

c1950   40.25in (102cm) long

$120-180   RAON

A 1980s Canadian 'Pattern' wool hooked runner rug, from Quebec.

50.5in (128cm) long

$70-80   RAON

A Canadian 'Pattern' hooked rug from New Brunswick.

The regularity and symmetry of the pattern helps identify this as the 'Pattern' rug.

c1950   32.75in (83cm) long

$50-70   RAON

A Canadian 'Freehand' hooked rug, made for the 1967 centenary of Canada.

Some of the motifs on this rug show the different nationalities living in Canada, such as the thistle for Scotland and native tipis and canoes, as well as the Canadian national symbol of the maple leaf and other symbols associated with Canada.

c1967   48.5in (123cm) long

$220-280

A Canadian wool 'Freehand' hooked rug, from Ontario, showing an Easter scene.

c1980   37.5in (95cm) long

$120-180   RAON

CANADIANA

A Canadian Nova Scotian 'Buttocks' woven basket, with pink painted finish.

This shape is known as 'buttocks' due to the double bulbous shape of the base.

c1950   13.75in (35cm) wide

$70-90   **RAON**

A Canadian Ontarian basket, with painted canes in stripes.

Baskets with original colour are sought-after, especially if the pattern is comparatively complex.

c1950   9in (23cm) wide

$30-40   **RAON**

A Canadian tribal tapering basket, with band of woven raffia.

c1930   9.5in (24cm) high

$25-35   **RAON**

A Canadian carved pine pumice box for sharpening knives, from Ontario.

The pumice is stored in the box. When it is needed, the box was taken off the wall, laid down and knives are sharpened on the extending part. Those that have been well-used have razor-thin back plates. Examine wear (or lack of it!) closely as reproductions are known, but it is hard to create the patina and wear correctly and together.

c1860   27.5in (70cm) high

$120-180   **RAON**

A late 19thC Canadian pine box, with a sliding lid over a smaller compartment, possibly a saleman's sample.

This piece retains its original paint, which was intended to brighten up daily life and is highly desirable as most furniture was stripped down in the 1960s when fashion favored stripped pine.

8in (20cm) long

$120-180   **ING**

A Canadian hand-forged cast iron boot jack, with decorative piercing.

c1880   13.75in (35cm) long

$70-90   **RAON**

A Canadian hand-forged cast iron boot jack, with two tear drop-shaped piercings.

c1880   12.25in (31cm) long

$70-90   **RAON**

A Canadian cast iron flat iron, moulded "WOODYATT GUELPH CANADA", from the Woodyatt foundry, Ontario.

6.5in (16.5cm) long

$12-18   **RAON**

A cast iron trivet for clipping on the side of a stove, with registered number 764765 for 1931.

c1932   4.75in (12cm) wide

$30-40   **RAON**

A Canadian 300th Anniversary of the Foundation of Canada bronze medal, by Henri Dubois, the obverse with Central figure of Jacques Cartier stepping from boat onto rock with crowns and cyphers of H.IV and E.VII either side, the reverse with female figures representing France and Great Britain sitting under maple tree, in extremely fine condition.

1908   *1.5in (3.5cm) diam*

$180-220   **BLO**

A CLOSER LOOK AT A HUDSON'S BAY BLANKET COAT

Blankets were introduced into the fur trade by the company in 1780 - although colors and patterns vary, this is the most recognisable and is often known as the 'traditional'.

Horizontal stripes are more common, vertical stripes are more unusual.

One of the best ways to date a blanket or coat is from the label - this label indicates a date from the early 1940s to the mid-1950s.

Look at the style, and for extra details such as peaked lapels, pocket flaps and buttons, as they can add value – here the buttons have been replaced.

A Hudson's Bay blanket double-breasted coat.

1941-55   *31in (79cm) high*

$70-100   **TYA**

A bronze medal commemorating the 60th anniversary of the Canadian Federation, by Raymonde Delamarre, the obverse with crowned bust of George V facing left, the reverse with central figure of Liberty with arms outstretched standing on tablet (dated 1867-1927) with map of Canada behind and wheat and maple leaves at her feet, in fine condition.

1927   *3in (7.5cm) diam*

$250-350   **BLO**

A 1950s reproduction Karl Rothammer Royal Canadian Mounted Police wooden plaque.

A noted wood carver and sculptor, particularly of religious items, Rothammer trained in Bavaria, Germany and emigrated to Canada in 1951.

13.25in (34cm) diam

$50-70   **TCF**

A molded silver-plated City Hall, Winnepeg souvenir spoon, with enameled shield and motto.

4.25in (11cm) long

$15-20   **TFR**

A silver-plated Windsor souvenir spoon, with molded terminal in the shape of a girl with a snowball and a maple leaf.

4.5in (11.5cm) long

$15-20   **TFR**

COLLECTORS' NOTES

■ The family-run Beswick pottery firm was set up by James Wright Beswick in 1894. Animal figures were made before 1900, but early pieces are hard to identify as the Beswick backstamp was only generally used from 1934; this was also when shape numbers began to be impressed in the base of figures.

■ Names of note include long-serving moldmaker and modeler Albert Hallam, who joined Beswick in 1926 aged 14, and decorating manager and art director James Hayward, who designed almost 3,000 decorations and patterns, and was instrumental in developing glazes. Arthur Gredington is probably Beswick's most famous designer. He is known for designing and making both realistic and stylized animal models.

■ Many models are available in different colorways and matte or gloss finishes. The value of a piece is often dependent upon the rarity of the colorway or finish, so invest in a specialist guide for detailed information. Certain ranges are prized, such as the Spirit horse collection, introduced in 1981 by Graham Tongue, and the accurately modeled Connoisseur range.

■ The firm was sold to Royal Doulton in 1969, but Beswick animals continued to be produced. In 1989 most animal models in production became 'Doulton Animals' and the pieces were issued with DA numbers. In 1999 Royal Doulton moved their range of animals, excepting limited editions, to the Beswick backstamp. The factory closed in 2002, and prices on the secondary market have consequently risen.

A Beswick 'King Eider Duck', 1521, designed by Colin Melbourne, from the Peter Scott Wildfowl series.

1958-71   *4in (10cm) long*

$180-280   **GORW**

A Beswick 'Mallard' small duck, 1518, designed by Arthur Gredington, first version.

The second version, made from 1962-71 is worth about two-thirds of this earlier version.

1958-62   *4.5in (11.5cm) wide*

$180-280   **GORW**

A Beswick large 'Goldeneye Duck', 1524, designed by Colin Melbourne, from the Peter Scott Wildfowl series.

1958-71   *6.5in (16.5cm) wide*

$200-300   **GORW**

A Beswick medium 'Pochard Duck', 1520, designed by Arthur Gredington, from the Peter Scott Wildfowl series.

1958-71   *4.5in (12cm) long*

$200-300   **GORW**

A Beswick 'Shoveler' duck, 1528, designed by Colin Melbourne, from the Peter Scott Wildfowl series.

1958-71   *3.5in (9cm) long*

$200-300   **GORW**

A Beswick 'Tufted Duck', 1523, designed by Colin Melbourne, from the Peter Scott Wildfowl series.

1958-71   *2.75in (7cm) long*

$180-280   **GORW**

A Beswick 'Widgeon Duck', 1526, designed by Colin Melbourne, from the Peter Scott Wildfowl series.

1958-71   *3.5in (9cm) long*

$150-200   **GORW**

A Beswick 'Grouse (pair)', 2063, designed by Albert Hallam.

1966-75   5.5in (14cm) high

$600-800   **PSA**

A Beswick 'Leghorn Cockerel', 1892, designed by Arthur Gredington.

1963-83   9in (23cm) high

$200-300   **PSA**

A Beswick 'Great Tit', 3274, designed by Martyn Alcock.

1990-95

$350-450   **PSA**

A Beswick 'Lapwing' figure, 2416A, designed by Albert Hallam, first version with split tail feathers.

The second version with the tail feathers together, made until 1982, is worth about 25 per cent less.

1972-unknown   5.5in (14cm) high

$400-500   **PSA**

A Beswick 'Lesser Spotted Woodpecker', 2420, designed by Graham Tongue.

1972-82   5.5in (14cm) high

$350-550   **PSA**

A Beswick 'Whitethroat', 2106A, designed by Graham Tongue, first version with mouth open and green mound base.

1967-73

$200-300   **PSA**

A Beswick 'Courting Penguins', 1015, designed by Arthur Gredington.

This model was produced in this traditional black and white colorway as well as a slightly more desirable blue version.

1945-65   5.5in (14cm) high

$300-400   **PSA**

A Beswick 'Penguin', 2357, designed by Albert Hallam, from the Fireside Model series.

As well as being unusually large, this figure would have been expensive in its day, meaning fewer are likely to have been sold.

A Beswick 'Penguin Chick Sliding', 2434, designed by Graham Tongue.

1971-76   12in (30.5cm) high

$1,200-1,500   **PSA**

1972-76   8in (20cm) long

$550-700   **PSA**

CERAMICS

A Beswick 'Girl on Jumping Horse', 939, designed by Arthur Gredington.

1941-65   *9.75in (24.5cm) high*

$550-700   **PSA**

A CLOSER LOOK AT A BESWICK HORSE AND RIDER

The pony was available on its own as Girl's Pony (1483) from 1957 to 1967.

Most other colours found are worth about 50 per cent of this example.

There are two variations to the shape as well, one with the girl down and one with her looking straight ahead. There is no difference in value.

The similar brown and white Skewbald version is the most common, and is worth about a tenth of this black and white version.

A Beswick 'Girl On A Pony', 1499, designed by Arthur Gredington, on rare Piebald (black and white) colourway pony.

1957-65

$6,500-8,000   **PSA**

A rare Beswick 'Cowboy on a Rodeo Horse' matt finish trial piece, made by Royal Doulton and decorated at the Beswick factory in the 1970s, unmarked.

$1,800-2,800   **PSA**

A Beswick 'Psalm with Ann Moore Up', 2535, designed by Graham Tongue, from the Connoisseur Horses series.

1975-82   *12.75in (32.5cm) high*

$600-800   **PSA**

A Beswick 'Boy On Pony', 1500, designed by Arthur Gredington, with Palomino pony.

The brown colorway is over twice as valuable, and other colors worth more than four times as much, as this Palomino example.

1957-76   *5.5in (14cm) high*

$500-600   **PSA**

A Beswick 'Cantering Shire', 975, designed by Arthur Gredington, in brown.

1943-89   *8.75in (22cm) high*

$70-100   **PSA**

A limited edition Beswick 'Przewalski's Wild Horse' figure, designed by Amanda Hughes-Lubeck, from an edition of 1,000 made exclusively for Sinclairs, boxed with certificate.

2005   *6.25in (16cm) high*

$200-300   **PSA**

A Beswick 'Shire Mare', 818, designed by Arthur Gredington, in Rocking Horse gray, first version without harness, slight restoration to one ear.

Unusually for an equine model, the rocking horse gray version is not one of the most valuable. Blue and iron gray are much rarer.

c1940-62

$800-1,200   **PSA**

CERAMICS

A Beswick 'Aberdeen Angus Cow', 1563, designed by Arthur Gredington, matt version.

The gloss version was introduced in 1959 and was retired at the same time as this matt example. The gloss version is worth about a third less.

1985-89   *4.5in (11cm) high*

$350-550   **PSA**

A Beswick 'Ayrshire Bull Ch. "Whitehill Mandate"', 1454B, designed by Colin Melbourne, second version with thick leg and tail.

1957-90   *5.25in (13.5cm) high*

$550-700   **GORW**

A Beswick 'Ayrshire Cow Ch. Ickham Bessie', 1350, designed by Arthur Gredington, matt version.

The gloss version was issued from 1954 and is worth about 25 per cent less than this matt version.

1985-89   *5in (12.5cm) high*

$350-500   **PSA**

Left: A Beswick 'Highland Calf', 1827D, designed by Arthur Gredington.

1962-90   *3in (7.5cm) high*

$100-150   **GORW**

Right: A Beswick 'Highland Cow', 1740, designed by Arthur Gredington.

1961-90   *5.25in (13.5cm) high*

$180-280   **GORW**

Left: A Beswick 'Fresian Calf', 1249C, designed by Arthur Gredington.

1956-97   *2.75in (7cm) high*

$100-150   **GORW**

Right: A Beswick 'Fresian Cow Ch. "Claybury Legwater"' 1362A, designed by Arthur Gredington.

1954-97   *4.5in (12cm) high*

$180-280   **GORW**

A Beswick 'Fresian Calf', 1249C, designed by Arthur Gredington, matt version.

1987-89   *2.75in (7cm) high*

$250-350   **PSA**

A Beswick 'Wessex Saddleback Sow "Merrywood Silver Wings 56tH"', 1511, designed by Colin Melbourne.

1957-69   *2.75in (7cm) high*

$700-900   **PSA**

A Beswick 'Middle White Boar', 4117, from the Rare Breeds series, boxed.

2001-02   *4in (10cm) high*

$50-90   **PSA**

A Beswick 'Nigerian Pot Bellied Pygmy Goat', G223, designed by Amanda Lughes-Lubeck.

1999-   *5.25in (14cm) high*

$20-40   **PSA**

A Beswick 'Greyhound "Jovial Roger"' figure, 972, designed by Arthur Gredington.

1942-90   *6in (15cm) long*

$70-90   **PSA**

A Beswick 'Whippet "Winged Foot Marksman of Allways"', 1786A, designed by Arthur Gredington, first version with tail curled between legs.

Designs were often changed to remove delicate, protuding parts, such as this dog's tail, which would have been prone to damage during manufacture. Today, earlier versions are usually more sought-after, as they are the original design, and are harder to find especially in undamaged condition. Compare this version to the second version to the right.

1961-unknown   *4.5in (12cm) long*

$200-300   **PSA**

A Beswick 'Whippet "Winged Foot Marksman of Allways"', 1786B, designed by Arthur Gredington, second version with tail attached to leg.

Unknown-1989   *4.5in (12cm) long*

$150-200   **PSA**

A Beswick large 'Corgi', 1299B, designed by Arthur Gredington.

The black version (1229A) available from 1953-82 is worth about twice this version.

1953-94   *5.5in (14cm) long*

$70-100   **PSA**

A Beswick 'Caught It', 2951, unknown designer, from the Playful Puppies series.

This figure was produced by Royal Doulton from 1934-85 as HN1097, which is worth about the same as the Beswick version.

1986-89   *2.75in (7cm) wide*

$50-70   **PSA**

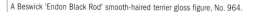

A Beswick 'Endon Black Rod' smooth-haired terrier gloss figure, No. 964.

$550-700   **PSA**

A Beswick 'Bull Terrier Romany Rhinestone' white figure, 970.

$80-120   **PSA**

CERAMICS

A Beswick 'Cheetah On Rock' figure, 2725, designed by Graham Tongue, with satin finish, from the Connoisseur series.

1981-89   *6.5in (16.5cm) high*

$300-400   **PSA**

A Beswick 'Seated Leopard', 841, designed by Arthur Gredington.

1940-c1954   *6.25in (16cm) high*

$700-900   **PSA**

A Beswick 'Lion On A Rock', 2554A, designed by Graham Tongue, satin finish, from the Connoisseur series.

This figure was also produced as 2554B in a gloss finish and without the base. It is worth about a third less than this example.

1975-84   *8.25in (21cm) high*

$180-280   **PSA**

A Beswick 'Siamese Cat', 1882, designed by Albert Hallam, from the Fireside Model series, seal point colorway.

The copper luster version, made only for export is the most desirable at nearly double the value of this colorway.

1963-89   *9.5in (24cm) high*

$120-180   **PSA**

A Beswick 'Siamese Cat – Climbing', 1677, designed by Albert Hallam.

1960-97   *6.5in (16.5cm) high*

$25-45   **PSA**

A Beswick 'Marlin', 1243, designed by Arthur Gredington, restored.

1952-70   *5.5in (14cm) high*

$550-700   **PSA**

A Beswick 'Barracuda', 1235, designed by Arthur Gredington.

1952-68   *4.75in (12cm) high*

$550-700   **PSA**

FIND OUT MORE...

Beswick Animals, *by Diana & John Callows and Marilyn & Peter Sweets, published by Charlton Press, 8th edition, 2005.*

COLLECTORS' NOTES

- Founded in 1894 to produce ornamental vases and other decorative objects, the John Beswick factory became known for its high quality character figures from the late 1940s. Talented ceramic artist Arthur Gredington joined the company to model finely realized animals, such as portraits of famous horses. In 1947, he began to mold characters from Beatrix Potter tales at the suggestion of Lucy Beswick, wife of the managing director, who had been inspired by a trip to the famous writer's home.

- Albert Hallam gradually took over from Gredington during the 1960s and continued to expand the range of Beatrix Potter characters. In 1968, he launched a 'Winnie the Pooh and the Blustery Day' series, based on the Disney cartoon. In 1975, Graham Tongue succeeded Hallam as head modeler and produced classic Beatrix Potter characters in new poses as well

as introducing 'double figures' such as 'Tabitha Twitchet and Miss Moppet'.

- Beswick's cartoon figures are becoming increasingly popular. Characters from David Hand's Animaland were produced from 1949 to 1955 and are extremely sought-after today. Introduced in 1968 following the release of the Disney cartoon, Winnie the Pooh has also become a favourite. A second series of Winnie the Pooh characters were introduced in 1996.

- Discontinued Beatrix Potter figures, and examples with early molds or color variations, attract the highest prices. Early and rare variations often have the desirable gold Beswick mark, used before 1972. Other popular ranges include Brambly Hedge, introduced in 1983, and the Snowman, produced between 1985 and 1994.

A Beswick 'Rupert Bear' figure, 2694, designed by Harry Sales, style one, from the Rupert Bear series.

This was the first figure released from the Rupert Bear series and the most desirable of the four of Rupert himself.

1980-86

$300-400   PSA

A Beswick 'Pong Ping' figure, 2711, designed by Harry Sales, from the Rupert Bear series.

1981-86   *4.25in (11cm) high*

$100-150   PSA

A Beswick 'Algy Pug' figure, 2710, designed by Harry Sales, from the Rupert Bear series.

1981-86   *4in (10cm) high*

$150-200   PSA

A Beswick 'Rupert Snowballing' figure, 2779, designed by Harry Sales, from the Rupert Bear series.

1982-86   *4.25in (11cm) high*

$400-500   PSA

A Beswick 'Bill Badger' figure, 2720, designed by Harry Sales, from the Rupert Bear series, style one.

1981-86   *2.75in (7cm) high*

$200-300   PSA

A Beswick 'A Good Read' figure, 2529, designed by David Lyttleton, from the Kitty MacBride series.

1975-83   *3.5in (9cm) high*

$100-150   PSA

A Beswick 'Winnie The Pooh' figure, 2193, designed by Albert Hallam, from the Winnie The Pooh series.

These figures are based on the Walt Disney cartoons, rather than the original illustrations by E.H. Shephard, although these did form the inspiration for the cartoons. All the figures are therefore marked "© Walt Disney Prod." on the base.

1968-90   *2.5in (6.5cm) high*

$50-70   **PSA**

A CLOSER LOOK AT A BESWICK CHARACTER FIGURE

Although virtually unknown today, the limited series of 'Animaland' animated short films was successful enough at the time for Beswick to release this series of animal figures based on the characters.

Hand previously worked for Walt Disney on projects including Bambi and Snow White & the Seven Dwarves.

The Animalands series was the first from Beswick to be based on a cartoon.

All the figures from the Animaland series are sought-after today.

A Beswick 'Loopy Hare' figure, 1156, designed by Arthur Gredington, from the David Hand's Animaland series.

1949-55   *4.25in (11cm) high*

$500-600   **PSA**

A Beswick 'Tigger' figure, 2394, designed by Graham Tongue, from the Winnie The Pooh series.

1971-90

$60-90   **PSA**

A Beswick 'Rabbit' figure, 2215, designed by Albert Hallam, from the Winnie The Pooh series.

1968-90   *3.25in (8.5cm) high*

$50-70   **PSA**

A Beswick 'Owl' figure, 2216, designed by Albert Hallam, from the Winnie The Pooh series.

1968-90   *3in (7.5cm) high*

$40-60   **PSA**

A Beswick 'Dusty Mole' figure, 1155, designed by Arthur Gredington, from the David Hands Animaland series.

1949-55   *3.5in (9cm) high*

$200-300   **PSA**

A Beswick 'Oscar Ostrich' figure, 1154, designed by Arthur Gredington, from David Hand's Animaland series.

1949-55   3.74in (9.5cm) high

$400-500   **PSA**

A Beswick Beatrix Potter figure 'Amiable Guinea-Pig', style one, designed by Albert Hallam, printed brown mark.

1967-83

$120-180   **WW**

A Beswick Beatrix Potter 'Anna Maria' figure, BP3b, modeled by Albert Hallam.

1974-83   *3in (7.5cm) high*

$100-150   **PSA**

A Royal Albert Beatrix Potter 'Babbity Bumble' figure, BP5, modeled by Warren Platt, boxed.

1989-93   *2.75in (7cm) high*

$200-300   **PSA**

A Beswick Beatrix Potter 'Benjamin Bunny', BP3, modeled by Arthur Gredington, first version with shoes and ears out.

1973-74   *4in (10cm) high*

$300-400   **GOR**

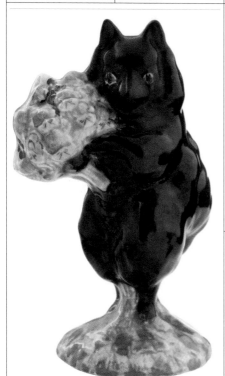

A Beswick Beatrix Potter 'Cecily Parsley' figure, BP2, modeled by Arthur Gredington, first version with head down, boxed.

1965-72   *4in (10cm) high*

$200-300   **PSA**

A Beswick Beatrix Potter 'Hunca Munca' figure, BP1, modeled by Arthur Gredington, style one.

1951-54   *2.75in (7cm) high*

$300-400   **PSA**

A rare Beswick Beatrix Potter 'Duchess' figure, BP2, modeled by Graham Orwell, style one holding flowers.

Duchess with flowers was the first Beatrix Potter figure to be retired and tended to be unpopular when on sale.

1955-67

3.75in (9.5cm) high

$1,500-2,000   **WW**

A Beswick Beatrix Potter 'Mr Alderman Ptolemy' figure, BP3b, modeled by Graham Tongue, boxed.

1974-85   *3.5in (9cm) high*

$60-90   **PSA**

A Beswick Beatrix Potter 'Mr Benjamin Bunny' figure, BP2, modeled by Arthur Gredington, first version with pipe out, boxed.

1971-72   *4.25in (11cm) high*

$200-300   **PSA**

CERAMICS

A Beswick Beatrix Potter 'Mr Jackson' figure, BP3a, modeled by Albert Hallam, first variation with green body, boxed.

1974   2.75in (7cm) high

$200-300   PSA

A Beswick Beatrix Potter 'Mrs Tiggy-Winkle' figure, BP2, modeled by Arthur Gredington, first version, second variation, boxed.

1972   3.25in (8.5cm) high

$120-180   PSA

A Royal Albert Beatrix Potter 'Old Mr Pricklepin figure, BP6, modeled by David Lyttleton.

This figure was also released with backstamp BP3 and, although earlier, is less desirable than this edition.

1989

$500-700   PSA

A Beswick Beatrix Potter 'Pig-Wig' figure, BP3a, modeled by Albert Hallam, boxed.

Although all versions are sought-after, the first version with backstamp BP2, is the most desirable. It can be easily identified by the grey colored body.

1973-88   4in (10cm) high

$150-200   PSA

A Beswick Beatrix Potter 'Simpkin' figure, BP3b, modeled by Alan Maslankowski, boxed.

This is the only backstamp that this figure was released with.

1975-83   4in (10cm) high

$300-400   PSA

A Beswick Beatrix Potter 'Sir Isaac Newton' figure, BP3b, modeled by Graham Tongue.

The size and color of this figure does vary, but the value is the same.

1974-84   3.75in (9.5cm) high

$200-300   PSA

A Beswick Beatrix Potter 'Susan' figure, BP3b, modeled by David Lyttleton, boxed.

Look for this figure with the Royal Albert backstamp, it can be worth upto six time more than this one.

1983-85   4in (10cm) high

$200-300   PSA

A Beswick Beatrix Potter 'Timmy Tiptoes' figure, BP2, modeled by Arthur Gredington, first version with red jacket.

1955-72   3.75in (9.5cm) high

$120-180   PSA

A Beswick Beatrix Potter figure 'Tommy Brock', BP3a, modeled by Graham Orwell, first version with spade handle out, first variation with small eye patches.

1973-74   3.5in (9cm) high

$80-120   WW

FIND OUT MORE...

Beswick Collectables, by Diana & John Callows and Hank Corley, published by The Charlton Press, 9th edition, 2005.

COLLECTORS' NOTES

■ The Brannam Pottery was founded in 1847 by Thomas Brannam in Barnstable, Devon, England and is still in production today. Along with many other 19thC potteries, such as Doulton, it initially made utility wares such as tiles and piping. In 1879, the pottery's most notable chapter began when Charles Brannam, Thomas' artistic son, who also worked at the pottery, eventually persuaded his father to allow him to design and produce art pottery.

■ The new range became very successful and in 1882, London department store Liberty & Co. became their sole agent. Grotesque and 'fantastical' animal designs, ranging from birds to dragons, were produced to much

acclaim into the 1930s. When Charles Brannam died in 1937, artistic direction was lost and the company moved into plainer domestic wares, which are not as desirable or as sought-after today.

■ Marks vary widely and can include the name 'Royal Barum Ware' registered in 1886, but in general, early marks are usually signed in script, often with a date. Initials usually indicate the skilled designers John Dewdney or William Baron. Large and visually appealing pieces, such as vases, tend to fetch the highest sums, but always look for typical designs and ideally the animal forms, for which the pottery became so well-known.

A C.H. Brannam jug, the pouring lip in the form of a fish, with sgraffito decoration in cream and blue against terracotta, incised marks and dated "1898".

1898	12in (30cm) high
$500-600	**GORL**

A C.H. Brannam cream and blue glazed vase, with three bird panels, incised marks and dated "1888".

1888	11in (28cm) high
$450-550	**GORL**

A large C.H. Brannam three-handled vase, decorated with sgraffito fish and pond flowers against a pitted ground, dated "1902", restored.

1902	7in (18cm) high
$400-500	**GORL**

A pair of C.H. Brannam novelty spill vases, modeled as a heron beside bamboo shoots.

	9.5in (24cm) high
$280-320	**GORL**

A pair of C.H. Brannam vases, with three handles, painted with scenes of Dutchmen running by a waterside, on blue ground.

	11in (28cm) high
$550-650	**B&H**

A C.H. Brannam for Liberty & Co. tyg, decorated with a fish in sgraffito, incised monogram and impressed mark.

	6in (15cm) diam
$150-200	**GORL**

A C.H. Brannam novelty chamberstick, modelled as a griffin holding a flowerhead, marked "Rd 44561" and dated.

1912	7in (18cm) high
$300-400	**GORL**

A C.H. Brannam puffin jug, with all-over green glaze, impressed marks.

	6.5in (16.5cm) high
$180-220	**GORL**

A C.H. Brannam four-piece wash set, each with a simple orange and white ground, impressed marks.

	Large bowl 15in (38cm) diam
$70-100	**GORL**

CERAMICS

COLLECTORS' NOTES

■ Carlton Ware was initially the trade name of Wiltshaw & Robinson Ltd of Stoke on Trent, England, which was established in 1890. Carlton Ware became the official company name for the pottery in 1958.

■ Inspired by Wedgwood's popular Fairyland Lustre range, designed by Daisy Makeig-Jones, Carlton Ware produced a range of lustrous and fanciful decorative wares. Popular with collectors today, the patterns were often influenced by Oriental, Egyptian and Persian designs, and were laid on rich, deeply colored grounds.

■ Another popular line was the 1930s molded range decorated with flowers, leaves and fruit against pastel grounds. Certain motifs and colors are scarce, as are some combinations. For example, Buttercup is easy to find in yellow, but much scarcer in pink.

■ The company also produced some striking designs in the 1950s and '60s, such as the 'Orbit' range. These later ranges, while not as valuable as the 1920s lustre pieces, are growing in popularity and value.

■ Carlton Ware fakes are on the market, so examine pieces closely and check the backstamp is appropriate for the item and its period of manufacture.

A Carlton Ware 'Lacecap Hydrangea' pattern tall vase, pattern no. 3967, designed by Violet Elmer, enameled and gilded on a red lustre ground, printed script mark, minor enamel loss.

This pattern can also be found on a pale green ground. Elmer was also responsible for the 'Bell', 'Explosions' and 'Fantasia' patterns for Carlton Ware.

c1937   8.5in (21.5cm) high

$700-900   **WW**

A Carlton Ware 'Honest' pattern sleeve vase, pattern no. 3278, shape no. 217.

6in (15cm) high

$80-120   **BAR**

A Carlton Ware Rouge Royale 'Mikado' pattern baluster vase.

12.5in (32cm) high

$100-150   **CA**

A 1930s Carlton Ware 'Hydrangea' pattern vase, with embossed decoration.

5in (12.5cm) high

$150-200   **BEV**

A Carlton Ware baluster vase, signed Geo. Roberts and dated 1922, painted with blue-tits amid blackberry canes, gilt rims, brown printed mark.

8.25in (21cm) high

$150-200   **BONR**

A Carlton Ware Chinoiserie small round bowl, the interior decorated with a Chinese river landscape.

$40-60   **LFA**

A Carlton Ware 'Swallow and Cloud' pattern ginger jar and cover, pattern no. 3073, with printed and painted marks.

8in (20cm) high

$300-400   **WW**

A Carlton Ware Chinoiserie jardinière, decorated with Oriental figures in a landscape, printed mark.

During the 1920s and '30s Carlton Ware produced a wide range of patterns on the Oriental theme, known collectively as Chinoiserie. The first pattern was 'Kang Hsi' in c1916. Certain motifs and decorations were copied across the different patterns, sometimes making it difficult to tell one pattern from another. Look for characteristics, such as two lovebirds in flight as seen on the Mikado pattern, and study the pattern on larger pieces to see it in full.

6in (15cm) high

$80-120   **WW**

A CLOSER LOOK AT A CARLTON WARE BOWL

This pattern was designed at the height of the West's fascination of all things Egyptian, following Howard Carter's discovering of Tutankhamen's tomb in Egypt in 1922.

Egyptian Fan' was also produced on mottled red, and dark blue ground.

The delicate, protruding feet and handles are easily damaged – undamaged examples such as this one command a premium.

Although the form is not particularly Egyptian, it displays the pattern well due to its large surface and ornate form.

A Carlton Ware 'Egyptian Fan' pattern pedestal bowl, pattern no. 3698, printed and painted in colors and gilt, printed mark.

Look for the range of commemorative 'Tutankhamen' wares produced by Carlton Ware not long after the tomb's discovery, as they are sought-after by collectors.

12.5in (31.5cm) wide

$800-1,200   **WW**

A Carlton Ware 'Tutankhamen' pattern bowl, printed and enameled in colors and gilt, printed marks.

5.5in (14cm) diam

$400-500   **WW**

A Carlton Ware 'Heron and Magical Tree' pattern bowl, pattern no. 4160, designed by Rene Pemberton, shape no. 1577, painted script mark.

c1938   10.5in (26.5cm) wide

$500-600   **WW**

A Carlton Ware 'Hollyhocks' pattern circular bowl, pattern no. 3973, printed and painted marks.

10in (25cm) diam

$150-200   **L&T**

A Carlton Ware 'Bird of Paradise' pattern square serving dish, decorated with a paradise bird, printed and painted marks.

9.75in (24cm) wide

$320-380   **L&T**

A Carltonware 'Cubist Butterfly' pattern square dish, pattern no. 3195.

Also produced on a red, blue and green ground.

11.25in (28.5cm) wide

$120-180   **BAD**

CERAMICS

A Carlton Ware 14-piece coffee set, each piece with a green ground and scrolling bands, the saucers in brown.

$70-100   **SWO**

A 1950s Carlton Ware hand-painted 'Windswept' pattern asymmetric mustard pot.

4in (10cm) wide

$20-30   **BAD**

A rare 1960s Carlton Ware 'Orbit' pattern gravy boat and tray.

The Orbit pattern, together with the Windswept pattern also on this page, are typical of 1960s design, with the bold use of color using a limited palette, and simple, stylized decoration, clearly influenced by the space race.

Tray 6in (15cm) diam

$80-120   **BAD**

A Carlton Ware Walking ware 'seated' soup bowl and cover.

The popular Walking Ware range was developed by Roger Mitchell and Danka Napiorkowska in 1974 and comprised a complete tea service. The range expanded to include 'running' and 'sitting' and pieces were also produce at the Mitchell's own Lustre studio. Today the range is produced by the Price Kensington pottery.

5.5in (14cm) high

$60-80   **BAD**

A Carlton Ware 'Lucy May' novelty tea pot, modelled as a bi-plane, printed Carlton Ware mark.

c1985   *6in (15cm) high*

$150-200   **WW**

A Carlton Ware 'Red Baron' novelty teapot, modelled as a bi-plane.

Part of a series of novelty teapots, including the green 'Lucy May' seen on this page and a blue 'Blue Max'. Fakes are being produced but do not have the name or the plane motifs on the nose.

8.25in (21cm) long

$220-280   **BAD**

A Carlton Ware 'Humpty Dumpty' musical jug, printed mark, paint wear, movement not working.

8in (20cm) high

$200-250   **WW**

A Carlton Ware 'Glacielle Ware' figure, modeled as a seated terrier, unmarked.

Glacielle Ware range was developed at Carlton Ware in the 1920s by a former Sevrès potter. Due to its high retail price it proved unpopular with the buying public and was withdrawn from production after six months.

7.25in (18.5cm) high

$200-250   **WW**

A Carlton Ware earthenware molded model of an English blue roan spaniel.

4.25in (11cm) high

$70-100   **BIG**

FIND OUT MORE...

Collecting Carlton Ware, by David Serpell, published by Krause Publications, 1999.

Collecting Carlton Ware, by Francis Joseph & Francis Salmon, published by Kevin Francis Publishing, 1994.

COLLECTORS' NOTES

- Clarice Cliff (1899-1972) was born in the potteries town of Tunstall, Staffordshire, England. She joined A.J Wilkinson's of Burslem in 1916, after studying and working for a local pottery from 1912. The pottery was impressed with her skill and soon promoted her to a position of more influence and artistic control.

- In 1925, managing director Colley Shorter gave Cliff her own studio. It was based in the newly purchased Newport Pottery, which had a large stock of defective blank wares, many in old-fashioned shapes. Cliff was encouraged to experiment, and to hide the faults in the blanks, covered them in brightly colored and thickly applied patterns. This new range, named 'Bizarre', was launched in 1928 and proved so successful that the entire pottery was moved over to its production. The similar 'Fantasque' line was launched in 1928.

- Over time, both the 'Bizarre' and 'Fantasque' range developed, with patterns becoming more elaborate, abstract and bold. By 1935 both the ranges had been phased out.

- Cliff continued designing when the pottery restarted after WWII, but her designs were not as popular with the public. Cliff sold the pottery to Midwinter after Shorter, by now Cliff's husband, died in 1963.

- Today, collectors look for Art Deco patterns in Cliff's trademark bright colors, which are thickly applied with visible brushstrokes. Large plates, jugs and vases are popular as they display the pattern well. Atypical patterns and muted colors are less desirable.

- Fakes and reproductions do exist, so always buy from a reputable source. Crude painting, as opposed to Cliff's hallmark visible brushstrokes, smudges, and thickly applied and uneven glazes could indicate a fake.

A Clarice Cliff Bizarre 'Acorn' pattern vase, shape 602.

This pattern is quite hard to find as it was only made during 1934.

1934   6.75in (17cm) high

$300-400   GHOU

A Clarice Cliff Banded ware 'Bonjour' shape Honeyglaze teapot and sugar bowl, printed registration mark only, No.776243.

Introduced 1937

$100-150   CHEF

A Clarice Cliff Bizarre 'Pastel Autumn' pattern conical sugar sifter.
1930-34   5.5in (14cm) high

$1,500-2,000   GHOU

A Clarice Cliff Fantasque 'Red Autumn' pattern side plate.

Red was the first version of this pattern to be released.

1930-34   5.5in (14cm) wide

$350-550   GHOU

A Clarice Cliff Fantasque Bizarre 'Berries' pattern tankard coffee pot and cover.

1930-32   7.5in (19cm) high

$800-1,000   GHOU

A Clarice Cliff Fantasque Bizarre 'Berries' pattern Leda shape plate.

1930-32

9in (23cm) diam

$500-600   GHOU

A Clarice Cliff Bizarre 'Blue W' pattern octagonal side plate.

1929-30

5.75in (14.5cm) diam

$600-800 **GHOU**

A Clarice Cliff Bizarre 'Orange Bridgwater' pattern Bonjour shape preserve pot and cover.

1934 4in (10cm) high

$600-800 **GHOU**

A Clarice Cliff Bizarre 'Yellow Branch and Squares' pattern bowl.

Introduced 1930 7.5in (19cm) diam

$600-800 **GHOU**

A Clarice Cliff Fantasque Bizarre 'Bobbins' pattern vase, shape 342.

1931-33 8in (20cm) high

$1,000-1,500 **GHOU**

A Clarice Cliff 'Cabbage Flower' pattern Bizarre vase, shape 602.

1934 6.75in (17cm) high

$600-800 **GHOU**

A Clarice Cliff Fantasque Bizarre 'Orange Chintz' sandwich tray, printed mark.

Introduced 1932 11.5in (29cm) wide

$250-450 **WW**

A Clarice Cliff Bizarre 'Blue Chintz' pattern Stamford teapot, cover restored.

This popular pattern was also produced in orange and in green, the latter is rare.

Introduced 1932 5in (12.5cm) high

$700-1,000 **GHOU**

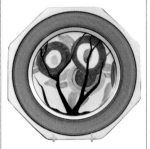

A Clarice Cliff Fantasque 'Circle Tree' pattern octagonal plate, printed marks.

1920-30 9.5in (24cm) wide

$800-1,000 **SWO**

A Clarice Cliff Fantasque 'Circle Tree' pattern octagonal plate.

1929-30 9.5in (24cm) diam

$800-1,000 **GHOU**

A Clarice Cliff Fantasque 'Comets' pattern plate.
1929-30   8.75in (22cm) diam
$600-800   **GHOU**

A Clarice Cliff 'Crocus' bowl, with printed mark in green.
7.75in (19.5cm) diam
$100-150   **GORL**

A Clarice Cliff Bizarre 'Autumn Crocus' pattern Bonjour shape preserve pot and cover.
1928-63   4in (10cm) high
$400-500   **GHOU**

A Clarice Cliff 'Autumn Crocus' pattern Bizarre candlestick, early painted green mark, shape 310.
1928-63   3in (7.5cm) high
$450-650   **GHOU**

A CLOSER LOOK A CLARICE CLIFF SUGAR SIFTER

Conical sugar sifters are a popular shape and are highly recognisable Cliff designs.

The tips of these sugar sifters are often damaged. The value would have been greater if it had not been restored.

This is the same pattern, but in a different colorway, as 'Devon' and 'Moonlight'.

The Moonlight colorway, with blue and pink trees and orange trunks, is the hardest to find.

A Clarice Cliff Bizarre 'Cornwall' pattern conical sugar sifter, tip restored.
Introduced 1933   5.5in (14cm) high
$1,000-1,500   **GHOU**

A Clarice Cliff 'Blue Crocus' pattern conical salt pot, lacks factory mark.
Introduced 1935   3.25in (8.5cm) high
$200-300   **GHOU**

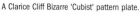

A Clarice Cliff Bizarre 'Cubist' pattern plate.
1929-30   8.75in (22cm) diam
$500-700   **GHOU**

A Clarice Cliff 'Diamonds' partial pattern Bizarre circular ashtray.

4.5in (11.5cm) diam

$300-400 GHOU

A Clarice Cliff Fantasque Bizarre 'Farmhouse' pattern conical jug.

1931 *6in (15cm) high*

$1,000-1,500 GHOU

A Clarice Cliff Bizarre 'Delecia' ware stepped candlestick, shape 391.

The Delecia range was originally just decorated with a thin wash of color, which was then covered in enamel color diluted with turpentine and allowed to run randomly over the piece. The effect was later combined with patterns such as Poppy, Citrus and Nasturtium.

3.5in (9cm) high

$350-550 GHOU

A Clarice Cliff 'Feathers and Leaves' pattern Fantasque fluted side plate.

6in (15cm) diam

$250-450 GHOU

A Clarice Cliff Fantasque Bizarre 'Coral Firs' pattern conical sugar sifter.

1933-38 *5.5in (14cm) high*

$800-1,000 GHOU

A Clarice Cliff Bizarre 'Blue Firs' pattern conical cup and saucer.

Rarer than the Coral version, the blue color caused problems during firing and the colorway was only produced during 1933.

1933 *Cup 2.25in (5.5cm) high*

$800-1,000 GHOU

A Clarice Cliff 'Football' pattern Bizarre biscuit barrel and cover with wicker swing handle, shape 335.

Introduced in 1929 *6in (15cm) high*

$1,500-3,000 GHOU

A Clarice Cliff 'Fruitburst' pattern Fantasque Bizarre plate.

10in (25.5cm) diam

$500-700 GHOU

A Clarice Cliff Fantasque Bizarre 'Orange Gardenia' pattern plate.

Introduced 1931

10in (25.5cm) diam

$500-700 GHOU

A Clarice Cliff Bizarre 'Gibraltar' pattern plate.

Introduced 1931

9in (23cm) diam

$1,000-1,500   **GHOU**

A Clarice Cliff Fantasque Bizarre plate 'House and Bridge', painted in colors, printed mark.

1931-35   9in (22.5cm) diam

$500-600   **WW**

A Clarice Cliff Fantasque Bizarre 'Orange House' pattern octagonal plate.

This is a rarer version of the 'Green House' pattern.

Introduced 1930

8.5in (21.5cm) wide

$1,500-2,000   **GHOU**

A Clarice Cliff Bizarre 'Honolulu' pattern biscuit barrel, shape 336.

'Rudyard' is an alternative colorway of this pattern.

Introduced 1933   6.5in (16.5cm) high

$1,500-2,500   **GHOU**

A Clarice Cliff Bizarre 'Latona Floral' pattern Dover jardinière.

1929-30   6in (15cm) high

$1,500-2,000   **GHOU**

A Clarice Cliff Bizarre 'Latona Pink Tree' pattern stepped vase, shape 369.

1929-30 7.75in (19.5cm) high

$1,500-2,500   **GHOU**

A Clarice Cliff 'Liberty' Havre shape bowl, printed and painted marks.

The name 'Liberty' refers to the fact that the paintresses were at liberty to decorate these banded bowls in any colors they liked. These simple designs were usually produced to bulk out orders as they were quick and easy to produce.

1929-34

$200-300   **CHEF**

A Clarice Cliff Fantasque Bizarre 'Limberlost' pattern Daffodil shape bowl, shape 475.

1932   12.5in (31.5cm) wide

$700-900   **GHOU**

A Clarice Cliff 'Lorna' pattern single-handled Lotus jug.

1936   11.5in (29cm) high

$800-1,000   **GHOU**

CERAMICS

A Clarice Cliff Bizarre 'Luxor' pattern Drum shape preserve pot and cover.

1929-30   *2.75in (7cm) high*

$600-800   **GHOU**

A Clarice Cliff Fantasque Bizarre 'Melon' pattern octagonal plate.

1930-32   *8.5in (21.5cm) wide*

$700-900   **GHOU**

A Clarice Cliff Fantasque 'Melon' pattern bowl.

This orange colorway is the most common, it was also produced in pastel, red, green and blue.

1930-32   *8.5in (21.5cm) diam*

$450-650   **GHOU**

A Clarice Cliff Bizarre 'Mondrian' pattern side plate.

There are a number of color variations to this pattern, it is also very similar to Cubist and Orange Blue Squares.

Introduced 1929   *5.75in (14.5cm) diam*

$600-800   **GHOU**

A Clarice Cliff Bizarre 'New Flag' pattern beehive preserve and cover, printed mark.

1929   *4in (10cm) high*

$450-650   **WW**

A Clarice Cliff Fantasque Bizarre 'Moonlight' pattern Bonjour shape sugar sifter.

Introduced 1932   *5in (12.5cm) high*

$1,000-1,500   **GHOU**

A pair of Clarice Cliff Bizarre 'My Garden' vases, shape 685, one with crack to rim.

'My Garden' is a range of shapes, each with the same molded flower decoration and painted in a range of colors. The range was not very original and is not particularly sought-after today.

Introduced 1934

$100-150   **DNT**

A Clarice Cliff 'Moonlight' pattern jug, shape 563, with printed marks and facsimile signature.

Introduced 1932   *9in (23cm) high*

$600-800   **SWO**

A Clarice Cliff Fantasque Bizarre 'New Fruit' pattern square ashtray.

This pattern is also referred to as 'Apples'.

1931-32   *4.75in (12cm) diam*

$350-450   **GHOU**

A Clarice Cliff Fantasque Bizarre 'Blue Newport' pattern conical sugar sifter.

1934   5.5in (14cm) high

$700-900   GHOU

A Clarice Cliff Bizarre 'Oranges and Lemons' pattern circular ashtray.

1931-32   5in (12.5cm) diam

$300-400   GHOU

A Clarice Cliff 'Original Bizarre' vase, shape 265.

c1928   6in (15cm) high

$800-1,000   GHOU

A Clarice Cliff 'Original Bizarre' Isis shape vase.

c1928   9.5in (24cm) high

$800-1,000   GHOU

A CLOSER LOOK AT A CLARICE CLIFF GLOBE VASE

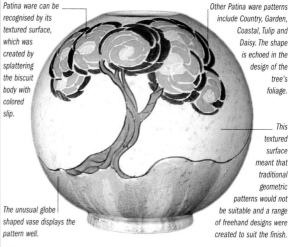

Patina ware can be recognised by its textured surface, which was created by splattering the biscuit body with colored slip.

Other Patina ware patterns include Country, Garden, Coastal, Tulip and Daisy. The shape is echoed in the design of the tree's foliage.

This textured surface meant that traditional geometric patterns would not be suitable and a range of freehand designs were created to suit the finish.

The unusual globe shaped vase displays the pattern well.

A Clarice Cliff Bizarre 'Patina Tree' pattern globe vase, shape 370.

1932-33   6in (15cm) high

$2,000-3,500   GHOU

A Clarice Cliff Bizarre 'Delecia Pansies' pattern conical sugar sifter, restored.

1932-34   5.5in (14cm) high

$450-650   GHOU

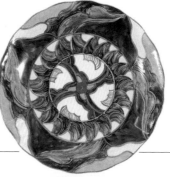

An early Clarice Cliff 'Persian' pattern plate, printed and painted mark, impressed 1927 date mark.

1927   9in (23cm) diam

$1,500-2,000   GHOU

CERAMICS

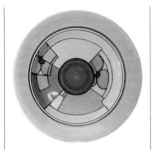

A Clarice Cliff Bizarre plate.

This is possibly a variation of 'Orange Picasso Flower'.

10in (25.5cm) diam

$600-800 GHOU

A Clarice Cliff 'Red Picasso Flower' pattern vase, shape 356.

This pattern was originally known as Red Flower.

4.5in (11.5cm) high

$2,000-3,000 GHOU

A Clarice Cliff Bizarre 'Orange Picasso Flower' pattern vase, shape 361.

1930 8.25in (21cm) high

$1,500-2,000 GHOU

A Clarice Cliff Fantasque Bizarre 'Poplar' pattern beehive honey pot and cover.

1930 3in (7.5cm) high

$600-800 GHOU

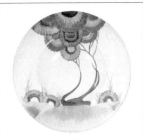

A Clarice Cliff Bizarre 'Rhodanthe' pattern wall charger.

Introduced 1934 18in (45.5cm) diam

$1,000-1,500 GHOU

A Clarice Cliff Bizarre 'Rudyard' pattern poppy bowl, rim restored.

The poppy bowl was probably a 1920s Newport factory shape that was used for Bizarre and phased out in the early 1930s.

1933-34 12in (30.5cm) diam

$1,000-1,500 GHOU

A Clarice Cliff Bizarre 'Sliced Fruit' pattern Coronet shape jug.

1930 7in (18cm) high

$450-650 GHOU

A Clarice Cliff Bizarre 'Rhodanthe' pattern vase, shape 358.

Introduced 1934 8in (20cm) high

$500-700 GHOU

A Clarice Cliff Fantasque Bizarre 'Secrets' pattern Havre shape bowl, printed mark.

7.5in (18.5cm) diam

$200-300 WW

A Clarice Cliff 'Sliced Circle' pattern Bizarre plate.

1929   *10in (25.5cm) diam*

$800-1,000   **GHOU**

A Clarice Cliff 'Stile and Trees' pattern pedestal bowl, printed mark.

c1937

$200-350

12in (30.5cm) diam

WW

A Clarice Cliff Fantasque Bizarre 'Summerhouse' pattern octagonal bowl.

This pattern is also used for the 'Café au Lait' range.

1931-33   *8.5in (21.5cm) diam*

$600-800   **GHOU**

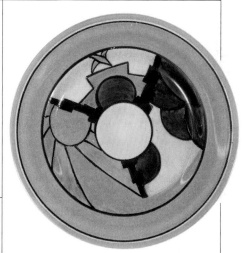

A Clarice Cliff Bizarre 'Sunray' pattern plate.

1929-30   *9in (23cm) diam*

$1,000-1,500   **GHOU**

A Clarice Cliff Bizarre 'Sunray' pattern candlestick, shape 310.

1929-30   *3in (7.5cm) high*

$800-1,000   **GHOU**

A Clarice Cliff Fantasque 'Green Sunrise' pattern vase, shape 341, rim restored.

1929   *5.5in (14cm) high*

$800-1,000   **GHOU**

A Clarice Cliff Bizarre 'Tennis' pattern Havre shape bowl.

1930   *8in (20cm) diam*

$800-1,000   **GHOU**

A Clarice Cliff Bizarre 'Tralee' pattern Gaiety shape basket.

1935-36   *14in (35.5cm) high*

$700-900   **GHOU**

A Clarice Cliff Bizarre 'Tennis' pattern plate.

c1930   *10in (25.5cm) diam*

$1,000-1,500   **GHOU**

A Clarice Cliff Fantasque Bizarre orange 'Trees and House' pattern Leda plate.

Orange is by far the most common colorway for this pattern, although it was initially produced in red.

Introduced 1930

8in (20cm) diam

$700-900   **GHOU**

A Clarice Cliff Fantasque 'Umbrellas and Rain' pattern Meiping vase, restored.

Introduced 1929

12in (30.5cm) high

$700-900   **GHOU**

A Clarice Cliff 'Viscaria' pattern Leda plate.

This is the pink colorway of the Rhodanthe pattern.

1934-36   9in (23cm) wide

$200-300   **GORL**

A rare Clarice Cliff Fantasque 'Triangular Flowers' pattern vase, shape 342, printed gold backstamp.

7.75in (19.5cm) high

$2,500-3,500   **GHOU**

A Clarice Cliff Fantasque Bizarre 'Windbells' pattern wall plate.

1933-34   10in (25.5cm) diam

$800-1,000   **GHOU**

A Clarice Cliff Bizarre circular ashtray, shape 503, painted with bands in shades of orange, blue, green and black.

4.5in (11.5cm) diam

$120-180   **GHOU**

A Clarice Cliff ashtray, shape 902, the top decorated with a house and a tree.

4in (10cm) diam

$100-150   **CA**

A Clarice Cliff Fantasque Bizarre 'Windbells' pattern conical sugar sifter, tip restored.

1934-35   5.5in (14cm) high

$800-1,000   **GHOU**

FIND OUT MORE...

www.claricecliff.com – *The Clarice Cliff Collectors' Club website.*

www.claricecliff.co.uk

Comprehensively Clarice Cliff, *by Greg Slater and Jonathan Brough, published by Thames & Hudson, 2005.*

Clarice Cliff – The Bizarre Affair, *by Leonard Griffin and Louis K. & Susan Pear Meisel, published by Thames & Hudson, 2000.*

COLLECTORS' NOTES

■ Susie Cooper (1902-95) ranks alongside Clarice Cliff as one of the key 20thC British ceramics designers. She began working as a paintress at A.E. Gray & Co. Ltd in 1922 before founding her own company in 1929. In 1931 she worked from the Crown Works at Woods & Sons in Burslem, England, initially using their shapes before designing her own from 1932. The Crown Works closed in 1979.

■ Her highly recognisable 1920s-30s Art Deco shapes and patterns are the most sought-after and are typified by stylized flowers or geometric patterns in bold colors. Her gentle floral designs from the late 1940s and 1950s are popular but do not fetch as high prices. In 1950, Cooper acquired a bone china factory and began to produce in bone china. These tend to be the least valuable, but reflect design tastes of the period well and represent an affordable entry point to her designs.

A Susie Cooper Falcon shape teapot, with a printed star pattern and molded "42" and painted "1680" to base.

c1939   *8.25in (21cm) high*

$150-200   **BAD**

A Susie Cooper Productions Kestrel shape coffee set, comprising coffee pot, three cups, five saucers and a milk jug, with ochre and black banded pattern.

c1933   *Teapot 7.5in (19cm) high*

$250-450   **ING**

A Susie Cooper 'Printemps' pattern milk jug, marked "2205" and impressed "42" on the base.

4.25in (11cm) high

$80-120   **BAD**

A Susie Cooper Productions 'Patricia Rose' pattern jug.

6.25in (16cm) wide

$70-100   **BAD**

A 1930s-50s Susie Cooper 'Dresden Spray' pattern 29-piece part dinner service, comprising: dinner, dessert, side plates and soup bowls, tureen and cover.

$300-400   **SWO**

A Susie Cooper Production platter, with foliate design and graduated pink rim.

$50-80   **BAD**

A Susie Cooper printed 'Wild Strawberry' pattern Quail shape bone china trio set.

c1958   *Plate 6.5in (16.5cm) diam*

$70-100   **BAD**

A Crown Devon Lustrine 'Summer' pattern lustre vase, by S. Fieldings & Co.

Simon Fielding formed S. Fielding & Co. in the early 1870s. It was renamed the Devon Pottery in 1912, but is better known by its trade name Crown Devon.

9.5in (24cm) high

$150-250   **BAD**

A Crown Devon luster ginger jar, painted by D. Cole, with enameled ship at sea pattern, signed by the artist.

7in (17.5cm) high

$220-280   **BAD**

A Crown Devon 'Orient' pattern coffee pot and cover, pattern 2115, printed and painted marks.

8.25in (21cm) high

$500-600   **WW**

A 1930s Crown Devon earthenware vase, of ovoid form decorated with orange, yellow and silver grey lozenges.

7.5in (19cm) high

$70-100   **BIG**

A Crown Devon 'Stockholm' pattern Karen shape bowl, designed by Bill Kemp.

The green colourway is known as Greenland.

Introduced 1955   8.75in (22.5cm) diam

$50-70   **BAD**

A Crown Devon 'Stockholm' Karen shape sugar sifter, with designed by Bill Kemp, leaping gazelle.

Introduced 1955   4.25in (12cm) high

$100-150   **BAD**

A 1950s Crown Devon 'Oceania' pattern moulded and painted salt pot.

5.5in (14cm) high

$10-20   **MTS**

A late 1970s Crown Devon 'Curry' storage jar, with wooden lid and printed decoration.

4.25in (11cm) high

$22-28   **MTS**

A Crown Devon 'Memphis' vase, by Colin Melbourne, with signature and impressed "CM", restored.

Sculptor and designer Colin Melbourne worked with a number of potteries, perhaps most significantly with Beswick, for who he produced his CM range. Other potteries include Midwinter, Royal Norfolk and Bossons. He was head of Ceramics at the Burslem School of Art from 1958-86 and he formed the Drumlanrig Melbourne design consultancy with Lord Queensberry in 1954. His work is sought-after today.

8.25in (21cm) high

$35-55   **GAZE**

A Doulton Lambeth stoneware teapot and cover, by Hannah Barlow, incised with dogs hunting a deer.

Hannah Barlow is one of Doulton's most popular of stoneware artists and is renowned for her animal designs.

4.5in (11cm) high

$1,000-1,500 WW

A Doulton Lambeth stoneware milk jug, by Hannah Barlow, incised with grazing deer, silver mount to rim.

3.5in (8.5cm) high

$800-1,200 WW

A Royal Doulton 'Huntsman' series water jug, D2778.

7in (18cm) high

$70-100 PSA

A Royal Doulton 'Titanian' glaze Egyptian tea caddy, D4263.

This range was released in 1924 to commemorate the opening of Tutankhamen's tomb.

1924-c1930 5in (13cm) high

$100-150 PSA

A Royal Doulton 'Flambé Veined' oviform vase, decorated with high-temperature glazes, printed mark and number "1619".

11.5in (29cm) high

$250-350 DN

A limited edition Royal Doulton 'Treasure Island' jug, designed by Charles J. Noke and Harry Fenton, from an edition of 600, with printed factory mark.

1934 7.75in (19.5cm) high

$1,000-1,500 GHOU

A Royal Doulton 'Lobster Man' large toby jug, D6617, designed by David B. Biggs.

1968-71

$100-150 KCS

A Royal Doulton coffee can and saucer, with a hand-painted floral design.

4.5in (11.5cm) diam

$60-80 BAD

A Royal Doulton hand-painted bud vase, impressed "7349" and printed "DS4971".

3.75in (9.5cm) high

$60-80 BAD

COLLECTORS' NOTES

■ Doulton had produced figurines during the 19th century, but the first Doulton figurines as we recognise them were launched in 1913 by the company's Art Director Charles Noke.

■ Many people choose to collect by type such as 'fair ladies', children or literary and historical characters. Ranges such as 'Dickens' and 'The Lord of the Rings' remain popular. Others collect by period or artist. Leslie Harradine, Mary Nicoll, Bill Harper and Peggy Davies – who spent 40 years with Royal Doulton and produced about 250 different figures – all have their own distinctive style and a significant following.

■ Over 4,000 different models and color variations are known to exist. A figure may have been produced in a number of different colorways, and each variation has an allocated 'HN' number. Each colorway is often worth a different amount, usually depending on rarity and length of production time.

■ Pieces without a 'Made In England' reference mark on the base are usually pre-1920 and can be rare and valuable. Figurines discontinued before WWII are also sought after, as are those produced for short periods of time. Figurines produced continuously for long periods like 'The Balloon Man', or those that are still in production today tend to be less desirable.

■ Condition directly contributes to value. Chips, cracks and restoration reduce value considerably, so examine all examples carefully. Take care when handling or cleaning – use a small soft brush to dust figurines and avoid getting water inside pieces.

A Royal Doulton 'A Country Lass' figurine, HN1991A, designed by Leslie Harradine.

This was first released as 'Market Day' HN1991 from 1947-55, which can be worth 20 per cent more than this example.

1975-81 7.25in (18.5cm) high

$150-250   **L&T**

A Royal Doulton 'Autumn' figurine, HN2085, designed by Margaret Davies, style two from The Seasons series.

1952-59   7.5in (19cm) high

$200-300   **L&T**

A Royal Doulton 'A Winters Walk' figurine, HN3052, designed by A. Hughes, from the Reflections series.

This figure was released one year earlier in the US.

1988-95 12.25in (31cm) high

$150-250   **L&T**

A Royal Doulton 'Boudoir' figurine, HN2542, designed by E.J. Griffiths, from the Haute Ensemble series.

1974-79 12.25in (31cm) high

$250-350   **L&T**

A Royal Doulton 'Carmen' figurine, HN2545, designed by E.J. Griffiths, from the Haute Ensemble series.

The original figurine named Carmen was designed by Leslie Harradine, and released in 1928. The early version can be worth upto four times this example.

1974-79   11.5in (29cm) high

$150-250   **L&T**

A Royal Doulton 'Cherry Blossom' figurine, HN3092, designed by P. Parsons, from the Reflections series.

This figurine was released a year earlier in the US.

1987-89 12.75in (32cm) high

$100-200   **L&T**

A limited edition Royal Doulton 'Eastern Grace' blue flambé figurine, HN3683, designed by Pauline Parsons, from an edition of 2,500.

Also available in red flambé and in traditional colours. The flambé versions are more desirable.

1995   12.5in (31.5cm) high

$300-400   **PSA**

A limited edition Royal Doulton 'Eliza Farren, Countess Of Derby' figurine, HN3442, designed by Peter Gee, from an edition of 5,000, with certificate, issued for the Royal Doulton International Collectors Club.

1993   *8.75in (22cm) high*

$150-250   **PSA**

A CLOSER LOOK AT A FIGURINE

This shape was also released in pink as HN1741, and was produced for one less year. It is usually of a similar value to HN1740.

Leslie Harradine was a prolific designer of 'Fair Lady' figurines and collectors often specialise in examples of his work.

Lawleys By Post commissioned the re-release of this figurine in 2000 in a limited edition of 2,000. It is worth about 20 per cent of this version.

The style of this figure is unusual: 'Fair Ladies' are usually full-length figures, either standing or seated.

A Royal Doulton 'Gladys' figurine, HN1740, designed by Leslie Harradine.

1935-49   *5in (12.5cm) high*

$550-750   **SWO**

A Royal Doulton 'Enigma' figurine, HN3110, designed by R. Jefferson, from the Reflections series.

1987-95   *12.75in (32cm) high*

$150-250   **L&T**

A Royal Doulton 'Genevieve' figurine, HN1962, designed by Leslie Harradine.

1941-75   *7in (18cm) high*

$150-250   **PSA**

A Royal Doulton 'Lori' figurine, HN2801, designed by Margaret Davies, from the Kate Greenaway series.

1976-87   *5.75in (14.5cm) high*

$100-180   **L&T**

A Royal Doulton 'Midsummer Noon' figurine, HN2033, designed by Leslie Harradine.

The blue version released 1939-49 is the most desirable version, worth upto double this one.

1949-55 5in (12.5cm) high

$300-500   **PSA**

A Royal Doulton 'Penelope' figurine, HN1901, designed by Leslie Harradine.

The lavender and green version, released as HN1902 in 1939 was only issued until 1949 and can be worth over three times as much.

1939-75   *7in (18cm) high*

$150-250   **L&T**

A Royal Doulton 'Ruth' figurine, HN2799, designed by Margaret Davies, from the Kate Greenaway series.

1976-81   *6in (15cm) high*

$120-180   **L&T**

A limited edition Royal Doulton 'Sophie Charlotte, Lady Sheffield' figurine, HN3008, designed by P. Gee, from the Gainsborough Ladies series, from an edition of 5,000, with certificate.

1990   *10in (25.5cm) high*

$100-150   **PSA**

A Royal Doulton 'Spring' figurine, HN2085, designed by Margaret Davies, style four, from The Seasons series.

1952-59   7.75in (19.5cm) high

$150-250   **L&T**

A Royal Doulton 'Strolling' figurine, HN3073, designed by A. Hughes, from the Reflections series.

This figure was released two years earlier in the US.

1987-95   13.5in (34.5cm) high

$150-250   **L&T**

A Royal Doulton 'Sweet Anne' figurine, HN1318, designed by Leslie Harradine, style one.

The most valuable version of this figure is HN1631, only issued between 1934-38 and in a green, red, pink and yellow colourway.

1929-49   *7.5in (19cm) high*

$200-300   **L&T**

A Royal Doulton 'Top O' The Hill' figurine, HN1834, designed by Leslie Harradine, style one.

Introduced 1937   *7in (18cm) high*

$90-150   **L&T**

A Royal Doulton 'Vivienne' figurine, HN2073, designed by Leslie Harradine.

1951-67   *7.75in (19.5cm) high*

$100-150   **PSA**

A Royal Doulton 'Water Maiden' figurine, HN3155, designed by Adrian Hughes, from the Reflections series.

1987-91   *12in (30.5cm) high*

$100-200   **L&T**

A Royal Doulton 'Cavalier' figurine, HN2716, designed by Eric J. Griffiths, style two.

1976-82   10in (25.5cm) high

$150-250   **L&T**

A Royal Doulton 'Ko-Ko' figurine, HN2898, designed by William K. Harper, from The Gilbert & Sullivan series.

1980-85   11.5in (29cm) high

$250-350   **PSA**

A Royal Doulton 'The Laird' figurine, HN2361, designed by Mary Nicoll.

At some point the base was made larger and the HN number was changed to HN2361A. The value is the same for either version.

1969-   8in (20cm) high

$100-150   **L&T**

A Royal Doulton 'Lambing Time' earthenware figurine, HN1890, designed by W.M. Chance, style one.

1938-81   9.25in (23.5cm) high

$250-350   **PSA**

A Royal Doulton 'The Carpenter' figurine, HN2678, designed by Mary Nicoll.

Nicoll is known for her portrayal of traditional British crafts and pastimes, with other designs including 'The Clockmaker', as well as marine characters.

1986-92   8in (20cm) high

$300-400   **PSA**

A Royal Doulton 'Aragorn' figurine, HN2916, designed by David Lyttleton, from the Middle Earth series.

1981-84   6.25in (16cm) high

$70-120   **PSA**

A Royal Doulton 'Bilbo' figurine, HN2914, designed by David Lyttleton, from the Middle Earth series.

1980-84   4.5in (11.5cm) high

$50-100   **PSA**

A Royal Doulton 'Gandalf' figurine, HN2911, designed by David Lyttleton, from the Middle Earth series.

1980-84   7in (18cm) high

$70-120   **PSA**

A Royal Doulton 'Owd Willum' figurine, HN2042, designed by Leslie Harradine.

1949-73   6.75in (17cm) high

$250-350   **L&T**

A Royal Doulton 'The Bedtime Story' figurine, HN2059, designed by Leslie Harradine.

1950-96   *4.75in (12cm) high*

$150-250   **L&T**

A Royal Doulton 'The Patchwork Quilt' figurine, HN1984, designed by Leslie Harradine.

1945-59   *6in (15cm) high*

$200-300   **L&T**

A Royal Doulton 'Ruth The Pirate Maid' figurine, HN2900, designed by W.K. Harper, from The Gilbert & Sullivan Series.

1981-85   *11.75in (30cm) high*

$350-550   **PSA**

A CLOSER LOOK AT A ROYAL DOULTON FIGURINE

Sculptor Phoebe Stabler is perhaps best known for her association with Carter, Stabler and Adams, which became Poole Pottery, through her husband Harold Stabler.

It was the first Doulton figurine to feature a 'street vendor'. Later additions include the Old Balloon Seller, the Carpet Vendor and The Potter.

This figure, which was designed in 1911, was also produced by Poole as 'The Lavender Woman' in a different colorway.

The shape was first issued as HN10 in 1913, one of the earliest from the HN series. All the variations are desirable, the last HN2034 (1949-51) is the least valuable, at less than half this version.

A Royal Doulton 'Madonna of the Square' figurine, HN613, designed by Phoebe Stabler, impressed "Phoebe Stabler", printed Doulton mark, restored neck.

1924-36   *8in (20cm) high*

$800-1,000   **WW**

A Royal Doulton 'Pierrette' figurine, HN643, designed by Leslie Harradine, style one.

This is one of a number of colourways; only one was produced after WWII. They are all sought-after.

1924-38

$2,000-3,000   **PSA**

A Royal Doulton 'The Wardrobe Mistress' figurine, HN2145, designed by Margaret Davies.

1954-67   *5.75in (14.5cm) high*

$350-550   **PSA**

A Royal Doulton 'Schoolmarm' figurine, HN2223, designed by Margaret Davies.

1958-81   *6.75in (17cm) high*

$200-350   **L&T**

FIND OUT MORE...

Royal Doulton Figurines, by Jean Dale, published by Charlton Press, 10th Edition, 2005.

COLLECTORS' NOTES

■ Royal Doulton have been producing animal character figures since the 1880s. Ranges have included Aesop's Fables, The Wind in the Willows and Beatrix Potter.

■ In 1969 the firm acquired the Beswick factory and benefited from Beswick's expertise in creating ceramic character animals. Modelers and designers Albert Hallam, Graham Tongue and Harry Sales helped further Royal Doulton's reputation for producing fine quality, collectible pieces.

■ Brambly Hedge mouse figures, based on the books by Jill Barklem, have remained popular since their introduction in 1983. Their poses were carefully designed so that different figures would appear to react well with each other when grouped together. Look out for rare models or color variations. The first

Brambly Hedge range was retired in 1997, but a new collection was introduced in 2000.

■ Bunnykins figures were first produced in 1939 and early figures are rare. The range was relaunched in 1972 with DB pattern numbers, and Harry Sales expanded the range in the early 1980s to appeal more to adult collectors. In 1987 the Royal Doulton International Collectors' Club issued a figure exclusively for its members and this 'Collector Bunnykins' DB54 is one of the most prized pieces.

■ Early discontinued models are sought-after, and figures are withdrawn regularly from the range, increasing value. Though limited editions have increased in size, demand often outstrips supply for many new Bunnykins figures as soon as they are launched.

A Royal Doulton Brambly Hedge 'Basil' figure, DBH14, style one, designed by Harry Sales.

1985-92   3.25in (8.5cm) high

$120-180   PSA

A Royal Doulton Brambly Hedge 'Clover' figure, DBH16, designed by Graham Tongue.

1987-97   3.25in (8.5cm) high

$30-60   PSA

A Doulton Brambly Hedge 'Mrs Toadflax' figure, DBH11, designed by Harry Sales.

The contents of the bowl varies in color, but this does not affect the value.

1985-95   3.25in (8.5cm) high

$50-90   PSA

A Royal Doulton Brambly Hedge 'Old Mrs Eyebright' figure, DBH9, designed by Harry Sales.

1984-95   3.25in (8.5cm) high

$50-90   PSA

A Royal Doulton Brambly Hedge 'Primrose Entertains' figure, DBH22, designed by Graham Tongue.

1990-95   3.25in (8.5cm) high

$80-120   PSA

A Royal Doulton Brambly Hedge 'Old Vole' figure, DBH13, designed by Harry Sales.

1985-92   3.25in (8.5cm) high

$200-300   PSA

A Royal Doulton Brambly Hedge 'Wilfred Entertains' figure, DBH23, designed by Graham Tongue.

1990-95   3.25in (8.5cm) high

$80-120   PSA

CERAMICS

A limited edition Royal Doulton 'Arabian' Bunnykins, DB315, designed by Caroline Dadd, from an edition of 1,000 commissioned by UKI Ceramics, boxed with certificate.

2004

$100-150 PSA

A CLOSER LOOK AT AN EARLY BUNNYKINS

Bunnykins figures are based on the drawings of Sister Mary Barbara Vernon, the daughter of Royal Doulton's Stoke-on-Trent manager at the time.

The first six figures are believed to have been designed by Charles Noke as there are similarities to his animal figures.

These first figures bear little resemblance to Barbara's drawings, which may explain why they were redesigned by Walter Hayward when the range was relaunched in 1972.

Production was interrupted by WWII meaning this version was only made for a short period of time. This makes them among the the rarest Bunnykins today.

A lively trade on the internet has seen more of these early figures come to light, meaning prices have dropped slightly, particularly for Billy and Mother.

A Royal Doulton earthenware 'Billy' Bunnykin, D6001, designed by Charles Noke.

1939-40   *4.5in (12cm) high*

$600-800 PSA

A Royal Doulton 'Daisie Bunnykins Spring Time' Bunnykins, DB7, modelled by Albert Hallam based on a design by Walter Hayward.

1972-83   *3.5in (9cm) high*

$150-200 PSA

A limited edition Royal Doulton 'Detective' Bunnykins, DB193, designed by Kimberley Curtis, from an edition of 2,500 exclusively for UKI Ceramics, boxed with certificate.

1999   *4.75in (12cm) high*

$80-120 PSA

A limited edition Royal Doulton 'Dutch' Bunnykins, DB274, from an edition of 2,000 from the Bunnykins of the World series, boxed with certificate.

2003

$80-120 PSA

A Royal Doulton 'Irishman' Bunnykins, DB178, designed by Denise Andrews, from a limited edition of 2,500 exclusively for UKI Ceramics, boxed with certificate.

1998

$150-200 PSA

A limited edition Royal Doulton 'Judy' Bunnykins, DB235, designed by Kimberley Curtis, from an edition of 2,500 exclusively for UKI Ceramics, boxed with certificate.

2001

$70-100 PSA

A limited edition Royal Doulton 'Juggler' Bunnykins, DB164, designed by Denise Andrews, from a limited edition of 1,500 exclusively for UKI Ceramics, boxed.

1996   *4.5in (12cm) high*

$200-300 PSA

A rare Royal Doulton earthenware 'Mary' Bunnykins, D6002, designed by Charles Noke.

1939-40   6.5in (16.5cm) high

$1,200-1,800   **PSA**

A limited edition Royal Doulton 'Mandarin' Bunnykins, DB252, designed by Caroline Dadd, from an edition of 2,500 exclusively for UKI Ceramics, boxed with certificate.

This one of 15 Bunnykins of the World, a range produced exclusively for UKI Ceramics.

2001   4.25in (11cm) high

$70-100   **PSA**

A limited edition Royal Doulton 'Matador' Bunnykins, DB281, designed by Caroline Dadd, from an edition of 2,000, boxed with certificate.

2003   4.75in (12cm) high

$80-120   **PSA**

A limited edition Royal Doulton 'Mexican' Bunnykins, DB316, designed by Caroline Dadd, from an edition of 1,000 exclusively for UKI Ceramics, boxed with certificate.

2004

$80-120   **PSA**

A limited edition Royal Doulton 'Mr Punch' Bunnykins, DB234, designed by Kimberley Curtis, from an edition of 2,500 exclusively for UKI Ceramics, boxed with certificate.

2001   4.75in (12cm) high

$70-100   **PSA**

A Royal Doulton 'Parisian' Bunnykins, DB317, from an edition of 1,000 for UKI Ceramics, boxed with certificate.

This was the last of the Bunnykins of the World series.

2005

$100-150   **PSA**

A limited edition Royal Doulton 'Rugby Player' Bunnykins, DB318, from an edition of 1,000, boxed with certificate.

2005

$80-120   **PSA**

A limited edition Royal Doulton 'Samurai' Bunnykins, DB280, from an edition of 2,000 exclusively for the UKI Ceramics series Bunnykins of the World, boxed with certificate.

2003

$100-150   **PSA**

A limited edition Royal Doulton 'Witch's Cauldron' Bunnykins, DB293, designed by Caroline Dadd, from an edition of 1,500 exclusively for UKI Ceramics, boxed with certificate.

2004

$100-150   **PSA**

FIND OUT MORE...

Royal Doulton Collectables, by Jean Dale and Louise Irvine, published by The Charlton Press, 4th edition, 2006.

CERAMICS

COLLECTORS' NOTES

■ Marcello Fantoni (b.1915) studied ceramics and sculpture at the Institute of Art in Porta Romana, Florence from 1927 onwards, before gaining commercial experience and then founding his own studio in 1936. His work met with instant critical and commercial success, and after WWII this continued, with the factory employing 50 employees by 1946. Both unique pieces, and 'production ranges' designed by Fantoni were made and his success reached a high point between the 1950s and '70s.

■ His style closely links modern and contemporary art movements with ceramics, but also takes some of its inspiration from ancient or archaic sources, such as Etruscan works. Forms tend to be simple and are often a modern take on ancient baluster or amphora forms. Glazes can either be bright or earthy and reminiscent of the Italian landscape, but are all applied in a truly modern, painterly manner on bodies with rough surfaces. Where designs appear, they are often scratched into the surface using the sgraffito process.

■ From the late 1950s-70s, the company produced a range of ceramics for US importer and distributor Raymor. For more information on Raymor, please see p118. Following many of Fantoni's key design themes, pieces often have extravagantly applied glazes that are dripped in a volcanic-like manner. These have become increasingly sought-after recently, but higher prices are reserved for his large, unique or limited production sculptural works. Examples of his work can be found in many museums including the Metropolitan Museum of Art, New York.

An Italian Fantoni for Raymor vase, with hand-painted green and blue bands on a rough cream ground, the base painted "Fantoni for Raymor ITALY", with Raymor labels.

11.25in (28.5cm) high

$350-450   **HLM**

An Italian Fantoni for Raymor beige, yellow, red and green mottled hand-painted baluster vase, the base marked "Fantoni for Raymor ITALY" to base, and with paper label.

11in (28cm) high

$320-380   **HLM**

A Italian Fantoni for Raymor large vase, the bulbous body with tall cylindrical neck hand-painted with a dripped brown glaze, the base painted "Fantoni for Raymor ITALY".

11in (28cm) high

$300-400   **HLM**

An Italian Fantoni for Raymor jug vase, with brown and yellow driped glazes and wide circular applied handle, the base unmarked.

Like those found on many West German Ceramics, which may have been partly inspired by Fantoni's work, the handle is not intended to be functional, but rather decorative.

11.25in (28.5cm) high

$350-450   **HLM**

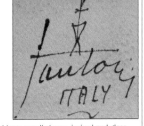

A 1960s Italian Fantoni large panelled vase, incised and gloss glazed with stylized geometric patterns and a horse and rider, the base marked "Fantoni ITALY".

Stylized geometric forms are typical of Fantoni. The figures are reminiscent of both prehistoric cave paintings and early, Etruscan murals, but are yet quintessentially mid-century modern in their handling and colors.

6.25in (41cm) high

$2,200-2,800   **TOJ**

A Italian Fantoni for Raymor 'Vesuvio' bowl, with 'volcanic' glazes, painted "Fantoni Italy for Raymor" mark and Raymor label.

9.75 (24.5cm) diam

$280-320   **HLM**

COLLECTORS' NOTES

■ Flow Blue was made in Staffordshire, England, for export to the US from the 1830s onwards. Inspired by the designs of popular imported Chinese porcelain, patterns were inexpensively printed rather than hand-painted. From the 1870s Flow Blue wares were also produced in the US.

■ Some experts believe that the distinctive Flow Blue finish was developed by accident when a problem with the glazing process caused blue transfer-printed designs to blur, although others argue that it was intentional. After it had proven popular in the US, lime or chloride of ammonia was added to the kilns to enhance the pleasing 'flow' effect. This design proved immensely popular, and also had the added benefit of concealing errors in the earthenware blank or transfer pattern.

■ Patterns can help with the dating. Chinese designs and landscapes were popular in the early Victorian period until c1860. Floral patterns were found mostly in the 1860-70s and Japanese patterns of shapes with raised designs and gilt details or scalloped edges were most popular from the late 1880s to the early 20thC.

■ Look for examples with a deep cobalt blue colouring against a clean, crisp white background. Avoid examples with gray tones. An even flow of blue across the piece is also more desirable than a patchy finish.

■ Certain shapes are rarer or more complex than others and these tend to be more valuable. For example, plates were bought more frequently than lidded tureens. The desirability of the pattern will also determine the value. The maker and the pattern name are usually found on the reverse.

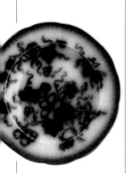

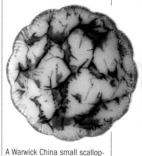

A Gustavsberg impressed Flow Blue soup bowl, with deep blue floral and foliate decoration, "9 A" and anchor mark.

9.5in (24cm) diam

$100-150   **FBS**

A mid-19thC Indian Stone China 'Lily' pattern Flow Blue dinner plate.

10.75in (27cm) diam

$220-280   **FBS**

A Warwick China small scallop-edged Flow Blue dish, with sprinkled gold dust sponged on to the edge.

6in (15.5cm) diam

$60-80   **FBS**

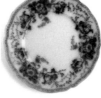

A Davenport 'Amoy' pattern Flow Blue soup bowl, of 12-sided form, the flowers being typically over-sized, impressed anchor mark to reverse.

c1844   10.25in (26cm) diam

$200-250   **FBS**

A New Wharf Pottery 'Cambridge' pattern Semi Porcelain Flow Blue soup bowl.

c1891   8.75in (22.5cm) diam

$80-120   **FBS**

A Johnson Bros. 'Richmond' pattern Flow Blue dinner plate.

c1900   10in (25.5cm) diam

$100-140   **FBS**

A Johnson Bros. 'St Louis' pattern Flow Blue side plate, with flowers superimposed over a graduated blue background.

c1900   7in (18cm) diam

$60-80   **FBS**

A W.H. Grindley 'F.B.' pattern Flow Blue kidney-shaped dish, no. 250387.

6in (15cm) long

$80-120   **FBS**

A Ridgway's 'Josephine' pattern Flow Blue shaped dish.

c1910   *6in (15cm) long*

$80-120   **FBS**

A Stanley Pottery 'St Domaine' pattern Flow Blue shaped dish.

6.5in (16.5cm) long

$80-120   **FBS**

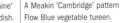

A Meakin 'Cambridge' pattern Flow Blue vegetable tureen.

c1891   *11.5in (29cm) wide*

$300-400   **FBS**

A Johnson Bros. 'Holland' pattern Flow Blue gravy boat and attached tray, with shaped handle, feet and rim.

c1891   *Tray 8in (20cm) long*

$200-300   **FBS**

A Johnson Bros. 'Oregon' pattern Flow Blue pitcher, with fancy handle and shaped rim.

c1900   *8.25in (21cm) high*

$400-600   **FBS**

A mid-19thC Flow Blue large jug, unmarked, with fine, deep blue decoration.

The deep blue decoration, combined with the shape, large size and the appealing pattern, make this example highly desirable.

10.5in (27cm) high

$850-950   **FBS**

A Prussian hand-sponged 'Spinach' pattern Flow Blue cup and saucer.

5.75in (14.5cm) diam

$80-120   **FBS**

A Henry Alcock & Co 'Touraine' pattern Flow Blue teacup and saucer.

Cup 4in (10cm) diam

$80-120   **FBS**

COLLECTORS' NOTES

- The designs of Italian Piero Fornasetti (1913-88) have become increasingly popular over the past five years. His first exhibition was in Milan in 1933 and he went on to become a notable interior decorator during the 1940s and '50s, and designed many ceramic, glass and furniture items as well.

- Fornasetti's love of surface ornamentation set him apart from his contemporaries in the mid-century Modern movement who aimed to unite form and function over surface decoration. Disregarded by his contemporaries, his work was popular with the buying public in the 1950s, and began to undergo a renaissance in the 1980s.

- Motifs are typically taken from the Classical Roman and Greek world and include elements of architecture and statuary. Others include suns, moons, playing cards and fish, and many have a integral sense of

humour or wit. Patterns are applied by lithographed transfers, typically in black, or gold, on a white background. Stronger, primary colors are known but are less common.

- Always look for the Fornasetti transfer-printed mark, that includes a painter's hand or brush on the reverse of ceramics, as reproductions and fakes are known. Also examine pieces carefully as wear, particularly to the gilt surface, is common and devalues a piece. Aim to buy complete sets, as finding a replacement, especially in similar condition, can be very hard.

- Pieces produced until Fornasetti's death in 1988 are considered vintage. Many designs are still being produced today as re-editions, or otherwise are being released by the company that still exists, run by his son Barnaba. Always aim to buy from an experienced dealer or consult reference works to ensure the piece is vintage.

Two German Eschenbach 'Strumenti Musicali' porcelain plates, designed by Piero Fornasetti, numbered "1" and "2".
1955-56   *8.25in (21cm) diam*
$180-220   GAZE

A set of eight late 1960s to early 1970s 'Adam' transfer-printed plates, designed by Piero Fornasetti.
Note the clever positioning of Adam's naked body over the set to avoid 'embarrassment'.

$280-320   P&I

One of set of 12 plates, designed by Piero Fornasetti, all with black ink mark on reverse.
10in (25.5cm) diam
$800-1,200 (set)   SK

A 'match man' transfer-printed dish or ashtray, designed by Piero Fornasetti.
5.5in (14cm) high
$120-180   HLM

A 'match dog' transfer-printed dish or ashtray, designed by Piero Fornasetti.
5.5in (14cm) high
$120-180   HLM

A pair of bathroom covered jars, designed by Piero Fornasetti, with gilt and black transfer-printed design.
7in (18cm) high
$120-180   ROS

A chocolate mug and cover, designed by Piero Fornasetti, with gilt and black portrait medallion transfer-printed pattern.
$50-70   GAZE

A 'Pumpkin' white ceramic lidded pot, designed by Piero Fornasetti, with hand-painted gilt decoration, lid cracked.
13in (33cm) long
$35-45   GAZE

COLLECTORS' NOTES

- Like many art pottery producers, Fulper began by producing utilitarian wares after they were founded in 1815, and utilised the local New Jersey clay.

- When the founder Samuel Hill died in 1858, the family sold the pottery to Hill's partner Abraham Fulper who changed the name to reflect the new ownership. It became the Fulper Pottery Company in 1899 when Fulper's grandson took control.

- The company's first art pottery line was launched in 1909 under the name Vasekraft and was primarily the result of William Fulper Hill's experimentation with glazes.

- To keep costs down, the bodies were almost exclusively slip-cast or molded, with only the extensive range of glazes being hand-applied.

- As a result, the type and quality of the glaze is the main indicator to value. Early, pre-WWII examples are usually the most desirable as they show the best range of glazes and creativity in application. In 1930 Johann Stangl acquired the firm and the name changed to the Stangl Pottery Company in 1955.

A CLOSER LOOK AT A FULPER VASE

Items made for exhibits display design and production at its best, and are highly sought-after and rare.

As is typical of Fulper, the shape and surface decoration is minimal – the glaze is all.

The simple form displays the glaze at its best. The factory won an award at the exposition.

Fulper pieces are rarely dated and the different marks seem to have been used, at least partially, concurrently. The labels help to date this piece fairly accurately.

A Fulper cat's eye flambé and blue sky glaze Edam vase, with exhibition labels to base.

c1915   5.5in (14cm) high

$1,500-2,000   **TOJ**

A Fulper baluster vase, with three handles to lip, stamped mark.

This vase displays an interesting glaze combination, including Chinese blue, taupe elephant's breath flambé and mahogany.

6.5in (16.5cm) high

$500-700   **TOJ**

A Fulper baluster vase, with all over amethyst coloured glaze with green around the neck, stamped mark.

1922-28   9in (23cm) high

$500-600   **TOJ**

A Fulper mirror black glazed urn vase, impressed mark.

The mirror glaze is one of Fulper's most collected, and black is a rare color. This is a particularly interesting example with a thickly applied glaze.

c1916-22   8in (20cm) high

$800-1,000   **TOJ**

A Fulper green-ish brown cat's eye flambé vase, with printed mark.

1922-28   7in (17.5cm) high

$400-500   **TOJ**

A Fulper small olive green and mirror black glazed vase, with attenuated neck.

1909-16   6in (15cm) high

$500-600   **TOJ**

A Fulper green 'leopard skin' glaze vase.

8in (20cm) high

$650-750   **TOJ**

COLLECTORS' NOTES

■ Hazle Boyles founded her pottery in 1990, drawing on her previous careers as an interior designer and as a Craft, Design & Technology teacher. It was while teaching that she began to develop her low-relief clay models.

■ The company's main product is the 'A Nation of Shopkeepers' series of flatback models of shops, often based on existing historic British buildings. Popular with tourists, this range is predominately hand-painted, with the use of decals having been phased out completely.

■ Look for limited production models; some editions were as low as five. Event pieces from the 10th and 15th anniversary celebrations are also collectible. Look out for examples signed 'Hazle Boyles' on the front, as this was only used between 1990-92. In 1993, it was replaced with the simplified 'Hazle', which can be signed by senior painters as well as Hazle herself.

A CLOSER LOOK AT A HAZLE CERAMICS WALL PLAQUE

The plaque takes its title from the Charles Dickens' book of the same name. The design is based on the Old Curiosity Shop, Portsmouth Street, London, England, which claims to be the inspiration for the book.

It was launched at a Dickens' Event in 2003 where it was signed on the flatback by Hazle Boyles and Cedric Charles Dickens, great grandson of the famous author.

The shape was also used to portray a modern-day version of the shop, which was produced from 1999-2005.

Date codes were introduced in 1995, starting with 'a'. This example is marked 'i' for 2003.

A limited edition Hazle Ceramics 'The Old Curiosity Shop' wall plaque, from an edition of 30, together with a certificate of authenticity.

2003   *7in (17.5cm) wide*

$500-600   **JEG**

A limited edition Hazle Ceramics 'Chinese Restaurant' wall plaque, from an edition of 100 from the Hazle 2000 series.

Based on a Boot's the Chemist building in Nottingham, England, built in 1877.

2003   *9in (22.5cm) high*

$500-700   **JEG**

A Hazle Ceramics 'The Florist' wall plaque.

Based on a building in Maldon, Essex, England. This is the early version signed "Hazle Boyles", which is worth up to 50 per cent more than the later "Hazle" version.

1990-92   *8in (20.5cm) high*

$220-280   **RA**

A Hazle Ceramics 'Post Office' wall plaque.

Based on a building in Colchester, England the blank was decorated as 'Corner Shop' from 1991-97 and as 'Post Office' from 1998.

7.75in (19.5cm) high

$180-220   **RA**

A limited edition Hazle Ceramics 'Royal Regalia' wall plaque, from an edition of 300.

Based on a building in Windsor, England. The first 100 pieces produced were used as part of a five-piece Jubilee Parade set, issued in 2002 to celebrate Queen Elizabeth II's golden jubilee.

8in (20cm) high

$220-280   **JEG**

A limited edition Hazle Ceramics 'A Pet is for Life' wall plaque, from an edition of 800.

Based on a 16thC farmhouse in Epping, England, currently used as a master saddlers.

1997-2001   *6.5in (16.5cm) high*

$350-450   **JEG**

FIND OUT MORE...

www.hazle.com, *official company website.*

COLLECTORS' NOTES

- Inspired by drawings of children by a nun, Sister Berta Hummel, Goebel's 'Hummel' figurines were first produced in 1935. Over the years, more than 500 different figurines have been released. Marks on the base help identify the name and the period in which a particular piece was made.

- Since 1935, there have been many changes to the Hummel trademark. Early pieces, denoted by 'Crown' marks and marks with a large bee motif, can be particularly valuable. From 1950, the bee design became smaller in size and its position was altered to sit inside the V shape. The bee motif was dropped after 1964, in favour of text, and a large 'G' dominated the mark from 1972.

- Unusual and rare variations are sought-after and can fetch high prices. Look for variations in color of certain parts of clothing. Early Hummel examples from the 1930s-50s are also popular. Larger examples – above 6in (15cm) in size – are also more valuable.

- The dates for pieces shown here relate to the period each piece was produced in, using its mark, and often its size, to help date it. Buyers should remember that some designs are still in production today.

- The bisque chips and cracks easily, so examine figurines carefully for damage or repair, as this will reduce value. Pieces can bruise when stored against each other, so care must be taken in display.

A Hummel 'Little Gardener' figure, No. 74, marked "Germany" in black.

1940-59   4.25in (11cm) high

$50-90   AAC

A Hummel 'A Stitch in Time' figure, No. 255.

1964-72   6.25in (17cm) high

$80-120   AAC

A Hummel 'Sister' figure, No. 98, marked "Germany" in black, no decimal.

1940-59 5.75in (14.5cm) high

$70-100   AAC

A Hummel 'School Girl' figure, No. 81/2/0, marked with an incised circle and "Germany" in black.

1940-59   4.25in (11cm) high

$60-80   AAC

c1949   6in (15.5cm) high

$120-160   EAB

A Hummel 'The Weary Wanderer' figure, No. 204, full bee mark, some restoration to the back of the head, stamped "204".

Look for the rare variation with blue coloured eyes as they can be worth over $1,800.

A Hummel 'Valentine Gift' figure, No. 387, exclusive special edition for the Hummel Collectors' Club, crazing under base.

1977-79 5.75in (14.5cm) high

$80-120   AAC

A late 1930s Hummel 'Happiness' figure, No. 86, marked "Germany" in black, repaired.

4.75in (12cm) high

$30-40   AAC

A Hummel 'Little Gabriel' figure, No. 32/0, incised circle, marked "Western Germany" in black, damage.

1958-72   5in (12.5cm) high

$40-70   **AAC**

A Hummel 'Mother's Helper' figure, No. 133, incised circle, marked "Germany" in black.

1940-59   5in (12.5cm) high

$100-150   **AAC**

A Hummel 'Signs of Spring' figure, No. 203/2/0, incised circle, marked "Western Germany" in black.

1958-1972   4in (10cm) high

$70-100   **AAC**

A Hummel 'Friends' figure, No. 136/I, incised circle.

1958-72   5in (12.5cm) high

$100-150   **AAC**

A Hummel 'Favorite Pet' figure, No. 361.

All examples carry a 1960 copyright date, although the model was not released for sale until the 1964 New York City World's Fair. Examples with earlier stamps can be found and are often worth significantly more.

c1964   4.25in (11cm) high

$280-320   **MAC**

A Hummel 'Doll Mother' figure, No. 67, marked with an incised circle and "Germany" in black.

1940-59   4.75in (12cm) high

$120-160   **AAC**

A Hummel 'Farewell' figure, No. 65/I.

1958-72   4.75in (12cm) high

$80-120   **AAC**

A Hummel 'Angel Serenade' figure, No. 214D.

1958-72   3in (7.5cm) high

$30-40   **AAC**

A Hummel 'Book Worm' figure, No. 8, base chip.

1972-79   4in (10cm) high

$40-60   **AAC**

A Hummel 'Street Singer' figure, No. 131.

1960-72   4.75in (12cm) high

$60-80   **WDL**

A Hummel 'Baker' figure, No. 128, crazing and some rubbing.

1958-72   4.75in (12cm) high

$50-70   **AAC**

A Hummel 'Soldier Boy' figure, No. 332, with blue cap badge, painter's signature for 1994.

1994   *6in (15cm) high*

$120-160   **WDL**

A Hummel 'Village Boy' figure, No. 51.

c1972   4.75in (9.5cm) high

$80-120   **EAB**

A larger Hummel 'Doctor' figure, No. 127.

1991-99   5.25in (13cm) high

$80-100   **WDL**

A Hummel 'Lost Sheep' figure, No. 68 2/0, marked with painter's signature.

1991-99   4.75in (12cm) high

$40-50   **WDL**

A Hummel 'Little Hiker' figure, No. 16/2/0, marked with an incised circle and "Germany" in black.

1940-59   4.25in (11cm) high

$50-90   **AAC**

A Hummel 'Chimney Sweep' figure, No. 12/2/0, base crazing.

1972-79   4in (10cm) high

$30-40   **AAC**

A Hummel 'Merry Wanderer' figure, No. 11, slight scratch to the umbrella, stamped "11".

c1964-72   4.5in (11cm) high

$80-120   **EAB**

A Hummel 'The Builder' figure,
No. 305.

1964-72   5.5in (14cm) high

$60-80   **AAC**

A Hummel 'Good Hunting'
figure, No. 307.

1972-79 5.25in (13.5cm) high

$120-160   **AAC**

A Hummel 'Begging His Share' figure, No. 9, with hole in cake.

1958-64   5.5in (14cm) high

$70-100   **AAC**

A Hummel 'The Artist' figure, No.
304, some crazing.

1972-79 5.25in (13.5cm) high

$70-100   **AAC**

A Hummel 'Little Pharmacist'
figure, No. 322, painter's
signature for 1998.

1991-99   6in (15cm) high

$100-130   **WDL**

A Hummel 'Grandpa's Boy'
figure, No. 562, wrong color
trousers, mark since 1991,
painter's signature from 1994.

1991-99   4.5in (11cm) high

$80-120   **WDL**

A Hummel 'She Loves Me, She
Loves Me Not' figure, No. 174,
incised crown mark, marked
"Made in U.S. Zone Germany" in
black in an oval, repaired.

1945-50   4.25in (11cm) high

$50-90   **AAC**

A Hummel 'Apple Tree Boy'
figure, No. 142/3/0, some
rubbing.

1958-72   4in (10cm) high

$45-65   **AAC**

A Hummel figurine 'Playmates',
No. 58 2/0, painter's signature
for 1998.

1991-99   3.75in (9.5cm) high

$60-80   **WDL**

CERAMICS

A Hummel 'Culprits' figure, No. 56/B, full bee mark appearing below the tips of the 'V'.

Later examples are painted with the boys eyes downcast towards the dog, there is no significant difference in value between these two versions.

1972-79   *6.75in (17cm) high*

$200-300   **AGO**

A Hummel 'Bird Duet' figure, No. 169.

1972-79   *4in (10cm) high*

$70-100   **AAC**

A CLOSER LOOK AT A HUMMEL FIGURE

The Merry Wanderer was one of the original 46 figures released in 1935.

This figure was made in a range of sizes, the larger sizes are generally more valuable.

The jumbo 32in figure, often used as a promotional figure, is the most sought-after.

It was modelled by master sculptor Arthur Moeller.

A Hummel 'Merry Wanderer' large figure, No. 7/II.

1972-79   *9.5in (24cm) high*

$350-550   **AAC**

A Hummel 'Volunteers' figure, No. 50/2/0, marked "Germany" in black, chip to base.

1940-59   *5in (12.5cm) high*

$50-90   **AAC**

A Hummel 'Smart Little Sister' figure, No. 346.

1964-72   *4.75in (12cm) high*

$80-100   **AAC**

A Hummel 'Forest Shrine' figure, No. 183, base crazing.

1972-79   *9in (23cm) high*

$150-220   **AAC**

A Hummel 'Guardian Angel' holy water font, No. 29/0, incised circle, marked "Western Germany" in black, discontinued.

1958-72 5.75in (14.5cm) high

$100-150   **AAC**

COLLECTORS' NOTES

- The Glidden Pottery was founded in Alfred, New York in 1940 by Glidden Parker (1913-80). Parker had studied at The New York State College of Ceramics, under Don Schreckengost and was highly entrepreneurial. The company grew quickly to be the most successful New York ceramics company, and had 55 employees by 1946 and was producing 6,000 pieces per week in 1953, which were sold in department and ceramic stores across the US.

- Both functional tablewares and decorative pieces were produced in over 200 shapes, all of which were slip-cast or press-molded before being decorated and glazed by hand. Pieces were robust, fashionable and inexpensive and proved extremely popular. Glidden also featured on TV shows, such as Lucille Ball's 'I Love Lucy', further promoting it to the public.

- Parker himself was responsible for many designs, although he did employ other designers such as Fong Chow, from 1953-57, Ernest Sohn and Sergio Dello Strologo. The company closed in 1957 as sales declined dramatically. Most pieces are marked with an impressed stamp of a stylized ram's head in a shield on the base, together with a shape number. As so much survives, prices are still comparatively low for much of their production, but interest and prices are rising, particularly after an exhibition in 2001.

A Glidden mottled green glazed teapot, the base impressed "GLIDDEN 140".

7in (18cm) high

$80-120　　　　**HLM**

A Glidden mottled green glazed creamer, the base impressed "GLIDDEN 143".

6in (15cm) wide

$70-90　　　　**HLM**

A Glidden 'Poodleware' lidded casserole, with hand-painted poodle, the base impressed "GLIDDEN 165".

Poodles were popular and fashionable motif during the 1950s and summoned thoughts of the elegance of Paris. They appeared on all manner of objects, including clothing.

8.5in (21.5cm) long

$60-80　　　　**HLM**

A Glidden 'Sandstone' cylinder vase, with hand-painted bands, the base with blue ram mark and incised "4004 USA".

9.5in (24cm) high

$180-220　　　　**HLM**

A Glidden 'Gulfstream' large blue and deep green squared ashtray, with cigarette rests and hand-painted target design, the base with impressed ram mark and "272".

This pattern was designed by Fong Chow, and was produced a short time before Glidden closed, making it hard to find today.

c1954-57　　　　*10in (25.5cm) wide*

$100-150　　　　**HLM**

A Glidden serving platter, with hand-painted lion and palm tree designs, the back impressed "GLIDDEN 300".

Glidden also aimed to create wares that looked like studio pottery but were actually mass-produced. Many designs are by Ernest Sohn, with animals being typical.

12in (30.5cm) long

$100-150　　　　**HLM**

FIND OUT MORE...

Glidden Pottery, by Dr. Margaret Carney, published by the Schein-Joseph Museum of International Ceramic Art, 2001 (www.ceramicsmuseum.alfred. edu/publications.html).

COLLECTORS' NOTES

■ Italian ceramics of the 1950s-70s are growing in popularity along with West German ceramics. They are typified by bright colors reminiscent of the Mediterranean and the use of sgraffito – where a design is engraved into the surface using a stylus. However, even less is currently known about most Italian ceramics than their West German cousins.

■ The most commonly found examples have a strong aqua blue glaze, often with a green tinge. The surface is decorated with bands of impressed symbols including crosses and ovals. These are from the Rimini Blu range, designed by Aldo Londi (1911-2003) in 1953 and today are still produced by Bitossi of Montelupo, Italy. A large number of different, modern shapes, some based on the baluster form were produced, as well as characteristic rectangular vases. A wide range of highly stylized, and often humorous, animal forms was also made. These tend to be the most valuable and desirable today.

■ Bitossi use an impressed shield-shaped mark but most examples found tend to be stamped or painted 'Made in Italy' and bear a series of numbers. These were made to be exported, with Hutcheson & Sons Ltd of London responsible for the UK market and Raymor for the US, during the 1960s.

■ Raymor, known first as Richards Morgenthau, were founded by Irving Richards (1907-2003) and his partners, and had showrooms on Fifth Avenue, New York, and Chicago. They became known throughout the 1950s-70s for bringing affordable modern designs to the public, such as Russel Wright's 'American Modern' ceramics range. Italy was also a focus and they imported pieces by Fantoni and others, which are often found with Raymor labels.

■ Look for large undamaged examples with eye appeal. The market is still emerging and will undoubtedly develop over the next few years as more information is discovered. Colorful designs that take more skill to create are more likely to be of value in the future.

A 1960s-70s Bitossi 'Rimini Blu' vase, designed by Aldo Londi, impressed "727/21 Made in Italy", with Hutcheson & Sons importer's label.

8.5in (21.5cm) high

$70-100   **GC**

A 1960s-70s Bitossi 'Rimini Blu' large baluster vase, designed by Aldo Londi, decorated in the 'Spagnolo' pattern, with "Made in Italy" paper label.

14in (35.5cm) high

$80-120   **GC**

A 1960s-70s Bitossi 'Rimini Blu' large rectangular vase, designed by Aldo Londi, with bands of impressed symbols, the base with painted marks "727/30 TTR".

12in (30.5cm) high

$80-120   **GC**

A 1960s-70s Bitossi 'Rimini Blu' lampbase, designed by Aldo Londi, with plain bands and bands of impressed symbols.

10.5in (26.5cm) high

$80-120   **GC**

A 1960s-70s Bitossi 'Rimini Blu' lampbase, designed by Aldo Londi, impressed with bands of symbols.

6in (15cm) high

$40-60   **GC**

A 1960s-70s Bitossi 'Rimini Blu' large round bowl, designed by Aldo Londi, with bands of impressed symbols, the base with painted marks "501/24 Tiny".

9in (23cm) diam

$70-100   **GC**

A pair of 1960s-70s Bitossi 'Rimini Blu' small dish candlesticks, designed by Aldo Londi, impressed with bands of symbols, both bases impressed "Italy".

4.25in (10.5cm) diam

$50-70 GC

A 1960s-70s Bitossi 'Rimini Blu' hippopotamus figurine, designed by Aldo Londi, and decorated in the 'Spagnolo' pattern.

8.25in (21cm) long

$70-100 GC

A 1960s-70s Bitossi 'Rimini Blu' cylindrical cat, designed by Aldo Londi, with disc-shaped face, impressed with bands of symbols.

15.75in (40cm) long

$200-300 GC

A 1950s-60s Italian tapering bullet-shaped vase, hand-painted with random multicolored, textured squares outlined with black lines on a pastel blue ground, the base painted "Italy 6679".

Along with many other examples marked simply "Italy" and a number, the makes are not yet know.

8.75in (22.5cm) high

$30-50 GC

A 1960s-70s Bitossi 'Rimini Blu' bird figurine, designed by Aldo Londi, inscribed by hand to mimic feathers.

6in (15cm) long

$70-100 GC

A 1960s-70s Bitossi 'Rimini Blu' stylized hen sculpture, designed by Aldo Londi, impressed with bands of symbols.

8.75in (22cm) high

$100-150 GC

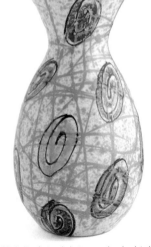

A 1950s-60s Italian factory tapering vase, hand-painted with random multicolored, textured squares outlined with black lines on a pastel pink ground, the base painted "Italy 6807".

8.25in (21cm) high

$30-50 GC

A 1950s-60s Italian factory gourd-shaped vase, hand-painted with random cross hatched lines and multicolored spots, the base painted "013 Italy 5/11".

5.5in (14cm) high

$35-45 GC

A 1950s-60s Italian factory baluster vase, hand-painted in glossy glazes with random grey lines and multicolored swirls, the base painted "Italy 7965".

8in (20cm) high

$40-50 GC

A 1950s-60s Italian factory tapering cylinder vase, incised and hand-painted with a central floral band, scored cross hatched areas and lines, and green bands, the base painted "Italy 6648".

This incised or scored technique, speckled textured background and thickly laid on colored glaze is typical of these types of Italian ceramics of the period, as are the bright, Mediterranean colors.

8in (20cm) high

$35-45 **GC**

A 1950s-60s Italian factory baluster vase, hand-painted with white, red, yellow and blue glazed stripes and circles, each with black outlines, the base painted "Italy".

8.5in (21.5cm) high

$50-80 **GC**

A 1950s-60s Italian factory small waisted vase, with satin finish, hand-painted zig-zag, dash and circle design on a white ground, the base painted "Italy 7456".

6in (15cm) high

$35-45 **GC**

A 1950s-60s Italian factory cylindrical jug, brightly hand-painted with stylized suns and linear, crennelated designs in bands, inscribed "M" or "W" on the base.

11.5in (29cm) high

$40-60 **GC**

A 1950s-60s Italian factory baluster vase, with hand-painted design of stylized Mediterranean houses on a textured matte beige ground, the base painted "Italy".

10in (24.5cm) high

$80-120 **GC**

A 1950s-60s Italian factory vase, with hand inscribed and hand-painted stylized Africans, glossily glazed over a brown ground with incised lines, the base painted "Italy 7894".

7.75in (19.5cm) high

$60-90 **GC**

A 1950s-60s Italian factory ceramic dish, hand-painted with a tree and house design, with a volcanic base.

West German factories such as Ruscha were also producing similar ceramics decorated with exotic scenes at this time. West German examples tend to be marked on the back with inscriptions and pattern names.

11.5in (29.5cm) wide

$30-40 **MTS**

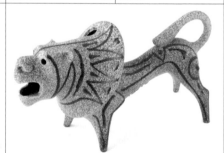

A 1950s-60s Italian factory lion-shaped ceramic vase, with mottled stone-effect glazed decoration and painted multicolored lines, the underbelly marked "RR ITALY".

12.25in (31cm) long

$60-90 **MTS**

COLLECTORS' NOTES

- Founded in 1953 in Almacera, Spain, by three brothers, Lladró has produced over 4,000 designs since its inception. Over 1,200 are still available, with figurines being retired annually. The Nao company was established in 1968 as part of the Lladró group.

- Pastel colors and a high gloss glaze are typical. The scarcer matte glaze is prized. A third 'Gres' finish, similar to stoneware, is often used for large pieces. Early pre-production pieces have a plain creamy finish and are sought-after and valuable, as are early pieces from the 1950s-70s. Limited editions, retired designs, or pieces with a short production period can fetch higher prices due to their comparative rarity.

- Fakes are known to exist, so check the base for marks. Pieces from the 1950s are rare and usually have incised marks. Standardized impressed and incised marks were used from c1960. From 1971 the familiar blue stamp was used, but lacked the accent over the 'o' until 1974, when the version still used today was introduced.

- Examine pieces carefully for damage or repair, as this reduces value considerably. Consider the facial expression, which should be full of character and individuality, something Lladró is known for. Lladró never use black to mark out eyes, brows and lids, a fact that can help identify fakes.

A Lladró large bust modeled as a young girl, in pastel tones of brown, gray and cream, printed mark to underside.

16.5in (42cm) high

$250-350   **ROS**

A Lladró 'Little Jester' figurine, 5203M, designed by Juan Huerta.

1984-92 7.75in (19.5cm) high

$250-350   **KCS**

A Lladró 'Baby with Pacifier' limited edition figure, 5102G, designed by Salvador Debón.

1982-85 6.5in (16.5cm) high

$250-350   **KCS**

A Lladró 'Reclining Angel' figure, 4541, designed by Fulgencio García.

Intro. 1969 2.5in (6cm) high

$30-50   **AAC**

A Lladró 'Angels Wondering' figure, 4962G/M, with matte finish, designed by Salvador Debón.

1977-91

5.5in (14cm) high

$50-70   **AAC**

A Lladró 'Soldier on Stand' figure, 1163G, designed by Vincento Martinez.

1971-78   *12in (30.5cm) high*

$500-600   **KCS**

A Lladró 'Soccer Player Puppet' figure, 4967, designed by Juan Huerta.

1977-85   8.25in (21cm) high

$250-450   KCS

A Lladró 'Olympic Puppet' figure, 4968G, designed by Juan Huerta, commemorating the Madrid Olympics, with stand.

1977-83   9.75in (25cm) high

$1,200-1,800   KCS

A Lladró 'Hang On!' figure, 5665, designed by Francisco Catalá.

1990-95   6in (15cm) high

$80-120   AAC

A Lladró 'Boy with Dog' figure, 4522, designed by Vincente Martínez.

1970-77   7.5in (19cm) high

$220-280   KCS

A Lladró 'Pick of the Litter' figure, 7621, an 'event' piece, designed by Salvador Debón.

1993   7.5in (18cm) high

$120-180   AAC

A CLOSER LOOK AT A LLADRÓ FIGURE

Based on the TV cartoon character 'Sport Billy', this figure is from a range featuring Billy playing a range of sports, as well as a 'Lilly Football Player' figure for his companion, 'Sport Lilly'.

This is one of Lladró's 'puppet' figures, which differ from their traditional, more natural figures. They can be overlooked as they bear such little resemblance to other Lladró examples.

They are particularly sought-after in the US, where the cartoon was fairly popular, although collectors often favour the more traditional figures.

Production was limited to only one year, making these figures harder to find.

A Lladró 'Billy Football Player' figure, 5135G, designed by José Roig, for the US Market, production limited to one year.

c1982   9in (23cm) high

$450-550   KCS

A Lladró 'Behave!' figure, 5703, designed by Juan Huerta.

1990-94   6in (15cm) high

$80-120   AAC

A Lladró 'New Playmates' figure, 5456G, designed by Antonio Ramos.
1988-2004   *4.75in (12cm) high*
$200-300   **KCS**

A Lladró 'Study Buddies' figure, 5451, designed by Regino Torrijos.
Introduced 1988   *4in (10cm) wide*
$180-220   **AAC**

A Lladró 'Bedtime Buddies' figure, 6541, designed by José Javier Malavia.
1998-2004   *3.5in (9cm) high*
$70-100   **AAC**

A Lladró 'Dog' figure, 4583G, designed by Fulgencio Garcia.
1969-81   *7in (18cm) high*
$200-300   **BIG**

A Lladró 'Dog' figure, 4583G, designed by Fulgencio Garcia.
1969-81   *7in (18cm) high*
$200-300   **BIG**

A Lladró 'Sea Lore' pipe, 5613, designed by Julio Ruiz.
1989-93   *3in (7.5cm) high*
$450-650   **KCS**

A Lladró 'Dog in Basket' figurine, 1128G, designed by Juan Huerta.
1971-85 7.25in (18.5cm) high
$400-600   **KCS**

A Lladró 'Heaven's Lullaby' figurine, 6583, designed by Antonia Ramos.
Introduced 1998
$200-300   **KCS**

FIND OUT MORE...

Collecting Lladró: Identification & Price Guide, *by Peggy Whiteneck, published by Krause, 2003.*

Lladró Authorised Reference Guide, *by Lladró, published by Lladró US Inc., 2000.*

www.lladro.com – official company website, with searchable 'historic' catalogues.

CERAMICS

COLLECTORS' NOTES

■ After the end of WWII, the allies occupied Japan. In order to help the country regenerate and rebuild its economy, Japan was allowed to export its ceramics and other items providing that it was clearly marked. This rule was in place from 1947 until April 1952. Only the marks 'Occupied Japan' and 'Made in Occupied Japan' guarantee that a piece was made and exported during this short period. It is these marks that serious collectors look for and all pieces shown here bear one of these authentic marks.

■ Ceramics made up the vast majority of objects, most of them functional kitchenware or dinnerware, but many decorative items, such as vases and figurines, were also exported. Items made from celluloid and transfer-printed tinplate, such as toys, were also exported. Most pieces are stamped on the base with printed marks in red, but beware of fakes. The marks on glazed ceramics are always under the glaze.

■ Ceramics were produced in molds on a factory production line process and then decorated in color by hand. Key indicators to value include the type, shape and size of the object and how well it is painted. The detail of the object is also important. A more finely detailed, well-painted example is always going to be more desirable than one that is not so well painted or modeled.

■ Many were based on existing European or American forms or styles that were already desirable. This took advantage of an existing market and allowed many to buy into a look at a more affordable price. Condition is also very important. Unglazed bisque should be clean and is generally an off-white color. Chips and glued repairs reduce value considerably as collectors only seek out pieces in undamaged condition, unless a piece is exceptionally rare. Always examine delicate protruding parts for signs of repair.

A pair of 'Made In Occupied Japan' mantelpiece figurines, each with male lute player and seated lady, with hand-painted detailing.

These are often found as lamp bases, and exact style and form differ widely, as does the value. This is a comparatively appealing pair, loosely based on fine 19thC Meissen porcelain from Germany.

6in (15cm) high

$70-100 (pair) TOA

A Paulux 'Made in Occupied Japan' hand-painted seated lady figurine, with gilt highlights.

5.75in (14.5cm) high

$35-45 TOA

A Paulux 'Made in Occupied Japan' hand-painted bisque flower holder, with a lady leading a swan shaped-carriage.

6.75in (17cm) high

$120-180 TOA

A Lenwile Ardalt 'Made in Occupied Japan' 'Fallen Skater' hand-painted bisque figurine, also painted "2350" on the base.

This figurine is hard to find in perfect condition as the legs, skate blades and particularly the delicate fingers are usually broken in some way or repaired.

5.5in (14cm) wide

$100-150 TOA

A pair of fine quality Andrea 'Made in Occupied Japan' hand-painted ceramic mantelpiece busts, marked "23/66" on the base.

As well as being an unusual shape, both the molded details and the painting on these busts is comparatively fine, hence their higher value.

9.75in (25cm) high

$350-450 TOA

A rare pair of 'Made in Occupied Japan' historical hand-painted ceramic figurines.

8in (20cm) high

$100-150 TOA

A CLOSER LOOK AT A PAIR OF FIGURINES

These figures are direct copies of those made by Florence of California, a highly successful company founded by Florence Ward in Pasadena in 1942. It is known for its desirable and decorative historical or literary figurines.

They appealed to those looking for a more affordable alternative to the sought-after 18thC and 19thC figurines by notable factories such as Meissen in Germany and Derby in the UK.

The poses, hand-painting and molded details are comparatively finer than other Japanese examples, and include textured areas, gilt highlights and well-painted faces.

They are in excellent condition with no damage or wear to the paint. They lack the wooden bases on which they would have been mounted for sale, although this does not affect the value.

A pair of Royal Sealy 'Made in Occupied Japan' hand-painted ceramic figurines of a Victorian or early 20thC couple, with gilt highlights.

9.5in (24cm) high

$80-120 TOA

A 'Made in Occupied Japan' hand-painted ceramic figurine of Little Bo Peep, with her shepherdess' crook.

As with the figurines above, this is a direct copy of a figurine designed and made by Florence of California.

6.25in (16cm) high

$40-50 TOA

A 'Made in Occupied Japan' hand-painted bisque sleeping baby, painted "434" on the base.

4.75in (12cm) long

$25-35 TOA

A 'Made in Occupied Japan' hand-painted bisque figurine, of a small boy playing a fiddle.

Popular figurines made in the US were not the only target for post war Japanese manufacturers. This charming boy is a copy of German factory Goebel's 'Little Fiddler' Hummel figure, designed for Goebel by Arthur Moeller in 1935 and still in production today. Other children figures from the 'American Children's Series' are more valuable and can be worth up to $150.

4.75in (12cm) high

$25-35 TOA

A 'Made in Occupied Japan' hand-painted bisque figurine, of a seated baby with his hands held aloft.

As with the Hummel figurine to the left, this is a copy of German doll and ceramic maker Heubach's range of 'Piano Babies'. Although this is a finely molded and painted example, with a good facial expression, better examples closer to the high quality associated with Heubach can be found.

5in (12.5cm) high

$100-150 TOA

A U.C.A.G.CO China 'Made in Occupied Japan' hand-painted bisque Bacchanalian putto figurine, with grapes and cup.

U.C.A.G.CO stands for United China & Glass Company, which was a distributor of china and glassware based in New Orleans and New York. Their agent S. Stolaroff signed the first contract allowing Japanese imports into the US. During the 1950s, they were one of the biggest importers of Japanese ceramics.

6in (15cm) high

$50-60 TOA

A 'Made in Occupied Japan' hand-painted bisque 'Uncle Sam' figurine.

4.25in (11cm) high

$50-60   **TOA**

A 'Made in Occupied Japan' hand-painted ceramic Mickey Mouse figurine, playing a bassoon.

Mickey Mouse was a popular character for the Japanese to copy. Most were not licensed by Walt Disney, hence he can look very different to the real Mickey Mouse, as here. Note the mark on the base, which is typical of 'Made In Occupied Japan' pieces. If there is more space between the words, it is likely to be a later reproduction.

3.25in (8cm) high

$70-120   **TOA**

A Lenwile China Ardalt 'Made in Occupied Japan' hand-painted ceramic clown, printed "6141" on the base.

5in (12.5cm) high

$50-60   **TOA**

A 1950s 'Made in Occupied Japan' hand-painted ceramic tribesman figurine.

This figurine crosses two collecting areas – Occupied Japan and Black Americana.

4.75in (12cm) high

$45-55   **TOA**

A 'Made In Occupied Japan' hand-painted bisque humorous monkey figurine.

The 'fur' on this example is made using small flakes of the ceramic, giving a rough texture. Although it has been used for centuries, this technique is commonly found on early to mid-20thC German bisque 'snow baby' novelty figurines.

4in (10cm) high

$30-40   **TOA**

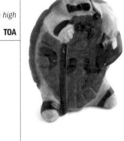

A 'Made in Occupied Japan' hand-painted ceramic standing 'business-turtle', with cane, monocle, hat and briefcase.

4.25in (10.5cm) high

$35-45   **TOA**

A pair of 'Made in Occupied Japan' turkey-shaped salt and pepper shakers.

These would also appeal to collectors of Thanksgiving holiday memorabilia.

2.5in (6.5cm) high

$20-25   **TOA**

A pair of 'Made In Occupied Japan' bear shaped salt and pepper shakers.

The form, color and particularly the closed eyes of these shakers indicate US maker Shawnee was the inspiration. However, Shawnee are better known for their pigs and cookie jars.

2.5in (6.5cm) high

$15-25   **TOA**

A 'Made in Occupied Japan' recumbent duck figure.

This is likely to be an un-licensed version of Donald Duck's girlfriend Daisy Duck, who made her debut in 1937.

4.25in (10.5cm) long

$35-45   **TOA**

A 'Made in Occupied Japan' hand-painted ceramic bassoon-player liquor bottle.

5in (13cm) high

$40-60   TOA

A 'Made in Occupied Japan' hand-painted ceramic centaur-shaped liquor bottle.

4in (10cm) high

$50-70   TOA

A 'Made in Occupied Japan' hand-painted ceramic 'Mexican' liquor bottle.

Liquor bottles are a popular area for collectors. They can be found in a wide variety of novelty shapes. Colorful and humorous shapes and recognisable characters are sought-after, as are finely painted or molded examples. The original contents does not add to the value.

6in (15cm) high

$50-70   TOA

A 'Made in Occupied Japan' hand-painted seated satyr-shaped liquor bottle.

Classical forms related to Greek and Roman Bacchanalian festivals, such as putti and satyrs are typical for liquor bottles.

4in (10cm) high

$55-65   TOA

A 'Made in Occupied Japan' hand-painted liquor bottle in the form of a Scottie dog and yellow puppy.

Dogs are one of the most common shapes for liquor bottles. The Scottie dog is the most popular and desirable breed to be featured, with examples usually being more valuable.

3.25in (8cm) high

$50-60   TOA

A 'Made in Occupied Japan' hand-painted ceramic liquor bottle, in the form of a Scottie dog and sorrowful looking puppy.

3.25in (8cm) high

$50-60   TOA

A 'Made in Occupied Japan' hand-painted ceramic liquor bottle, in the form of a squirrel holding a nut.

4in (10cm) high

$50-60   TOA

COLLECTORS' NOTES

■ William Moorcroft (1872-1945) began working at James McIntyre's Staffordshire, England, ceramics factory in 1898. His first major designs were the 'Aurelian' and 'Florian' ranges, with their often symmetrical and Moorish-inspired floral and foliate designs, which exemplified the prevalent Art Nouveau style in ceramics.

■ Moorcroft split from McIntyre's in 1912, founding his own company with backing from London retailer Liberty & Co., who had previously sold his designs with great success. His success grew, with the company being awarded the Royal Warrant in 1929. Stylized floral designs executed in a tube-lined process with rich and deep glaze colors became the company's hallmarks.

■ Tube-lining uses liquid clay piped on to the surface of the body forming enclosed 'cells' that are filled with

liquid glaze. William died in 1945 and his son Walter took over, continuing many of his father's designs, as well as introducing designs of his own. Here, the designer of the pattern is given, if known.

■ Early ranges, including 'Florian', 'Claremont' and 'Eventide', and limited production ranges tend to be the most valuable. However, more modern and even contemporary ranges by designers such as Sally Tuffin and Rachel Bishop are also becoming sought-after.

■ Pieces can be dated to a period from the shape, size, pattern, colors and type of marks on the base. Damage affects value considerably, so inspect a piece very carefully. Patterns produced for long periods of time tend to be the least valuable, particularly if on small sized pieces.

A 1980s Moorcroft 'Anemone' pattern baluster vase, designed by William Moorcroft, die-stamped "Moorcroft made in England" on the base and signed "WM" in green slip.

10.25in (26cm) high

$280-320 **BEL**

A Moorcroft 'Anemone' pattern shallow dish, signed to the base and with paper label.

9.5in (24cm) diam

$280-320 **MAX**

An early Moorcroft 'Claremont' pattern bowl, designed by William Moorcroft, typically decorated in shades of blue, green and red, with painted signature and date.

Claremont is a highly desirable range, registered in 1903 and named, and initially sold, by Liberty. It was produced for nearly 40 years. Later pieces have bolder rendering and stronger colors. This is also an unusual shape.

1914 *7in (18cm) wide*

$3,200-3,800 **GORL**

A Moorcroft 'Eventide' pattern baluster vase, designed by William Moorcroft, with a landscape design of trees against an ochre ground, cracked.

Landscape themes were popular in the 1920s and '30s. Eventide was launched in 1923.

c1925 *9in (23cm) high*

$1,200-1,800 **GORL**

A Moorcroft 'Coral Hibiscus' pattern baluster vase, designed by Walter Moorcroft, die-stamped "Moorcroft made in England", with a circular Moorcroft paper label.

'Hibiscus' was designed c1949 and 'Coral Hibiscus', with a single-colored flower, was introduced in 1968.

8.25in (21cm) high

$200-300 **BEL**

A Moorcroft 'Leaf & Berries' pattern bowl, with a blue foot, impressed facsimile mark "Potter to HM The Queen".

1929-49 *9in (23cm) diam*

$350-450 **SWO**

A Moorcroft 'Flambé Leaves and Fruit' pattern shouldered vase.

c1928-45 *4.25in (11cm) high*

$700-900 **GHOU**

CERAMICS

A CLOSER LOOK AT A MOORCROFT VASE

This range was designed by Philip Gibson, and was launched in 1999 to great acclaim.

The designs were complex to produce, particularly the long, flowing lines of the trout's body and the freehand dots used to create the trout's scales.

Although there are always two trout, a new design was created for each shape meaning there is more variation in design between shapes than in any other range.

The range was also expensive to produce, leading to a high retail price. The skill needed to decorate it, the low numbers produced and the great appeal of the design is likely to make it a Moorcroft classic.

A Moorcroft 'Trout' pattern squat vase, with two trout chasing a dragonfly, marked "Moorcroft Made in Stoke on Trent England" in green, the artist's mark "LB", "Copyrighted in 98" and a black "GP" stamp.

1999   8in (20cm) wide

$600-800   **BEL**

A Moorcroft 'Magnolia' pattern jardinière, designed by Walter Moorcroft, impressed and signed in green.

This pattern was introduced in 1976, initially in pink on blue and later also in pink on ivory, yellow and green backgrounds.

7in (18cm) high

$320-380   **MAX**

A pair of Moorcroft 'Meknes Night and Day' large vases, designed by Beverley Wilkes, dated "11-9-2002" and "24-3-2003".

15.5in (39.5cm) high

$1,500-2,000   **GHOU**

A Moorcroft ovoid 'Orchids' pattern vase, designed by William Moorcroft, with a design of multi-colored flowers against a deep green ground, incised facsimile signature and impressed "Potter to HM The Queen".

c1935   5in (12.5cm) high

$350-450   **GORL**

A 1930s Moorcroft 'Pomegranate' pattern vase, of flared cylindrical form, with triple handles, impressed and signed in green.

7.5in (19cm) high

$800-1,200   **MAX**

A Moorcroft 'Pomegranate' pattern posy vase, designed by William Moorcroft, painted initials and impressed marks including "M32", cracked.

2.75in (7cm) high

$320-380   **GORL**

A small Moorcroft 'Spring Flowers' pattern vase, designed by William Moorcroft, with a colorful array of flowers against a deep blue ground.

4.25in (11cm) high

$280-320   **GORL**

FIND OUT MORE...

Moorcroft, by Paul Atterbury, published by Richard Dennis, 1998.

CERAMICS

COLLECTORS' NOTES

■ Carter & Co. Pottery of Poole, Dorset, England, began producing domestic ware in 1921, through their subsidiary company, Carter, Stabler & Adams. Pieces by key designer Truda Adams (later Carter), typically hand-painted with Art Deco or floral designs, are desirable.

■ After WWII, Alfred Burgess Read became chief designer. He worked with thrower Guy Sydenham and painter Ruth Pavely to create effectively unique hand-thrown and hand-decorated pieces. Read's Swedish-inspired 1950s Contemporary range, with its bold stripes and wavy lines, is prized by collectors.

■ In 1958 Robert Jefferson became resident designer.

With Sydenham and Tony Morris he developed the Delphis range, bridging the gap between commercial ware and studio pottery. Typifying the 1960s and '70s with its bright colors and organic, abstract designs, Delphis has become popular with collectors today.

■ The Craft Section, set up in 1966, increased production of studio pottery and other decorative ranges such as Aegean, Ionian and Atlantis. Aegean, introduced in 1970, featured a dark color palette and a variety of decorating techniques.

■ Poole Studio Pottery underwent a renaissance in the mid-1990s. Look out for pieces by Sir Terry Frost, Sally Tuffin, Janice Tchalenko and Charlotte Mellis.

A Poole Pottery 'KS' pattern vase, by Eileen Prangnell, impressed "Poole England", painted artist cipher and "KS", small nick to base rim.

1924-37   6in (15cm) high

$180-220   **WW**

A Poole Pottery 'ED' pattern vase, shape 267, painted by Phyllis Ryall, with water staining.

Water staining is common, as these vases were bought to be used. Perfect examples are very sought-after.

1928-37 5.75in (14.5cm) high

$70-100   **KCS**

A Poole Pottery 'HE' pattern vase, shape 203, painted by Ruth Pavely, with the early swastika mark.

This pattern is better known as the 'Bluebird' pattern and was designed by Truda Adams. Popular paintress Pavely used a swastika painter's mark from 1922 until 1937 when she changed it, presumably due to its adoption by Nazi Germany. Pieces bearing this mark are more desirable those with the mark she used afterwards.

1922-37

$450-550   **KCS**

A 1930s Carter, Stabler & Adams Poole Pottery vase, with floral decoration.

6.5in (16.5cm) high

$50-70   **GOR**

A Poole Pottery 'CO' pattern trial vase, shape 969, pattern designed by Truda Carter, painted by Hilda Hampton, with hexagonal trial mark.

Trial pieces are more desirable than standard pieces and may show extreme or very subtle variations on the standard line.

1930-34

$280-320   **KCS**

A pair of Poole Pottery 'BF' pattern sprig vases, shape 443, painted by Hazel Allner.

These traditionally decorated vases were first made in the early 1920s. These later examples would have been made alongside more modern designs developed after WWII.

1946-57   7in (18cm) high

$220-280   **KCS**

A Carter, Stabler & Adams Poole Pottery 'EN' pattern vase, shape 380, painted by Margaret Holder.

This example only has painted decoration on the lower half of the vase. Examples that are fully covered with the pattern are more valuable.

1925-34   6.5in (16.5cm) high

$180-220   **KCS**

A Poole Pottery 'PC' pattern vase, shape 803, painted by Sheila Jenkins.

This is a rare shape to find as it has molded, banded decoration.

1949-61   5.75in (14.5cm) high

$70-100   **KCS**

A 1930s Poole Pottery 'BN' pattern vase, shape 596, painted by Myrtle Bond (1927-42).

This is a rare shape and also displays the pattern well due to its size.

9in (23cm) high

$280-320   **KCS**

A Carter, Stabler & Adams Poole Pottery 'Bluebird' pattern earthenware cylindrical vase, painted by Anne Hatchard.

1922-37   10in (25.5cm) high

$100-150   **CA**

A rare and early Poole Pottery 'VE' pattern red earthenware jam pot, shape 288, painted by Dorothy James.

This rare 'Jazz' pattern is desirable. A more standard patterned jam pot would be worth upto $70. The red earthenware body was used from 1922 until 1934 when it was changed to a white body.

1924-34   4in (10cm) high

$100-150   **KCS**

A Poole Pottery 'V' pattern jam pot, shape 286, painted by Marjorie Cryer.

1934-37   4in (10cm) high

$70-100   **KCS**

A Poole Pottery 'AP' pattern bowl, shape 432, painted by Vera Mills.

1936   8in (20cm) wide

$180-220   **KCS**

A rare Carter, Stabler & Adams Poole Pottery 'RP' pattern red earthenware footed bowl, shape 495, painted by Ruth Pavely, with impressed mark.

1922-34 9.25in (23.5cm) wide

$220-280   **KCS**

A Poole Pottery 'MD' pattern red earthware trial shallow bowl, shape 413, painted by Eileen Prangnell.

It is rare to find this pattern with a bird included.

1924-37   8in (20cm) diam

$250-350   **KCS**

CERAMICS

A 1920s Carter, Stabler & Adams 'Sheep in Meadow' tile, by Dora Batty, from the Nursery Toys series.

5in (12.5cm) wide

$220-280   **KCS**

A 1920s Carter, Stabler & Adams 'Little Miss Muffet' tile, by Dora Batty, NR6, from the Nursery Rhyme series.

5in (12.5cm) wide

$220-280   **KCS**

A 1920s Carter, Stabler & Adams tile, by Joseph Rouelants, from the Dutch series.

6in (15cm) wide

$280-320   **KCS**

An early 1920s Carter & Co. Architectural Keramic Works, Poole ceramic advertising paperweight, possibly unique.

3in (7.5cm) wide

$180-220   **KCS**

An early 1930s Poole Pottery red earthenware footed bowl, designed by John Adams, shape 463, with unusual embossed and impressed marks.

This range was the forerunner to the Sylvan Ware line.

6.5in (16.5cm) diam

$120-180   **KCS**

A Poole Pottery Sylvan Ware 'M22' jug, shape 319, designed by John Adams.

M22 refers to the glaze color.

1934   5.5in (14cm) high

$80-120   **KCS**

A 1920s/30s Poole Pottery green luster slipware glaze beaker.

This late beaker displays a glaze that was used between 1900-18 and was developed by Owen Carter.

3in (7.5cm) high

$100-150   **KCS**

A 1930s Poole Pottery three-branch grape candlestick, designed by John Adams, with white glaze.

Available as single, double, triple or quadruple candlesticks, and in different colored glazes, an example was shown at the British Industries Fair in 1931.

8.5in (21.5cm) high

$180-220   **C**

A mid-to late 1930s Poole Pottery model of a fish, no. 314, probably designed by John Adams and modeled by Harry Brown, with Picotee green and blue glazes.

8.5in (21.5cm) high

$600-700   **C**

A 1950s Poole Pottery 'Freeform' plain carafe, shape 690, designed by Guy Sydenham.

10.5in (26.5cm) high

$220-280 **KCS**

A 1950s Poole Pottery 'Freeform' 'PJ.B' pattern vase, shape 703, the shape designed by Guy Sydenham and Alfred Read, the pattern designed by Alfred Read.

7.75in (19.5cm) high

$150-200 **GAZE**

A 1950s Poole Pottery 'PL.T' pattern waisted vase, shape 669 designed by Guy Sydenham and Alfred Read, the pattern by Read, printed mark and painted monogram.

7.75in (19.5cm) high

$280-320 **LFA**

A 1950s Poole Pottery 'PL.C' pattern Contemporary vase, shape 686 by Claude Smale and Guy Sydenham, the pattern designed by Alfred Read, impressed "98", painted marks.

9.75in (24.5cm) high

$180-220 **GAZE**

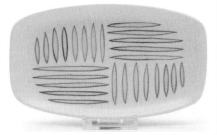

A Poole Pottery 'ROC' pattern cucumber dish, shape 555, the shape designed by John Adams c1935, the pattern designed by Ruth Pavely in 1954.

c1955 16in (40.5cm) wide

$50-70 **C**

A Poole Pottery 'UIL' pattern tray, shape 361, the shape designed by Alfred Read and Guy Sydenham, the pattern designed by Ruth Pavely and Ann Read, with pre-1959 back stamp.

1956-58 7in (18cm) wide

$40-60 **NPC**

A Poole Pottery 'Poole Whaler 1783' deep dish plate, painted by Gwen Haskins, from a design by Arthur Bradbury.

Being based in a coastal town, ships have featured on a number of pieces. Ship plates were introduced in the 1930s and can still be commissioned from the pottery today.

1950 15in (38cm) diam

$1,000-1,500 **C**

A Poole Pottery display plaque, designed and first painted by Ann Read in 1956.

14in (35.5cm) wide

$700-1,000 **C**

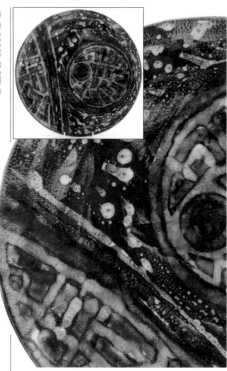

A Poole Studio Pottery small pin tray, painted in an abstract architectural green and blue design.

5in (12.5cm) wide

$120-180   C

A Poole Studio Pottery hand-thrown dish, by Guy Sydenham, with an orange ship's wheel design, marks to base.

12in (30.5cm) diam

$500-600   C

A Poole Studio Pottery charger, by Tony Morris, finished in an abstract architectural design in blue and green on a white ground, impressed "Poole Studio" to back and Tony Morris monogram to back.

1962-82   *13.5in (34.5cm) diam*

$3,200-3,800   C

A Poole Studio Pottery plate, shape 58.

1964-66   *13in (33cm) diam*

$700-800   KCS

A Poole Studio Pottery bowl, decorated by Thelma Bush.

1966   *5in (12.5cm) wide*

$220-280   KCS

A Poole Studio Pottery plate, designed by Robert Jefferson.

1964-66   *8in (20cm) diam*

$180-220   KCS

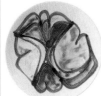

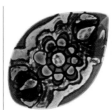

A 1960s Poole Pottery Delphis plate, painted in a swirl of colors, unknown artist.

A late 1960s Poole Pottery Delphis plate, with rare white background.

A late 1960s Poole Pottery Delphis plate, shape 4, with textured decoration.

Textured decoration is unusual, adding to the value.

A 1960s Poole Pottery Delphis shield dish, shape 91.

10.5in (26.5cm) diam

8in (20cm) diam

10.5in (26cm) diam

12in (30.5cm) long

$220-280   C

$100-150   KCS

$180-220   KCS

$100-150   KCS

A Poole Pottery Delphis bowl, painted by Thelma Bush.

The Delphis range developed out of the Studio line and this early example shows the range's heritage – the colors and design are both from the Studio line and were not officially part of the Delphis range.

1967-68   5.5in (14cm) wide

$280-320   KCS

A CLOSER LOOK AT A POOLE POTTERY CHARGER

This large charger is typical of later examples from the Delphis range.

Despite each piece being hand-painted, this symmetrical, stylized floral decoration is commonly found on later Delphis pieces.

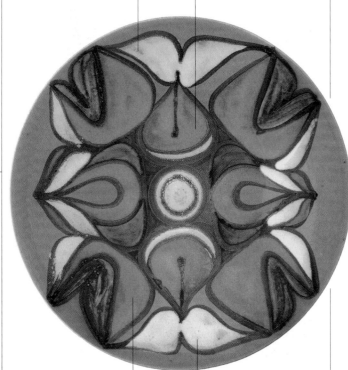

A Poole Pottery Delphis shield dish, painted by Carol Cutler, shape 91.

Carol Cutler is one of Poole's most sought-after Delphis paintresses. The stylized 'alien face' is typical of her work.

1969-75   12in (30.5cm) long

$100-150   KCS

In 1971, the color palette was refined to yellow, orange, green and red.

The large size format is ideal for displaying the pattern.

A Poole Pottery Delphis charger, painted by Cynthia Bennett.

1971-77

16in (40.5cm) diam

$450-550   KCS

A Poole Pottery Delphis small vase, shape 31, painted by Carol Kellett (née Cutler), with blue and green decoration.

This vase has been decorated with two linking Cs, which are typical of Cutler's work. The use of blue and green together is unusual.

A Poole Pottery 'Delphis' vase, shape 90, painted by Jean Millership.

This is a rare shape.

1966-69   8in (20cm) high

$450-550   **KCS**

c1969

$70-100   **KCS**

A Poole Pottery Delphis vase, factory and painters mark to base.

5.5in (14cm) high

$220-280   **JN**

An early and unusual Poole Pottery Delphis carved vase, painted by Geraldine O'Meara.

This is a very early Delphis vase, O'Meara only worked at Poole for one year. The use of carved decoration in two directions is rare.

1966   9in (23cm) high

$220-280   **KCS**

A rare Poole Pottery 'Delphis' hand-potted vase, shape 83, by Christine Tate.

1964-70   6in (15cm) high

$100-150   **KCS**

A rare Poole Pottery 'Delphis' carved vase, painted by Irene Kirton.

Carved decoration and the use of purple are both rare.

1968-69 15.5in (39.5cm) high

$600-800   **KCS**

An early Poole Pottery 'Delphis' textured vase, painted by Angela Wyburgh.

The use of blue and green indicates this is from the start of the Delphis range and the textured finish is desirable. Wyburgh is a sought-after artist and her pieces are rising in value.

A Poole Pottery 'Delphis' vase, shape 84, painted by Ingrid Hammond.

This is a rare shape.

1971-73   9in (23cm) high

$220-280   **KCS**

A late 1960s Poole Pottery Delphis vase, shape 83, unmarked.

The use of deep red indicates this is an early example from the Delphis range.

5.75in (14.5cm) high

$70-100   **KCS**

c1968

$600-800   **KCS**

15.5in (39.5cm) high

KCS

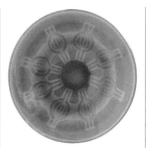

A Poole Pottery Aegean large bowl, pattern number 58.

13.5in (34.5cm) diam

$180-220 FD

A unique 1970s Poole Pottery Aegean charger, by Ros Sommerfelt.

Sommerfelt is a sought-after Aegean range paintress.

13in (33cm) diam

$600-800 KCS

A Poole Pottery Aegean charger, marked "A" for trial piece.

1974-75 12.5in (31.5cm) diam

$220-280 KCS

A 1970s Poole Pottery Aegean 'Yacht' pattern plate, shape 4.

Leslie Elsden was responsible for the creation of the Aegean range. He also designed this, one of a series of 'Yacht' patterns.

10.5in (20cm) diam

$70-100 KCS

A Poole Pottery Aegean sweet dish, shape 82.

17.25in (44cm) long

$35-45 GAZE

A Poole Pottery Aegean vase, shape 84, potted by Alan White and painted by Julie Wills.

1972-78 9in (23cm) high

$220-280 KCS

A 1970s Poole Pottery Aegean vase, shape 85, with sgraffito decoration, and 'mosaic' band.

16in (40.5cm) high

$350-450 KCS

A Poole Pottery Aegean gray vase, by Carol Kellett (née Cutler), based on shape 84.

The use of gray is rare and the pattern is unusual.

1976-78

$700-900 KCS

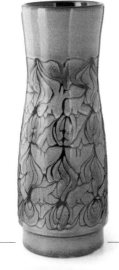

A late 1970s Poole Pottery 'Aegean' vase, hand-potted by Alan White, with sgraffito decoration.

Alan White is considered one of Poole's best potters. The use of sgraffito to create a 'silhouette' design is common to the Aegean range.

15.75in (40cm) high

$250-350 KCS

CERAMICS

A rare Poole Pottery Atlantis A20/3 vase, by Carol Kellett (née Cutler), marked with artist's cipher and "Poole, England".

Developed by Guy Sydenham out of the Craft Section, the Atlantis range was launched in 1969. The 'studio' style pieces were produced in muted colors on red, gray or black bodies that were often carved. Many pieces were produced by Sydenham himself.

1972-77   5.5in (14cm) high

$450-550   **FD**

A Poole Pottery Atlantis A14/1 bowl, thrown and painted by Catherine Connett.

1973-76

$50-70   **GAZE**

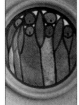

A Poole Pottery Ionian small stoneware bowl, with a stylized design.

This short-lived range was produced between 1974-75 and was an elaborate variation on the Aegean range. It is comparatively rare and sought-after today.

1974-75   5.75in (14.5cm) diam

$45-55   **FD**

A CLOSER LOOK AT A POOLE POTTERY VASE

The Olympus range was only produced for one year and is gaining in popularity.

The shapes and patterns were designed by Ros Sommerfelt and all feature a band of decoration, the themes usually being fruit, flowers, seeds or the seashore.

Ros Sommerfelt began working in 1970 as a paintress on the Delphis range and also painted the Aegean range. She was also responsible for developing the Beardsley and Dorset ranges.

Carol Kellett is a popular and collectable paintress.

A Poole Pottery Atlantis A14/1 bowl, thrown and painted by Catherine Connett.

1973-76

$120-180   **GAZE**

A Poole Pottery Ionian vase, carved with sunrise motif, printed marks.

1974-75   12.5in (32cm) high

$350-450   **WW**

A Poole Pottery Olympus hand-potted stoneware vase, shape 63, painted and potted by Carol Kellett (née Cutler).

1975-76   6in (15cm) high

$100-150   **KCS**

A Poole Studio Pottery bottle vase, hand-potted and decorated by Alan White, with seal to bottom.

The tradition of studio-type wares began in the 1920s and proved particularly successful in the 1960s when it spawned successful ranges such as Delphis and Aegean. The Poole Studio was re-established in 1995 and produces unique pieces, such as this, as well as limited editions. White has added his seal to this vase, which was reserved for special pieces.

c1995   8in (20cm) high

$250-350   **KCS**

A Poole Studio Pottery 'HX' pattern vase, by Karen Brown.

Based on the traditional patterns from the 1920s and '30s, these vases are made to order. Karen Brown first worked in the Traditional Decoration department when she joined Poole in 1973.

2004   10in (25.5cm) high

$280-320   **KCS**

A Poole Studio Pottery 'HX' pattern vase, by Sue M. Pottinger, made to order.

2004   10.25in (26cm) high

$280-320   **KCS**

A Poole Studio Pottery 'Old Harry Rocks' Athens vase, from the 'Isle of Purbeck' series designed by Karen Brown.

Introduced in 1997, the Athens vase was made exclusively for the Poole Collectors' Club.

10.5in (26.5cm) high

$150-200   **CHEF**

A limited production Poole Studio Pottery 'Fish' vase, designed by Sally Tuffin.

This vase was only made from one year.

1996   8in (20cm) high

$220-280   **KCS**

A Poole pottery terracotta owl plate, thrown and glazed by Alan White.

c1996   12in (30.5cm) diam

$280-320   **C**

A 1990s Poole Studio Pottery Egyptian plate, designed and painted by Nicola Massarella, with "NN15" date mark.

8in (20cm) diam

$120-180   **KCS**

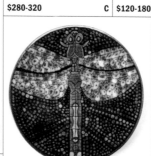

A late 1990s Poole Studio Pottery limited edition plate, designed by Tony Morris and painted by Nicola Massarella, from an edition of 100.

14in (35.5cm) diam

$600-800   **KCS**

A Poole Pottery 'Seagull' pattern dish, designed by Sally Tuffin, dated "10/06/1998".

Made in three sizes, this, the largest size dish is the rarest and the most valuable.

1998   14in (35.5cm) diam

$400-500   **KCS**

FIND OUT MORE...

Poole Pottery, *by Leslie Hayward, published by Richard Dennis, third edition 2002.*

COLLECTORS' NOTES

■ The Postmodern movement, led by architects such as Ettore Sottsass, developed at Studio Alchimia during the late 1970s and boomed with the Memphis Group in the 1980s. Ceramics were an integral part of the movement. Typical styles include the use of traditional architectural and historical references and forms, bright colors, geometric designs, the use of unusual materials and a certain type of wit in combining these themes.

■ Bitossi in Italy produced many of these designers' works, and some have been re-issued since. Production is kept to a small amount, keeping prices relatively high. However, as the movement is not currently considered fashionable, bargains can still be found. In its time the movement was highly popular and representative, and is arguably yet to reach its peak on the secondary market. See p183-4 for Postmodern ceramics by Swid Powell.

An Italian Bitossi 'Vaso Calice' hand-painted ceramic goblet vase, designed by Ettore Sottsass.

This is a contemporary re-issue of Sottsass' 1960 design.

18.25in (46.5cm) high

$300-400   **GM**

An Italian Bitossi 'Vaso Ossidante Turch' blue and oxidised copper glazed vase, designed by Ettore Sottsass, with unglazed white band under the rim and signed underneath.

This vase has been recently re-issued.

8.75in (22cm) high

$250-350   **GM**

An Italian Giotto 'JG4' blue ceramic vase, designed by Johanna Grawunder in 1992, in a 'sprung' steel holder.

The Giotto range, designed by Grawunder and Sottsass was intended to be made inexpensively in the Far East, opening this style of design up to more people. However, the deal never took off and very few examples were made, making them rare today.

c1992   9.25in (23cm) high

$1,000-1,500   **GM**

A Peter Shire hand-painted and handmade ceramic studio teapot, signed on the base "P.X. SHIR.E 1996".

1996   9in (23cm) wide

$700-1,000   **GM**

A 1990s Italian Bitossi 'E-Vaso' double vase, designed by Paola Palma and Carlo Vannicola in 1990, the central urn-shaped vase sliding out of the main body.

This was available in a range of colours including black and white, and burgundy and white. This green 'verdigris' glazed finish recalls weathered bronze garden urns.

9.75in (24.5cm) high

$220-280   **GM**

A set of German Ritzenhoff 'Dinner For Two' transfer-printed dinner plates, designed by Alessandro Guerriero in 1990, with original card box.

Note the use of (neo) classical sculpture as imagery.

Largest 12.75in (32cm) wide

$120-180   **GM**

COLLECTORS' NOTES

■ Maria Longworth Nichols founded the Rookwood pottery as a continuation of her interest in painting ceramics, a popular hobby with high society Cincinnati ladies. The pottery was established in 1880 with money from the Longworth family and initially was not a commercial success. In 1883, William Watts Taylor was employed as business manager and began to make the pottery more commercially viable. By 1888 the pottery was turning a substantial profit and, following Nichols' remarriage, Taylor took control of Rookwood in 1890.

■ With the employment of a number of talented artists such as Albert R. Valentien, Artus Van Briggle, Kataro Shirayamadani and Matt Daly, the pottery gained a reputation for high quality hand-decorated art pottery. Taylor also hired pioneering chemists to rediscover

ancient glaze techniques or to develop new ones including the brown Standard glaze, Iris and Vellum, all of which are sought-after by collectors today. Due to the quality of the glazes, crazing, particularly on high-gloss examples, can effect value considerably.

■ The Great Depression lead to the quality of production decreasing at the Rookwood pottery and in 1932 the majority of staff were laid-off. The company changed hands a number of times before finally closing in 1960.

■ Given the quality of the artists involved with Rookwood, signed examples are always desirable. Large-sized pieces and those decorated with landscapes, portraits or other unusual subject matter also tend to be more desirable.

A Rookwood Vellum bulbous vase, decorated by Ed Diers, with white and pink cherry blossoms on a blue ground, burst glaze bubbles to interior, with flame mark, date mark XXVI, shape no. 2831 and artist's mark "ED".

Ed Diers was an artist at Rookwood from 1896 to 1931.

1926   5.75in (14.5cm) high

$1,000-1,500   DRA

A Rookwood Vellum bulbous vase, decorated by Margaret H. McDonald, with white and pink trumpet vines on apricot ground, uncrazed, with flame mark, date mark XXX, shape no. 927F and artist's initials "MHM".

1930   6in (15cm) high

$1,200-1,800   DRA

A Rookwood Vellum baluster vase, decorated by Ed Diers, with pink roses on an ivory-to-green ground, seconded mark for glaze miss near base, with flame mark and "VII/935D/K1/88X/ED/V/XXX".

1907   7.5in (19cm) high

$1,200-1,800   DRA

A Rookwood Scenic Vellum vase, decorated by Fred Rothenbusch, with a band of ships, seconded for unknown reason, minor glaze flake, with flame mark, date mark VIII, shape no. 946, artist's mark "FR" and seconded mark "X".

Despite being marked as a 'second', this is still a desirable piece. The ship decoration is unusual, the size is large, being over 10in (25.5cm) high and Rothenbusch is a sought-after artist. The value would have been higher if the decoration had covered more of the vessel, rather than just a band of decoration around the body.

1908   10.75in (27.5cm) high

$2,800-3,200   DRA

A Rookwood Scenic Vellum tall vase, decorated by Fred Rothenbusch, with a moody landscape under a gray sky, with flame mark, date mark XIV, shape no. B951 and artist's mark "FR".

1914   12.75in (32.5cm) high

$2,800-3,200   DRA

A Rookwood Green Vellum tall vase, decorated by Fred Rothenbusch, minor bruise to rim, with flame mark, date mark XVI, shape no. 952D, Vellum mark "V" and artist's mark "FR".

1916   9.5in (24cm) high

$2,500-3,000   DRA

A massive Rookwood Double Vellum matte glaze vase, by Louise Abel, hand-decorated with large, stylized blooms in brick red on top of green and blue leaves and foliage on a mustard yellow background, with flame mark, date mark XXVII, shape no. 324 and artist's mark, some light peppering to the glaze.

Vellum pieces in this large size are very unusual.

1927   17in (43cm) high

$3,000-4,000   BEL

A Rookwood Vellum glaze tapered vase, decorated by Kataro Shirayamadani, with water lilies on a pond, with flame mark, date mark VII, shape no. 950D, "V" for Vellum and the artist's Japanese cipher, uncrazed, some very light peppering to the glaze and a slightly thin area of color near the base.

As well as being by celebrated artist Kataro Shirayamadani, this example displays no crazing, which is highly unusual for early Vellum pieces.

1907   9in (23cm) high

$5,500-6,500   BEL

A Rookwood Scenic Vellum tapering vase, decorated by Sallie Coyne, with a river landscape in greens, purples and vermillion, seconded mark probably for unobtrusive short glaze separations, with flame mark, date mark XX, shape no. 1655E, "V" for Vellum and artist's mark "SEC".

1920   8.5in (21.5cm) high

$2,000-3,000   DRA

A CLOSER LOOK AT A VELLUM VASE

A Rookwood Scenic Vellum bulbous vase, decorated by Ed Diers, with trees in a landscape, with flame mark, date mark XXI, shape no. 2066, "V" for Vellum and artist's mark "ED".

1921   7.75in (19.5cm) high

$1,800-2,200   DRA

Vellum is one of Rookwood's most collected ranges.

Landscapes are complex patterns – here the sense of perspective and light and shade is captured atmospherically.

Kataro Shirayamadani was perhaps Rookwood's most talented artist and pieces by him are always highly sought-after.

At 15in (38cm) high, this is taller than the average Vellum piece making it more desirable.

Vellum produced prior to 1915 are prone to crazing, which can reduce the value by around 40 per cent.

A Rookwood Scenic Vellum vase, decorated by Kataro Shirayamadani, with a scene of a wooded pond, with flame mark, date mark XII, shape no. 1369B, the letter "V" for vellum and the artist's incised Japanese signature, minor nick to the glaze.

1912   15in (38cm) high

$10,000-15,000   BEL

A rare Rookwood carved Iris glaze tall tapering vase, decorated by John D. Wareham, with hummingbirds in flight, uncrazed, restoration to base and to the surface of one bird, with flame mark, shape no. 807, artist's mark "JDW" and "L78".

Birds are an unusual subject matter for Iris glaze pieces. Flowers and plants are much more common.

1900   12.75in (32.5cm) high

$2,500-3,000   **DRA**

A Rookwood Iris glaze cylindrical vase, decorated by Sallie Coyne, with pink roses on a shaded ground, uncrazed, but seconded for grinding inconsistency on base, with flame mark, date mark VI, shape no. 952E, artist's mark "SEC", "W" for Iris and seconded mark "X".

1906   7in (18cm) high

$1,000-1,500   **DRA**

A Rookwood Iris glaze ovoid vase, decorated by Ed Diers, with purple violets on a slate gray ground, small scratch to glaze on front, with flame mark, date mark II, shape no. 917D, artist's mark "ED" and "W" for Iris glaze.

1902   6.75in (17cm) high

$1,200-1,800   **DRA**

A Rookwood Iris glaze vase, decorated by Sara Sax, with yellow and purple pansies on a yellow ground, with flame mark, date mark II, shape no. 77C, "W" for Iris glaze and artist's cipher.

1902   5in (12.5cm) high

$1,800-2,200   **DRA**

A CLOSER LOOK AT AN IRIS GLAZE VASE

Matthew Andrew Daly (1860-1937) worked at Rookwood from 1882 until 1903. He was a highly talented, and now sought-after, artist.

This vase was decorated the year that the Iris glaze was introduced.

Due to the colors used, other glazes are sometimes mistaken for the more desirable Iris glaze. Look for the "W" backstamp and the use of white clay, which was predominately used on the range.

The clear high gloss of the glaze means that crazing has a detrimental effect on the decoration and so the value.

A rare Rookwood carved Iris Glaze vase, by Matthew A. Daly, decorated with four heavily carved acanthus leaves finished in a frothy beige and green over a pale green to chartreuse background, with Rookwood logo and 14 flames, shape no. 907E, "M.A. Daly" and "W" for Iris Glaze, remnants of red crayon cataloging numbers from the Cincinnati Art Museum, in mint condition with lighter-than-average crazing.

1900   8.5in (21.5cm) high

$3,500-4,500   **BEL**

A Rookwood Iris Glaze vase, decorated by Olga Geneva Reed, with clovers applied in heavy slip on a light brown background, with flame mark, date mark III, shape no. 907F, "W" for Iris glaze and the artist's initials, with crazing.

1903   7in (18cm) high

$1,000-1,500   **BEL**

A Rookwood Standard glaze spherical vase, attributed to Caroline Steinle, with branches of amber cherry blossoms, with flame mark, shape no. 880 and artist's mark "CS".

1899   *6in (15cm) high*

$450-550   **DRA**

A Rookwood Standard glaze vase, by Edith Felten, with floral decoration, with flame mark, date mark IV, shape no. 914F and the artist's initials, top rim professionally restored.

1904   *4.25in (11cm) high*

$150-250   **BEL**

An early Rookwood dark Standard glaze ovoid vase, painted by A.R. Valentien, with apple blossoms, a few small burst bubbles, marked "ROOKWOOD", date, shape no. C271 and artist's mark "A.R.V. "

1886   *8.5in (21.5cm) high*

$700-800   **DRA**

A Rookwood Standard glaze narrow vase, painted by Sara Sax, with red poppies on a shaded ground, a few shallow scratches to surface, with flame mark, shape no. 829 and artist's mark "SAX".

Sara Sax is another desirable Rookwood artist.

1899   *9.25in (23.5cm) high*

$800-1,000   **DRA**

A Rookwood Celadon Green glaze vase, decorated with a South American scene, with Rookwood logo, date mark XLIV and shape no. 6762.

1944   *5.5in (14cm) high*

£180-220   **BEL**

A Rookwood Celadon Green high glaze vase, with molded iris decoration, with Rookwood logo, date mark XLVI and shape no. 6830.

1946   *6.5in (16.5cm) high*

$100-150   **BEL**

A Rookwood bright green high glaze vase, with stylized floral decoration, with Rookwood logo, date mark LI and shape no. 6363.

1951   *5.75in (14.5cm) high*

$120-180   **BEL**

A Rookwood bright green high glaze vase, with Rookwood logo, date mark XXV and shape no. 2905, opposing lines to the body of the vase.

1925   *9.25in (23.5cm) high*

$80-120   **BEL**

A Rookwood green gloss console bowl, with Rookwood logo, date mark LIV and shape no. 6826, with a wheel ground seconds mark "X" for no apparent reason.

1954   *13in (33cm) wide*

$80-120   **BEL**

A Rookwood high glaze bowl, decorated by Sara Sax, with blueberries around the rim over a background of light blue and a deep cobalt interior, with Rookwood logo, date mark XXII, shape no. 955 and artist's mark, uncrazed.

1922   *4.75in (12cm) wide*

$700-900   **BEL**

A Rookwood tapering vessel, decorated by Caroline Stegner, with silhouette of a rabbit in gray, with Rookwood logo, "XLVI", shape number 6569, numbers 3318 and 62 and the artist's mark.

1946   *7in (18cm) wide*

$600-800   **BEL**

A Rookwood vase, with stylized leaves finished in an unusual deep aqua-colored crystalline high glaze, with olive spots throughout, with Rookwood logo, date no. XXXI, shape no. 6233 and fan-shaped 50th Anniversary mark.

1931   *5in (12.5cm) high*

$180-220   **BEL**

A Rookwood beige semi-gloss glaze vase, with stylized floral decoration, with Rookwood logo, date mark XLVI, and shape no. 6777, in mint condition and uncrazed.

1946   *11.75in (30cm) high*

$220-280   **BEL**

A Rookwood bright sky blue high glaze vase, with Rookwood logo, date mark XL and shape no. S2169, uncrazed.

7.5in (19cm) high

$100-150   **BEL**

A Rookwood high glaze vase, decorated by Margaret McDonald, with oak leaves, branches and acorns, with Rookwood logo, date mark, shape no. 6211 and artist's cipher, uncrazed.

This is a large size piece, well-covered in decoration and in clean, uncrazed condition.

1936   *10in (25.5cm) high*

$2,500-3,000   **BEL**

A Rookwood Black Opal glaze vase, decorated and finished by Harriet Wilcox, with Rookwood logo, date mark XXVII, shape no. 2989 and the artist's initials in black slip, uncrazed, unobtrusive factory flaw at the base.

1927   *6.75in (17cm) high*

$600-800   **BEL**

A Rookwood pitcher, decorated by Harriet Wilcox, with purple wisteria, the entire design outlined in gold with gold spider webs, with Rookwood logo and four flames, shape no. 343 and "W. HEW" painted in gold at the base, professional restoration to handle and rim.

7.25in (18.5cm) high

$220-280   **BEL**

A Rookwood trivet tile, in handcrafted Mission oak frame.

Tile 5.25in (13.5cm) wide

$250-300   **BEL**

A Rookwood matte blue vase, with Rookwood logo, date mark XLIII and shape no. 6432, with a wheel ground "X" due to a stilt pull at the base.

1943　　　　*4in (10cm) high*

£100-150　　　　　　**BEL**

A Rookwood matte blue vase, decorated with butterflies, with Rookwood logo, date mark XLV and shape no. 6457.

1945　　*4.75in (12cm) high*

$150-200　　　　　**BEL**

A Rookwood matte blue vase, decorated with molded irises, with Rookwood logo, date mark XXVIII and shape no. 2476.

1928　　*8.5in (21.5cm) high*

$280-320　　　　　**BEL**

A Rookwood matte vase, decorated by John Welsey Pullman, with Rookwood logo, date mark XVII, shape no. 1016C and artist's mark.

1927　　*8.5in (21.5cm) high*

$1,000-1,500　　　　**BEL**

A Rookwood graduated bell flower vase, decorated by Charles Todd, with blue flowers with burgundy rim, date mark for 1919, and artist's mark "CST".

7in (18cm) high

$1,000-1,500　　　　**TOJ**

A Rookwood Production ware beige vase, #2217, Rookwood flame mark, date mark XIX, shape no. 2142.

1921　　　*7.5in (19cm) high*

$500-700　　　　　**TOJ**

A Rookwood matte glaze vase, by Janet Harris, with atypical decoration of vining leaves and fruit on a trellis background, with Rookwood logo, date mark XXX, shape no. 2734 and artist's cipher.

1930　　*8.5in (21.5cm) high*

$1,000-1,500　　　　**BEL**

A rare Rookwood Painted Matte glaze vase, decorated by Charles S. Todd, the tapered, closed lip vase encircled in a vine of bleeding heart flowers in browns, greens and maroons, with Rookwood logo, date mark XI, shape no. 1865 and the artist's mark in slip.

1911　　　　　*7.5in (19cm) high*

$1,500-2,000　　　　　**BEL**

A Rookwood rich pink glaze vase, with window pane ovals and drip effect, with Rookwood logo, date mark XXIII and shape no. 2433.

1923　　　*9in (23cm) high*

$250-350　　　　　**BEL**

COLLECTORS' NOTES

■ Rosenthal was founded as a porcelain decorating company in 1879, and began producing its own ceramics in 1891. Products were first marked with the company name in 1907. Quality has always been high and after WWII it began working with many notable designers, producing innovative designs, many under its higher end 'Studio Linie' brand.

■ Danish designer Bjørn Wiinblad (b.1918) began designing for the company in 1957 and continues today. He is known for his poster, glass and theatrical designs as well as his ceramic designs for his own studio and Nymølle. For examples of these, please see p177. Most patterns are transfer-printed and focus on his core themes of legends, fairy tales or stories.

A 1970s/80s German Rosenthal Studio Linie vase, from the 1001 Nights series designed by Bjørn Wiinblad, with printed Rosenthal backstamp in green and Wiinblad's facsimile signature to base.

6in (15cm) high

$180-220   **RWA**

A 1970s/80 German Rosenthal Studio Linie vase, from the 1001 Nights series designed by Bjørn Wiinblad, with printed Rosenthal backstamp in green and Wiinblad's facsimile signature to base.

8in (20cm) high

$220-280   **RWA**

A 1990s German Rosenthal Studio Linie vase, from the '1001 Nights' series, designed by Bjørn Wiinblad, with printed round Rosenthal mark and Wiinblad's facsimile signature to base.

Produced from 1976-96, this was one of Wiinblad's most popular designs for Rosenthal, particularly in blue. Large vases, such as this, were expensive at the time making them rare today.

9.5in (24.5cm) high

$350-450   **RWA**

A 1970s/80s German Rosenthal Studio Linie vase, by Bjørn Wiinblad, decorated with a female figure, with Henning Hansen retailers sticker, with printed Rosenthal mark.

14.25in (36cm) high

$220-280   **RWA**

A German Rosenthal Studio Linie porcelain bottle vase, designed by Bjørn Wiinblad, with gold transfer pattern of a Chinaman in a landscape, the base with printed mark.

10.75in (27cm) high

$150-200   **L&T**

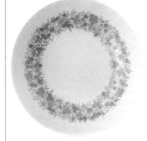

A German Rosenthal 'Romanze' ceramic vase, designed by Bjørn Wiinblad, with gold transfer floral pattern, printed marks and signature.

6.25in (16cm) high

$80-120   **TCM**

A German Rosenthal 'Romanze' ceramic dish, designed by Bjørn Wiinblad, with gold transfer floral pattern, with printed marks and signature.

$100-150   **TCM**

A German Rosenthal Studio Linie figural candlestick, designed by Bjørn Wiinblad, with circular impressed stamp to base.

More valuable blue and white handmade designs, similar to this, were also produced at Wiinblad's personal studio in Denmark.

13in (33cm) high

$70-90   **GAZE**

A Roseville 'Futura' range star-shaped vase, in green and gray glaze, unmarked.

8in (20cm) high

$550-650 DRA

A CLOSER LOOK AT ROSEVILLE FUTURA VASE

The unusual geometric base and clean-lined form is typical of the unique shapes Frank Ferrell designed for this range.

The stylized fruit 'balloons' are also typically Art Deco, as is the use of bright colours.

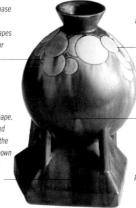

This is a sought-after shape. The asymmetric base and solid form recall one of the rarest Futura shapes, known as the 'Tank', which can fetch over $10,000.

If it had not had a hole drilled through the base, for possible conversion into a lamp base, it could have been worth upto 50 per cent more. Blue is also a desirable color.

A Roseville 'Futura' range blue 'Balloon' vase, the spherical top decorated with 'balloons' in polychrome, all on a faceted base with buttresses, paper label.

Futura was introduced in 1928 and is Roseville's most Art Deco styled range, it is also one of its most sought-after today.

8.5in (21cm) high

$1,000-1,500 DRA

A Roseville 'Futura' range two-handled vase, in orange with green accents and geometric band near stepped rim, unmarked.

$250-350 DRA

A Roseville 'Futura' range Blue Triangle vase, 388-9", unmarked, restorations to edges and waist of vase.

9.25in (23.5cm) high

$300-400 BEL

A Roseville 'Futura' range flat vase, with radiating blue design on a pale blue ground, unmarked.

$180-220 DRA

A Roseville 'Futura' range vase, decorated with green geometric designs along the curved top, covered in an orange and blue mottled glaze, unmarked.

$220-280 DRA

A Roseville 'Futura' range two-handled vase, with green squat base and orange stepped body, unmarked.

$350-450 DRA

A Roseville 'Futura' range Twist vase, 398-6 1/2", unmarked, small area at the rim has been professionally restored.

6.75in (17cm) high

$280-320 BEL

CERAMICS

A Roseville brown 'Montacello' pattern bulbous vase, unmarked.

As can be discerned from the geometric line and arrowhead pattern, Montacello was introduced in 1931 at the height of the Art Deco movement. It came in mottled tan, blue and green. Try to look for examples with clear painted patterns. Pieces are unmarked.

7.5in (19cm) high

$500-600   **DRA**

A Roseville brown 'Montacello' pattern vase, faintly marked "561" in red crayon.

7.25in (18.5cm) high

$500-600   **BEL**

A Roseville brown 'Montacello' pattern vase, 558-5", unmarked, professional restoration to rim.

5.25in (13.5cm) high

$400-500   **BEL**

A Roseville brown 'Montacello' pattern vase, 556-5", unmarked, professional restoration to rim.

5.25in (13.5cm) high

$120-180   **BEL**

A Roseville brown 'Montacello' pattern vase, 579-4 2/4", with two wide handles, marked "579" in red crayon, chip to the inside edge of one handle.

4.75in (12cm) high

$150-200   **BEL**

A pair of Roseville brown 'Montacello' pattern candleholders, each marked "1085" in red crayon, both pieces broken and restored at the waist and one with second break at the neck.

4.75in (12cm) high

$200-300   **BEL**

A Roseville blue 'Montacello' pattern double-handled vase, faintly marked "579" in red crayon, both handles restored at some time and three glaze skips, two on the rim and one at the waist.

4.75in (12cm) high

$150-200   **BEL**

A Roseville blue 'Montacello' pattern vase, marked "557" in red crayon, pinholes to glaze below one handle and inside the rim.

5.25in (13.5cm) high

$350-450   **BEL**

A scarce Roseville 'Montacello' pattern blue handled basket, 332-6", unmarked.

This is a scarce shape and has a very delicate handle, which is often damaged. The handle on this example has been professionally restored, if it were in mint condition the value would rise considerably.

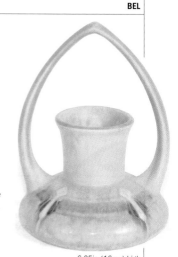

6.25in (16cm) high

$250-300   **BEL**

A Roseville green 'Baneda' pattern squat vase, with foil label.

7in (17.5cm) wide

$600-800   **DRA**

A Roseville green 'Baneda' pattern bulbous vase, showing a soft mold, unmarked.

8.5in (21cm) high

$450-550   **DRA**

A Roseville green 'Baneda' pattern vase, with crisp mold and strong color, paper label, original china and glass store label.

7.5in (19cm) high

$450-550   **DRA**

A Roseville pink 'Baneda' pattern bulbous vase, crisp mold and good color, unmarked.

Baneda was introduced in 1932 and was available in green, pink or blue. Pink is generally the preferred color; the color on this example is very even and strong, and the molding is visibly crisp. The blue version is very rare.

9.25in (23cm) high

$850-950   **DRA**

A Roseville 'Blackberry' pattern vase, 572-6", unmarked, rim professional restored.

6.25in (16cm) high

$300-400   **BEL**

A Roseville 'Blackberry' pattern vase, 576-8", unmarked, bruise at the rim with a slight flake.

8.5in (21.5cm) high

$400-500   **BEL**

A Roseville 'Blackberry' pattern vase, 574-6", with two small handles in a bulbous form, unmarked.

Blackberry was introduced in 1933 in this color combination only.

7.5in (19.cm) wide

$500-600   **BEL**

A Roseville 'Blackberry' pattern tapered vase, unmarked.

5.5in (14cm) high

$400-500   **DRA**

A Roseville blue 'Bleeding Heart' pattern basket, marked "USA 359-8".

8.5in (21.5cm) wide

$250-350   **BEL**

A Roseville blue 'Bushberry' pattern vase, marked "USA 32-7".

7.25in (18.5cm) high

$250-350 BEL

A Roseville blue 'Bushberry' pattern console bowl, marked "USA 416-12".

14in (35.5cm) long

$220-280 BEL

A Roseville 'Carnelian I' (Drip) pattern vase, marked with "RV" ink stamp.

5.5in (14cm) high

$100-150 BEL

A Roseville 'Carnelian I' (Drip) pattern broad vase, marked with "RV" ink stamp and "318" in red crayon, filled shallow chip at the base.

Carnelian I was introduced in c1910 and has either a smooth glaze with a darker dripped over-glaze or a single heavier glaze with some dripping. Colors included blue, aqua, turquoise and pink. Ornate handles are also a typical feature of this range.

9.25in (23.5cm) wide

$180-220 BEL

A Roseville blue 'Bushberry' pattern jardinière and pedestal set, raised mark.

Bushberry was released in 1941 and is typical of the floral ranges of the later period of Roseville's production. Large sets such as this example are scarce. The bowl is more common than the stand.

$1,200-1,800 DRA

A Roseville 'Carnelian I' (Drip) pattern vase, 319-9", with drip glaze in shapes of green, unmarked.

9.5in (24.5cm) high

$200-250 BEL

A Roseville 'Carnelian II' (Glaze) pattern vase, 331-7", unmarked.

7.25in (18.5cm) high

$250-300 BEL

A Roseville 'Carnelian II' pattern bulbous two-handled vase, covered in rose, ochre, and green dripping glazes, unmarked.

9.5in (24cm) wide

$400-500 DRA

A large Roseville 'Carnelian II' pattern bulbous two-handled vase, with collared rim, covered in a foamy blue and green glaze, unmarked.

Carnelian II was introduced in c1915 and is typified by a single, heavy glaze with some dripping. Forms also tend to be simpler and less detailed.

12in (30cm) high

$450-550 DRA

A Roseville 'Pink Cherry Blossom' pattern ovoid vase, with collared rim, unmarked.

10.5in (26cm) high

$750-850   **DRA**

A Roseville 'Chloron' range pitcher, unmarked.

Chloron was released in 1905 in matte green only and is rare today. Note the similarities to Van Briggle pottery, which was being produced, and was popular, at the same time.

7.5in (19cm) high

$400-500   **DRA**

A Roseville blue 'Cosmos' pattern flower pot, with matching saucer, pot marked "USA 650-5", the saucer marked "Roseville", saucer with line from rim through to base.

Cosmos was released in 1940 in blue, green or tan and is a relatively collectible range.

5.75in (14.5cm) high

$350-450   **BEL**

A Roseville brown 'Columbine' pattern vase, with green base and blue flowers, marked "USA 20-8".

8.25in (21cm) high

$200-300   **BEL**

A Roseville blue 'Cosmos' pattern bowl, marked "371-10".

12.5in (32cm) wide

$200-300   **BEL**

A Roseville green 'Cosmos' pattern two-handled jardinière, faintly marked "649-6" in red crayon, small area of rim repaired.

7in (18cm) high

$150-200   **BEL**

A Roseville 'Dahlrose' pattern triple bud vase, 76-6", unmarked.

6.25in (16cm) high

$350-450   **BEL**

A Roseville 'Dahlrose' pattern pedestal, unmarked.

Dahlrose was designed by Frank Ferrell and George Krause and was introduced in 1928. It is one of the most popular patterns to collect today, and is typical of Roseville.

21in (52.5cm) high

$650-750   **DRA**

A Roseville 'Dawn' pattern squat vase, with buttress handles, marked "315-4", two small glaze flakes to base and one to each handle.

4.25in (11cm) high

$70-100   **BEL**

A Roseville 'Earlam' pattern vase, 89-8", unmarked.

10.5in (26.5cm) wide

$300-350   **BEL**

A CLOSER LOOK AT ROSEVILLE FERELLA PLANTER

Ferella was released in 1931, and was designed by and named for Frank Ferell, Roseville's art director at the time.

As it was a functional piece, examples were often damaged through use. This piece is in excellent condition.

This is a rare shape - the tray is attached to the vase.

The pierced areas are typical of the design and the colors on this are bold and evenly applied.

A Roseville brown 'Ferella' pattern footed vessel, unmarked.

5.75in (14cm) wide

$450-550   **DRA**

A rare Roseville red 'Ferella' planter, unmarked.

6.5in (16cm) wide

$1,000-1,500   **DRA**

A Roseville 'Foxglove' pattern vase, marked "USA 47-8", shallow flake to base.

8.25in (21cm) high

$150-200   **BEL**

A Roseville blue 'Foxglove' pattern flower pot and saucer, pot marked "USA 660-5", saucer marked "USA", glaze skip from a mold flaw at the base.

6.5in (16.5cm) high

$180-220   **BEL**

A Roseville pink 'Foxglove' pattern tray, 424-14", marked "USA".

15in (38cm) long

$150-200   **BEL**

A Roseville green 'Freesia' pattern bowl, marked "USA 463-5", line to rim and repairs to flowers and base.

5in (12.5cm) high

$35-45   **BEL**

A Roseville blue 'Freesia' pattern basket, marked "USA 390-7".

7.25in (18.5cm) high

$120-180   **BEL**

A Roseville brown 'Fuchsia' pattern fan vase, marked "896-8", a broad, shallow chip from the base reglued in place.

8.25in (21cm) high

$150-200   **BEL**

A CLOSER LOOK AT ROSEVILLE IMPERIAL VASE

Introduced in 1930, Imperial II is loved by collectors due to the quality and visual appeal of the numerous glazes found on the range, that are akin to later studio pottery.

The simple form and linear decoration maximise the effects of the superb and strongly colored glaze on this example.

Its less sought-after and more common predecessor, Imperial I, is known for its textured finishes.

Both ranges were designed by Roseville's art director Frank Ferrell.

A Roseville 'Imperial II' pattern flaring vase, with threaded design, covered in a mottled pink and blue glaze, overglazed, unmarked.

6.5in (16cm) wide

$1,500-2,000   **DRA**

A Roseville brown 'Fuchsia' pattern vase, marked "893-6".

6.5in (16.5cm) high

$180-220   **BEL**

A Roseville green Hexagon vase, with "RV" ink mark.

8.25in (20.5cm) high

$500-600   **DRA**

A Roseville blue 'Iris' pattern vase, marked "921-8", three minute flakes off of base.

8.5in (21.5cm) high

$250-350   **BEL**

A Roseville pink and green 'Iris' pattern vase, 358-6", marked to base.

Introduced in 1939.

6.25in (16cm) high

$150-200   **BEL**

A Roseville pink 'Ixia' pattern vase, with Art Deco handles, marked "857-8" and "3" on the base in blue slip.

Introduced in 1937.

8.5in (21.5cm) high

$150-200   **BEL**

A Roseville red 'Laurel' pattern vase, 673-8", unmarked, six small chips to the base, heavy lime deposit to inside rim.

8.25in (21cm) high

$150-200   **BEL**

A large Roseville 'Luffa' pattern vase, 689-8", unmarked.

Luffa was introduced in 1934 in brown and green. It is not one of the most sought-after ranges today. Far Eastern fakes have been seen in blue, which was not a Roseville color for this range.

8.25in (21cm) high

$400-500 BEL

A Roseville 'Luffa' pattern vase, 683-6", unmarked with remnants of old retail label.

6.5in (16.5cm) high

$220-280 BEL

A Roseville 'Luffa' pattern vase, marked "685" in red crayon.

7.25in (18.5cm) high

$300-400 BEL

A Roseville brown 'Magnolia' pattern vase, marked "USA 97-14", crescent-shaped line across the top of the base.

14.25in (36cm) high

$120-180 BEL

A Roseville blue 'Magnolia' basket, marked "USA 385-10" on base, glaze flake or pop colored-in on one branch.

13in (33cm) wide

$250-350 BEL

A Roseville white 'Ming Tree' pattern vase, with high glaze finish, marked "USA 572-6".

6.5in (16.5cm) high

$70-100 BEL

A Roseville brown 'Panel' pattern fan vase, with "RV" ink mark.

This dramatic form and design is strongly Art Deco in inspiration. It is a comparatively scarce and sought-after range.

8.5in (21cm) high

$700-900 DRA

A very large Roseville pink 'Poppy' pattern vase, marked "877-12", four repaired chips.

Introduced in 1938 in yellow, blue, green and orange-pink combinations.

12.25in (31cm) high

$280-320 BEL

A Roseville 'Rozane Light' pattern footed vase, with blue pansies on a greenish background, unmarked, restoration to feet, base and rim.

5in (12.5cm) high

$45-55 BEL

CERAMICS

A Roseville light blue 'Silhouette' pattern vase, with two nudes, one on each side, marked "Roseville USA 763-8".

Despite being a late range introduced in 1950, Silhouette is sought-after in appealing shapes and good colors such as this.

8.25in (21cm) high

$650-750 BEL

An early Roseville 'Velmoss' pattern corseted vase, embossed with broad green leaves on a yellow-green ground, unmarked.

Velmoss was introduced in 1935 and is sought-after in stylized patterns such as this. Earlier examples are not marked, with later pieces being stamped 'Roseville' and with the shape number.

c1937 12in (30cm) high

$1,000-1,500 DRA

A Roseville 'Vista' pattern vase, with buttresses around rim, unmarked.

Introduced in 1920, Vista is very desirable due to its Arts & Crafts style and patterns, as is evident in this example.

17.75in (44cm) high

$650-750 DRA

A Roseville brown 'Water Lily' pattern cookie jar, lacks lid, marked "USA 1-8", small flake at base.

8.25in (21cm) high

$150-200 BEL

A Roseville blue 'Wincraft' pattern window box, with geraniums on each side, marked "Roseville USA 268-12".

13.75in (35cm) wide

$120-180 BEL

A Roseville brown 'Wisteria' pattern vase, 632-5", unmarked.

4.75in (12cm) high

$450-550 BEL

A Roseville 'White Rose' pattern floor vase, in pink and green, marked "USA 992-15".

15.5in (39.5cm) high

$400-500 BEL

A Roseville brown 'Wisteria' pattern vase, 631-6", with lavender blooms, unmarked.

6.25in (16cm) high

$400-500 BEL

A Roseville blue 'Zephyr Lily' pattern vase, raised mark.

$400-500 DRA

FIND OUT MORE...

Collectors Encyclopaedia of Roseville Pottery, *by Sharon & Bob Huxford and Mike Nickel, published by Collector Books, 2001.*

Warman's Roseville Pottery & Price Guide, *by Mark Moran, published by Krause Publications, 2004.*

COLLECTORS' NOTES

- Founded by Franz Heinrich Müller in 1775, the Royal Copenhagen Porcelain Manufactory gained the patronage of Queen Juliane Marie in 1779 after severe financial problems.

- Müller's obsession with finding the secret of hard paste porcelain lead to the company being prized by collectors for its fine, Meissen-inspired pieces. Today, collectors also look to its later works of stoneware and porcelain art ceramics. With designers such as Axel Salto and Nils Thorsson, works from the 1950s and '60s are typical of post war Scandinavian design with inspiration often being taken from the local landscape and nature. Decoration tends to be in muted, earthy or cool colors, with stylized natural or geometric designs.

- Pieces are usually marked with the factory's three wavy line or crown marks, together with initials or a number for the painter, which can help to date a piece. Examples by popular designers are desirable, as are hand-painted pieces and those of a larger size.

A Danish Royal Copenhagen bottle with stopper, no. 4494, decorated with molded low-relief quince and Danish crown and three line logo to each side.

$70-90   **MHT**

A Danish Royal Copenhagen crackle glaze vase, the baluster shape with flared rim decorated with iron red foliage and gilt highlights, printed and painted marks.

8.5in (21.5cm) high

$120-180   **CHEF**

A Danish Royal Copenhagen 'Tenera' bottle vase, designed by Kari Christensen.

c1969-74   9in (22.5cm) high

$70-100   **RWA**

A Danish Royal Copenhagen 'Baca' bottle vase, designed by Nils Thorsson, with tribal design in brown glaze, marked to base with printed Royal Copenhagen Crown mark, Nils Thorsson monogram, shape number 3259 and date code.

Nils Thorsson (1898-1975) worked for Royal Copenhagen from 1912 until his death. He was their most prolific and important designer and became Artistic Director.

c1969-74   9in (22.5cm) high

$120-180   **RWA**

A Danish Royal Copenhagen 'Fayance' bottle vase, designed by Nils Thorsson, painted "712/3529" and "S", and impressed "3259".

8.75in (22.5cm) high

$100-150   **GAZE**

A Danish Royal Copenhagen 'Fayance' bottle vase, designed by Nils Thorsson, painted "712/3529", impressed "3259", painted "S" and printed mark.

8.75in (22.5cm) high

$100-150   **GAZE**

A Danish Royal Copenhagen 'Fayance' pillow vase, designed by Bengt Jacobsen, painted "436/3121", impressed "3259", painted marks.

7.5in (19cm) high

$120-180   **GAZE**

A Danish Royal Copenhagen 'Tenera' pillow vase, decorated with stylized fruit and foliage, painted and printed marks.

7.5in (19cm) high

$150-200   **CHEF**

A Danish Royal Copenhagen 'Tenera' fayance vase, designed by Kari Christensen, the compressed bottle form with hand-painted abstract design, printed and painted marks.

8.25in (21cm) high

$80-120   **CHEF**

A CLOSER LOOK AT A ROYAL COPENHAGEN ANNUAL MUG

Royal Copenhagen have produced a commemorative mug every year since 1967.

The larger version has a metal disc set into the base for presentation inscriptions. The disc was silver until 1980 when it was replaced with pewter and then later a shiny base metal.

They are available in two sizes, this being the larger. The smaller version is 3in (7.5cm) high.

Examples from the first years of production are the most desirable and could be worth double.

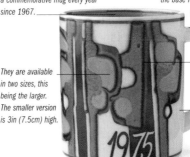

A Danish Royal Copenhagen large annual mug for 1975, designed by Bodil Buch, decorated with an abstract design and dated 1975, with silver plaque set into base for inscription, printed marks.

4.5in (11.5cm) high

$150-200   **CHEF**

A Danish Royal Copenhagen Aluminia moon vase, by Kari Christensen, with beehive and three waves mark.

The Aluminia faïence factory acquired Royal Copenhagen in 1882, explaining the use of two names and marks.

5.25in (13.5cm) high

$30-50   **GAZE**

A Danish Royal Copenhagen 'Tenera' mug, by Inge-Lise Koefoed, with blue glazed design, marked to base with printed Royal Copenhagen backstamp, painted pattern number 454, shape number 3113, Inge-Lise Koefoed monogram and decorator's mark.

c1986-89   5.5in (14cm) high

$100-150   **RWA**

A Danish Royal Copenhagen large annual mug for 1976, designed by Anne Marie Trolle, with silver plaque in base with Danish hallmark "AMT 9255 DM", printed, painted and impressed marks.

c1976   4.5in (11.5cm) high

$20-40   **TCM**

A Danish Royal Copenhagen 'Fayance' large square-form dish, marked "156/2885", painted mark "4".

10.5in (26.5cm) wide

$50-70   **GAZE**

A Danish Royal Copenhagen Aluminia 'Tenera' wall relief, by Beth Breyen, with stylized bird design, with painted marks and printed Aluminia backstamp, Beth Breyen monogram and decorator's mark "BA".

c1961   11.75in (30cm) high

$120-180   **RWA**

A CLOSER LOOK AT A ROYAL COPENHAGEN VASE

Scandinavian ceramic and glass design is often influenced by nature, as can be seen in this rough, organic and bark-like texture.

As was often typical of Royal Copenhagen, the surface decoration is kept to a minimum allowing the form and the solfatara glaze to come to the fore.

Axel Salto (1889-1961) studied painting before working for Bing & Grøndahl from 1923-25 and Royal Copenhagen from 1933.

Salto, Jais Nielsen and Knud Kyhn (well-known for his stoneware models of animals), were particularly skilled at working with stoneware.

A Danish Royal Copenhagen stoneware budding vase, by Axel Salto, with brown and fawn solfatara glaze.

c1957

3.5in (9cm) high

$1,800-2,200   **RWA**

A 1950s/60s Danish Royal Copenhagen Aluminia Marselis vase, by Nils Thorsson, with incised under-glaze stylized leaf design, marked with printed Marselis Aluminia beehive mark, Nils Thorsson monogram and pattern number 2648.

10.75in (27.5cm) high

$200-300   **RWA**

A 1950s/60s Danish Royal Copenhagen (Aluminia) Marselis vase, by Nils Thorsson, with incised under-glaze diamond design, marked to base with printed Marselis Aluminia beehive mark, Nils Thorsson monogram and pattern number "2634".

6.5in (17cm) high

$200-300   **RWA**

A rare Danish Royal Copenhagen stoneware vase/pot, by Kari Christensen, with incised line decoration, marked to base with printed backstamp, incised CK monogram, painted "22162" and three wavy lines.

Kari Christensen was one of the 'Tenera' range designers and it is very unusual to find pieces other than her 'Tenera' designs.

c1965   5.25in (13.5cm) high

$200-300   **RWA**

A 1950s/60s Danish Royal Copenhagen Aluminia Marselis vase, by Nils Thorsson, with incised under-glaze leaf design, marked to base with printed Marselis Aluminia beehive mark and Nils Thorsson monogram.

10.75in (27.5cm) high

$200-300   **RWA**

A Danish Royal Copenhagen stoneware vase, designed by Jørgen Mogensen, in unusual celadon glaze with relief owl decoration, with printed Royal Copenhagen backstamp, painted pattern no. 21488 and three wavy lines and JM monogram.

c1957   7in (17.5cm) high

$300-400   **RWA**

A 1930s Danish Royal Copenhagen studio bowl, designed by Carl Halier, with stag design in celadon glaze, marked to base with "CH" monogram and three blue wavy lines.

8.7in (22cm) diam

$200-300   **RWA**

COLLECTORS' NOTES

■ Scandinavian ceramics proved to be both popular and influential as styles became more modern from the early 20thC onwards. The 1930s and 1950s-'70s were particularly important periods, with many innovative and influential designs being created. In all instances, aim to buy pieces that best represent the movement's core themes, and preferably those by notable designers.

■ Major factories included Sweden's Gustavsberg and Finland's Arabia. Key designers were Wilhelm Kåge and Stig Lindberg at Gustavsberg and Ulla Procopé and Kaj Franck at Arabia. Both introduced and popularised modern forms, colors and patterns, exemplified in one aspect by Lindberg's colorful faience designs and on the other by Kaj Franck's cooler, more classical and functional pieces.

■ Also look to other, smaller factories such as Saxbo and Palshus for good examples of the design ethic of the time, particularly in terms of form and strong colors. Although lines are generally clean and modern, a strong functional aspect pervades all designs. Nature also provided strong inspiration, with asymmetric, bud-like forms. Whimsical designs were also popular and often took animal forms, furthering this natural inspiration.

■ Unique Scandinavian hand-made studio ceramics are an interesting sector of the market. Names such as Arne Bang, during the 1930s and '40s, and Connie Walther are hotly sought-after. Stig Lindberg and others also experimented with studio ceramics, and their miniature vases, usually with fine and complex glazes, are desirable with surprisingly high values, given their small size.

A Swedish Gustavsberg 'Argenta' vase, designed by Wilhelm Kåge, decorated in silver with a fish, painted marks with anchor.

6.25in (16cm) high

$200-300   **WW**

A Swedish Gustavsberg 'Argenta' charger, designed by William Kåge, decorated with stylised fish in silver, with painted mark including Kåge's signature, hairline to rim.

Argenta ware was introduced as a luxury range in 1930 at the Stockholm 'Stockholmsutställingen', the major exhibition of art and industrial design. It was produced into the 1950s in a variety of shapes.

18in (46cm) diam

$600-800   **WW**

An early 1950s Swedish Gustavsberg vase, designed by Stig Lindberg, with a silver basket of flowers, with painted marks and paper label.

10.5in (26.5cm) high

$400-600   **SWO**

A Swedish Gustavsberg 'Karneval' faïence slab vase, designed by Stig Lindberg, with hand-painted figure of a lute-playing centaur on front and sunflowers on the back, with painted Gustavsberg studio hand, model number "230.1", and star monogram for decorator Giovanni Pugno to base.

c1958-62   *8in (20.5cm) high*

$280-320   **RWA**

A Swedish Gustavsberg 'Karneval' faïence slab vase, designed by Stig Lindberg, with hand-painted fantasy figure caged girl on front and a bird on the back, with painted Gustavsberg studio hand, original Stig Lindberg label, model number "R.199", and monogram for unknown decorator to base.

c1958-62   *7in (17.5cm) high*

$180-220   **RWA**

A Swedish Gustavsberg 'Bohus Bersa' dish, designed by Stig Lindberg, with stylized leaf transfer decoration.

This varied and popular range of oven-to-tableware was designed by Lindberg in 1960 and was produced until 1974.

12.25in (31cm) long

$80-120   **MHT**

A 1950s Swedish Gustavsberg faïence dish, designed by Stig Lindberg, with hand-painted lattice pattern.

This is typical of Lindberg's modern faïence designs from this period. They influenced many potteries outside of Scandinavia, such as England's Poole Pottery.

8in (20.5cm) wide

$280-320   **GGRT**

A CLOSER LOOK AT A MINIATURE VASE

Miniature vases were made by many Scandinavian factories as part of their hand-made 'studio' ranges.

Gustavsberg's studio pieces were marked with an inscribed hand motif. The style of this and the placement of the artist's name changed each year and helps to date them.

Both Stig Lindberg and Berndt Friberg designed miniatures for Gustavsberg, they were signed "Stig L", and "Friberg" respectively.

They differ from standard production in their comparatively traditional forms and fine, highly detailed, subtly colored glazes.

A Swedish Gustavsberg Studio miniature vase, by Stig Lindberg, with dark red glaze.

Although the presence of the inscription "Stig L" does not guarantee that that piece was by Lindberg personally, it is highly likely.

c1980   3in (8cm) high

$250-350   **RWA**

A 1950s Swedish "Gustavsberg small leaf tray, designed by Stig Lindberg, marked to back with painted Gustavsberg studio hand, "G/86, 30, Sweden" and decorator's mark for Franca Pugno.

4.75in (12cm) long

$100-150   **RWA**

A 1950s Swedish Gustavsberg indigo vase, by Karin Björquist, with hand-painted blue decoration, marked to base with painted Gustavsberg studio hand, Karin Björquist monogram and decorator's mark.

Björquist was inspired by her predecessors Kåge and Lindberg, as can be seen in the style of decoration, and guided Gustavsberg's designs through the 1960s and '70s. Her work is arguably yet to be fully appreciated.

9.5in (24cm) high

$180-220   **RWA**

A 1960s Swedish Gustavsberg Granada vase, designed by Lisa Larson.

The cylinder was a popular form for ceramics during the 1960s – for transfer-printed wares it allowed easy application of the transfer and maximised display of the pattern.

9in (23cm) high

$180-220   **RWA**

A 1960s/70s Swedish Gustavsberg vase, designed by Britt-Louise Sundell, with brown mottled glaze and band of white rings, marked to base with original Gustavsberg "B.-L SUNDELL" label and Gustavsberg paper label.

9.5in (24cm) high

$180-220   **RWA**

A 1960s/70s Swedish Gustavsberg large bowl, designed by Britt-Louise Sundell, with dark green mottled glaze and white ring decoration, marked to base with original "Gustavsberg B.-L SUNDELL" label and Gustavsberg paper label.

11.75in (30cm) diam

$120-180   **RWA**

A Swedish Gustavsberg Studio miniature globe vase, designed and possibly made by Stig Lindberg, with dark red mottled glaze, signed on the base.

c1978   3.5in (8.5cm) diam

$300-400   **RWA**

A Swedish Gustavsberg Studio miniature vase, designed and possibly made by Stig Lindberg, signed on the base.

This is a typical inscribed mark found on such miniature vases.

$80-120   **GAZE**

2.25in (5.5cm) high

A Swedish Gustavsberg Studio pottery miniature vase, designed and possibly made by Berndt Friberg, with caramel striated glaze, signed on the base.

Friberg (1899-1981), was awarded a gold medal at the Milan Triennale in 1948 along with Stig Lindberg. Note the subtlety of the glaze and the delicacy of the rim on this high quality, hand-made miniature.

2.25in (6cm) high

$180-220   **GAZE**

A Swedish Gustavsberg Studio thin-walled footed bowl, designed and possibly made by Berndt Friberg, with green and brown shiny glazes, marked to base with incised Gustavsberg studio hand, "Friberg" and "42".

c1942   5in (12.5cm) wide

$300-500   **RWA**

A 1960s/70s Swedish Gustavsberg horse, designed by Stig Lindberg, with green glaze, marked to base with printed Gustavsberg anchor mark and 'Sweden'.

4.5in (11.5cm) high

$220-280   **RWA**

A 1960s/70s Swedish Gustavsberg horse, designed by Stig Lindberg, with speckled brown glazes and white to mane and tail, marked to base with printed Gustavsberg anchor mark and "Sweden".

5.25in (13.5cm) high

$280-320   **RWA**

A Swedish Gustavsberg bulldog, designed by Lisa Larson, from the Kennel series.

This popular range of stylised dogs included a white poodle, a black and white bull terrier and a boxer.

1972-83

$70-100   **RWA**

A 1950s Swedish Gustavsberg stoneware cat, designed by by Stig Lindberg, with darkened sgraffito decoration.

7.5in (19cm) long

$250-350   **FD**

A Swedish Rorstrand hand-painted tall cylindrical 'Sarek' vase, designed by Olle Alberius.

12in (30.5cm) high

$80-120　　　　　　　**MTS**

A 1950s/60s Swedish Rorstrand vase, designed by Carl-Harry Stålhane, with shiny brown glaze, marked to base with incised "R" with three crowns, "C.H.S.", "Sweden" and "S A E".

4.5in (11.5cm) high

$120-180　　　　　　　**RWA**

A 1950s Swedish Rorstrand tall vase, designed by Gunnar Nylund, with brown and coffee-coloured glaze, horizontal shallow flutings and unglazed vertical flutings to base, marked to base with incised "R", three crowns, "Sweden" and "GN", stamped "5".

Rorstrand was founded in 1926 at Rorstrand, Stockholm and has been part of the Rorstrand-Gustavsberg group since 1988. The 20thC saw the employment of many innovative designers working in porcelain and stoneware. After training at Bing & Grøndhal, Nylund (1904-97) joined as art director in 1931, until 1958. He then freelanced at Nymølle and worked with glass at Strombergshyttan.

11.25in (28.5cm) high

$180-220　　　　　　　**RWA**

A 1960s Swedish Rorstrand squat stoneware vase, designed by Carl-Harry Stålhane, with gray and brown glaze, marked to base with incised "R" with three crowns, "Atelje, C.H.S. - c" and "Sweden".

5.5in (14cm) diam

$180-220　　　　　　　**RWA**

A 1950s Swedish Rorstrand bowl, designed by Gunnar Nylund, in coffee-colored glaze with brown glazed incised decoration and unglazed vertical fluting around base, marked to base with incised "R" with three crowns, "Sweden" and "GN".

6.5in (16.5cm) high

$80-120　　　　　　　**RWA**

A Swedish Rorstrand miniature tri-lobed bowl, designed by Gunnar Nylund, hand-incised "Sweden GN ASH" to base.

2.25in (5.5cm) high

$100-150　　　　　**GAZE**

A Swedish Rorstrand bowl, designed by Carl-Harry Stålhane, with spiral relief pattern.

Stålhane worked for Rorstrand from 1939-73, leaving to start his own studio. His harmonically formed stoneware pieces with their subtle glazes inspired many period studio pottery designs and are much loved.

8in (20cm) long

$100-150　　　　　**GAZE**

A Swedish Rorstrand heavy brown mottled and petrol blue dish, by Gunnar Nylund, scored "R Sweden GN KN' on the base.

8in (20.5cm) diam

$120-180　　　　　**GAZE**

A Swedish Rorstrand cube-shaped candle holder, designed by Sylvia Leuchovius, with painted mark and impressed initials.

2.5in (6.5cm) high

$30-40　　　　　**TCM**

CERAMICS

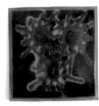

A 1970s Danish Søholm stoneware wall plaque, with abstract design under a heavy high-fired glaze, marked to back with impressed Søholm factory mark and pattern number 3559, painted with paintress mark "K".

The underglaze crazing and slight warping is normal and does not indicate a faulty 'second'. Søholm Stentoj is based on the island of Bornholm, Denmark.

13.5in (34cm) wide

$120-180 RWA

A 1970s Danish Søholm stoneware wall relief, designed by Noomi Backhausen, with flower design, marked to front left-hand bottom corner with incised "Noomi", marked to back with impressed "Søholm" factory mark, impressed pattern number "3573", painted paintress mark "A".

15.25in (39cm) high

$70-100 RWA

A CLOSER LOOK AT A SØHOLM TILE

Although it is unsigned, it is likely to be by Noomi Backhausen due to the strong linear decoration and heavily moulded pattern.

The inclusion of a bird also indicates it is by Backhausen, who designed for the company from 1966-90.

Like so many tiles and studio pieces produced by Søholm, it is thick and very heavy for its size.

Ceramic wall plaques were popular during the 1960s and '70s and were also produced by other Scandinavian and West German ceramics companies.

A Danish Søholm Stoneware wall relief, unsigned but almost certainly designed by Noomi Backhausen, with bird design partly glazed in matt and shiny black, brown and red, marked on back with impressed Søholm factory mark, pattern number 3592.1 and date "14 Juli 1981" and painted paintress mark "K".

c1981 13.5in (34cm) wide

$180-220 RWA

A Danish Søholm moulded blue gloss glaze lamp base, with low relief abstract decoration, the base inscribed "Søholm Denmark S Tenty 1018".

10.5in (26.5cm) high

$50-70 PSI

Søholm
DANMARK
NOOMI

A 1970s/80s Danish Søholm studio large stoneware vase, designed by Noomi Backhausen, with heavy applied relief decoration in brown glazes, painted marks to base 'Søholm Danmark Noomi'.

10.25in (26cm) high

$220-280 RWA

A Danish Søholm miniature lampbase, with printed marks to base.

4.75in (12cm) high

$30-50 GAZE

A Danish Søholm Stentoj earthenware bowl, with glazed stylised floral decoration, painted marks to base for "Søholm Stentoj, Denmark".

11.75in (30cm) long

$30-50 GAZE

A 1950s Finnish Arabia oxblood glazed ginger jar, designed by Francesca Mascitti-Lindhl.

4in (10cm) high

$50-70　　　　　**GAZE**

A 1940s/50s Swedish Höganäs miniature vase, designed by John Andersson, with blue glaze.

2.5in (6.5cm) high

$100-150　　　　**RWA**

A Swedish Höganäs stoneware vase, designed by John Andersson, with blue glaze, marked to base with printed "Höganäs Keramik" back-stamp with centre entwined "AJ".

Höganäs was founded in 1797 and Berndt Friberg worked there as a thrower from 1915-18.

c1956-67　　5in (12.5cm) high

$120-180　　　　**RWA**

A 1960s/70s Danish Laholm Keramik tall vase, with floral design.

11.25in (28.5cm) high

$40-60　　　　**RWA**

A 1950s Danish Nymølle tall vase, designed by Gunnar Nylund, with matt blue glaze, marked to base with painted "Nymöelle Denmark. N" with three hearts/crowns, "G Nylund".

This is similar in form and decoration to many Palshus pieces.

13in (33cm) high

$220-280　　　　**RWA**

A Swedish Rolf Palm Studio bottle vase, with mottled brown glaze.

Rolf Palm works from his own studio in Mölle.

5.75in (14.5cm) high

$220-280　　　　**RWA**

A 1950s Danish Palshus stoneware vase, designed by Per Linnemann-Schmidt, with olive haresfur glaze, marked to base with incised "Palshus Denmark", "PL-S" and "PR6VF".

4.25in (11cm) high

$300-350　　　　**RWA**

A 1950s Danish Palshus teapot, by Frode Bahnsen, with blue haresfur glaze and wicker handle, marked to base with impressed "Palshus Denmark", monogram for Frode Bahnsen and pattern number T3.

Sculptor Frode Bahnsen (1923-83) is also well-known for his coin and medal designs. The 'haresfur' glaze is a sought-after hallmark of the factory, particularly in this deep blue.

8in (20.5cm) high

$300-350　　　　**RWA**

A Norwegian Porsgrund porcelain vase, the white ground with transfer-printed blue birds and flowers, blue and green printed marks, including an anchor and numbered "M231" and "D.78084".

5.5in (14cm) high

$30-50   **GAZE**

A 1930s-40s Danish Saxbo teapot, with cane handle and cobalt blue semi-matte glaze.

Saxbo was founded by Nathalie Krebs in 1930 and closed in 1968. Krebs developed the glazes and Eva Stæhr-Nielsen developed the shapes. Oriental style glazes and simple, clean-lined shapes are typical of the factory's production.

6.5in (16.5cm) long

$250-350   **FD**

A 1950s Danish Palshus 'Torpedo' vase, designed by Per Linnemann-Schmidt, with blue haresfur glaze.

8.5in (21.5cm) high

$350-450   **RWA**

A Danish Saxbo miniature footed dish, with silvery green glaze, hand inscribed on base "Saxbo Denmark 73 (S) 4 E.S.E.N. X".

$50-70   **GAZE**

A Danish Saxbo square-sided vase, designed by Eva Stæhr-Nielsen, with impressed panels on front and back in shiny brown glazes, marked to base impressed Saxbo Zing Yang mark, number "228" and "6" and incised E.ST.N. monogram.

c1951-68   *3.25in (8cm) high*

$150-200   **RWA**

A Swedish Upsala-Ekeby vase, by Mari Simmulson, with leaf design.

Estonian-born Simmulson (b.1911) worked for Upsala Ekeby from 1949-72.

9in (23cm) high

$70-100   **RWA**

A Swedish Upsala Ekeby vase, designed by Ingrid Atterberg, with swirling design.

Atterberg (b.1920) worked for Upsala Ekeby from 1944-63 and won a gold medal for her designs at the Milan Triennale in 1957. It is rare to find the original label on these pieces.

c1951-56   *8.25in (21cm) high*

$100-150   **RWA**

A Swedish Upsala Ekeby pot, designed by Ingrid Atterberg, with swirling decoration.

c1951-56   *5in (12.5cm) diam*

$70-100   **RWA**

A 1960s Danish Conny Walther studio chamotte dish, with brown and fawn glaze, marked to the base with impressed "CW" Conny Walther own studio mark (partially hidden by sticker).

Chamotte is a type of high-fired clay.

11in (28cm) wide

$180-220 RWA

A CLOSER LOOK AT BJØRN WIINBLAD

These are from Wiinblad's studio, which made unique hand-made and hand-decorated pieces, rather than being produced by one of the factories he designed for, such as Nymølle and Rosenthal.

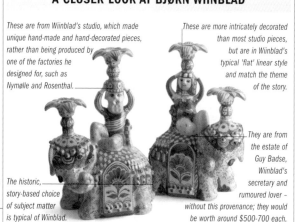

These are more intricately decorated than most studio pieces, but are in Wiinblad's typical 'flat' linear style and match the theme of the story.

They are from the estate of Guy Badse, Wiinblad's

The historic, story-based choice of subject matter is typical of Wiinblad.

secretary and rumoured lover – without this provenance; they would be worth around $500-700 each.

A Danish Bjørn Wiinblad studio 'King Solomon' and 'Queen of Sheba' pair of candleholders, from the estate of Wiinblad's secretary Guy Badse, dated.

1979 & 1987

35cm (14in) high

$700-1,000 (each) RWA

A 1960s Danish Conny Walther studio large chamotte stoneware vase, with a brown running glaze along top edge and down front, hairline firing crack on base, marked to the base with impressed "CW" Conny Walther own studio mark.

7in (8cm) high

$300-400 RWA

A 1960s Danish Conny Walther studio squat vase, with brown running glaze and partially exposed body, base marked with impressed "CW".

5in (12.5cm) diam

$100-150 RWA

A 1960s Danish Conny Walther stoneware bowl, with applied, glazed motif and glazed interior.

5.25in (13.5cm) high

$120-180 RWA

Five from a set of 12 Danish Nymølle ceramic 'Month' plaques, designed by Bjørn Wiinblad.

Wiinblad worked at Nymølle from 1946-56 and then again when he acquired the financially troubled company in 1976 until its closure in the 1990s.

6in (15cm) diam

$80-120 (set) GAZE

A Danish Nymølle circular dish, designed by Bjørn Wiinblad, number 3029-1285, with T.H. Torntoft of Aarhus retailer's paper label.

8.75in (22.5cm) diam

$30-50 GAZE

A 1960s Danish Bjørn Wiinblad Studio pair of male and female centaur candleholders, in a heavy brown glaze.

These are unmarked, which is quite common for these figures. The choice of glazes is unusual for Wiinblad, who usually worked with more ornamented and enriched designs. Wiinblad also designed for German pottery Rosenthal, see p153-4

13.75in (35cm) high

$1,200-1,800 RWA

CERAMICS

A Shelley three-piece nursery tea set, designed by Mabel Lucie Attwell, comprising a teapot and cover, a milk jug and a sugar bowl, each forming the shape of a mushroom and painted in green, orange and yellow, painted marks and Rd. no.724421.

5in (12.5cm) high

$500-800 | **L&T**

A CLOSER LOOK AT A SHELLEY FIGURE

Book illustrator Mabel Lucie Attwell joined Shelley in 1926 and designed a range of popular nursery ware, that even reached the nurseries of Princesses Elizabeth and Margaret, and later Prince Charles.

They typically featured rosy cheeked children or playful elves, which appealed to adults and delighted children.

The range included teapots, cups and saucers, and sugar bowls, but the figures are the most desirable and among the rarest today.

Fakes are found, so check the marks and the quality of the paintwork carefully. Also check for damage as many were broken.

A Shelley 'I's Shy' figure, by Mabel Lucie Attwell, printed mark in green.

6in (15cm) high

$2,00-3,000 | **LFA**

A Shelley 'Harrogate' crested cup and saucer.

Saucer 6in (15cm) diam

$35-55 | **BAD**

A Shelley 'Syringa' pattern teapot, marked "W12070".

8in (20cm) wide

$220-280 | **BAD**

A Shelley 'Mode' shape teapot and cover, pattern no. P11754, in shades of green and gold, printed and painted marks.

High Art Deco shapes such as Mode, Eve and Vogue are popular. The combination of green, gilt and black is also a typical Art Deco colour combination.

5in (13cm) high

$450-650 | **WW**

A Shelley 'Melody' pattern chintz preserve pot and cover, pattern no. 13453.

c1930   3.5in (9cm) high

$100-200 | **BEV**

A Shelley Harmony Ware ginger jar and cover, printed factory mark.

The Harmony Ware range was available on a wide variety of shapes. The color was applied by hand and the piece was then spun to blend the colors together. Some pieces just show bands of color, others, such as this, combine drips and bands. Color combinations abound.

9in (23cm) high

$250-350 | **WW**

A Shelley Harmony Ware ginger jar and cover.

5in (13cm) high

$220-280 | **BAD**

COLLECTORS' NOTES

- The pottery that became known as Stangl was founded by Samuel Hill in Flemington, New Jersey in 1814. It was then acquired by Abraham Fulper, whose family ran it as the Fulper Pottery until 1930 when it was acquired by Johann Martin Stangl. The company is known for its wide ranges of dinnerware and decorative birds. Stangl died in 1972 and the company was acquired by Wheaton Industries, before closing in 1978, when the rights were bought by Pfaltzgraff.

- Their birds were produced from 1940-72 and are hotly sought-after. Some reissues were made from 1972-77, but are dated on the base and can fetch up to half the value of vintage examples. The range was based on illustrator and naturalist John Audubon's famous 'Birds of America' folios and was designed by August Jacob. They were popular during the 1940s and '50s, but began to wane from the late 1950s.

- Look for large, complexly molded examples, with detailed painting in bright colors. Models produced for shorter periods of time, or that were expensive in their day are likely to be worth more, as less would have sold. Artist's signatures do not add to value, but can help to date a model, as can the style of other marks. Carefully examine protruding areas such as beaks and tails as these are susceptible to damage, which reduces value, as does restoration.

A Stangl running duck, in brown, green, and blue, marked.

5in (12.5cm) high

$450-550 DRA

A Stangl standing duck, no. 3431, in brown and blue, marked.

8in (20cm) high

$1,000-1,500 DRA

A Stangl adult verdin, no. 3921, marked and with original label.

4.5in (11cm) high

$1,500-2,000 DRA

A Stangl vermillion fly catcher, base printed "Stangl" and "MW", hand-painted twice in black and red.

6in (15cm) high

$800-1,200 DWG

A rare Stangl porcelain single scarlet tanager, no. 3723, marked.

6in (15cm) high

$700-800 DRA

A rare Stangl Della-Ware pheasant, in natural colors, marked.

15.5in (39cm) wide

$1,500-2,000 DRA

A Stangl passenger pigeon, no. 3450, marked.

18in (45cm) wide

$1,500-2,000 DRA

CERAMICS

COLLECTORS' NOTES

■ Studio pottery began to emerge as a force in the first decades of the 20thC. The term is defined by a single potter producing wares, which can be functional or decorative, or a combination of the two. Individualistic and expressive artistic elements run through many designs. A potter will usually take on students, often for commercial reasons, who will help to produce pots as well as learning techniques. Each piece is typically handmade, although molds may also be used.

■ After WWII the movement boomed and has continued to grow rapidly. Pottery has become considered an art form and is one of the most diverse and vibrant art markets today. The work of many pioneers such as

Bernard Leach, Shoji Hamada, Otto & Gertrud Natzler and Peter Voulkos usually fetches high prices today, but much mid-late 20thC studio pottery by less well-known potters is also becoming increasingly sought-after.

■ Much work is still comparatively inexpensive and arguably 'yet to be discovered'. Always look for quality in terms of period feel, form, glaze and overall design. Larger pieces are often scarcer. Always look for marks as these will help identify the potter. Investing in a book showing potters' marks is essential. Also aim to learn about contemporary potters, who they studied under, and where they worked as they may go on to be considered as classic potters of the future.

An American Rose Cabat 'Feelie' vase, with a white over blue glaze, signed "CABAT" inscribed on base.

3in (7.5cm) high

$400-500   **TOJ**

An American Rose Cabat 'Feelie' spherical vessel, covered in a brown crystalline vellum glaze, signed "Cabat".

Self-taught Arizona potter Rose Cabat (b.1914) and her late husband Erni developed the 'Feelie' vessels, with their smooth, highly tactile glazes and characteristic hand-thrown teardrop shapes. They are highly sought-after today, particularly in large sizes, glazed in appealing colors.

4in (10cm) high

$700-1,000   **SDR**

An American Michael Connelly studio pitcher, with printed mark.

Michael Connelly's work is commanding increasing respect from a growing number of collectors. He studied and still works in New York, and has lectured, taught and exhibited around the US. His work can be found internationally, including in the China Yaoware Museum and the Schein-Joseph International Museum of Ceramic Art.

12in (30.5cm) high

$200-300   **TOJ**

An American Michael Connelly studio vessel, with printed mark.

5.25in (13.5cm) high

$60-80   **TOJ**

An American Michael Connelly beige and green dripped glaze studio vessel, with printed mark.

5.25in (13cm) high

$60-80   **TOJ**

An American Rising Fawn Pottery tapered barrel vase, by Charles Counts, with hand-inscribed pattern, the base hand-inscribed "Tribute Beaver Ridge 1993".

1993   *9in (23cm) high*

$400-500   **TOJ**

CERAMICS

A vintage American Charles Counts floor vase, with inscribed grass-like design, signed on the base "charles counts".

Charles Counts, who died in 2000, was a noted and influential potter. His first pottery was opened in 1959 and he went on to found the notable Rising Fawn Pottery, near Lookout Mountain, Georgia. As well as writing books on pottery, he taught widely with students including Mark Issenburg and Sue Cannon. His work is found in many public collections, including the Smithsonian in Washington, D.C.

14.25in (36cm) high

$600-800 TOJ

An American Malcolm Davis chimney vase, with applied abstract slip bamboo-like pattern, Shino-type glaze and four feet.

8in (20.5cm) high

$400-500 TOJ

An American Otto Heino squat globe vase, with a white glaze spattered and dripped with deep gray-green markings.

Otto Heino (b.1915) trained under esteemed pioneer potter and ceramicist Glen Lukens (1887-1967), and made decorative and functional wares in partnership with his wife Vivika (1909-96) until her death. Their work is widely respected and much collected.

5in (12.5cm) diam

$500-600 TOJ

A Mark Hewitt vase, with leaf and dot pattern, and printed "MH" monogram.

10in (25.5cm) high

$250-350 TOJ

A Sylvia Hyman jug, with green dripped glaze, based inscribed "Hyman".

6in (15cm) high

$100-150 TOJ

An American Fred Johnston floor vase, with splashed and dripped green glaze over an uncolored clay ground, signed in glaze "Fred Johnston" on the base.

This is a large piece with eye-catching decoration, and is by a notable potter.

14in (35.5cm) high

$400-500 TOJ

An American Sequoia Miller faceted textured studio vase, with impressed "SQ" mark.

Miller is interested in faceted shapes – note how the glaze colors change on every facet to give the impression of light and shade.

9.75in (25cm) high

$100-150 TOJ

CERAMICS

A contemporary Sequoia Miller ovoid form, rectangular section glazed studio vase, impressed "SM" mark.

This shows two other key aspects of Miller's work; shapes which are flattened or altered after being thrown and potted on a wheel, and a strong Japanese influence derived from the 'mingei' crafts movement, whose followers include Shoji Hamada and Bernard Leach.

c2006   7.5in (19cm) high

$250-350   **TOJ**

A CLOSER LOOK AT A STUDIO POTTERY BOWL

Oestreich (b.1947) studied under notable US ceramicist Warren McKenzie, and also under influential potter Bernard Leach in England for two years from 1969.

A teaching position in the city of Napier, New Zealand with its Art Deco buildings led to an interest in the Art Deco style, which can be seen in the patterning on this bowl.

As well as his 'J.O.' stamp, this bowl has a section of the foot cut out and rejoined, furthering his aim to alter functional pieces in a decorative way.

Oestreich's current work is altered through stretching and other techniques after being thrown – this bowl deviates from the utilitarian circular form in terms of the impressed curves.

An American Jeff Oestreich studio bowl, with "J.O." mark and cut base.

5.75in (14.5cm) wide

$80-120   **TOJ**

An American David Stuempfle double-gourd wood-fired floor vase.

This is an exceptionally large example and demonstrates Stuempfle's inspirations from natural forms.

18.5in (47cm)

$500-600   **TOJ**

An American Ben Owen III studio vase, hand inscribed with a curving, cloud like pattern, the base inscribed "Ben Owens III 1995".

Owen's grandfather, also called Ben Owen, was head potter for Jugtown pottery from 1923-59. Owen's father was also a potter. This vase has a strong Asian feel and is reminiscent of Chinese burial urns.

1995   7.2in (18.5cm) high

$300-400   **TOJ**

An American Malcolm Wright studio vase, with Karatsu leaf design against a cream Shino-type glaze ground, inscribed on the base.

9in (23cm) high

$400-500   **TOJ**

Two Henry Varnum Poor pitchers, one with daisies on an ivory ground, the other with yellow and white stripes, both marked.

Henry Varnum Poor (1887-1970) was an artist as well as a potter, as can be seen in his painterly decoration that often includes people.

c1926   Larger 7.75in (19.5cm) high

$220-280   **SDR**

COLLECTORS' NOTES

■ Swid Powell was founded in New York in 1983 by Nan Swid and Addie Powell. Both had previously been employed by furniture makers Knoll International to produce a range of architect-designed functional objects for the home. These included transfer-printed ceramics and metalware, such as candlesticks and salt and pepper shakers. In c1994 the company became known as Nan Swid Design, with Swid also designing for other manufacturers and notable labels. The company closed c2000.

■ The company produced works by some of the major designers of the day, many of whom were also architects and leaders of the prevalent 'Postmodern' style. They included eminent names such as Michael Graves, Ettore Sottsass, Zaha Hadid and Robert Venturi.

■ These Postmodernists rejected the functional and plain ideals of the Modern movement, begun in earnest during the first decades of the 20thC. They introduced historical, cultural and Pop motifs and references, as well as a feeling for color and surface pattern. No longer was design dictated purely by function.

■ Quality was very high, with ceramics being finely transfer-printed. All ceramics bear a facsimile signature of the designer on the back, underneath the company name and the pattern name. They were expensive and were aimed at the growing numbers of style-conscious urban professionals. They also influenced many other less costly, lower quality wares during the 1980s and '90s.

■ The market is still emerging, as the style had fallen out of fashion. Despite its importance to 20thC design, it is yet to come to the attention of larger numbers of collectors. The nearest equivalent is Italy's Alessi, who also employed similar design ethics, but has enjoyed more appeal amongst collectors. Aim to buy examples in the best condition possible as many were were worn or damaged through use. Items shown here are in unused and mint condition.

An American Swid Powell 'Medici' pattern transfer-printed teacup and saucer, designed by Ettore Sottsass in 1984.

Ettore Sottsass is perhaps the best known and most prolific Italian Postmodernist. After taking part in the radical and experimental Alchimia design group, he helped found the more successful and influential Memphis group. He then went on to design products and buildings, on his own behalf and for many other notable companies.

Saucer 5.75in (14.5cm) diam

$220-280   **GM**

An American Swid Powell 'Medici' pattern transfer-printed soup bowl, designed by Ettore Sottsass in 1984.

9.25in (23.5cm) diam

$150-200   **GM**

An American Swid Powell 'Medici' pattern transfer-printed dinner plate, designed by Ettore Sottsass in 1984.

12in (30.5cm) diam

$150-200   **GM**

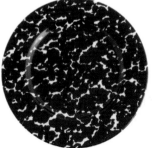

An American Swid Powell 'Notebook' pattern transfer-decorated ceramic dinner plate, designed by Robert Venturi in 1984.

Venturi took this design from the front cover of a school notebook. As well as the black being typically 1980s, the pattern's unexpected use on dinnerware makes a strong Postmodern statement.

12in (30.5cm) diam

$220-280   **GM**

An American Swid Powell 'Medici' pattern transfer-printed side plate, designed by Ettore Sottsass in 1984.

9.25in (23.5cm) diam

$150-200   **GM**

An American Swid Powell 'Beam' pattern transfer-printed dinner plate, designed by Zaha Hadid in 1988.

12in (30.5cm) diam

$150-200   **GM**

A CLOSER LOOK AT A SWID POWELL PLATE

Robert Venturi (b.1925) is a Philadelphia-based architect who was one of the founding fathers of the late 20thC Postmodern movement, criticising the plain and functional Modern principle of design.

The pattern is known as 'Grandmother' and is an ironic statement about a grandmother's favourite old chintzy tablecloth updated with black lines and stylization. It was based on a tablecloth belonging to the grandmother of one of Venturi's associates.

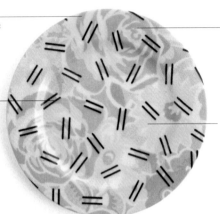

It also relates to one of Venturi's principles that we consider the styles of our immediate (our mother's) past as being bad taste, but after the 'buffer' of one generation, our grandmother's styles can be appealing.

It represents the Postmodern style as it brings in colorful surface decoration that has historical and cultural references – ideals the Modernists had baulked at and rejected.

An American Swid Powell transfer-decorated 'Grandmother' pattern ceramic plate, designed by Robert Venturi in 1984.

9in (23cm) high

$120-180 GM

An American Swid Powell transfer-decorated 'Grandmother' pattern ceramic mug, designed by Robert Venturi in 1984.

3.75in (9.5cm) high

$30-50 GM

An American Swid Powell 'Black Stripes' pattern transfer-printed mug, designed by Robert and Trix Haussmann in 1984.

Although considered strictly Postmodern, the design is very similar to the Op Art movement of the 1960s, championed by those such as painter and printmaker Bridget Riley.

4in (10cm) high

$220-280 GM

An American Swid Powell 'Broken' pattern transfer-printed dinner plate, designed by Robert and Trix Haussmann in 1984.

12in (30.5cm) diam

$220-280 GM

An American Swid Powell 'Volumetric' pattern transfer-printed dinner plate, designed by Steven Holl in 1986.

12in (30.5cm) diam

$150-200 GM

An American Swid Powell 'Planar' pattern transfer-printed dinner plate, designed by Steven Holl in 1986.

12in (30.5cm) diam

$150-200 GM

An American Swid Powell 'Calla Lily' pattern transfer-printed plate, designed by Robert Mapplethorpe in 1984 after one of his photographs, with original card box.

1984 12in (30.5cm) diam

$600-800 GM

FIND OUT MORE...

Swid Powell, by Sarah Nolan and Annette Tapert, published by Rizzoli, 1990.

A Grimwades Art Deco form cube-shaped teapot, with dragon decorated band and gilt trim.

c1930   *4in (10cm) wide*

$80-120   **BAD**

A Grimwades 'Royal Winton' yellow teapot, with a floral handle and finial, marked with patent number "301262".

$120-180   **BAD**

A Price Bros. 'Ye Olde Inn' cottageware teapot and cover.

The purple/orange/green colorway is rarer than other colorways.

c1930s

$450-600   **JF**

A Price & Kensington Potteries 'Ye Olde Cottage' teapot, marked.

Price Brother was formed in 1896, becoming Price Bros. Ltd in 1903. In 1962 the company amalgamated with Kensington Pottery Ltd (established c1922) becoming Price & Kensington. They are known for their production of cottageware.

9in (22.5cm) wide

$60-80   **JL**

A Till majolica teapot and cover, of baluster form with weeping widow finial, in brown green and mustard glazes.

$150-200   **ROS**

A German teapot, with molded and floral swag decoration and gilt highlights.

$70-100   **JL**

A Wade transfer-printed 'Paisley' pattern chintzware-style teapot.

c1930   9.75in (25cm) wide

$80-120   **BAD**

An English sepia transfer-printed teapot, depicting Bragham Castle, impressed "Made in England", one chip.

9in (22.5cm) wide

$70-90   **JL**

An early 20thC Whieldon-type cabbageware teapot and cover, naturalistically modeled and glazed in shades of green.

Master potter Thomas Whieldon (1719-95) is associated with the production of tortoiseshell ware and agateware that was decorated with green, brown or blue translucent glazes applied with a mottled effect.

5.5in (14cm) high

$280-320   **ROS**

CERAMICS

A Wade Heath jug, pattern no. 3397, marked with Reg'd design 787794 for 1933 and "VV" painter's initials.

Compare this to the similar Myott jug on p119 of the Myott section in last year's book. Which came first...?

7.75in (19.5cm) high

$70-90   **NAI**

A Wade green-glazed molded jug, no. 567.

8.75in (22cm) high

$30-60   **GAZE**

A Wade 'Zena' figurine, designed by Jessie Hallen, factory marks.

Jessie Hallen was responsible for the majority of Wade's 1930s lady figurines, inspired by Doulton's Fair Ladies. In 1930 she was given her own studio within Wade's Manchester Pottery and eventually had studios in all three of the Wade potteries.

8.75in (22cm) high

$200-300   **SWO**

A 1940s Wade Harvest Ware vase.

9in (21.5cm) high

$70-90   **GAZE**

A Wade Heath 'Big Bad Wolf & The Three Little Pigs" musical jug.

This was inspired by the Disney animation The Three Little Pigs, featuring the wolf as the villain. It was released in 1933.

c1933   10.25in (26cm) high

$500-900   **NAI**

A Wade panda bear plaque, size 195.

From the Wade Extravaganza, held at Alton Towers in 1998. It was produced in other colors for other events.

1998   8in (20.5cm) high

$80-120   **CA**

A 1940s Wade cockatoo spirit container.

5in (12.5cm) high

$70-100   **GAZE**

A Wade 'Jock Blow Up' figure, from Disney's Lady and the Tramp'.

The name 'Blow Up' comes from the fact they are enlarged versions of the smaller 'Hat Box Series' that preceded them. Jock is one of the hardest to find of the 10 Blow Up figures from 'Lady and the Tramp', and 'Bambi' and was released 18 months after the initial four.

1962-65

$250-350   **WW**

An early Wade Mambo dish, later renamed Zamba.

Africa and African art had a great influence on 1950s design, perhaps aided by the reduction of cost in international air travel and films such as African Queen in 1951.

c1957   9.5in (24cm) wide

$80-120   **NPC**

A set of five Wade Mambo plates.

c1957   4.25in (11cm) wide

$80-120   **NPC**

A Wade Harmony Ware 'Shooting Star' pattern fruit bowl, shape 440, with tripod base.

The space race between the USSR and US at this time had a significant influence on design and motifs, such as the shooting stars on this bowl, are commonly seen.

c1957-62   9in (23cm) wide

$100-150   **NPC**

A 1950s Wade Harmony ware 'Carnival' pattern bowl, with pierced rim.

12.25in (31cm) wide

$100-150   **NPC**

A 1950s Wade Harmony Ware 'Carnival' pattern fruit bowl, shape 440, with pierced rim and tripod base.

9in (23cm) long

$25-35   **GAZE**

A Wade Harmony Ware 'Parasols' pattern fruit bowl, with pierced rim.

1957-62   12.25in (31cm) wide

$120-180   **NPC**

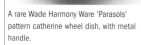

A rare Wade Harmony Ware 'Parasols' pattern catherine wheel dish, with metal handle.

7in (18cm) wide

$80-120   **NPC**

A Wade 'Quack-Quacks' pattern nursery mug, by Robert Barlow.

3in (7.5cm) high

$20-30   **CHS**

COLLECTORS' NOTES

■ Samuel A. Weller established his pottery business in 1872 in his hometown of Fultonham, Ohio and initially produced flowerpots and other household wares. He transferred the pottery to Zanesville in 1888 and not long after acquired the Lonhuda Pottery of Steubenville.

■ It was also about this time that Weller began to produce art pottery utilizing techniques learnt from W.A. Long, the former head owner of Lonhuda, who worked at Weller for a year after his company was bought.

■ Early ranges included Louwelsa, taken from his daughter Louise's name, Tourada and Dicken's Ware. Aiming to compete with the neighbouring potteries of Rookwood and Roseville, Weller employed the services of a number of noted artists and designers such as

Frederick Rhead; responsible for the tube-lined Jap Birdimal and L'Art Nouveau, and Frank Ferrell.

■ Many early lines were hand-painted, but high production costs meant that these were slowly replaced between 1910-14 by molded, production line pottery. However, Weller was one of the last potteries to fully remove art pottery from their catalog, which they did in 1935. The pottery closed in 1948.

■ Fierce competition between the Zaneville potters meant that Weller often produced similar lines to directly compete against the likes of Rookwood and Roseville but often failed to win.

■ The early, hand-painted ranges, such as Hudson, Eocean, Sicard and Dicken's Ware are the most sought-after, particularly large and signed examples.

A Weller 'Ardsley' bowl and flower frog set, unmarked.	A Weller light blue 'Atlas' squat vase, with a star opening, marked "Weller C-3" in script, chip to one of the star's corners and two darkened lines at the rim.	A Weller Barcelona vase, with wide, swooping handles, marked "A Weller" on base in yellow slip.	A pair of Weller 'Blue Drapery' candleholders, with dark pink roses and green leaves, both marked 'Weller', one bruised with two flakes at the base. *'Blue Drapery' was a popular pattern in the 1920s.*
Bowl 14.5in (36cm) high	*6.25in (16cm) wide*	*8.25in (21cm) wide*	*8in (20cm) high*
$400-500 DRA	**$22-28** BEL	**$180-220** BEL	**$100-150** BEL

A Weller 'Blue Drapery' bowl, with dark pink roses and green leaves, unmarked, glaze skip on the rim, showing through as a darker blue.

6in (15cm) wide

$100-150 BEL

A Weller 'Bonito' handled vase, with blue lilies of the valley, marked "A Weller Pottery" in script, overall crazing and an unobtrusive glaze skip at the rim.	A rare Weller Camelot yellow footed dish, dark crazing around foot, unmarked. *This is a hard pattern to find, the version with a rose pink glaze is even rarer.*
5.75in (14.5cm) high	*8in (20cm) diam*
$80-120 BEL	**$600-800** DRA

A Weller 'Coppertone' frog figure, incised mark.

4.5in (11cm) wide

$220-280 **DRA**

A Weller 'Cornish' vase, in brown with berries and leaves, marked "Weller" in script.

7in (18cm) high

$200-300 **BEL**

A Weller 'Delsa' tall vase, with three branch-like handles, marked "A Weller Pottery Since 1872 17".

12.25in (31cm) high

$120-180 **BEL**

A fine Weller Fru Russet two-handled squat vessel, decorated with white blossoms on one side, bright blue berries on the other, all on a curdled pink and green ground, impressed "Weller".

5.5in (14cm) wide

$800-1,000 **DRA**

A CLOSER LOOK AT A WELLER VASE

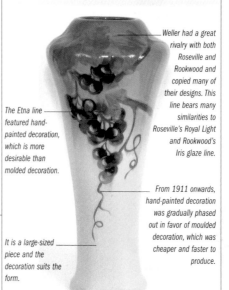

Weller had a great rivalry with both Roseville and Rookwood and copied many of their designs. This line bears many similarities to Roseville's Royal Light and Rookwood's Iris glaze line.

The Etna line featured hand-painted decoration, which is more desirable than molded decoration.

From 1911 onwards, hand-painted decoration was gradually phased out in favor of moulded decoration, which was cheaper and faster to produce.

It is a large-sized piece and the decoration suits the form.

A Weller 'Etna' large vase, with grape decoration front and rear, marked on the base "A Weller Etna" in block letters and signed "A Weller" in the body below the decoration.

14.75in (37.5cm) high

$800-1,000 **BEL**

A Weller Forest handled pitcher, in a high gloss finish, marked with number "11" in green slip, repaired rim including the spout and repair to two lines.

5.25in (13.5cm) high

$120-180 **BEL**

A Weller 'Glendale' vase, depicting birds tending to their nest, unmarked.

6.75in (17cm) high

$550-650 **BEL**

A Weller 'Glendale' baluster vase, embossed with birds, flowers, and butterflies, stamped mark.

12in (30cm) high

$650-750   **DRA**

A CLOSER LOOK AT A WELLER HUDSON VASE

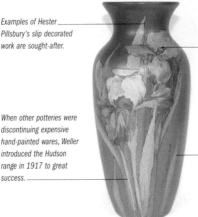

Examples of Hester Pillsbury's slip decorated work are sought-after.

Flowers are a typical motif, although portraits and scenic versions are also found.

When other potteries were discontinuing expensive hand-painted wares, Weller introduced the Hudson range in 1917 to great success.

The large size of the vase encourages the artist to cover the majority of the ground with a bold design.

A Weller 'Hudson' vase, by Hester Pillsbury, decorated with irises, marked "Weller" and signed "HP" at the base, professional restoration to the rim and body.

15.5in (39.5cm) high

$1,500-2,000   **BEL**

A Weller Hudson ovoid vase, painted by Sarah Timberlake, with lily-of-the-valley, artist's initials, impressed mark.

9in (22.5cm) high

$550-650   **DRA**

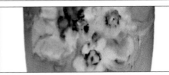

A Weller Hudson vase, painted by Hood, with blue, pink, and yellow blossoms on a shaded blue to green ground, impressed mark, artist's mark.

8.25in (20.5cm) high

$400-500   **DRA**

A fine Weller 'Jap Birdimal' hair receiver, decorated in squeezebag with Viking ships on a blue ground, impressed "812".

A hair receiver, although archaic today, would have been commonly found on a Victorian lady's dressing table. They were used to collect hair taken from brushes or combs, which would be saved up and used to stuff items such as pin cushions, small pillows or for 'ratts', small balls of hair sewn into a sheer hairnet and used to bolster elaborate Victoria hairstyles. They were produced in a variety of materials, and can usually be identified by the finger-sized hole in the top.

4in (10cm) diam

$600-700   **DRA**

A Weller 'Knifewood' vase, carved with butterflies and daisies on a black ground, impressed mark.

4.25in (10.5cm) high

$350-450   **DRA**

A Weller 'L'Art Nouveau' vase, decorated with orange flowers and flowing leaves, unmarked.

8.75in (22cm) high

$200-300   **DRA**

A Weller 'Marvo' green double-bud gate, marked with Weller Pottery half kiln stamp.

5in (12.5cm) high

$120-180 BEL

A Weller 'Marvo' tan and green wall pocket, unmarked, chip inside hang hole.

7.75in (19.5cm) high

$120-180 BEL

A Weller 'Louella' vase, painted with yellow irises, impressed "Weller".

9.5in (24cm) high

$250-350 DRA

A Weller 'Muskota' flower frog, modeled as a finely detailed crab, marked "Weller", tips of the two longest claws have been repaired.

5.25in (13.5cm) wide

$100-150 BEL

A Weller 'Muskota' flower frog, with a frog sitting in a lotus flower on his lily pad, unmarked, small factory flaw near one of the open holes in the base.

4.5in (11.5cm) high

$150-200 BEL

A Weller 'Muskota' flower frog, with a brick-orange lobster, marked "Weller".

6.5in (16.5cm) long

$200-300 BEL

A Weller brown 'Oak Leaf' vase, marked "Weller".

10.75in (27.5cm) high

$70-100 BEL

A Weller brown 'Oak Leaf' vase, marked "A Weller" in script, with small flake from the base.

6.5in (16.5cm) high

$40-60 BEL

A Weller 'Orris' wall pocket, embossed with flowers and columns under a dark brown and green glaze, unmarked.

8in (20cm) high

$120-180 DRA

A Weller 'Patra' bowl, with scalloped rim, marked "Weller Pottery" in script, small rim chip and a very tight, short line.

7.5in (19cm) wide

$100-150   **BEL**

A CLOSER LOOK AT A WELLER SICARD VASE

Jacques Sicard joined Weller in 1902 and developed this metallic, iridescent glaze that was produced until 1907.

This is one of Weller's best glazes, together with the Standard Brown glaze. Consequently these glazes are popular with collectors.

Sicard learnt the glaze technique from Clement Massier, who developed his 'Reflets Metalliques' glaze by 1889.

This is a relatively simple shape with subtle decoration, larger and more elaborate examples could be worth significantly more.

A Weller Sicard corseted vase, decorated with berries and leaves, signed in script.

6.25in (15.5cm) high

$350-450   **DRA**

A rare Weller 'Rochelle' vase, painted by Claude Leffler, with pink and yellow nasturtium, marked in script, artist's initials.

Rochelle was a variation on Weller's successful Hudson range. Claude Leffler is a desirable Weller painter.

6.25in (15.5cm) high

$400-500   **DRA**

A Weller 'Roma' wall pocket, decorated with Dupont motif, impressed mark.

Introduced in 1912, Roma was one of Weller's first molded lines, developed to cut manufacturing costs. It was produced in large amounts, so look for undamaged examples with crisp details, as the molds wore out over time.

10.25in (25.5cm) high

$200-300   **DRA**

A Weller 'Roma' bottle-shaped vase, unmarked.

13.5in (34cm) high

$180-220   **DRA**

A Weller 'Silvertone' vase, with a squat base and narrow opening, marked with Weller Pottery full kiln stamp.

6.5in (16.5cm) high

$200-300   **BEL**

A Weller 'Silvertone' double-handled vase, with yellow and blue butterflies amongst lavender and fuchsias, marked with Weller Ware stamp.

The Silvertone line was created by Dorothy England Laughead.

10.75in (27.5cm) high

$550-650   **BEL**

A Weller 'Silvertone' bulbous vase, with flared rim, embossed with blooming irises, stamped mark.

5.5in (14cm) high

$350-450   **DRA**

A Weller 'Souevo' handled jug, shape number 17, with geometric decorations in white on a reddish clay, marked "WELLER".

The Souevo line was introduced in 1907 and was based on Native American pottery, a popular motif for the Arts & Crafts movement. It is sometime known as 'Indian Ware'.

6.25in (16cm) high

$180-220   **BEL**

A Weller 'Tutone' triangular vase, in purple with green accents, faintly marked with Weller Pottery half kiln stamp, restored chip at base and some flat flakes off the underside.

11.75in (30cm) high

$150-200   **BEL**

A Weller 'Tutone' chalice vase, in purple with green highlights, marked with Weller Pottery full kiln stamp, three tight lines at the rim.

5.5in (14cm) high

$20-30   **BEL**

A Weller 'Tutone' basket-form vessel, in green over purple glazes, marked with Weller Pottery half kiln stamp, glaze pop at the bottom rim.

8in (20cm) long

$120-180   **BEL**

A Weller 'Warwick' bowl with handles, marked with Weller Pottery full kiln stamp.

10in (25.5cm) wide

$100-150   **BEL**

A Weller 'Woodcraft' vase, with three foxes peering out of their hole, unmarked, one nose chipped off and chip to rim.

5.75in (14.5cm) high

$150-200   **BEL**

A Weller 'Woodcraft' bowl, with a squirrel perched on the side, marked with Weller Pottery kiln stamp.

5.25in (13.5cm) high

$220-280   **BEL**

A scarce Weller 'Woodcraft' tall log vase, with an owl peering out of its hole at a squirrel, unmarked, repairs to the base and rim, and a slight touch-up to the ears.

18.5in (47cm) high

$400-500   **BEL**

COLLECTORS' NOTES

■ Although West German ceramics from the 1950s have been a recognised collecting field for some years, their later, very different 1960s and '70s younger siblings have largely been ignored. Over the past few years, this has begun to change and interest is growing.

■ Much research is still to be done, but the lack of official company records, which were not kept or were destroyed, makes it hard. Handling as many identified pieces, preferably with labels, is the best way of learning. The name and period of manufacture can be gained from considering the shape, color of clay used, color and type of glaze and the marks on the base.

■ The most desirable designs are known as 'fat lava' by collectors and are brightly colored with thick, dripped, and cratered textured glazes that look like molten or dried lava, or the moon's surface. Many of these were complex to produce and are rare. Shapes were all

molded, and those that were typical of their time are also desirable. Simple, glossy glazes in dull colors on simply molded bodies are generally less desirable.

■ Many of the more sought-after 'wild' glazes were only produced in limited numbers, with the 'tamer' designs being exported widely in much larger numbers. Size is important, with large, floor standing vases being sold in smaller quantities at the time, making them less numerous today. Many collectors collect by shape, glaze or company.

■ Always buy in the best condition possible, as many perfect examples can still be found on the market. Most companies closed, or discontinued their decorative ranges, from the mid-1970s to early 1990s as tastes changed and less expensive imports from the Far East affected them.

A 1970s West German Scheurich vase, with repeated 'sliced onion' like molded design and cream glaze, the base molded "285-18 W. Germany".

7in (18cm) high

$25-35 DTC

A 1970s West German Scheurich vase, with repeated 'sliced onion' like molded design and brown glaze, the base molded "285-15 W. Germany".

6in (15cm) high

$25-35 DTC

A 1970s West German Scheurich vase, with repeated 'sliced onion' like molded design, the base molded "285-30 W. GERMANY".

This is one of the most commonly seen patterns and can be found in a wide variety of sizes and colors.

11.75in (30cm) high

$50-80 DTC

A West German Scheurich tapering cylinder vase, with dripped purple lava-type glaze over painted green bands on a matte brown ground, the base molded "205-32 W.Germany".

12.5in (31.5cm) high

$70-90 GC

A 1970s West German Scheurich vase, the base molded "202-22 W.Germany".

9in (23cm) high

$30-40 L

A West German Scheurich vase, with alternating bands of volcanic textured orange and brown glaze, the base molded "205/32 W.Germany", with paper label.

Note the shape of the rim and neck, which is a typical Scheurich feature.

12.5in (32cm) high

$50-80 GC

A West German Scheurich large floor vase, with creamy brown mottled and textured top and base, and orange band with brown lava-type glaze dripped design, the base molded "517-30 W.Germany".

On Scheurich pieces, the first figure indicates the shape number, the second the size in centimetres.

A West German Scheurich vase, with matte brown lava 'tartan' pattern effect glaze over a glossy red ground, the base molded "200-28 W.Germany", and with paper label.

11in (28cm) high

$40-60 GC

A West German Scheurich vase, with orange lava glaze dripped over a glossy ultramarine blue glazed body, the base molded "200-22 W.Germany".

8.75in (22.5cm) high

$40-60 GC

11.75in (30cm) high

$70-90 GC

A late 1970s West German Scheurich large floor standing vase, with a painted design of a stylised flower stem and random brushstrokes in brown, the base molded "Scheurich-Keramik 291-45 W.Germany".

17.75in (45cm) high

$220-280 GC

A West German Scheurich vase, with handle, with green, orange and black glossy glazed bands, the base molded "401-28 W.Germany".

Like many of Scheurich's handled jug vases, this shape can also be found without a handle.

11in (28cm) high

$25-35 GC

A 1970s West German Scheurich jug vase, with handle and wavy and straight line design, the base molded "408-40 W.Germany".

This is typical of 1970s Scheurich production in its colour, form and decoration. The base markings and label are also typical of the maker.

15.75in (40cm) high

$60-80 DTC

A West German Scheurich jug vase, with handle, unmarked.

This is one of the harder to find Scheurich jug forms.

15.5in (39.5cm) high

$50-70 GAZE

A West German Scheurich ovoid jug vase, with handle, with wide central band hand-painted with a green and black volcanic textured glazed stylised flower, with creamy brown top and base, the base molded "484-30 W.Germany".

11.75in (30cm) high

$50-70 GC

CERAMICS

An enormous West German Scheurich floor standing vase, with a wide band of hand-painted and carved yellow diamonds and circles between two bands of textured black and white glaze, the base molded "553-52 W.Germany".

20in (51cm) high

$280-320 GC

A West German Scheurich vase, the bronze glaze overlaid on the flanges with drips of purple lava glaze, the base molded "267-25 W.Germany".

The thin, raised areas of glaze damage has occurred when bubbles have burst as the piece has been moved and handled.

9.75in (24.5cm) high

$70-90 GC

A West German Scheurich square floor bottle, molded with the 'Montignac' pattern of a bull and a stag with hand-painted detail, dripped brown lava glaze, the base molded "281-30 W.Germany".

This pattern is inspired by the French Lascaux caves, which contain some of the best prehistoric cave paintings known.

11.5in (29.5cm) high

$120-180 GC

A huge West German Scheurich floor vase, with a 'stained glass window' design of different coloured cells bordered by raised black glaze lines, with matte black top and 'volcanic' textured brown areas, the base molded "517 45 W.Germany".

17.25in (44cm) high

$220-280 GC

A huge West German Bay Keramik floor jug vase, with handle, with all-over dripped glossy yellow lava-type glaze, the base molded "BAY 218-50 W.Germany".

The Contura label is likely to be for a distributor or a retailer.

19.25in (49cm) high

$280-320 GC

A huge West German Bay Keramik floor vase, the body and rim with rows of molded berry-like bosses, with textured cream and brown brushed glazed waisted neck, the base molded "BAY 44 50 W.Germany".

19.25in (49cm) high

$150-200 GC

A West German Bay Keramik vase, with thick cream glaze dripped over the matte black glazed body, the base molded "BAY 630 40 W.Germany".

15.75in (40cm) high

$70-100 GC

A West German Bay Keramik globe vase, with semi-iridescent glossy speckled blue, brown and cream glazes with painted circular and wavy line patterns, the base molded "64 17 BAY W.Germany".

6.5in (16.5cm) high

$60-80 GC

A CLOSER LOOK AT A CARSTENS VASE

It is a very large, floor standing size.

This label indicates Carsten's high-end 'Luxus' range, many designed by Dieter Pieter, Trude Carstens or Gerda Heuckeroth.

The color and design are very similar to Scandinavian designs, which would have been fashionable at the time.

The Luxus range was more expensive and less were made, making examples harder to find today.

A West German Carstens 'space capsule' tapered vase, with central band printed with orange and white glazed shapes, the top half with mottled bronze and brown gloss glaze, the bottom half with textured brown glaze, the base molded "1253-15 W.Germany".

6.25in (16cm) high

$50-70   GC

A West German Dümler & Breiden vase, with molded pebble design in red and yellow over a glossy blue-green glazed ground, the base impressed with the factory motif and "613/22 Germany".

8.75in (22cm) high

$80-120   GC

A West German Carstens 'Luxus' range floor vase, with molded brown glazed stylised flower design on a textured cream glazed ground, the base molded "7690-50 W.Germany".

20in (51cm) high

$280-320   GC

A West German Dümler & Breiden square footed vase, from the 'Relief' range, with dripped snow-like textured white glaze over a satin finish royal blue glazed body, the base impressed with a factory motif and "RELIEF 84/36 Germany".

14.25in (36.5cm) high

$80-120   GC

A West German Dümler & Breiden vase, with tapering orange top section with molded runic designs and paper label, the base impressed with factory motif and "10 30 Germany".

Runic designs were also popular with studio potters of the period.

11.5in (29.5cm) high

$100-150   GC

A West German Dümler & Breiden two-handled pot, from the 'Relief' range, in glossy glazes, molded with circular bosses and impressed on the base with factory motif and "RELIEF 90/15 Germany".

10.25in (26cm) high

$80-120   GC

A fine and large West German ES-Keramik amphora-type vase, with 'Bombay' red and blue-grey lava glaze over a blue-grey ground, unmarked.

ES Keramik was the name used by Emons & Söhne.

10.5in (26.5cm) high

$150-200   GC

A West German ES-Keramik jug vase, with tall neck and handle and dripped matte red and blue-grey lava effect glaze over a blue-grey ground, unmarked, with shield-shaped foil label.

11.25in (28.5cm) high

$100-150   GC

A West German Fohr baluster vase, the satin finish glazed purple body overlaid with a dripping, glittering bronze coloured glaze, the base molded "W.Germany 312-20".

8in (20.5cm) high

$70-100   **GC**

A CLOSER LOOK AT A WEST GERMAN BOWL

The bright color with the black lava glaze bubbling through it is a typical hallmark of Otto Keramik pieces from the 1970s.

The craters show where the glaze has bubbled through and popped - this example has a good range of sizes and dense clustering.

Otto Keramik is still in business today, producing tamer designs.

The bases of Otto Keramik pieces are most often covered in felt.

A West German Otto Keramik small bun-shaped bowl, with matte black glaze bubbling through the thick matte yellow lava glaze, unmarked, with felt base.

3.25in (8.5cm) high

$70-100   **GC**

A West German Jasba ovoid vase, with molded knobbly, pebble-like effect and orange glaze brushed over a matte black glazed body, the base impressed "N 9001125", with English language gold foil label.

9.75in (25cm) high

$70-100   **GC**

A West German Jopeko octagonal jug, with yellow and black mottled glossy lava-type glaze dripped over a smooth black speckled purple glazed ground, the base impressed "1305".

6in (15.5cm) high

$50-70   **GC**

A West German Jopeko small footed circular vase, with light covering of smooth lime green glaze on a black ground, the base with textured matte black glaze, indistinctly marked.

The combination of smooth, bright glazes and a black lava glaze is typical of Jopeko.

6in (15.5cm) high

$70-90   **GC**

A 1970s West German Otto Keramik cylinder vase, the glossy red glaze with matte cratered textured black glaze bubbling through, unmarked, with felt base.

9.5in (24cm) high

$50-70   **GC**

A West German Roth Keramik rectangular section oval vase, with molded red gloss glazed concave areas between bubble textured black glazed strands, with paper label, the base molded "W.Germany 310".

Roth Keramik are based in Ebernhahn, and this design, found in yellow, purple and red with black, is one of their best known and loved by collectors. Look out for the taller jug vases with ring handles, as these can fetch over $120 in large sizes.

6.25in (16cm) high

$70-90   **GC**

A West German Roth Keramik shaped vase, molded with concave purple glossy glazed ovals between white and black textured bubbled strands, the base molded "W.Germany".

10.25in (26cm) high

$70-100   **GC**

A West German Ruscha rounded rectangular footed vase, with dripped and graduated brown, lime green and purple lava type glazes, unmarked.

9.75in (25cm) high

$70-100 GC

A West German Ruscha footed vase, with small, flared rim, with 'Vulcano' orange-red lava glaze over a black ground, the base molded "805".

The form and even finish of this vase recall antique Oriental ceramics and also the works of some modern ceramicists. 'Vulcano', developed in 1959, is one of the most sought-after and famous West German glazes of the period.

7in (18cm) high

$100-150 GC

A CLOSER LOOK AT A WEST GERMAN VASE

This design was by Cari Zalloni, who went on to found the fashionable Cazal eyewear company.

It is part of a range of differently shaped vases with similar glazes and decoration.

It was designed in the early 1960s and forsees the Op Art movement, championed by Bridget Riley.

Steuler Keramik pieces are often marked on the base with a molded 'S' and 't' monogram within a shield.

A West German Steuler Keramik 'Zyklon' pattern rectangular vase, the base molded and numbered "215/25".

9.75in (24.5cm) high

$50-70 GC

A West German Schlossberg rectangular section vase, the textured cream glazed body with molded ovals filled with glossy blue, the base molded "296/25".

9.75 (24.5cm) high

$100-150 GC

A West German Schlossberg rectangular vase, with glossy orange drips over a glossy brown lava-type glaze, the base molded "298 25".

As well as the company name, the label reads "Handarbeit", which indicates the piece is 'hand-made'.

9.75in (24.5cm) high

$80-120 GC

A West German Spara Keramik gourd vase, with gloss green and black glaze, the base stamped "SPARA 266/15".

The form of this vase closely resembles antique Chinese 'double gourd' forms.

6in (15cm) high

$40-60 GC

A West German Ü-Keramik square section jug, with inset handle and dripped and mottled glaze, the top with small off-centre opening, unmarked.

11.75in (30cm) high

$100-150 GC

A West German Ü-Keramik vase, with dripped cream satin finish and speckled orange-red gloss glazes, the base indistinctly impressed, with gold foil label.

10.25in (26cm) high

$50-70 GC

FIND OUT MORE...

Fat Lava West German Ceramics of the 1960s & 70s, *by Mark Hill, www.markhillpublishing.com, 2006, ISBN: 978-0-95528-650-6.*

COLLECTORS' NOTES

■ Russel Wright (1904-76) was diverted from a career in law by a part-time job in industrial designer Norman Bell Geddes' workshop. After visiting the 'Art Deco' exhibition in Paris in 1925, he returned and designed furniture, as well as the first jukebox for Wurlitzer. He continued creating innovative designs in many different media throughout his life.

■ He designed ceramics from 1937, but could not find a company to manufacture them, due to their radical shapes, which were influenced by his education as a sculptor and his restrained Quaker upbringing.

■ When the bankrupt Steubenville factory in Ohio reopened in 1940, it produced his 'American Modern' range in 11 colours until 1961. The range became one of the most successful ever produced.

■ The 'Casual China' range was designed in 1946 for Iroquois China Co. of Syracuse, NY. It was advertised as being a 'revolution in china' and was guaranteed against breakage for one year. Shapes were designed to allow them to stack and store easily. Available into the 1960s, it too was highly successful and was less prone to damage than 'American Modern'.

A Steubenville 'American Modern' Coral teapot, designed by Russel Wright, the base with impressed mark.

10in (25.5cm) wide

$80-120   **HLM**

A Steubenville 'American Modern' Bean Brown creamer, designed by Russel Wright, the base unmarked.

7in (18cm) wide

$10-20   **HLM**

A Steubenville 'American Modern' Coral long dish, designed by Russel Wright, the base unmarked.

10.5in (26.5cm) long

$15-25   **HLM**

A Steubenville 'American Modern' long leaf-shaped green dish, designed by Russel Wright, the base with impressed marks.

13.5in (34cm) long

$40-50   **HLM**

A Steubenville 'American Modern' green-beige teacup and saucer, designed by Russel Wright, the base with stamped mark.

Saucer 4.25in (11cm) diam

$15-25   **HLM**

A Steubenville 'American Modern' Grey small espresso coffee cup, designed by Russel Wright, the base unmarked.

Saucer 4.25in (11cm) diam

$15-25   **HLM**

An Iroquois 'Casual China' Charcoal gray wine pitcher, designed by Russel Wright.

Designed 1946 and available until the 1960s.

4.75in (25cm) high

$300-400   **HLM**

A Iroquois 'Casual China' two-piece combined creamer and sugar bowl, designed by Russel Wright, with blue printed mark to base.

4.25in (11cm) high

$60-80   **HLM**

An Iroquois 'Russel Wright China' Sugar White glazed creamer, designed by Russel Wright, with printed mark to base.

5in (12.5cm) high

$35-45   **HLM**

An Iroquois 'Casual China' Sugar White covered pitcher, designed by Russel Wright, with printed mark to base.

Sugar White, Ice Blue and Lemon Yellow were the first colors used by Iroquois, with Nutmeg, Charcoal, Ripe Apricot and Pink Sherbet coming later. Cookware is difficult to find. Look out for the rare turquoise color known as 'Deep Aqua'.

5in (12.5cm) high

$180-220   **HLM**

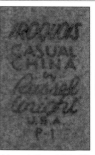

A 1950s Iroquois 'Casual China' Lemon Yellow teapot, designed by Russel Wright, with red printed mark to base.

This is from the redesigned range.

9.25in (23.5cm) wide

$70-100   **HLM**

A pair of Iroquois 'Casual China' Nutmeg Brown glazed stacking salt and pepper shakers, designed by Russel Wright.

3.25in (8cm) high

$20-30   **HLM**

An Iroquois 'Casual China' small green dish, designed by Russel Wright.

5in (13cm) diam

$15-20   **HLM**

A Iroquois 'Casual China' Nutmeg Brown dish, designed by Russel Wright.

8.25in (21cm) wide

$40-60   **HLM**

A Sterling China restaurant ware Cedar Brown 2qt water pitcher, designed by Russel Wright, with molded mark.

Designed in 1949, the range was available in green, gray, brown, yellow and white and was not produced for long. It is often hard to find today, especially if unmarked.

6in (15.5cm) high

$150-200   **HLM**

A Sterling China yellow creamer, designed by Russel Wright, with molded marks to base.

5.75in (14.5cm) long

$30-40   **HLM**

CERAMICS

A 1960s Bellaire California dish, with hand-inscribed and hand-painted motif of two Native Americans, the base with hand-painted mark.

15.25in (39cm) long

$180-220 HLM

A Bennington Pottery black vase, designed by David Gil, with petal-type opening, the base impressed "bennington pottery vermont *1994 ds".

1994 12.5in (31.5cm) high

$250-350 HLM

A Bennington Pottery small white globe vase, designed by David Gil, with petal-type opening, the base impressed "bennington pottery vermont *1994 ds".

1994 6in (15cm) high

$80-120 HLM

A pair of Bennington Pottery hand-painted candleholders, with a blue stylized flower pattern.

Note the similarity to Scandinavian designs.

3.5in (9cm) high

$80-120 HLM

A Sascha Brastoff rectangular lidded box, with hand-painted stylized leaf pattern and "Sascha B", the base with rooster mark.

8in (20cm) wide

$100-150 HLM

A Sascha Brastoff Rooftop series 'canoe' bowl, hand-painted with houses, and "Sascha B", the base with gilt rooster stamp and "F21".

7.25in (18.5cm) wide

$70-100 HLM

A CLOSER LOOK AT AN EVA ZEISEL TEAPOT

A Sascha Brastoff vase 'Star Steed' vase, hand-painted with a prancing horse design on a green ground and "Sascha B" base with gilt mark and painted in gilt "F20".

This horse design is typical of Brastoff's work. Brastoff (1918-93) was an artist who, backed by Wintrop Rockefeller, founded his first factory in 1948. He attracted the Hollywood glitterati to the launch of his second factory in 1953, after a fire destroyed the first. They continued to support him and his glitzy 1960s and '70s designs, many bearing his hallmark 'Sasha B' gilt signature.

5.5in (14cm) high

$60-80 HLM

This teapot was designed by Hungarian designer Eva Zeisel (b.1906), whose prolific and influential designs are currently being reassessed and more firmly appreciated by design historians and collectors.

It was part of a range designed from 1942-43 at the suggestion of Eliot Noyes, the director of the Industrial Design department at the Museum of Modern Art in New York, which is how it received its name.

It claimed to be the first opaque china dinnerware produced in the US and, despite similarities, was different to European imports. It was also a breakthrough in terms of its warmer white color, and less geometric and more elegantly curving design.

Due to WWII, it was finally launched in 1946 and was available nationally in 1947, however sales only began to take-off once patterns were added, in around 1949.

A late 1940s Castleton China Co. 'Museum' range white teapot, designed by Eva Zeisel, unmarked.

9.75in (25cm) high

$300-400 HLM

A Clifton Pottery of New Jersey 'Tirrube' pattern hand-painted slip vase, the base impressed with factory mark, "Clifton" and hand-incised with "148".

10in (25.5cm) high

$400-600   **TOJ**

A Clifton Crystal Patina small beige vase, the base hand-inscribed "Clifton NJ 1906".

The Crystal Patina range, with its glittering micro-crystalline glaze and often unusual forms is one of the most desirable range produced by Clifton.

1906   3.5in (9cm) high

$400-500   **TOJ**

A Clifton Pottery of New Jersey 'Tirrube' pattern hand-painted slip vase, the base hand-inscribed "Clifton 153".

The pottery was founded in Clifton in 1905 by William Long and celebrated decorator Albert Haubrich. Although the company only lasted a few years, they produced a wide range of molded pottery, and Tirrube is one of their most collected lines. Long left Clifton to join Weller in 1909 and art pottery was produced until 1911, after which manufacture moved over fully to tiles.

c1908   8in (20cm) high

$400-600   **TOJ**

A limited edition vase, made to commemorate the 1989 Pottery Festival, decorated with grapes and gilt trim, from an edition of 100, marked "Crooksville CP USA Pottery Festival 1989" on the base.

1989   10.75in (27.5cm) high

$100-150   **BEL**

A Fiesta small yellow juice pitcher.

6in (15cm) high

$70-100   **TM**

A late 1950s Gladding McBean & Co. 'Oven Safe Color-Seal' Franciscan Eclipse shape 'Starburst' pattern transfer-printed teapot.

Designed in 1953, this was one of Franciscan's most successful and widely sold ranges during the 1950s. The shape was designed by George T. James, and the pattern by Mary Brown.

8in (20.5cm) wide

$150-250   **HLM**

A late 1950s Hall China Co. Hallcraft transfer-printed 'Fantasy' pattern coupé soup dish, designed by Eva Zeisel.

13in (33cm) long

$80-120   **HLM**

A Hall China Co. yellow tapered cylinder pitcher.

4.75in (12cm) high

$40-50   **TM**

A Japanese hand-painted cat-shaped string holder, with "Japanese Holt Howard 1958" printed to base.

1958   5in (13cm) wide

$35-45   **TM**

CERAMICS

A Peters & Reed Moss Aztec 'Vestal Virgin' jardinière, unmarked.

Peters & Reed was founded in 1899. In 1912 it released its first art pottery range, Moss Aztec, developed by Frank Ferrell. It became the Zane Pottery Co. in 1921, and continued to produce many art pottery lines until 1941, when the pottery closed.

c1920   6in (15cm) high

$320-380   TOJ

A CLOSER LOOK AT AN OWENS VASE

The J.B. Owens Pottery was founded in 1885 and only produced art pottery for a short period between 1896 and 1907, before moving onto the production of tiles.

It is hand-painted by Charles Chilcote, who is also known for his flower designs at Weller, and also worked for Roseville and Zanesville.

Owens' first range was known as Utopian – Lotus is similar but has paler backgrounds, later it was offered in a matte finish.

At over 16ins in height, it is a large, and as such rare, piece and the design is skillfully painted.

A rare Owens Lotus tall vase, by Charles W. Chilcote, decorated with lotus blossoms on a graduated background, marked "Owens 1249" on the base, signed "Chilcote" n the side in slip, overall even crazing.

16.5in (42cm) high

$3,000-4,000   BEL

A 1920s Peters & Reed green dripped Shadow Ware vase, unmarked.

Unmarked wares are typical for Peters & Reed, particularly early examples.

6.75in (17cm) high

$250-350   TOJ

A Pfaltzgraff for Raymor 'Country-Time' deep cobalt blue pitcher, designed by Ben Seibel.

10in (25.5cm) high

$100-150   HLM

A 1950s-60s Red Wing 'Smart Set' dinner plate, with hand-painted yellow and black linear design, the base impressed "RED WING USA".

10.75in (27.5cm) diam

$15-25   HLM

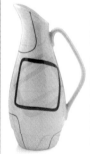

A 1950s-60s Red Wing 'Smart Set' pitcher, with hand-painted yellow and black linear design, the base impressed "RED WING USA".

12.75in (32.5cm) high

$180-220   HLM

A 1950s-60s Red Wing 'Smart Set' boomerang-shaped divided bowl, with hand-painted yellow and black linear design, impressed "RED WING USA".

Shapes such as this are typical of the period, making them sought-after by collectors. Red Wing closed in 1967.

13.75in (35cm) long

$120-180   HLM

A 1950s-60s Red Wing 'Smart Set' small lidded bowl with handle, with hand-painted yellow and black linear design, the base impressed "RED WING USA".

6.75in (17cm) widest

$70-90   HLM

A green Red Wing baluster vase, the base impressed "900 RED WING".

10in (25.5cm) high

$120-180   HLM

A Schmid International 'Think' head condom holder, designed by Tarck, with transfer-printed design.

This was used in bars and is a particularly early example of contraception awareness campaigns.

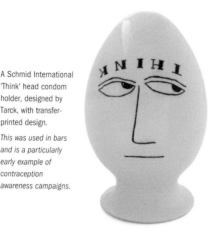

1959   8.5in (21.5cm) high

$150-250   HLM

A Steubenville for Raymor Contempora range 'Mist Gray' milk jug, designed by Ben Seibel, with grey linear pattern.

Little is known about Ben Seibel, but the success of his Contempora range for Steubenville led Raymor to request a line, which was called Raymor Modern Stoneware and was manufactured by the Roseville Pottery Co.

4in (10cm) high

$35-45   HLM

A Harris Strong small dish, impressed "Harris G. Strong B80" on the base.

8in (20cm) long

$80-120   TOJ

A Harris Strong elliptical dish, impressed "Harris G. Strong B-81" and molded "A".

10.5in (26.5cm) long

$100-150   TOJ

A CLOSER LOOK AT A PUZZLE JUG

Puzzle jugs emit water from the holes on the rim, soaking the unaware user when he or she tries to pour the liquid inside, out.

The 'puzzle' is how to stop this happening – here, covering a hole on the inside of the handle with a finger makes a seal, meaning the liquid can be poured safely.

This example also holds a surprise – when the base is held to the light a reclining nude is seen in the base.

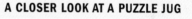

This decoration is known as a lithophane, with the light and dark areas being created by different thicknesses of the porcelain – thicker parts appear darker.

A 1950s Harris Strong hand-painted bowl, decorated with a horse, impressed "B51 Strong".

The design is very similar to Picasso's drawings, etching and paintings.

9in (22.5cm) wide

$80-120   TOJ

An American York Pottery red-glazed baluster urn, with applied ring handles, the base impressed "YORK P 145".

13in (33cm) high

$150-250   HLM

A mid-to late 19thC German white porcelain 'puzzle jug', with molded naturalistic motifs, the base with a lithophane of a reclining naked woman.

These 'amusements' were popular from the Middle Ages onwards, but saw a second peak in the 18thC and 19thC.

7in (17.5cm) high

$100-150   DWG

A Batman mirror, licensed to Creative Accessories Ltd, Bellmore NY, by DC Comics 1987.

c1987 18in (46cm) high

$20-30 **NOR**

A Batman & Robin molded plastic 'talking' alarm clock, marked "1974 Janex Corp".

c1974 7in (17.5cm) high

$70-100 **NOR**

A Batman bat logo machine-cut perspex clock, by Creative Accessories Ltd.

13.75in (35cm) wide

$50-80 **NOR**

A Batman & Robin Melmac printed plate, with "National Periodical Publications Inc" wording.

7.25in (18.5cm) diam

$30-40 **NOR**

A Batman 'Super Plants' ceramic planter, printed "©National Publications 1975" and impressed "JAPAN".

From a set of four 'Super-Hero Planters' featuring Superman, Batman, Wonder Woman, and Shazam! (Captain Marvel – see two pages on for an example). These 'pot' plant holders perhaps held 'Super Plants'.

3.25in (8cm) high

$30-40 **NOR**

A 44-card set of Topps Batman 'Blue Bat' series cards, in original case, marked "1966 ©National Periodical Publications Ltd".

Topps issued five sets of Batman cards in 1966, three of which had painted illustrations. They are differentiated by the colour of the bat logo which can be found in blue, red and black. They are all about the same value and are the most common of the 1966 cards.

1966 3.75in (9.5cm) wide

$30-50 **NOR**

A 55-card set of Topps Batman 'Black Bat' series cards, in original case, marked "1966 ©National Periodical Publications Ltd".

1966 3.75in (9.5cm) wide

$30-40 **NOR**

A box of Topps Batman deluxe reissue edition cards.

In 1989 Topps reissued the three painted series of cards from 1966. They can be confused with the originals, but have a glossy front and the backs are printed with "reissue 1982".

1989 3.5in (9cm) wide

$12-18 **NOR**

An American 'Adventures of Batman, Chapter 4: Poison Peril' Super 8 reel, boxed, Columbia Pictures Home Movie.

1943 5in (13cm) wide

$30-50 **NOR**

An American Toy Biz Co. Superman action figure, '©1989 Superman DC Comics".

It is rare to find a figure with the cape. A carded example is worth up to $200.

c1989

$50-80   NOR

A Burger King Superman figural cup holder.

This was produced as a promotional give-away for stores.

1988   4.25in (10.5cm) high

$10-15   NOR

A Superman the Movie promotional double-walled plastic mug and cup set, by Dawn, Passaic NJ, marked "©1978 DC Comics".

c1978   4.25in (10.5cm) high

$15-20   NOR

A large Superman screen-printed glass.

This is a very unusual shape and size.

1971   6.75in (17cm) high

$20-30   NOR

A Pepsi Collectors' Series Superman screenprinted glass.

6.25in (16cm) high

$20-25   NOR

An American Superman laminated card, 78-record single 'Supercase', "©DC Comics Inc 1976".

7.75in (19.5cm) high

$50-70   NOR

A rare Superman Thermos flask, "©1967 National Periodical Publications Inc.", in great condition.

This rare Superman Thermos will appeal to collectors of Thermos and those wanting to complete a set with a lunchbox.

7.25in (18.5cm) high

$80-120   NOR

A pair of Superman licensed plastic child's rollerskates, "©1975 DC Comics".

7in (18cm) long

$15-20   NOR

An early Superman printed Valentine card.

1940   4.25in (11cm) high

$20-25   NOR

An American Popeye WWII propaganda postcard, marked "© King Features Syndicates".

1942   *5.5in (14cm) high*

$30-50   **LDE**

An American Popeye jointed wood doll, with transfer-printed and carved decoration, the foot printed "Made in USA".

5in (13cm) high

$200-250   **MG**

A 1940s unmade-up Captain Marvel Club 'Shazam' printed tin pin.

There is another, scarcer version of this pin where the superhero is looking off to one side.

1in (3cm) wide

$40-60   **LDE**

A Captain Marvel 'Shazam!' 'Super-Hero Planter', "©National Publications 1975" and impressed "JAPAN".

A number of comic book publishers have characters called Captain Marvel. This version was created by Fawcett Publications in 1939. The character was then licensed to DC Comics in 1972 but the name had been copyrighted by Marvel. To get around the issue, DC marketed the character under the trademark 'Shazam!'

c1975   *3.25in (8cm) high*

$20-30   **NOR**

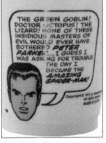

An Amazing Spider-Man promotional 7-Eleven Slurpee cup, marked "©1975 Marvel Comics Group".

5in (12.5cm) high

$7-10   **NOR**

A box of Marvel Superhero 'Adventure Cookies', with Spider-Man promotional money bank, unopened.

1991   *9.75in (25cm) high*

$15-20   **NOR**

A Barbie as Wonder Woman Collector Edition doll, by Mattel, mint, boxed.

This Barbie doll will be popular with Barbie collectors as well as Wonder Woman fans. The planned 2007 film by Joss Whedon should help to increase interest in the character.

1999   *13.5in (34.5cm) high*

$50-80   **NOR**

A pair of Wonder Woman plastic scissors, for Dyno MDDSE corp, made in Hong Kong.

1978   *5in (13cm) high*

$8-12   **NOR**

A Corgi Magic Roundabout 'Dylan' plastic figure.

The Magic Roundabout was originally a French children's programme (Le Manège Enchanté), created by Serge Danot in 1963. It was shown in the UK by the BBC who commissioned Eric Thompson (father of actress Emma Thompson) to provide an English voiceover which he based not on the original script but soley on the visuals. The show proved a huge hit with both adults and children and numerous interpretations exist to the 'true' meaning of the show.

2in (5cm) high

$20-30 **RBC**

A Magic Roundabout 'Florence' plastic figure.

8.25in (21cm) high

$20-30 **MTS**

A Corgi Magic Roundabout 'Dougal' plastic figure

3in (7.5cm) long

$12-18 **RBC**

A Magic Roundabout printed tin kaleidoscope, by Green Monk Combex, dated.

1968 *9in (23cm) high*

$30-40 **MTS**

A Deans Playtime 'My Magic Roundabout Pop-Up Book'.

1975 *9.25in (23.5cm) wide*

$25-35 **RBC**

A box of Magic Roundabout Crackers, by Tom Smith & Co Ltd., Norwich, England, each containing a tissue party hat, balloon, a 'character' badge and a snap, box marked "BBC TV 1971".

A complete and unused box of crackers, such as this, is very rare.

Box 16.75in (42cm) wide

$220-280 **MTS**

A 1970s Magic Roundabout printed paper party plate.

7.5in (19cm) diam

$3-5 **MTS**

A Magic Roundabout printed plastic lampshade.

8.75in (22cm) high

$50-70 **MTS**

A Snoopy soft toy.

Charlie Brown's beagle Snoopy first appeared in the Peanuts comic strip on October 4th, 1950, two days after the very first strip. Initially a silent, supporting character, Snoopy came into his own when writer Charles Schultz began to draw thought balloons for the character. From the 1960s the strip focused more on Snoopy and his various alter-egos which included a WWI flying ace. Today he is arguably one of the most recognisable comic strip characters in the world.

c1950   8in (20cm) high

$15-20   **RBC**

A 1970s Snoopy 'Another Determined Production' vase.

5in (12.5cm) wide

$20-30   **MTS**

A Snoopy painted wood money box, marked "©1958, 1966".

6in (15cm) high

$30-40   **RBC**

A 1990s Snoopy electric hairdryer, by Clariol Appliances, marked "© 1958, 1966".

9.5in (24cm) high

$25-35   **RBC**

A 1970s Peanuts diecast car, with Snoopy driving and Woodstock as a passenger.

4.25in (11cm) long

$100-150   **RBC**

An American Peanuts Belle Fun & Fashion Dress-Up doll, by Knickerbocker, with Woodstock figure, mint and boxed, marked "© 1958, 1965".

Belle, a little seen character in the Peanuts strip, is Snoopy's sister. She is mostly known through merchandise rather than the comic strip, leading occasional readers to mistake her for Snoopy's girlfriend.

Box 10.25in (26cm) high

$70-100   **RBC**

A Snoopy 'Tea for Two' transfer-printed mug, marked "FOREIGN".

3.25in (8.5cm) high

$15-20   **RBC**

A Peanuts cartoon graphic printed silk tie.

$30-40   **S&T**

A 'Bendy' foam Kermit the Frog Muppet figure, with indistinct marks.

c1970   8.5in (21.5cm) high

$25-35   **RBC**

A 1970s 'Bendy' foam Miss Piggy Muppets figure, in karate outfit.

8in (20cm) high

$15-20   **RBC**

A CLOSER LOOK AT A PAIR OF LONE RANGER DOLLS

These examples are in mint, original condition. As they would have been bought to play with, most examples show wear, damage or missing parts ⎯

The painted composition is in excellent condition and shows no signs of cracking or crazing on the face.

They retain their clothing, accessories and moreover their weapons, which is very unusual. ⎯

A rare pair of 1930s Dollcraft Novelty Lone Ranger and Tonto composition dolls, clothed.

These large size figures would have been relatively expensive when originally made, meaning fewer would have been sold.

The Lone Ranger and Tonto were based on characters created by George W. Trendle and developed by writer Fran Striker. They first appeared on radio in 1933, beginning a hugely successful run of nearly 3,000 episodes. The series moved to television in 1949 and the duo also appeared in comic books, novels and movie serials.

c1938   20in (51cm) high

$800-1,200   **SOTT**

A Fozzie Bear Muppets soft toy, by Fisher Price Toys, copyright 1976, with moulded rubber hat and plastic eyes.

c1976   12in (30.5cm) high

$30-50   **RBC**

A Little Miss Chatterbox, by Holland Studio Craft Ltd, copyright 1998.

2.75in (7cm) high

$10-15   **RBC**

A Li'l Abner 'Shmoo' moulded brass pin.

The selfless Shmoo first appeared in Al Capp's *L'il Abner* comic strip in August 1948. The perfect herd animal, the Shmoo delighted in being eaten and tasted of different meats depending on the cooking method. A vast amount of licensed Shmoo merchandise was created, particularly in the late 1940s and early '50s and is still desirable today.

1.5in (4cm) high

$40-60   **LDE**

A Li'l Abner 'Kigmy' brass hollow pin.

In 1949, Al Capp followed up his popular Shmoo character with the Kigmy (Kick-Me) creature, which was similar in shape to the selfless Shmoo and loved to be kicked. Capp stated that he was inspired by two ethnic groups who were 'kicked around' by American society: the African Americans and Jews, but the L'il Abner readership did not take to the new character and it was soon dropped. Despite the Kigmy's short run, merchandise including kickable inflatable toys was produced, but in smaller amounts than for the Shmoo.

c1949   1in (2.5cm) wide

$30-50   **LDE**

CHOCOLATE MOLDS

COLLECTORS' NOTES

- Metal chocolate molds were widely used from the late 1800s, reaching their height of popularity during the 1920s and 1930s. Germany was a centre of production, but molds were also made in France and the US. Metal chocolate molds were replaced by less costly plastic molds in the 1950s.

- Makers included H.Walter of Berlin, Sommet of Paris and Eppelsheimer of New York. Many examples carry stamped numbers which were used in the ordering process to indicate a catalog number. Although many molds do not have maker's names, their style, manufacture and position of the catalog number can help to identify makers.

- A variety of symbols were used by the different makers. Sommet, for example, used a stylised fish and Eppelsheimer, a spinning top. Marked, and particularly dated, examples are more desirable in

general. Materials can also indicate date of manufacture. Tin-plated copper was used until the late 1890s, when it was largely replaced by tin-plated steel (the most commonly found material). Later examples used nickel-plated steel and nickel silver and have a shiny silvery appearance.

- Molds by German maker Reiche are particularly popular. Founded in 1870, the company produced over 50,000 designs. T.C Weygandt of New York imported Reiche molds from 1885 until 1939, when WWII broke out. The factory re-opened in Communist East Germany in 1950 after the original plant was destroyed in the war. It closed in 1972.

- Large molds and fine detailing attract higher prices. Unusual details or forms can add value. Clips are rarely original as they were interchanged many times during use.

An unmarked cockerel hugging a chicken chocolate mold, no. 6537.

3.5in (9cm) high

$100-200   **DF**

A chicken in a basket chocolate mold, no. 6558.

Makers' numbers and marks are often worn away by the clips being pulled on and off.

3.75in (9.5cm) high

$40-50   **DF**

A French Sommet chocolate and 1 liter ice cream mold, no. 1417, in the form of a cockerel.

The presence of a pull-off lid on the base shows this is also an ice cream mold. It is stamped with a stylised fish showing it was made by Sommet and also has a '49' in a diamond stamping, dating it precisely.

1949   *10.5in (27cm) high*

$300-400   **DF**

An American Eppelsheimer dressed chick mold, no. 8037.

5in (12.5cm) high

$80-120   **DF**

A German Anton Reiche cockerel, chicken, and chick chocolate mold, with date mark and agency copyright wording "Ohne Unsere Genehmigung Darf Dieses Muster Anderen Nicht Unterbrietet Werden" and "George Diltoer Agent Generale Berchem Bruxelles".

1933   *6in (15cm) long*

$80-120   **DF**

A French Letang Fils pelican chocolate mold, no. 3611.

8in (20cm) high

$280-320   **DF**

A penguin chocolate mold, no. 4270, stamped "F.Q". or "F.O". on the base.

4.75in (12cm) high

$100-150   **DF**

An unmarked elephant chocolate mold, with raised trunk.

A raised trunk was meant to bring or indicate good luck.

8.5in (21.5cm) wide

$200-300 DF

A CLOSER LOOK AT A CHOCOLATE MOLD

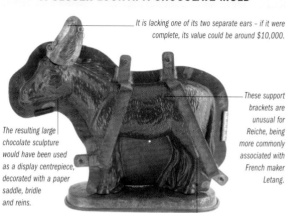

It is lacking one of its two separate ears - if it were complete, its value could be around $10,000.

These support brackets are unusual for Reiche, being more commonly associated with French maker Letang.

The resulting large chocolate sculpture would have been used as a display centrepiece, decorated with a paper saddle, bridle and reins.

Weighing in at over 11kg, this chocoholics' dream would also have been dressed with chocolate baskets filled with individual chocolates.

A large German Anton Reiche donkey chocolate mold.

16.5in (42cm) high

$6,000-8,000 DF

A German Walter chocolate mold of a dromedary.

2.25in (6cm) high

$80-120 DF

A postwar American T.C. Weygandt Scottie dog nickel-plated chocolate mold, no. 383.

Weingandt was originally an importer for German maker Anton Reiche. After the war, it also made its own molds, but these do not have the sharpness and detail of Reiche's originals.

4.75in (12cm) high

$70-90 DF

A postwar Dutch Vormenfabriek dog nickel-plated chocolate mold, no. 16164, stamped "JKV Tilburg".

4.25in (11cm) high

$30-40 DF

A 1930s French Letang Fils fish chocolate mold.

The remarkable condition of this mold can be explained by the fact that many Letang molds, made just before the war, languished in a warehouse during the war. They were distributed later, during the 1940s and 1950s, but many were not used.

12.5in (31.5cm) long

$150-200 DF

A German Anton Reiche crocodile chocolate mold, no. SB1156.

8in (20.5cm) long

$250-350 DF

An unmarked frog chocolate mold, no. 8435.

3.5in (9cm) long

$120-180 DF

A French Letang Fils Santa chocolate mold, with clasped hands and long coat, no. 2040.

6.5in (16.5cm) high

$80-120   **DF**

An American nickel-plated Santa chocolate mold, no. 1042.

This more rounded form is the other most common form for Santa to take, and is more American in style.

8in (20.5cm) high

$350-450   **DF**

A CLOSER LOOK AT A CHOCOLATE MOLD

This size of mold, at over 13 inches high, is very rare – most were half this size.

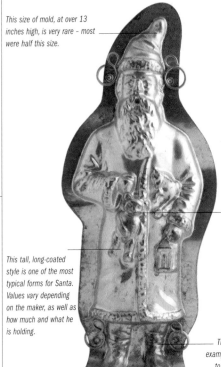

This tall, long-coated style is one of the most typical forms for Santa. Values vary depending on the maker, as well as how much and what he is holding.

This specific type of Santa is usually found without the teddy and horse, just holding the lantern

This is one of only a few examples of this type known to collectors, making him extremely rare.

A German Anton Reiche Santa chocolate mold, no. 13133.

13.75in (35cm) high

$2,500-3,500   **DF**

A German Anton Reiche 'postcard' chocolate mold, with Santa and children in front of a Christmas tree, no. 522.

Rectangular 'postcard' molds are highly collectible. Values vary depending on the maker, size, image shown and level of detail in the image. This is a highly detailed example by a known maker in a sought-after theme.

7in (17.5cm) high

$700-900   **DF**

A postwar BM nickel silver chocolate mold of Santa on a running rabbit, stamped "34 Solid Nickel Silver".

4.25in (11cm) high

$500-600   **DF**

A German Walter Santa on a motorbike chocolate mold, numbered inside "9599".

Walter was the only company to stamp its mold numbers on the inside.

4.25in (10.5cm) wide

$150-250   **DF**

A German Anton Reiche angel chocolate mold, no. 13053.

5.25in (13cm) high

$180-220 DF

A French Letang Fils angel chocolate mold.

This example and the near identical example on the left show how often makers copied each other. However, the finishing on the Letang is not as fine, note the badly cut 'overlap' on the middle left corner. The detail is also less fine than on Reiche's example.

4.75in (12cm) high

$120-180 DF

A large French Letang Fils turkey chocolate mold, unmarked, no. 274.

7.5in (19cm) high

$400-500 DF

A small unmarked turkey chocolate mold.

4.5in (11.5cm) high

$50-70 DF

A German Anton Reiche witch on a broomstick chocolate mold, no. 22167S, marked and imported into the US by T.C Weygandt.

6.25in (16cm) high

$300-400 DF

A German three-piece turkey chocolate mold, stamped "Germany" and "93".

It is rare to find a chocolate mold with three pieces as here.

8in (20cm) high

$700-900 DF

A German Anton Reiche Halloween 'scaredy cat' chocolate mold, dated and stamped no. 17473.

Note the clips, which are clearly not original. This does not affect the value as clips were never original, being interchanged many time over by the chocolatiers as they used the molds.

1930 *3.5in (9cm) long*

$150-200 DF

An unmarked Easter egg with rabbit chocolate mold.

4.5in (11.5cm) high

$100-150 DF

CHOCOLATE MOLDS

A Belgian car chocolate mold, stamped "Cer ... ernard S.A. Bruxelles".

5.25in (13.5cm) long

$80-120   **DF**

A German small car chocolate mold, stamped "Made in Berlin Germany".

4.25in (10.5cm) long

$40-60   **DF**

An unmarked German chocolate mold of an armored car.

4in (10cm) long

$80-1210   **DF**

A German postwar nickel-plated tractor chocolate mold, imported and stamped by "E. Hahn Buffalo N.Y." and "Made in Germany".

4.75in (12cm) long

$40-60   **DF**

A rare German F.W. Kutzscher of Schwarzenberg Zeppelin chocolate mold, no. 5551.

Due to its quality, this mold was once thought to have been made by Walter or Anton Reiche, but a recently discovered catalog has now identified it as being by short-lived maker Kutzcher. The Zeppelin is also a desirable form and it is very well detailed, adding to its desirability.

9in (23cm) wide

$400-500   **DF**

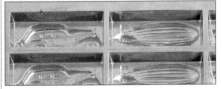

A German Anton Reiche flat chocolate mold of various modes of transport, no. 29907-10, with T.C. Weygandt importers and date stamps.

The maker, date, large size and form make this a desirable and valuable mold. It would have been used to create 48 individual flat-backed chocolates and includes a desirable Zeppelin.

1934   *16.5in (42cm) long*

$300-400   **DF**

A postwar Dutch Vormenfabriek kettle chocolate mold, no. 16014, also marked with retailer's stamp for "Jos Boyen Bruxelles".

23.5in (60cm) high

$40-60 **DF**

A pre-war German Walter coffee grinder nickel-plated chocolate mold, no. 9574.

Unusually for Walter, the number is stamped outside. The use of nickel shows that the mold was in use before the war.

2.25in (6cm) high

$80-120 **DF**

A German Anton Reiche shop scales chocolate mold, no. 28409, with date stamp.

1935 *3.75in (9.5cm) high*

$70-100 **DF**

An unmarked very large and heavy key chocolate mold.

It is the size as well as the unusual shape that make this so valuable – a smaller 6in example may fetch around $70-100.

16.25in (41cm) long

$250-350 **DF**

An American Eppelsheimer shell chocolate mold, no. 7470.

7.75in (19.5cm) long

$150-200 **DF**

A French Letang Fils fiddle and bow four-piece mold, no. 3917.

Complete sets of molds like this are rare, and the size and shape is also rare and desirable.

10.75in (27cm) high

$250-350 **DF**

An unmarked postwar nickel-plated rocking horse chocolate mold.

4.25in (11cm) high

$70-100 **DF**

A Dutch De Smedt Willebroek teddy bear chocolate mold, no. 16159.

5.25in (13.5cm) high

$70-100   **DF**

A postwar Dutch Vormannfabriek teddy bear nickel-plated chocolate mold, no. 16055.

4.25in (10.5cm) high

$70-100   **DF**

An unmarked German teddy bear chocolate mold, no. 23989, with hinged clips.

The teddy bear is a highly collectible subject and so can fetch high prices, even for simpler, later molds. This example is valuable because it is finely detailed, is in a different and charming pose and is more three-dimensional than others.

4in (10cm) high

$550-650   **DF**

An unmarked defecating monk chocolate mold, stamped "43".

As well as being aimed at children, some subjects appealed to adults. A series of unusual, sometimes bizarre, subjects can be found and are highly collectible among today's collectors.

4.5in (11.5cm) high

$45-55   **DF**

A German Laur ... 'Paul on the Pot' chocolate mold, no. 13055, with oval maker's stamp.

4.25in (11cm) high

$40-50   **DF**

A postwar Hansel & Gretel nickel chocolate mold, no. 2597, also stamped "121".

5.25in (13.5cm) high

$100-150   **DF**

A French Sommet tin-plated copper horse and jockey chocolate mold, no. 1811.

Sommet molds are typified by overlapping edges.

9.5in (24cm) high

$500-600   **DF**

COLLECTORS' NOTES

- Due to the sheer range of types available, most coin collectors concentrate on one area such as the ancient world, commemoratives, error coins, or examples from one specific period and/or place.

- Beware of facsimile collectors coins, which are common. Although not necessarily made to deceive, it can be hard to tell them from the genuine article. The abundance of facsimiles may lower the value of rare coins.

- When buying commemoratives, note the edition number. Those produced in large numbers will appreciate less than strictly limited issues.

- As condition is very important, coins should be handled as little as possible. Always hold coins by the edges or wear gloves, and invest in a good quality album and mounts to display and store your collection. Do not clean coins, as collectors generally prefer coins with an 'original' appearance. Cleaning might reduce values by half or more.

A Paxs type penny of Winchester, minted by William I, in good to very fine condition with light gold and gray tones.

1066-87

$700-800   **BLO**

A rare class D groat, minted by Edward III, fourth coinage with normal 'R', reversed 'N', with some original color, one of the finest known examples.

1327-77

$800-1,000   **BLO**

A rosette-mascle groat of Calais, minted by Henry VI, with reverse with plain cross, in very fine condition, struck on a large flan.

1422-61

$150-200   **BLO**

A light coinage ryal of Bristol mint, minted by Edward IV, in extremely fine condition, slightly small flan.

During the reign of Edward IV, the face value of his coinage became less than that of the metals they were made from. To counter this the amount of metal in the coins was reduced by approximately 20 per cent. This is known as light coinage.

1461-70

$1,800-2,200   **BLO**

A scarce groat, minted by Henry VII, with profile portrait, in extremely fine condition, dark gray tones.

1485-1509

$600-800   **BLO**

A third coinage groat, minted by Henry VIII, second bust, light gray tones, in extremely fine condition, rare as such.

1509-47

$1,200-1,800   **BLO**

A sixpence, minted by Elizabeth I (1558-1603), the obverse with a bust in plain dress with rose, toned, weak impression around forehead, very fine condition.

1562

$280-320   **BLO**

A third issue threepence, minted by Elizabeth I (1558-1603), gray tones, in extremely fine condition.

1571

$120-180   **BLO**

A third coinage shilling, minted by James I, the obverse with sixth bust, in extremely fine condition, scarce in this condition.

1603-25

$550-650   BLO

A type 3a3 halfcrown of Tower mint under Parliament, minted by Charles I, rainbow-toned, in good condition.

1625-49

$220-280   BLO

A lozenge-shaped halfcrown of Newark mint (beseiged), minted by Charles I (1625-49), in fine condition, weak area of strike.

1646

$1,500-2,000   BLO

A shilling, minted by Oliver Cromwell (1649-58), in extremely fine condition, with superb blue and gold toning, scarce as such.

1658

$1,800-2,200   BLO

A second bust shilling, minted by Charles II (1660-85), in good condition.

1668

$120-180   BLO

A guinea, minted by James II (1685-88), in good condition.

1687

$2,200-2,800   BLO

A CLOSER LOOK AT A GOLD COIN

The obverse and reverse of this coin were designed by John Roettier (1631-c1700), the notable German-English engraver known for the veracity of his portraits.

Five guineas was a significant amount of money at the time of issue. Fewer coins of this large denomination were therefore produced.

This coin contains over an ounce of gold, giving it an intrinsic value as well.

Due to the large gold content, the edge was milled to deter clipping or filing of the coin.

A five guineas coin, minted by Charles II (1660-85), the obverse with second bust, in very fine condition, with some edge bruising, a die crack at base of King's hair.

1679

$7,000-8,000   BLO

A plain crown septimo, minted by Anne (1702-14), with second bust portrait, in good condition with some light field scratches.

1707

$600-800 BLO

A guinea, minted by George III (1767-1820), with fourth bust portrait, in very fine condition.

1774

$450-550 BLO

A scarce proof halfcrown, minted by George IV (1820-30), lightly garnished shield, in as struck condition, some obverse abrasions.

1820

$1,000-1,500 BLO

A scarce shilling, minted by George IV (1820-30), in as struck condition, with full radiant luster.

1825

$220-280 BLO

A scarce halfpenny, minted by William IV (1830-37), in as struck condition, with rainbow and chocolate tones.

1837

$350-450 BLO

A rare plain-edged proof sovereign, minted by William IV (1830-37), with second bust portrait, once mounted with trace of solder to left of bust, some edge bruising.

1831

$1,000-1,500 BLO

A penny, minted by Victoria (1837-1901), with young head portrait, in as struck condition, 20 per cent red-brown luster.

1858

$180-220 BLO

A shilling, minted by Victoria (1837-1901), die no.54, with young head portrait, in as struck condition, with full radiant luster.

1865

$280-320 BLO

A wreath crown, minted by Edward VII (1902-10), in as struck condition, with full radiant luster.

1928

$400-500 BLO

COINS

An American Connecticut penny, with "ET LIB" on the reverse, in fair condition, date illegible.

1787

$18-22   BLO

A Canadian two dollar gold coin, from Newfoundland, in as struck condition with full luster, rare as such.

1885

$800-1,000   BLO

A scarce Republic of China dollar coin, with bust of Sun Yat-sen, the reverse with a junk with birds above and a rising sun, in extremely fine condition, with much luster.

1932

$350-450   BLO

A CLOSER LOOK AT A CURAÇAON FIVE REAL

The island of Curaçao was an open port and traders from Europe and Latin America met to exchange goods.

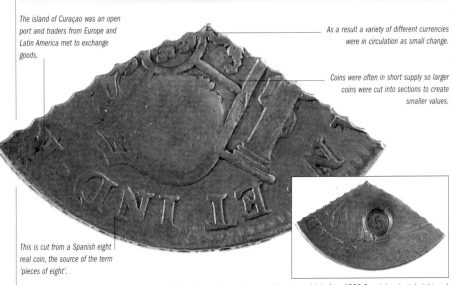

As a result a variety of different currencies were in circulation as small change.

Coins were often in short supply so larger coins were cut into sections to create smaller values.

This is cut from a Spanish eight real coin, the source of the term 'pieces of eight'.

A rare Curaçaon five real, ND countermark for 1818, '5' in circle struck on crenellated cut third of an 1809 Spanish colonial eight real coin, in fair condition, mark in extremely fine condition.

$3,200-3,800   BLO

A Filipino shipwrecked peso, light corrosion of surfaces and adherences in ear, probably in as struck condition before being wrecked.

1897

$120-180   BLO

A French gold proof 100 franc coin, with bust of Marie Curie 1934/1984, in mint condition.

This was produced in a low mintage of only 5,000 gold coins.

$280-320   BLO

A scarce German five reichmarks, from the Weimar Republic, in extremely fine condition.

1913

$120-180   BLO

A German States 24 Mariengroschen, from Brunswick, with bust of George II of England, in good condition, with superb rainbow tones.

1705

$120-180   **BLO**

An Guatemalan half real, die countermark struck on Peru Peso 1893, coin and mark in extremely fine condition.

1894

$80-120   **BLO**

A Hong Kong 50 cents, in very fine condition, with light gray to blue tones.

1891

$100-150   **BLO**

A Hungarian ducat, in extremely fine condition.

1765

$280-320   **BLO**

An Indian Kushan gold stater, from the Kidarite Kingdom, Kushan Empire, the obverse with King standing left, the reverse with Ardoksho seated facing, in fine condition.

c360-380 AD

$150-200   **BLO**

An Indian gold mohur, in extremely fine condition.

1841

$800-1,000   **BLO**

A Maltese 30 tari, with bust of Emmanuel de Rohan, in good condition, with uneven toning, scarce as such.

1795

$350-450   **BLO**

A Scottish thirty shilling coin, minted by Charles I, grainy as though from the ground, slightly off center, in good-to-fine condition.

1625-49

$280-320   **BLO**

A rare Maltese four tari, minted by Jean de Valette, period of Turkish siege, toned, in very fine condition with areas of flat strike.

c1565

$1,200-1,800   **BLO**

COLLECTORS' NOTES

■ Comics have long since ceased to be just for kids and many are now collectors' items. Rarity and condition are crucial to value, as are age and featured characters. Collectors may focus on one era, or may prefer to collect the complete run of a title.

■ The first issue of a title is usually the most desirable, with values dropping considerably for subsequent issues. Other sought-after issues often feature the first appearance or death of a character. Historical topicality, such as the appearance of of the first nuclear explosion, can also increase value.

■ The most prized comics date from the Golden Age (1938-c1955). This era began with the publication of

Action Comics No.1, featuring Superman, and a mint condition copy of this issue could now fetch up to $400,000! A host of rival publications and characters followed. Superman and Batman are generally the most sought-after today from this period.

■ Spider-Man is probably the most desirable of the Silver Age (c1956-c1969) characters, which also include X-Men and The Fantastic Four. Marvel titles of that period are currently more popular than titles from the other big publisher, DC Comics.

■ Mainstream comics, even early examples, have large print runs. However, scarcities, such as the 1984 first issues of Teenage Mutant Ninja Turtles, exist.

"All Star Comics", No.3, Winter 1940, published by DC Comics, fine to very fine condition (7), off-white to white pages, featuring the origin and the first appearance of the Justice Society of America.

The Justice Society of America were the first superhero team and was initially put together as a marketing ploy to increase the exposure of a number of characters. The title was canceled in 1951 with issue 57 and many fans mark this as the end of the Golden Age of Comics and the decline of superhero titles. DC Comics issued a reprint of this issue in 1974 with the cover titled "Famous First Edition". Beware of later versions with their covers removed being offered as the original version.

1940

$12,000-18,000   MC

"The Amazing Spider-Man", No.4, Sept. 1963, published by Marvel Comics, fine to very fine condition (7), off-white pages, featuring the first ever appearance of the Sandman.

$700-1,000   MC

"The Amazing Spider-Man", No.8, Jan. 1964, published by Marvel Comics, near mint condition (9.4), off-white pages.

$4,500-5,500   MC

"The Amazing Spider-Man", No.17, Oct. 1964, published by Marvel Comics, near mint condition (9).

1964

$1,500-2,000   MC

"The Amazing Spider-Man", No.39, Aug. 1966, published by Marvel Comics, very fine to near mint condition (9).

1966

$450-550   MC

"The Amazing Spider-Man", No.6, Nov. 1963, published by Marvel Comics, fine to very fine condition (7), featuring the first appearance of The Lizard.

$750-850   MC

"The Amazing Spider-Man", No.9, Feb. 1964, published by Marvel Comics, near mint condition (9.4), off-white pages, featuring the origin and first appearance of Electro.

$5,000-7,000   **MC**

"The Avengers", No.2, Oct. 1963, published by Marvel Comics, very fine to near mint condition (9), off-white pages.

1963

$700-1,000   **MC**

"The Avengers", No.57, Oct. 1968, published by Marvel Comics, near mint condition (9.6), cream to off-white pages, featuring the first appearance of the Silver Age Vision.

$750-850   **MC**

"Batman", No.6, Aug/Sep. 1941, published by DC Comics, very fine to near mint condition (9).

$4,500-6,500   **MC**

"Batman", No.7, Oct./Nov. 1941, published by DC Comics, very fine condition (8), white pages, features a Bullseye cover, with artwork by Bob Kane.

$2,500-3,500   **MC**

"Captain America Comics", No.1, Mar. 1941, published by Marvel Comics, fine condition (6), red ink not printed, cream to off-white pages, featuring the origin and first appearance of Captain America, with cover artwork featuring Hitler and by Joe Simon.

A correctly printed copy of this comic, in similar condition, would be worth up to $7,000-10,000, depending on condition.

$12,000-18,000   **MC**

"The Defenders", No. 1, Aug. 1952, published by Marvel Comic Group, near mint condition (9.4), off-white to white pages.

$300-400   **MC**

A CLOSER LOOK AT A DETECTIVE COMICS ISSUE

This issue features the first appearance of Robin, the Boy Wonder.

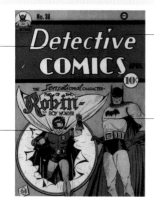

The idea of a young sidekick was originally disliked, but this issue sold double the usual amount of issues and the character remained.

This is one of the top three most sought-after Batman era Detective Comics issues.

The character of Robin was created by Bill Finger and Bob Kane, who were also responsible for the creation of Batman.

"Detective Comics", No.38, published by National Periodical Publications, very fine condition (7.5), off-white pages.

$20,000-30,000   **MC**

"The Fantastic Four", No.4, May 1962, published by Marvel Comics, near mint condition (9.4), off-white pages, featuring the first appearance of the Sub-Mariner.

$18,000-22,000 MC

"The Fantastic Four", No.48, Mar. 1966, published by Marvel Comics, very fine to near mint condition (9), off-white pages, featuring the first appearance of Galactus.

$700-1,000 MC

"The Fantastic Four", No.50, May 1966, published by Marvel Comics, near mint condition (9.2), off-white to white pages, featuring the first Silver Surfer cover.

$700-1,000 MC

"The Incredible Hulk", No.5, Nov. 1974, published by Marvel Comics, near mint condition (9.2), graded.

$3,000-5,000 MC

"The Incredible Hulk", No.181, published by Marvel Comics, near mint condition (9.6), off-white pages, featuring the first full story with Wolverine.

This issue is worth significantly more than any other issue from the second series due to the introduction of Wolverine, a firm fan favourite and X-Men regular.

$3,000-5,000 MC

"More Fun Comics", No.54, published by National Periodical Publications, very fine condition (8), featuring classic Specter cover artwork.

$7,000-10,000 MC

"Superman", No.5, published by National Periodical Publications, near mint condition (9.4), off-white pages.

$20,000-30,000 MC

A CLOSER LOOK AT RED RAVEN COMIC

This was the first and only issue of this title, the name was changed to "The Human Torch" with issue two.

This cover is the first signed cover art work by the hugely influential and prolific comic book artist, Jack Kirby.

Although the title only lasted one issue, Red Raven was the first superhero character to debut with his own title. Captain America is often thought to be the first, with" Captain America Comics" debuting in March 1941.

The character of Red Raven was resurrected in issue 44 of the X-Men, May 1968 and has made odd appearances since.

"Red Raven", No.1, Aug. 1940, published by Timely Publications, very fine to near mint condition (9), off-white pages.

$20,000-30,000 MC

"Crypt of Terror", No.19, Jun.-Jul. 1950, published by E.C. Comics, very fine condition (8.5).

Called Crime Patrol until issue 16, only three issues of this title were produced before the name was changed again to Tales from the Crypt.

$1,200-1,600 MC

"Dark Mysteries", No.21, Apr. 1955, published by Merit Publications, very fine to near mint condition (9), off-white to white.

$500-700 MC

"The Haunt of Fear", No.11, Jan.-Feb. 1952, published by E.C. Comics, near mint condition (9.2), off-white pages.

$500-800 MC

"The Haunt of Fear", No.18, Mar./Apr. 1953, published by E.C. Comics, near mint condition (9.4), white pages.

$1,500-2,000 MC

"Haunted Thrills", No.5, Oct. 1952, published by Ajax/Farrell Publications, near mint condition (9.6), off-white pages.

$1,200-1,800 MC

"Shock SuspenStories", No.14, published by E.C. Comics, near mint condition (9.6), off-white to white pages.

$1,000-1,500 MC

"Spook", No.24, Mar. 1953, published by Star Publications, near mint condition (9.4).

This issue was cited with others by Dr. Fredric Wertham in his book Seduction of the Innocent, which partially blamed comics for juvenile delinquency.

$800-1,200 MC

"Strange Terrors", No.4, Sep. 1952, published by St. John Publishing Co., very fine condition (8), cream-off-white pages, with cover artwork by William Ekgren.

$700-1,000 MC

"Tales From The Crypt", No.24, Jun./Jul. 1952, published by E.C. Comics, very fine to near mint condition (9), off-white pages.

$700-1,000 MC

COMICS

"Tales To Astonish", No.27, Jan. 1962, near mint condition (9.4), off-white to white, featuring the first appearance of the Ant-Man.

$1,500-2,000 **MC**

"The Thing!", No.8, Sep. 1952, published by Captiol Stories, near mint condition (9.2).

The Thing! was particularly notorious for the level of gore and violence included, before the Comic Code Authority was formed.

$800-1,200 **MC**

A CLOSER LOOK AT A HORROR COMIC

The title Vault of Horror started with issue 12, and was previously called War Against Crime.

Together with Crypt of Terror, also by E.C. Comics, Vault of Horror was the first horror comic produced.

E.C. Comics are particularly well known for their gory, violent crime and horror comics and were particularly affected by the introduction of the Comic Code Authority in 1954.

The cover art work was painted by Johnny Craig who was responsible for the covers for the entire run and introduced a naturalistic approach to the series.

"The Vault of Horror", No.12, Apr./May 1950, published by E.C. Comics, near mint condition (9.4).

$22,000-28,000 **MC**

"The Vault of Horror", No.18, Apr./May 1951, published by E.C. Comics, near mint condition (9.4).

$1,200-1,800 **MC**

"The Vault of Horror", No.22, Dec. 1951/Jan. 1952, published by E.C. Comics, near mint condition (9.2).

$600-800 **MC**

"The Vault of Horror", No.23, Feb./Mar. 1952, published by E.C. Comics, near mint condition (9.4).

$1,500-2,000 **MC**

"Weird Terror", No.7, Apr. 1953, published by Allen Hardy Associates, very fine to near mint condition (9), off-white to white.

$700-900 **MC**

"Witchcraft", No.5, Oct./Nov. 1952, published by Avon Periodicals, very fine condition (8.5), off-white pages.

This was the penultimate issue of this title. The cover artwork is by award-winning illustrator Frank Kelly Freas (1922-2005).

$1,500-2,000 **MC**

"Mad", No.15, Sep. 1954, published by E.C. Comics, very fine to near mint condition (9).

$1,200-1,800   MC

"Mad", No.16, Oct. 1954, published by E.C. Comics, near mint condition (9.6).

$2,000-3,000   MC

"Famous Funnies", No.209, Dec. 1953, published by Eastern Color, near mint condition (9.4), cream-off-white pages, with cover artwork by Frank Frazetta.

$2,200-2,800   MC

"Mad", No.19, Jan. 1955, published by E.C. Comics, very fine to near mint condition (9).

$750-850   MC

"Mad", No.20, Feb. 1955, published by E.C. Comics, very fine to near mint condition (9), artist file copy.

$400-600   MC

A CLOSER LOOK AT A COMIC

Even before the US joined WWII, a number of patriot superheroes appeared to defend the world against evil.

Uncle Sam first appeared in "National Comics", No. 1, issued July 1940. His own title ran for eight issues until 1943 and he would not appear again until 1973.

Issue one came with two cover variations, this, darker one with the price and a lighter one without the price. The values are the same.

The superhero version of Uncle Sam as created by the renowned comic artist and writer Will Eisner, who also did the cover artwork for this issue.

"Uncle Sam Quarterly", No.1, Autumn 1941, published by Quality Comics Group, near mint condition (9.6).

1941

$15,000-20,000   MC

"Mad", No.21, Mar. 1955, published by E.C. Comics, near mint condition (9.4), off-white to white pages.

$1,200-1,800   MC

FIND OUT MORE...

Official Overstreet Comic Book Price Guide, by Robert M. Overstreet, published by House of Collectibles, 2006, 36th Edition.

www.dccomics.com, official DC Comics website.

www.marvel.com, official Marvel Comics website.

COSTUME & ACCESSORIES

COLLECTORS' NOTES

■ Vintage fashion attracts interest from both collectors and those looking for a unique or classic look, away from the proliferation of 'mall' styles. As such, values have risen sharply, particularly in the past decade. However every budget is catered for, particularly away from the top fashion houses pieces.

■ Important names such as Christian Lacroix, Chanel, Dior and Yves Saint Laurent will generally always attract high prices, particularly for 'couture' garments made to exacting standards in small quantities for specific personal orders, or examples of classic collections. Always consider the label design, as many designers such as Versace have had long established 'diffusion' lines that were originally less expensive and more mass-produced.

■ Aim to look for iconic classics, such as Chanel's famous tweed suit or dresses in Dior's revolutionary 'New Look' of the 1950s. The 1950s and 60s are two particularly 'hot' decades, although the 1980s is rapidly gaining ground, particularly Punk, minimal and 'power dressing' designs by those such as Vivienne Westwood, Giorgio Armani and Lagerfeld at Chanel.

■ Always consider the shape, construction, material, pattern and color. Pieces by top houses will usually be very well made, using fine quality materials. Look at fashion books to learn how to recognise the key looks of the decade you wish to collect or wear. Stained or torn pieces should be ignored unless very rare (or intended!), and thoroughly examine a piece before buying as repairs can be expensive and unsightly.

A Bill Blass couture floor-length silk satin gown, with wide waist band, and fine tulle covering the entire skirt and forming a halter overlaying the strapless bodice, approx size 12.

$500-700 FRE

A Bill Blass couture silk evening ensemble, with coordinating woven tapestry iridescent silk bustle skirt and burgundy silk cinch-waist jacket, size 12.

$500-700 FRE

A Chanel silk and wool evening skirt ensemble, with a collarless wool blend metallic-flecked tweed jacket and a cranberry iridescent silk long skirt and camisole, size 44.

$800-1,200 FRE

A Chanel off-white cotton and linen beaded skirt suit, with red woven lines and glass beads and matching knitted and beaded cotton camisole, lined in silk.

$800-1,200 FRE

A fine Chanel evening gown and matching jacket, in silk chiffon with translucent green sequins, the silk dyed in very pale vertical stripes in pink, yellow and green and creating an ombre effect, with a sewn insert creating a gathered area at left side and split at hem, the jacket with no closure and quilted with tiny embroidered 'plus' signs with loose threads and stand-up collar, size 40.

2000

$1,000-1,500 FRE

A Christian Dior oversized knitted sweater coat, in dark grey heather wool and cream colored contrasting fringe knit pattern, marked size small.

$400-500　　　　**FRE**

A vintage 1970s Gucci fur wrap calf length coat, with a thin leather tie-belt, with a full fox collar, lined in brown signature "Gucci" acetate, approx. size 4.

$1,000-1,500　　　　**FRE**

A CLOSER LOOK AT A CHANEL DRESS

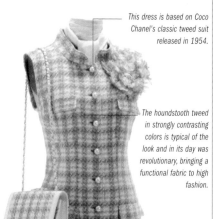

This dress is based on Coco Chanel's classic tweed suit released in 1954.

The houndstooth tweed in strongly contrasting colors is typical of the look and in its day was revolutionary, bringing a functional fabric to high fashion.

The modern and tailored profile, rounded, almost collarless, neck and the bold buttons are other hallmarks of the style.

The matching handbag with its hallmark Chanel gold metal chain and form has a value of its own, fetching around $700.

A Chanel orange and white houndstooth tailored sleeveless dress and matching handbag, with faux pearl buttons and four pockets, short stand-up collar, falling to below the knee, with a large camelia brooch in same fabric, size 42.

$1,800-2,200　　　　**FRE**

A Christian Lacroix chartreuse cropped jacket, with gold iridescent lace overlay and gold and rhinestone buttons, size 42.

$120-180　　　　**FRE**

An Andre Laug couture embroidered metallic rayon dress, with silk cording, beaded and embroidered cuff trim, waist and fold-over neckline, approx. size 12.

$400-600　　　　**FRE**

A Thierry Mugler tailored grey woven silk skirt suit, the jacket with sculptural silhouette and futuristic pin-tuck pleated details, two snap closure and no lapels, with a straight matching skirt, size 46.

$150-200　　　　**FRE**

A 1970s Emilio Pucci 'Queen Anne's Lace' pattern pink and black printed silk jersey gown, with banded V-neck and gathered under the centre/bust, approx size 8.

Although the use of a banded bust collar and hem is typical of Pucci, the length and particularly the style of the print are very unusual.

$600-800　　　　**FRE**

A 1960s-70s Emilio Pucci printed silk dress.

This is more typical of Pucci in terms of the printed pattern and the form. Always look for the 'Emilio' signature within the print.

$300-400   **HP**

A Mary Quant 'Ginger' label black and white short dress, size 11.

Quant's more mass-produced 'Ginger Group' clothing was aimed at a less wealthy buyer.

c1967   34.25in (87cm) long

$100-150   **GAZE**

A CLOSER LOOK AT A CAMPBELL SOUP DRESS

Although it feels like paper, this dress is made from 80 per cent cellulose and 20 per cent cotton, and made a Pop Art statement about disposability as it was meant to be thrown away after use.

The design is taken from Andy Warhol's iconic Pop Art soup can artworks, which summed up 1960s popular and consumer culture.

The simple sleeveless A-line shape of the dress is also typically 1960s.

It was mass-produced but proved unpopular, meaning few were sold and making survivors rare today.

A late 1960s Campbell's Soup 'The Souper' paper dress, designed Andy Warhol, labelled with care instructions, in bright, clean and undamaged condition.

$1,200-1,800   **SDR**

An Oscar De La Renta couture lace evening tuxedo suit ensemble, consisting of a long black lace coat, with satin ribbon trim at waist, matching black lace tuxedo trousers, and a cream silk chiffon ruffled halter blouse. approx size 12.

$800-1,200   **FRE**

A 1960s Castaways 'Disposable Dress', sealed in its original bag, made from printed paper.

Paper clothing, meant to be thrown away after use, enjoyed a brief period of popularity in the late 1960s. Although it allowed fashionable ladies to buy up to the minute shapes in up to the minute patterns, it was not terribly practical and somewhat uncomfortable. Original packaging is rare.

An Oscar De La Renta couture powder blue felt coat, with large fox collar, in a heathered wool or wool blend with a felted surface, with a single button and additional hook closure on the large full dyed fox collar, size 12.

$700-1,000   **FRE**

A late 1960s 'Paperdelic' four-piece paper cloth beach outfit.

Packet 10in (25.5cm) high

$20-30   **NOR**

10in (25.5cm) high

$25-35   **NOR**

A 1960s denim bikini, with dungaree-style top.

$60-80   **SM**

A 1950s Estrava bikini, made from Tootle fabric decorated with an Emilio Pucci fish design.

Pants 12.5in (31.5cm) wide

$220-280   **SM**

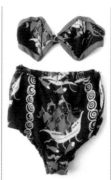

A 1970s printed cotton bikini, with ships and sea decoration, unmarked.

Pants 15in (38cm) wide

$120-180   **SM**

A pair of Levi's 501 'red line' jeans, size W32 L33.

Red Line jeans have a red line down each side of the selvage on the inside leg seams and this feature helps to date the jeans. Red lines were discontinued in 1983, which is also the cut off date for Levi's jeans to be considered as 'vintage'.

$80-120   **BR**

A pair of vintage Bronks jeans, by Oshkosh B-Gosh, size 34.

OshKosh B'Gosh introduced Bronks jean in 1951. Vintage examples can be rare and sought-after.

$400-600   **BR**

A hand-painted silk tie, by Jones of New York, with stylized decoration.

$12-18   **BR**

A modern gentleman's tie, made to a 1950s design using unused, original 1950s printed 'showgirl' silk.

5.25in (13.25cm) long

$280-320   **SM**

A 1950s printed cotton cravat, with rock 'n' roll design.

When seeing the combination of this traditional form of neckwear with the avant garde pattern of rock'n'rollers, surely the practical, yet slightly caddish, cravat is due for a revival?

40in (101cm) long

$60-90   **SM**

A 1950s Gossard black lace and stretch 'all in one' corset.

$100-150   **SM**

COSTUME & ACCESSORIES

COLLECTORS' NOTES

- Handbags have been an essential accessory for 100 years, but have now also become hotly sought-after collectibles, charting changing styles and fashions. Values depend on a number of factors: quality of materials and manufacture, the maker, condition of the bag and its date and style.

- Always look for high quality materials. Some, such as lizard or snakeskin, can be scarcer than others and can add to the value. Details such as straps and metal clasps should also be made from good quality materials that will withstand usage. Examine stitching and construction carefully as a well-made piece is likely to indicate a good maker and have a higher value.

- Makers' names are important, with those such as Hermes, Gucci, and Judith Leiber leading the field. However, many bags by unknown makers are also desirable, if they are of a good quality and design. Look for bags made for fine retailers in prestigious locations, such as Bergdorf Goodman, as this is likely to indicate a good example.

- Date and style are important. Look for examples that sum up the fashions of the period in terms of the materials, color and overall design. These are likely to appeal to collectors, as well as followers of fashion keen to acquire a particular period look.

- Condition is vital, as so many collectors buy their bags to use, as well as to build a collection. Style icons such as Kate Moss and popular TV characters such as Carrie Bradshaw from 'Sex In The City' have widened the popularity of vintage style. Bags in truly mint condition will command a premium, so examine edges, corners, linings and metal fittings for signs of wear or damage.

- Bags have always been widely exported and imported, and today this continues with a lively trade over the internet. Online auction sites such as eBay, vintage fashion shops and charity shops are ideal places to look for examples – but always keep an eye on fashion magazines to try to spot the 'next big thing'.

A 1950s Nettie Rosenstein black box calfskin handbag, made in Florence, Italy.

12.25in (31cm) wide

$600-900   **MGL**

A 1950s American Holzman black calfskin handbag, with Lucite handles and satin lining.

Holzman were known for their sculptural handles, as on this example.

9.5in (24cm) wide

$300-500   **MGL**

A late 1950s American Murray Kruger rectangular calfskin-covered box purse, decorated with faux airline travel stickers, with typical blue leather fitted interior and matching change purse.

The 1950s saw a boom in air travel as the number of airlines grew and prices fell, encouraging tourism. However, flying was still comparatively expensive and was synonymous with glamor and 'life in the fast lane'.

13in (33cm) wide

$400-600   **MGL**

A late 1950s Gucci handbag, with ruched black silk covering and gilt clasp.

7.5in (19cm) wide

$220-280   **LB**

A 1950s Nettie Rosenstein black silk box purse, with an unusual clasp.

American fashion designer Rosenstein is also well known for her costume jewelry. Note how this aspect of her designs are included here in the costume jewelry style of the clasp.

9.5in (24cm) wide

$400-600   **MGL**

A 1950s American Bienen-Davis enamelled and pleated box purse, with mirror inside lid and original purse.

Bienen-Davis produced very fine quality bags.

8.75in (22cm) wide

$150-200   **MGL**

A 1940s American Bogan black calfskin handbag, the accordion top with recessed base and green satin lining, retains original patent tag.

c1949   *8in (20.5cm) wide*

$400-600   **MGL**

A 1950s Nettie Rosenstein brown crocodile handbag, made in Florence, Italy.

10.5in (26.5cm) wide

$800-1,200 **MGL**

A 1950s British L. & M. Edwards tapestry bag, with Lucite handle and change of cover.

This bag has a detachable cover, which can be replaced with other patterned or plain examples that were often made at home. This is a typical design feature of many 1950s handbags.

9in (23cm) wide

$80-120 **MGL**

A CLOSER LOOK AT A HANDBAG

This unique, custom-made bag was designed and made by Martin van Shaak, who designed opulent bags for wealthy New York socialites.

The cast metal poodle clasps are unusual - the poodle was a popular motif during the 1950s, evoking the elegance of Paris.

Van Shaak did not use a shop, but preferred to visit his clients personally. His bags were always very well made from fine and expensive materials.

The exterior is covered with alligator skin and the interior is lined with red leather - all parts are in excellent condition.

A 1950s alligator bag, with poodle clasps, the interior signed "Martin van Schaak".

8.5in (21.5cm) wide

$700-1,000 **MGL**

A 1950s rare, reversible woven plaid bag, with black trim and interior, unsigned, with glove holder vinyl strap.

The shape, pattern, presence of a glove holder in the strap and reversible design are all hallmarks of 1950s handbag design.

14.5in (5.5cm) wide

$100-150 **MGL**

An unusual 1950s woven basket bag, with applied fabric rosebuds and flowers, with Lucite details and velvet ribbon.

10in (25.5cm) wide

$80-120 **FAN**

An early 1950s American 'Dorset Rex 5th Avenue' woven metal strips box bag, with Lucite lid and red fabric lining.

Although not as collectible as Lucite-bodied or beaded bags, woven metal bags are growing in desirability.

6in (15cm) wide

$150-200 **DJI**

A 1950s Nettie Rosenstein lizard skin box bag, the lizard covering with gold wash, made in Florence, Italy.

8.25in (21cm) wide

$350-450 **MGL**

An unsigned 1960s bag, with psychedelic swirling pattern, plastic handle and matching purse.

10in (25.5cm) wide

$100-150   **MGL**

A 1960-1970s Emilio Pucci velvet handbag, with waterfall front and geometric design.

An American 1960s Ingber bag, of classic psychedelic pattern and typical form.

11.5in (29cm) wide

$80-120   **MGL**

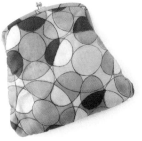

Designer Emilio Pucci's iconic 1960s-70s swirling or geometric designs in bright, often acid, colors have legions of fans, ensuring high prices.

7.5in (19cm) wide

$800-1,200   **MGL**

A 1960s Emilio Pucci box handbag, with black, purple and blue swirled velour fabric, leather interior, gold metal handles and clasp.

This bag is worth less as the hallmark Pucci design only covers a part of the bag.

7.5in (19cm) wide

$250-350   **RR**

An 1960s American Kadin faux cowhide or pony skin handbag.

12in (30.5cm) wide

$100-150   **MGL**

A 1960s American Ronay faux pony skin bag, unsigned.

c1960   *16in (40.5cm) wide*

$300-350   **MGL**

A 1960s American Ronay faux-leopard skin handbag, with leather covered handle.

15.75in (40cm) wide

$250-300   **MGL**

A 1960s American Enid Collins handbag, beige canvas with a bowl of fruit and floral design highlighted with gold and clear plastic cabochons.

A 1960s American Enid Collins handbag, in beige canvas decorated with a bird pattern with applied plastic cabochons.

9.5in (24cm) wide

$150-200   **LB**

Enid Collins was based in Texas and signed her bags with an EC monogram or her name and an internal label. Instantly recognisable and much sought-after, her wood box bags are the most desirable.

10.25in (26cm) wide

$280-320   **LB**

A CLOSER LOOK AT AN HERMÈS KELLY BAG

The Kelly bag was named after film star and style icon, Grace Kelly, Princess of Monaco who favoured this style of bag.

It has been ultra-fashionable since its introduction in 1956, being a 'holy grail' for both collectors and fashionistas.

They are crafted from the finest materials by luxury brand Hermès – always look for complete examples with their padlock, keys and key cover, as here.

A 1960s black box calf 'Kelly' handbag, by Hermès, with lock, keys and clochette.

In 2005 a Hermès 'Etrusque' crocodile Kelly bag sold for over $12,000 at auction in New York.

The Kelly bag can be found in many different finishes and leathers, some rarer and more expensive than others. Beware of fakes which are common – they use lower quality materials and display poorer detailing, stitching and finishing.

11.25in (28.5cm) wide

$2,000-3,000   **MGL**

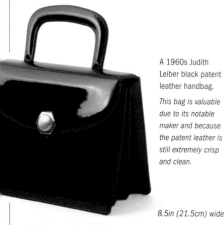

A 1960s Judith Leiber black patent leather handbag.

This bag is valuable due to its notable maker and because the patent leather is still extremely crisp and clean.

8.5in (21.5cm) wide

$300-500   **MGL**

A 1960s unsigned classic black crocodile bag, with gilt chain shoulder strap and clasp.

The form and chain in particular are inspired by Chanel's iconic 2.55 bag, which celebrated it's 50th anniversary in 2005.

10.25in (26cm) wide

$350-450   **LB**

A 1960s American Bobbie Jerome black velvet structured bag, with brown Lucite circle handles and satin interior.

15.25in (38.5cm) wide

$200-300   **MGL**

A 1960s yellow leather faux crocodile handbag, with gilt clasp.

8.75in (22cm) wide

$120-180   **LB**

A 1960s unsigned patent white and gold-finished leather handbag, with gilt metal handle and clasp.

9.5in (24cm) wide

$220-280   **LB**

A 1960s American Gaylene red corduroy and black leather cylinder bag, with matching black purse.

12in (30.5cm) wide

$250-350   **MGL**

A 1970s Gucci black handbag, with shoulder strap.

10.25in (26cm) wide

$400-600   **MGL**

A 1970s-80s dark brown crocodile bag, by Gucci, in as new condition.

This bag is so valuable as it is extremely unusual to find such bags in truly mint, unused condition.

10in (25.5cm) wide

$2,000-3,000   **MGL**

A 1960-70s Gucci black lizard handbag, with bamboo handle.

This bag is rarely found in lizard skin and the handle has a pleasing patina built up through careful use, giving it a good finish and color.

10.5in (26.5cm) wide

$800-1,200   **MGL**

A 1980s French Charles Jourdain purple leather shoulder bag, with gilt frame and clasp.

8.75in (22cm) wide

$220-280   **LB**

A 1980s black crocodile backpack, possibly by Ralph Lauren.

11.75in (30cm) wide

$220-280   **LB**

A 1970s American Morris Moskiwitz multicolored, sculpted chenilled bag, signed "MM", of doctor's bag form with leather piping and trim.

14in (35.5cm) wide

$300-500   **MGL**

A 1970s Carpet Bags of America brown and black chenille carpet bag.

8in (20.5cm) wide

$100-150   **MGL**

A unusual 1970s Judith Leiber leather tote bag, with needlework of whale and floral designs to exterior, unsigned.

This is an extremely unusual bag for Leiber, who is more famous for his jeweled 'minaudieres' in novelty shapes.

16in (40.5cm) wide

$700-1,000   **MGL**

A 1970s Chanel cocoa color lambskin clutchbag, with lizard trim, with retractable chain strap.

11.5in (29cm) wide

$700-1,000   **MGL**

COLLECTORS' NOTES

■ Lucite bags are one of the most popular areas of handbag collecting. Lucite is a form of early plastic and can be found in clear, opaque, 'pearlised' and mottled finishes. The components for each bag were molded individually and assembled and decorated by hand. Production declined sharply in the late 1950s as injection molding led to less expensive imports and the fashion for leather bags returned.

■ The majority were made in the US in the 1950s and were exported widely. Names such as Rialto, Wilardy and Llewelyn are among the most popular due to their fine quality and variety of superb forms and designs. Black and pearlised white and gray are the most common colors. Others colors such red, blue

and yellow are rarer and often more valuable.

■ Look for extra exterior detailing, such as inset rhinestones or molded or carved patterns, in appealing and period designs. Unusual shapes also command a premium. Some have fabric lining, but those with rigid fitted interiors are more desirable.

■ Avoid storing Lucite bags in high temperatures or strong sunlight as this can lead to the plastic degrading completely, or to 'fogging' where the plastic becomes misty. Examine bags for signs of 'crazing' as this indicates irreversible degrading. If the interior has a strong chemical smell, avoid the bag as this is an indication that the plastic has started to deteriorate.

A 1950s Florida mottled gray Lucite hexagonal handbag.

c1953   9.5in (24cm) wide

$280-320   **DJI**

An early 1950s Myles Originals clear Lucite handbag, with internal copper and silver threads.

7in (18cm) wide

$280-320   **DJI**

A 1950s Wilardy Lucite handbag, decorated with shells, pearls and tiny gray beads in floral patterns.

6in (15cm) wide

$400-600   **DJI**

A late 1950s Wilardy pearl white Lucite handbag, with pleated design and black fabric lining.

10.5in (26.5cm) wide

$400-600   **DJI**

A Wilardy gray swirl Lucite handbag.

This bag has been nicknamed 'the rocket' because of its shape.

c1953   9in (23cm) wide

$400-600   **DJI**

A late 1950s Wilardy pearl white pearlised Lucite handbag, with gold and rhinestone clasp.

This bag is from the collection of Will Hardy who started the Wilardy range.

7.5in (19cm) wide

$400-600   **DJI**

An unsigned rectangular Lucite handbag, by Shoreham, the glitter plastic shell with gray and silver confetti and rhinestones at the base of the handle.

The unusual, flat shape and high level of decoration make this bag more sought-after.

c1955   8in (20.5cm) wide

$700-1,000   **DJI**

A CLOSER LOOK AT LUCITE HANDBAG

American maker Wilardy is one of the most respected and sought-after names in vintage Lucite handbags.

Blue is a rare color, making this example more desirable and valuable.

The handle has an attractive twist and the clean-lined oval box shape is popular with collectors.

The lid has a design of small shells and beads imitating pearls, set into a ground of small gray beads to look like sand on a beach.

A 1950s Wilardy blue pearl Lucite handbag, with pattern of shells, pearls and beads on top.

c1955

7in (18cm) wide

$700-1,000   DJI

A 1950s Wilardy black Lucite oval handbag, with bands of inset rhinestones.

The almost Art Deco appearance and the inset rhinestones make this an especially appealing bag.

c1952

$1,200-1,800   DJI

An early 1950s Weisner black Lucite handbag, with a thick band of inset pearls and rhinestones at the base.

8in (20.5cm) wide

$400-600   DJI

A 1950s Charles Kahn of Miami, Florida, shiny satin white Lucite handbag, with moulded criss-cross design on the clear lid.

8in (20.5cm) wide

$280-320   DJI

A mid-1950s Rialto of New York pearl white Lucite handbag, with 'aurora borealis' and milk glass rhinestone decoration.

Aurora borealis stones are so named as they contain and reflect numerous colors, just like the polar sky phenomenon.

c1955   6.25in (16cm) wide

$800-1,200   DJI

An early 1950s Wilardy Lucite handbag, of tambourine design, inset with rhinestones.

6.25in (16cm) wide

$800-1,200   DJI

A Wilardy pearl white Lucite handbag, the lid with gold and rhinestone decoration.

This is a rare shape, designed to fit around and 'hug' the hips.

c1958   7.75in (19.5cm) wide

$600-900   DJI

COLLECTORS' NOTES

■ The general costume jewelry market has enjoyed significant growth recently, and demand for vintage pieces has continued to rise. Named pieces and high-quality jewelry from the 1930s-1940s are sought after. Many people buy to wear, so even unsigned pieces can command high prices if they are particularly attractive, unusual or fashionable.

■ Trifari is one of the most collectible names. Among the most coveted pieces are the Jelly Belly figural pins, crown pins and designs by Alfred Phillippe. Other names to look out for include Miriam Haskell, Coro, Joseff, Chanel and Schiaparelli.

■ Kenneth Jay Lane jewelry has been worn by high-profile figures such as Jackie Kennedy Onassis, Audrey Hepburn and Diana, Princess of Wales, but has remained affordable to most. Inspired by a diverse range of traditional styles from around the world from Art Deco to Asian, pieces made before the late 1970s are the most sought after.

■ Coro's prodigious and diverse output caters to most income brackets and tastes. Designs by Adolph Katz and the double-pin Coro Duettes are particularly prized.

■ Fakes and forgeries have become more common, especially at the upper end of the market, such as pieces by Chanel. Learn to recognise makers' styles and marks. The latter also helps with dating a piece.

A 1970s Kenneth Jay Lane umbrella pin, cast in gold-tone metal with pavé-set clear crystal rhinestones and red, blue and green glass stones and drops.

2.5in (6.5cm) long

$80-120 JJ

A 1980s Kenneth Jay Lane umbrella pin, cast in gun metal and set with polychrome and clear glass stones of various cuts, including round and baguette.

2.5in (6.5cm) long

$70-100 JJ

A Kenneth Jay Lane coach pin, gold-tone metal set with green, blue and red rhinestones, amethyst-coloured glass drops and sapphire blue glass cabochons.

3in (7.5cm) wide

$80-120 ABIJ

A 1970s Kenneth Jay Lane 'Catwalk' or 'Runway' chain necklace and pendant, in gilt base metal with smaller ruby red and larger dark emerald green glass beads.

A 1980s Kenneth Jay Lane Buddha pendant necklace, cast in gold-tone metal with a serpent above the Buddha, embellished with mother-of-pearl and emerald green glass cabochons, and with diverse metal and faux stone pendants.

Pendant 5.5in (14cm) long

$180-220 JJ

Kenneth Jay Lane (b.1930) began his career in design in the Art Department of Vogue magazine in the mid-1950s. After designing shoes and jewelry for others, he set up his own company, K.J.L., in 1963. Early pieces are the most sought-after and are distinguished by their "K.J.L." mark, which changed to "Kenneth Jay Lane" or "Kenneth Lane" in the late 1970s. He is still designing today.

29in (73cm) long

$350-450 JJ

A 1970s Kenneth Jay Lane twin ram's head bangle, in gold-tone metal set with clear, ruby red and emerald green rhinestones.

3in (7.5cm) long

$180-220 ABIJ

A pair of 1970s Kenneth Jay Lane pendant hoop earrings, in antique gold-tone metal with purple-red glass drops and cabochons and clear rhinestones.

2.5in (6.5cm) long

$100-150 ABIJ

COSTUME JEWELRY

A 1940s Coro clown pin, in vermeil sterling silver with tiny polychrome rhinestone highlights.

3in (7.5cm) long

$100-150   **ABIJ**

A 1930s Coro hobo pin, cast in gold-tone metal with polychrome rhinestone highlights.

1.25in (3cm) high

$60-90   **JJ**

A 1940s Coro circus girl-on-a-trapeze pin, cast in vermeil sterling silver, set with blue, pink and clear crystal rhinestones.

3in (7.5cm) long

$120-180   **JJ**

A Coro 'Oriental' pin, comprising a Buddha-like figure cast in vermeil sterling silver and embellished with carved 'fruit salad' stones and clear crystal rhinestones.

Established in 1901, Coro came to prominence under the design directorship of Adolph Katz who joined in 1924. The company was hugely prolific and produced jewelry for every pocket. Look for pieces from the Corocraft and Vendome ranges, which were aimed at the high-end market. Vendome became a subsidiary company in 1953, see p.234 for examples.

c1945   *1.5in (3.75cm) high*

$450-550   **JJ**

A 1930s Coro umbrella pin, cast in gold-washed metal with a girl, dog and palm tree, all under an arch of wheatsheaves, and with green and red enameling and clear rhinestone highlights.

1.5in (4cm) wide

$70-100   **JJ**

A Corocraft umbrella pin, cast in vermeil sterling silver, set with pink and clear crystal rhinestones.

1938   *2.5in (6.5cm) long*

$220-280   **JJ**

A 1960s Coro green enameled artichoke pin.

2in (5cm) long

$40-60   **ABIJ**

A 1950s Corocraft peach pin, in brushed vermeil with European crystal rhinestone accents.

2in (5cm) long

$80-120   **ABIJ**

Two 1940s Coro squirrel-under-umbrella pins, one cast in silver, the other in vermeil silver with selective black enameling.

2.75in (7cm) long

$60-90 each   **JJ**

An early 1950s Coro 'Duette' owl clip, in sterling silver set with faceted green glass eyes and pavé-set clear and green crystal rhinestones.

1.5in (4cm) long

$250-350 JJ

A CLOSER LOOK AT A CORO DUETTE PIN

The double pin mechanism was invented by Louis Cartier in 1927.

Initially of Art Deco design, Coro found great success with their figural pins featuring birds, other animals or characters, such as this Dutch couple.

Coro began making their own version, the Duette, in 1931.

The highly versatile double pin could be worn as a single piece, or divided into two and worn on either side of a neckline, for example.

A 1940s Coro Dutch couple 'Duette' pin, in rose vermeil sterling silver set with ruby red, aquamarine and clear crystal rhinestones.

2in (5cm) wide

$600-900 CRIS

A late 1940s/early 1950s Coro floral 'Duette' pin, in vermeil sterling silver, with jade green enameling and clear crystal rhinestone highlights.

2.5in (6.5cm) long

$280-320 CRIS

A late 1950s Coro 'Space Age' starburst pendant necklace, in yellow gold-tone metal with turquoise rhinestone highlights.

2.25in (5.5cm) diam

$35-45 MILLB

A late 1940s Coro bolo-style necklace, in white metal with a rosette set with green and red rhinestones.

20in (51cm) long

$50-70 MILLB

A 1950s/60s Coro foliate motif necklace, in silver-tone metal.

7.5in (19cm) long

$35-45 MILLB

COSTUME JEWELRY

A 1940s Denbe by J.J. Denberg of New York necklace and bracelet, in rhodium-plated metal set with clear and ruby red rhinestones.

Necklace 16in (40.5cm) long

$180-220　　　**ABIJ**

A pair of Mitchell Maer for Dior floral motif earrings, with clear rhinestones in rhodium-plated settings.

One of a number of designers licensed by Dior, Maer produced pieces for Dior's collections for four years from 1952. Maer was responsible for some of Dior's most sought-after designs. Other designers working with Dior include Henry Schreiner, Kramer and Josette Gripoix.

1952-56　　　*1.25in (3cm) diam*

$350-450　　　**FM**

A late 1970s Florenza stylized floral motif pendant necklace, in gold-tone metal set with turquoise and amethyst glass cabochons.

Pendant 3in (7.5cm) long

$35-45　　　**ABIJ**

A pair of 1960s Florenza clover motif earrings, in gold-tone metal with aurora borealis rhinestones and jade green glass beads set against a black enameled ground.

1in (2.5cm) wide

$40-60　　　**JJ**

A 1950s Leo Glass bracelet, in silver-tone metal with blue glass stones.

6.75in (17cm) long

$80-120　　　**ABIJ**

A pair of 1990s Dinny Hall 'Diffusion Line' silver clip earrings.

0.75in (2cm) diam

$70-100　　　**PC**

A 1990s Dinny Hall gold and white topaz pendant cross necklace.

Necklace 9.5in (24cm) long

$120-180　　　**PC**

A 1950s Har fortune-telling genie pin, in gilt base metal with round-cut clear and star-cut sapphire blue rhinestones.

Little is known about Har other than the fact that they operated in New York during the 1950s. This mystery seems to add to the desirabilty of their exotic designs, often showing Oriental influences.

2.5in (6.5cm) long

$800-1,200　　　**SUM**

A 1950s Har exotic pendant necklace, with a silver-tone metal chain, aurora borealis rhinestones, and other fantasy stones.

Pendant 4in (10cm) wide

$400-600　　　**SUM**

A 1950s Har rabbit-on-a-carrot pin, cast in gold-tone metal with green and red enameling and crystal rhinestones.

1.5in (4cm) high

$180-220 JJ

A 1950s Har swirling wheat-sheaves pin, in brushed gold-tone metal.

2.25in (5.5cm) diam

$35-45 MILLB

A pair of 1970s Miriam Haskell pendant hoop earrings, in antiqued gilt metal, and each with a faux pearl drop.

2.75in (7cm) long

$120-180 ABIJ

A 1940s/early 1950s Miriam Haskell umbrella pin, cast in vermeil sterling silver and set with polychrome glass beads and faux pearls.

1.5in (4cm) long

$180-220 JJ

A 1960s Hollycraft floral motif necklace, with a gilt metal chain and castings, the latter set with pink and clear crystal rhinestones.

Established as the Hollywood Jewelry Manufacturing Company in 1938 and operating until the mid-1970s, Hollycraft's 1950s pieces and Christmas tree pins are some of its most collected pieces. Unusually, all examples are marked, adding to their collectibility.

15in (38cm) long

$300-400 JJ

A 1940s Harry Iskin of Philadelphia pin and pair of matching earrings, in vermeil sterling silver with blue glass stones.

Pin 2.75in (7cm) long

$50-70 ABIJ

A 1960s Jewelerama floral pin, of antiqued white metal casting with a pewter-tone refractive disc centre.

2.5in (6.5cm) long

$35-45 JJ

A late 1950s Kramer choker, with textured yellow metal leaves edged with faux pearls.

15in (38cm) long

$60-90 MILLB

A pair of 1980s Karl Lagerfeld stylized plant-form earrings, in gold-washed metal, each with a faux pearl highlight, with original packaging.

1in (2.5cm) long

$50-70 MILLB

A Lanvin hinged bangle, of gilt metal casting with Classic key motif border against red enameling.

c1970s/80s   *8in (21cm) wide*

$120-180   **LB**

An early 1970s Lisner necklace, in burnished gold-tone metal with foliate green rhinestones.

16.5in (42cm) long

$80-120   **ABIJ**

A 1940s Lisner umbrella pin, cast in gold-washed metal with yellow enameling and clear, faceted glass bead drops.

2in (5cm) long

$40-60   **JJ**

A pair of 1980s Lunch At The Ritz 'Happy Hour' earrings, in gold-tone metal with black beads and enamelling.

5in (12.5cm) long

$220-280   **JJ**

A Lucinda house pin, in black and white plastic.

2.5in (6.5cm) long

$25-35   **JJ**

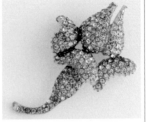

A 1930s Marvella lion-tamer pin, in gold-washed metal with white and red enameling.

2in (5cm) wide

$40-60   **JJ**

A 1940s Mazer Brothers bow pin, in vermeil sterling silver set with clear and polychrome rhinestones, and with a prong-set, ruby-colored glass stone centre.

2.25in (5.5cm) long

$220-280   **ABIJ**

A 1970s Mimi Di N (Niscemi) flower pin, cast in gold-tone metal with pavé-set rhinestones.

2.25in (6.5cm) long

$100-150   **ABIJ**

A 1960s Napier 'ethnic' necklace, bracelet and earrings parure, with gold findings and diverse polychrome beads and stones of various cuts, including blue aurora borealis rhinestones.

Necklace 60in (152.5cm) long

$100-150   **ABIJ**

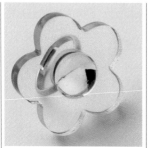

A 1960s Mary Quant flower ring, in green and clear plastic, together with its original box, not shown.

1.5in (3.5cm) diam

$220-280   **LB**

A CLOSER LOOK AT A SCHIAPARELLI PIN

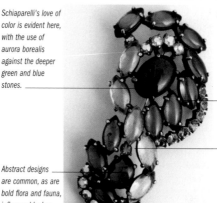

Schiaparelli's love of color is evident here, with the use of aurora borealis against the deeper green and blue stones.

Pieces dating from the 1940s and later are more easily found, making them popular with collectors. Earlier pieces are extremely scarce and therefore valuable.

Not all pieces are signed and copies do exist, so be sure to buy from a reputable source.

Abstract designs are common, as are bold flora and fauna, influenced by her connection with the Surrealist movement.

A 1950s Elsa Schiaparelli pin, in gilt metal with prong-set glass stones in shades of blue and green, and with small aurora borealis rhinestone highlights.

3.5in (9cm) long

$600-800   **SUM**

A 1970s Robert Originals elephant pendant necklace, cast in gold-tone metal and with small, purple rhinestone highlights.

Pendant 3in (7.5cm) wide

$35-45   **ABIJ**

A 1960s Sandor floral pin, in orange and yellow enameled base metal.

2in (5cm) diam

$50-70   **JJ**

A 1950s Elsa Schiaparelli necklace, with three strands of contrasting-colored glass beads and faux pearls.

16in (40.5cm) long

$220-280   **ABIJ**

An early 1950s Selro necklace and earrings, in gilt metal with prong-set red and emerald green glass stones with opaque white beads and aurora borealis rhinestones.

Necklace 17in (43cm) long

$300-500   **JJ**

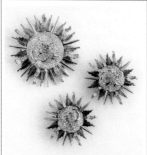

A 1990s Swarovski sun motif pin and pair of earrings, cast in gilt metal pavé-set with clear Swarovski crystal rhinestones.

Pin 2.25in (7cm) wide

$220-280   **RITZ**

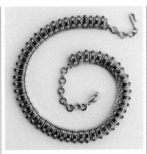

A 1960s Vendome necklace, of brushed gold-tone metal set with magenta, white and blue crystal rhinestones.

16in (40.5cm) long

$60-90 ABIJ

A 1950s Vendome necklace and earrings, made with glass beads in various shades of coral, and clear crystal rhinestones.

Necklace 15in (38cm) long

$180-220 JJ

A CLOSER LOOK AT A VIVIENNE WESTWOOD NECKLACE

Vivienne Westwood opened her first shop with partner Malcolm McLaren in 1970. McLaren also famously managed the Sex Pistols who wore her designs at their first gig.

Royal motifs are commonly part of Westwood's witty designs, subverting symbols of the British establishment. This was a common theme of the punk movement of which Westwood was a key player.

The use of gold-tone metal with clear rhinestone highlights are also typical of her work.

As with other high fashion designers, Westwood's vintage accessories are much more affordable than her highly sought-after and iconic costumes, making them accessible to a larger number of collectors.

A 1980s Vivienne Westwood pendant orb necklace, in gold-tone metal with rhinestone highlights.

Pendant 1.25in (3.5cm) long

$300-400 LB

A Warner 'night and day' flower pin, in gold-tone metal with an open-and-shut mechanism.

This 'night and day' flower pin has two settings; open (day), as here, and night (closed). Warner's mechanical pins such as this one are relatively rare and have been rising in value.

c1960   2.25in (5.5cm) long

$180-220 LB

A Warner 'sun and rain' umbrella pin, in gold-tone metal set with floral motifs of colored and clear crystal rhinestones.

c1960   3in (7.5cm) long

$50-70 JJ

A 1980s Vivienne Westwood triple-strand faux pearl choker, the clasp and royal orb in silver-tone metal pavé-set with clear crystal rhinestones.

13.5in (34.5cm) long

$180-220 REL

A 1960s Whiting & Davis coiled snake bangle, in gold-tone, expandable metal mesh, with a solid punched and engraved head.

12in (30.5cm) circ

$50-70 JJ

A 1950s unsigned elephant pin, cast in gold-tone metal and set with turquoise and ruby red glass stones.

2.25in (6cm) wide

$50-70 CRIS

A 1950s unsigned cat pin, cast in textured gold-tone metal with blue and green enameling and green glass cabochon eyes.

1.5in (4cm) high

$35-45 CRIS

A 1950s unsigned bassett hound pin, cast in gold-tone metal with pavé set clear crystal rhinestones.

$25-35 CRIS

An unsigned English 'jelly belly' penguin pin, in silver-mounted clear glass with diamanté highlights.

c1910 2.25in (5.5cm) high

$350-450 LYNH

A 1940s unsigned 'jelly belly' fish pin, in vermeil sterling silver with a Lucite body.

Jelly belly pins were originally conceived by Alfred Phillippe, Trifari's chief designer, who used smooth Lucite pebbles to form the bodies of whimsical animal, bird or insect-shaped pins. The value depends on the motif used, and original Trifari examples are more desirable than unsigned ones.

A 1950s unsigned French bird-on-a-branch pin, cast in gold-tone metal and set with turquoise glass beads.

2in (5cm) long

$30-50 CRIS

3.5in (9cm) long

$250-350 ABIJ

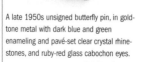

A 1950s unsigned Siamese goldfish, cast in gold-tone metal with selective dark blue enameling.

2.5in (6.5cm) wide

$50-70 CRIS

A late 1950s unsigned butterfly pin, in gold-tone metal with dark blue and green enameling and pavé-set clear crystal rhinestones, and ruby-red glass cabochon eyes.

3.25in (8cm) wide

$40-60 CRIS

A late 1930s unsigned beetle pin, cast in rhodium-plated metal with a large blue glass cabochon abdomen and green glass cabochon eyes.

2in (5cm) long

$120-150 CRIS

A 1950s Austrian fruit pin, with gilt metal stalks, pale green enameled glass leaves, and foil-backed red glass cherries.

Always marked "Austria", these fruit pins were made by a number of factories across Austria and occasionally have matching earrings. Fruits commonly found include strawberries, cherries, pears and bunches of grapes and are formed from brightly colored glass that is foil-backed to reflect the light and enhance the richness of the colors.

1.75in (4.5cm) wide

$100-150   **ECLEC**

A 1940s unsigned Alpine motif chatelaine pin, cast in gold-washed metal and set with red, blue and turquoise glass stones.

Chalet 1.75in (4.5cm) wide

$100-150   **JJ**

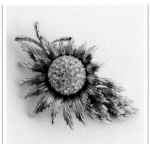

A 1950s unsigned floral pin, in textured gold-tone metal, with pavé-set clear crystal rhinestones.

3in (7.5cm) wide

$60-80   **CRIS**

A 1930s unsigned floral, fruit and foliate basket pin, cast in rhodium-plated metal and set with baguette-cut red glass stones.

2.5in (6cm) wide

$120-160   **CRIS**

A 1950s unsigned pair of floral scatter pins, in white metal set with clear crystal rhinestones.

1in (2.5cm) long

$60-90   **JJ**

A 1940s unsigned scrolling bow pin and pair of earrings, in rose-vermeil sterling silver with large, prong-set aquamarine glass stones.

Pin 1.25in (3.5cm) long

$280-320   **CRIS**

A 1940s unsigned crown pin, in vermeil sterling silver with fleur-de-lys finials, sapphire blue, ruby red and emerald green glass teardrops, and small clear crystal rhinestones.

2in (5cm) wide

$100-150   **CRIS**

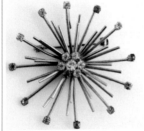

A late 1950s unsigned 'Space Age' starburst pin, in white metal with rhinestone highlights.

2.25in (5.5cm) diam

$35-45   **MILLB**

A mid-1950s unsigned hyacinth pin and pair of earrings, in antiqued gold-tone metal set with amber, citrine and red faceted glass stones.

Pin 3.25in (8cm) long

$100-150   **CRIS**

A 1940s unsigned Aborigine pin, cast in gold-tone metal.

2.25in (5.5cm) long

$80-120 JJ

An unsigned watch pin, resembling the Tin Man from 'The Wizard of Oz', in gold-tone metal with articulated arms and legs, and rhinestone highlights.

Despite being unsigned, the addition of a watch and the pin's whimsical form add to the value.

2.5in (6cm) long

$450-550 LB

A late 1950s unsigned clown-on-a-bicycle pin, cast in gold-tone metal with selective red, blue and green enameling, and glass cabochon eyes.

3in (7.5cm) high

$35-45 CRIS

A 1940s unsigned 'Manneken Pis' style umbrella pin, probably a souvenir piece, cast in vermeil silver, with enamel highlights.

1.5in (4cm) long

$220-280 JJ

An unsigned umbrella pin, with a tree and two sheltering figures, in polychrome painted plastic.

c1920 *1.75in (4.5cm) high*

$50-70 JJ

A late 1950s courting couple pin, with articulated revolving umbrella, in polychrome plastic.

2.25in (5.5cm) long

$40-60 JJ

A 1930s unsigned dog-walking-dog pin, cast in gold-washed metal set with rectangular, navette and round-cut clear crystal rhinestones.

5in (12.5cm) wide

$220-280 JJ

A 1940s theatrical dancing couple pin, cast in base metal and enameled in red, green and gold.

3in (7.5cm) long

$60-90 ECLEC

A pair of 1950s earrings, with clusters of turquoise glass stones banded by, and set in, gold-tone castings.

1in (2.5cm) long

$45-55 CRIS

A pair of 1950s Czech Republic earrings, with large purple glass cabochons and pale blue rhinestone highlights.

1in (2.5cm) long

$40-60 CRIS

A pair of 1950s crescent moon earrings, cast in gold-tone metal and set with peridot glass stones.

1.25in (3cm) long

$45-55 CRIS

A pair of 1950s plastic poodle earrings.

Poodles are a common 1950s decorative theme, echoing the chic Paris of the time, and seen as the epitome of good taste.

1in (2.5cm) long

$25-35 ECLEC

A pair of 1940s triangular-pendant gold-tone metal earrings.

2.25in (5.5cm) long

$60-90 ECLEC

A pair of 1920s unsigned pendant earrings, with carved, shell-shaped, clear crystal drops.

3in (7.5cm) long

$220-280 ECLEC

A 1960s unsigned necklace, with rows of mauve-colored plastic beads and a gold-tone metal clasp.

15.75in (40cm) long

$50-70 ECLEC

A 1960s mother-of-pearl necklace, with faux pearl centre.

14.25in (36cm) long

$50-70 ECLEC

An Austrian silver necklace, set with clear crystal rhinestones and pendant polychrome glass beads.

13in (33cm) long

$280-320 ECLEC

COSTUME JEWELRY

An early 1940s American silver necklace, set with mother-of-pearl and clear crystal rhinestones.

16.5in (42cm) circ

$100-150 ECLEC

A 1920s French unsigned necklace, with cut crystal beads of graduated size and jade green glass spacers.

15.75 (40cm) long

$250-350 CRIS

A 1950s unsigned bracelet, in japanned black metal with opaque white glass floral motifs, with clear rhinestone centres.

7.5in (19cm) diam

$100-150 CRIS

A 1920s unsigned silver bracelet, set with three faceted, emerald-green crystal stones.

7.25in (18.5cm) long

$180-220 CRIS

An unsigned bracelet and pair of earrings, in gold-tone metal with prong-set aurora borealis rhinestones.

Bracelet 7in (18cm) long

$100-150 CRIS

A 1980s unsigned leopard bracelet, in textured gold-tone metal with ruby red crystal rhinestone eyes.

This was probably made by Sphinx for Saks of Fifth Avenue.

6.75in (17.5cm) circ

$40-60 CRIS

A 1950s unsigned expandable bracelet, in textured gold-tone metal set with emerald green, ruby red and clear crystal rhinestones.

6.5in (17cm) circ

$120-180 CRIS

A late 1940s unsigned copper bangle, with comedy and tragedy masks.

Although unsigned, this bangle was made by Francisco Rebajes who worked almost exclusively in copper. A signed example would be worth twice as much.

6.5in (16.5cm) circ

$220-280 CRIS

A 1940s wooden bracelet, with a copper clasp and a carved wooden horse's head set on a disc of caned leather and wood.

Disc 2in (5cm) diam

$120-180 CRIS

FIND OUT MORE...

DK Collectors' Guide: Costume Jewelry, by Judith Miller, published by Dorling Kindersley, 2003.

COLLECTORS' NOTES

■ Bakelite jewelry became popular in the 1920s, allowing ladies of all incomes, particularly during the difficult years of the Depression, to share in the glamorous fashions of the era. Victorian ideals had downplayed the use of jewelry, but the Jazz age saw no need for such restraint, and flamboyant women adorned themselves with brightly colored pieces.

■ Color, form, size and the type and level of decoration are the main indicators to value. In general, the brighter the color, the more valuable a piece will be. Strong cherry reds, bright oranges and vibrant greens are particularly sought-after. Although less typical, black can make a bold statement, particularly with large pieces with similarly bold Art Deco designs.

■ Plastics were also ideal for carving. Geometric patterns are sought after, as are other highly stylized motifs. Many are based on flowers, leaves or other natural forms. The most desirable forms tend to be either deep and dramatic, or intricate and detailed.

■ Always consider how a piece was made as this will also indicate value. Look closely at the decoration as hand-carving adds value. Machine carving tends to be shallower and more regular. Examine pieces for cracks, which often show up as thin dark lines, or filed down areas of damage, which reduce value.

■ Although many different plastics, such as cast phenolics, were used, they are commonly grouped under the term 'bakelite', a term which is used here.

A 1930s heavily carved and pierced yellow cast phenolic bangle, with stylized flowers.

3in (7.5cm) diam

$800-1,000   **MG**

A 1930s carved and pierced bakelite bangle, with a 1960s appearance.

3in (7.5cm) diam

$500-800   **MG**

A hand-carved yellow bakelite bangle, carved with stylized feathers.

3in (7.5cm) diam

$300-500   **MG**

A wide carved green bakelite ribbed bangle.

The same carved ribbing was also used on small dressing table accessories, such as lidded pots for rings.

3in (7.5cm) diam

$100-150   **MG**

A 'creamed corn' carved cast phenolic bangle, with curving and twisting pattern

3.25in (8.5cm) diam

$120-180   **MG**

A 1930s hand-carved tortoiseshell-patterned bangle, carved with stylized roses.

2.75in (7cm) diam

$800-1,200   **MG**

A 1950s turquoise green Lucite bangle, made from a single curled piece.

3.25in (8.5cm) diam

$300-500   **MG**

A heavily carved and pierced cherry red cast phenolic bangle.

Pieces in bright colors, and particularly cherry red, are often more desirable. Strong levels of carving and piercing are sought-after features.

3in (8cm) diam

$2,000-3,000   **MG**

A CLOSER LOOK AT A PLASTIC BANGLE AND MATCHING EARRINGS

These are known as 'Philadelphia' bangles, possibly after the city they were first sold in. Summing up the bright colors of the Jazz Age, they are rare today.

The colored cast phenolic sections had to be carefully cut, assembled and laminated together and finally worked to give a seamless surface finish. This took many hours of work.

A 'Philadelphia' laminated bangle and matching earrings.

Other examples are found with carved 'fins'. Although plastics were generally used to create more affordable pieces, high quality pieces such as these were expensive in their day.

A 'Philadelphia' bracelet sold for over $15,000 at auction in 1998, demonstrating their rarity and great desirability.

3.25in (8.5cm) long

$2,000-3,000　　　　　　　　　　　**MG**

A large laminated yellow and black zig-zag bakelite bangle.

3in (8cm) diam

$1,500-2,000　　　　**MG**

A 1980s light wood-effect bangle, engraved with black stained bands , with 'df' gilt decal for Diane von Furstenburg.

Diane von Furstenburg is famous for designing the 'Wrap Dress', which she launched in 1976 with the slogan "Feel like a woman – wear a dress". This style of dress is currently enjoying a revival.

3.5in (9cm) diam

$30-50　　　　　　**BB**

Three yellow cast phenolic bangles, with wood corners.

Wood applied to bakelite bodies is more unusual and more valuable than the more commonly found bakelite mounted on wood.

$700-1,000 (each)　　　**MG**

A black bangle, with heart, made from a single piece of bakelite.

This bangle was carved from a single very thick piece of plastic rather than being bent into shape or made from assembled separate pieces. Bangles were rarely carved in this way as the amount of waste material this generated was uneconomical. This factor and the heart design makes this piece valuable.

3in (8cm) diam

$1,500-2,000　　　　　　**MG**

A late 1920s large mottled red bakelite bangle.

Despite being made in the 1920s, this bangle has a 1960s look. The shape, size and color combine to make it desirable.

3.5in (9cm) high

$1,800-2,200　　　**MG**

A 1930s reverse-carved and painted clear Lucite bangle.

Lucite was invented in 1931 by chemists at DuPont. It was often carved and painted with designs.

3in (8cm) diam

$700-1,000　　　**MG**

A translucent dark-green bakelite hinged bracelet.

The textured pattern on this bangle is reminiscent of snake skin. Snakes are popular motifs.

3in (7.5cm) diam

$800-1,200   **MG**

A 1940s chocolate brown bakelite bracelet, with razor blade effect.

This bracelet is from the Donald Alvin collection.

3in (8cm) diam

$800-1,200   **MG**

A CLOSER LOOK AT A CARVED PLASTIC BRACELET

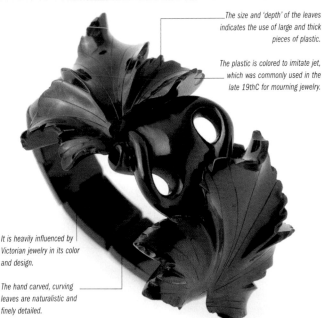

The size and 'depth' of the leaves indicates the use of large and thick pieces of plastic.

The plastic is colored to imitate jet, which was commonly used in the late 19thC for mourning jewelry.

It is heavily influenced by Victorian jewelry in its color and design.

The hand carved, curving leaves are naturalistic and finely detailed.

An articulated black bracelet, hand-carved with a curling motif and two leaves.

2.75in (7cm) diam

$1,000-1,500   **MG**

A Czechoslovakian 'apple juice' bakelite and Czech glass bracelet.

Note the Egyptian styling. Egypt was a major influence on Art Deco design, fuelled by Howard Carter's discovery of Tutankhamen's tomb in 1922.

2.75in (7cm) diam

$200-300   **MG**

An Art Deco 'apple juice' and black bakelite stretch-open articulated bracelet.

3in (8cm) diam

$500-700   **MG**

A hand-carved green 'apple juice' bakelite bracelet.

Transparent 'apple juice' bakelite comes in a range of colors. It was made by injecting a form of Lucite with pigment. It is most often carved and is highly sought-after today.

2.5in (6.5cm) high

$500-700   **MG**

A red 'over-dye' yellow bakelite horse racing or hunting themed charm bracelet, with brass insets.

The red color is an 'over-dye', a secondary process which involves the shaped bakelite being washed with color. The 'over-dye' is often worn away through use, revealing the true color of the bakelite beneath. The theme of this bracelet adds to the value.

7in (18cm) long

$350-450   **ELI**

A carved cherry red Catalin stylized leaf bar pin.

2.75in (7cm) wide

$80-120 **ELI**

A large and deeply hand-carved cherry red leaf pin.

3.75in (9.5cm) long

$700-1,000 **MG**

A very deeply carved and pierced cherry red Catalin pin, with leaves and flowers.

This is very deeply carved and pierced piece, with a well composed, and typically highly stylized design, hence its high value.

3in (7.5cm) high

$2,000-3,000 **MG**

A carved cherry red Catalin 'pinwheel' design flower pin.

Catalin is a trade name for a form of cast phenolic resin, known for its strong colors and shiny surfaces.

2.25in (6cm) diam

$120-180 **ELI**

A carved red Catalin clip, with stylized floral or foliate pattern.

This lighter level of carving and shaping, with no piercing, is the most commonly found.

2in (5cm) high

$60-90 **ELI**

A 1940s cherry red bakelite 'bleeding heart' and cherry pin with original beads.

The 'bleeding heart' has great sentimental appeal for collectors. It is unusual to find these with their original beads intact as they easily crack or break off and are replaced.

3in (8cm) high

$600-900 **MG**

A hand-carved burgundy cast phenolic stylized flower and leaf design oval pin.

3in (7.5cm) long

$200-300 **MG**

A burgundy bakelite and carved wood stylized pineapple pin.

3in (8cm) high

$120-180 **MG**

A transparent tortoiseshell Lucite pin, with carved geometric pendant on metal.

3.25in (8.5cm) high

$200-300 **MG**

A rare Lucite hand-shaped pin, with enamelled metal flower.

This design is strikingly similar to a Schiaparelli hand pin, and the flower resembles an orchid pin by Chanel.

3.5in (9cm) long

$1,200-1,800   **MG**

A CLOSER LOOK AT A PORCELAIN AND LUCITE PIN

The curving pieces of Lucite resemble scarves twirling around the dancer as she moves.

Josephine Baker (1906-75) was a famous nightclub dancer of the 1920s. She performed her popular Banana Dance routine at the Folies Bergère in Paris.

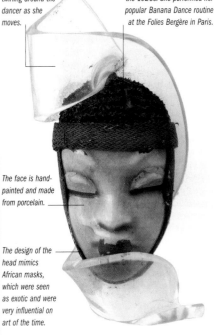

The face is hand-painted and made from porcelain.

The design of the head mimics African masks, which were seen as exotic and were very influential on art of the time.

A very rare painted porcelain and bent Lucite pin, in the form of Josephine Baker's head.

3in (8cm) high

$800-1,000   **MG**

A large carved and painted Lucite Indian's head pin, with metal pin fixing to reverse.

The placing of the pin fixing on the back is unusual here, as it is so visible.

3.25in (8.5cm) high

$150-250   **MG**

A 1950s French large Lucite cicada bug pin, hand painted on the exterior and interior.

5in (13cm) high

$700-1,000   **MG**

A pair of reverse-carved and injected oval bakelite dress clips, with flower motif.

Dress clips were popular from the 1920s to the 1950s. They were worn at the neckline of a dress to highlight the outfit.

2in (5cm) high

$300-500   **MG**

A pair of bakelite-on-wood dress clips, with flower and leaf design.

This combination of bakelite on wood is more commonly found than wood on bakelite.

2.25in (6cm) high

$100-150   **ELI**

A 1920s black hand-carved bakelite peacock necklace and pendant.

The skill that has gone into carving the detailed and delicate pendant makes this valuable.

3in (7.5cm) diam

$2,000-3,000　　　　　　　**MG**

A CLOSER LOOK AT A BAKELITE NECKLACE

The reverse carving is done by hand while the piece is hot so that the injected paint adheres to the surface. The deeper the carving, the better and more desirable the piece.

The original chain is attached and is still in excellent condition, despite its delicacy.

The colour filling in the clear plastic gives the impression of real flowers under a glass.

It has a Victorian feel and is strongly reminiscent of a locket.

A 1930s Prystal and black bakelite necklace, with reverse-carved and injected pendant.

Prystal is a synthetic clear crystal-like plastic material developed in Italy during the 1930s.

Pendant 2.25in (6cm) diam

$800-1,200　　　　　　　**MG**

A 1920s sterling silver and red bakelite pendant, with original red bakelite chain.

A design has been cut out of the, now tarnished, sterling silver allowing the red bakelite beneath to show through.

Pendant 3.75in (9.5cm) high

$700-1,000　　　　　　　**MG**

A mottled orange and black Catalin pendant, swivelling open to reveal a mirror.

This Art Deco necklace with small vanity mirror conjures up images of glamorous flapper girls 'powdering their noses' at wild parties.

2.75in (7cm) high

$800-1,200　　　　　　　**MG**

A 1920s necklace with red and black Catalin cube pendants and metal chain.

8in (20cm) diam

$500-700　　　　　　　**MG**

A 1940s Napier green bakelite and white metal necklace and earrings.

7in (18cm) diam

$500-800　　　　　　　**MG**

A 1950s two-tone bakelite necklace.

Geometric patterns and combinations of colors are very popular. Here, amber transparent and opaque yellow bakelite has been laminated together to form the beads.

6.25in (16cm) diam

$700-1,000　　　　　　　**MG**

A green and beige carved bakelite necklace, with metal fittings.

8in (20cm) long

$300-500   **MG**

A hand-carved 'apple juice' bakelite necklace, with cylindrical and barrel beads.

7in (18cm) diam

$700-1,000   **MG**

A 1950s multi-coloured laminated Lucite ring.

The size of this ring makes it a very showy and desirable item. It is layered with multiple colors so that it changes appearance when seen from different angles.

1.5in (4cm) high

$30-50   **MG**

A laminated square yellow and brown-streaked bakelite ring.

1.25in (3cm) high

$200-250   **MG**

A hand-carved 'creamed corn' bakelite stylized rose and triangle ring.

1in (2.5cm) high

$70-100   **MG**

A green and yellow carved cog ring.

1in (2.5cm) high

$30-50   **MG**

A hand-carved 'creamed corn' bakelite stylized curving leaf ring.

1in (2.5cm) high

$100-150   **MG**

A hand-carved green bakelite and stylized leaf ring.

1in (2.5cm) high

$70-100   **MG**

FIND OUT MORE...

DK Collectors' Guide: Costume Jewelry, by Judith Miller, published by Dorling Kindersley, 2003.

COLLECTORS' NOTES

■ Acme Studios is an American product design company and was founded in 1985 by Adrian Olabuenaga and his wife Lesley Bailey. It produces writing instruments, stationery, personal accessories and other items, all with a strong design focus. It has since worked with many important late 20thC designs and designers and has exported its products around the world.

■ Pins and jewelry were amongst the first items offered, with the 'Memphis Designers For Acme' range, comprising over 100 designs by 14 notable Postmodern designers, being released in 1985. The following year, the 'Architects for Acme' range was released. Designers included Ettore Sottsass, Michele De Lucchi, Peter Shire and Marco Zanini.

■ All represent the Postmodern movement strongly, with references to architecture rendered in bright colours being typical. All pieces are of high quality and are marked on the reverse. In recent years, the tools and dies used to make certain jewelry ranges have been destroyed and the ranges withdrawn from general sale. As interest in Postmodernism of the 1980s and early 1990s grows, these are likely to become desirable collectables of the future.

A 1980s Acme Studios 'Circulus' enameled metal pin, designed by Ettore Sottsass, from the 'Memphis Designers For Acme' range.

One of these pins is in the permanent collection of the Brooklyn Museum, New York.

2in (5cm) high

$200-350 QU

An Acme Studios 'Madras' enameled metal pin, designed by Ettore Sottsass, from the 'Architects For Acme' range.

2in (5cm) high

$200-350 BWH

An Acme Studios 'Optima' enameled metal pin, designed by Ettore Sottsass, from the 'Memphis Designers For Acme' range.

2.75in (6.5cm) high

$250-350 BWH

An Acme Studios 'Grids 4' enameled metal pin designed by Cesar Pelli in 1986, from the 'Architects For Acme' range.

2in (5cm) wide

$200-300 BWH

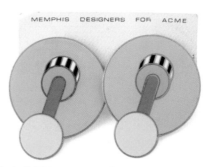

A pair of ACME Studios 'Aristotele' enameled metal earrings, designed by Michele de Lucchi, mounted on an original card, from the 'Memphis Designers For Acme' range.

Like many designs, this was also made as a pin and a 'bolo' tie pull.

2in (5cm) high

$200-300 MTS

A pair of Acme Studios 'Tahiti' enameled metal earrings, designed by Ettore Sottsass, mounted on an original card, from the 'Memphis Designers For Acme' range.

These take the form of Sottsass' notable 'Tahiti' table lamp design of 1981.

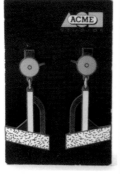

Earrings 1.75in (4.5cm) high

$250-350 BWH

An ACME Studios 'Euphoria' enameled metal pendant on original necklace, designed by Ettore Sottsass, from the 'Memphis Designers For Acme' range.

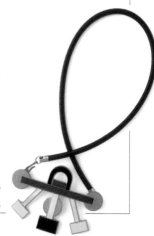

Pendant 3in (7.5cm) wide

$300-400 MTS

COLLECTORS' NOTES

■ 19thC items, such as pottery plates, specially made to commemorate famous trading ships have long appealed to collectors and now give an insight into a lost era. Objects that were actually used on the ships are equally popular, particularly if connected to a well-known historical figure.

■ Ocean Liner memorabilia from the golden age of luxury sea travel is also very popular. Many collectors concentrate on a single ship or line, or a specific category such as menus or advertisements. Objects relating to the best-known shipping companies, such as Cunard, White Star Line, Union Castle, P&O and Canadian Pacific, are highly sought after and items showing the ship or logo are particularly prized. The most collectable cruise ship items are associated with the 'Titanic'.

■ Not all souvenirs were made to be used or sold on a particular ship and some commemorative items were produced many years after a ship took its last voyage.

A pearlware plate, commemorating the steam ship 'The Robert Bruce', within a border of flowers of the Union.

In 1819, The Robert Bruce ran the first regular route that called at the Isle of Man from the mainland. She was transferred to the Liverpool-to-Dublin run in 1820 but after only a few months she caught fire and was sunk to extinguish the flames.

c1819

$600-800   SAS

A pink lustre-banded earthenware plate, printed in gray with a cartouche of two sailing vessels, hairline crack.

c1820   8.5in (21.5cm) diam

$40-70   SAS

A 'Transatlantic Steam Ship Company' ironstone plate, the center printed in puce with a paddle steamer under sail, rim chip.

The Transatlantic Steamship Company operated in the North Atlantic from 1838 running only one ship, the Liverpool. The company was disbanded in 1840 and the ship was sold to P&O who renamed her the Great Liverpool.

c1838   8.5in (21.5cm) diam

$250-450   SAS

A steam passenger list from the North German Lloyd Line 'Rhein' steamship, sailing from New York to Bremen on 30th May 1874, exhibits minor soiling.

1874   8.5in (21.5cm) high

$120-180   AAC

A 'Victoria and Albert Yacht' commemorative pink lustre banded soup bowl, decorated in colored enamels with the named paddle steamer.

The first vessel to carry the name 'Victoria and Albert, she was designed by Sir William Symonds and was launched in 1843. She made over 20 voyages with the royal couple aboard and was renamed Osbourne in 1854. She was broken up in 1868.

c1854

$200-300   SAS

A Victorian stevenograph bookmark, commemorating Captain H.R.H. Alfred, Duke of Edinburgh.

In 1867, Prince Alfred visited the island of Tristan da Cunha while on a world tour aboard the royal yacht Britannia. The main settlement on the island was named Edinburgh of the Seven Seas in his honour.

c1867   9.25in (23.5cm) long

$120-180   COB

A pair of HMS Raleigh leaves, each painted with a warship under sail, framed.

The HMS Raleigh was an iron frigate built at Chatham in 1873. The ship enjoyed a long overseas commission and in 1899 led the last squadron of Naval ships to put to sea under sail.

8.75in (22.5cm) wide

$150-200   SAS

An interesting Continental porcelain plaque, the green body overlaid in white with a ship thought to be the Kaiserin Augusta.

Kaiserin Augusta was a luxurious German North Atlantic liner of 1906. After WWI she was surrendered to the British and subsequently became the Canadian Pacific's 'Empress of Scotland'. She was scrapped in 1930.

c1900   8in (20cm) wide

$70-100   **SAS**

A small Titanic commemorative jug, by Carlton China, inscribed on the reverse.

Despite its small size and plain decoration, its connection to the most famous of cruise liners makes it desirable.

1912   2.25in (5.5cm) high

$250-350   **SAS**

A White Star Line silver-plated wine bottle stopper.

c1930   3.25in (8.5cm) high

$250-350   **F**

A 1930s Clyde-Mallory Lines cruise line brochure, for trips to and from Miami to Havana.

9.5in (23.5cm) high

$80-120   **DD**

An S.S. Normandie commemorative ceramic dish.

c1935   5in (13cm) diam

$100-150   **COB**

A 1930s pack of P&O playing cards.

3.5in (9cm) long

$35-45   **COB**

A 1950s pack of Orient Line S.S. Orcades playing cards.

3.5in (9cm) long

$22-28   **COB**

An RMS Queen Elizabeth menu, for Sunday, October 20th, 1968.

This was used during the liner's final voyage.

1968   10.5in (16.5cm) high

$18-28   **COB**

A 1950s P&O 'Arcadia' eggcup, marked "Mappin & Webb" and "Mappin Plate".

3.25in (8.5cm) high

$22-28   **DH**

DISNEYANA

COLLECTORS' NOTES

■ Walter Elias Disney (1901-66) founded a pioneering animation studio in 1922 with his brother Roy. Mickey Mouse was developed in 1928, and the film 'Snow White & The Seven Dwarfs' in 1937 had an enormous impact on cinema. Values for the vast amount of memorabilia produced around his characters and films is largely based on the character, the type, the date it was made and the condition and rarity.

■ Memorabilia began to be produced from c1930 onwards, and it is memorabilia from the 1930s that is generally the most valuable today. Marks are important and help to date a piece. Early marks may include George Borgfeldt's name, as he was the first to receive a license from Disney to produce his characters. Star salesman and marketeer Kay Kamen was another early name. He signed a deal with Disney in 1939 that was cut short by his death in 1949.

■ Before 1939, most pieces were marked "Walt Disney Enterprises" or, more rarely, "Walter E. Disney". British-made pieces of the 1930s may also feature "Walt Disney Mickey Mouse Ltd". From 1939-84, the marking changed to "Walt Disney Productions" and after 1984 the marking "© Disney" or "© Disney Enterprises" tended to be used.

■ Characters such as Mickey Mouse will have a broad and lasting appeal amongst the widest variety of generations of collectors. Earlier, more short-lived and obscure characters, such as Horace The Horse, will be less desirable to many, despite being rare. However, the small group of collectors who do collect rare characters will often pay large sums for good examples. Certain characters have also changed in appearance over time. Mickey Mouse lost his toothy grin in the early 1930s and became rounder, and less rodent-like by the 1950s.

A 'Bendy' foam Mickey Mouse figure, marked "©WD".

c1970   7in (18cm) high

$15-25   **RBC**

A Walt Disney Production Mickey Mouse Disneyland nodder, labels.

6.5in (16.5cm) high

$60-80   **PA**

A 1930s Steiff Mickey Mouse small soft toy, in excellent and clean condition, complete with Steiff ear button and foot stamp.

7in (17.5cm) high

$800-1,200   **SOTT**

A 1980s Walt Disney Minnie Mouse 'Bendy' foam figure, marked "1981 (c) Walt Disney Co.", original cotton and lace bib.

Damage reduces value dramatically.

8in (20cm) high

$15-25   **RBC**

An R. Dakin & Company Walt Disney Productions soft vinyl Mickey & Minnie.

8in (20cm) high

$100-150   **NOR**

A 1960s-70s Donald Duck painted wood money bank.

The paintwork is still in surprisingly good condition.

13.5in (34cm) high

$60-90   **MEM**

A 1980s Donald Duck painted wood money bank, with lock and key, marked "© Disney".

11.75in (30cm) high

$60-90   **MEM**

A CLOSER LOOK AT MICKEY & MINNIE MOUSE TOYS

Dean's introduced character memorabilia in 1930, but gaining the right to make the first ever Mickey Mouse dolls from Walt Disney in 1930 was a real coup.

The design with printed teeth is the earliest; in 1934 a softer version without 'scary' looking teeth was introduced.

It is very rare to find Minnie, let alone a pair together, and both are in mint condition, being very clean with unfaded printed facial features and clothes.

A smaller 6in (15cm) high Mickey with a clip can be found. Known as a 'jigger' or 'jazzer' and costing two shillings at the time, he could be attached to the arm of a gramophone where he would dance around as the music played.

A pair of rare Dean's Rag Book Mickey & Minnie 'Evripose' fabric and velvet wire-framed dancing dolls, with printed Regd No.750611 for late 1929.

These toys were voted the 'Boom' toy of the year in February 1930.

c1931

12.5in (32cm) high

$900-1,300 (PAIR)

TCT

A 1980s 'Bendy' foam Donald Duck figure, marked "1984 copyright Walt Disney Co.", with original fabric bowtie.

8in (20cm) high

$20-25   **RBC**

A 1980s Thumper molded plastic figure, marked "©Disney China".

4.5in (11.5cm) high

$15-20   **RBC**

A 1980s Flower molded plastic figure, from 'Bambi', marked "©Disney China".

4.5in (11.5cm) high

$15-20   **RBC**

A 'Lady' hand-painted ceramic figurine, from 'Lady and the Tramp', marked "Disney Japan".

4in (10cm) high

$20-25   **TSIS**

A 1950s-60s Walt Disney Snow White hand-painted ceramic figurine, marked "©Walt Disney Prod. Japan".

7.25in (18.5cm) high

$50-70   **RBC**

A 1960s Walt Disney Productions plastic Goofy on a tricycle toy.

5in (13cm) high

$20-25   **NOR**

A Bambi hand-painted ceramics figural flower pot, impressed "Bambi Walt Disney ®".

9.5in (24cm) wide

$50-80   **TM**

A Marx Toys plastic and soft vinyl Pinnochio 'Pip Squeek' figure, mint in box.

1970   *5in (12.5cm) high*

$8-12   **MEM**

A 1970s Walt Disney Productions Pluto battery-operated 'Mystery Action' figure, in mint condition with original box.

'Mystery Action' was a term used frequently in the 1950s and 1960s by Japanese makers to describe the moving or flashing elements on their toys.

10.75in (27.5cm) high

$40-60   **MEM**

An American Walt Disney Mickey Mouse Club wind-up fireman toy, by Durham, in mint condition with unopened box.

Box 11in (28cm) high

$60-90   **MEM**

An AHI Walt Disney Productions Mickey Mouse in car toy, in mint condition in blister pack.

It is rare to find these toys still unopened in their blister packs. The 'Fast Wheels' were made to compete with Corgi's 'Whizz Wheels' and Mattel's 'Superfast' Hot Wheels models.

1977   *5in (13cm) high*

$12-18   **MEM**

An AHI Walt Disney's Productions Donald Duck in car, in mint condition in unopened blister pack.

1977   *5in (13cm) high*

$12-18   **MEM**

A Herbert George & Co. 'Donald Duck' black Bakelite camera, for Walt Disney Productions.

The survival of the original card box is very rare, and makes the camera many times more desirable. This is due also to its appealing and colourful graphics. Without the box, a used camera usually fetches under $50.

c1946   *4.75in (12cm) wide box*

$200-300   **MEM**

An Ensign Ltd. Mickey Mouse battery-powered toy lantern set, consisting of a viewer, 11 sets of slides, spare battery and bulbs, with "Walter E. Disney" licensing wording, all in original labelled boxes.

The use of the wording "Walter E. Disney" implies licensed merchandise made in Britain during the 1930s and its appearance is rare.

c1935   *Box 10.5in (26.5cm) wide*

$200-300   **GORL**

A set of 1950s Mickey Mouse Picture Cubes, each wooden cube covered with printed paper, "Walt Disney Productions Made in West Germany".

Box 7in (18cm) wide

$30-40   **NOR**

A 1950s-60s American 'Donald Duck' lithographed tin paint box, by Transogram Co. Inc, marked "© Walt Disney Productions.

8in (20cm) wide

$30-50 SOTT

A 1950s Walt Disney Productions Snow White hand-painted ceramic mug.

From the lightweight, white, granular ceramic used and style of the hand-painted design, this was probably made in Japan.

3.75in (9.5cm) high

$30-50 NOR

A 1930s Donald Duck hand-painted jug, the base impressed either "Walter Disney" or "Walt E. Disney".

6in (15.5cm) high

$80-120 NOR

A 1960s-70s Walt Disney Productions Mickey Mouse plastic cup, with 'blinking' eyes.

4in (10cm) high

$30-50 NOR

A 1960s Walt Disney Production Jiminy Cricket plastic cup, with 'blinking' eyes.

4in (10cm) high

$15-25 NOR

A 1950s Walt Disney Productions child's lampshade, in excellent clean condition.

8.5in (21.5cm) high

$20-30 MA

A 1950s American box of Walt Disney Productions Mickey Mouse '100 Sunshine Straws', unopened and complete.

It is the rarity of the unopened nature of this box, as well as the colorful and comparatively early artwork on the box, that makes this valuable.

8.75in (22cm) long

$60-80 TRA

A 1950s American box of Walt Disney Productions Donald Duck 'Sunshine Straws' unopened and complete.

8.75in (22cm) high

$60-80 TRA

An American Warren Biggs Co. calendar card for July 1947, with Walt Disney's Donald Duck with Mrs. Jumbo and Dumbo.

1947 *9in (23cm) high*

$40-60 LDE

An American Warren Biggs Co. calendar card for December 1947, with Walt Disney's Mickey, Minnie, Huey and Duey.

1947   *9in (23cm) high*

$30-50   **LDE**

A CLOSER LOOK AT A FANTASIA SCARF

Fantasia memorabilia is rarer than that for other Disney films as the world was at war when the film was released in 1940.

The film is deemed one of Disney's high points and has many fans who are eager to collect original items relating to the film.

It is very large and in excellent, clean condition with no tears or stains and original, bright colors, which is unusual for items made for children to wear.

It is also unusual as it does not feature Mickey Mouse, but shows other characters such as Mademoiselle Upanova, cupids and Melinda the Centaurette, who is featured in the Pastorale Symphony part of the film.

A rare 1940s Walt Disney Productions 'Fantasia' rayon scarf.

         30.25in (77cm) wide

$200-300   **NOR**

A 1950s-60s Walt Disney Productions 'Disneyland' rayon and silk-mix handkerchief, the corner signed or printed "Hillegas".

         16.5in (42cm) wide

$15-20   **NOR**

A late 1960s-70s Walt Disney Productions Jungle Book printed cotton handkerchief, featuring Shere Khan.

         9in (23cm) high

$20-30   **NOR**

A rare 'Yoo Hoo' Mickey Mouse badge, printed with "©1930 Walter E. Disney All Rights Reserved For Great Britain", but made in the 1960s.

         3.5in (9cm) diam

$100-150   **LDE**

An Ingersoll Mickey Mouse child's wristwatch, with articulated metal strap, inoperative.

Ingersoll began producing these watches in 1933, this example dates from the late 1930s and has its original strap with molded and painted Mickey Mouses. Value, particularly for less expensive later examples from the 1950s-60s, is dependant on whether the watch works, as the movements were typically of poor quality and are hard to find in working order.

$180-220   **SAS**

A Walt Disney World Minnie Mouse plastic wallet.

         3.75in (9.5cm) wide

$12-18   **NOR**

COLLECTORS' NOTES

■ Bisque dolls can be identified by looking for impressed or incised marks, which indicate a mold number and sometimes a maker, on the nape of the neck. The facial characteristics of a doll can also act as a guide to makers. Armand Marseille (AM) was one of the most prolific makers, with production peaking from c1900-30. Their '390' doll is one of the most commonly seen. Look for well-painted, lively and characterful features, and clean bisque. Cracks and mismatched bodies devalue a doll, and the presence of original clothes adds value.

■ Composition and fabric dolls are also widely collected. Always examine the painted surface of composition dolls as damage to the surface or cracks will devalue a doll. Composition is a mixture of plaster, wood pulp, glue and other ingredients that can

be molded. It was used from c1900 to the 1950s when it was superseded by the more economical and versatile plastic. Early fabric dolls from the early to mid-19thC can be rare as most have been worn or fallen apart. Many were home-made, or sewn together and stuffed using self assembly kits bought from shops.

■ Plastic dolls have risen in value dramatically over the past decade as the generation who remember them as children has begun to collect. Examples in clean, un-played with condition, complete with their original clothes, boxes and tags (ie; in shop-sold condition) are the most valuable. Look out for examples that also retain their original hairstyles. Madam Alexander, Pedigree, Terri Lee and American Character Doll Co. are among the many collectable makers.

A German Armand Marseille bisque doll, with sleeping blue eyes, open mouth, blonde wig and jointed body in original white dress and underclothes, marked "A8M 996".

22.5in (57cm) high

$200-300   **SAS**

A German Armand Marseille bisque doll, with sleeping blue eyes, blonde wig and composition body with wooden limbs dressed in cream nightwear, marked "1894".

15.25in (39cm) high

$200-300   **SAS**

A German Armand Marseille doll, with sleeping brown eyes, brown wig and composition body dressed in cream nightdress, marked "390".

21in (53cm) high

$200-300   **SAS**

A German Armand Marseille child doll, with fixed blue eyes, pierced ears, long blonde wig and jointed composition body, dressed in a white and red dress and under-clothes, marked "1894", one foot detached.

17in (43cm) high

$150-200   **SAS**

A German Heinrich Handwerck girl doll, with brown sleeping eyes, pierced ears, open mouth with four teeth, mohair wig, jointed body, wearing a pink dress with hat and shoes, marked "109/11 3/4", some wear.

c1900   *22in (55cm) high*

$800-1,000   **LAN**

A German Schoenau & Hoffmeister bisque child doll, with blue sleeping eyes, blonde wig and jointed composition body wearing a cream dress with matching bonnet, underclothes and black leather shoes.

1909   *24in (61cm) high*

$200-300   **SAS**

A German Schoenau & Hoffmeister child doll, with sleeping blue eyes, brown wig and wood and composition body wearing a lilac dress, marked "1923".

23.25in (59cm) high

$250-350   **SAS**

An American Kellogg's 'Papa Bear' printed fabric doll.

These promotional cloth dolls were given away by Kellogg's as kits to be cut out, sewn and stuffed at home. 'Papa Bear' was only made in 1925, with the other characters from the Goldilocks story being produced only in 1926 .

1925   13.25in (33.5cm) high

$70-90   **HGS**

An American Kellogg's 'Goldilocks' printed cloth doll, with "©1926 Kellogg Co. Battel Creek Mich." printed fabric label.

12.75in (32.5cm) high

$70-90   **HGS**

An 1920s American Kellogg's Nursery Rhymes 'Little Bo Peep' cloth doll.

14.25in (36.5cm) high

$70-90   **HGS**

A late 19thC Judy printed cloth doll.

15.25in (38.5cm) high

$70-90   **HGS**

A late 19thC American Arnold Printworks 'Our Soldier Boys' printed fabric doll.

This self-assembled cloth doll kit was advertised in 'The Youth's Companion' in October 1894, together with a variation holding a sword.

c1894   8in (20cm) high

$30-40   **HGS**

A rare set of ten American Arnold Printworks printed fabric skittles, weighted at base area with heavy beads.

The complete set of different, characterful faces and the complexity of printing makes this set especially appealing.

1904-05   9.75in (24.5cm) high

$400-600   **HGS**

A Steiff German soldier felt doll, with button and original tag.

This complexly made cloth doll is both very hard to find, and in mint condition, with its tag and with no wear or damage, which makes it exceptionally rare. It is unlikely that a boy would have wanted such a cloth doll, and the same certainly rings true for girls. Despite this, its great rarity and fine condition make it highly desirable to collectors today.

c1930s   8.5in (22cm) high

$4,000-6,000   **TCT**

A Käthe Kruse fabric boy doll, with painted hair and face, dressed in a pair of trousers, jacket and shoes.

16in (40cm) high

$800-1,000   **LAN**

An Italian Lenci pressed felt girl doll, with brown painted side-glancing eyes, blond mohair wig, jointed felt and cloth body, some damage to dress, lacks shoes.

13.75in (35cm) high

$150-250   **SAS**

A Norah Wellings fabric boy doll, with molded felt face, painted features, and velvet hands and legs, marked "Norah Wellings made in England" on wrist.

c1950   *11in (28cm) high*

$120-180   **RBC**

A late 1930s American Effanbee Playmate Anne Shirley composition doll, with original clothes, card tag and box.

21.25in (54cm) high

$300-400   **MEM**

An Effanbee 'Skippy' composition soldier doll, with side-glancing eyes, military outfit and cap, fine crazing and minor chipping to face paint.

'Skippy The All American Boy' was a 1920s newspaper character drawn by Percy Crosby. He was a playmate for the popular Patsy doll.

14in (35.50cm) high

$400-500   **JDJ**

A Campbell Kid composition and cloth-bodied doll, with composition hands, dressed in original checker board dress and shoes.

11.75in (30cm) high

$120-180   **MEM**

An American Madame Alexander Sonja Henie composition doll, complete with original hairstyle, tagged dress and leatherette ice skates.

Sonja Henie (1912-69) was a Norwegian champion figure skater who won 10 consecutive world championships from 1927. Moving to the US, she turned professional in 1936. During the 1950s she performed in shows, TV programmes and films.

1939-42   *15in (38cm) high*

$300-400   **MEM**

A 1940s British Mark Payne composition doll, with wind-up disc playing mechanism.

Mark Payne also released a 'Queen Elizabeth' speaking/singing doll for the 1953 Coronation, using the same face and body as this example.

26in (66cm) high

$120-180   **DSC**

A 1940s Frank Popper pot doll, in bridal outfit and mohair wig, marked "FP210", in original box.

Pot is a material similar to composition but more chalky. British manufacturer F. Popper is best known for making 'pot' dolls.

21in (53.5cm) high

$60-90   **GAZE**

A German Schildkröt celluloid headed doll, with a leather body and celluloid arms, blue sleeping eyes and open mouth with teeth, marked "SiR Germany 13 1926".

1926   17.25in (43cm) high

$100-150   WDL

A CLOSER LOOK AT A PLASTIC DOLL

Madame Alexander dolls are renowned for their authentic clothes and well-modeled and 'made-up' faces. Jacqueline Kennedy is a highly sought-after character.

She is complete and in mint condition, even retaining her delicate stockings, card tag and her original hair style and 'make-up'.

A French celluloid baby doll.

c1920   20in (51cm) high

$150-250   BEJ

Jacqueline, along with her daughter Caroline, was only produced from 1961-62. They are hard to find today.

This outfit is rare and perfectly matches popular styles of fashionable young women of the day.

A 1930s French Petitcolin celluloid boy doll.

21in (53.5cm) high

$70-100   DSC

An American Madame Alexander Jacqueline Kennedy vinyl doll, with original clothes and in original condition, with card hand tag.

1961-62   21in (53.5cm) high

$600-800   MEM

A rare American Madame Alexander Caroline Kennedy doll, in mint condition, in original box.

This scarce doll is rare in mint condition, and rarer still with her original box and card tag.

$400-500   MEM

A late 1950s American Character Doll Co. Betsy McCall hard vinyl doll, in her original blue dress with her original hairstyle, in excellent condition.

Betsy McCall began life as a paper doll in McCall's magazine. American Character Doll released this highly popular version in 1957.

8in (20.5cm) high

$150-200   MEM

An American Character Doll Co. 'Sweet Sue' hard plastic doll, with original clothes, hair style and card hand tag.

Sweet Sue's hair is rooted in a skull cap, which was an exclusive patent owned by the American Character Doll Company.

20.5in (52cm) high

$300-350   **MEM**

A CLOSER LOOK AT A REVLON DOLL

The Revlon doll was issued by the renowned Ideal Toy Corporation in 1956 and used the famous Revlon name and a lower price to compete against other fashion dolls.

She was available with an extensive range of hairstyles and in many different outfits, all named after Revlon products of the time, such as 'Queen of Diamonds'.

She is complete with all her clothes, earrings and shoes and retains her original red-painted nails and lips

The upswept hair retains its original style and is said to be scarce.

An American Ideal 'Little Miss Revlon' hard vinyl doll, complete with clothing and accessories, lacks box.

If she had her box and tag in mint condition, she could fetch up to 50 per cent more.

c1958   11in (28cm) high

$150-200   **DIM**

A 1970s British Burbank Alexandra Rose vinyl doll, with soft body and legs.

22in (56cm) high

$25-45   **DSC**

A 1950s Palitoy girl doll, the plastic head with painted features and cloth body, reg. design no. 824 206 for 1937.

c1938   19in (48.5cm) high

$15-20   **GAZE**

A 1950s 'Girl' hard plastic 'walker' doll, by Palitoy.

Her cheek coloring is not worn and her mohair wig is still curled. She is a 'walker' doll meaning she turns her head as she walks. Palitoy released her in conjunction with 'Girl' comic, published by Hulton Press which is why she has the logo on her belt, dress and hair ribbon. Hard plastic dolls by Palitoy typically have lilac eyes.

14in (35.5cm) high

$150-200   **DSC**

A 1970s Tri-ang Pedigree 'Mam'selle' vinyl doll, in mint condition with original box.

19.5in (49.5cm) high

$40-70   **GAZE**

A 1950s Pedigree Delite hard plastic baby doll.

14in (35.5cm) high

$80-120   **DSC**

A CLOSER LOOK AT A PLASTIC DOLL

Her body and limbs are made from a form of thin rubber or latex, stuffed with kapok, to emulate real skin.

The latex tended to split over time, making complete, undamaged dolls rare today - this example has only one split on her hand.

Her head is made from hard plastic and is very clean.

Pedigree dolls have been collectable for years, but are becoming increasingly desirable in finer condition.

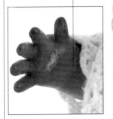

A Sasha doll, with blonde hair, dressed in blue cord dress, tights and shoes.

c1985   *16in (40.5cm) high*

$150-200   **GAZE**

A rare 1950s Pedigree 'Beauty Skin Delite' doll, in replaced clothes.

18in (45.5cm) high

$120-180   **DSC**

An American Terri Lee ballet dancer doll, in original condition with her original pink dress.

The presence of the original dress is rare as they were often lost and replaced.

10.25in (26cm) high

$100-150   **MEM**

A 1960s American vinyl 'Go-Go' doll, with original clothing, shoes and sunglasses.

19.75in (50cm) high

$30-50   **NOR**

An Elizabeth Taylor plastic fashion doll, in mint condition in original box, with MGM licensing wording, in mint condition with original box.

These dolls, made after her role as a prostitute in the 1960 film 'Butterfield 8', are very rare as Taylor is said to have disallowed dolls to be made of her until a deal with Mattel in 2000.

Box 14in (35.5cm) high

$300-400   **DIM**

A 1930s Princess Elizabeth paper doll, with 11 outfits.

12in (30.5cm) high

$250-350   **BEJ**

A 1930s 'Princess Margaret Rose' paper doll with 11 outfits.

Doll 12in (30.5cm) high

$150-250   **BEJ**

A CLOSER LOOK AT A HALF DOLL

Half dolls were attached to fabric 'dresses' at their waists, which were used as pin cushions or to cover powder boxes or other objects.

Her face is charming and full of character, and the flowers and extra detail are painstakingly modeled, attached and painted.

This large doll is complexly modeled - the arms would have been separately molded and attached.

Most half dolls were made in Germany from the late 19thC to the 1930s - this example is attributed to the prestigious Capodimonte factory.

A 1930s porcelain half-lady or pin doll wearing a red bonnet.

4.5in (11.5cm) height

$70-100   **CSO**

An Italian large half doll, in the form of a lady, attributed to Capo Di Monte.

6in (15cm) high

$1,000-1,500   **JDJ**

An American Bliss two-storey printed paper-on-wood doll's house, some bubbling to paper, but overall bright, lacks front steps and a piece of railing paper possibly replaced.

Bliss are a sought-after name in doll's houses, and are known for their attention to detail and use of traditional American domestic architectural features.

16.50in (42cm) high

$800-1,000   **JDJ**

An early 20thC homemade, scratch-built model of 'Rose Cottage', with detailed decoration including lean-to and pig sty, with penny-operated lighting mechanism.

13.75in (35cm) high

$450-650   **ROS**

A group of ebonised wooden doll's house furniture, displayed in a wooden room setting; together with additional mahogany finished doll's house furniture.

The label shows that this was made in 1912 by a craftsman, probably at home, to display at an exhibition of furniture at Maples store in London, England.

Setting 11.5in (29cm) high

$300-400   **F**

An unusual leather and painted metal doll's watch, with moveable metal hands.

c1910   *Face 0.5in (1.5cm) diam*

$100-200   **BEJ**

COLLECTORS' NOTES

■ The popularity of vintage eyewear has risen dramatically over the past five years, as people looking for an individual, often 'retro', personal look have begun to compete against collectors. As such, prices have risen and even contemporary designers look to the styles of past decades for inspiration amid a flurry of coverage in fashion magazines.

■ The value of much vintage eyewear lies in the style or look of the frames, the name of the maker or designer, the material and the condition. Always aim to buy frames that are most representative of the period they were produced in. The 1950s and '60s are currently the most popular decades, with highly stylized cat's-eye and bug-eyed, or cupped shapes, being the most desirable.

■ Fashions change regularly, but currently, large lensed frames such as the ever-popular 'Jackie O' style and certain 1960s and '80s designs are also in vogue. Colorful or complex plastics, and those with appealing or period printed or carved designs, are also popular.

■ Condition is important. Values are not usually affected too seriously by missing or scratched lenses, as many wearers and collectors will prefer to fit lenses of their own. However, if the original lens were unusual, such as having a graduated (or gradient) tone, value will be affected as these can be hard to replace.

■ Split, cracked, brittle or glued frames should be avoided, as these are very difficult, if not impossible to repair, especially invisibly. Those that have bent over time can be reshaped by professionals using heat. However, this can only be done providing the curving is not too great. Look for 'dead' unused shop stock, which is unworn.

■ Look out for famous names, not just those such as Alain Mikli and Emmanuelle Khahn in the world of eyewear, but also in the world of fashion, including Christian Dior, Emilio Pucci and Pierre Cardin. As well as all the above, look out for frames that have that extra 'something', which is perhaps best summed up as 'specs appeal'.

A pair of 1950s-60s American plain black gent's frames, marked "US Optical MADE IN USA".

5in (12.5cm) wide

$30-40   **BB**

A pair of French grey and silver striated plastic frames, with "CA" monogram, marked "Frame France YVAN".

5.25in (13.5cm) wide

$30-50   **BB**

A pair of 1950s silver and white grey pearlescent plastic frames, the corners inset with two small metal stars.

5in (12.5cm) wide

$30-40   **BB**

A pair of 1950s American Raybert 'Baccara' triple-laminated brown, white and clear plastic frames, hand-cut down on brows in a flame-like pattern.

The three colors of plastics are shown to dramatic effect in the typically 1950s carved areas.

5.75in (14.5cm) wide

$250-300   **VE**

A pair of American white plastic sunglasses, with pink lenses, marked with "Suntimer AA" motif.

5.5in (14cm) wide

$150-200   **VE**

A pair of French Alain Mikli black plastic and gilt metal frames, with moulded textured pattern, marked "Hand Made in France".

5in (13cm) wide

$250-350   **VE**

A pair of 1960s yellow opalescent plastic hexagonal frames, with 'O-O' motif.

5in (13cm) wide

$30-50   **BB**

A pair of 1960s French 'blonde tortoiseshell' plastic sunglasses, with blue lenses.

A pair of 1960s French large oval 'blonde tortoiseshell' plastic sunglasses.

This over-sized, almost 'bug-eyed' look has become popular once again after the style was reintroduced by Dior and Blinds and popularised by Madonna and U2's Bono.

A pair of American white and pale brown laminated 'bug-eyed' sunglasses, with graduated (or gradient) lenses and matching side lenses, marked "Mod Twist".

The side lenses have no real purpose apart from extending the 'Op Art' look of these shades. The color of the lenses cleverly mirrors the color of the brown base plastic, under the white lamination.

6in (15.5cm) wide

5.75in (14.5cm) wide

$250-300 VE | **$250-350** VE | **$350-450** VE

A CLOSER LOOK AT A PAIR OF CARDIN GLASSES

The frames are by Pierre Cardin, who was a major international designer during the 1960s and was responsible for many key fashion movements of the period.

While the round frames are typical of the 1960s, the shape, straight-style of the arms and use of tortoiseshell plastic strongly resemble early 19thC frames.

Unusually, they fold down into a small and strong structure, making them ideal for carrying around safely. The folded arms also protect the lenses.

A pair of 1960s French Pierre Cardin 'tortoiseshell' plastic folding frames.

6in (15cm) wide

$250-350 VE

A pair of Emilio Pucci 'Portofino' printed black plastic sunglasses.

Fashion designer Emilio Pucci was known for his brightly, often psychedelically, colored geometric and swirling printed patterns. Here fabric has been laminated under plastic. Interestingly, Pucci has a famous branch of its boutiques in Portofino.

A pair of 1960s American laminated red white and blue plastic sunglasses, stamped "MAY USA" with "BGN SPORTS STRIPE" sticker.

This fashionable style of frame is often known as 'Jackie O' after Jackie Onassis Kennedy, who was seen regularly sporting this look. The coloring of this pair makes them highly patriotic. May & Co. are a collectible name.

A pair of 1960s blue striated and clear plastic frames, unmarked.

6.5in (16.5cm) wide

5.25in (13.5cm) wide

5.25in (13.5cm) wide

$300-400 GAZE | **$250-350** VE | **$250-350** VE

A pair of 1960s French red plastic frames, with integral grid 'lenses', marked "Made in France".

The 1960s saw a wide variety of highly unusual shapes and decorative treatments, many inspired by the 'future' and outer space, including thin slits and such 'grids'.

6in (15cm) wide

$120-180 VE

A pair of 1960s French white square sunglasses, with original lenses, marked "Made in France".

These frames were inspired by the shapes of TV screens, as televisions became regular and much-loved features in most homes around the world.

6in (15cm) wide

$200-250 VE

A pair of late 1950s-early 1960s pearlised 'champagne' plastic laminated on black plastic sunglasses, the top rim carved by hand with lines, marked "Made in France".

These highly stylized retro specs have the color and shape of the 1950s but have been affected by the slightly eccentric style of the coming 1960s.

6.25in (16cm) wide

$150-250 VE

A pair of 1960s French laminated white, pearlised grey plastic and black plastic diamond-shaped sunglasses, marked "Made in France".

The geometric form and contrasting colors of the frames were inspired by the growing 'Op Art' movement of the 1960s, championed by artists such as Bridget Riley and Viktor Vasarely.

6in (15.5cm) wide

$350-450 VE

A pair of 1960s large green plastic sunglasses, with light blue lenses, marked "135 852 506".

The wide top edge of the frame both covered and imitated eyebrows.

2.75in (7cm) high

$150-250 VE

A pair of 1960s French Pierre Cardin 'Renée' large hexagonal 'light tortoiseshell' plastic frames, marked "Hand Made in France Renee".

The famous designer name, popular in his day, increases the value of these visually striking frames.

6.25in (16cm) wide

$250-350 VE

A pair of 1970s Ted Lapidus gold polka-dot on black and metal 'bamboo' sunglasses, marked "TL 07 48".

6in (15cm) wide

$250-350 VE

A pair of American graduated green and yellow plastic large unisex frames, unmarked.

5.75in (14.5cm) wide

$30-50 BB

A pair of Christian Dior sunglasses, with curving metal frames and Optyl graduated lenses, marked "Made in Austria".

Optyl is a lightweight plastic.

5.25in (13.5cm) wide

$250-350 VE

A pair of 1950s American Victory black 'cat's-eye' sunglasses, with new lenses and inset metal V-shapes, the arms marked "USA".

5.5in (14cm) wide

$30-50 BB

A pair of 1950s French 'fantasy' rhinestone-inset frames, the top edge with moulded curves, the arm marked "France".

These fabulous hand-cut one piece 'fantasy' styles are hotly sought-after, particularly if completely carved and embellished with rhinestones.

4.5in (11.5cm) wide

$250-350 VE

A CLOSER LOOK AT A PAIR OF MAKE-UP GLASSES

Frames made for special uses are scarcer than standard frames, but appeal mainly to eyewear collectors.

The shape of the frame is typically 1950s, being similar to the popular and fashionable 'cat's-eye' styles. The straight arms are unusual, allowing them to be put on and taken off easily.

The lens holders are hinged allowing them to be flipped down to help with the application of make-up and flipped up for distance viewing.

The heavy look, often using bold, single colors was popular at the time.

They are well-made, using fine quality materials and are in mint condition with no wear and strong and intact brass hinges.

A pair of 1950s black plastic 'cat's-eye' hinged make-up frames, marked "FRAME FRANCE".

5in (13cm) wide

$50-70 BB

$60-80 BB

A pair of 1960s French striped 'tortoiseshell' Lucite laminated on black Lucite 'bug-eyed' frames.

6.5in (16.5cm) wide

$60-80 BB

A pair of 1960s Italian Samco wire frames, with a set of interchangeable colored circular lenses in a folding plastic case, the case marked "Samco Italy".

Depending on your mood you could look at the world through rose, blue or even grey tinted spectacles.

Case 12.25in (31cm) high

$50-70 BB

A pair of 1980s Swatch sunglasses, with two interchangeable fronts, laminated grey pearl plastic backs, the arms moulded "Swatch".

Typically 1980s in terms of color, different 'fronts' could be clipped onto the standard frames. The bottom shot shows the inside of the frames with a front clipped on.

5.5in (14cm) wide

$120-180 VE

FIND OUT MORE...

Specs Appeal – Extravagant 1950s & 60 Eyewear, by Leslie Pina and Donald-Brian Johnson, published by Schiffer Books, 2002.

Eyeglass Retrospective – Where Fashion & Science Meet, by Nancy Schiffer, published by Schiffer Books, 2000.

COLLECTORS' NOTES

■ The 1950s saw a rejuvenation of design after emerging from the restrictions and privations of WWII.

■ New materials, developed in part because of the war, meant that man-made products such as vinyl, formica, Draylon and nylon were very much the vogue. Colors were bright, but often in pastel cheerful tones, black and white were a common combination, and decoration was stylish and whimsical.

■ These new materials also meant that items could be mass-produced like never before and saw the emergency of the 'throw away' culture. This means that pieces were often produced in large numbers, for example Ridgway's Homemaker dinnerware, making them affordable and easy to find. Examples by known designers are more likely to hold and rise in value as are those in the best condition.

■ The emergence of the teenager meant much was aimed at this youthful audience with frivolous designs to the fore. Glamour was also in after the drab war years, and popular motifs include pin-up girls, scenes of Paris and elegant, elongated women. With the continuing rise of celebrity movie stars and singers such as Marilyn Monroe and Elvis Presley, items or endorsed by or featuring famous people are also desirable.

A 1950s Beswick 'Circus' pattern toast rack, decorated with underglaze color transfer.

6.25in (16cm) long

$60-80   **BAD**

A 1950s Beswick 'Circus' pattern sugar bowl, decorated with underglaze color transfer.

4.75in (12cm) wide

$40-70   **BAD**

A 1950s Beswick 'Ballet' pattern mustard pot, decorated with underglaze color transfer.

This pattern was later renamed Pavlova'. The ballet and the circus were both popular themes during the 1950s.

2.75in (7cm) high

$20-30   **MA**

A 1950s Burleigh ware 'Viscount' transfer-printed pattern sauce boat.

8in (20cm) long

$30-40   **BAD**

A 1950s Foley China 'The Gay Nineties' fancy dish, designed by Maureen Tanner.

c1956   *5in (13cm) high*

$20-30   **GROB**

A 1950s 'Teenage Caper' cup, with gilt trim, marked "Made in England" to the base.

This cup sums up the 1950s in many ways with the arrival of the teenager and rock 'n' roll. The reverse shows a Gaggia espresso machine, which helps to date this piece to c1957 when coffee bars began appearing in London.

c1957   *3.25in (8.5cm) diam*

$35-45   **MA**

A Ridgway Potteries Ltd 'Homemaker' pattern part coffee service, the pattern designed by Enid Seeney in 1956-57, comprising a coffee pot and cover, six coffee cups and saucers and a two-handled soup dish and plate, high, printed marks.

Homemaker plates are commonly found as they were produced and sold in the thousands. Coffee pots are much harder to find as people only tended to buy one. They also display the pattern well, making them more valuable.

1957-70   *Coffee pot 7.5in (19cm) high*

$250-350   **DN**

A 1950s Swedish JIE, Ganiopta ceramic biscuit barrel, designed by Anita Nylund, with wooden lid, labelled "Gogay tableware", impressed "J I E - SWEDEN 22-3".

6.25in (16cm) high

$60-80　　　　　　　　　　　TCM

A CLOSER LOOK AT A LADY HEAD VASE

She retains her original eyelashes, earrings and necklace, adding to her value.

Lady head vases were initially sold in florists as gifts containing flowers and were often thrown away once the flowers had died.

Named examples are not necessarily more desirable; the quality of the design and moulding, and the elegance of the form and facial expression are more important.

The protruding bow and tail of her scarf could be easily damaged, but in this case are complete.

A 1950s NAPCO lady head vase, with necklace and eyelashes, marked "NAPCO 1956 C2633C" printed mark and National Potteries Co. Cleveland "MADE IN JAPAN" silver foil label.

5.25in (13.5cm) high

$80-120　　　　　　　　　　　TSIS

A 1950s Arthur Wood cylindrical hand-painted storage jar.

6.5in (16.5cm) high

$20-30　　　　　　　　　　　MTS

A set of five late 1950s/early 1960s Cortendorf 'boomerang' shaped dishes, marked "Made in West Germany".

Boomerang or kidney shapes, such as seen on these dishes, are typical of 1950s design.

5.25in (13.5cm) wide

$20-30 (each)　　　　　　　　GROB

A 1950s German Goebels poodle salt and pepper set in shaped dish, marked "foreign", with bee in V mark.

Poodles call to mind elegant Parisian ladies and feature in many 1950s designs.

Tray 4.75in (12cm) wide

$120-180　　　　　　　　　　　BAD

A 1950s Japanese Freemo lady head vase, with original eye lashes and necklace, but lacking original earrings.

5.5in (14cm) high

$100-150　　　　　　　MAC

A 1950s Japanese Napco lady head vase, her green bonnet decorated with flowers, transfer mark "NAPCO C3812C 1959".

5.5in (14cm) high

$150-200　　　　　　　MAC

FIFTIES

A CLOSER LOOK AT A FREDERICK WEINBERG SCULPTURE

American sculptor Frederick Weinberg was active from the 1950s onwards and is known for his abstract figural designs.

From the mid-1940s and through the 1950s designs became for organic, rejecting the stark angular lines of early Modernism.

Weinberg was also influenced by Africa and tribal art, as can be seen in his other works on this page.

As well as sculpture, he also produced lighting and pieces for shop window displays.

A Frederick Weinberg wall relief, reinforced fibreglass casting, depicting stylized Trojan warriors, signed "F. Weinberg" on the back.

34in (85cm) high

$1,000-1,500   **SDR**

A Frederick Weinberg salmon-colored molded plaster abstract figural sconce, with some chips.

36in (90cm) high

$700-1,000   **SDR**

A Frederick Weinberg spray-painted cast iron figural sculpture.

9in (23cm) high

$200-250   **MG**

A Frederick Weinberg cast iron giraffe figural sculpture, painted orange later.

11.5in (29.5cm) high

$200-250   **MG**

A Frederick Weinberg spray-painted cast iron horse figural sculpture, stamped "©F.W."

7.75in (19.5cm) high

$200-250   **MG**

A 1950s '****ocraft' teak headrest or stool, with triangular Design Center sticker.

This small piece of furniture is based on an African headrest that meets Mid-Century Modern in terms of material and line.

14.25in (36cm) high

$25-35   **GAZE**

An American Alamo Savings & Loan Association 'The Satellite Bank' plated metal rocket-shaped money bank, marked "Duro Mold & Mfg. Inc. Detroit 34 Mich".

A set of six transfer-printed tall glasses, each decorated with a different scene of an ethnic couple dancing and playing instruments, with gilt rims.

These were produced by the same manufacturer as the following set.

5in (12.5cm) high

$80-120 **MA**

A set of six 'Hawaiian Melody' tall glasses, with transfer-printed scenes, each glass different, and gilt rims.

5in (12.5cm) high

$80-120 **MA**

The 'Space Race' between the US and the Soviet Union began around the launch of Russia's Sputnik 1 satellite on October 4th, 1957. It was to have a huge influence on design with motifs such as rockets, spaceman helmets, flying saucers and shooting stars appearing on all manner of objects.

10in (25cm) high

$150-200 **CVS**

A 1950s Celebrity 110-volt Coffee Clutch instant tea and coffee kit for home, travel and office, containing two melamine cups, two melamine milk or water containers, a heating element and a melamine spoon, contained in a printed bag.

8in (20.5cm) wide

$120-180 **MTS**

Four 1950s music-themed paper bags, for holding 45rpm singles.

8in (20cm) wide

$1-1.50 (each) **MA**

FILM & TV

A Marx Toy battery-operated red Dalek, in excellent condition and in original box marked "©BBC 1974".

c1974

$220-280 SAS

A Marx Toys battery-operated yellow Dalek, in excellent condition and in original box marked "©BBC 1974".

c1974

$220-280 SAS

A Denys Fisher Doctor Who Tardis, in excellent condition and in original box.

The two buttons on the top of Tardis worked a mechanism that could make an action figure seem to disappear inside the toy. This toy did not sell particularly well at the time, perhaps due to the two additional and distracting buttons, and can be hard to find today.

c1977

$220-280 SAS

A CLOSER LOOK AT TWO DOCTOR WHO ACTION FIGURES

This was the only one of Denys Fisher's Doctor Who range to be issued by Italian company Harbert.

The Doctor also retains his sonic screwdriver and extra-long scarf.

The Giant Robot only appeared in one storyline but resulted in an extremely accurately modeled action figure. He retains his shoulder shields, which is unusual.

Denys Fisher's Doctor Who figures were manufactured by US firm Mego whose film, TV and music related figures are collectable in their own right.

Two Denys Fisher Doctor Who action figures, comprising the Doctor in a Harbert Italian language box and the 'Giant Robot', both complete and in excellent condition and in original boxes.

c1976

$300-500 SAS

A Codeg 'Mechanical Dalek' silver and blue plastic clockwork figure, 117-22, in excellent condition, with original box marked "©BBCTV 1965".

Dalek toys were also made by Palitoy and Marx, which can also be seen on this page. The Codeg versions are usually the most valuable.

c1965

$700-1,000 SAS

A Palitoy Talking Dalek battery-operated figure, in original box marked "©1975 British Broadcasting Corporation".

c1975 7in (18cm) high

$280-320 GAZE

A Palitoy Doctor Who battery-operated Talking K-9 toy, 73009, in excellent condition and in original box.

Following the success of their Talking Dalek toys, Palitoy released the Talking K-9 soon after. The audio is supplied by a crude miniature record player inside.

c1978

$250-350 SAS

"Doctor Who: The Missing Adventures – The Ghosts of N-Space", by Barry Letts, published by Virgin Publishing.
1995

$10-15　　　　　　　TP

"Doctor Who: The Missing Adventures – Downtime", by Marc Platt, published by Virgin Publishing.
1996

$10-15　　　　　　　TP

"Doctor Who – The Handbook: The First Doctor", by Howe, Stammers and Walker, published by Virgin Publishing.
1994

$12-18　　　　　　　TP

"Doctor Who – The Handbook: The Sixth Doctor", by Howe, Stammers and Walker, published by Virgin Publishing.

1993

$12-18　　　TP

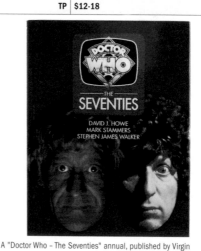

'Doctor Who Annual 1982', published by BBC TV and distributed by World Distributors.
1981

$10-15　　　　MTS

A "Doctor Who – The Seventies" annual, published by Virgin Publishing.
1994　　　　*12in (30.5cm) high*

$30-50　　　　　　　TP

'Doctor Who Annual 1984', published by BBC TV and distributed by World Distributors.

1983　　*10.5in (27cm) high*

$20-30　　　　　MTS

A Doctor Who 'Get Well Soon' greeting card, the inside with "What the Doctor ordered", the back marked "A Dennis A. Ian print licensed the BBC Enterprises Ltd.", in original plastic wrapper.
7.25in (18.5cm) high

$3-5　　　　　　MTS

A Doctor Who greeting card, the inside with "Always happy days", the back marked "A Dennis A. Ian print licensed the BBC Enterprises Ltd.", in original plastic wrapper.
7.25in (18.5cm) high

$3-5　　　　　　MTS

A Walt Disney's Black Hole 'V.I.N.Cent' plastic action figure, by Mego, lacks white plastic arms to front.

This film was not a great success for Disney at the time. The Mego toys were equally unpopular making them hard to find today. V.I.I.N.Cent was part of the first wave of figures released in 1979. The second series, released in 1980 is much scarcer. This example is incomplete and is lacking its 'arms'. Boxed examples could be worth up to $80.

1979   *2.25in (6cm) high*

$8-12   **KNK**

'Blow Up', soundtrack stereo LP, MGM E/SE-4447.

1966

$40-60   **GAZE**

A 'The Blues Brothers' pin.

Although John Belushi and Dan Aykroyd performed, in character, as a real band, the Blues Brothers started in a sketch on a tv show.

1.5in (3.5cm) diam

$20-25   **LDE**

A 1960s A.C. Gilbert for Sears James Bond figure.

3.5in (9cm) high

$10-15   **KNK**

A 1960s A.C. Gilbert for Sears James Bond's Auric Goldfinger figure.

One of a set of 10 Bond figures including Dr. No, Miss Moneypenny, M and Bond in three different poses.

3.25in (8.5cm) high

$10-15   **KNK**

An MB 'James Bond Thunderball' 007 Jigsaw puzzle, complete with 1,000 pieces.

c1965   *Box 14.25in (36cm) wide*

$30-50   **NOR**

A 'The Real James Dean Story' magazine.

11.25in (28.5cm) high

$60-80   **NOR**

A 'James Dean Album' magazine, produced to commemorate the life of the actor, with black and white images.

c1956   *11in (28cm) high*

$150-200   **NOR**

A 1960s 'I Like Richard - Dr Kildare' pin.

The character of Dr James Kildare first appeared on the silver screen in 1937 played by Joel McCrea. When the TV series was created in 1961, the character was taken over by Richard Chamberlain who became a teen idol. The series ended in 1965.

2.25in (5.5cm) diam

$60-80   LDE

A 'The Loves of Hercules' advertising laminated pocket calendar, with full-length portrait of Jayne Mansfield.

1964   4.25in (10.5cm) high

$25-35   LDE

A 'Jerry Lewis in The Nutty Professor' pin.

c1963   3.25in (8cm) high

$30-40   LDE

A 'Saturday Night Fever' pin, the back marked "Paramount Pictures".

c1977   1.5in (4cm) diam

$80-120   LDE

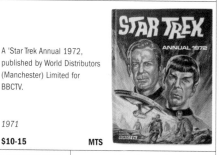

A late 1970s Starsearcher bubblebath/shampoo and sponge bath set, by K.L. Harris Ltd. England, boxed in Star Wars imitation packaging.

8in (20cm) high

$30-40   MTS

A 'Star Trek Annual 1972, published by World Distributors (Manchester) Limited for BBCTV.

1971

$10-15   MTS

A Kenner Terminator 2 'Secret Weapon' Terminator carded action figure.

1991   11.75in (30cm) high

$3-5   KNK

'The Thomas Crown Affair', original soundtrack LP SULP 1218, released by United Artists.

1968

$10-15   GAZE

A Mae West signed Grauman's Chinese Theatre program.

Grauman's Chinese Theatre is probably Hollywood's best known movie theatre and is home to a famous collection of Hollywood star footprints.

9.5in (24cm) high

$70-100   LDE

GLASS

COLLECTORS' NOTES

■ Machine-made pressed glass was produced from the early 19thC. It was perfected by the 1880s when developments allowed for complex molds and sophisticated machinery, that were often fully automated. Due to this, and the nature of the material itself, identical pieces could be mass-produced inexpensively, opening glass up to the masses.

■ Imitation cut glass was a popular, early style. The glass in this section was made from the 1920s-'30s, between the World Wars, and was largely inspired by the work of Lalique. Due to this comparatively short period of manufacture, certain pieces can be hard to find today.

■ Jobling and Bagley in Britain were two notable manufacturers, although many Czechoslovakian factories also produced similar pressed glass, often in strongly Art Deco styles. Both Jobling and Bagley began producing this type in the early 1930s, with Jobling, who had molds made by continental factory Franckhauser, ceasing at the outbreak of WWII.

■ Colors affect value, with opalescent glass being the most desirable. The stronger the opalescence, the more valuable it will usually be. British companies generally used green, pink, blue, amber and clear 'flint', while Czechoslovakian companies had a wider range of colors and tones, such as turquoise. German examples, such as those by Walther & Sohn, are usually stronger in tone.

■ There are many different shapes, with most being both decorative and functional. Centerpieces are a mainstay and were highly popular at the time, particularly as wedding gifts amongst the middle classes. Vases were the next most popular object.

■ Condition is important. Scratches, scuffs, chips and cracks will reduce value considerably. All values given here reflect items in mint condition with no damage unless stated, in which case the price reflects the damage. Surprisingly, mold lines, internal bubbles and even internal ash (workers were allowed to smoke while working) do not affect value. However, a collector will always prefer a perfect piece.

■ Modern reproductions do exist but are of little interest. They are generally lighter and smaller, and sometimes in different colors. Frosted areas can also be rougher as they are sandblasted rather than acid-etched.

A 1930s 'Seated Lady Holding Torch' pink pressed glass comport, by an unknown maker, with registered number 755635 for 16th June 1930.

Although the design was registered by M. & J. Guggenheim Ltd, the maker is not known. This is the sister piece to the blue 'Four Cherubs' also on this page.

10.5in (26.5cm) high

$200-300   **AAB**

A 1930s pink pressed glass two-piece compote, of a dancing girl holding her dress aloft.

From the shade of pink used, this is likely to be Czechoslovakian.

10.25in (26cm) high

$300-400   **AAB**

A 1930s two-piece pressed glass comport, possibly by Brockwitz, with molded floral arcs and floral garland decoration to bowl.

10.75in (27.5cm) high

$300-400   **AAB**

A 1930s German Walther 'Nymphen' green pressed glass two-piece comport.

As the bowl was often damaged or lost, the base is often sold as a candlestick due to the recess that would hold the bowl fitment.

12.5in (30.5cm) high

$200-300   **AAB**

A 1930s light blue pressed glass 'Four Cherubs Comport', by an unknown maker, with registered number for 15th July 1930.

This is comparatively common. The version with roses on the bowl is worth around 25 per cent more.

7.5in (19cm) high

$200-300   **AAB**

A German Walther 'Luttich' pink pressed glass four-piece centerpiece, with black glass base.

This is also known as 'Hollander' or 'Undine' depending on the style of the bowl the figure comes in.

8.5in (22cm) high

$120-180   **AAB**

A 1930s Sowerby 'Flora' Rosalin pink pressed glass three-piece centerpiece, with molded pattern of roses on the dish.

This is a comparatively common centerpiece.

8.5in (22cm) high

$70-100   **AAB**

A 1930s German Walther 'Schwalben' pink pressed glass three-piece centerpiece.

9in (23cm) high

$150-200   **AAB**

A 1930s German Walther 'Pelicans' pink pressed glass two-piece centerpiece.

The bowl is highly susceptible to damage, this example is intact.

11.5in (29.5cm) diam

$120-180   **AAB**

A CLOSER LOOK AT A CENTERPIECE

The figurine is more desirable than the bowl, and can be more desirable than the complete piece.

The figurine is worth nearly the same value on her own as the complete piece.

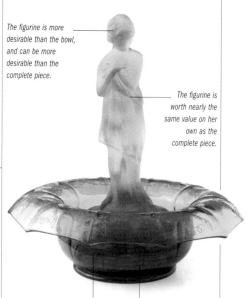

A 1930s amber pressed glass 'Windy Wendy' three-piece centerpiece, by an unknown maker, with molded hobnail bowl.

Guggenheim figurines also fit this bowl, perhaps indicating it was made by that factory.

9.75in (25cm) high

$220-280   **AAB**

A 1930s Jobling 'Dancing Girl & Block' yellow pressed glass three-piece centerpiece.

From the catalogue number of 11900, it appears that this would have been designed in the summer of 1934. It is rare to find matching colored bases, rather than black, as fewer were made.

9.5in (24cm) high

$200-300   **AAB**

This is the tallest of the lady figurines made, with her visual impact making her desirable.

Examples seen in the US often have opaque figurines and clear bowls.

A 1930s American Cambridge Glass Co. 'Draped Lady' centerpiece, the Depression glass-type bowl molded with a grape pattern.

Bowl 12.5in (31.5cm) diam

$300-400   **AAB**

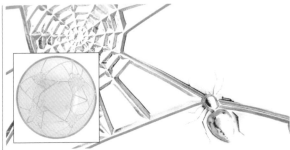

A 1930s Jobling amber pressed glass 'Fir Cone' bowl, catalogue no. 5000, registered design no. 777133 for 29th Sept 1932.

This was the first decorative (rather than functional) glass design Jobling registered.

8.5in (22cm) high

$45-65 AAB

A 1930s Jobling 'Uranium' green pressed glass 'Spider Web Bowl', with the spiders forming the three low feet, catalogue number 2567, registered design number 792167 for 21st April 1934.

Uranium green is generally more desirable than other colors, which are worth up to $180.

8.25in (21cm) diam

$150-200 AAB

A 1930s German Walther 'Lydia' blue and clear pressed glass powder puff jar, shape no.41228.

This is also available in Cloud glass, but it is very rare. See the DK Collectibles Price Guide 2006 by Judith Miller and Mark Hill for examples of Cloud glass.

5.5in (14cm) high

A 1930s Jobling opalescent pressed glass 'Bird Design Bowl', catalogue number 7000 with registration number 780717 for 17th February 1933.

This design and color strongly resembles French designs, however the opalescence on this example is very weak.

7.45in (19cm) diam

$200-300 AAB

A 1930s Sowerby 'Ladye Pot' lime green pressed glass powder puff pot.

Pale blue is usually worth less, at up to $180.

6.75in (17cm) high

$200-300 AAB

$200-300 AAB

A 1930s Art Deco frosted, clear pressed glass figurine of a draped nude, possibly French, by an unknown maker, mounted on a wooden base.

This is a large, well-molded and appealing figurine, with a naturalistic pose and good proportions.

9.25in (23.5cm) high

$200-300 AAB

A 1930s Czechoslovakian Art Deco green pressed glass figurine of a draped nude, mounted on a matching pedestal.

There is also a long-haired version of this figurine, which is of roughly the same value.

9.5in (24cm) high

$100-150 AAB

A 1930s Czechoslovakian Hoffman frosted clear pressed glass seated boy figurine, with butterfly mark.

This is usually found with a flat base and no protrusion. The butterfly mark on pressed glass indicates Hoffman as the manufacturer, not Baccarat as some books have erroneously indicated.

3.75in (9.5cm) high

$150-200 AAB

A 1930s Bagley blue pressed glass 'Tulip Lamp', no. 3025.

This shape is also found as a vase, the only difference being there is no hole for the wire.

8.25in (21cm) high

$200-300   **AAB**

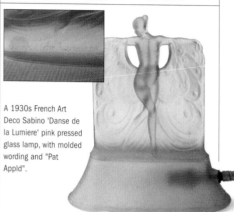

A 1930s French Art Deco Sabino 'Danse de la Lumiere' pink pressed glass lamp, with molded wording and "Pat Appld".

A 1930s Bagley green pressed glass star-shaped lamp, no. 934.

The condition is very important on these lamps, as the corners are easily chipped or cracked.

15in (38cm) high

$350-550   **AAB**

11.5in (29cm) high

$2,000-3,000   **AAB**

A 1930s Czechoslovakian Art Deco clear frosted pressed glass mantel clock.

Egyptian forms influenced the Art Deco movement. This design also appears on a similar dressing table set.

6.5in (16.5cm) high

$350-550   **AAB**

A 1930s German Walther & Sohn blue pressed glass 'Windsor' clock and 'Rheingold' vases garniture.

The clock is the rarest and most desirable component and is worth around $180 alone.

Vases 6in (15cm) high

$200-300   **AAB**

An American 'Bottom's Up' jade green pressed glass stirrup cup, molded "Patent 77725", mounted on a black glass base.

This is more common in clear 'flint', being worth up to $180, and rarest in opalescent jade green, being worth up to $350.

Cup 3.5in (9cm) high

$200-300   **AAB**

A late 1930s Bohemian Carlshutte pink pressed glass two-piece sailing boat flower display, registered number 812656 for 3rd June 1936.

10.75in (27.5cm) long

$120-180   **AAB**

A 1930s Czechoslovakian clear and frosted pressed glass 'polar bear on ice' ashtray, for the French market, marked "Tchecoslovaquie" on the base.

c1933   9.25in (23.5cm) long

$200-300   **AAB**

COLLECTORS' NOTES

■ Blenko was founded in 1922 in Milton, West Virginia by British-trained glass designer William John Blenko (1854-1933). Blenko's training and experience had been in stained glass for windows, but when demand fell, he used his experience to make decorative glass, which was introduced in 1929. It is this background that led to the strong and bright colours that are so loved by many today. Their glass proved successful and by the early 1930s it was being stocked in department stores such as Macy's of New York.

■ Although Blenko and his son William H. Blenko designed shapes, other designers were also employed. The first was Winslow Anderson, who designed for the company from 1947-53. He was followed by Wayne Husted (1952-63), Joel Myers (1963-70), John Nickerson (1970-74), Don Shepherd (1974-88), Hank Adams (1988-94) and others. Anderson is known for his Scandinavian-inspired forms, while Husted is known for his curving, sculptural shapes.

■ All pieces are hand-blown, most often using molds. The bases bear 'broken' pontil marks, where the piece was snapped off the glass blower's pontil rod after being finished. Labels and acid-etched marks were also used. Colour and form can be used to identify Blenko pieces. Some forms were only made in certain colours for certain periods of time, so it is best to learn typical Blenko colours and forms. Designs were copied widely by other West Virginia glassmakers.

■ Look out for vibrant colours and large pieces in unusual and eccentric sculptural forms, as these usually prove to be the most valuable and desirable. Examples with lime deposits from water are very hard to clean and are best avoided, unless rare. Handle stoppers with care as many are hollow. Also always examine decanter rims carefully for chips.

A Blenko Persian Blue conical decanter, shape 920, "Blenko Handcraft" silver foil hand-shaped label, designed by Winslow Anderson.

17.75in (46cm) high

$150-200   **HLM**

A Blenko green conical decanter, shape number 920, with teardrop-shaped stopper, designed by Winslow Anderson.

16.5in (42cm) high

$150-200   **HLM**

A Blenko Ruby conical decanter, shape number 920, with teardrop-shaped stopper, designed by Winslow Anderson.

16.25in (41cm) high

$150-200   **HLM**

A Blenko Tangerine amberina-type tall cased glass bottle, shape number 6427, with freeform rim and attenuated neck, designed by Joel Philip Myers in 1963.

A Blenko Tangerine conical decanter, shape number 920, with teardrop-shaped stopper, designed by Winslow Anderson.

22.75in (58cm) high

$250-300   **HLM**

A rare Blenko Tangerine decanter, shape number 5826, with bulbous stopper, designed by Wayne Husted in 1957.

c1959-60 16in (40cm)

$280-320   **HLM**

A Blenko Turquoise 'shotglass' decanter, with tall thin neck and hollow stopper with open top, designed by Wayne Husted.

17in (43cm) high

$300-400   **HLM**

Many of Myers' designs are similar to those of other studio glassmakers of the period. The studio glass movement began to take hold in the US from the early 1970s.

22.75in (58cm) high

$350-450   **HLM**

A Blenko Persian Blue bottle, shape number 9114L, with molded circle pattern, designed by Hank Adams in 1990.

Many of Adams' design feature molded textured surfaces, as here.

15in (38cm) high

$120-180   **HLM**

A Blenko Teal rectangular bottle, shape number 9029, molded with knobbles, designed by Hank Adams in 1990.

15.75in (40cm) high

$120-180   **HLM**

A Blenko Tangerine rectangular vase, with molded textured surface and concave discs.

12.5in (32cm) high

$200-250   **HLM**

A Blenko Tangerine vase, with mold-blown knobbly prunts and wavy rim, the base with broken pontil mark and 'Blenko' acid stamp, designed by Wayne Husted.

8in (20cm) high

$70-90   **HLM**

A Blenko Tangerine vase, shape number 6223, with horizontal bark-textured pattern and flared rim, designed by Wayne Husted in 1962.

12.75in (32.5cm) high

$120-180   **HLM**

A CLOSER LOOK AT A BLENKO DECANTER

At over 27.75in (50cm) in height it is a large and complex form with many bulbous curves, which are hallmarks of Husted's designs.

The cupped neck covering the bottom half of the hollow stopper is again typical of Husted's designs.

A large Blenko Turquoise footed bottle, shape number 6212, with elongated hollow teardrop-shaped stopper, designed by Wayne Husted in 1961 for the 1962 catalogue, the base with broken pontil and silver foil 'Blenko Handcraft' label.

20.5in (52cm) high

$150-250   **PC**

It is marked with a 'Blenko' acid stamp, which was used from 1958-61 and the silver foil Blenko label, which was used from the 1930s-1982, although remainders were used after this date until they were exhausted.

A Blenko Turquoise bottle, shape number 5922, designed by Wayne Husted in 1958, with silver foil Blenko hand-shaped label, the base broken pontil mark and 'Blenko' acid stamp.

1959-61

20.5in (52cm) high

$500-600   **HLM**

GLASS

A Sowerby amber cloud glass vase.

This is probably the only known example of Sowerby amber cloud glass. This shape was usually produced in clear 'flint' glass.

7.5in (19cm) high

$120-180 STE

A Davidson briar cloud glass 'Ripple' vase.

Cloud glass was introduced by George Davidson & Co. in 1923 and was largely discontinued after WWII, going completely out of production during the early 1960s. It is made by adding trails of a darker glass to a lighter glass base and then pressing the piece, causing random, abstract swirls to be created. Each piece is uniquely patterned. It was also produced by S. Reich & Co. and Walther in Europe, and Sowerby and Jobling in Britain.

1957-61   7in (18cm) high

$100-150 STE

A CLOSER LOOK AT A CLOUD GLASS FLOWER SET

This shape of flower bowl was produced from 1922 into the early 1960s.

All components of flower sets are usually in a matching color - this example has black components as no matching clear blue examples have yet been found.

This is in the very rare clear blue color - blue streaks on matte clear 'flint' glass - produced in the early 1960s only. Davidson's standard blue, made from 1925-34, had purple streaks on blue glass.

It is differentiated from the more common pattern no. 21 as it has either no recess to hold the flower holder or, on later examples, four short protrusions to do that job.

A Davidson clear blue cloud glass three-piece flower set, pattern no. 20.

Davidson cloud glass can be dated to a period from the shape and the color.

c1962   10.5in (27cm) diam

$1,200-1,800 STE

A Davidson tortoiseshell cloud glass vase, pattern no. 293.

Not commonly seen, tortoiseshell is actually amber cloud glass with both sides polished – most cloud glass has one matte side.

1931-36   6.5in (16.5cm) high

$40-60 STE

A Davidson 'Good Companion' amber cloud glass lamp, pattern no. 804, design number 804952 for 31st July 1935.

Davidson made two electric lamps, this model being named after J.B. Priestley's book. Green and purple versions are rare. The design number relates to the pattern on the shade, rather than the base.

1935-57

$600-700 STE

A Davidson amber cloud glass barleytwist candlestick, pattern no. 283.

c1912-30   3in (7.5cm) high

$50-70 STE

A Davidson briar cloud glass vase, pattern no. 1907TD.

The 'T' in the shape number stands for 'Tiny'.
'D' was used for 'Downturned rim'.

1957-60   4.75in (12cm) wide

$25-35   STE

A Davidson green cloud glass 'Everest' ashtray, registered May 1938, made for T.H. Lawley & Company Ltd.

1938-41 5in (12.5cm) wide

$100-150   STE

A Walther 'Malachit' cloud glass 'Rotterdam' plate.

1935-39   8.75in (22cm) diam

$180-220   STE

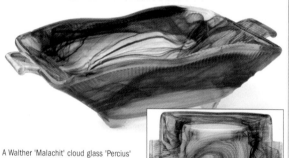

A Walther 'Malachit' cloud glass 'Percius' dish.

1935-39   12.25in (31cm) diam

$180-220   STE

An S. Reich & Co. pink cloud glass chamberstick.

1925-30   4in (10cm) wide

$120-180   STE

An S. Reich & Co. light green cloud glass chamberstick.

1925-30   4in (10cm) wide

$120-180   STE

FIND OUT MORE...

www.cloudglass.com

Davidson Glass – A History by Chris & Val Stewart, 2005, ISBN 0955036305.

A rare S. Reich & Co. cobalt blue cloud glass 'Viktoria' trinket set.

The 'Viktoria' is the only trinket set known to have been produced in cloud glass. The vase, water jug, tumblers, sugar and cream are missing from this set.

1925-30   11in (28cm) wide

$1,000-1,500   STE

COLLECTORS' NOTES

■ Modern glass design, produced in the former Communist country of Czechoslovakia from c1945-c1989, has becoming increasingly popular and sought-after over the past five years. Previously, very little was known about developments as the country was behind the 'iron curtain' or was restructuring after the 'velvet revolution' of 1989. Information is now emerging and cooperation is growing, enabling researchers and collectors to learn more.

■ Leading names include Stanislav Libensky, Frantisek Vízner, Pavel Hlava, René Roubícek and Jirí Harcuba. Although some problems existed, the Communist regime generally allowed them to work freely, enabling them to experiment and produce innovative, modern designs, which are only just being widely understood. Many also trained the next generation of designers, who continue to push the boundaries of glass design and technique today.

■ As well as the unique, studio-type or architectural pieces produced by these designers, mass-produced, often hand-pressed, glass was also made in the many factories that made up the historic Bohemian glass

industry. The largest included Crystalex and the Sklo Union, the latter a conglomerate of existing glass factories that was created in 1965. They produced very high quality hand-pressed glass in quintessentially modern designs by leading, specially trained, glass designers of the time such as Frantisek Peceny and Adolf Matura.

■ Most of the designs were produced for long periods, from the 1950s-80s, and in large numbers, with much being exported. Many designs date from the early 1960s, but some pieces were made from existing pre-WWII molds. Always aim to buy pieces in the best condition possible as comparatively large numbers of examples survive and prices are also comparatively affordable.

■ Many designs have been identified, but work is still being undertaken to identify all the designs, makers and designers. Look out for a shiny shallow depression on the base with a flat machine-cut rim and good quality molding. Although these are not truly reliable hallmarks, it is a good indication that the piece is certainly Central European in origin.

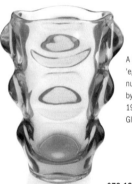

A Sklo Union light blue 'egg' vase, pattern number 20047, designed by Frantisek Vízner in 1962 for the Hermanova Glassworks.

7.75in (19.5cm) high

$70-100   **GROB**

A Sklo Union small brown lobe rimmed vase.

This design is similar to those of James Hogan for Whitefriars, and pressed glass from some French factories. The base, however, clearly identifies it as being from the Sklo Union factories. From known drawings of a similar vase, it is probably an early design by Frantisek Vízner.

5.75in (14.5cm) high

$30-50   **GC**

A Sklo Union vase, pattern number 13162, with curved rim and bark textured exterior, designed by Frantisek Vizner for the Hermanova Glassworks in 1962.

5.5in (13.5cm) high

$70-100   **MHC**

A Sklo Union green lobed and waisted vase.

This is also found in other colors such as yellow and blue.

6in (15cm) high

$25-35   **GC**

A grey glass vase, possibly by Sklo Union or a Scandinavian factory, with molded concentric squares.

9.75in (24.5cm) high

$50-70   **GC**

A Sklo Union vase, with protruding bands with concave 'lenses', designed by Frantisek Peceny in 1961.

This was still available from distributors into the early 1970s, and came in three sizes.

8in (20cm) high

$30-50   **MHC**

A Sklo Union wide clear hobnail jardinière, pattern number 13236, designed by Rudolf Jurnikl in 1964.

This pattern is also found in tall vases, low vases and ashtrays in various different colors including a strong purple.

8.5in (21.5cm) long

$30-50 GC

A Sklo Union amethyst glass ashtray, pattern number 983/17, with molded cigarette rests, designed by Adolf Matura for the Libochovice Glassworks in 1962.

6in (15.5cm) diam

$20-30 GC

A Harrachov Glassworks (Borske Sklo) 'Harttil' glass bowl, with internal webbing of woven glass fibres.

These ashtrays are often mistaken for Murano. The development of this technique of casing glass fibres in glass by Milos Pulpitel and Milan Metalek was revolutionary. Organic forms and pulled rims are typical.

1955-60   5.25in (8cm) wide

$40-60 AG

A CLOSER LOOK AT A SKLO UNION VASE

The molded pattern is cleverly designed to be read two ways – as a face looking at the viewer or as two profiles kissing one another.

Press moulding was not the only technique used here. After being molded, it has been fire-polished to give a shiny, reflective finish and then parts have been treated with acid to produce a matte, frosted appearance.

It was also available as a lower, wider footed vase, which is worth around the same value.

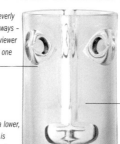

A Sklo Union 'Head' series vase, pattern number 3484/145, designed by Adolf Matura for the Libochovice Glassworks in 1972.

Adolf Matura is considered an important modern Czech glass designer and is known for his functional tableware such as the 'Praha' range designed in 1971.

9in (23cm) high

$80-120 MHC

A Jurnikl amethyst glass ashtray, pattern number 1045/17, with undulating rim, designed by Rudolf Jurnikl for the Rosice Glassworks in 1962.

6.75in (17cm) diam

$30-40 GROB

A Cesky Kristal mold blown glass vase, designed by Pavel Hlava in 1959, with internal conical forms and graduated red to yellow colouring, and with engraved signature to base.

This questions the distinction between a sculptural object and a practical vase.

Tallest 14.25in (36cm) high

$350-450 WW

A Novy Bor (Crystalex) mold-blown lidded jar, with green body, pink lid and blue knop, designed by Eric Hoglund, signed and dated "E. Hoglund-92 Novy Bor".

Hoglund is better known for his 1960s-70s designs for Swedish factory Boda.

$60-90 GAZE

GLASS

A CLOSER LOOK AT AN ENGRAVED VASE

Jiří Harcuba (b.1928) is one of the most respected and experienced glass engravers in the world, and has both studied and taught at numerous prestigious institutions.

This piece is dated 1965, the year Harcuba won first prize at the national Czechoslovakian glass exhibition and, unusually for the time, lectured at the Royal College of Art, London.

The geometric pattern of lines and shapes of different widths and depths is typical of Harcuba's spontaneous approach to engraving, where he almost 'draws' onto the surface.

The back has a polished concave 'lens' which magnifies the designs when it is viewed through it.

A Jiří Harcuba hand-cut glass pillow-shaped vase, with a deeply cut cross-hatched pattern in the form of an abstract tree, the reverse with concave cut polished 'lens' to view main panel, signed "J. Harcuba 1965".

1965

8.25in (21cm) high

$3,000-5,000

PC

A 1930s Moser of Karlsbad waisted and facet-cut vase, with thick applied gilt rim.

5.25in (13.5cm) high

$100-150 MHT

A set of six Moser of Karlsbad hand-engraved amber shot glasses, each with a similar tree, kingfisher and rushes design, in an "Bohemia Moser Praha" card box.

As they are hand-engraved, each glass has a slightly different design.

2.25in (6cm) high

$100-150 MHT

A Novy Bor vase, with internal dark and light blue spiralling vertical veins and horizontal white lines.

8in (20cm) high

$180-220 MHT

A Palme König green spiralling ribbed glass vase, with slight fumed iridescence.

This colour and form with its frilled rim are typical of the company's designs, which were similar to Loetz designs.

c1905 6.5in (16.5cm) diam

$100-150 MHT

A Skrdlovice Glassworks purple heart-shaped vase, with random internal bubbles, designed by Vladimir Jelínek.

c1960 5.75in (14.5cm) high

$500-700 MHT

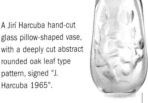

A Jiří Harcuba hand-cut glass pillow-shaped vase, with a deeply cut abstract rounded oak leaf type pattern, signed "J. Harcuba 1965".

1965 8.25in (21cm) high

$3,000-5,000 PC

FIND OUT MORE...

Czech Glass 1945-1980: Design In An Age Of Adversity, by Helmut Ricke, published by Arnoldsche, 2005.

An American Hazel Atlas Glass Co. 'Royal Lace' pattern green dessert dish.

2.75 (7cm) high

$12-18   **GROB**

An American Hazel Atlas Glass Co. 'Royal Lace' pattern green Depression glass trio set.

Plate 5.75in (14.5cm) diam

$20-30   **GROB**

An American Hazel Atlas Glass Co. 'Royal Lace' pattern green Depression glass pitcher.

Depression glass was mass-produced inexpensively during the 1920s and '30s using a mechanical pressing technique. Its bright colors and low prices made it attractive in difficult times. Today, most collect by patterns, which cross natural, geometric and historical themes. Always aim to buy in the best condition possible as large quantities were made.

6.75in (17.5cm) high

$25-45   **GROB**

An American Hazel Atlas Glass Co. 'Royal Lace' pattern cobalt blue Depression glass twin-handled cup.

Royal Lace was made from 1934-41.

4.25in (10.5cm) high

$15-20   **GROB**

An American Hazel Atlas Glass Co. 'Royal Lace' pattern pink Depression glass plate.

6in (15cm) diam

$7-9   **GROB**

An American Jeanette Glass Co. 'Cherry Blossom' pattern pink Depression glass twin-handled cup.

3.25in (8.25cm) high

$20-30   **GROB**

An American Jeanette Glass Co. 'Cherry Blossom' pattern pink Depression glass cup and saucer.

Cherry Blossom was produced from 1930-39. Crystal, Jadeite and red are the rarest colors.

5.5in (14cm) diam

$35-45   **GROB**

An American Jeanette Glass Co. 'Cherry Blossom' pattern pink Depression glass milk jug.

3.25in (8.5cm) high

$22-28   **GROB**

An American Hazel Atlas Glass Co. 'Moderntone' pattern colbalt blue Depression glass trio set.

Moderntone was made from 1934-42 and again in the late 1940s and '50s.

Plate 6in (15cm) diam

$40-60   **GROB**

COLLECTORS' NOTES

■ The Higgins Studio was founded in 1948 by Frances and Michael Higgins. They had met at the Chicago Institute of Design, with Frances first experiencing the slumping technique they became renowned for at a ceramics course in Cincinnati in 1942. She then decided to slump plate glass into molds, decorating the surface with molten glass strands. Later, Frances introduced the technique of fusing layers of glass in the kiln, while Michael brought the idea of including pieces of coloured glass between these layers.

■ Their deep love of colour is clear in their work, which is typically bold and strong, focusing on round or square dish forms. An early distributor was Richard Morgenthal, who founded Raymor, but their breakthrough was when they worked at Dearborn

Glass Co. in Chicago from 1957-64. Pieces produced there can be recognised from the gilt transfer "higgins" facsimile signature, with earlier and later pieces usually having an engraved name.

■ After Dearborn, they worked with Haeger until 1966 before returning to their own independent studio, where they worked until Michael died in 1999 and Frances died in 2004. Their striking and individual work is becoming increasingly sought-after, particularly large strongly coloured pieces, which make bold visual statements typical of the period. Examine pieces closely for scratches or chips. Examples can be found in the Metropolitan Museum of Art, New York and the Victoria & Albert Museum, London, England.

A Higgins blue and green on purple ground slump and sandwich glass bowl, with gilt transfer "higgins" signature.

12in (30.5cm) diam

$150-250   **HLM**

A Higgins small circular slump and sandwich glass dish, with gilt spiral, circles and gilt transfer signature.

4.25in (11cm) diam

$60-80   **HLM**

A very large Higgins light blue and green slump and sandwich glass charger, with gilt "higgins" signature.

17in (43cm) diam

$300-400   **HLM**

A Higgins 'Classic Line' slump and sandwich glass bowl, with white line and dot and gilt spiral pattern and gilt "higgins" signature.

The lines were applied with a syringe, which allowed control of the flow and thus the thickness of the line itself.

12.25in (31cm) diam

$200-250   **HLM**

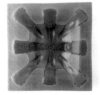

A Higgins 'Siamese' blue, violet and green slump and sandwich glass square dish, with gilt transfer "higgins" signature.

7in (17.5cm) wide

$100-150   **HLM**

A Higgins 'Mandarin' slumped sandwich glass ashtray, with molded cigarette rests and gold "higgins" transfer signature.

Large numbers of Mandarin pieces were made at Dearborn, as was this example.

10in (25.5cm) high

$120-180   **HLM**

A Higgins 'Patchwork' yellow, red and orange slump sandwich glass rectangular dish, with gilt overlay and gilt transfer "higgins" signature.

7in (17.5cm) long

$100-150   **HLM**

COLLECTORS' NOTES

■ Mdina was founded on Malta in 1968 by ex-Royal College of Art tutor Michael Harris (1933-94). Studio glass techniques has just arrived in the UK from the US and Harris quickly adapted them to function on a commercial basis. Colors are typically in the greens, blues and sand of the Mediterranean landscape and examples are chunky, being rendered in thick glass. Shapes include vases, bowls, dishes and paperweights.

■ Characteristic shapes, such as the 'Fish' vase, are the most desirable, as are large pieces. Production was aimed at the tourist market, as well as export, and tended to be focused on smaller, portable pieces. Harris did not approve of signing pieces with his name, making those that are signed in this way rare. Most other pieces are simply signed with the studio name. Harris left in 1972 and pieces produced after this date are currently slightly less desirable, although all Mdina glass has become increasingly sought-after in recent years.

■ After leaving Malta, Harris founded his second studio on the Isle of Wight in the same year. Ranges from the 1970s tend to be executed with broad swirls of color, in deep blues, ochres, browns and pink. The turning point in the studio's history came in 1978, when Harris and RCA student William Walker devised the 'Azurene' range, where surfaces are decorated with silver and 22ct gold leaf. This became one of most popular and collected ranges produced and is still sought-after today.

■ Other popular, best selling ranges include 'Meadow Garden' and 'Golden Peacock'. However, as the market is still growing, look out for rarities produced for short periods of time, as these can be valuable. The level of experimentation begun by Harris has been continued by his widow Elizabeth and son Timothy, and many innovative and colorful ranges have been produced. As with Mdina, both values and the number of collectors are increasing, making this a vibrant collecting area.

A 1970s Mdina vase, in amethyst-tinted glass with applied blue-green trails.

7.25in (18.5cm) high

$50-70   **GAZE**

A Mdina 'Tricorn' vase, with turned-over rim and polished base.

The slightly off-centre and bulbous nature of this vase reinforces the handmade nature of Mdina glass. This is a large and uncommon Tricorn form.

c1970   7in (18cm) high

$280-320   **ART**

A Mdina deep purple 'Fish' vase, the purple core cased in clear and then purple glass.

These smaller Fish vases are early and were likely to have been made by Harris himself. Purple is a rare, early color – in more standard colors they can be worth up to $200.

1968-69   6in (15cm) high

$280-320   **MHC**

A large Mdina glass 'Sculpture', designed, made and signed on the base by Michael Harris.

In a spectacle for the audience, Harris trailed molten glass onto a surface to create these visually impactful sculptures. The size and his signature make this even more valuable.

c1970   12.25in (31cm) high

$500-700   **CHEF**

A scarce Mdina glass large 'Tricorn' dish, with swirling green/beige pattern and polished base.

It is difficult to control the glass to form this tricorn shape. This shape was only produced towards the end of Harris' time at Mdina, and in very small numbers. The green swirls turn a sandy brown when light passes through them.

c1971   14.5in (37cm) widest

$300-400   **PC**

A 1970s Isle of Wight Studio Glass 'Lollipop' vase, with internal green and blue swirls cased in clear glass.

6.5in (16.5cm) high

$120-180 **GAZE**

A CLOSER LOOK AT AN ISLE OF WIGHT GLASS CHARGER

Pink & Blue Swirls is a comparatively scarce range as it did not prove as popular as other ranges, such as 'Aurene' and particularly 'Tortoiseshell'.

This example is signed by Michael Harris on the base, which adds further to its rarity and value.

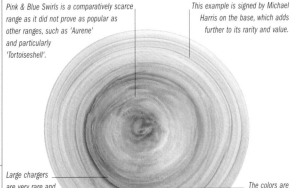

Large chargers are very rare and could only be made by Michael Harris himself. They were also very expensive at the time and very few were produced for sale.

The colors are deep and strong, which is unusual for such a large piece where the colored enamels became paler as the piece was blown outwards.

An Isle of Wight Studio Glass 'Pink & Blue Swirls' charger, made by Michael Harris, with polished base, signed "Michael Harris Isle of Wight".

c1974-76 — 19in (48.5cm) diam

$800-1,200 **GAZE**

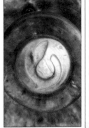

An Isle of Wight Studio Glass 'Aurene' cylinder vase, the base with impressed 'flame' pontil mark.

This is much more typical of the rich and bold coloring of this range. The iridescent streak is left when salts escape from the join near the pontil rod and is not a sign of fumed iridescence.

c1975-c1982 — 8in (20cm) high

$120-180 **ART**

An unusual Isle of Wight Studio Glass 'Aurene' globe vase, with impressed 'flame' pontil mark to base.

This example is unusual as it is primarily in clear glass. The light coating of enamels at the top and base gives a delicate feel to the piece.

c1975-c1982 — 5in (12.5cm) high

$70-100 **TGM**

An Isle of Wight Studio Glass black 'Azurene' low bowl, with silver and gold leaf and flat polished base.

This example is from the studio's archive room and was used as a 'model' piece for other glassmakers to copy due to its superb Azurene finish. This shape is sometimes known as the 'Doughnut'.

c1979 — 4.75in (12cm) diam

$100-150 **ART**

An early Isle of Wight Studio Glass pre-Minimal range Azurene dove, with silver and gold leaf and triangular label to base.

1981-82 — 1.5in (4cm) high

$40-50 **ART**

An Isle of Wight Studio Glass 'Blue Azurene' Lollipop vase, with flat polished base.

1979-88   9in (23cm) high

$120-180   **TGM**

A CLOSER LOOK AT AN ISLE OF WIGHT STUDIO GLASS VASE

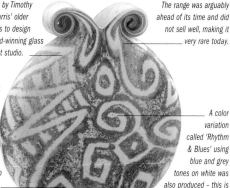

Jazz was designed by Timothy Harris, Michael Harris' older son, who continues to design and produce award-winning glass at the Isle of Wight studio.

Colored powdered enamels were laid on a surface and a finger drawn through them to give the pattern – the hot glass body was then rolled over them to coat the surface.

The range was arguably ahead of its time and did not sell well, making it very rare today.

A color variation called 'Rhythm & Blues' using blue and grey tones on white was also produced - this is even rarer than 'Jazz'.

An Isle of Wight Studio Glass 'Jazz' vase, designed and made by Timothy Harris, with opaque white glass background and pulled, curling rim.

1992-93   6in (15cm) high

$300-400   **PC**

An Isle of Wight Studio Glass 'Golden Peacock Royale' perfume bottle, with gold foil and trailed iridescent swirls.

The trailed stopper is a hallmark of this range, which was one of the most popular at the time, selling in large numbers.

1987-98   4in (10cm) high

$80-120   **PC**

An Isle of Wight Studio Glass 'Nightscape' glass paperweight, with triangular black sticker.

c1990   3in (7.5cm) high

$80-120   **GAZE**

An extremely rare Isle of Wight Studio Glass 'Pink Fizz' paperweight.

This is a variation of 'Golden Rain' designed by Timothy Harris. The surface is slightly fumed to give a gentle iridescence bringing the gold foil and mottled pink to life.

1987   2.25in (5.5cm) high

$150-200   **MHC**

An Isle of Wight Studio Glass Meadow Garden 'Poppy' globe vase, with flat polished base.

Globe vases in this size from this range were produced for one year only

1988   4in (10cm) high

$80-120   **PC**

FIND OUT MORE...

Michael Harris: Mdina Glass & Isle of Wight Studio Glass, by Mark Hill, published by Mark Hill Publishing, www.markhillpublishing.com, ISBN 978-0-9552865-1-3.

www.isleofwightstudioglass.co.uk

COLLECTORS' NOTES

- The Morgantown Glassworks was founded in 1899 in Morgantown, West Virginia. Its tableware products were hand-blown and remained primarily colorless until c1918, when color was introduced. Sales offices existed across the US but much of the production was exported to Australia, Mexico and Europe.

- In 1903, the company became known as the 'Economy Tumbler Company' and produced functional wares for domestic, industrial and commercial uses. During the 1920s and '30s, new colors were introduced to the range, which was largely inexpensive. The popular 'Continental Line' was developed during the early 1920s and, in 1929, the company became known as Morgantown once again.

- The factory closed from 1937-39, but went on to introduce a rainbow of new colors during the 1940s and '60s. Modern designs accompanied this, often in starkly geometric clean-lined shapes reminiscent of Scandinavian glass of the period. These pieces, like those shown here, were mold-blown and usually have thin bodies. In 1965, the company was acquired by Fostoria Glass Company. The factory closed in 1971.

- Many sought-after earlier works feature distinctive etched or cut designs. Look out for modern forms produced from the 1960s onwards, particularly in strong colors. Avoid examples with chips, internal bubbles or with excessive liming from water as these destroy the inherent clarity of the glass.

A 1960s Morgantown Peacock blue 'American Modern' mold-blown compote or footed dish, designed by Russel Wright.

6in (15cm) diam

$30-40   **HLM**

A 1960s Morgantown Peacock blue mold-blown 'Susquehanna' footed vase or bowl, with angular form.

Morgantown are situated in the same West Virginia area as Viking and Blenko.

5.5in (14cm) high

$40-50   **HLM**

A 1960s Morgantown Peacock blue 'Tuscany' waisted double conical mold-blown glass vase.

5in (13cm) high

$25-35   **HLM**

A Morgantown Peacock blue 'Federal' mold-blown and cased patio light or footed vase.

8.5in (21.5cm) high

$30-40   **HLM**

A Morgantown yellow 'Federal' mold-blown and cased patio light or footed vase.

8.5in (21.5cm) high

$30-40   **HLM**

A Morgantown large yellow 'Wheatley' mold-blown bottle vase.

17.25in (44cm) high

$150-200   **HLM**

Six Morgantown Chartreuse 'American Modern' small stemmed sherbet glasses, designed by Russel Wright.

Russel Wright designed a number of shapes for Morgantown that accompanied his 'American Modern' ceramic designs for Steubenville. They came in five colours; Chartreuse, Granite, Gray, Coral and Seafoam.

2.25in (5.5cm) high

$120-180   **HLM**

FIND OUT MORE...

Morgantown Glass, by Jeffrey B. Snyder, published by Schiffer Books, 2000

Be in the know and pocket the profit

With Judith Miller's authoritative visual guides.

"DK has made it easy for buyers, sellers and collectors to identify and value antiques and collectibles quickly with these beautiful, full-color guides from internationally renowned expert, Judith Miller."

—*BookPage*

For additional titles, visit **www.dk.com**

GLASS

COLLECTORS' NOTES

■ Glass has been made on the Venetian island of Murano since the 13thC. During the 1950s, designs underwent a radical transformation, breaking away from the traditional forms and patterns made for centuries. Old techniques were not abandoned, but were used in innovative ways. Colors became brighter, more exuberant, and almost painterly. Forms and patterns grew ever more abstract, often being sculptural.

■ At the forefront of this design renaissance were historic, leading factories such as Venini, Seguso, Salviati and A.V.e.M. (Arte Vetreria Muranese). They employed new designers such as Dino Martens, Fulvio Bianconi and Flavio Poli to breathe new 'modern' life into their hand-blown glass. Today, pieces by these factories and designers tend to fetch the highest values, particularly landmark designs such as the 'fazzoletto' or 'Oriente' vases.

■ Many of these designs were copied in subsequent decades by the vast number of smaller factories producing glass for the tourist market. Along with novelty forms such as clowns and fish, these tend to be less valuable but make an accessible and visually rewarding entry to the market. Examine pieces carefully as chips, scratches and errors such as internal bubbles (unless intended as part of the pattern) devalue a piece. Look out for wildly colorful and exuberant forms and read reference books to help you spot hidden but notable designer treasures.

An A.V.e.M clear cased vase, in the shape of a seated llama, designed by Manfredo Brosi and Ferdinando Toso, with stripes of opaque yellow, purplish-black and white glass.

c1954   7.6in (19cm) high

$150-200   **VZ**

An A.V.e.M vase, designed by Giulio Radi, with an opaque white body cased in amber and purple-black glass, the exterior with gold foil inclusions.

c1950   8.5in (21.5cm) high

$1,500-2,000   **VZ**

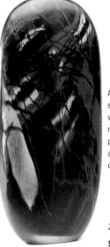

A Michele Burato hand-blown sculptural glass 'Pietra Focaia' vessel, of elliptical form with marbelized red and chartreuse pattern on black ground, with aventurine accents, signed, dated and titled on base.

2002   20in (51cm) high

$1,800-2,000   **SDR**

A Cenedese 'D' vase, designed by Antonio da Ros, the dark turquoise core heavily cased in flashed yellow glass, with, manufacturer's label to base .

c1962   10.6in (26.5cm)

$1,500-2,000   **VZ**

A Salviati incalmo vase, with a bottle green base and a wide clear glass lip with white spirals.

1960   10in (25.5cm) high

$800-1,200   **JN**

A Seguso Vetri D'Arte sommerso glass vase, the amethyst bowl cased in red and cased again in clear glass, possibly designed by Flavio Poli.

1960   7in (18cm) high

$700-900   **JN**

A Seguso Vetri D'Arte tapering red glass vase, with aventurine inclusions, the base acid etched "Seguso, Murano".

15in (37.5cm) high

$300-500   **WW**

A CLOSER LOOK AT A MURANO GLASS VASE

A Venini amber 'Corroso' glass amphora vase, with acid-etched stamp to base.

The lightly textured, almost matte 'corroso' effect is obtained by treating the surface of the glass with acid.

10.25in (26cm) high

$200-300 GC

This form is also known as a 'fazzoletto', the Italian word for 'handkerchief'.

This example is marked with the Venini acid stamp – the form was widely copied and if you want to collect Venini examples always look for this mark.

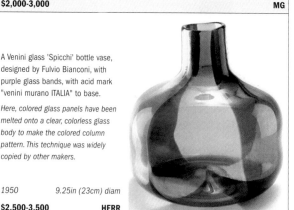

The witty form was designed by Paolo Venini and Fulvio Bianconi around 1949-50 and was meant to represent a dropped handkerchief 'frozen' in time and space.

As well as being executed in an unusual bold red-cased white, typical of the 1960s and '70s, it is very large, hence its high value.

A 1960s Venini large red cased opaque white handkerchief vase, the base with "Venini Murano" acid stamp and Venini round gold foil label.

10.25in (26cm) high

$2,000-3,000 MG

A Venini brown bottle vase, designed by Tony Zuccheri.

1966-70 9in (23cm) high

$600-800 JN

A Venini glass 'Spicchi' bottle vase, designed by Fulvio Bianconi, with purple glass bands, with acid mark "venini murano ITALIA" to base.

Here, colored glass panels have been melted onto a clear, colorless glass body to make the colored column pattern. This technique was widely copied by other makers.

1950 9.25in (23cm) diam

$2,500-3,500 HERR

A Venini amber glass pitcher, with pulled lip and acid etched mark to base.

7.75in (20cm) high

$150-200 TCM

A Venini red and blue glass 'Clessidre' hourglass sculpture, designed by Paolo Venini in 1955, unmarked.

5in (12.5cm) high

$700-1,000 SDR

A Zanetti Vetreria Artistica glass pelican sculpture, designed by Licio or Oscar Zanetti, with applied purple glass beak and feet, the base signed "Zanetti" in vibropen.

Zanetti was founded on Murano in 1959 by glassmaker Oscar Zanetti and his son Licio. Sculptural forms such as birds and other motifs from nature are typical of the company's production.

9.25in (23.5cm) high

$800-1,000 MG

A Murano sommerso glass vase, with blue/green and green glass layers heavily cased in clear glass, and pulled rim.

Such asymmetric, curving and almost organic forms were typical of the 1950s and '60s and were inspired by Flavio Poli's work with the sommerso technique during the 1940s and '50s at Seguso Vetri D'Arte.

6.25in (16cm) high

$350-550 HLM

A Murano small purple, blue and clear cased asymmetric teardrop-shaped glass vase, with pulled rim.

6.25in (16cm) high

$180-280 HLM

A Murano sommerso glass vase, the ovoid red body heavily cased in yellow and with two pulled wings.

10.25in (26cm) high

$300-550 HLM

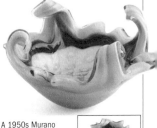

A Murano sommerso large blue, amber and clear cased glass vase.

Note how the many cut facets add an optical element to the sommerso design. This style can also be found on ashtrays, which tend to be less popular and valuable than vases. This example is also large.

9.75in (24.5cm) high

$120-180 GAZE

A Murano glass vase, with applied red and blue stripes and gold inclusions.

Compare this to the 'Spicchi' vase on the previous page, as it is made in a similar manner.

3.25in (8cm) high

$40-50 GC

A 1950s Murano glass ashtray, with pulled, curled rim and controlled internal bubbles.

8.5in (21.5cm) wide

$50-70 GC

A Murano yellow and green glass bird sculpture, with elongated 'S' shaped neck and green striped body.

12.5in (32cm) high

$100-150 MG

A Murano glass cobalt blue tricorn-shaped ashtray, with internal controlled bubbles.

5.5in (14cm) wide

$30-40 GROB

A very large Murano glass glass clown-shaped decanter, with applied bow tie, 'buttons', shoes, hands and facial features.

16.5in (42cm) high

$300-400 MG

FIND OUT MORE...

DK Collectors Series: 20th Century Glass, *by Judith Miller, published by DK, 2004.*

A CLOSER LOOK AT A SCANDINAVIAN VASE

A Danish Kastrup blue vase, designed by Jacob Bang.

c1960   *9.75in (24.5cm) high*

$120-180   **GC**

The 'Naebvase' or 'Beak Vase' was designed by Lütken in 1951 and can be found in different forms and sizes, this being the most commonly seen.

The name comes from the shape of the rim, which is created by pulling the molten glass with tongs and then swinging the piece, with gravity elegantly elongating the pulled areas.

The asymmetric, organic form is typical of both 1950s Scandinavian glass design and Lütken's designs during this period – it is also typically found in this color or clear, colorless glass.

Beware of unmarked examples, and those marked "H2" as they often bear faults, which disturb the design. Until 1962 pieces were dated around the monogram.

A 1960s-70s Danish Holmegaard aqua 'Beak' vase, designed by Per Lütken, the base engraved with artist's monogram and factory production number "15272".

6.5in (16.5cm) high

A Danish Kastrup antique green vase, designed by Jacob Bang.

c1960   *5.75in (14.5cm) high*

$60-80   **GC** | **$70-90**   **FD**

A Danish Kastrup capri blue angular vase, designed by Jacob Bang, with original label.

Jacob Bang (1899-1965) joined Holmegaard as Chief Designer in 1927. He left the glass industry in 1941 but rejoined Kastrup in 1957. He is known for his clean-lined, ultra-modern forms with no surface decoration.

c1960   *8.25in (21cm) high*

$70-100   **GC**

A Danish Kastrup smoke gray conical vase, designed by Jacob Bang.

c1960   *10in (25.5cm) high*

$40-60   **GC**

A Danish Kastrup small green conical vase, designed by Jacob Bang.

8in (20.5cm) high

$35-45   **GC**

A Danish Holmegaard smoke grey 'Aristocrat' decanter, designed by Per Lütken, with six 'Scanada' glasses.

Designed in 1956, this was produced until 1990. The decanter alone can be worth up to $180.

15in (38cm) high

$220-280   **FD**

A Finnish Iittala 'Kalvolan Kanto' vase, designed by Tapio Wirkkala, the base signed "_3241 Tapio Wirkkala".

'Kalvolan Kanto' means 'tree stump', demonstrating the influence the Scandinavian landscape had on Wirkkala's designs. It is an early modern Scandinavian glass design, dating from 1947, and was part of a range that caused great sensation at the Milan Triennale in 1951.

4.5in (11.5cm) high

$300-400 **MHT**

A Finnish Iittala 'Pinus' vase, designed by Tapio Wirkkala, the base signed "TW".

8.75in (22.5cm) high

$280-320 **MHT**

A 1970s Finnish Iittala 'Ultima Thule' textured glass beaker, designed by Tapio Wirkkala.

Ultima Thule was designed for Finnair to commemorate their first trans-Atlantic flights in 1967. A smaller tumbler was the first piece designed.

5in (12.5cm) high

$22-28 **MHT**

A Finnish Iittala large ribbed, bark-textured vase, designed by Timo Sarpaneva, the base engraved "TS".

14.75in (37.5cm) high

$280-320 **MHT**

A Finnish Iittala flanged glass vase, from the 'i-glass' range, designed by Timo Sarpaneva, etched "T.SARPANEVA 2318".

The i-glass range was launched in response to criticism that Iittala was moving away from functional tableware. All pieces were mold-blown in different colors, promoting colorful combinations.

c1958   9.5in (24cm) high

$220-280 **MHT**

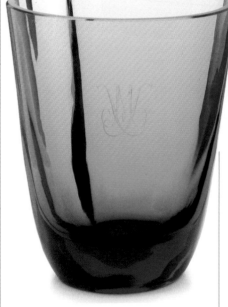

A Finnish Iittala blue-cased vase, designed by Erkki Versanto, the base signed "Erkki Versanto 3654".

Versanto (1915-90) worked as an in-house designer from 1936-80 and was responsible for many tableware designs.

c1960   6in (15cm) high

$80-120 **MHT**

A Finnish Karhula green vase, designed by Goran Hongell, with engraved Gothic 'MV' monogram.

Hongell was a designer for Karhula from 1932-57. His designs are more angular than the work of his contemporary Alvar Aalto. Cut rims and thick walls are also typical. Hongell won a Milan Triennale gold medal in 1954. Karshula had been part of the same company as Iittala since 1917.

c1937

$300-400 **MHT**

A Finnish Iittala clear dish, designed by Tapio Wirkkala, engraved with lines and "Tapio Wirkkala Iittala 3336".

5in (13cm) wide

$280-320 **MHT**

A CLOSER LOOK AT A KOSTA VASE

A Kosta smoke gray glass vase, designed by Vicke Lindstrand, engraved on the base "KOSTA A3141".

6in (15cm) high

$70-100   **MHT**

A Kosta vase, designed by Vicke Lindstrand, with thin and slightly thicker vertical cut lines, engraved "LG 198" on the side.

5.25in (13.5cm) high

$120-180   **MHT**

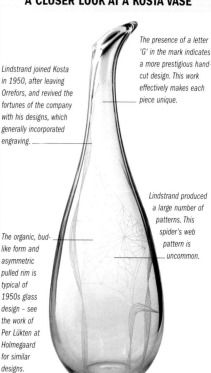

The presence of a letter 'G' in the mark indicates a more prestigious hand-cut design. This work effectively makes each piece unique.

Lindstrand joined Kosta in 1950, after leaving Orrefors, and revived the fortunes of the company with his designs, which generally incorporated engraving.

Lindstrand produced a large number of patterns. This spider's web pattern is uncommon.

The organic, bud-like form and asymmetric pulled rim is typical of 1950s glass design – see the work of Per Lükten at Holmegaard for similar designs.

A Kosta 'Sunflower' bottle, designed by Goran Warff, engraved "KOSTA 477190 Warff" on the base.

4.75in (12cm) high

$70-100   **MHT**

A 1950s Kosta vase, designed by Vicke Lindstrand, engraved with a spider's web hanging between reeds, signed to the base "KOSTA LG 2384".

15.75in (40cm) high

$550-650   **MHT**

A Kosta blue/gray glass dish, heavily walled, signed "KOSTA WH 5596" on the base.

10.5in (26.5cm) diam

$220-280   **MHT**

A Kosta rectangular section vase, designed by Goran Warff, with two bands of cut diamonds.

8in (20.5cm) high

$100-150   **MHT**

A 1980s Kosta Boda multi-coloured cast, cut and polished glass sculpture, designed by Kjell Engman and engraved "K. Engman" on the base.

Engman joined Boda in 1978, two years after the merged Boda, Afors and Kosta companies were renamed Kosta Boda AB.

5.25in (13.5cm) high

$220-280   **GAZE**

A Riihimaën Lasi Oy yellow 'Pompadour' candlestick, designed by Nanny Still in 1966.

Nanny Still (b.1926) joined the company in 1949. 'Pompadour' can be found in a number of shape and color variants.

9in (23cm) high

$70-100   **NPC**

A 1970s Riihimaën Lasi Oy straw yellow vase, the design attributed to Tamara Aladin.

Tamara Aladin (b.1932) joined the company in 1959 and is known for her strongly geometric, flanged forms.

11in (28cm) high

$70-100   **FD**

A Riihimaën Lasi Oy large honey colored vase, designed by Tamara Aladin.

During the 1930s and '50s a group of talented designers were taken on as freelance designers by Riihimaën Lasi Oy and dominated design into the 1970s. Pieces were modern in appearance and were generally mold-blown using spinning molds to ensure an even distribution of glass. Colors were strong and jewel-like and forms were typically geometric with clean surfaces. Due to a drop in quality and the closure of certain glass manufacturers, many retailers, such as Britain's Boots the Chemists, ordered glass from Riihimäki during the 1970s. These designs do not appear in Riihimäki's catalogues, possibly as they were made solely for export. As such, these designs can currently only be attributed to designers based on their style.

11in (28cm) high

$100-150   **FD**

A Riihimaën Lasi Oy yellow vase, the design attributed to Tamara Aladin.

7in (18cm) high

$50-70   **NPC**

A Riihimaën Lasi Oy yellow vase, the design attributed to Tamara Aladin, pattern no. 1939.

9.75in (25cm) high

$40-60   **NPC**

A Riihimaën Lasi Oy yellow 'Stromboli' range vase, designed by Aimo Okkolin in 1963, with factory label.

Aimo Okkolin (1917-82) trained as an engraver and cutter and worked for Riihimäki from 1937. He was related to the company's owners.

8.75in (22cm) high

$50-70   **NPC**

A Riihimaën Lasi Oy deep blue vase, the design attributed to Tamara Aladin, pattern no. 1939.

9.75in (25cm) high

$40-60   **NPC**

A Riihimaën Lasi Oy blue vase, the design attributed to Nanny Still.

25in (63.5cm) high

$40-60   **NPC**

A 1970s Riihimaën Lasi Oy flanged vase, the design attributed to Helena Tynell, in an unusual light blue glass.

Examine pieces carefully as chips, scratches and liming reduce desirability, as they detract from the purity and strength of the color. Some colors are more desirable and scarcer than other, with striking, stronger examples often being more sought-after. Some shapes are rarely found in certain colors.

11in (28cm) high

$70-100 **FD**

A 1970s Riihimaën Lasi Oy mould-blown blue 'Ahkeraliisa' vase, designed by Helena Tynell in 1968, with factory label to rim.

Tynell joined the company in 1946, three years before the Scandinavia-wide competition was held in 1949. This is one of her most sought-after designs and was available in a number of colors. Ahkeraliisa is the Finnish name for the 'Busy Lizzie' flower.

8.5in (21.5cm) high

$120-180 **GAZE**

A 1970s Riihimaën Lasi Oy 'Grapponia' bottle, designed by Nanny Still in 1968.

Although often used today decoratively as a 'solifleur', this bottle was intended to be functional tableware.

c1970 7.5in (19cm) high

$100-150 **FD**

A Riihimaën Lasi Oy green 'Tuuliki' vase, the design attributed to Tamara Aladin.

8in (20cm) high

$50-70 **NPC**

A Riihimaën Lasi Oy tapered green 'Stromboli' range vase, designed by Aimo Okkolin.

7in (18cm) high

$30-50 **NPC**

A 1960s-70s Riihimaën Lasi Oy red waisted vase, by an unidentified designer.

7in (18cm) high

$30-40 **NPC**

A Riihimaën Lasi Oy amethyst bullet-shaped vase, the design attributed to Aimo Okkolin.

9.5in (24cm) high

$50-70 **NPC**

A 1970s Riihimaën Lasi Oy 'Quadrifolio' glass vase, designed by Nanny Still in 1967.

This is often attributed to Tapio Wirkkala for littala, due to its texture. However, the shape and knobbly effect is different to his work.

7.75in (19.5cm) high

$100-150 **FD**

COLLECTORS' NOTES

■ As Scandinavian glass is renowned for the clarity and purity of its transparent color, cased glass tends to be largely under-rated and ignored. Its importance was noted by the important Czech glass artist Stanislav Libensky as early as 1972, who admired both the visual effect and the fact that it could be mass-produced cost effectively, which he felt could not be done as efficiently in Czechoslovakia at the time.

■ Holmegaard of Denmark is the most notable factory that produced such cased glass, with the 'Carnaby' range designed by Per Lütken in 1968 and produced from 1969-76, being currently the most desirable and valuable. Michael Bang's similar 'Palet' range designed in 1970 is also sought-after. In 1965, the Holmegaard, Kastrup and Odense factories were amalgamated under the Holmegaard name.

■ In all examples shown here, opaque white glass was overlaid with colored transparent glass to give a bright and appealing visual effect, with the color sometimes varying due to the thickness of the colored overlay. Pieces were blown into molds and spun at high speed to ensure an even distribution of glass around the mold. Shapes were clean-lined and modern, and colors bright, reacting against 1950s forms that were inspired by nature and placing them firmly in the 1970s aesthetic.

■ A number of other Scandinavian factories including Alsterfors also produced cased glass and the origin of many pieces is yet to be identified. Look for clean-lined modern forms that exemplify the movement, large sizes and brighter 'Pop' colors.

A Danish Holmegaard 'Carnaby' yellow cased vase, designed by Per Lütken, with original factory sticker.

1969-76   9in (23cm) high

$180-220   **FD**

A Danish Holmegaard 'Carnaby' light blue cased vase, with bulbous neck.

Note the rounded rim on Holmegaard pieces, which is not machine-cut and flat.

1969-76   9in (23cm) high

$220-280   **GC**

A Danish Holmegaard 'Carnaby' light blue cased carafe or pitcher, designed by Per Lütken.

1969-76   8in (20.5cm) high

$100-150   **GC**

A 1970s Danish Holmegaard white and yellow cased hanging lampshade, possibly designed by Michael Bang.

17in (43cm) high

$50-70   **FD**

A CLOSER LOOK AT A CASED GLASS VASE

This vase is part of a range of glass designed in 1968 and named after the most popular street in 'Swinging London' that set the trend for many fashions of the 1960s and '70s.

Although made from glass, the shiny opaque appearance and curving form recalls plastic, which was a popular material of the period, being used particularly for furniture.

The strong red color fits with the prevalent 'Pop' fashion of the period and would have complimented period room interiors.

The 'Carnaby' range is often confused with the 'Palet' range, which was designed by Jacob Bang's son Michael in 1970. The shape identifies which range a piece is from.

A Danish Holmegaard 'Carnaby' red and white cased vase, designed by Per Lütken, with original factory sticker.

c1969-76   8.75in (22cm) high

$280-320   **FD**

A Danish Kastrup purple and white cased torpedo-shaped vase, designed by Jacob Bang.

13in (33cm) high

$150-200 GC

A Swedish Alsterfors green cased 'UFO' shaped vase, possibly designed by Per-Olaf Strom.

The 1960s styled 'space-aged' form and bright color makes this a desirable piece. Note the subtle variation in the color from the base to the 'UFO', created by the differing thickness of the green glass. Also note the rim is machine-cut flat, unlike Holmegaard pieces.

8in (20cm) high

$80-120 GC

A Danish Kastrup large purple tear drop-shaped cased white vase, designed by Jacob Bang.

The austere cased glass forms designed by Jacob Bang echo his earlier designs from the 1930-50s. For other examples, please see p 317 of this book.

16.5in (42cm) high

$180-220 GC

A 1970s Swedish Alsterfors blue and white cased vase, designed by Per-Olaf Strom, etched on the base "PO Strom 70".

Strom's designs are characterised by highly modern geometric and angular forms.

9.75in (25cm) high

$60-80 GC

A 1970s Swedish green cased ribbed and flared vase, by an unidentified factory.

11in (28cm) high

$30-50 GC

A 1970s Swedish green-blue cased, flared and stepped vase, possibly by Alsterfors.

7.5in (19cm) high

$40-60 GC

A 1970s Swedish red cased vase, possibly by Alsterfors, with large hollow base.

6in (15cm) high

$40-60 GC

A 1970s Swedish deep blue cased stepped/ribbed vase, possibly by Alsterfors.

7in (17.5cm) high

$70-100 GC

A pair of 1970s Scandinavian yellow cased candlesticks or vases, with plated metal rims.

These are probably Danish and possibly made by Kastrup's sister factory at Odense.

6.5in (16.5cm) high

$70-100 GC

A Swedish Afors Glasbruk bottle, with molded band of vertical lines, designed by Bertil Vallien.

Vallien joined Afors in 1963, the year before it merged with Kosta. He has since become one of Sweden's most avant garde and revolutionary glass designers, known particularly for his sculptural works.

7.25in (18.5cm) high

$70-100   **MHT**

A Swedish Afors Glasbruk deep blue vase, designed by Bertil Vallien, with molded band of vertical ribs.

c1965   7in (17.5cm) high

$70-100   **MHT**

A Swedish Alsterfors opaque blue glass geometric vase, designed by Per-Olof Strom, the base with etched signature and date.

1968   9.5in (24cm) high

$100-150   **FD**

A Swedish Alsterfors abstract molded and textured glass vase, designed by Per-Olof Strom, the base with etched signature and date.

1968   10in (25.5cm) high

$80-120   **FD**

A Swedish Alsterfors goblet, designed by Per-Olof Strom.

7.25in (18.5cm) high

$25-35   **GC**

A Swedish Aseda clear glass vase, with white spiralling internal threading, designed by Bo Borgstrom.

This design is usually found in red.

9.5in (24cm) high

$45-55   **MHT**

A Swedish Aseda knobbly vase.

11in (28cm) high

$40-60   **NPC**

A 1970s Dansk Design Ltd. clear glass decanter, with teak stopper, designed by Gunnar Cyren, the base marked "DENMARK".

12in (30cm) high

$80-120   **MHT**

A CLOSER LOOK AT A JOHANFORS GOBLET

A Swedish Flygsfors 'Coquille' vase, designed by Paul Kedelv.

The Coquille range, named after the French word for 'shell', is usually found in low bowl forms, rather than tall vases, making this piece comparatively rare.

c1960   11.75in (30cm) high

$100-150   **GC**

A Johanfors etched teardrop-shaped goblet vase, designed by Bengt Orup, etched with a stylized skyscraper design, the base hand-inscribed "Johanfors Orup" and with Johanfors label.

11.5in (29cm) high

$220-280   **GC**

Bengt Orup (1916-96) worked as the leading artist for Johanfors from 1951 until 1972, when the factory was sold to Orrefors.

It is very finely blown and of a large size, and is meant for display rather than a specific usage.

The acid-etched design is very modern – Orup's experience as an engraver and graphic designer no doubt came into play with this design.

Orup ran his own studio where he worked as a painter, engraver and sculptor.

A Johanfors goblet-shaped vase, designed by Bengt Orup, acid-etched and sandblasted with a design of stylized people.

11.5in (29cm) high

$220-280   **GC**

A Norwegian Hadeland heavily cased purple bowl, designed by Willy Johansson, with internal green blob in foot, and signed "WJ 54 HADELAND".

Willy Johansson joined Hadeland in 1936 as an apprentice under his glassblower father Wilhelm. In 1947, he became a designer, remaining there until 1988. He was interested in color contrasts, as shown in this design.

c1956   3.5in (9cm) high

$70-90   **MH**

A Norwegian Hadeland gray bowl, probably designed by Willy Johannsson, with applied white enameled rim.

These bowls are often thought to be made by Whitefriars, due to the clean lines and color. However, the glass on these bowls is much thicker, the color is different and the applied opaque rim is a feature of many of Johansson's designs.

11in (28cm) diam

$220-280   **MHT**

A Swedish Gullaskruf goblet, designed by Arthur Percy.

Percy (1886-1976) worked for Gullaskruf from 1951-70. Many of his designs are thinly blown and elongated. This goblet is blown in one hollow piece down to the separate solid, cylindrical stem.

9.5in (24cm) high

$70-100   **MHT**

A Swedish A.B. Kalmar Glasbruk lobed vase, with amethyst internal banding and original label.

4.75in (12cm) high

$40-60   **MHT**

GLASS

A Finnish Nuutajärvi Nöstjo yellow vase, designed by Kaj Franck, with dimpled base and machine-cut rim and signed "KF Nuutajärvi Nöstjo 64".

Franck (1911-89) brought about a design revolution at Nuutajärvi when he became art director in 1950. He was responsible for the company's first modern designs and remained pre-eminent until his departure in 1976. From 1965-68 his designs were not marked at his request, with his name appearing on most of his designs after this date.

c1964   10.25in (26cm) high

$300-400   MHT

A Finnish Nuutajärvi Nöstjo yellow vase, designed by Kaj Franck, with dimpled base and machine-cut rim and signed "KF Nuutajärvi Nöstjo 64".

c1964 10in (25.5cm) high

$180-220   MHT

A Norwegian Magnor graduated electric blue and clear vase, with original label.

5in (12.5cm) high

$25-35   MHT

A Finnish Nuutajärvi Nöstjo blue molded vase, designed by Kaj Franck, with flared rim and foot.

c1966   5in (12.5cm) high

$100-150   MHT

A Finnish Nuutajärvi Nöstjo clear 'Pikku-Majakka' vase, designed by Oiva Toikka.

Although very similar to Nanny Still's 'Pomapdour' range, the use of clear glass and a wider, shorter rim shows this to be different. The name means 'little lighthouse'.

c1965   9in (23cm) high

$100-150   NPC

A Swedish Pukeberg pink bowl, designed by Staffan Gellerstedt, with label.

As with most factories, Pukeberg designers came to prominence during the 1950s. The Pukeberg logo of a gather of glass on a rod was designed in the 1960s by Ann Warff, wife of Goran, who also worked for Kosta.

c1976   6in (15cm) diam

$50-70   NPC

A Norwegian Randsfjord brown, black and cream swirling clear-cased vase, designed by T. Torgersen, with blue paper label to base.

5.75in (14.5cm) high

$120-180   GC

A Swedish F.M. Ronneby lampbase, with European light fittings.

Due to the coloring, this glass is often confused with Mdina glass. Ronneby was founded independently in Sweden in 1961 by Josef and Benito Marcolin. Mats Jonasson produced some signed paperweights at the factory before its closure in 1990.

10.25in (26cm) high

$80-120   MHT

A CLOSER LOOK AT A STROMBERG VASE

A Swedish 1960s Skrufs Glasbruk AB textured clear glass vase, with bark-like finish.

This is similar to some of Tapio Wirkkala's designs for littala, but has thicker glass and a flat, machine-cut rim and base. Textured glass was very fashionable from the late 1960s-70s, with designs inspired by the rugged Scandinavian landscape.

7.5in (19cm) high

$60-80 **MHT**

The use of strong color is unusual for this factory - more typical designs are in cool colored or clear glass.

The asymmetric, bud-like form is typically 1950s, but is again unusual for Stromberg, whose designs are usually more like the oval bowl also on this page.

This piece is likely to have been designed by Gunnar Nylund (1904-89) who designed for the factory from 1952-75 and introduced more typical 1950s forms.

These heavily cased forms are scarcer, more technically complex and more visually appealing than more typical designs, and have probably not yet reached their peak in value and desirability.

A Strombergshyttan curved heavily cased yellow glass vase, engraved "Stromberg 973". c1959

4.25in (10.5cm) high

$120-180 **MHT**

A Swedish Skrufs Glasbruk AB clear knopped, textured bottle, designed by Bengt Edenfalk, with polished pontil.

7.75in (19.5cm) high

$100-150 **MHT**

A Swedish Skrufs Glasbruk AB vase, designed by Bengt Edenfalk.

Edenfalk joined Skrufs as their first full-time chief designer in 1953.

7.75in (19.5cm) high

$80-120 **NPC**

A Smalandshyttan gray cased bowl.

Just as 'Lasi Oy' means 'glass company', 'hyttan' means hut, implying a factory. This factory was based in Smaland, Sweden, in the same area as Strombergshyttan, Kosta and many other glass factories.

3.75in (9.5cm) high

$40-60 **MHT**

A Strombergshyttan spherical heavily cased brown-gray vase, engraved "Stromberg 0937" on the base.

3.5in (9cm) high

$220-280 **MHT**

A Strombergshyttan ice blue oval dish, with curving machine-cut rim and heavy walls.

The austere form and color, thick walls and cut, polished rim are more typical Stromberg features. The majority were designed by Gerda Stromberg, the wife of the founder Edward, who worked as a designer from 1933-46. However, similar (but often more flowing) work was also designed by H.J. Dunne-Cooke, who was British importer Elfverson & Co.'s buyer and designer.

9.75in (25cm) wide

$100-150 **MHT**

COLLECTORS' NOTES

■ Schott was founded in 1884 in Thuringia, Germany by Otto Schott and began by making optical glass. The renowned Carl Zeiss was an early partner until his death in 1888. Bauhaus designer Wilhelm Wagenfeld was an early designer, who worked from 1931-35, with a clear glass teapot being among his notable designs.

■ One of his assistants was Heinrich Loffelhardt (1901-79), who was employed as a freelance designer from 1954. Many of his designs were for tableware, which was made at the Vereinigte Farbenglaswerke plant in Zweisel, Bavaria. The plant had been acquired by Schott in 1927 and used for optical glass manufacture.

■ In the 1970s, Loffelhardt and his colleague Wilhelm Kuchler augmented their growing and successful range of tableware with a range of art glass also made at Zweisel. The growth in popularity of studio glass from the late 1960s onwards undoubtedly influenced them in this decision. The majority are heavily cased in clear glass, with strong, vibrant colors including blue and green.

■ One popular range had streams of randomly sized internal bubbles trapped under the outer layer. Apart from distinctive colors, heavy casing and bubble patterning, Schott Zweisel pieces can be recognised by the large polished concave pontil mark on the base. Pieces were marketed under the Zweisel and 'Cristallerie Zweisel' brands. Large, bubbled designs in the characteristic blue are currently the most desirable and valuable.

A 1970s Schott Zweisel heavily cased tall vase, with pulled curving rim.

9.75in (24.5cm) high

$70-100 GC

A 1970s Schott Zweisel blue-cased bulbous vase, with lobed rim.

7in (17.5cm) high

$35-45 GC

A 1970s Schott Zweisel green glass vase, with applied clear glass flower.

7.75in (19.5cm) high

$70-100 GC

A 1970s Schott Zweisel green waisted vase, with heavily cased base.

9.25in (23.5cm) high

$60-100 GC

A 1970s Schott Zweisel vase, designed by Heinrich Loffelhardt, with densely packed random internal bubbles.

This is one of the more commonly found shapes from this factory, but also one of the more desirable shapes, particularly in larger sizes.

6in (15cm) high

$80-120 GC

A 1970s Schott Zweisel amber vase, with large internal bubbles.

975in (24.5cm) high

$70-100 GC

A 1970s Schott Zweisel tall vase, with large internal bubbles.

9.75in (24.5cm) high

$70-100 GC

A 1970s Schott Zweisel spherical candleholder, designed by Heinrich Loffelhardt, with internal bubbles.

The inside is hollow, with access gained from the machine-cut base.

4in (10cm) high

$60-100 GC

COLLECTORS' NOTES

■ The contemporary glass movement of spheres and orbs developed in the 1980s onwards from the creation of art glass marbles and paperweights by contemporary studio glass artists, who mainly work in the US. From such simple toys has sprung a new, exciting and dynamic art glass movement. Spheres tend to be larger than marbles, with the tag 'orb' being reserved for the largest examples.

■ The designs are not painted on the interior or exterior of the sphere, but are contained within the sphere, being carefully hand-worked in hot, colored glass and most often in more than one layer. The glass designs are then encased in a top layer of clear 'crystal' or 'borosilicate' glass.

■ Spheres really need to be handled and viewed in person to best appreciate the intricate detail within, and the myriad reflections and magnifications caused by the curving surface. The skill involved in their creation shows how far the studio glass movement has progressed since the late 1960s.

■ Names to look out for include Paul Stankard, Jesse Taj, David Salazar, Dinah Hulet, Rolf Wald and James Alloway. New artists come to the field every year, each bringing their own style and skill, making this a vibrant and ever-changing market. Prices are currently comparatively affordable for such detailed, unique works.

■ Watch out for new young makers, examining their work and comparing it to established names. Many artists make their own murrines, which are also known as 'milli', 'millifiori' or 'murrini'. Some artists such as Jesse Taj and David Strobel sell their murrines for others to incorporate into their own designs.

■ As well as established collectors, a new younger audience has been attracted to the market. Images from cartoons and sub-cultures are often included, making this art form highly relevant to today. Spheres are intricate, easy to display and offer great variety. Values should increase as the market grows.

A Nick Bartlett translucent burgundy and beige rake pull sphere, signed "NB05".

When held to the light, the interior reveals a crescent shaped 'veil', which is a characteristic feature of Bartlett's larger designs.

A Shane Caswell 'Sea Floral' sphere, signed with a signature cane.

The color is 'pulled' into the sphere with a vacuum process.

2005	2.75in (7cm) diam
$200-250	**BGL**

2005	1.5in (4cm) diam
$50-80	**BGL**

A Teri Conklin double-faced sphere, with dichroic fume and pulled stringers and a rake pull torsade.

2005	1.75in (4.5cm) diam
$60-80	**BGL**

A Drew Fritts banded swirl sphere, with dichroic and multicolored strands, signed and dated "AF 2005 7".

2005	1.75in (4.5cm) diam
$100-150	**BGL**

A Steve Hitt double-layered 'Cedars' sphere, with butterfly and floral murrines, signed "SH03".

The decoration is applied in separate layers, giving depth and perspective to the design.

	1.75in (4.5cm) diam
$150-200	**BGL**

A Josh Howard hollow marble or sphere, the surface with applied glass 'stringer' designs.

This piece is actually hollow, so is very light in weight.

2004   1.5in (4cm) diam

$60-80   **BGL**

A CLOSER LOOK AT A SPHERE

Dustin Morell is well known for his Vortex spheres, which are extremely well executed in bright colors.

They are complex to make and give the impression that the centre of the concave vortex is deeper than the corresponding outside surface of the sphere.

Vortex spheres started off being very, very small marbles, and only grew in size as glass artists became more skilled – larger examples such as this are sought-after.

The back is executed very carefully as the hot glass used to decorate it can burn through the thin, opaque background layer into the vortex when dripped onto the surface.

A Dustin Morell orange 'Vortex' sphere, with honeycomb back, signed "DKM 2004".

2004   2.25in (6cm) diam

$120-180   **BGL**

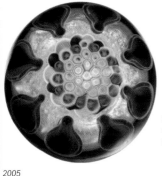

2005   2in (5cm) diam

$100-150   **BGL**

A Jerry Kelly 'Millfiori' sphere, with self-made murrines and pulled 'stringers', signed "JK05".

A Shawn Messenger gathered millefiori 'Flora' marble.

Each of the millefiori is made from a sliced glass cane and is placed in position by hand.

2005   2in (5cm) diam

$100-150   **BGL**

A Kris Parke rake pull swirl sphere, in black, red, purple and orange on a white base.

2005   1.5in (4cm) diam

$70-100   **BGL**

A Tony Parker marble or sphere, with internal twisted ribbon and dichroic band, with applied heart murrines.

1990   2in (5cm) diam

$80-120   **BGL**

A Tony Parker 'Marilyn Monroe' sphere.

Marilyn's face is composed of black frit, which is trailed onto the white surface and then melted into it.

1990   1.5in (4cm) diam

$80-120   **BGL**

GLASS

A Jim Hart torchworked sphere, with dichroic base under curving patterns applied to the surface, and a signature heart-shaped cane.

1.5in (4cm) diam

$60-80 BGL

A CLOSER LOOK AT A SPHERE

Cathy Richardson (b.1949) is a noted glass artist who has studied at the respected Pilchuck and Corning glass schools.

She assembles many lampworked glass elements before encasing them in clear glass with a complicated and difficult vacuum process.

Richardson's love of nature is clear – she holds a doctorate in geology, which shows in her detailed seabeds, and she grew up in Virginia where she gained her love of the seaside.

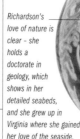

This is a comparatively large sphere and has two layers of designs, which add depth and perspective. Three layer spheres are even more valuable.

A Cathy Richardson double layered 'Coral Reef' orb, signed "C. RICHARDSON 2004".

2004 *2.75in (7cm) diam*

$200-250 BGL

A Josh Sable 'Reticello' sphere, with rake pull base and sides, and stained glass window-like reticello double vortex, signed "SABLE 2003".

2003 *2in (5cm) diam*

$120-180 BGL

A David Salazar experimental paperweight-style sphere, with 'painted' glass butterflies, flora and fauna on a surface.

Salazar is one of the best known proponents of the Californian style of 'painting' with glass and has over 25 years of experience of glassmaking.

1.5in (4cm) diam

$120-180 BGL

A Jesse Taj 'Flora' sphere, with self-made murrines of a butterfly, sun, dragonfly and lion's head within a torsade, signed "TAJ 03 3/03 Wilkinson".

Jesse Taj is well known for his wide variety of finely made murrines.

2003 *1.5in (4cm) diam*

$150-200 BGL

A Beth Tomasello paperweight style sphere, with lampwork flora and berries on a ground glass base.

2004 *1.5in (4cm) diam*

$100-150 BGL

FIND OUT MORE...

Contemporary Marbles & Related Art Glass, by Mark Block, published by Schiffer Books, 2001.

The Encyclopaedia of Modern Marbles, Spheres & Orbs, by Mark Block, published by Schiffer Books, 2005.

COLLECTORS' NOTES

■ The studio glass movement developed in the US during the 1960s after glassmakers Harvey Littleton and Dominick Labino found ways to free glass making from the confines of the factory in 1962. This allowed artists to make glass themselves, although many still choose to work in teams.

■ The movement spread to the UK and Europe in the late 1960s and '70s, and as artists and makers practiced techniques, the level of skills developed and pieces became more appealing and more finely made. The breadth of techniques mastered also developed and glass became increasingly seen as an art form rather than a craft during the 1980s.

■ Originators such as Dale Chihuly, William Morris, Marvin Lipofsky and Dan Dailey have become legendary and their works are valuable. However, works by successive 'generations' can be affordable. Date is not always an indicator of value, and some early examples are crudely formed although they do reflect this important development in glass history.

■ Buy a reference book and look out for names that have strong collecting bases behind them, or who have works featured in public collections. The secondary market at auctions and dealers is still developing and bargains can be had. Recent graduates can make an interesting contemporary gamble, but one that will always pay off if you buy because you like the piece.

■ Today the market is extremely diverse and vibrant, and crosses Europe, the UK and the US. Boundaries are constantly being pushed, resulting in a myriad of different designs in a rainbow of colors across many price ranges. The increasing solid interest in the area that developed during the 1990s is sure to continue and studio and contemporary glass should become a hot collecting area.

■ Signatures can be hard to read, so try and learn how to recognise particular artists' styles. Only a single price is given for some pieces as this reflects the retail price of that individual contemporary piece.

'Alfred's Mirror', by Keith Cummings, kiln-formed opaque glass inlaid and decorated with copper wire, copper bands and glass faux pearls.

This piece was inspired by the 9thC 'Alfred's Jewel' in the Ashmolean Museum, Oxford, which was made for King Alfred.

2003   14.5in (37cm) long

$4,500   **CG**

'Aesculus', by Kate Jones and Stephen Gillies, from cased, sandblasted and cut glass, signed on the base "Gillies Jones Aesculus 2004/08 Rosedale".

This is formed from glass coated with a layer of colored glass, which is then masked off and sandblasted to create the pattern.

2004   11.5in (29.5cm) diam

$3,400   **CG**

A Sam Herman vase, with swirled inclusions of mauve, ochre and blue, the base with incised marks.

American Sam Herman is one of the founding fathers of studio glass and was the first to bring the ideas to the UK. His work is typified by a painterly approach to color and pattern, and is rising in value and desirability today.

1980   6in (15.5cm) high

$120-180   **CHEF**

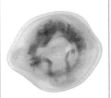

A large Sam Herman glass bowl, of irregular, freeblown form, streaked with green glass, the base with etched signature.

1971   18in (46cm) wide

$320-380   **WW**

A Glasform iridescent vase, designed and made by John Ditchfield, with waterlily leaves pattern, the base signed "Glasform1=8/L".

4.25in (11cm) high

$120-180   **GAZE**

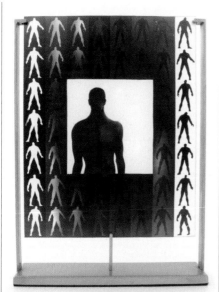

'Eclipse', by Alison Kinnaird, engraved, sandblasted and cased glass panel, with figural designs, mounted on a metal stand.

Kinnaird is an important glass engraver internationally and was awarded an MBE in 1997. Her work is in many museums and galleries including the Victoria & Albert Museum, London.

2001   Panel 11.5in (29.5cm) high

$6,400   **CG**

A unique Skyline 'pebble' form, designed by Peter Layton.

Although the form is more typical of Layton's designs, the color and pattern was from a new and experimental range. The delicate and varied coloration is particularly appealing.

2004   11.5in (29cm) wide

$2,700   **PL**

A Paradiso disc, by Peter Layton.

The Paradiso range was inspired by painters such as Howard Hodgkin, emulating their color and abstract 'brushed on' patterns.

2004   11.5in (29cm) diam

$4,300   **PL**

A large Mirage 'stone form', designed by Peter Layton.

Mirage was inspired by the landscape seen by Layton on a visit to the ancient city of Petra in Jordan. Layton is one of Britain's most respected glass artists, with a varied and long experience. Today he runs the London Glass Blowing studio with a team of glass makers and designers.

2004   13.5in (34cm) wide

$5,400   **PL**

A rare Peter Layton dropper bottle, made at the London Glassblowing Workshop.

This is an extremely unusual shape for this range and may have been an experimental piece. The clear 'bubbles' are arranged in a spiral pattern, but appear to be banded. The skill of the glassmaker has meant that as this piece was blown out the internal pink lines in each bubble shape have not been widened.

c1989   20cm (8in) high

$120-180   **PC**

An Annette Meech goblet, with clear stem and spotted green and blue on a white background bowl, signed "Annette Meech 1978" to the base.

1978   7in (17.5cm) high

$180-220   **MHT**

A Simon Moore vase, the flared and waved green body bordered and decorated with clear swirls, on a black glass pedestal, engraved "Simon Moore 88" to rim.

1988   9in (23cm) high

$70-90   **ROS**

A 'Stream Bowl' by Keïko Mukaïdé, in kiln cast blue glass with enameled powder surface.

This was possibly cast in a sand mould as grains of sand are bonded to the outside.

2003   12.5in (31.5cm) widest

$2,000   **CG**

An American Michael Nourot glass perfume bottle, with a central band of gold foil on a black ground.

2004   *5in (13cm) high*

$150-200   **AGW**

'Dog Days A Sun Fetish' by Ronald Pennell, amethyst glass cased vessel made by Karl Nordbruch and engraved by Ronald Pennell, signed with an "RP" monogram.

Of this work, Pennell says 'There are many ways to connect with past civilisations and cultures. In this work a man and his dog are confronted by three strange figures including one who is holding a symbolic sunburst'.

2003   *8in (20.5cm) high*

$6,800   **CG**

A large blown 'Seascape' bowl, designed and made by Anthony Stern.

These reveal a landscape effect as the bowl is turned and light passes through it.

2003   *8.75in (22cm) high*

$2,500-3,500   **ASG**

An Okra perfume bottle and stopper, designed and made by Richard Golding, with iridescent and trailed design with floral detail, the base engraved "Okra 87 WS LSB No. 9".

1987   *6.5in (16.5cm) high*

$100-150   **GAZE**

'Europe - The Past Is Not Enough' by Ronald Pennell, green overcased glass vase made by Karl Nordbruch, then engraved on a diamond wheel by Ronald Pennell, signed with an "RP" monogram.

Pennell is one of Britian's most important glass engravers, whose designs are based on stories and are engraved onto the bodies without preparatory drawings.

2003   *8.25in (21cm) high*

$6,500   **CG**

A CLOSER LOOK AT A DAVID REEKIE HEAD

David Reekie (b.1947) is an internationally renowned glass artist known for his cast glass works of the human form, which often convey emotions or highlight the human predicament.

Even though pieces are cast in molds, each piece is unique and is not repeated.

The simple head form is related to Reekie's early landmark work 'Construction with Guarding Figures' from 1977.

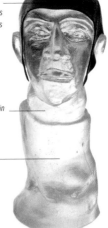

This was part of a series of four similar heads sold to a London gallery, with this being the only example looking upwards.

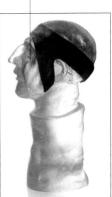

A David Reekie cast soda/barium glass head, with hand-made lead head cap, the base hand inscribed "D.REEKIE 1986".

As well as in key private collections, Reekie's work can be found in the Victoria & Albert Museum, London, and museums in the US, Denmark and France.

1986   *6.5in (16.5cm) high*

$800-1,200   **PC**

A large 'African Vase', by Anthony Stern, made from lightly iridised light blue glass blown into a cone made from woven reclaimed African telephone wire woven in Kwazululand and accented with cowrie shells by Stern.

The glass is blown into the wire cone while still molten.

2004   11.75in (30cm) high

$2,800-3,200   **ASG**

An American cameo and engraved glass lamp base, designed and made by Valerie Surjan, the black glass with engraved and cameo floral design.

2004   12in (30.5cm) high

$2,800-3,200   **AGW**

A tapering blue glass vase, designed and made by David Traub, signed "Traub 93".

1993   7.75in (19.5cm) high

$30-50   **GAZE**

'Jug & Cup', by Koichiro Yamamoto, of cast and polished glass, signed on base "Koichiro C Jug & Cup 2001".

It is hard to polish such convex surfaces as they can't be left on a machine, meaning each piece has to be polished by hand. In the largest piece, the 'handles' are cavities running through the piece, giving an optical illusion. Yamamoto was shortlisted for the Jerwood Prize.

A Rachael Woodman cased vase, with hot-worked striated deep gray exterior and yellow interior.

c1990   8in (20cm) high

$1,000-1,500   **JH**

2001   6in (15.5cm) high

$2,800   **CG**

An American Zelique Studio heart-shaped 'Hanging Wisteria' perfume bottle, designed and made by Joseph Morel, with 'painted flamework', signed "J.M. 2001 WHK8".

The internal pattern is made by 'torchwork' where a small blowtorch is used to partially melt the glass, allowing it to be bent, joined and formed before being cased in clear glass.

4.25in (11cm) high

$280-320   **BGL**

A small 20thC blown studio glass bottle, with surface enamel decoration and applied colored bands, with impressed maker's pontil mark.

5in (13cm) high

$35-45   **PC**

FIND OUT MORE...

Collectors Guide: 20th Century Glass, by Judith Miller, published by DK, 2004.

Artists in Glass, by Dan Klein, published by Mitchell Beazley, 2001.

GLASS

COLLECTORS' NOTES

- The 'Blown Soda' range was introduced by Whitefriars at the 1962 annual Blackpool, England trade fair. It was designed by Geoffrey Baxter, who had joined as assistant designer in 1954. Their jewel-like colors and simple, often geometric, forms show Baxter's modern design ethics, as well as the prevailing influence of Scandinavian glass designs at that time.

- The soda glass used is typically thin, meaning pieces are light in weight, and were blown into a mold to give a uniform shape. Some shapes were adapted from molds made for lighting. They were originally launched in midnight blue, shadow green and amethyst, then ruby, golden amber, twilight, and finally pewter.

- The range was very popular and can be easily found today, although smaller examples are more common than larger examples. Certain shapes, such as the decanter and glass are rare, and some shapes are rare in certain colors. The range was long-lived and its modern design still has great appeal today, and is largely more affordable than Baxter's later 'Textured' range.

A Whitefriars ruby 'Blown Soda' range medium bulbous vase, pattern no. 9599, designed by Geoffrey Baxter.

Note the different shapes and neck lengths on these similar looking vases.

c1963   *7in (17.5cm) high*

$50-70   **GC**

A Whitefriars midnight blue 'Blown Soda' range vase, pattern no. 9602, designed by Geoffrey Baxter.

c1963   *6.75in (17cm) high*

$120-180   **GC**

A Whitefriars amethyst 'Blown Soda' bulbous vase, designed by Geoffrey Baxter.

c1962-64   *4in (10cm) high*

$70-100   **MHT**

A Whitefriars midnight blue 'Blown Soda' range bulbous vase, pattern no. 9597 designed by Geoffrey Baxter, with tall, slightly flared neck.

c1963   *5in (14cm) high*

$70-90   **GC**

A Whitefriars amethyst 'Blown Soda' range vase, designed by Geoffrey Baxter, with cylindrical neck.

7in (18cm) high

$120-180   **GC**

A Whitefriars pewter 'Blown Soda' range waisted vase, pattern no. 9638, designed by Geoffrey Baxter.

Note the applied white enamel rim. This is a rare feature as the enamel rarely bonded to the soda glass successfully. These vases can also be found in shadow green.

c1963   *7.5in (19cm) high*

$100-150   **TCS**

A Whitefriars ruby 'Blown Soda' waisted vase, pattern no. 9594, designed by Geoffrey Baxter, with later label.

c1963   *8in (20.5cm) high*

$35-45   **GC**

A Whitefriars amethyst 'Blown Soda' range vase, pattern no. 9474.

This shape, similar to a hyacinth vase, was introduced during the 1950s in golden amber, sea green, twilight and ruby.

A Whitefriars midnight blue 'Blown Soda' range 'bow tie' vase, pattern no. 9591, designed by Geoffrey Baxter.

c1963   5.5in (14cm) high

$50-70   GC

c1963   7.75in (19.5cm) high

$80-120   GC

A Whitefriars amethyst 'Blown Soda' range 'stem cup', pattern no. 9593, the design attributed to Geoffrey Baxter.

c1963   6in (15.5cm) high

$120-180   GC

A Whitefriars ruby 'Blown Soda' range vase, pattern no. 9596, designed by Geoffrey Baxter.

It is easy to imagine that this form was derived from a lampshade design.

c1963   9.5in (24cm) high

$60-90   GC

A Whitefriars amethyst 'Blown Soda' range vase, pattern no. 9553, designed by Geoffrey Baxter.

This is the early label. In 1962 Whitefriars changed their label, making it more stylized.

1962   4.75n (12cm) high

$22-28   GC

A Whitefriars ruby 'Blown Soda' range large 'pinched' or 'dented' vase, pattern no. 9362, designed by Geoffrey Baxter.

These were introduced in the 1966 catalog.

c1967   10.5in (27cm) high

$100-150   MHT

A Whitefriars midnight blue 'Blown Soda' range mushroom vase, pattern no. 9639, designed by Geoffrey Baxter, with white enameled rim.

c1963   7in (18cm) high

$280-320   TCS

A scarce Whitefriars shadow green decanter and glass, pattern no. M122, with later label.

The glass fits over the neck to form a cover, but is often missing leading many to assume these decanters are rare vases.

6.75in (17cm) high

$70-100   GC

GLASS

COLLECTORS' NOTES

- Whitefriars was founded in London, England in the 1600s and was acquired by James Powell in 1834 when it became known as 'Powell & Sons'. In 1926, the factory moved to Wealdstone, Middlesex, England. It became known as Whitefriars once again in 1962. Most collectors, however, refer to much of the 20thC glass as 'Whitefriars'.

- 19thC and early 20thC pieces by designers such as Harry Powell, William Wilson and James Hogan are sought-after. But it is the post war designs, mainly designed by Geoffrey Baxter that have increased the most. He remained with the company until its demise due to financial problems in the harsh economic climate of 1980.

- Baxter's quintessentially modern designs reflected the influences of the times they were made in, but were also innovative, with a unique British direction. During the 1950s, they took on a modern Scandinavian influence in terms of form and clarity of color, with clean lines, casing, strong or cool colors

and lack of surface decoration. Scandinavian glass was popular at the time and many other British factories also followed these principles.

- 1967 saw the unveiling of Baxter's 'Textured' range that was to become the pinnacle of his achievements and the most sought-after range today. Molds with internal textures were used to create glass with strong surface textures and in bright colors that matched the interiors of the time. The 'Studio' range, designed by Peter Wheeler and Baxter, and inspired by the growing studio glass movement of the late 1960s, is also highly collectible, with each piece being unique.

- Always consider the form, size and color of a piece as these affect value considerably. New colors were introduced in 1969. Key designs such as the 'Banjo' and 'Drunken Bricklayer' have become iconic. Smaller pieces from the 'Late Textured' range of the 1970s are not as desirable as they lack the visual impact, large sizes and 'freshness' of the late 1960s designs.

A Whitefriars large footed vase, designed by James Hogan.

c1948   7.75in (20cm) high

$70-100   **TCM**

A Powell & Sons bulbous clear 'Flint' glass decanter, probably designed by Harry Powell.

Cut glass examples are more valuable and can fetch up to $450.

c1880-90   13in (33cm) high

$120-180   **GC**

A Whitefriars ocean blue glass vase, designed by Geoffrey Baxter in 1957, with square base and four side ribs.

9.5in (24cm) high

$70-100   **GC**

A Whitefriars golden amber glass vase, designed by William Wilson in 1935, with square cut base.

1935-c1938   8in (20cm) high

$120-180   **GC**

A Whitefriars kingfisher blue cased vase bud vase, designed by Geoffrey Baxter.

8.5in (21.5cm) high

$40-50   **MHT**

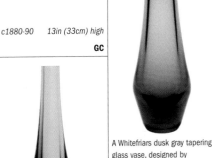

A Whitefriars dusk gray tapering glass vase, designed by Geoffrey Baxter.

7.5in (19cm) high

$30-40   **NPC**

A Whitefriars arctic blue tall 'Beak' vase, designed by Geoffrey Baxter in 1957, pattern number 9437, with organic, pulled rim.

The cool color and organic bud-like form show the influence of contemporary Scandinavian designs, particularly Per Lütken's 'Naebvase' or 'beak' vase of 1952.

22in (56cm) high

$450-550 GC

A CLOSER LOOK AT A WHITEFRIARS BOTTLE

The white enamel streaks did not adhere to the blue surface easily, causing technical problems.

The manufacturing problems meant the range was only made for a very short period of time in 1961. As a result, very few pieces were made.

The range was also made in ruby red, with the same problems.

The range was due for launch at the important 1962 Blackpool, England sales fair. Its failure led to the development of the much ignored Blown Soda range.

A very rare Whitefriars blue cylindrical bottle, designed by Geoffrey Baxter, with white striations.

1961 11.25in (28.5cm) high

$550-650 GC

A very rare Whitefriars lichen heavily clear-cased vase, designed by Geoffrey Baxter.

This color combination of green-streaked pewter is very rare. A number of Baxter's designs were influenced by nature.

c1970 5in (12.5cm) high

$350-450 GC

A Whitefriars full lead crystal 'Cirrus' small baluster vase, with complex aqua internal streaks and heavily gold colored cased foot.

Although this appears similar to Baxter's early 1970s 'Streaky' range, it was a later range, appearing in the 1980 catalog.

c1980 4.75in (12cm) high

$120-180 GC

A Whitefriars orange-streaked Studio range bulbous vase, designed by Geoffrey Baxter, pattern number 9803, with 'iridescent' silver chloride streaks.

1972-80 7in (18cm) high

$450-550 GC

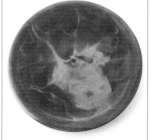

An experimental Whitefriars Studio range charger, designed by Peter Wheeler and Geoffrey Baxter, with white enamel back and gray and green marbled front.

c1968-69 10.5in (27cm) diam

$600-700 TCS

A Whitefriars ruby red dish, designed by Geoffrey Baxter, with inverted lip and asymmetric opening.

5.5in (14cm) diam

$45-55 NPC

A Whitefriars kingfisher blue 'Banjo' textured vase, designed by Geoffrey Baxter in 1966, pattern number 9681.

Kingfisher and tangerine were launched later, in 1969.

1969-c1973 13in (33cm) high

$1,200-1,800 GHOU

A Whitefriars tangerine orange 'Banjo' textured vase designed by Geoffrey Baxter in 1966, pattern number 9681.

1969-c1973 13in (33cm) high

$1,000-1,500 GC

A Whitefriars willow gray 'Banjo' textured vase, designed by Geoffrey Baxter in 1966, pattern number 9681.

1967-c1973 12.5in (32cm) high

$1,500-2,000 BIG

A Whitefriars tangerine orange 'Bamboo' textured vase, designed by Geoffrey Baxter in 1966, pattern number 9669.

1969-c1970 8in (20cm) high

$200-300 CHEF

A Whitefriars cinnamon brown 'Bamboo' textured vase, designed by Geoffrey Baxter in 1966, pattern number 9669, with label.

1967-c1970 8.25in (21cm) high

$280-320 GAZE

A Whitefriars aubergine tall 'Greek Key' textured vase, designed by Geoffrey Baxter, pattern number 9810.

1972-74 8in (20cm) high

$180-220 GC

A Whitefriars sage green tall 'Greek Key' textured vase, designed by Geoffrey Baxter, pattern number 9810.

1972-74 7.75in (19.5cm) high

$150-200 GAZE

A Whitefriars ruby red 'Chess' textured glass vase, designed by Geoffrey Baxter, pattern number 9817.

1972-74 5.75in (14.5cm) high

$100-150 GAZE

A Whitefriars aubergine small 'Drunken Bricklayer' textured vase, designed by Geoffrey Baxter in 1966, pattern number 9673.

Although this popular shape, inspired by a pile of bricks, was available from 1967-c1977, it was only shown in aubergine in the 1972 catalog, the year it was introduced. Baxter was said to have disliked this color.

1972 8in (20.5cm) high

$450-550 GC

A Whitefriars aubergine 'Aztec' textured vase, designed by Geoffrey Baxter, pattern number 9816.

1972-74   *7in (18cm) high*

$100-150   **GAZE**

A Whitefriars 'Haemorrhoid' textured full lead crystal vase, designed by Geoffrey Baxter, pattern number 9829, with multicolored streaks in aqua green.

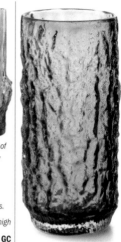

This colorway is a unique 'end of day' type experiment, probably made by a glass blower in his spare time. It was available as part of the standard range in sage, kingfisher and lilac colors.

c1974   *12.5in (30.5cm) high*

$600-700   **GC**

A Whitefriars pewter gray 'Bark' textured vase with tapered foot, designed by Geoffrey Baxter, pattern number 9734.

These are the largest of the bark textured cylindrical 'Log' vases, and are distinguished by the tapered foot. They were not popular at the time and were only produced in pewter, tangerine, ruby and kingfisher for a couple of months in 1969, making them rare today.

10.5in (26.5cm) high

$350-450   **GC**

A very rare Whitefriars kingfisher blue 'Teardrop' textured vase, designed by Geoffrey Baxter, pattern number 9848.

c1974   *11in (28cm) high*

$700-900   **GC**

A very rare Whitefriars kingfisher blue 'Poppy' textured vase, designed by Geoffrey Baxter, pattern number 9827.

These rare and heavy vases were produced in two sizes, this being the larger, and in kingfisher, lilac and sage colors.

c1974   *11in (28cm) high*

$600-700   **GC**

A Whitefriars indigo 'Fish Scale' or 'Onion' textured vase, designed by Geoffrey Baxter, pattern number 9758.

This texture was made using overlapping large headed tin tacks nailed into wood.

1971-74   *5in (12.5cm) high*

$70-100   **GC**

A Whitefriars sage green 'Pot Belly' textured vase, designed by Geoffrey Baxter, pattern number 9832.

1974-80   *5in (12.5cm) high*

$70-90   **GC**

A Whitefriars ruby red flared textured vase, designed by Geoffrey Baxter, pattern number 9831.

c1974   *8in (20cm) high*

$80-120   **GC**

A Whitefriars kingfisher blue 'Hourglass' textured vase, designed by Geoffrey Baxter, pattern number 9836.

c1974   *6in (15cm) high*

$70-100   **GAZE**

FIND OUT MORE...

Whitefriars Glass, by Lesley Jackson, published by Richard Dennis, 1996.

GLASS

A Maurice Heaton sag-molded glass plate, with brown enamels of seated people.

Heaton produced a series of pieces decorated with linear designs of people, which are commonly found today.

8.25in (21cm) wide

$300-400 HLM

A Maurice Heaton sag-molded glass figural dish, with molded pattern of musicians and green and brown enamelled decoration, marked "M.H".

9.5in (24cm) wide

$320-380 HLM

A Maurice Heaton sag-molded glass plate, enamelled with red-brown sunburst-style pattern and white lines, one side marked "M.H."

8.25in (21cm) wide

$250-300 HLM

A Maurice Heaton slumped glass 'chip and dip' plate and bowl set, with screen-printed white foamy striations and red mottled interior, marked "M.H."

Glass artist Maurice Heaton (1900-89) was a forerunner of the studio glass movement, and specialised in working with colored enamels and 'scratched' linear designs on kiln-slumped glass. In 1933, he began working with enamels, perfecting a technique of bonding them to the bottom surface of plate glass in 1947. In 1961, he adapted the technique to lamination, allowing 'sandwiches' of glass to be made. Much of his work focuses on sunburst designs and bears a small 'M.H' monogram somewhere in the design, usually near the rim.

14.25in (36cm) diam

$400-500 HLM

A 1960s-70s Rainbow Glass large purple decanter, with optic-type body and oversized, elongated teardrop-shaped stopper, the base with broken pontil mark.

Rainbow Art Glass was founded in 1942 by Henry Manus in Huntington, West Virginia and was known for its crackle glass and for decorating glass for other companies. The factory burnt down in 1960 and after rebuilding, crackle glass was discontinued with production focusing on popular modern forms similar to those by Blenko, for which Rainbow's piece are often mistaken. Decanters in strong colors such as this are particularly sought-after.

17.25in (44cm) high

$150-250 HLM

A 1960s-70s Rainbow Glass small green decanter, with optic-type body and elongated teardrop-shaped stopper, the base with broken pontil mark.

11in (28cm) high

$70-90 HLM

A 1960s Rainbow Glass mold-blown ribbed blue bottle, with broken pontil mark to the base.

Note the similarity to many Scandinavian forms, particularly those by Finnish company Riihimaki.

10.25in (26cm) high

$60-80 HLM

A 1960s American Greenwich Flint Works amberina-style large bottle, with spun rim.

9in (23cm) high

$100-150 HLM

GLASS

Four 1950s Imperial Glass Co. Smoke grey 'Pinch' juice glasses, designed by Russel Wright in 1949.

These were intended to go with the Iroquois Casual dinnerware line and can be found with thick or thin walls.

4in (10cm) high

$80-120 **HLM**

A 1960s American large mold-blown orangey red 'flame' textured bottle vase, with broken pontil mark, by an unknown maker.

The size and rich coloring make this desirable, and the textured surface is typical of the 1960s.

19in (48.5cm) high

$120-160 **HLM**

A set of six 1930s-40s green Cambridge Glass Co. wine glasses, the silver-plated metal holders by Farber Bros., New York.

5.75in (14.5cm) high

$70-100 **BB**

A pair of rare graduated Opaline opaque white 'Theme Formal' water goblets, designed by Russel Wright.

The graduated Opaline glass also incorporates a very delicate blue. Reputedly, demand was so low that the line was never put into full production by Japanese manufacturer Yamato, making them very rare today.

6in (15.5cm) high

$500-600 PAIR **HLM**

A 1930s-40s green Cambridge Glass Co. ice bucket, with silver-plated handle and holder by Farber Bros. New York NY, the base marked with "PAT 87496 1924011".

4.75in (25cm) high

$150-250 **BB**

An American Phoenix Glass light blue pressed glass 'Freesia' pattern vase, with frosted finish and machine cut base.

8.25in (21cm) high

$250-300 **MAC**

A CLOSER LOOK AT A GLASS DECANTER

Farber Bros. was founded in 1915 and produced hollow metal wares. In 1932, they developed a chrome-plated metal 'clip on - clip off' holder that meant that a broken glass insert could be replaced easily.

Although most glass was supplied by Cambridge, others such as Fenton, Fostoria and Imperial also supplied inserts. Examples can also be found in other typically strongly contrasting colors such as purple or black.

Silver-plated metal finishes were offered from 1935 with the purchase of the Sheffield Silver Company, who outlived Farber and were sold to Reed & Barton in 1973.

A 1930s-40s green Cambridge Glass Co. cocktail decanter, with silver-plated metal holders, by Farber Bros., New York.

Despite being successful, tastes changed during the 1950s and a number of the glass companies that supplied the inserts closed down. Both factors led to Farber closing in 1965.

11in (28cm) high

$150-250 **BB**

COLLECTORS' NOTES

■ The customs and iconography relating to celebrating holidays have a rich and lengthy history resulting in images that we may no longer associate with that particular event.

■ The rosy-cheeked Santa Claus in his white-trimmed red suit was popularized (but not created) by Haddon Sundblom working for Coca-Cola in the 1930s and many today consider this the traditional depiction of Santa. However, early illustrations from the turn of the century depict him in a variety of outfits, examples of which are sought-after today. Early pieces in general are desirable and were usually produced in Germany from papier-mâché until the beginning of WWII. Later examples were produced in Japan and the US, often in plastic. From the 1960s onwards,

memorabilia was more likely to be mass-produced and lower quality, making examples from this period less desirable.

■ Much Halloween memorabilia reflects its rural roots in Scotland – the custom was brought over by Scottish immigrants in the 1880s. Vegetable-shaped candy containers, figurines and centerpieces are common. The more frightening objects, ghouls and the like, are always popular. Halloween postcards are a popular collecting area and appeared in the late 1880s in the US and Germany. Embossed and ornate examples in mint condition are the most desirable, as are those by Brundage, Clapsaddle and Schmucker. However unsigned examples are a great way to amass an affordable collection that is easy to store and display.

A 'Jolly Hallowe'en' vegetable man falling in tub postcard.

5.5in (14cm) wide

$20-30   **SOTT**

A Halloween embossed postcard, of a boy and girl carrying a pumpkin.

1908   *5.5in (14cm) wide*

$25-35   **SOTT**

A 'Happy Hallowe'en' embossed postcard, printed by International Art Publishing Co, with 1908 copyright.

5.5in (14cm) wide

$25-35   **SOTT**

A Halloween Greetings' card, with red border, pumpkins, lady and hand mirror, "Made in Saxony".

5.5in (14cm) wide

$20-30   **SOTT**

A Halloween embossed postcard, with vegetable head figures, and gilt highlights.

5.5in (14cm) wide

$15-25   **SOTT**

A 'Jolly Hallowe'en May Fortune Smile on You' silver painted embossed postcard, with witch.

5.5in (14cm) wide

$35-45   **SOTT**

A 'Joyous Hallowe'en' gate postcard.

5.5in (14cm) wide

$20-30   SOTT

A 'Best Hallowe'en wishes' embossed postcard, decorated with pumpkin and girls and gold foil highlights.

5.5in (14cm) wide

$22-28   SOTT

A 'Jolly Hallowe'en' lady in mirror postcard, by Fred C. Lounsbury, with 1907 postmarks.

5.5in (14cm) wide

$15-25   SOTT

A 'Halloween Greetings', embossed gold postcard.

1912   5.5in (14cm) wide

$25-35   SOTT

A German 'With All Hallowe'en Greetings' postcard, dated October 31st, 1909.

5.5in (14cm) wide

$20-30   SOTT

A 'Happy Halloween' postcard, with boy and pumpkin.

1911   5.5in (14cm) wide

$15-25   SOTT

A Halloween embossed postcard, with gilt detailing and Vegetable heads in car.

5.5in (14cm) wide

$22-28   SOTT

An 'All Halloween' embossed postcard, by TR Co., with large pumpkin, and witch flying above.

5.5in (14cm) wide

$20-30   SOTT

A Halloween moon embossed postcard.

5.5in (14cm) wide

$25-35   SOTT

A 1920s German small vegetable man composition 'roly poly', weighted base.

2.25in (5.5cm) high

$200-250   **SOTT**

A pressed pulp card roly-poly jack-o-lantern vegetable man lantern.

9in (22.5cm) high

$500-600   **SOTT**

A CLOSER LOOK AT A JACK-O-LANTERN MAN

This delicate automated figure has survived in relatively good condition given his age.

Wind-up Halloween figures are unusual and this would have been more expensive than static examples at the time of manufacture.

His head is made from clay-sprayed papier-mâché and has its original painted features. It also display bright colours.

His original clothes are in complete and unfaded condition.

A 1920s German wind-up walking jack-o-lantern man, with fabric clothes.

7in (18cm) high

$800-1,200   **SOTT**

A German large composition vegetable man, with black fabric-covered squeaker hat.

The hat would be pushed down to make a noise and would eventually stay compressed. This example is in original condition although the squeaker isn't working any longer.

$450-550   **SOTT**

A German clay-sprayed card egg-shaped vegetable man, on springy legs on candy box.

9.5in (24cm) high

$650-750   **SOTT**

A German wooden and papier-mâché cat rackett clacker.

See the Black Cat Collectibles section of this book for more examples of feline memorabilia.

10.25in (26cm) high

$200-250   **SOTT**

A very rare 1920s German gauze-covered card candy holder, with painted plaster/chalk skeleton.

4.25in (11cm) high

$400-500   **SOTT**

A CLOSER LOOK AT A SANTA CLAUS FIGURE

The term belsnickle comes from the Pennsylvania Dutch and is a corruption of Pelz-Nickel or Pelts Nicholas meaning 'St. Nicholas in fur.'

The red-suited figure we are used to seeing today was popularized through Haddon Sunblom's depictions of the character for Coca-Cola. Other colored figures were produced, such as the brown examples on this page, but the blue mohair coat is unusual.

These early figures were made from papier-mâché, a fragile material meaning few examples survive.

He retains his wooden backpack, which is unusual.

A 1920s German ceramic dressed Santa Claus candy container, with early tree, good luck mushroom, and sack.

7.5in (19cm) high

$700-900   **SOTT**

A rare and early German blue mohair coat Santa Claus belsnickle figurine, with wooden backpack. *c1918*

8.5in (21.5cm) high

$1,200-1,600   **SOTT**

An early Belsnickle Santa Claus, on wooden base, with long coat and feather tree.

A number of things point to this being an early example. His stuffed hat, lined coat and the tree made from a feather.

7.5in (19cm) high

$600-800   **SOTT**

A 'Merry Christmas' advertising clicker, with Santa Claus, marked "Kirchhof USA".

1.75in (4.5cm) high

$60-80   **LDE**

A 'Grants Toy Dept.' Christmas advertising clicker.

1.75in (4.5cm) high

$60-80   **LDE**

A red, white and green roly-poly rabbit candy container, card base printed "Germany".

Look at the font on the marked base as well as the material as these help to date a piece. This can also be dated to pre-WWII as it is marked simply "Germany" rather than "West Germany".

5.5in (14cm) high

$200-300 SOTT

A hand-painted composition girl bunny candy container, printed "Germany".

6.25in (16cm) high

A very early hand-painted pressed card and plaster-dipped candy container, of a bunny in clown suit, base printed "Made in Germany".

c1915   7.5in (19cm) high

$500-600 SOTT | **$120-180** SOTT

A German pink and blue plaster Easter rabbit candy container, marked "MADE IN GERMANY US Zone".

Unusual color combinations for an Easter bunny are rare and make them more desirable. This mark was only used between 1945-53.

A green and white plaster candy container rabbit, base printed "Germany".

This green and white color combination is unusual and is worth more than the pastel version also on this page.

A 1920s German composition nodding head rabbit, with glass eyes, dressed in suit, the card base printed "Germany".

6.75in (17cm) high

6.75in (17cm) high

6.75in (17cm) high

$220-280 SOTT | **$120-180** SOTT | **$200-250** SOTT

A 1930s Japanese rabbit in a basket candy container, with cotton bunting rabbit.

2.75in (7cm) high

A 1920s German squeaky body candy container, with sprung gauze-covered body and plaster-dipped card head.

6in (15cm) high

A very rare 1930s Japanese cotton ball chick, with crêpe hat, with "MADE IN JAPAN" label.

7.75in (19.5cm) high

$120-180 SOTT | **$250-300** SOTT | **$50-60** SOTT

A CLOSER LOOK AT A PLAYBOY MAGAZINE

"Playboy", May 1954, with Joanne Arnold as Playmate of the month, feature on 'Fahrenheit 451' (part 3) by Ray Bradbury; 'Kill the Umpire' by Jack Strausberg; 'How to Apply for a Job' by Shepherd Mead, his first article.

11in (28cm) high

$300-500   **NOR**

Vintage Playboy magazines are a popular collecting area, the value depending on a number of factors.

The popularity of the featured playmate adds desirability – in this case Marilyn Waltz, in her second of three appearances. She was one of only four woman to be Playmate of the month more than once.

The quality of the short stories and features is also important. This issue features Ray Bradbury's Fahrenheit 451, other popular authors include Arthur C. Clarke.

Other factors include the appearance of controversial celebrities and important interviews. Early issues are also desirable – this is the first anniversary issue, which adds to the value.

"Playboy", April 1954, with Marilyn Waltz as Playmate of the month, features including Ray Bradbury's Fahrenheit 451 (part 2) and Jaaz: The Metronome All Stars featuring photos and story on Benny Goodman, Count Basie, Jack Teagarden, Harry James, Bob Haggert, Gene Krupa and others; 'Advice on the Choice of a Mistress' by Benjamin Franklin and 'Pleasures of the Oyster' by Thomas Mario.

11in (28cm) high

$750-850   **NOR**

"Playboy", January 1955, with short stories including 'The Concrete Mixer' by Ray Bradbury, 'The Ears of Johnny Bear' by John Steinbeck.

This issue's Playmate of the month was model Bettie Page (b.1923). She is best known for her ground-breaking fetish and bondage modelling for Irving Klaw and Bunny Yeager. Interest in her revived in the 1980s and she inspired a number of models including Dita von Teese. A biographical film titled 'The Notorious Betty Page' was released in 2006, which should introduce her to a wider audience.

11in (28cm) high

$300-500   **NOR**

"Playboy", May 1955, with Marguerite Empey as Playmate of the month, and featuring pictorials showing Bunny Yeager taken by herself, Terry Shaw and Bettie Page.

Bunny Yeager was a pin-up model who went on to become a famous pin-up photographer herself, working with famous models including Bettie Page. She won 'Photographer of the Year' in 1959 and was nominated as one of the top 10 photographers in the US. She is still working today.

11in (28cm) high

$300-400   **NOR**

"He", March 1956, articles including 'Hollywood's Lush set, are Women masochists?'.

5.75in (14.5cm) high

$70-100   **NOR**

"Risk", March 1957, featuring 'Nights of Sin & Gin' and a Bunny Yaeger cover photo.

5.75in (14.5cm) high

$15-25   **NOR**

LIFE', Feb 21st 1964, the cover apparently showing Lee Harvey Oswald holding a copy of Communist paper 'Daily Worker' and the Mannlicher Carcano rifle later used to assassinate President John F. Kennedy.

This photograph is considered by some to be fake and Oswald himself claimed his head had been superimposed over someone else's body. Conspiracy theorists point to the fact that the shadow cast by the body is in the 11 o'clock position, while the shadow under the nose would result from the sun being overhead. Also that the rifle is too long in comparison for Oswald's height and that there appears to be a splice line under his lip. Despite these claims, photograph experts and the House Select Committee on Assassinations in the 1970s maintained the photograph is genuine.

13.75in (35cm) high

$35-45   **NOR**

"Newsweek", Nov 13 1967, with Jane Fonda as Barbarella on the cover.

10.75in (27.5cm) high

$25-35   **NOR**

"Photoplay", October 1958, with Elvis Presley and Jerry Lewis on the cover.

The appearance of big name stars like Elvis on the cover will increase the value of a vintage magazine.

10.75in (27.5cm) high

$80-120   **NOR**

"TV Guide", vol. 1, no. 26, Sept 1953, featuring George Reeves as Superman, in near mint condition.

TV Guides are a popular collecting area. This example is one of the most collectible.

8.25in (21cm) high

$650-750   **NOR**

"Vanity Fair", October 1927, cover art by 'Benito', original price 35 cents a copy.

It is the Art Deco style of the art work as well as the title that makes this magazine valuable.

12.75in (32.5cm) high

$80-120   **DD**

"Vogue", June 1946.

The uncluttered cover of this issue, with its minimal use of text and simple image are typical of earlier covers.

11.5in (29cm) high

$50-70   **VM**

"Vogue", September 15, 1965.

12.75in (32.5cm) high

$30-50   **VM**

"Vogue", June 1998, with Kate Moss cover.

Covers featuring supermodels and famous faces are more likely to retain, or increase their value.

11.25in (28.5cm) high

$50-70   **VM**

COLLECTORS' NOTES

■ Handmade marbles can be identified by the presence of a rough 'pontil' mark where the marble was removed from the glass rod during its manufacture. The earliest handmade marbles are traditionally the most desirable and valuable, but due to the scarcity of fine examples and rising prices, later machine-made and contemporary marbles from the 1920s onwards are eclipsing them. Notable manufacturers to look for include Peltier, Akro Agate and particularly The Christensen Agate Company.

■ The 1950s-60s saw Far Eastern and South American glass marbles take over. Of poorer quality and produced in large numbers, very few are sought-after today. From the 1990s, a market in contemporary glass marbles has developed and continues to grow

strongly. Other materials such as china, earthenware and stones usually date from the mid-late 19thC.

■ The type of marble affects value considerably. Look at the pattern and color as well as the size. Minute differences can re-categorise a marble and affect value. Symmetry in design and unusual or bright colors are important considerations, along with 'eye-appeal', which can vary from collector to collector.

■ Condition is important, particularly on machine-made marbles. Chips, scuffs and play wear that affects the pattern will reduce value. Marbles in truly mint condition can sell for up to double the value of a used marble. Packaging can also have a value of its own, as so much was thrown away. Marbles shown here are in near-mint to mint condition.

A German handmade oxblood 'Opaque' marble.

Other colours such as black and white (often used for voting in a ballot box) are more common.

c1860-c1920 0.5in (1.5cm) diam

$60-80   **AB**

A German handmade end-of-day 'Submarine' marble.

Submarine marbles are rare, and have alternating multilayer sub-surface and surface panels over or under ribbons and on a transparent base. Those with mica chips are even rarer.

c1860-c1920 0.75in (2cm) diam

$70-100   **AB**

A German handmade 'Striped Transparent' marble.

c1860-c1920 1in (2.5cm) diam

$7-10   **AB**

A German handmade 'Slag' marble.

Here the pontil mark is clearly visible on the right-hand side. The number of and the appealing colours make this desirable.

c1860-c1920 0.5in (1.5cm) diam

$40-60   **AB**

A German handmade green 'Mica' marble.

c1860-c1920 0.75in (2cm) diam

$15-25   **AB**

A German handmade end-of-day 'Cloud' marble.

Cloud marbles have splodges of colour, that have not been stretched into bands, on a transparent base.

c1860-c1920   0.75in (2cm) diam

$100-150   **AB**

A handmade German 'Cane End' marble and a handmade 'Swirl Ribbon' core marble.

The marble on the right comes from the end of a glass cane, part of which is still attached. The marble on the left comes from within a cane as the swirl appears through the entire marble.

c1860-c1920   1in (2.5cm) diam

$30-50   **AB**

A Christensen Agate Company 'Peach Slag' machine-made marble.

Although slags were produced by all marble companies, this very scarce peach colour is unique to the Christensen Agate Company.

1927-29   0.5in (1.5cm) diam

$300-400   AB

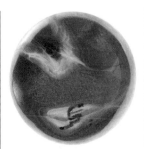

A Champion Agate Company 'New Old-Fashioned' machine-made marble.

This style of marble was produced from the company's founding in 1938 until the 1970s and was reintroduced in the 1980s.

c1984   0.5in (1.5cm) diam

$10-15   AB

A Christensen Agate Company 'American Agate' machine-made marble.

'American Agates' can be distinguished from 'Swirls' by the bright 'electric' colours, which range from red to orange, on an opaque or opalescent base.

1927-29   0.75in (2cm) diam

$100-150   AB

A 1930s-40s Peltier Glass Company 'Experimental Rainbo' machine-made marble.

Colours tend to be less vibrant on Peltier's 'Rainbos', with colours lying in the surface only.

1in (2.5cm) diam

$70-100   AB

An Akro Agate Company 'Carnelian' machine-made marble.

Carnelian and 'ade' marbles are fluorescent under UV lighting due to the presence of uranium in the base glass.

0.75in (2cm) diam

$25-35   AB

An Akro Agate Company 'Lemonade Oxblood' machine-made marble.

Lemonade refers to the translucent yellowy white colour. A combination with oxblood is one of the more common variations of a Lemonade swirl.

0.75in (2cm) diam

$100-150   AB

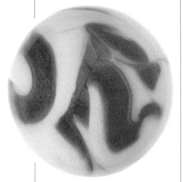

A Christensen Agate Company 'Swirl' machine-made marble.

0.75in (2cm) diam

$15-25   AB

A 1920s-30s Peltier Glass Company 'National Line Rainbo Ketchup & Mustard' machine-made marble.

Vibrant 'National Line Rainbo' marbles are among the most popular produced by Peltier, with collectors giving them names based around their colours.

0.75in (2cm) diam

$200-300   AB

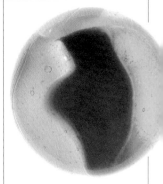

A Peltier Glass Company 'Clear Rainbo' machine-made marble.

0.5in (1.5cm) diam

$30-40   AB

A rare M.F. Christensen & Son Company 'Persian Turquoise Opaque' machine-made marble.

c1910   0.5in (1.5cm) diam

$80-120   **AB**

A CLOSER LOOK AT A MARBLE

Marble King's 'Rainbow' marbles usually have only two colors – this example is a rare variation combining two different types of coloring.

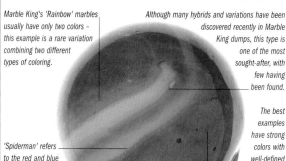

Although many hybrids and variations have been discovered recently in Marble King dumps, this type is one of the most sought-after, with few having been found.

'Spiderman' refers to the red and blue coloring and 'Watermelon' to the red and green coloring. Watermelon is also a rare variation in itself.

The best examples have strong colors with well-defined patches and ribbons - those with blended, less distinct colors are less sought-after and valuable.

A 1950s Marble King Inc. 'Watermelon/Spiderman Hybrid Rainbow' machine-made marble.

0.5in (1.5cm) diam

$650-750   **AB**

A Champion Agate Company 'Swirl' machine-made marble.

0.75in (2cm) diam

$15-25   **AB**

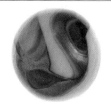

An American 'Metallic Swirl' machine-made marble, by an unknown West Virginia maker.

0.5in (1.5cm) diam

$15-25   **AB**

A Peltier Glass Company 'National Line Rainbo Blue Galaxy' marble.

This is an extremely rare and desirable marble with superb ribbons and coloring.
The black and yellow ribbons contain aventurine (minute copper flakes), making them sparkle.

0.75in (2cm) diam

$1,000-1,500   **AB**

An American 'Aventurine Swirl' marble, by an unknown West Virginia maker.

0.5in (1.5cm) diam

$10-15   **AB**

An Akro Agate Company 'Silver Oxblood' marble.

0.5in (1.5cm) diam

$25-35   **AB**

A Vitro Agate Company 'Parrot' marble.

With four or more bright colors, 'Parrots' are the most popular Vitro Agate Company marbles. Look out for the colors forming a 'V' shape, which adds value. Large sizes such as this are typical.

1 in (2.5cm) diam

$70-90   **AB**

A Ravenswood Novelty Company 'Swirl' marble.

c1931-c1955

0.75in (2cm) diam

$15-25 **AB**

A Christensen Agate Company 'Chocolate Pistachio Swirl' marble.

0.75in (2cm) diam

$60-80 **AB**

A rare Akro Agate Company box of 'Swirl' marbles.

This early card box with sliding window lid contains a metal insert, which is extremely rare. The marbles within it are worth around $20, the rest of the value being for the box in this condition.

c1925

$100-150 **AB**

An Alley Agate Company 'Swirl' marble.

0.75in (2cm) diam

$10-20 **AB**

A 'Pinwheel' hand-painted china marble, with rough pink band and a flower motif.

China marbles, made from porcelain typically have white bodies. Look out for landscape scenes, which are very rare. Brown and lavender are scarce colors.

0.75in (2cm) diam

$70-100 **AB**

A rare larger hand-painted china marble, with bands and a flower motif.

$400-500 **AB**

A large hand-painted china marble, with blue flower motifs.

The flowers are comparatively well-painted and more numerous on this marble, as well as being in better condition, meaning a higher value.

1.5in (4cm) diam

$150-250 **AB**

A 'Doughnut Bullseye' hand-painted china marble.

Bullseye motifs are slightly more commonly found than flowers, but the thick 'doughnut' motifs indicate early production.

1840s-1870s

0.75in (2cm) diam

$60-80 **AB**

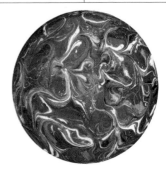

An extremely rare and large gutta percha marble.

Most non-glass marbles are made from clays, china or stone. Gutta percha, made from a tree gum, was developed in 1843 by Dr William Montgomerie and is considered the first true plastic of importance. Golf balls are commonly found in this material and are known as 'gutties'. Marbles are scarcely found and it is also the large size, color, condition and patterning that make this example so valuable.

c1850

1.5cm (4in) diam

$450-550 **AB**

FIND OUT MORE...

www.marblecollecting.com

Marbles: Identification & Price Guide, by Robert Block, published by Schiffer Publishing, 2002.

COLLECTORS' NOTES

■ Mechanical music devices take a number of forms; a musical box with a revolving metal cylinder, boxes containing a flat metal disc, the phonograph and the gramophone. The majority were produced from the mid-19thC to the early 20thC, and were clockwork-driven by winding springs.

■ Musical boxes are among the earliest, dating generally from the mid-19thC to the 1900s. They contain cylinders with protruding pins that strike metal teeth of different lengths on a metal comb to produce the sound. The decorative quality of the case, the complexity of the movement, the number of tunes, its size and maker affect value considerably.

■ Thomas Edison's 'phonograph' uses a needle, 'soundbox' and horn to make sounds picked up from fine grooves in a wax-like cylinder. The same system was used with flat discs by Emile Berliner, who developed the 'gramophone' in 1887. By the turn of the century, the gramophone had overtaken the phonograph in terms of popularity.

■ Again, the decorative appeal of the case, the size and the maker count towards general value. The model is also worth considering. The horn also adds to desirability and value, particularly if decorated and original. Beware of the many reproductions on the market, which tend to use tropical woods and have bright yellowy brass horns.

■ Children's gramophones, most often made from tinplate, can be sought-after. Look for charming scenes in bright colors and notable makers, such as Bing. In all instances, condition is important. Replaced or broken teeth on a comb reduce value. Beware of winding seized mechanisms as this can cause serious and expensive damage.

An American 'Graphophone Champion' horn gramophone, in an oak case with four turned corner columns, the funnel hand-painted with floral designs.

Horn 19.25in (48cm) diam

$700-1,000 ATK

An American Durable Toy and Novelty Corp. of New York toy projector, with 'Durotone' gramophone, the tin plate body printed to simulate wood, hand crank-operated but with electric projecting light.

$600-800 ATK

A German Bing child's clockwork gramophone, in a yellow 'crocodile skin' lithographed tin case formed as a suitcase.

c1925

$150-250 ATK

A late 1940s-to-early 1950s American Lindstrom Corporation, of Bridgeport Conn., printed metal child's electric gramophone.

13.5in (34cm) long

$100-150 NOR

An American Edison 'Model D' phonograph, with 'H' reproducer for four-minute cylinders, housed in an oak case with lid and horn.

1909-14

$500-700 ATK

1902

$600-800 ATK

An American Edison 'Gem Model A', with 'C' reproducer and black horn, contained in an oak case, with three cylinders.

The popular and affordable Gem was produced by Edison from 1899 to 1914 in various models.

A German Symphonion Musikwerke disc musical box, for 5.25in discs, with 76-teeth in duplex comb, with one disc.

c1900

$500-900 ATK

A German Polyphon Musikwerke 'Euphonion' disc music box, for 8.5in discs, 42 teeth in music comb, contained in a walnut case with lithographed picture in lid.

Symphonium or Polyphon cases with serpentine fronts, inlaid wood and original prints set into the lid are more valuable.

10.5in (26cm) wide

$700-1,000   **ATK**

A CLOSER LOOK AT A MUSICAL BOX

Symphonium are renowned for their large floor standing or wall-monted disc musical boxes that produced complex and wonderful, resonant sounds.

A clockwork mechanism revolves a large metal disc pierced with holes. The pierced and bent parts strike metal 'teeth' of different widths on 'combs' to produce the sound.

The carved walnut case is typically highly ornate and is in excellent condition, with the original gilt transfer lettering on the glass door.

They were originally made to be played in stores or at events and are operated by putting a penny in the slot - the larger the discs and the more ornate the case, the rarer it is likely to be.

A German Symphonion Model No. 33 'Lyra' upright disc musical box, with 84 teeth on two music combs, complete with winding key and one disc.

c1900   *34in (85cm) high*

$3,500-5,500   **ATK**

A Swiss B.A. Brémond cased brass cylinder musical box, with eight melodies and hidden bells, the comb with 98 teeth, eight teeth to operate the bells, the front and lid inset with inlays.

25.25in (63cm) wide

$400-500   **ATK**

A Swiss Mermod Frères brass cylinder musical box, with four airs, steel comb with 102 teeth, with original tune sheet.

c1875   *15.25in (38cm) wide*

$700-1,000   **ATK**

An American musical photograph album, with brass clasp and celluloid cover depicting a U.S. warship, probably the U.S.S. Olympia, playing 'The Liberty Bell' and 'Manhattan Beach' marches, on felt-covered base with folding stand with 1895 patent date, tune card and instruction sheet.

c1900   *12.5in (31.5cm) wide*

$220-280   **EG**

A mechanical singing bird cage, probably French, both birds with heads and beaks moving as the sound plays, unmarked.

10.5in (26cm) high

$450-650   **ATK**

A rare German felt-covered pig music box, wind the tail and he plays music, with painted wooden trotters.

c1910   *6.75in (17cm) long*

$250-450   **SOTT**

COLLECTORS' NOTES

■ Examples of items documenting our planet's natural history and prehistory have been collected for centuries and reached an apex during the Georgian and Victorian periods. The 'wunderkammer' or 'cabinet of curiosities' often contained interesting fossils and minerals, sometimes collected on travels, that were seen as signs of education and distinction.

■ Although the area is a highly specialized one, attracting keen collectors interested in geological phenomena and the exploration of prehistoric life, a market based around the decorative appeal of specimens is often highly active. As a result, values today are based as much around the visual impact and eye-appeal of specimens as other criteria.

■ Collectors or those wishing to add an unusual piece to an eclectic interior should also consider the type of mineral or fossil, as some are rarer than others, and the size as large examples are nearly always worth more than smaller ones. Fakes are known, including those cast from molds or comprized of many parts of fossils assembled on a rock 'matrix' base. Always buy from reputable dealers or auction houses.

■ The preparation is also important, particularly with fossils. Fossils that have been sandblasted or acid-etched, to remove excess rock will usually have less detail or damaged specimens. Some are still covered with rock particles, which can obscure the fossil or interrupt its visual appearance. Smaller pieces are very affordable and can be found easily, making the market accessible, but larger and finer examples as seen here are much rarer and fetch high prices.

A Triassic period fossilized Kiechousaur specimen, from China, 230 million years ago.

This is a well-positioned specimen, and has a further specimen disarticulated next to it.

11.5in (29cm) high

$1,500-2,000   **BLO**

An American Eocene period fossilized fresh water ray, collected from Green River, Wyoming, 55 million years old.

22.5in (57cm) high

$1,500-2,500   **BLO**

An American Eocene period 'mass mortality' fossilized fishplate, containing Knightae and Diplomystus species, collected from Green River, Wyoming, 55 million years old.

27.5in (70cm) high

$1,500-2,500   **BLO**

Two Permian period fossilized mesosaurs in their own matrix, collected in Brazil, 260 million years old.

To find two complete specimens on the same matrix is rare.

28.25in (72cm) wide

$3,500-5,500   **BLO**

An Eocene period fossilized Harpactocacinus species crab on its own matrix, 55 million years old.

7in (18cm) wide

$450-650   **BLO**

A Carboniferous period fossilized Scaphocrinites species crinoid (sea lily), collected in Morocco, 360 million years old.

47.25in (120cm) wide

$8,000-10,000   **BLO**

A rare Triassic period fossilized Traumatacrinus species crinoid (sea lily), collected in Hunan, China, 230 million years old.

This large specimen features exquisite preparation work and shows very fine detail, hence its high value.

25.5in (65cm) high

$10,000-15,000   **BLO**

A CLOSER LOOK AT A FOSSIL

Mass mortality refers to the fact that a number of creatures died at the same time and are contained in the same 'matrix' rock closely together.

This example has been very well prepared and exhibits fine detailing. It has also not been abrasively cleaned or over-painted, and is in original condition.

It is very rare due to its extremely large size and the large number of densely packed and intact fossils it contains.

Trilobites are one of our planet's first complex life forms and became extinct before the dinosaurs - they attract many keen collectors today.

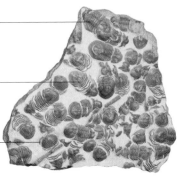

A rare Middle Ordovician period 'mass mortality' Xenasaphus species trilobite specimen, collected in Volhov, St Petersburg, Russia, 470 million years old.

Beware of fakes made up from a number of different species, or overly reconstructed trilobites, particularly from Morocco.

25.5in (65cm) wide

$15,000-25,000   **BLO**

A Jurassic period silver iridescent Cleoniteras species ammonite, collected in Madagascar, 160 million years old.

7in (18cm) wide

$700-1,000   **BLO**

A Carboniferus period large polished Goniatite specimen on its own matrix, collected in Morocco, 360 million years old.

21.5in (55cm) high

$1,500-2,000   **BLO**

A fossilized Arietites species Ammonite, collected in Schoppenstedt, Braunschweig, Germany.

17in (43cm) high

$2,500-3,500   **BLO**

A Miocene period fossilized Charcharadon Megalodon species shark's tooth, collected in Atacama, Chile, 12 million years old.

4.75in (12cm) high

$1,000-1,200   **BLO**

An Oligocene period Oreodont skull, collected in Badlands, South Dakota, United States of America, 35 million years old.

This skull is very well prepared.

8in (20cm) wide

$1,000-1,200   **BLO**

A fossilized dinosaur's egg, mounted on a Chinese wooden stand, collected in outer Mongolia, 60-70 million years old.

6in (15cm) high

$400-500   **OG**

A smokey quartz cluster, from Madagascar.

13.5in (34cm) high

$600-800   **BLO**

An interesting quartz point specimen, with mica and gem-grade aquamarine, from Pakistan.

This quartz crystal displays a beautiful Tourmaline crystal inclusion. This is a very rare combination.

7.5in (19cm) high

$800-1,000   **BLO**

A pair of Bolivian amethysts.

These are far less common than their Brazilian counterparts and of a far better quality in terms of size, color and structure.

Largest 6.75in (17cm) high

$300-400   **BLO**

An amethyst 'cathedral', from Brazil.

Cathedral is the term used to describe these tall, arching geodes. The value of this lies in its large size, shape and the fact that it is not broken.

27.25in (69cm) high

$3,000-4,000   **BLO**

A polished orbicular jasper freeform, Madagascar.

The unusual coloring include pinks, yellows and greens adds to the value of this piece.

6.75in (17cm) high

$600-800   **BLO**

A fine polished amber specimen, from Chiapas, Mexico.

2.25in (6cm) long

$250-450   **BLO**

A large malachite freeform, from the Democratic Republic of Congo.

14.25in (36cm) high

$3,000-4,000   **BLO**

A nickle-iron meteorite, from Campo Del Cielo, Argentina.

Meteorites are usually composed of iron as stone usually breaks up upon entry. Composition, size, weight and form affect value.

3.25in (8cm) wide

$800-1,200   **BLO**

A Jurassic period septarian concretion mudstone, one face polished and cut with a flat base, from Madagascar. (160 million years ago).

Septarian concretions or nodules are hard masses of sedimentary rock containing angular cavities that typically contain crystals, usually Calcite. They are typically broken open to reveal their contents, and are often polished flat.

10.75in (27cm) high

$350-550   **BLO**

COLLECTORS' NOTES

- Sought-after brands including Waterman, Parker, Montblanc and Dunhill Namiki still lead the market, particularly large examples, and those with precious metal overlays. The best of Dunhill's 1930s maki-e lacquer models occupy the very high end of the market, but prices have dropped recently so now is a good time to buy.

- In the past, collectors tended to concentrate on pens produced in their own country. As the market matures and prices rise, collectors are looking further afield and formerly less appreciated brands are becoming

sought-after. For example, England's brightly colored and highly useable Conway Stewarts are now proving popular on both sides of the Atlantic.

- As many collectors use their pens, condition and completeness is very important. Replaceable parts such as nibs and clips should be original, and cracked or damaged examples should be avoided.

- As modern limited editions are often bought for investment, many are kept in pristine condition – values for used examples are therefore unlikely to rise.

An American Parker model 25 eyedropper-filling pen, smooth black hard rubber with Parker Fountain Pen 5 nib with triangular vent hole, polished and one nib tine lacks iridium, but in very good condition.

c1905

$150-200   **BLO**

An American Parker model 16 eyedropper-filling pen, the gold-filled filigree overlay signed on the barrel overlay, with Parker Lucky Curve 'lazy S' nib, overlay slipped, in fair to good condition.

c1905-15

$320-380   **BLO**

A rare American Parker model 16 Jack-Knife Safety baby eyedropper-filling pen, with gold-filled filigree over smooth black hard rubber, 'turban cap' and Parker Lucky Curve Pen 3 keyhole nib, in very good condition.

The name 'turban cap' comes from the shape of the top of the cap, which is found on some early Parker pens.

1912-16

$600-800   **BLO**

A Canadian Parker Lucky Curve Duofold Special button-filling pen, jade green Permanite with Duofold 'P' medium nib, even but not unattractive darkening, otherwise in very good condition.

The Parker Duofold came in a wide range of colors and a number of sizes. Early examples, larger sizes and rare colors such as 'Mandarin yellow' are the most sought-after.

1927

$150-200   **BLO**

A Canadian Parker oversize Vacumatic filling pen, emerald pearl hooped celluloid with Parker Vacumatic two-color arrow medium nib, in very good condition, but barrel threads lengthened.

Much like the earlier Duofold, the Vacumatic was made in a wide range of variations, which differ greatly in value. This oversized model is popular with collectors, while smaller models are generally worth under $70.

1935

$250-350   **BLO**

A 1930s Canadian Parker Premiere button-filling pen, marbled blue and black, Canadian 14K medium nib, in very good to excellent condition.

$120-180   **BLO**

An English Parker Duofold Senior button-filling pen, light and dark burgundy pearl marble celluloid, with Parker Duofold 'N' medium nib, slight fading, otherwise in very good condition.

c1945

$180-220   **BLO**

A new-old-stock American Parker Blue-Diamond Major Vacumatic filling pen, silver pearl celluloid with gold Parker Arrow USA 6 nib, in mint condition, with two stickers, nib possibly inked.

1946

$120-180   **BLO**

An American Parker 51 Blue-Diamond Vacumatic-filling pen, Buckskin with gold-filled Custom cap, double jewels and medium nib, otherwise generally very good condition.

This is the earlier version of the 51 with a Vacumatic filling system. This is indicated by the screw-off section at the end of the barrel, which covers the filling plunger. It was replaced by the Aerometric system in 1948.

1945

$350-450   BLO

A new-old-stock 1950s American Parker 51 Custom pen, burgundy Aerometric-filler, with gold-filled Insignia design cap and fine nib, in mint condition.

Probably Parker's best known and most popular pen, this version of the 51 was produced in vast numbers from 1948 until 1968. The majority of surviving examples were made in the 1950s and '60s and, in standard colors and well-loved condition, are worth under $50.

$150-200   BLO

A new-old-stock mid/late-1960s American Parker 61 cartridge-filling pen, turquoise with chrome trim, Lustaloy cap and medium nib, in mint condition with 61 cartridge barrel chalk marks, and 61 convertible $12.50 swinger tag with nib grade, rare in this condition.

$120-180   BLO

A English Parker 61 'Cumulus' pen set, gold-plated 'Cloud' design (plain clouds on heavy wavy-line background) with medium nib, and matching push-cap ballpoint, in Parker hard duo box, in near mint condition, pen excellent.

1976-80

$300-400   BLO

A late 1960s American Parker 75 vermeil 'Crosshatch Grid' pattern pen, marked "Sterling & 14K GF" and "Made in U.S.A.", with flat tassies, section ring with '0' reference and Parker 14K Point USA code 69 fine stub nib, in excellent condition.

$180-220   BLO

A French Parker 75 Laqué duo pen set, Jasper Red Quartz lacquer with Parker .585 France fine nib, matching push-cap ballpoint, in mint condition, with tag on pen.

1979

$200-300   BLO

An American Parker Falcon 50 stainless steel pen, brushed steel with medium nib, in mint condition with swinger tag.

c1980

$70-100   BLO

A CLOSER LOOK AT A PROTOTYPE PARKER PEN

This brass prototype was produced by Devlin to show the finish and final design of the pen, which was produced in 18ct gold.

It is believed that Parker intended an edition limited to only 1,000 pieces but as only one gold example has been seen, it is probable that the line never went into full production.

Although the shape of the pen was based on the existing budget 'Arrow' range, the textured finish is the typical of the work of contemporary goldsmith Stuart Devlin.

Devlin was born in Australia in 1931 and awarded a scholarship to the Royal College of Art, London in 1958. He was responsible for designing the new Australian decimal coinage in 1963.

A prototype Parker 'Limited Prestige Range' pen, designed and made by Stuart Devlin, the brass body with textured, sculptured finish, guide for positioning of hallmarks, and Parker Arrow medium nib, in mint condition.

1982

5in (13cm) long

$300-500   BLO

PENS & WRITING EQUIPMENT

An extremely rare American Waterman's 'second model' No. 5 straight-holder eyedropper filling pen, smooth black hard rubber with two line imprint with "Feb 12" and "Nov 4 1884" patent dates, three-fissure feed and Waterman's Ideal New York 5 nib with arrow-head vent and second breather hole, in excellent/near mint condition.

This is an extremely rare large-size early Waterman in superb condition with an unusual nib.

1884-89

$800-1,200   **BLO**

A rare American Waterman's 222 'Barleycorn with Nameplate' pattern eyedropper-filling pen, with white-metal half-overlay with nameplate space, taper cap, three fissure feed, and (later) Waterman's 2 nib, in excellent condition with a crisp overlay, boxed.

The Barleycorn pattern is a surprisingly difficult overlay to find on a Waterman's pen, possibly because the company chose to promote more flamboyant styles.

1899

$600-800   **BLO**

A scarce American Waterman's 18 eyedropper-filling pen, chased black hard rubber with Waterman's 8 nib, some mild oxidation.

Despite this small image, the model 18 was the largest standard production Waterman at the time.

1900-07

$300-400   **BLO**

An American Waterman's 414 'Filigree' pattern eyedropper-filling pen, three-leaf filigree overlay signed "Sterling" on the barrel, with Clip-Cap and Waterman's 4 nib, in Waterman's hard eyedropper box, in very good condition.

1908-15

$300-400   **BLO**

A new-old-stock American Waterman's 45 safety filling pen, chased black hard rubber with Waterman's 5 fine nib, possibly with pre-owned nib.

Although early, standard plain black pens, such as this, are not generally valuable, the fact it is in unused condition makes it desirable.

c1910

$120-180   **BLO**

An American Waterman's 5-size 'Sheraton' pattern gold-filled rotary pencil, with black hard rubber nozzle, ball of clip brassed.

These pencils are hard to find in this size

c1917

$80-120   **BLO**

An American Waterman's 05521/2 L.E.C. 'Pansy Panel' pattern lever-filling pen, gold-filled, fully covered overlay, with 'Clip-Cap' and Waterman's medium flexible 2 nib, light wear on post.

1925-27

$180-220   **BLO**

A rare large-size American Waterman's 456 'Basketweave' pattern lever-filling pen, marked "Sterling" on cap, barrel and clip, with Waterman's 6 medium nib, some oxidation and wear from use on hard rubber, otherwise in very good condition.

Large size pens are generally harder to find and more valuable. It is likely that less were made as the large size was not as comfortable to use for most people and they would have been more expensive to buy at the time.

1924-27

$1,800-2,200   **BLO**

An American Waterman's 4521/2 L.E.C. 'Basketweave' pattern lever-filling pen, marked "Sterling" on clip, cap, barrel, and lever, with Waterman's Reg US 2 nib, in very good condition.

1928-30

$200-300   **BLO**

An American Waterman's 4521/2 LEC 'Hand-Engraved Vine' pattern lever-filling pen, marked "Sterling" with Waterman's 2 nib, some wear from use, generally in very good/excellent condition.

L.E.C. stands for Lower End Covered and indicates a fully overlaid pen.

1928-30

$300-400   **BLO**

A 1920s American Waterman's 56 Cardinal lever-filling pen and pencil, Cardinal red hard rubber with Clip-Cap and Waterman's 6 medium nib, with similar rotary pencil, boxed, both in excellent condition, clips differ slightly.

$500-700

BLO

An extremely rare American Waterman's 51V Ripple lever-filling pen, red and black hard rubber with Waterman's Ideal Reg US 1 medium-broad nib, minor oxidation, otherwise in excellent condition.

1928-30

$120-180

BLO

A Canadian Waterman's 92 'Silver Lizard' lever-filling pen, silver pearl 'lizardskin' celluloid with Waterman's Canada 2 oblique medium nib, in excellent condition.

1931-34

$350-450

BLO

A Canadian Waterman's Lady Patricia lever-filling pen, Nacre (pearl and black) celluloid with Waterman's 2 'ballpoint' nib, in excellent condition, a rare color to find in the Lady Patricia.

A rigid 'ballpoint' nib has a smooth, round ball of iridium on the tip of the nib, which would have made it suitable for making carbon copies.

1932-33

$120-180

BLO

A Canadian Waterman's 94 'Steel Quartz' (red-flecked grey marble) lever-filling pen, with chrome trim and Waterman's 4 medium nib, engraved name and light surface marks, generally in good/very good condition.

1934-39

$70-100

BLO

A Canadian Waterman's 3V lever-filling pen, burgundy pearl marble celluloid with Waterman's Canada 2 broad nib, with box and papers, in near mint condition, a great example.
1935-38

$180-220

BLO

A Canadian Waterman's 3 lever-filling pen, red-flecked dark blue-grey pearl marble celluloid, with Waterman's Ideal 2 medium-stub nib, in excellent condition.

1935-39

$70-100

BLO

An American Waterman's Hundred Year lever-filling pen, smooth red transparent lever-filler with triple cap band, with medium Hundred Year Pen nib, cap lip shortened.

The thin lip of the cap on this model is often cracked or has been shortened, as in this example. An undamaged example would command a premium.

c1941

$120-180

BLO

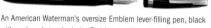

An American Waterman's oversize Emblem lever-filling pen, black with replaced standard-size Emblem medium nib.
c1942

$120-180

BLO

A 1970s French Waterman CF silver 'Barleycorn' pattern cartridge-filling pen and ballpoint, marked "Argent Massif" and with French control marks, 18ct fine nib, with box, leaflet and tags and card sleeve, in inked mint to mint condition.

Often mistakenly thought of as Waterman's first cartridge-filling (CF) pen, it was actually preceded by a 1936 model that used refillable glass cartridges and ink pellets that were mixed with water.

$150-200

BLO

A rare American A.A. Waterman 291M-3+ eyedropper filling pen, chased black hard rubber with "Not Connected With..." barrel imprint, A.A. 14k No.2 medium flexible nib, in very good condition.

Arthur A. Waterman, unrelated to Lewis Edson Waterman, started his pen company prior to 1900. In 1907, L.E. Waterman sued the company for trademark infringement and won, resulting in all further A.A. Waterman pens being imprinted with "Not Connected with the L. E. Waterman Company".

c1915

$40-60   BLO

A rare American Chilton 77S pneumatic-filling pen, pearl and black celluloid with Greek-key design cap band and Chilton Pen 14K nib, with only minor yellowing to the celluloid.
c1930

$180-220   BLO

An American Conklin 5 NL crescent-filling pen, wave-chased black hard rubber with Conklin 4 Toledo nib, in very good condition.

1910-18

$80-120   BLO

An American Conklin 5000-word Nozac piston-filling pen and pencil set, facetted green herringbone Pyrolin, with word gauge and Conklin Toledo medium nib, with matching pencil, pen professionally overhauled, pencil cap slips and needs attention.

1934-38

$350-450   BLO

An American Dunn 8-size Camel pump-filling pen, smooth black hard rubber, red Casein pump handle, plain clip, Dunn Pen Camel medium-fine nib, in very good condition, a rare and large pen.

c1921-24

$320-380   BLO

A 1920s Canadian Eclipse 'Mandarin Yellow' flat top, oversize Lucky Curve Senior-style pen in yellow celluloid with green ends and Warranted 14K medium nib, in very good to excellent condition.

This is very similar to Parker's Lucky Curve Duofold Senior, which was much copied at the time. A Mandarin yellow Parker Duofold, one of the rarest colors in that range, in a similar size and condition could be worth up to $1,000.

$180-220   BLO

A late 1920s American John Holland 4-size Jewel lever-filling pen, pearl and black celluloid lever-filling pen, with 'Bell' clip and Jewel John Holland 'Cin O' nib, lacks iridium, but rare and in decent condition.

'Pearl and black' marbled plastic was used by a number of pen manufacturers. The 'pearl' sections often become discolored to a muddy brown/green, which reduces the value, but this example has a nice, clean color.

$180-220   BLO

A late 1920s American Le Boeuf Unbreakable 65 lever-filling pen, grey-white swirl celluloid with Le Boeuf Springfield Mass 6 fine nib, in excellent condition.

Although a relatively small company, in existence for little more than 10 years, Le Boeuf pens are highly sought-after. Frank Le Boeuf developed a new manufacturing process in 1918, which meant pens could be produced in colored and patterned plastics found on no other pens.

$400-600   BLO

An American Wahl-Eversharp Coronet lever-filling pen set, the lined gold-filled body with jet Pyralin inlay, Eversharp Manifold fine nib with ink shut-off valve, matching repeater pencil, in unmarked hard duo presentation box, in very good condition, light ring of wear on pen from cap.

1936-38

$700-1,000   BLO

A very rare English Burnham rolled gold button-filler, marked rolled gold around the clip screw, with rectangular chequer and plain line design and Burnham nib, ding in blind cap, otherwise in excellent condition.

Metal-covered Burhams are rare, they are also more commonly found as lever-fillers.

c1935

$320-380 BLO

A rare 1920s English Conway Stewart Dinkie No. 540, striated light blue and turquoise ('toothpaste') Casein with Conway Stewart medium nib, discoloration by cap band and barrel threads, in excellent condition.

Small ringtop pens, such as this, were designed for ladies to wear on a ribbon around their necks or on a chatelaine. They are usually more affordable than larger examples making them ideal for collecting on a budget.

$100-150 BLO

A rare English Conway Stewart 60 lever-filling pen, black with Duro medium-fine nib, in excellent condition, rare in black.
1958-63

$80-120 BLO

A rare 1920s Scottish De La Rue rolled gold Onoto, fully covered fine barley design, with metal section and De La Rue 3 medium nib, professionally restored overlay on cap crown and plunger cover, otherwise in very good condition.

$100-150 BLO

A 1950s English Conway Stewart 58 'Cracked Ice' lever-filling set, silver pearl-veined black marble celluloid with Duro Conway Stewart medium nib, and The Conway No 33 pencil, in Conway Stewart duo-box, mild brassing on pen clip, otherwise in excellent condition.

The scarce 'Cracked Ice' finish, named by collectors, is one of the most popular with Conway Stewart enthusiasts.

$400-600 BLO

A Scottish De La Rue Onoto [5235-93] plunger-filling pen, light and dark burgundy pearl marble celluloid, with De La Rue Onoto 5 two-color medium nib, in very good condition.
c1948

$100-150 BLO

An early 1930s English Esterbrook 'Relief' No 22-L midsize lever-filling pen, light and dark blue pearl marble celluloid with red band and Esterbrook Relief 14ct 2 medium-oblique nib, in very good condition.

$100-150 BLO

A 1920s English Mabie, Todd & Co 'Blackbird' safety filling pen, chased black hard rubber with later Blackbird nib, "made by the 'Swan' Pen People", in very good condition, a few teeth marks.

$120-180 BLO

A rare 1920s English Mabie, Todd & Co Swan Eternal 444B/61 lever-filling pen, mottled red and black hard rubber with Swan Eternal 4 medium nib, in very good condition.

$280-320 BLO

An English Mabie, Todd & Co. Blackbird Self-Filler BB2/46 lever-filling pen, 'Oriental Blue' (blue and light blue with bronze marble), Blackbird 14 ct medium nib, in excellent condition.
1934-37

$320-380 BLO

PENS & WRITING EQUIPMENT

A German Montblanc 1-M safety filling pen, smooth black hard rubber with Simplo 1 fine nib, in excellent condition.

Montblanc were known as the Simplo Filler Company from their founding in 1908 until after WWII when the brand name Montblanc was phased in.

1920-25

$350-450   BLO

A German Montblanc L25 Meisterstück push-knob filling pen, luxury pearl and black marble celluloid, with later Montblanc 14ct broad-oblique nib, in mint condition.

Colored Montblanc pens are very rare. This luxury example is in mint condition and also has a scarce broad oblique nib making it more desirable.

1931-34

$1,000-1,500   BLO

A German Montblanc 224 'PL' push-knob filling pen, platinum pearl striated celluloid with Montblanc 4 nib, in slightly later Montblanc kidney-shaped card box, scratch on blind cap and mild oxidation, otherwise in near mint condition.

1935-37

$800-1,200   BLO

A Danish Montblanc 2 button-filling pen, coral red with 14ct M fine nib, in very good condition, slight wear and brassing.

1937-46

$200-300   BLO

A German Montblanc 3341/2 M piston-filling pen, black with broad steel 41/2 Montblanc nib, the cap with Stöffhaus cap imprint, in excellent condition.

Stöffhaus was a German retailer.

1937-38

$280-320   BLO

A CLOSER LOOK AT A MONTBLANC PEN

It is in near mint condition. As pens are intended for use, dings and dents are common on metal overlaid pens.

Initially, Montblanc did not make their own metal overlays so they commissioned German silversmith Sarastro to produce them. They can be identified by the 'S' mark.

Metal overlaid Montblancs are exceedingly rare.

Overlays made or commissioned by the manufacturer are the most desirable, followed by contemporary overlays produced for importers or individuals. Modern overlays are also added to old pens, some with the intention to deceive.

A very rare German Montblanc 14ct gold octagonal 132 piston-filling pen, with eight-sided engine-turned and polished overlay, two-color 4810 P nib, in black leather Stöffhaas case with mother-of-pearl button, in near mint condition, one pinhead ding; signed "S 585 (Sarastro)".

c1938

$2,800-3,200   BLO

A rare Danish Montblanc 25 push-knob filling pen, green marble celluloid, 12-sided with 4810 medium-fine nib, in very good condition with light wear, although clip screw possibly glued on.

Faceted Montblancs are rare.

1939-43

$600-800   BLO

A German Montblanc 242-B 'PL' piston-filling pen, platinum pearl striated celluloid with Montblanc broad nib, in near mint condition.

1950-54

$350-400   BLO

A CLOSER LOOK AT A NAMIKI PEN

Maki-e lacquer decorated pens are some of the most valuable and desirable ever produced. Those made by Namiki are particularly finely made.

Value of maki-e pens depends on size, condition, subject matter and the quality, type and level of lacquer decoration.

The quality of the hand-painted decoration is exceptional. It would have taken many months of painstaking work to complete.

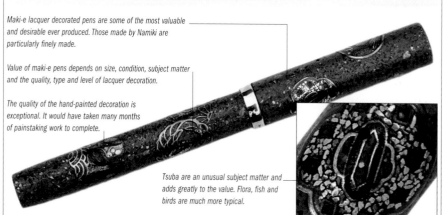

Tsuba are an unusual subject matter and adds greatly to the value. Flora, fish and birds are much more typical.

A mid-1920s Japanese Namiki maki-e lacquer lever-filling pen, medium-large 6-size, the unusual red raden ground inlaid with iridescent aogai (mother-of-pearl) shell and decorated with sakura (plum) blossom, five different tsuba (sword guards) in high relief using a variety of maki-e and lacquer techniques, a red seal kao hidden amongst the decoration of the fifth, with Namiki 6 14K nib, in superb condition.

$18,000-22,000 **BLO**

A late 1920s Japanese Namiki maki-e lacquer ringtop lever-filling pen, decorated with a temple amongst trees in a mountain landscape and inlaid with aogai, with (replaced) warranted nib, cap ring and posting wear.

$700-1,000 **BLO**

A 1930s Japanese Platinum maki-e lacquer balance lever-filling pen, decorated in gold and red with uguisu (nightingale) in a flowering plum tree, with silver clip and similar lever, with 14K Highclass nib, in very good/excellent condition.

$800-900 **BLO**

A fine 1950s Japanese Pilot maki-e R-type piston-filling pen, decorated with a dragon emerging through storm-clouds and lightning, in gold, silver and red iroe-hiramaki-e and togidashi-maki-e; the dragon writhing as it moves through the rolling storm clouds, clutching the tama (sacred pearl) whilst ascending from the sea to the heavens, with gold-filled clip and Pilot 14K 4 fine nib, signed Keizo above a red seal kao, with Kokko-kai to the right of the signature, in near mint condition.

Dragons featured on a small series of 1950s Pilot pens made by a group of freelance maki-e masters. It is a bold and evocative subject matter, its sinuous shape ideally suited to the medium.

$5,000-7,000 **BLO**

A Japanese Pilot maki-e deluxe cartridge/convertor-filling pen, decorated with gold bamboo stems pruned to encourage new growth and with purple-bronze leaves in togidashi-hiramaki-e and nashiji and mura nashiji background, signed Ei with red seal kao and kokko-kai, with 14K 585 Pilot M 190 nib, in near mint/mint condition.

Bamboo is a common decorative theme on maki-e and is symbolic of fidelity, constancy, and long life in Japanese culture.

1978-1980s

$800-1,200 **BLO**

A CLOSER LOOK AT A LIMITED EDITION FOUNTAIN PEN

The Lorenzo de Medici was the first from Montblanc's limited edition 'Patrons of the Arts series and is the most sought-after.

The design and decoration is based on a c1920 Montblanc safety-filling fountain pen.

It is part of the annual 'Patron of Art' series, all of which are limted to 4,810 pieces.

This example is still sealed in the factory's plastic sleeve and retains all of its paperwork, boxes and card outers. Any other state would reduce the value considerably.

A German limited edtion Montblanc 'Lorenzo de Medici' piston-filling pen, from an edition of 4,810, with hand-engraved silver octagonal overlay, two-color 4810 18K M nib, in box with paperwork, pen sealed mint; some wear to box card outers.
1992

$6,000-7,000 BLO

A German limited edition Montblanc 'Hemingway' ballpoint, from an edition of 30,000, orange-red and brown, in mint condition, with box, papers, fountain pen outer box.

The first release from Montblanc's Writers edition, the fountain pen and ballpoint were produced in relatively large numbers compared to the Patron of Art edition.

1992

$600-800 BLO

A German limited edition Montblanc 'Oscar Wilde' 0.9mm propelling pencil, from an edition of 12,000, pearl and black resin with vermeil clip marked "925", with box and papers, in near mint condition.

Limited edition pencils and ballpoints are a more affordable way to collect modern editions and are usually made in smaller numbers.

1994

$220-280 BLO

A German limited edition Montblanc 'F.M. Dostoevsky' piston-filling pen, from an edition of 17,000, decorated black resin barrel, polished black cap with decorated trim and blue cabochon stone set in clip, dated and decorated 4810 M nib, in box with paperwork, in 'inked mint' condition.
1997

$500-700 BLO

A German limited edition Montblanc 'F. Scott Fitzgerald' piston-filling pen, from an edition of 18,500, white pearl barrel with contrasting silver-banded black cap and barrel end, silver 'Art Deco' clip, dated two-color 4810 M nib, in box with paperwork, in 'inked mint' condition.
2002

$500-600 BLO

A German limited edition Montblanc 'Jules Verne' piston-filling pen, from an edition of 18,500, blue guilloché lacquer cap and barrel, decorated 4810 M nib, in box with leaflet, no outer box or slipcase, in mint condition.
2003

$500-600 BLO

A German limited edition Pelikan 'Spirit of Gaudi' piston-filling pen, from an edition of 1,000, black resin with Gaudi-inspired silver overlay, 18C-750 white gold M nib, in box with paperwork, in mint condition.
2002

$800-1,200 BLO

A German limited edition Pelikan 'Xuan Wu' Asia 851/888, "Ag 925" mark, 18ct M nib, in box with paperwork, in mint condition.
2001

$1,000-1,500 BLO

A rare American limited edition Bexley Deluxe II model 2006 cartridge/convertor filling pen, from an edition of 250, Mandarin Yellow acrylic with faux button-filler, marked "Bexley" on wide cap band and "10k" on cap band and clip, numbered decal on blind cap, two-color Bexley 14k medium nib, in near mint condition.

This is inspired by Parker's iconic Lucky Curve Duofold, produced in the 1920s and '30s.

c2000

$200-250   BLO

An English limited edition Conway Stewart 'Churchill' lever-filling pen, from an edition of 500, red and black ripple hard rubber with 18ct gold band, Conway Stewart 18ct Gold medium nib, in mint condition with box, cigar, ink bottle, papers and card outer.

2000

$350-450   BLO

A French limited edition Waterman Edson Signé Boucheron cartridge/convertor-filling pen, from an edition of 3,741, sapphire blue Edson with 18ct-gold latticed overlay by Boucheron, 18k 750 M nib, in presentation box with paperwork, in near mint condition.

c1996

$800-1,200   BLO

An Italian limited edition Ancora 'Cielo' vacumatic-style filler demonstrator pen, from an edition of 204, transparent sky blue acrylic, with vermeil trim and 18ct 1919 fine nib, in mint condition with box and papers.

1998

$500-700   BLO

An Italian numbered edition Montegrappa 'Oriental Zodiac - The Dragon' pen set, with silver barrel overlay of a dragon, two-color medium nib and matching screw-cap rollerball, each with cloth, tray, papers, casket, card outer box and sleeves, in mint condition.

While not from a limited edition, pens are individually numbered.

1998

$1,200-1,800   BLO

A French limited edition OMAS 'Galileo Galilei' piston-filling pen, from an edition of 4,692, pearl-veined black marble acrylic, with broad two-color arrow nib, in near mint condition with silver-grey box, circular booklet and card outer.

1993

$400-500   BLO

An Italian limited edition Visconti 'Uffizi' pen, from an edition of 500, silver filigree over teal granite celluloid, with Visconti 18K white gold nib, box and outer, in 'inked mint' condition.

1993

$500-600   BLO

A very rare Italian limited edition Visconti 'D'Essai Platinum' pen, from an edition of 100, silver-pearl hooped laminated celluloid, with Visconti 18k .750 medium nib, inked, with certificate.

The four pens in the D'Essai series were Visconti's first limited editions and were made from a small cache of 1940s vintage celluloid.

1994

$300-400   BLO

A Japanese limited edition Namiki Emperor Collection 'Steppes Flowers' pen, signed Kyusai, decorated in togidashi maki-e with two quails in front of flowers and tall grasses and signed Kyusai and Kokko Kai with red seal kao and 18 Karat Namiki 50 fine nib, in leather pouch, with box, card cover and papers, inked.

c2000

$2,800-3,200   BLO

A Japanese Namiki 'The Panda' pen, from an edition of 700, maki-e lacquer, signed Kyusai with red seal kao and Kokokai broad 18k gold nib, in mint condition with papers and casket.

$800-1,200   BLO

An 1870s American ornate cast iron patent inkstand with thermometer, the square base decorated with a palmette frieze and similar feet, the shaped front with Sphinx figurine, cast patented "July 4 1876" on the base, with fitted glass inkwell.

$280-320   **BLO**

A CLOSER LOOK AT AN INKWELL

The 'Isobath' was an expensive inkwell made by Doulton in Lambeth, London for the notable printing company, and later fountain pen maker, De La Rue.

The hemisphere and lid are often lost or broken, but here they are complete and intact. There are only a couple of small chips to the frilled edge.

The main body contains the ink and a hard rubber, swinging hemisphere which forces the ink into the small side receptacle to keep it at a constant full level.

They are found in many different decorative designs and come with or without trays. This example has the more desirable frilled tray and fine decoration all over the body.

A very rare Doulton stoneware 'Chiné-ware' De La Rue Isobath inkwell, with decorators' marks including Fanny Sayers, Rosetta Hazeldine and Edith Herapath or E.Hibberd.

1888-1890   *6.25in (16cm) high*

$320-380   **BLO**

A rare English Perry & Co. patent Perryian gravitating inkstand, the shaped brass holder with an octagonal glass inkwell on swivel-mounts, on scallop-shaped base with sprung grip and penrest.

c1850   *2.25in (5.5cm) high*

$150-200   **BLO**

An Elkington Art Manufacturers Association inkwell, the central glass inkwell set in a copper surround modeled as a naturalistic tree-trunk, with three shield-shaped panels of leaves and berries and three different bearded faces with scroll support.

c1897

$70-100   **BLO**

A rare Morton's patent glass inkwell, with nickel-plated iris diaphragm, stamped "Morton's Patent" on the rotating cover.

1870s-1900   *2.25in (6cm) wide*

$150-200   **BLO**

A German patent automatic 'Constant Level' inkwell, molded glass with screw-in bulb-shaped reservoir and shaped well, with metal cover.

This design was protected under patent no. 4699, which was granted to Heinrich Gerhardt of Nuremberg on 17th August 1878.

1878-91   *3.75in (9.5cm) high*

$180-220   **BLO**

A mid-19thC William Mitchell ceramic 'Syphon' inkwell, the cylindrical white glazed stoneware well with spout and integral plinth base, with black stencilled "William Mitchell/London" within an ellipse on the base, and two incised characters or numerals, in very good condition.

$70-100   **BLO**

A novelty elephant inkwell, probably French, dark patinated spelter modeled as a lively elephant, hinged cover on the back over a glass liner, in very good condition, although probably originally gilded.

1860s-70s   *3in (7.5cm) high*

$120-180   **BLO**

A CLOSER LOOK AT A DESK BASE

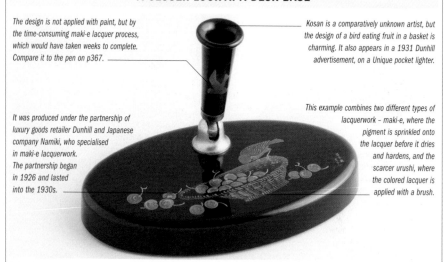

The design is not applied with paint, but by the time-consuming maki-e lacquer process, which would have taken weeks to complete. Compare it to the pen on p367.

Kosan is a comparatively unknown artist, but the design of a bird eating fruit in a basket is charming. It also appears in a 1931 Dunhill advertisement, on a Unique pocket lighter.

It was produced under the partnership of luxury goods retailer Dunhill and Japanese company Namiki, who specialised in maki-e lacquerwork. The partnership began in 1926 and lasted into the 1930s.

This example combines two different types of lacquerwork – maki-e, where the pigment is sprinkled onto the lacquer before it dries and hardens, and the scarcer urushi, where the colored lacquer is applied with a brush.

A 1930s Dunhill Namiki maki-e and urushi lacquer desk base, signed by Kosan and executed in takamaki-e and urushi on a roiro-nuri background.

6in (15cm) high

$550-650   **PC**

An American Parker Duofold bronzed metal desk set, with tulip and jade Permanite Duofold Junior pen with taper and additional cap.

c1930

$120-180   **BLO**

An unusual 1950s American Parker 51 Magnetix gold anodised aluminum desk set, with four pen rests, 'Magic Wand' tulip and black 51 Aerometric desk pen.

$150-200   **BLO**

A 1930s American Wahl-Eversharp Doric green marble double desk base, with two brass columns supporting an octagonal Elgin 8-day clock and two lined green Doric tulips and matching Gold Seal Doric lever-filling desk pens.

$550-650   **BLO**

A 19thC cold cast metal 'Wild Boar' shaped penwipe, probably German, painted in white and black, with painted brown and black eyes and pink snout.

$150-200   **BLO**

A late 19thC English silver-plated baby's bootee penwipe, with eyelets for the laces and black bristles.

4in (10cm) wide

$100-150   **BLO**

A English chrome-plated 'Boot Wipe' penwipe, set with white and black bristles.

1890s-c1910   3.5in (9cm) wide

$120-180   **BLO**

PENS & WRITING EQUIPMENT

A late 1950s/60s Parker 51 or 61 14-pen case, with dark red cloth cover, cream plush-lined tray and gold-colored Parker logo on the white satin lid lining.

8.5in (22cm) wide

$280-320   **BLO**

An early 1950s Parker 51 freestanding wooden shop display stand, with six grooves and three inset discs with card prices, stamped "The Parker Pen Company" and "Made in England" on the back.

$350-450   **BLO**

A Persian brass writing utensil box, with lid for writing utensils and a small ink pot, decorated with floral and fairy tale-like animals and figures.

Often known as a 'qualandan' and dating from the 18thC, examples of this type of portable penholder are generally much later, dating from even as late as the late 20thC.

10.5in (26cm) long

$18-22   **WDL**

A set of early 20thC brass postal scales, with calibrated pan and cantilever section on an oak base, with four loose weights.

$70-100   **BIG**

A late 1880s cast-iron folding pen rack, with two sprung sides and arms to hold six pens, marked "Pat'd. apl'13.1880 Jan 12. 1886 pat'd. in Europe".

3.5in (9cm) wide

$150-200   **BLO**

A 1960s Olivetti Synthesis 45 plastic letter rack, designed by Ettore Sottsass in 1973.

This was part of a range of stationery objects, designed by this notable Postmodern architect and designer. They could be mixed and matched in different colors.

7.25in (18cm) wide

$40-60   **GM**

A 1980s English Sheaffer brown glazed ceramic ashtray, made by Wade for the Arabic market, with gold lettering.

$70-100   **BLO**

An early 20thC MacNiven & Cameron Waverley white and brown enameled and embossed pen nib advertising sign, with some chips.

$320-380   **BLO**

A 1940s American Parker 'V-Mail' package, comprising a display card for Parker "Micro-Film Black" 'V-mail Quink', two boxed bottles of 'V-mail Quink', and a box of 'Wolf Envelope Co. V-mail' combined letters and envelopes.

'V-mail' was developed in the last years of WWII and replaced the slow process of sending bulky non-critical personal letters to troops by sea or air. Letters were microfilmed and then reproduced near the recipient's base, meaning 2lbs of microfilm replaced 100lbs of mail. To support this, Parker promoted their special 'Microfilm Black Quink', enabling letters to be reduced and enlarged by V-mail without losing definition.

9.75in (25cm) high

$100-150   **BLO**

COLLECTORS' NOTES

- Pez peppermint flavoured sweets were invented by Viennese confectioner Eduard Haas III in 1927. Originally sold in tins, Oskar Uxa designed a new dispenser shaped like a cigarette lighter in 1948. These are known as 'regulars' today.

- Pez was introduced to the US in 1952. To appeal to children, new fruit flavours were introduced and dispensers were enhanced with character heads.

- Early characters included Santa Claus, Space Trooper, and Popeye. The range was soon expanded with cartoon and film characters and holiday themes. Companies such as eBay and Nivea have also commissioned promotional dispensers.

- Many characters have been redesigned over the years and collectors often try to collect all the variations of their favourite dispensers. Pre-1987 dispensers lack feet and are generally more desirable. Plain 1950s 'regulars' and early figural designs are among the most sought-after types.

- Look for rare variations such as unusual colors. Pez now produce a range of dispensers and other merchandise aimed directly at collectors.

A 1960s 'Nurse' Pez dispenser, made in Austria, no hat, patent number 2 620 061.

The 'Nurse' pez dispenser with the hat can be worth up to $120

4.25in (11cm) high

$70-100   **SOTT**

An early 1970s 'Sheik' Pez dispenser, from the Pez Pals series, with red band around the burnoose and without feet.

Versions with a black headband are worth around 10% more.

4.5in (11.5cm) high

$60-80   **DMI**

An early 1970s Walt Disney's 'Mickey Mouse' Pez dispenser, first non-die-cut version, with removable nose, without feet.

4in (10cm) high

$15-20   **DMI**

An early 1970s 'Indian Chief' Pez dispenser, with a white headdress and without feet.

These dispensers came in a huge range of multicolored headdresses, but white is the most common.

4.5in (11.5cm) high

$70-100   **DMI**

A late 1970s Walt Disney's 'Scrooge McDuck' Pez dispenser, original version with feet.

This original version used the same mold as a Donald Duck dispenser, and includes applied glasses, sideburns and hat. These pieces were often lost, making complete examples relatively scarce.

A late 1970s Walt Disney's 'Dumbo' Pez dispenser, without feet.

4.25in (11cm) high

$30-50   **DMI**

4.5in (11.5cm) high

$15-20   **DMI**

A 'Bunny' Pez dispenser, made in Yugoslavia, with no feet and fat ears, patent number "3 942 683".

The patent number places the date of manufacture between 1976 and 1990.

4.25in (11cm) high

$15-20   **SOTT**

An MGM's 'Barney Bear' Pez dispenser, complete in original packaging.

Commissioned by toy store FAO Schwartz.

1999 9.5in (24cm) high

$5-7   **DMI**

An early 1970s 'Mr Ugly' Pez dispenser, with olive green face and without feet.

There are variations with differently colored heads, of these the chartreuse green face is the most valuable, usually fetching up to around $80. However, models with feet fetch considerably less.

4in (10cm) high

$30-50 DMI

A 1970s three-piece 'Witch' Pez dispenser, without feet.

This is a common color combination.

4.25in (11cm) high

$15-20 DMI

A 1990s 'Misfit Snowman' Pez dispenser, manufactured for a mail-in offer.

Misfits are standard characters produced in limited numbers in unusual colors.

4.5in (11.5cm) high

$3-5 DMI

A 'Jack-in-the-Box' promotional Pez dispenser, marked on the back of the head "Mfg for Jack in the Box restaurants".

Commissioned by the Jack-in-the-Box fast food chain.

c1999   4.75in (12cm) high

$5-7 DMI

A 'USA Hearts' Pez dispenser, manufactured after the terrorist attacks on 11th September 2001.

2002   4.5in (11.5cm) high

$2-3 DMI

A late 1990s 'Psychedelic Flower' Pez dispenser, collector's edition remake.

3.75in (9.5cm) high

$12-14 DMI

A 'Honey-Nut Cheerios' short-stem Pez dispenser.

Commissioned as a special offer with Honey-Nut Cheerios breakfast cereal.

2001 2.75in (7cm) high

$12-18 DMI

A Pez dispenser, commissioned for the FX Show collectors fair, "The Coolest Show On Earth".

2005   4.25in (11cm) high

$12-14 DMI

An early 1990s 'Truck' Pez dispenser, from the 'D' series, with glow-in-the-dark trailer.

4in (10cm) long

$8-12 DMI

FIND OUT MORE...

Collectors' Guide to Pez, by Shawn Peterson, published by Krause Publications, 2nd Edition, 2003.

The Museum Pez Memorabilia, 214 California Drive, Burlingame, California, 94010, USA.

www.pezcentral.com

www.pezcollectors.com

COLLECTORS' NOTES

■ The development of plastic has been of undoubted key importance to the 20thC – our world would be very different if it had not been developed. The first 'plastic' materials, such as celluloid, were used in the late 19thC but Bakelite, developed in 1907 by Belgian chemist Dr Leo Baekeland, is considered the first true synthetic plastic.

■ Dubbed the 'material of 1,000 uses', it is found primarily in darker colors such as brown and black, and occasionally in red, green and blue. Its development generated a boom in the plastics industry and led to a vast number of different plastics being made. Thus, not all plastics are true 'Bakelite' although the term 'bakelite' is commonly applied to many early plastics.

■ The 'golden age' lasted from c1910 to the 1950s, when cheaper injection molded plastics took over. The adaptability of the material in terms of color and form saw it being used for cost-effective mass production of many different objects from electrical insulators to kitchenware to jewellery.

■ Two key indicators to value are color and form. Plastic allowed domestic pieces to break away from the dominance of dull woods and plain metals, so brighter colors are more desirable, particularly in strong tones such as cherry red. 'Catalin' was a phenolic resin made by the Catalin Corporation in the US, and is known particularly for its vibrant colors. Blue, red and green Bakelite is generally rare.

■ The Art Deco style was dominant during this period and it is this that collectors seek out. Look for quintessential Deco designs, such as clean lines, stepped designs, streamlining and geometric forms. Condition is also all-important, with chips, cracks and repairs affecting value considerably, particularly for more common pieces, which should be avoided. Some colors have faded, darkened or changed over time, but this often does not affect value as seriously.

A 1930s butterscotch cast phenolic cylindrical cigarette box, the lid unscrewing to act as an ashtray.

3in (8cm) high

$200-300 **MG**

A 1930s slightly marbled cherry red Catalin cigarette box, with carved yellow Catalin cigarette shaped handle .

4in (10cm) high

$700-900 **MG**

A 1930s Art Deco amber and yellow marbled powder box, with molded vertical ribbing , the lid with triangular finial.

3.25in (8cm) high

$250-350 **MI**

A late 1930s-1940s mottled green cast phenolic round powder box, with elliptical, domed lid, some darkening.

5in (12.5cm) diam

$400-600 **MG**

A very rare reverse carved 'Apple Juice' bakelite powder box, with carved lines and flowers on the lid.

This form of Lucite is known as 'Apple Juice' due to the color. The flower has been carved into the lid from the underside, a technique used frequently with costume jewelry in this material. The resulting cavities can be filled with colored paste, the remains of which can be seen in the detail.

4.25in (11cm) diam

$500-700

MG

A 1930s Art Deco amber and yellow marbled cast phenolic cigarette box, the lid and handle made from a single piece of phenolic

4in (10cm) long

$500-700   **MG**

A 1950s Lucite and bakelite cigarette box, the Lucite finial reverse carved and injected with color to form a rose surrounded by leaves.

5.25in (13.5cm) long

$500-700   **MG**

A 1930s cream urea-formaldehyde jewelry box, molded with stylised acanthus leaves.

6in (15cm) long

$30-50   **JBC**

A CLOSER LOOK LOOK AT A PLASTIC BOX

This dressing table box was designed by famous and skilled glass designer Rene Lalique, who also designed perfume bottles and jewellery.

It is the only example of Lalique using plastics - liquid plastic acts very much like molten glass and Lalique was skilled at producing molded glass.

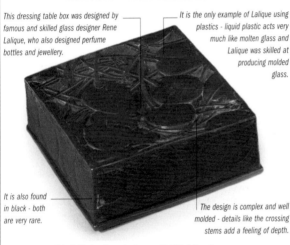

It is also found in black - both are very rare.

The design is complex and well molded - details like the crossing stems add a feeling of depth.

A Lalique red celluloid "Cerises" powder box, molded "R. Lalique".

c1923   *2in (5.5cm) diam*

$1,000-1,500   **DRA**

A 1930s American Art Deco molded red and black cigarette box, with stepped handle, the base molded "Made in USA".

8in (20cm) long

$600-900   **MG**

A 1930s clear and black Lucite cigarette holder and dispenser, with carved rope twist border.

Cigarettes lie horizontally in the box, and are viewed from the central vertical 'window'. To take a cigarette, the rope twist border is pulled up, moving the stack upwards, until a cigarette falls onto the concave ridges on either side.

5.25in (13.5cm) high

$150-200   **MG**

A 1930s Art Deco green and black cigarette box, with metal globe finials, the base with molded "GE" mark, for General Electric.

5in (12.5cm) long

$500-700   **MG**

A 1930s Art Deco design 'Cleopatra' phenolic resin box, with green lid and black base.

This sums up Art Deco very well in its choice of colors, geometric, fan decoration and curving form.

5.75in (14.5cm) long

$400-600   **MI**

BAKELITE & PLASTICS

A 1930s orange Catalin mantle clock pencil sharpener, with transfer-on-paper inset dial with metal retaining ring.

1in (3cm) high

$80-120 **MG**

A 1930s green Catalin mantle clock pencil sharpener, with transfer-on-paper inset dial with metal retaining ring.

2in (5cm) high

$80-120 **MG**

An early 1940s American carved marbled brown Catalin American tank pencil sharpener, with transfer decoration and black inserted Catalin tank barrel.

1.75in (4.5cm) long

$80-120 **MG**

An early 1940s American red and black carved WWII plane pencil sharpener, with transfer decoration.

2.25in (6cm) long

$80-120 **MG**

A CLOSER LOOK AT A DESK BASE

This was made by British company J.Dickinson, under the name 'Carvacraft' - pieces are marked with a stamp underneath.

The curving shape and stepped edges are typical of late Art Deco, when streamlining became a key style, particularly in the US.

It is part of a set of desk accessories including a stamp wipe, an ink stand, a small clip board, a rocker blotter and a rare picture frame and letter rack.

These are found in three colors; amber, yellow and the very rare green.

An amber Carvacraft double pen holder, with double pen tray to front.
c1948

6.5in (16.5cm) wide

$80-120 **MHC**

A late 1930s American orange carved Catalin 'Charlie McCarthy' pencil sharpener, with intact transfer decoration.

McCarthy was the brainchild of ventriloquist Edgar Bergen. Their radio debut was in 1936 and they became instantly popular, with McCarthy receiving an honorary degree from Northwestern University in 'Innuendo and Snappy Comebacks' in 1938. 1939 saw a popular film 'Charlie McCarthy, Detective'.

1.75in (4.5cm) high

$100-150 **MG**

An American Chase yellow cast and carved Catalin and chrome blotter.

The Chase Metalware company made domestic items in their characteristic chrome and brass finish during the 1930s - today they are highly sought-after.

5.25in (13.5cm) long

$50-80 **MG**

A 1930s red and clear Lucite tiered desk ornament, with applied gold plastic horsehead motifs.

2.5in (6.5cm) high

$100-150 **MG**

An Art Deco Brookes & Adams red and green marbled 'Bandalasta' ware teaset, with molded marks to base.

Bandalasta ware was made from molded urea thiourea formaldehyde by Streetly Manufacturing. Such colorful pieces were found primarily in picnic sets. Made in a variety of different colors, the red marbled example is the rarest and most desirable.

1927-32   *Teapot 6.75in (17cm) wide*

$1,000-1,500   **JES**

Two differently marbled Brookes & Adams 'Bandalasta' picnic 'horns' or beakers.

1927-32   *5in (12.5cm) high*

$20-30 (each)   **JBC**

A rare 1930s American cast clear and amber swirled Catalin cruet set on a tray, each piece overlaid with thin tiles of chromed metal to give a chequerboard effect.

Tray 3.5in (9cm) high

$300-350   **MG**

A pair of 1930s cast and carved orange Catalin salt and pepper shakers, with yellow Catalin inserts.

2.5in (6cm) high

$50-80   **MHC**

A 1930s Art Deco brown mottled Bakelite toast rack, with shaped handle and sprung metal holders.

5.5in (14cm) wide

$20-25   **MHC**

A 1920s-30s American unmarked green mottled urea formaldehyde revolving toothpick holder and dispenser.

This was probably made for use in restaurants.

4.75in (12cm) high

$8-12   **BH**

A 1950s Thermos Model no. 931 blue and cream ice bucket, with Thermos interior and plastic basket.

Found in a variety of colors, these are frequently missing their plastic basket or have damaged Thermos linings.

6in (15.5cm) high

$40-60   **GROB**

A late 1920s Bakelite Corporation mottled brown Bakelite dish, with molded V pattern to the outside, with molded mark to base.

Items with this mark are original products of Baekeland's 'Bakelite Corporation', with the infinity symbol intending to indicate the many uses of his plastic. This version, with a tri-lobed border, dates from after 1926, but before 1956 when the infinity symbol became larger.

5in (13cm) diam

$70-100   **MG**

A 1930s-40s Smiths brown mottled Bakelite key wound mantel clock, with hour striking.

Smiths, based in England, made a vast range of clocks in a great variety of colored plastics into the 1950s.

8in (20cm) high

$50-80 MHC

A French 1930s Art Deco Blangy brown mottled Bakelite key wound mantel clock.

The strong and distinctive Art Deco styling of this clock, and the detailing of ships at sea on the face, make it highly desirable.

5.25in (13cm) high

$250-350 PC

A CLOSER LOOK AT A CLOCK

The design exemplifies Art Deco, with its geometric shapes, clean lines and stepped 'skyscraper' appearance - it is also very similar to the famous 'Air King' radio design by Harold van Doren.

It was rumored to have been designed by notable Deco designer Paul Frankl, although no factory records directly link him with this design although they do very clearly with the chrome-plated, enameled metal and glass No.431 'Modernique' of c1928.

It was available in a walnut effect, white or green 'Vinylite' plastic - the marbled green is extremely rare.

As well as for its iconic design, it is celebrated as being the first Telechron alarm clock and the first self-starting electric alarm clock made.

An Art Deco Warren Telechron Co, of Ashland Massachusets, Telechron '700 Electroalarm' 'Vinylite' electric mantel clock with alarm and light bulb.

7.75in (19.5cm) high

$600-800 CAT

An American Art Deco Taylor yellow and green mottled and carved Catalin desk thermometer and hydrometer, the card face with company advertising for Steel Heddle Mfg Co.

4in (10cm) high

$150-250 MG

A late 1940s white urea-formaldehyde 'Rototherm' desk thermometer.

These can be found in a variety of different colors and as a matching barometer. The 'industrial' design is inspired by aircraft and car dashboard dials.

6.75 in (9cm) high

$30-40 MHC

A 1950s brown Bakelite and metal 45rpm holder, with lyre-shaped handle.

Brown Bakelite was used for domestic items as late as the 1950s. The lyre-shaped handle alludes to the musical contents of the case.

11.75in (30cm) long

$700-900 MG

A Wurlitzer Wireless bakelite speaker, of circular form on disk feet, molded "W" mark.

6.75in (17cm) high

$120-180 WW

PLASTICS & BAKELITE

A Bakelite desk lamp with magnifier, on a teardrop-shaped wood base with bent metal arm with a bakelite framed glass magnifier.

c1930   13.5in (34.5cm) high

$400-500   **SK**

A CLOSER LOOK AT A BAKELITE LAMP

This lamp was designed in 1945 and is typical of the streamlined styles of the 'Machine Age' period.

It was made by the French company Jumo, who are noted for their innovative lamp designs and it uses popular materials of the period such as chrome, brass and plastic.

It folds down to form a sleek, streamlined shell-like form that resembles the front of trains of the period - the pivoting shade can be angled and the arm bent low or pulled tall and straight.

It was available in black, green and cream versions - black is the most commonly found with cream, and particularly green, being much rarer.

A late 1940s 'Jumo' 'streamlined' late Art Deco phenolic desk lamp for Brevette, the black/brown bakelite case with internal extendible arm, factory stamp to the base, France.

17.75in (45cm) high extended

$1,200-1,800   **ROS**

A 1930s Art Deco pink and black urea formaldehyde plastic ashtray, made for the 'Queen Mary' cruise liner, marked "British Buttner Product".

4.5in (11.5cm) high

$120-180   **JES**

A 1930s German brown Bakelite CB Rotor Auto 1001 friction powered car, with chips, complete with original box.

4.75in (12cm) high

$100-150   **LAN**

An Art Deco Roanoid Ltd thiourea-formaldehyde and bakelite ashtray.

These were made for Dunlop in five different colors. The three cigarette rest arms fold inwards, tightly locking the ash in, and a weighted base also means the ashtray never falls over.

3.25in (8cm) high

$100-150   **SWO**

A 1930s small carved yellow Catalin desk sculpture, with applied carved birds.

Novelties like these are often unique, large and complex examples can fetch high prices.

2.25in (6cm) high

$70-100   **MG**

A 1930s circular cast marbled amber Catalin Catholic wall plaque, with inset diamante and Catholic 'IHS' motif.

5.25in (13.5cm) diam

$100-150   **MG**

A pair of 1930s cast butterscotch Catalin novelty dice, with black painted dots.

2in (5cm) wide

$300-500   **MG**

COLLECTORS' NOTES

■ Posters have become increasingly desirable to general buyers, as well as collectors, due to their visual impact, snapshot of social history and reflection of period design. Most buyers choose to collect or buy in one particular area, such as travel or product advertising posters. It is possible to concentrate on specific themes within these areas, for example the Art Deco style, airline posters or posters advertising food and drink.

■ The 'golden age' of the poster was arguably the period from the turn of the 20thC, when graphics began to be used by mainly French designers, until other media such as television took over in the 1950s. Styles such as Art Nouveau, Art Deco and Modernism are strongly represented and prove a draw today.

■ There are a number of factors to consider, including the brand depicted, the overall design and artwork and the artist. Eye appeal is also an important consideration, particularly for those who wish to buy posters to display. Posters for notable brands with a strong following or by famous artists, such as Adolphe Mouron (Cassandre), will be desirable and usually very valuable.

■ Also consider the condition as posters were made to be displayed and most often were used. Tears, especially to the image, will affect the value seriously. Folds and creases can be repaired, providing the surface of the image is not rubbed and removed. Backing posters on linen is a good idea for storage and display, but this should only be done by a professional.

■ With travel posters, consider the brand, mode of transport and the imagery. Bold colors, period stylized designs and major names in travel such as White Star, BOAC, Air France and Canadian Pacific will be a draw to many buyers. A notable artist will further enhance the value, as will popular destinations such as ski resorts or famous holiday locations.

■ Beware of reproductions, which are commonplace. Inspect originals at reputable dealers and auction houses carefully to learn how to distinguish between modern prints and originals. Thicker, glossy paper and the presence of pixels are an indication of a reproduction.

'London, St Pauls', designed by J. Bateman and published by the LNER.

The bottom strip with the text has been cut off and reattached, devaluing this poster.

'London, Trafalgar Square', designed by Donald Blake and printed for RE(ER) by Jordison & Co.

British railway posters came in two sizes and formats, to fit standard advertising hoardings.

50in (127cm) wide

$2,800-3,200   **ON**

40in (102cm) high

$800-1,000   **ON**

'Visit London, Travel by Train', designed by Gordon Nicol and printed for BR(WR) by Waterlow & Sons Ltd.

40in (102cm) high

$320-380   **ON**

'Cheltenham for Health and Pleasure', designed by Claude Buckle and printed for GWR and LMS by Lowe & Brydone, folds.

40in (102cm) high

$800-1,200   **ON**

'Essex, Travel by Rail', designed by Terence Cuneo and printed for the LNER by the Baynard Press.

1945   40in (102cm) high

$600-800   **ON**

'Old World Market-Places Boston', designed by Austin Cooper and printed for the LNER by Adams Bros., mounted on linen.

40in (102cm) high

$320-380 ON

'Bournemouth Go By Train', anonymous designer, published for the BR(SR).

c1970 *40in (102cm) high*

$120-180 ON

'Deal For Your Holidays' designed by P. Shine and printed for Deal Town Council and Belgian State Railways by David Allen & Sons Ltd., mounted on linen.

1924 *40in (102cm) high*

$600-800 ON

'Enjoy A Holiday In Northern Ireland', designed by Costelloe and printed for the Ulster Transport Authority by Stafford, mounted on linen.

40in (102cm) high

$500-700 ON

'Ulster, Northern Ireland', designed by Greene and printed for the BR(LMR) by Waterlow & Sons Ltd.

40in (102cm) high

$600-800 ON

'Isle of Man', designed by Peter Collins and printed for the BR(LMR) by Waterlow & Sons Ltd., folds.

50in (127cm) wide

$200-300 ON

'Littlehampton, Go by Train', designed by Studio Seven and printed for SR(BR) by Gilbert Whitehead & Co Ltd.

40in (102cm) high

$150-200 ON

'Hints for Holidays', designed by Ronald Brett and printed for the Southern Railway by Sanders Phillips & Co. Ltd., restored and mounted on linen.

This type of colorful, bold and highly suggestive imagery is sought-after.

1933 *40in (102cm) high*

$700-900 ON

A CLOSER LOOK AT A RAILWAY POSTER

This poster was designed by Terence Cuneo (1907-96), who is often considered the best railway painter in the world.

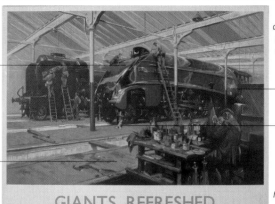

Cuneo was skilled at catching a moment in time and showing the grandeur of locomotives. This image depicts two powerful engines at rest with men working on them.

His realistic and dramatic style is loved and sought-after by collectors, and the streamlined A4 Pacific is perhaps the most loved LNER locomotive type.

He often included a mouse 'hidden' in his images as a trademark; here a cat sits inquisitively in front of the blue locomotive.

GIANTS REFRESHED

"PACIFICS" IN THE LNER LOCOMOTIVE WORKS, DONCASTER

'Giants Refreshed' designed by Terence Cuneo and printed for the L.N.E.R. by Waterlow & Sons Ltd. "Pacifics" in the LNER Locomotive Works Doncaster.

c1945   50in (127cm) high

$4,000-6,000   ON

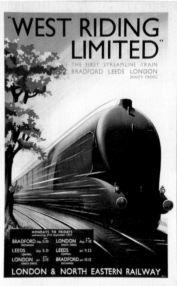

'West Riding Limited, The First Streamline Train', designed by Shep and printed for the LNER by the Baynard Press, folds.

Shep was the name used by Charles Shepherd (b.1892), who was head of the studio at the Baynard Press. He designed posters for London Transport as well as the LNER and SR. The style of the train and the feeling of movement make this especially desirable.

30in (76cm) high

$2,200-2,800   ON

'Hampton Court by Tram', designed by Herrick and printed for the London Underground by the Baynard Press.

40in (102cm) high

$180-220   ON

'At Your Service', designed by Leo Dowd and printed for London Transport by the Baynard Press.

40in (102cm) high

$200-300   ON

'Kew Gardens', designed by George Sheringham and printed for the London Underground by Vincent Day Brooks.

1924   40in (102cm) high

$150-200   ON

'Staggered Travelling Saves Busy Workers' Time', designed by Pat Keeley and printed for London Transport by Waterlow & Sons Ltd., mounted on linen.

An interesting and early example of promotion of flexi-time at work.

1945   40in (102cm) high

$200-300   ON

'Lake Tahoe Region, Southern Pacific', designed by Maurice Logan for the Southern Pacific railroad.

23.25in (59cm) high

$600-800   **ON**

'Shasta Route, Southern Pacific', designed by Maurice Logan for the Southern Pacific railroad.

Maurice Logan (1886-1977) was one of San Francisco's most influential artists and poster designers.

23.25in (59cm) high

$600-800   **ON**

'New Orleans, Southern Pacific' designed by Maurice Logan for the Southern Pacific railroad.

23.25in (59cm) high

$150-200   **ON**

'Martha's Vineyard, The New Haven Railroad', designed by Ben Nason for the New Haven Railroad.

After WWII, the railroad launched a publicity campaign to attract holidaymakers to the island. After arriving at Wood Hole, they were taken by ferry to the island. The masthead shown here represents local whaling history.

c1945   42in (106.5cm) high

$1,200-1,800   **SWA**

'The Royal York', by an anonymous designer for the Canadian Pacific Railway.

Built for the Toronto railway in 1929, the hotel was the largest in the British Commonwealth.

c1930   40in (102cm) high

$2,200-2,800   **SWA**

'Demain Matin Cote d'Azur', designed by Roland Hugon and printed for the SNCF by Paul Martial.

1938   39in (99cm) high

$600-800   **ON**

'Balaton', designed by Bereny Bortnyik, advertising a two-for-one travel deal.

Balaton, in Hungary, is the largest lake in Central Europe and is a popular tourist destination. The surreal Modernist collage style is desirable.

37.5in (95cm) high

$600-800   **SWA**

'Holland Bulbtime', designed by E.G. and printed for Netherlands Railways by L.Van Leer & Co, linen-backed.

39in (99cm) high

$80-120   **ON**

'Japan' designed by P. Irwin Brown for the Japanese Government Railways.

Brown also designed posters for British railway companies. The 'flat' design with broad areas of color recalls the style of Japanese prints.

1934   37.25in (94.5cm) high

$800-1,200   **SWA**

'Aberdeen & Commonwealth Line, England to Australia', designed by Longmate and printed by Gibbs & Gibbs Ltd.

The Aberdeen & Commonwealth Line was formed in 1932 when Shaw, Savill & Albion acquired the Aberdeen Line (founded 1825) and Australia's Commonwealth Line fleet from the bankrupt White Star Line. In 1936 Furness, Withy & Co. acquired Shaw, Savill & Albion and in 1938, the 'Aberdeen' name was dropped.

1930s   *40.5in (103cm) high*

$1,200-1,800   **ON**

'Aberdeen & Commonwealth Line, Australia via Malta, Port Said & Colombo', designed by P.H. Yorke and printed by Howard Jones Roberts Leete Ltd.

The presence of a Scottie dog makes this poster also appeal to other types of collector.

40.5in (103cm) high

$800-1,200   **ON**

'Aberdeen & Commonwealth Line England-Australia Malta', designed by E.J. Waters and printed by Gibbs & Gibbs Ltd.

40.5in (103cm) high

$400-600   **ON**

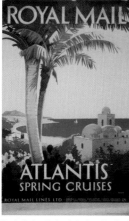

'Royal Mail Atlantis Spring Cruises', designed by Daphne Padden and printed for Royal Mail Lines Ltd. by Baynard Press.

Royal Mail Lines Ltd. was founded out of the crisis caused when the Kylsant Shipping Empire, which owned White Star and other lines, went bankrupt in 1932. It took on the Royal Mail Steam Packet Company's routes and survived as a name until the early 1970s. These 1930s posters are desirable due to the bright, colorful and idealised artwork that drew tourists to book tickets to these idyllic lands.

40in (102cm) high

$700-900   **ON**

'Shaw Savill Line New Zealand via Panama Canal', designed by E. Waters and printed by Gibbs & Gibbs Ltd.

40.5in (103cm) high

$1,000-1,500   **ON**

'Shaw Savill & Albion Line New Zealand Direct' designed by E. Waters.

This uses two New Zealand related icons, Mt. Taranaki, Egmont, and Captain Cook.

39.75in (101cm) high

$400-600   **ON**

'Royal Mail Atlantis Summer Cruises', designed by Daphne Padden and printed for Royal Mail Lines Ltd. by Baynard Press, small tears.

40in (102cm) high

$600-800   **ON**

'Royal Mail Atlantis Cruises', designed by Daphne Padden and printed for Royal Mail Lines Ltd. by Baynard Press, small tears.

40in (102cm) high

$600-800   **ON**

'Adriatica, Toute La Méditerranée Orientale, by an anonymous designer, with a ship on the horizon and its course across the globe.

The design is very similar to Cassandre in its choice of colors, lines and sense of movement.

c1938   39in (99cm) high

$600-800   **SWA**

A CLOSER LOOK AT A SHIPPING POSTER

This poster shows the famous Art Deco masterpiece the Normandie, which was once the fastest, largest and most luxurious cruise liner in the world.

Montague Black painted many famous White Star liners, including the Olympic and the ill-fated Titanic. His images are sought-after.

She first arrived in New York in 1935 and then completed 138 transatlantic voyages. Original period images are highly desirable today.

The scale of the ship is shown in a dramatic way and setting, hallmarks of Black's style.

'French Line C.G.T., An Express Luxury Service France-England-U.S.A. S.S. Ile de France E.S. Normandie', designed by Montague B. Black and printed in England.

The Normandie met a sad fate in 1942, while being converted into a troop carrier in New York, when she was accidentally set on fire and sunk. She was broken up in 1947.

                    40in (102cm) high

$5,000-7,000   **ON**

'Cruise on the Great Lakes Canadian Pacific', designed by Peter Ewart.

Ewart designed many posters for the vast Canadian Pacific company.

35in (89cm) high

$1,000-1,500   **SWA**

'Cunard White Star To Europe Via North America', designed by Tom Curr, showing the RMS Queen Mary leaving New York.

39.75in (101cm) high

$2,200-2,800   **SWA**

'French Line G.C.T. Paris, Paris All The Way To New York', designed by K. Herkomer and printed by Hill Siffken & Co.

1934   40in (102cm) high

$3,200-3,800   **ON**

'Hamburg Amerika Linie, Mediterranean Cruises', designed by Albert Fuss and printed by Muhlmeister & Johler.

39.75in (101cm) high

$400-600   **ON**

'Lloyd Triestino, Australia', designed by Gino Boccasile and printed by Pizzi & Pizio, Milan.

Lloyd Triestino was an Italian shipping line founded in 1937. This poster depicts the Romolo, which was scuttled in 1940 to avoid enemy capture.

c1938   37.5in (95.5cm) high

$1,000-1,500   **SWA**

'AOA to USA', designed by Jan Hewitt & George Him and printed by W.R. Royle & Son Ltd for American Overseas Airlines.

1948   *40in (102cm) high*

$280-320   **ON**

'AOA – USA Par Le Stratocruiser Deux Ponts', by an anonymous designer, printed by W.R. Royle & Son Ltd.

40in (102cm) high

$280-320   **ON**

'BOAC – Time is Money, Save it by Flying BOAC', possibly designed by Abram Games and printed in Great Britain, mounted on linen.

Notable designer Abram Games (1914-96) is known to have designed posters for BOAC, and this is very much in his style. He often takes an object related to the theme or subject of the service or item and gives it an almost surreal, stylized appearance on a graduated background.

30in (76cm) high

$500-700   **ON**

'Ship TWA Air Cargo' by an anonymous designer.

Air Cargo was formed in 1941 to carry freight from the four largest US airlines comprising United, American, Eastern and TWA. After WWII, most airlines set up independent freight services.

38.5in (98cm) high

$700-900   **SWA**

'Mexico Tomorrow Via Pan American', by an anonymous designer, showing a DC-3 and a Mexican woman in traditional dress.

c1940   *41in (104cm) high*

$800-1,200   **SWA**

'PAN AM, Rio' by an anonymous designer, showing Oba-Oba dancers from Oswaldo Sargentelli's famous night-club in Rio de Janeiro.

c1970   *36.5in (92.5cm) high*

$1,200-1,800   **SWA**

'TWA', by an anonymous designer, showing a woman gazing longingly at a cactus with a cowboy watching on.

37.75in (96cm) high

$2,000-3,000   **SWA**

'Swissair, Lisboa-Nova Iorque Sem Escala Con DC-7C', showing the Chrysler Building, New York.

SwissAir went bankrupt in 2001 and are now known as 'Swiss'.

1960s   *40in (102cm) high*

$200-300   **ON**

POSTERS

'Lenzerheide, Switzerland', designed by Heinze & Pedreff and printed by Anstalt C. J. Bucher, small tears.

40in (102cm) high

$200-300   **ON**

A CLOSER LOOK AT A TOURISM POSTER

Swiss designer and architect Daniele Buzzi is known for his poster designs produced to attract people to his home region of Ticino.

The image is of the Madonna del Sasso Sanctuary and the surrounding sub-tropical vegetation. It brings to mind more obviously popular tourist destinations such as the Mediterranean and South America.

The image is eye-catching, being bright, bold and colorful with stylized forms, which are typical hallmarks of Buzzi's work.

This poster dates from the 1920s. His post-WWII work is less desirable as it became less colorful and appealing.

'Locarno, Golf, Casino, Tennis', designed by Daniele Buzzi.

1926   39.5in (100.5cm) long

$800-1,200   **SWA**

'Montana Vermala, Valais Suisse Alt 1500m', by an anonymous designer and printed by A. Marsens.

Although advertising Swiss resorts known for their skiing, as indicated by the snowy mountains in the background, these do not usually appeal to skiing poster collectors, due to the lack of skiing imagery.

40in (102cm) high

$200-300   **ON**

'Kandersteg Switzerland', designed by 'CM' and printed by Orell Fussli.

39.5in (100cm) high

$180-220   **ON**

'Thun Plage Switzerland', designed by Clare and printed by Casserini-Aebi, small tears and loss.

40in (102cm) high

$400-600   **ON**

'Nassau in the Bahamas', color lithograph photographic image poster published by the Development Board Nassau.

1938   41in (104cm) high

$600-800   **ON**

'Join The Smart Set in Nassau and The Bahamas', by an anonymous designer.

c1960   42.5in (108cm) high

$500-700   **SWA**

'Carnaval 1937, Panama', by an anonymous designer, printed by Senefelder, Ecuador.

'Australia, The Tallest Trees in the British Empire', designed by Trompf and published by the Australian National Travel Association.

'Melbourne', designed by Max Forbes, published by the Australian National Travel Assoc.

Although not an official Olympics poster, the games are mentioned at the base and the boy holding sports equipment has a ticket to the games in his pocket.

'Leningrad', Russian-produced tourism poster for the city.

The 'Liberty Monument' to victims of the revolution can be seen in the centre of the park as the exaggerated statue of Lenin looks over Russians and tourists visiting the park.

1937 26.25in (66.5cm) high	*40in (102cm) high*	*c1956 39in (99cm) high*	*c1935 38.5in (98cm) high*
$600-800 **SWA**	**$800-1,200** **ON**	**$700-1,000** **SWA**	**$800-1,200** **SWA**

'Annecy La Plage', designed by Robert Falcucci and printed for PLM by Gds Ets de l'Imp Generale.

1935 39in (100cm) high

$1,000-1,500   ON

'USSR Health Resorts', Russian-produced poster for the Black Sea coast 'Russian Riviera' known for its vegetation, spas and resorts.

39.25in (99.5cm) high

$1,800-2,200   SWA

'Norway, The Land of the Midnight Sun', designed by Ivar Gull and printed by Norsk Lithografsk.

39.5in (100cm) high

$400-600   ON

'Spain Glorious Spring', by an anonymous designer and printed by Union Grafica SL Tolosa, mounted on linen.

39.5in (100cm) high

$500-700   ON

'NSU' racing motorcycle advertising poster, designed by H. Weiss.

1953   33.75in (86cm) high

$80-120   **ON**

The NEW
MICHELIN
tyre
durable, non-skid.

'The New Michelin Tyre, Durable, Non-Skid', by an anonymous designer and printed by L. Serre & Cie, mounted on linen.

This poster can be dated from the pattern of the tread as it is not shown in the Michelin poster reference work. Items showing the Michelin man are desirable.

c1927   78.75in (200cm) high

$1,000-1,500   **ON**

'Peugeot' advertising poster, designed by Andre Girard.

Andre Girard is best known for his work for Columbia Records. The sense of speed as a car zooms around a corner, as well as the bold colors and fame of the brand, make this a valuable poster.

c1929   63.75in (162cm) high

$2,800-3,200   **SWA**

'The Quick-Starting Pair, Shell Oil and Petrol', poster no. 132, designed by Jean d'Ylen and issued by Shell-Mex Ltd., restored and mounted on linen.

1926   44.5in (113cm) wide

$2,200-2,800   **ON**

'These Men Use Shell, You Can Be Sure of Shell', poster no. 506, designed by Derek Sayer and printed by Waterlow, small tears.

1937   45in (114cm) wide

$320-380   **ON**

LONGINES

'Longines', designed by Jean d'Ylen and printed by Vercasson, mounted on linen, restored.

21.5in (54.5cm) high

$1,000-1,500   **ON**

la rapidisima
Hispano-Olivetti

'La Rapidisima Hispano-Olivetti', printed by Llauger SA, Barcelona.

A rather odd contrast of a typewriter and steam train, the message is presumably that you'll be typing out work faster than a speeding steam train if you use an Olivetti.

52.5in (133.5cm) high

$2,000-3,000   **SWA**

'Zenith', designed by Jean d'Ylen and printed by Vercasson, mounted on linen.

1928   35.5in (90cm) high

$2,200-2,800   **ON**

A CLOSER LOOK AT AN ADVERTISING POSTER

This poster was designed by eccentric illustrator Louis Wain (1860-1939), known for his drawings and paintings of cats, which are now highly sought-after by collectors.

Wain is better known for his book illustrations and drawings, he created comparatively few advertising pieces.

This is typical of his style, with mad-eyed, personified cats engaging in human activities – here listening to an early Marconi radio set with headphones at a garden party.

Typical of his erratic style, it is amusing to note that none of the cats are wearing the hats or boots the poster is advertising.

'Jacksons' World Famous Hats & Boots For Ladies and Gents', color lithograph poster, printed by Tom G. Porter Printer, Leeds, folds.

30.5in (77.5cm) wide

$12,000-15,000   **ON**

'Need A Light? Get The Name Right', 1970s Brymay matches advertising poster, by an anonymous designer, folds.

59.5in (151cm) high

$100-150   **ON**

A 1980s Marlboro cigarettes advertising poster.

The rugged Marlboro man promotes the fact that 'real men' smoke. As smoking becomes increasingly unfashionable worldwide, ephemera related to it may rise in value, especially if typical.

22in (56cm) wide

$30-40   **CLG**

'Arrow Collars and Shirts', designed by J.C. Leyendecker.

This is typical of Leyendecker's elegant 1920s-30s style and is perhaps the forerunner of today's 'preppie' styled Abercrombie & Fitch advertising.

27.5in (70cm) high

$1,800-2,200   **SWA**

'Raviba, Pour Teindre Et Raviver Les Bas', French sock advertising poster designed by Jean d'Ylen and printed by Vercasson, with stains and damage.

17in (43cm) high

$320-380   **ON**

'La Maison Du Porte Plume', on a beige background, designed by Jean d'Ylen and printed by Publicite E. V. Ferdi, mounted on linen.

Showing 'unbranded' pens by Swan, Waterman and Parker, this will also appeal to writing equipment collectors. It is also available on a white background.

c1930   61in (155cm) high

$2,200-2,800   **ON**

'Robys Premier Fils', French alcohol advertising poster, printed by Affiches Stentor Paris, mounted on linen.

1936   76.5in (194cm) wide

$1,200-1,800   **ON**

'Men of London, Each Recruit Means Quicker Peace, Join To-Day', published by the Central Recruiting Office.

17in (43cm) high

$40-60   **ON**

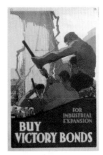

'Remember Belgium, Buy Bonds, Fourth Liberty Loan', designed by Ellsworth Young, mounted on linen.

This dramatic image showing a German soldier hauling a Belgian girl along as her village burns shocked many at the time.

30in (76cm) high

$600-800   **ON**

'Buy Victory Bonds, For Industrial Expansion', designed by Arthur Keelor, mounted on linen.

36.25in (92cm) high

$320-380   **ON**

'Tittle Tattle Lost The Battle', designed by G. Lacoste, American WWII propaganda poster, framed.

The style of the hidden Hitler listening in to conversations was also used by Kenneth Bird under the name 'Fougasse', and made famous in his 'Careless Talk Costs Lives' campaign during WWII.

21.25in (54cm) high

$320-380   **ON**

'War Loan, Back the Empire with your Savings, Invest Now', no. 21, by an anonymous designer, mounted on linen.

30in (76cm)

$100-150   **ON**

'It May Cost Life, Think Before You Write', designed by Noke and printed for HMSO by C&P.

19.75in (50cm) high

$80-120   **ON**

'El 11 Març Sortirà Companya Revista de La Dona', designed by I.G. Viladot.

This 1930s Spanish Civil War poster is very much in the style of artist Georges Braque.

39in (100cm) high

$800-1,200   **CL**

'In War And Peace We Serve', designed by Reginald Mayes and printed for GWR/LMS/LNER/SR by Jas. Truscott & Son Ltd.

This poster was meant to show how Britain's railways served the country equally well in war and in peacetime. Look out for Helen McKie's interiors of Waterloo station that have a similar message as these can fetch over $3,500.

40.25in (102cm) high

$350-450   **ON**

'Marionetten-Theater, Münchener Künftler', designed by Lucian Bernhard and printed by Hollerbaum & Schmidt, Berlin.

Designed to look like a stage, the poster is typical of Bernhard's (1883-1972) Modernism, with flat tones and no outlining.

'Minnie Dupree "A Rose O' Plymouth-town"', American poster for the Broadway production.

1902   80in (203cm) high

$800-1,200   **CL**

1910   36.75in (92cm) wide

$800-1,200   **SWA**

'Original American Barés', advertisement for the singer, dancer, equilibrist and musical imitator.

c1910   39in (99cm) high

$400-600   **CL**

'Count the First – Living Proof of The Darwin Theory', American animal show poster.

c1910   41in (104cm) wide

$600-900   **CL**

'A Gentleman from Mississippi', American theatrical or film advertising poster.

c1914   41in (104cm) high

$400-600   **CL**

'D'Oyly Carte Opera Company', designed by Dudley Hardy and printed by David Allen & Sons, mounted on linen.

30in (76cm) high

$100-150   **ON**

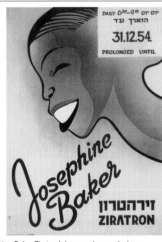

'Zu Ehren Pablo Casals', designed by B. Olonetzki, advertising a benefit concert to honour cellist Pablo Casals's 75th birthday.

'Josephine Baker Ziratron', by an unknown designer.

This rare and highly appealing poster advertises Baker's Israeli performances.

1951   50in (125cm) high

$800-1,200   **SWA**

1954   28in (70cm) high

$1,800-2,200   **SWA**

'Dzieje Grzechu' (Story of a Sin), designed by Jerzy Flisak, Polish film poster for the Waleriana Borowczyka film.

1975   33in (84cm) high

$180-220   **CL**

'Malzonkowie Roku II' (The Scarlet Buccaneer), designed by Andrzej Krajewski, Polish film poster for the Jean-Paul Rappeneau film.

1972   33in (80cm) high

$120-180   **CLG**

'Trema' (Stagefright), designed by Marek Freudenreich, Polish Film poster for the Alfred Hitchcock film.

'Morderca Samotnych Kobiet', designed by Andrzej Bertrandt, Polish film poster for the Helmut Nitzschke film.

1972   33in (84cm) high

$120-180   **CLG**

'Tango', designed by Maria Ihnatowicz, Polish film poster for the Stanislav Barabas film.

5,900 of these posters were printed.

1967   33in (84cm) high

$280-320   **CLG**

1966   33in (84cm) high

$300-500   **CL**

'Sanjuro Samuraj Znikad', (Sanjuro), 1960s Polish poster for the Akira Kurosawa film, designed by Andrzej Krajewski.

Printed in an edition of 4,200 copies for the 1962 film, this poster is rare today.

1968   33in (84cm) high

$320-380   **CLG**

'Zmoklá Nedele', designed by Richard Fremund, Czech film poster for the Marton Keleti film.

Fremund was one of the noted artists who gave birth to the avant garde Czech poster design movement.

1962   33in (84cm) high

$280-320   **CLG**

'Fortel a Jak ho Ziskat' (The Knack ... and How To Get It), Czech poster for a Richard Lester film.

1965   33in (84cm) high

$220-280   **CLG**

COLLECTORS' NOTES

- Colored printed pot-lids appeared in the mid-1840s, and are one of the earliest types of visually appealing packaging. Products include bear's grease (its many uses included rifle-cleaning and hair styling), and meat or fish paste. Major pot-lid makers were F.R. Pratt, T.J. & J. Mayer and Brown-Westhead & Moore.

- It is not usually possible to date pot-lids precisely as so many were produced over long periods, with no records remaining. Form, events depicted and certain makers' marks can help to date some to within a date range. Over 350 different images are known, many taken from watercolors by artist Jesse Austin.

- Earlier lids, from before 1860, are usually flat and light in weight, with fine quality prints, and often have a

screw thread. Lids from 1860 to 1875 are heavier and have a convex top. Later lids are heavier still, are often flat, and the printing tends to be of a lower quality. Run your finger over a lid and if you can feel the transfer, it is likely to be a later reproduction.

- Rare variations and designs and attractive, strongly colored examples fetch the highest prices. Chips to the flange and rim do not affect value seriously. Chips to the image, or restoration, can lower values by 50-75 per cent. Complex borders usually add value.

- Numbers given here relate to reference no. in K.V. Mortimer's book 'Pot-Lids and other Colour Printed Staffordshire Wares', published by the Antique Collectors' Club, 2003.

A Pratt 'The Listener' domed pot-lid, no. 130, with black marbled border, restored.

This is a later version – earlier examples have a yellow striped apron. Look out for the exhibition example with a wide gold band, as this can fetch over $1,000.

4.25in (10.5cm) diam

$100-150 SAS

A Pratt 'Lady, Boy and Goats' pot-lid, no. 276, with hairline crack.

This image was based on artist Sir Edwin Landseer's watercolor 'Harvest time in the Scottish Highlands'.

3in (7.5cm) diam

$40-60 SAS

A Cauldon 'Charity' pot-lid, no. 133.

This version with a line border is the most common and this example had considerable restoration, hence its low value. Had it not been so damaged it may have fetched around $80.

5in (12.5cm) diam

$50-70 SAS

A Pratt 'The Swing' pot-lid, no. 327.

4.25in (11cm) diam

$150-200 SAS

A Pratt 'The Wolf And The Lamb' pot-lid, no. 343.

This is a comparatively common lid.

4.25in (10.5cm) diam

$40-60 SAS

A Pratt 'On Guard' pot-lid, no. 334.

Two variations, both of the same value, are known. One has a bucket under the seat, the other a dog. It was produced for a long period after around 1860.

4.25in (10.5cm) diam

$80-120 SAS

POT-LIDS

A late 19thC 'Negro and Pitcher' pot-lid, no. 311.

4.75in (12cm) diam

$220-280 SAS

A CLOSER LOOK AT A POT-LID

This is an early lid and has some under-glaze hand painting. It is also from an unknown factory.

It can be found in a number of variations, with a green or red coat and with a gold band (as here), a marbled flange or vignetted. All are very rare.

The image is taken from 'Pleasures of Life' by famous British satirical caricaturist Thomas Rowlandson (1756-1827).

This example is from the Abe Ball collection. Ball was a pioneering and notable pot-lid collector and researcher.

A 'How I Love to Laugh' pot-lid, no. 367, with black mottled flange and tall matching base.

3in (7.5cm) diam

$3,200-3,800 SAS

A 'Tam-o-Shanter' pot-lid, no. 199, with shallow flange.

4.25in (11cm) diam

$180-220 SAS

A Bates, Brown-Westhead & Moore (Cauldon) 'Tam-o-Shanter and Souter Johnny' (346) pot-lid, no.198, with shallow flange and hairline crack.

4.25in (10.5cm) diam

$70-100 SAS

A Pratt 'Lady Brushing Hair' pot-lid, no. 111.

Look out for examples with a bared breast or a gold band as they can be worth more than twice this value.

2.75in (7cm) diam

$400-500 SAS

A Bates, Elliot & Co. 'Summer' pot-lid, no. 335.

The presence of a British registration mark underneath indicates an earlier and more valuable example.

4.5in (11cm) diam

$60-80 SAS

A 'The Matador' pot-lid, no. 78.

This may have been produced by Mayer and is a very rare lid.

3.5in (8.5cm) diam

$1,200-1,800 SAS

A later issue of Mayer's 'New Houses of Parliament, Westminster' pot-lid.

5.25in (13cm) diam

$200-300   **SAS**

A late 19thC Pratt 'Thames Embankment' pot-lid, no. 245.

4.25in (10.5cm) diam

$70-100   **SAS**

A late 19thC Pratt 'The New Blackfriars Bridge' pot-lid, no. 244.

4.5in (11cm) diam

$30-50   **SAS**

A Mayer 'Buckingham Palace' pot-lid, no. 174.

Beware of reproductions that are flat and heavier than the slightly domed originals.

5.25in (13cm) diam

$400-600   **SAS**

A late 19thC Pratt 'Albert Memorial' pot-lid, with coaches.

The version without coaches can be worth slightly more.

4.25in (10.5cm) diam

$120-180   **SAS**

A 'Windsor Castle and St. George's Chapel' pot-lid, no. 175, probably by Cauldon, chipped.

An undamaged example with rare advertising wording for S. Graftey may fetch up to around $800.

3.5in (9.5cm) diam

$80-120   **SAS**

A Mayer 'Osborne House' pot-lid, no. 179.

This version with a white border and crown is the most valuable.

5in (12.5cm) diam

$120-180   **SAS**

A Mayer 'Great Exhibition 1851' pot-lid, no. 142, restored.

c1851   *4.25in (10.5cm) diam*

$70-100   **SAS**

A Mayer 'The Interior of the Grand International Building of 1851' pot-lid, no. 143.

Look out for examples with the band but no wording and a different roof, which can fetch up to $1,500

c1852   5.25in (13cm) diam

$450-550   SAS

A Pratt 'Interior View of Crystal Palace' pot-lid, no. 145.

4.5in (11.5cm) diam

$600-800   SAS

A Pratt 'Philadelphia Exhibition 1876' circular pot-lid, no. 155.

A rare rectangular version of this lid, which does not show the coach and horses, can be worth over twice the value of this lid.

4.5in (11cm) diam

$80-120   SAS

A late 19thC Pratt 'Paris Exhibition 1878' pot-lid, no. 153, with hairline crack.

4.5in (11cm) diam

$80-120   SAS

A Mayer 'New York Exhibition 1853' pot-lid, no. 154, with minor hairline crack to rim.

This example with an oak-leaf band is one of the most valuable versions.

5.25in (13cm) diam

$800-1,200   SAS

A Pratt 'L'Exhibition Universelle de 1867' pot-lid, no. 152.

4.75in (12.5cm) diam

$120-180   SAS

A 'The Administration Building World's Fair, Chicago 1893' pot-lid, possibly by Pratt.

Gray is the most common color, buff or yellow prints are extremely rare – other colors are only rumored to exist.

4.25in (10.5cm) diam

$600-800   SAS

A 'Gothic Archway' pot-lid, no. 309.

This is a very rare lid and a number of variations are known. It was produced by an unidentified maker for medical supplies maker and retailer S. Maw & Sons of London.

3.25in (8cm) diam

$3,000-5,000   SAS

A Pratt 'Deer Drinking' pot-lid, no. 277, with hairline crack.

4.25in (10.5cm) diam

$80-120   **SAS**

A CLOSER LOOK AT A POT-LID

An example with a window behind the inkwell and quill is the least valuable, usually fetching up to $80.

This lid is paired with 'A Pretty Kettle of Fish' showing four dogs fighting over a cauldron of fish soup.

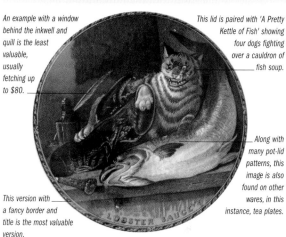

This version with a fancy border and title is the most valuable version.

Along with many pot-lid patterns, this image is also found on other wares, in this instance, tea plates.

A Pratt 'Lobster Sauce' pot-lid, no.57, first issue with title.

4.25in (10.5cm) diam

$320-380   **SAS**

A Pratt 'Country Quarters' pot-lid, no. 273.

4.75in (12cm) diam

$150-200   **SAS**

A 'The Snow-drift' (276) pot-lid, no. 267.

This image is based on Sir Edwin Landseer's 'Highland Shepherd's Dog In The Snow'. Usually values are the same whether the wording is present or not.

4.25in (10.5cm) diam

$50-70   **SAS**

An early and very rare 'Bear in a Ravine' advertising pot-lid, no. 14, with restored flange.

2.5in (6.5cm) diam

$2,800-3,200   **SAS**

A late 19thC 'The Swallow' pot-lid, no. 287, restored.

3.75in (9.5cm) diam

$220-280   **SAS**

A Mayer 'The Kingfisher' pot-lid, no. 286, gold line border, restored.

This very rare and beautiful example, from the Abe Ball collection, has a gold border. It is an early lid, later issues have greenish tinges.

5.25in (13cm) diam

$1,200-1,800   **SAS**

A Mayer 'Pegwell Bay, Ramsgate, Still Life Game' pot-lid, no. 43, with a hairline crack.

4.25in (10.5cm) diam

$70-100 SAS

A 'Shells' pot-lid, no. 75.

Shell pot-lids were made either by Pratt or Mayer. The number and type of shells shown helps identify these visually similar lids.

4.5in (11cm) diam

$100-150 SAS

A 'Shells' pot-lid, no.73, restored.

3.25in (8cm) diam

$100-150 SAS

A 'Shells' pot-lid, no. 72, framed.

This is the most common of the shell pattern pot-lids.

5in (12.5cm) diam

$40-60 SAS

A Pratt 'Rose & Convolvulus' pot-lid, no. 401, with gold line.

4in (10cm) diam

$320-380 SAS

A very rare Mayer 'Balaklava, Inkerman, Alma' pot-lid, no. 204.

This Crimean war commemorative lid shows (clockwise) the Earl of Cardigan, the Duke of Cambridge, Lord Raglan and General Simpson. It would have fetched more if it had not been damaged and restored. Beware of later examples that have weaker colors as these are generally worth about a quarter of this value.

5in (12.5cm) diam

$400-600 SAS

A very rare Mayer 'Alma' Crimean war commemorative pot-lid, no. 203.

This example, from the notable Cashmore collection, has a fancy border highlighted in gold. It is the rarest and most valuable variation.

5.25in (13cm) diam

$2,000-3,000 SAS

A 'Royal Coat of Arms' pot-lid, no. 173, without name, restored.

4.25in (11cm) diam

$800-1,200 SAS

COLLECTORS' NOTES

- Loose powder compacts first became popular in the 1920s when it became more acceptable for women to apply makeup in public. After World War II, the rise of the working woman meant more disposable income to spend on beauty products, such as face powder and lipstick, portable enough to be carried in handbags. Silver screen stars set the trend for powder compacts and increased their popularity.

- During the early years face powder was imported from France but many compacts were supplied by American makers. Most examples were made of sterling silver, silver plate, chrome plate, or gold plate. Other fashionable materials were also used such as Bakelite and tortoiseshell. Look out for examples that reflect the style of an era – Art Deco is hugely popular.

- Compacts came in many shapes, sizes and price brackets. Some had mechanisms that played music and others, such as a Schuco soft toy range, concealed a powder container inside novelty casing.

- When buying, look out for examples in excellent condition. Check that mirrors are intact and that exteriors have not been damaged through use. As many compacts were stored in purses and pockets and so were subject to wear, examples in good condition are hard to finder and thus are sought after.

- Desirable names include Stratton and Kigu in the UK and Elgin in the US. Stratton was particularly innovative, introducing a self-opening lid to prevent broken fingernails. Equally appealing is the Salvador Dali 'Bird-in-Hand' compact, designed for Elgin.

An Art Deco blue and green guilloché enamel and silver powder compact, Birmingham hallmark.

1937   2.75in (7cm) diam

$150-200   **SH**

A 1930s American La Mode yellow guilloché enamel compact, with flower embossed sides.

2.75in (7cm) diam

$200-300   **MGT**

A 1930s Coty white metal compact, decorated with an image of a sailing ship, from their Paris range.

2.5in (6.5cm) diam

$30-60   **MGT**

A 1950s Kigu black enamel compact, with cut-out ivorine insert of two dancers, marked "Made in England. Patented".

3.5in (9cm) diam

$70-100   **MGT**

A Japanese tri-color inlaid gold and silver powder compact.

c1920   2in (5cm) diam

$350-450   **SH**

A 1920s Vinolia Aralys satyr powder compact, with registered design mark "732540" for 1927.

2in (5cm) diam

$120-180   **SH**

A 1930s Atkinson's Art Deco white metal compact, for pressed powder.

$150-200   **MGT**

A 1930s Gwenda butterfly wing compact.

Butterfly wings have been used in jewelry and small decorative objects since the 1920s, initially in Europe. Use peaked in the 1950s, but they are still used in some places today. The material is often used to simulate the sky or sea with a reverse-painted design placed over the top. Older pieces are usually more desirable, as are examples with good quality decoration.

3.25in (8.5cm) diam

$80-120   **MGT**

A 1930s Coty butterfly wing powder compact, with unusual use of different types of wing.

2in (5cm) diam

$80-120   **MGT**

A 1930s Dubarry Baby-Jack compact, with foil design of a fairy, with Dubarry logo.

2.25in (5.5cm) diam

$120-180   **MGT**

A 1930s Gwenda powder compact, with foil-backed design of a courting couple, with original puff and sifter.

The addition of the original puff and sifter makes this example more desirable. The foil-backed sky effect can be mistaken for butterfly wings, so check pieces carefully.

2.25in (5.5cm) diam

$70-100   **SH**

A 1950s English Melissa gilt metal powder compact, with lucite swan insert.

2.75in (7cm) diam

$50-90   **MGT**

A 1930s/40s French powder compact, with silk flowers under a plastic dome.

2.75in (7cm) diam

$50-70   **SH**

A 1930s French plastic transfer printed compact, depicting romantic couple, enhanced with gilding and with brass frame.

$70-100   **MGT**

A Stratton R.M.S. Queen Mary liner powder compact.

This is likely to have been bought from an onboard shop.

c1960   *2.5in (6.5cm) diam*

$120-180   **MGT**

A 1960s 'The Beatles' gilt powder compact, no maker's mark.

This desirable compact appeals to collectors of Beatles memorabilia as well as compact collectors.

3in (7.5cm) diam

$200-300   **MGT**

A 1930s Japanese Princess Deco enameled clam shell-design powder compact, no maker's mark.

3.25in (8.5cm) high

$120-180 MGT

A 1950s Russian enameled silver shell powder compact, with gilt-washed interior, Russian hallmark.

3.25in (8.5cm) high

$200-300 MGT

A 1930s American Elgin Ford V8 advertising compact, with separate rouge and powder compartments.

3.5in (9cm) high

$70-100 MGT

A 1930s American Elgin oval guilloché enamel powder compact, with separate rouge and powder compartments.

3.25in (8.5cm) high

$150-200 MGT

A 1930s La Mode padlock powder compact, with tri-colored goldtones original puff and label.

3in (7.5cm) high

$180-220 SH

A La Mode heart guilloché enameled powder compact.

c1937 *2.5in (6.5cm) high*

$150-200 SH

A 1940s American Elgin tri-color teardrop powder compact, with original advertising booklet inside.

3.75in (9.5cm) high

$70-100 MGT

A French Jonteel white metal deep hexagon powder compact, with embossed ibis on the cover.

c1921 *1.5in (4cm) wide*

$70-100 SH

A 1930s hexagonal blue guilloche-on-brass tango powder compact, possibly Austrian, with rotating sieve mechanism, no maker's mark.

The appealing color, unusual form and great condition make this desirable.

2.25in (5.5cm) wide

$250-350 MGT

A 1910s/20s French girl-on-a-swing powder compact, decorated with stove-baked enamel signed "Gamel".

3in (7.5cm) wide

$150-250   **SH**

A late 1940s Stratton Pontoon-shape power compact, decorated with enameled bluebirds, marked "Pro PAT".

3in (7.5cm) wide

$50-70   **MGT**

A 1940s/50s Schildkraut square mother-of-pearl compact, with petite-point insert.

2in (5cm) wide

$70-100   **MGT**

A 1950/60s amber-colored powder compact, with glass jeweled top.

2.25in (5.5cm) wide

$40-60   **SH**

An Austrian Framus red enamel on gilt and red carved bakelite powder compact, with unusual spring action opening.

3.25in (8.5cm) wide

$200-300   **MGT**

A 1940s Zeigfeld Glorified Girl striped plastic compact.

4.5in (11.5cm) wide

$100-150   **MGT**

A 1930s Art Deco green enameled powder compact, with unusual clip fastening, no makers mark.

3in (7.5cm) wide

$100-150   **MGT**

A 1930s silver and enamel scenic tango powder compact.

2.25in (5.5cm) wide

$200-300   **SH**

A 1920s Art Deco silver-plated tango powder compact, decorated with a silhouette lady and with tassel and separate coin compartments.

2.5in (6.5cm) high

$150-200   **SH**

A CLOSER LOOK AT A POWDER COMPACT

This is an early example of a compact intended for use outside of the house.

The additional powder compartment and lipstick holder add appeal and the compact retains its original puffs and lipstick, increasing the value.

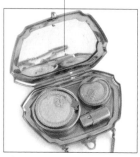

These compacts could be heavily used, resulting in wear. This example is in good condition and the decoration is well-executed

Guilloché enameled powder compacts are sought-after and the shape of this example is particularly attractive.

A 1920s blue guilloché enamel bag-shaped powder compact, with separate blush and lipstick, original puffs and lipstick.

3.25in (8.5cm) wide

$350-450   **SH**

A 1950s German Zast black plastic and goldtone metal handbag-shaped powder compact, marked "UO NR 7780".

3in (7.5cm) wide

$50-70   **SH**

A late 1930s/early 1940s Henriette black and gilt metal dragon design fan compact.

5in (12.5cm) wide

$120-180   **MGT**

A 1940s Volupte figural hand powder compact, known as the 'Gay Nineties Mitt', decorated with a printed black 'lace' mitten and floral bracelet.

4.5in (11.5cm) wide

$600-800   **MGT**

A Pygmalion Sonata gilt metal piano powder compact, with folding legs.

c1954   *2.75in (7cm) wide*

$220-280   **MGT**

A 1940s plastic army officer's cap powder compact, unmarked but probably by Henriette.

3in (7.5cm) wide

$100-150   **MGT**

An unusual 1920s French bottle-shaped powder compact, with powder in lid and mirror on base.

2in (5cm) high

$50-80   **SH**

POWDER COMPACTS

A 1940s/50s American Derneys 'Three Secrets' powder box and perfume, with original outer box.

6in (14.5cm) wide

$60-80   **SH**

A 1920s Art Nouveau L.T. Piver Poudre Pompia powder box.

This example is empty, a sealed box with its original contents could be worth around $150-200.

3.75in (9.5cm) high

$70-100   **SH**

A 1940s Richard Hudnut Lady Dubarry large oval powder box, opened but with outer box.

4in (10cm) high

$30-60   **SH**

A 1930/40s French Lenthérique Bal Masqué powder box, with theatrical mask decoration, sealed with outer box.

3in (7.5cm) diam

$50-80   **SH**

A 1920s French Jonteel Ibis Cold Cream powder box, empty.

3in (7.5cm) diam

$20-40   **SH**

A 1940s French Bourjois Soir de Paris powder box, open with contents.

3in (7.5cm) diam

$15-35   **SH**

An American Heather 'Geranium' rouge tin, by Heather Co. NJ USA, with original puff.

c1925   *1.75in (4.5cm) diam*

$30-40   **SH**

A 1930/40 Tangee 'Gay Red' dry rouge compact tin, by George Luft Co, with original puff.

1.5in (4cm) diam

$20-30   **SH**

A rare 1920s French Coty Falling Puffs design powder box, designed by Lalique.

3.25in (8.5cm) diam

$20-30   **SH**

FIND OUT MORE...

Collector's Encyclopedia of Compacts, Carryalls and Face Powder Boxes Vols. I & II, by Laura Mueller, published by Collector Books, 1993 & 1997.

Vintage and Vogue Ladies' Compacts, by Roselyn Gerson, published by Collector Books, 2001.

British Compact Collectors' Club, PO Box 131, Woking, Surrey, GU24 9YR.

Compact Collectors, P.O. Box 40, Lynbrook, NY 11563, USA.

COLLECTORS' NOTES

- Rock and pop memorabilia continues to make the headlines with million dollar items coming up for sale around the world. Despite this is there is something for every pocket, ranging from records, merchandise, autographs and even items owned by the stars themselves.

- It is this latter category that tends to garner the highest prices. Instruments or clothing used by an artist are always sought-after and a connection to a significant event lends a greater cachet. This area can mean high prices so check for a cast-iron provenance.

- Stars such as the Beatles and Elvis had their image attached to a mind-boggling array of merchandise, which is open to a wider market. Look for examples in mint condition or retaining original packaging.

- The punk movement is a hot collecting area, as the music and the fashions of the period are back in vogue. The outrageous Sex Pistols were only together for a few years, so tickets and posters from their concerts are desirable as are items connected to Sid Vicious who died in 1979 at the young age of 21.

- Autographs are another popular area, but always ensure they are genuine. The huge demand for autographs from performers like Elvis, the Beatles and the Rolling Stones meant that band members would often sign for each other, as would assistants or fan club staff.

A very rare 'Mersey Beat' music paper, volume I #4 August 17th 1961, featuring early Beatles content.

The 'Mersey Beat' had a close association with the Beatles, it was founded by one of Lennon's fellow students from the Liverpool Art College, Bill Harry. Brian Epstein, who went on to manage the band wrote a column for the paper.

1961

$100-150   **GAZE**

The Beatles, 'Love Me Do', UK single 45-R 4949, released by Parlophone, with red label.

The red label denotes the first pressing, later pressings have a black label and are worth slightly more. The red label version was re-released in 1982, but can be distinguished by the word 'mono' on the label.

1962

$70-100   **GAZE**

An American 'The Beatles Sound Best on KRLA' pin.

Californian radio station KRLA have the distinction of being the first first southland station to air the band.

2.25in (5.5cm) diam

$60-80   **LDE**

A 1964 The Beatles 'Beat Monthly' calendar.

11in (28cm) high

$120-180   **GAZE**

A Beatles lithographed tin tray, by Worcesterware, with some wear to the finish.

c1964   13in (33cm) wide

$40-60   **GAZE**

The Beatles with Tony Sheridan and Guests, 'My Bonnie', rare US LP SE4215, released by MGM, with inner.

1964

$100-150   **GAZE**

The Beatles Quiz Book, printed by William Collins Sons and Company Limited.

1964   11in (28cm) wide

$30-50   **GAZE**

ROCK & POP

A Foyles Luncheons guest list and table plan, for a lunch to mark the publication of John Lennon's 'In His Own Write', 23rd April 1964, bearing signatures of John Lennon, Lionel Bart and Alma Cogan.

$500-700 GAZE

A 1960s The Beatles pendant necklace, with small black and white press photograph of the group.

1in (2.5cm) wide

$50-70 GAZE

A 1965 Beatles pocket diary.

4.25in (11cm) high

$100-150 GAZE

The Beatles, 'Les Beatles dans Leurs 14 Plus Grands Succès', French LP OSX231, released by Odeon.

1965

$600-800 GAZE

A Saunders Enterprises card cut-out George Harrison coat hanger.

c1965 *15.25in (38.5cm) high*

$120-180 GAZE

A Paul McCartney guitar-shaped 'jewellery brooch', produced by Invicta Plastics, on the original card.

c1965

$40-60 GAZE

The Beatles, 'Beatles For Sale', Australian LP PMCO1240, released by Parlophone.

1965

$30-40 GAZE

A pair of 1960s Dutch Beatles stockings, patterned with rows of the Beatles heads and printed design to the top band.

$40-60 GAZE

A collection of Beatles memorabilia, comprising a Beatles fan club membership booklet bearing signatures, a 'Magical Mystery Tour' UK double EP MMT 1-2, released by Parlophone, 'Introducing the Beatles', US LP VJLP 1062, released by Vee-Jay, 'All My Loving', UK EP GEP 8891, released by Parlophone, and a Cavern Club membership card.

$1,500-2,000 ROS

The Beatles, 'Magical Mystery Tour' UK mono double EP MMT-1, released by Parlophone, in excellent condition.

1967

$70-100 GAZE

The Beatles, 'Penny Lane/Strawberry Fields' UK double A-side single R5570, released by Parlophone, with original picture sleeve.

250,000 copies of this single were released in the picture sleeve.

1967

$40-60 GAZE

A John Lennon and Yoko Ono pin.

This image was used as the controversial cover of the 'Unfinished Music No.1: Two Virgins' album released by John and Yoko in 1968. Outraged distributors sold the album in a brown paper wrapper and a number of copies were impounded for obscenity.

c1968 2.25in (5.5cm) diam

$60-90 LDE

The Beatles, 'Strawberry Fields', Dutch record club-issue LP DS018, released by Parlophone.

1968

$150-200 GAZE

The Beatles, 'Love Me Do', red vinyl 'For Juke Boxes Only!' single S7-56785, issued by Capitol.

The first of a series of juke box singles reissued by Capitol, this was intended to be in black vinyl only but the pressing machine still contained red vinyl from a previous pressing, and a number were printed by mistake. The exact number of red copies made is uncertain, but it is probably somewhere between 300 and 1,200.

1992

$20-30 GAZE

Four large Beatles plastic key rings, with press photography.

c1968 5in (12.5cm) high

$40-60 GAZE

The Beatles, 'Please Please Me', Japanese issue LP AP 8675, released by Apple, with different cover and color inserts.

c1969

$40-60 GAZE

A 'Best Wishes, Elvis Presley' badge, the back marked "Elvis Presley Enterprises 1956".

3in (7.5cm) diam

$120-180   **LDE**

Elvis Presley, 'Rock n' roll', first UK LP CLP 1093, released by HMV.

1956

$280-320   **GAZE**

An 'Elvis' badge.

3.75in (9.5cm) diam

$80-120   **LDE**

Elvis Presley, 'Got a Lot o' Livin' To Do!', Malaysian issue LP PR-101, by Pirate Records.

1976

$50-70   **GAZE**

An 'Elvis Monthly Special' book, published by Albert Hand, distributed by World Distributors (Manchester) Ltd.

1977

$10-15   **MTS**

A pack of Elvis Collectors Series bubble gum cards, by Boxcar Enterprises Inc.

1978   *4in (10cm) wide*

$15-20   **MTS**

An 'Elvis Monthly Special 1981' book, published by Albert Hand, distributed by World Distributors (Manchester) Ltd.

1981

$10-15   **MTS**

An packet of promotional Elvis Presley 'Tickle Me' feathers, sealed.

Released to promote Presley's western comedy-musical 'Tickle Me'.

1965   *11.5in (29cm) high*

$80-120   **LDE**

A 'Bay City Rollers' badge.

2.25in (5.5cm) diam

$25-35   **LDE**

The Beach Boys, 'LA Light', UK picture disc LP CRB 11-86081, released by Caribou Records.

1979

$12-18   **GAZE**

Jeff Beck, 'Boston Tea-Party', Japan acetate LP.

1969

$60-80   **GAZE**

A 'San Francisco likes Tony Bennett' badge, with ribbon.

3.25in (8.5cm) diam

$30-50   **LDE**

Marc Bolan, 'The Wizard', UK demo 45 single F 12288, released by Decca.

1965

$400-600   **GAZE**

David Bowie, 'Ragazzo Solo, Ragazza Sola', rare UK single, BW 704 208, released by Philips, second edition.

1969

$70-100   **GAZE**

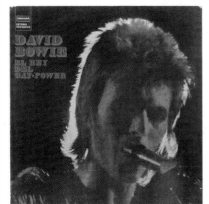

David Bowie, 'El Rey Del Gay Power', Spanish issue double compilation LP DCS 15044, released by Deram, with gatefold cover.

1973

$120-180   **GAZE**

A 'Maxine Brown Fan Club' badge.

2in (5cm) diam

$50-70   **LDE**

An early Kate Bush color photo, signed with dedication, with certificate of authenticity.

$100-150   **GAZE**

Johnny Cash, 'The Fabulous Johnny Cash', US LP BPG 62042, released by CBS, bearing signature on reverse.

Cash's death in 2003 re-ignited interest in his work and in memorabilia connected to him. The success of the Oscar-winning biopic 'Walk the Line' has also contributed to this.

1961

$60-80   **GAZE**

Dead or Alive, uncut picture disc featuring Pete Burns.

Burn's appearance on Celebrity Big Brother in 2005 has renewed interest in his band. It remains to be seen how long this interest will last.

$30-40   **GAZE**

Lonnie Donegan, 'Lonnie', 10in UK LP Nixa NPT 19027, released by Pye.

Lonnie Donegan, known as 'The King of Skiffle' was a huge influence on many 1960s UK bands including John Lennon and Paul McCartney.

1957

$12-18   **GAZE**

Donovan, 'A Gift From a Flower to a Garden', UK double LP boxed set NPL 20000, with navy blue box, released by Pye.

This was also produced with a black box, which is worth the same amount.

1968

$40-60   **GAZE**

The Doors, 'LA Woman', UK single K 42090, released by Elektra, the cover with rounded corners and die-cut PVC window.

1971

$20-30   **GAZE**

Eagles, 'One of These Nights', 12in LP, released by Asylum, bearing signatures of members of the band.

1975

$150-200   **GAZE**

Georgie Fame, 'Yeh Yeh', US LP LP 8292, released by Imperial, with white label promo.

1964

$15-20   **GAZE**

A 1950s 'Go Man Go! – Crazy Man Crazy!' Eddie Fisher badge.

1.75in (4.5cm) diam

$30-40   **LDE**

A late 1970s 'The Four Tops at The Sands', Atlantic City pin.

3in (7.5cm) diam

$40-60   **LDE**

Jimi Hendrix, 'Isle of Wight', Japanese LP MP2217, released by Polydor, with original cover and obi.

1971

$120-180 **GAZE**

Jimi Hendrix Experience, 'Band of Gypsys', LP released by Polydor.

1973

$20-30 **GAZE**

Jimi Hendrix Experience, 'Axis Bold as Love', French LP 0820167, first edition released by Barclay with unique cover.

1968

$200-300 **GAZE**

A 'Herman's Hermits' badge.

3.5in (9cm) diam

$30-50 **LDE**

A 'High Hopes – Emerald Room, Wildwood, NJ' card badge, with ribbon, marked "Aura Badge Co. Tommy Tatler Booking Management".

3.25in (8.5cm) diam

$60-90 **LDE**

INXS, 'Shabooh Shoobah', UK LP PRICE 94, released in Mercury, signed by all the group including Michael Hutchence, with certificate of authenticity.

1984

$120-180 **GAZE**

Joy Division, 'An Ideal For Living', rare picture disc album.

1978

$30-40 **GAZE**

A 1970s 'The Combined Led Zeppelin I & II', songbook, Kinney Music Ltd.

c1973

$30-40 **GAZE**

Led Zeppelin, 'The Song Remains the Same', Japanese double LP WPCR11619, released by Atlantic, with booklet and obi.

1976

$20-30 **GAZE**

ROCK & POP

Joni Mitchell, 'Court and Spark', UK LP SYLA 8756, released by Asylum, Half Speed Master album.

1974

$10-15 GAZE

The Modern, 'Industry', green vinyl single 9877069, released by Mercury, signed by the band in the sleeve.

Emerging band The Modern had this, their second single, banned from the UK charts due to fans and friends buying multiple copies in order to raise the band's position – the first time such action had been taken. It will be interesting to see how this effects the value of the single in the secondary market.

2006

$5-8 MHC

A 'The Monkees' pin, by Raybert Productions Inc 1966.

3.5in (9cm) diam

$40-60 LDE

Mott the Hoople, 'Live with David Bowie', rare German LP LTD 1073.

1973

$30-50 GAZE

Patti Smith Group, 'You Light Up My Life', LP PSG 44, live in Santa Monica.

1978

$20-30 GAZE

Pink Floyd, 'Psychedelic Games for May', limited edition picture disc, SNAP - 01.

$40-60 GAZE

A Pink Floyd Saville Theatre program, for October 1967, one of the earliest Floyd programs in existence.

$320-380 GAZE

A Pink Floyd 'See Emily Play' original sheet music book.

1967

$150-200 GAZE

Pink Floyd, 'A Saucerful Of Secrets/The Piper At The Gates Of Dawn', limited edition German set of the bands first two LPs 1C 062-04 190/1C 062-04 292, released by EMI/Columbia.

1973

$280-320 GAZE

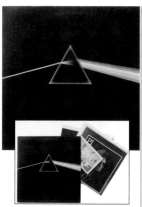

Pink Floyd, 'The Dark Side of The Moon', UK LP SHVL 804, released by Harvest with two sticker and two posters.

1973

$20-30   **GAZE**

A CLOSER LOOK AT A QUEEN SINGLE

To celebrate this award, EMI decided to release a special limited edition single and chose Queen for the honour.

In 1978 EMI were awarded the prestigious Queen's Award To Industry For Export Achievement. This was in part due to the success of Queen and their hit Bohemian Rhapsody.

The record was supposed to be purple, the band's signature color and was to match the sleeve. Due to a production error they were printed in blue and it was decided to keep the blue color.

EMI Records

This single was recently listed No. 5 on Record Collectors all time rarest 100 singles.

Queen, 'Bohemian Rhapsody', limited edition UK blue vinyl single PS EMI 2375, released by EMI in an edition of 200, special EMI In House "Queens Award For Export".

Although the edition was limited to only 200, un-numbered test pressings and end-of-run copies are on the market but lack the sleeve and the special illustrated label. They are usually worth up to $1,000.

1978

$4,000-5,000   **GAZE**

Queen, 'The Best of ...", rare 1980s Korean LP, with unique cover, long since deleted.

$60-80   **GAZE**

Queen, 'I Want It All', UK single QUEEN 10, released by Parlophone, the picture sleeve bearing signatures of the group, obtained from an official fan club member.

1989

$350-450   **GAZE**

Queen, 'Queen's First E.P.', very rare UK demo EMI 2623, released by EMI.

1976

$30-40   **GAZE**

Roxy Music, 'Manifesto', UK picture disc LP, EGPD 001, released by Polydor/E.G.

1979

$20-30   **GAZE**

Sex Pistols, 'No One Is Innocent/My Way ', Japanese single PC 1978, YK-109-AX, released by Virgin with lyric insert.

1978

$60-80   **GAZE**

ROCK & POP

Siouxsie and the Banshees, 'Cities in Dust', live in Brussels double LP, released by Wonderland.
1986
$50-70   **GAZE**

The Soft Machine, 'The Soft Machine', French issue LP, released by Barclay with unique cover.
1969
$50-70   **GAZE**

Soft Machine, 'Soft Space UK Harvest', 'A' demo, HAR 5155, released by Harvest.
1978
$20-30   **GAZE**

Bruce Springsteen, 'As Requested Around the World' LP, very rare US DJ only LP, Columbia AS 97.
1981
$50-70   **GAZE**

Tyrannosaurus Rex, 'Unicorn/Beard of Stars', re-issued double album TOOFA 9, released by Cube/Pye.
1978
$30-40   **GAZE**

A 'The Supremes Fan Club' badge.
2.5in (6.5cm) diam
$100-150   **LDE**

Roger Waters, 'Music From the Body', rare Italy issue LP 3C 064-04615, released by Harvest with unique Italy-only cover.
1974
$80-120   **GAZE**

The Who, 'Tommy', UK double LP 2657 002, released by Track with original booklet.
1973
$35-45   **GAZE**

The Yardbirds, 'The Yardbirds', rare Swedish LP SSX 1018, released by Columbia.

This LP was released first with this 'Studio Cover' and then with a second pressing 'Street Cover'. This cover was shot by photographer Dezo Hoffman, famous for shooting bands including The Beatles and cementing their carefully crafted image.
1965
$60-80   **GAZE**

COLLECTORS' NOTES

■ The development of transfer-printing in the late 18thC, along with improved manufacturing and distribution methods in the 19thC, allowed royal commemorative ceramics to become more widely available. Many items were produced from the reign of Queen Victoria onwards.

■ As there is a huge variety of items available, many collectors choose to limit their collection to a particular personality, subject area or time period.

■ The quality of an item is a key indicator to value, with those by well-known makers, made from high quality materials and with fine decoration usually being the most valuable. Designers to look for include Eric Ravilious, Charlotte Rhead and Richard Guyatt.

■ Condition is also vital as so many pieces were produced in large numbers. Always buy pieces in the best condition possible, as this will help to maintain or increase values.

■ As well as ceramics, many other different items have been produced for royal events such as coronations, jubilees, births and deaths. Trinkets and 'ephemeral' card and paper items can be found regularly at affordable prices and can make a satisfying collection.

■ With modern wares, look for limited editions and 'deluxe' versions made in low numbers. Some collectors tend to prize items with photographic images while others prefer those with just coats of arms or ciphers.

A Queen Victoria and Prince Albert Royal Wedding plate, unmarked.

1840   6.25in (16cm) diam

$700-800   **RCC**

A Staffordshire Queen Victoria Coronation six-sided plate, in excellent condition and bright colors.

Despite the ready availability of Queen Victoria Jubilee pieces, earlier coronation commemoratives are much harder to find.

1837   7.5in (19cm) wide

$800-1,000   **RCC**

A Prince Albert Victor, Duke of Clarence commemorative white parian bust, by Robinson & Leadbeater.

7.5in (19cm) high

$400-500   **RCC**

A silk of Prince Albert, the Prince Consort.

9in (23cm) high

$70-90   **RCC**

A Queen Victoria and Prince Albert commemorative plate, decorated in pink luster, printed in pink and enameled in colors with portraits entitled "Victoria and Albert".

c1851   8.75in (22cm) diam

$80-120   **SAS**

A Queen Victoria and Prince Albert commemorative cup and saucer, printed in pink and enameled in colors with portraits entitled "The Royal Family".

c1851

$100-150   **SAS**

A Prince Albert In Memoriam tall jug, with molded decoration and decorative handle, registered design mark.

1861   8in (20cm) high

$220-280   **RCC**

A Queen Victoria commemorative plate, featuring an unusual full-length portrait, possibly German.

10.5in (26.5cm) diam

$180-220   **RCC**

A CLOSER LOOK AT A COPELAND TYG

The plainer standard edition has no lip and is less desirable. It can be worth upto $2,500.

The portraits include Queen Victoria, Field Marshall Lord Roberts and the Most Honorable Marquis of Salisbury.

The Transvaal was incorporated into the British Empire in 1900, following the second Boer War.

This deluxe version was limited to only 100 pieces. The small edition means this tyg will always be sought-after.

A Copeland Edition De Luxe 'Transvaal Tyg', from an edition of 100, Thomas Goode subscribers copy.

c1900   6in (15cm) high

$3,000-4,000   **RCC**

A Doulton Burslem Queen Victoria Diamond Jubilee beaker.

c1897   3.75in (9.5cm) high

$200-300   **RCC**

A Doulton Lambeth Queen Victoria Diamond Jubilee stoneware mug, printed in brown with young and old portraits.

$70-100   **SAS**

A German Queen Victoria Diamond Jubilee beaker, with portraits of the Royal Family.

c1897

$120-180   **RCC**

A Copeland Queen Victoria Diamond Jubilee molded teapot, with green and gilt decoration.

c1897   9in (23cm) wide

$400-500   **RCC**

A Chown limited edition 'Royal Dynastic Plate', commissioned by Paul Wyton & Joe Spiteri to commemorate the centenary of Queen Victoria's Diamond Jubilee, from an edition of 50.

1997   10.5in (26.5cm) diam

$200-250   **RCC**

A Coalport King Edward VII Coronation plate, with wavy rim.

1902   10in (25.5cm) diam

$180-220   RCC

A Winton King Edward VII In Memoriam plate.

1910

$100-150   RCC

A Copeland King Edward VII In Memoriam two-handled vase, from an edition of 100, Thomas Goode subscribers copy.

1910   7in (18cm) high

$2,000-2,500   RCC

An English King George V & Queen Mary Coronation egg cup, with gilt rim.

1911   2.75in (7cm) high

$25-35   RCC

A Shelley late Foley King George V & Queen Mary Coronation teapot, with gilt trim.

1911

$220-280   RCC

A Wilkinson Ltd. 'HM King George V – Pro Patria' character jug, designed by Francis Carruthers Gould, issued by Soane & Smith Ltd during WWI, decorated in underglaze colors, enameled and gilded, with printed marks.

12.25in (30.5cm) high

$1,500-2,000   SAS

A Princess Mary, Princess Royal and Henry, Viscount Lascelles Royal Wedding beaker.

1922   4in (10cm) high

$280-320   RCC

A King George V & Queen Mary Silver Jubilee mug, with flag-shaped handle.

1935   7in (18cm) high

$50-70   RCC

A Crown Staffordshire King George V & Queen Mary Silver Jubilee lidded pot, in the form of a crown.

1935

$100-150   RCC

A Ridgway Prince Edward, Prince of Wales Investiture plate.

1911   *9in (23cm) diam*

$100-150   **RCC**

A Shelley cup and saucer set, commemorating Prince Edward, Prince of Wales' visit to South Africa, with gilt rims.

1925

$70-100   **SAS**

A Prince Edward, Prince of Wales tapering pottery beaker, with named naval portrait.

c1925

$70-100   **SAS**

A Melba China King Edward VIII globe, decorated in colors on an inscribed base.

1937   *3.5in (9cm) high*

$180-220   **SAS**

A Bovey Pottery 'The Three Reigns of 1936' three-handled mug, with portraits of George V, Edward VIII and George VI.

c1936   *3.5in (9cm) high*

$180-220   **RCC**

A Hammersley King Edward VIII Coronation mug, with the abdication date added.

Without the abdication the value would be $70-100.

c1936   *3.5in (9cm) high*

$220-280   **RCC**

A Shelley Edward VIII Coronation plate.

c1936   *9in (23cm) diam*

$70-90   **RCC**

A J. & J. May Wallis Simpson In Memoriam mug.

1986   *3.5in (9cm) high*

$70-100   **RCC**

A Lady Grace China limited edition 'The King's Dilemma' character jug, by Peggy Davies Ceramics, commemorating the 60th Anniversary of Edward VIII's abdication, from an edition of 350.

1997   *9.5in (24cm) high*

$250-350   **RCC**

A King George VI & Queen Mary plate, commemorating their visit to the Delhi Dunbar, India.

1911   5.5in (14cm) diam

$40-60   **RCC**

A Paragon King George VI & Queen Elizabeth Coronation preserve pot.

4in (10cm) high

$70-100   **RCC**

An Aynsley King George VI & Queen Elizabeth Coronation plate, with raised laurel wreaths to the centre.

1937   10.5in (26.5cm) diam

$180-220   **RCC**

A Royal Albert Crown China King George VI & Queen Elizabeth Coronation mug, with photographic portrait of the Royal Family by Marcus Adams.

1937   4in (10cm) high

$30-50   **RCC**

A Compton & Woodhouse Queen Elizabeth the Queen Mother commemorative plate.

8in (20cm) diam

A Royal Doulton King George VI & Queen Elizabeth Coronation mug, with 'G' shaped handle.

1937   3.5in (9cm) high

$220-280   **RCC**

$70-100   **RCC**

A Chown limited edition Queen Elizabeth the Queen Mother 101st birthday mug, commissioned by Paul Wyton & Joe Spiteri, from an edition of 70, with two portraits on a pink ground.

2001   3.75in (9.5cm) high

$40-60   **RCC**

A Chown limited edition Queen Elizabeth the Queen Mother In Memoriam plate, commissioned by Paul Wyton & Joe Spiteri, from an edition of 25.

2002   8in (20cm) diam

$80-120   **RCC**

A Creampetal Grindley Princesses Elizabeth and Margaret commemorative plate.

c1936   10.5in (26.5cm) wide

$100-150   **RCC**

A Paragon bowl commemorating the birth of Princess Elizabeth, printed in brown with named and dated portrait after Marcus Adams, lined in red and gilt.

1926   *5.5in (14cm) diam*

$60-80   **SAS**

A Crown Derby Queen Elizabeth II Coronation musical tankard, playing 'The National Anthem'.

1953   *5.5in (13.5cm) high*

$80-120   **SAS**

A Wedgwood Queen Elizabeth II Coronation mug, designed by Richard Gyatt.

1953   *4in (10cm) high*

$100-150   **RCC**

A Queen Elizabeth II Coronation mug, with E-shaped handle.

1953   *3.5in (9cm) high*

$30-50   **RCC**

A Paragon Queen Elizabeth II Coronation loving cup.

1953   *6in (15cm) wide*

$100-150   **RCC**

A Wedgwood 'Embossed Queen's Ware' Queen Elizabeth II Coronation milk jug.

1953   *6in (15cm) wide*

$40-50   **RCC**

A Mercian China Queen Elizabeth II Silver Jubilee plate, designed by A. Kitson Towler, DFA, from an edition of 60 commissioned by the Commemorative Collectors' Society.

This is from a series of 12 different plates.

1978   *10.5in (26.5cm) diam*

$70-100   **RCC**

A Mercian China Prince Philip, Duke of Edinburgh Silver Jubilee plate, designed by A. Kitson Towler, DFA, from an edition of 60 commissioned by the Commemorative Collectors' Society.

    10.5in (26.5cm) diam

$70-100   **RCC**

A tankard commemorating the restoration of Windsor Castle, from The Royal Collection.

1997   *3in (7.5cm) high*

$40-60   **RCC**

A Royal Stafford Queen Elizabeth II Golden Jubilee teapot.

2002 11in (28cm) wide

$70-90 RCC

A Paragon Princess Margaret plate, commemorating her birth.

1930 9.5in (24cm) diam

$180-220 RCC

A limited edition Princess Margaret 60th Birthday commemorative plate, commissioned by Peter Jones China, from an edition of 5,000.

1990 8.5in (21.5cm) diam

$60-80 RCC

A Halcyon Days Queen Elizabeth II Gold Wedding beaker.

1997 4in (10cm) high

$200-250 RCC

A Coronet Pottery 'The Ladies of August' commemorative plate, with portraits of Queen Elizabeth the Queen Mother, Princess Margaret and Princess Anne.

These three members of the Royal family have birthdays in August.

1990 10.5in (26.5cm) diam

$70-100 RCC

A Panorama Studios Ceragraphics Princess Anne and Captain Mark Phillips Royal Wedding mug.

1973 4.25in (11cm) high

$40-60 RCC

A Coalport Princess Anne 'Save the Children' commemorative plate, from an edition of 10,000.

The Princess Royal has been president of Save the Children since 1981.

9in (23cm) diam

$50-70 RCC

An Aynsley limited edition Princess Anne and Commander Timothy Laurence Royal Wedding mug, commissioned by Peter Jones China, from an edition of 2,000.

1992 3.75in (9.5cm) high

$70-100 RCC

A Wedgwood Prince Andrew and Sarah Ferguson Royal Wedding mug.

1986 3in (7.5cm) high

$50-70 RCC

A Paragon Prince Charles Souvenir mug.

This would have been released to coincide with his mother's coronation.

c1953   3in (7.5cm) high

$70-100   RCC

A Carlton Ware Prince Charles and Lady Diana Spencer Royal Wedding cup, with double-heart handle.

1981   4.5in (11.5cm) high

$70-100   RCC

A Crown Derby limited edition Prince Charles' Investiture as Prince of Wales dragon figurine, from an edition of 250, with original box.

The delicate extremities are easily damaged, so undamaged examples are sought-after. The addition of the original box adds to the value.

1969   5.25in (13.5cm) high

$1,000-1,500   RCC

A Coronet Pottery Prince William plate, commemorating his birth.

1982   10.5in (26.5cm) diam

$80-120   RCC

A Wedgwood mug commemorating the birth of Prince William, designed by Richard Guyatt.

1982   3in (7.5cm) high

$60-80   RCC

A Royal Doulton limited edition 'The Princess of Wales' commemorative plate, from an edition of 10,000, painted by John Merton.

1991   10.5in (26.5cm) diam

$180-220   RCC

A Chown limited edition Diana, Princess of Wales In Memoriam loving cup, commissioned by Paul Wyton & Joe Spiteri, from an edition of 400.

1997   3in (9.5cm) high

$100-150   RCC

A Crummles limited edition Prince William 21st birthday pill box, commissioned by Paul Wyton & Joe Spiteri, from an edition of 30.

2003

$100-150   RCC

A Chown Prince Charles and Camilla Parker-Bowles Royal Wedding mug, commissioned by Paul Wyton & Joe Spiteri.

The date of this wedding was postponed by one day so that Prince Charles could attend the funeral of Pope John Paul II.

2005   3.75in (9.5cm) high

$40-60   RCC

COLLECTORS' NOTES

■ Before the development of specially designed commercial bottles for individual perfumes, stylish ladies would buy perfume and decant it into a perfume bottle for use at their dressing tables. The vessel used to transport the perfume was plain and functional. These decorative bottles were popular during the late 19thC, and began to tail off during the 1910s and '20s as custom-designed perfume bottles began to proliferate.

■ The majority were produced in France and Czechoslovakia, with some French bottles being designed by notable makers such as Lefébure, Depinoix, Viard and Lalique. Most of these are made from pressed glass, sometimes stained with colour to highlight the molded design. Czechoslovakian examples can be in pressed or cut glass and often have large and extravagant stoppers etched or cut with figures or complex stylized floral motifs.

■ Companies in Italy and Germany also made examples that are collectible today. Materials include precious metals and ceramics, but the majority found are in glass. Large examples and those in the prevailing styles of the day, such as Art Nouveau and Art Deco, tend to be the most desirable, particularly if by a notable designer.

■ Look out for chips and damage, especially around the rim and on the stopper. Feel edges and designs with your finger, checking for chips or repaired polished areas, which will appear flat. Compare the stopper to the bottle as these can be replaced. Do not scrub stained areas as this may remove the applied stain.

An Art Deco Czechoslovakian cut-glass scent bottle, the stopper etched with a nude female figure.	An Art Deco clear glass scent bottle, the stopper decorated with dancing female figures.	A Czechoslovakian large cut-glass scent bottle, with cut-out and star cut stopper.
c1930　　Bottle 10in (25.5cm) high	c1920s　　9.25in (23.5cm) high	c1930s　　Bottle 10.5in (26.5cm) high
$220-280　　　LB	**$400-500**　　　TRIO	**$220-280**　　　LB

A 1930s Art Deco amber-coloured glass scent bottle, the smoky clear glass stopper featuring two herons, signed and marked "Czechoslovakia".

The mark in English shows that this was intended for export.

c1930　　　　8.25in (21cm) high

$400-500　　　　　　TRIO

A French Art Deco pressed glass atomiser, by Viard, with green stain, metal fittings and puffer.

Bottles by sculptor and glassmaker Julien Viard are similar in style to those of his contemporary, René Lalique. Viard also designed bottles for perfumier Dubarry.

c1930　　　　6in (15cm) high

$250-350　　　　TDG

An unmarked scent bottle, in frosted pressed glass with stain and painted details.

The design of this bottle is also very similar to Lalique and is both floral and feminine, suiting the contents.

c1920s　　　　5in (12.5cm) high

$1,200-1,800　　　RDL

A late 1920s Art Deco clear glass scent bottle, with black puffer.

6.75in (17cm) high

$300-400   **TRIO**

An Art Deco clear glass scent bottle and stopper, with black decoration.

c1920s   4.5in (11.5cm) high

$250-350   **TRIO**

A late 1920s Art Deco clear glass scent bottle, with black decoration and puffer.

4.75in (12cm) wide

$250-300   **TRIO**

A 1930s Czechoslovakian Art Deco cut-glass atomiser, the pyramid-shaped bottle with stepped sides and carved and painted decoration.

3.5in (9cm) high

$150-200   **LB**

An Art Deco clear glass scent bottle and stopper, with overlaid floral decoration.

3.5in (9cm) wide

$400-500   **TRIO**

A 1920s clear glass perfume bottle, possibly by Viard, with blue glass decoration and atomiser, with replaced tassel.

6.5in (16.5cm) high

$250-350   **LB**

A CLOSER LOOK AT A SCENT BOTTLE

Although it looks like glass, the bottle is actually made from a type of colorless plastic called Lucite that was popular from the 1930s.

The geometric, stepped form is typically Art Deco.

The squared sides of the cylindrical blue Lucite bottle reflect the color and give an interesting optical effect.

The form is architecturally inspired and brings to mind the skyscrapers that were being built at the time.

A 1930s Art Deco Lucite scent bottle, with asymmetrical faceted Lucite stopper.

6.75in (17cm) high

$400-500   **TDG**

A French scent bottle, by Lefébure & Cie glassworks, in frosted glass with sepia stain.

c1910   5.75in (14cm) high

$1,800-2,200   **RDL**

A 1920s/30s Czechoslovakian Art Deco scent bottle, with gilt detailing, metal fittings and puffer.

3.75in (9.5cm) wide

$350-450   **TRIO**

An early 20thC German elliptical glass scent bottle, of opaque milk glass with blue, yellow and orange trails, brass mounting and spherical stopper.

3.25in (8cm) high

$40-50   **KAU**

A French scent bottle, silver-cased clear glass with blue, green and orange bands, elliptical shape with brass mounting and spherical stopper.

c1930   2.5in (6.5cm) high

$45-55   **KAU**

An Italian scent bottle, clear glass with blue and white zanfirico spiral threads, and with an engraved, hinged stopper.

c1930   2in (5cm) high

$40-50   **KAU**

An early 20thC English zanfirico-style clear and white scent bottle, with a glass stopper.

c1910   2in (5cm) long

$120-180   **TRIO**

An Art Deco green glass ovoid scent bottle, with silver hinged lid and glass stopper.

c1920s   4.25in (11cm) high

$300-400   **TRIO**

A pair of 1930s hand-carved cast phenolic scent holders, with ivory stems.

These tribal sculpture-inspired bottles are rare, especially with their ivory stems. The style is typical of the exotic influences on the Art Deco movement.

4.75in (12cm) high

$500-700   **MG**

A 1930s Czechoslovakian novelty gold-plated atomiser, the metal fitment in the form of a small 'urinating' boy or cherub.

4.75in (12cm) high

$180-220   **LB**

A French Art Deco silver scent bottle, embossed with a serpent around the neck and a spider on the stopper.

c1928   3in (7.5cm) high

$180-220   **TDG**

A Victorian scrap of a Dutch boy holding a small cane and string.

3.25in (8cm) high

$5-8　　　　　　　　　　　　　**AOY**

A Victorian scrap of a Dutch boy holding a goose.

3.25in (8cm) high

$5-8　　　　　　　　　　　　　**AOY**

A Victorian scrap of a lady holding a fan.

3.5in (9cm) high

$10-15　　　　　　　　　　　　**AOY**

A small Victorian scrap of an elegant lady.

Scraps were produced from the early 19thC until the 1930s, with the 'golden age' being 1860s-1900s. They were collected and stored in albums, or used to decorate greetings cards, boxes or large room screens. Note the protruding tabs of white paper on this example. These were used to hold scraps together on a printed sheet, the blank areas of the sheet having been mechanically stamped out. Each scrap would be torn gently away from the sheet for use. The lady on this scrap also shows Victorian ideals of beauty with her gentle eyes, small nose, rosebud lips, porcelain-like skin and flower encrusted dress.

2.25in (5.5cm) high

$8-12　　　　　　　　　　　　　**AOY**

A Victorian or Edwardian scrap of cricketers.

3.25in (8cm) wide

$8-12　　　　　　　　　　　　　**AOY**

A Victorian scrap of Santa Claus in a black suit.

It is unusual to find Santa Claus in a black suit, revealing its early date. Haddon Sundblom's 1930s advertising campaign for Coca-Cola lays claim to popularising a red-suited Santa.

2.75in (7cm) high

$7-10　　　　　　　　　　　　　**AOY**

A Victorian scrap of Santa Claus and child bearing gifts.

2in (5cm) high

$5-8　　　　　　　　　　　　　**AOY**

A large Victorian scrap of a parrot or macaw.

4in (10cm) high

$5-8　　　　　　　　　　　　　**AOY**

COLLECTORS' NOTES

■ Look out for 1960s & '70s memorabilia which makes a bold visual statement in terms of form, color and pattern. The work of leading companies and notable designers may fetch higher prices, but even un-named designs can be desirable if they capture 'the look'. Items which inspire fond memories or, for younger buyers, a sense of fascination for this colorful and exciting time, are the most sought after.

■ Bright, acid and often clashing colors dominate - look for hot pinks, oranges and yellows. Designs explode in psychedelic or 'flower power' patterns, and the sinuous Art Nouveau style of the 1900s was given a lurid makeover. Pop, and Op, art inspired designs are also popular.

■ Other recurring themes include youth, love and peace. Items relating to 'Swinging' London, where images of Union jacks, marching bands and old military iconography were repackaged in an anti-establishment manner, are also prized. Most were aimed at, and were popular with, tourists.

■ Continuing from the 1950s, the development of plastics and laminates was closely related to themes of the future, but also convenience. The new informality saw fun and functional ceramics being used – mugs replaced cups and saucers and functional, and often fun, oven-to-tableware became fashionable.

■ Condition is important as most pieces were used and worn - truly mint examples will be more desirable.

An English Ironstone Tableware flower power plate, by Washington Potteries, Staffordshire, England.

7.25in (18cm) diam

$8-12   **MTS**

An English Ironstone Tableware flower power plate, by Washington Potteries, Staffordshire, England.

7.25in (18cm) diam

$8-12   **MTS**

An American Deka Plastics Inc. printed plastic tray, by Deka, Elizabeth, NJ.

13in (32.5cm) diam

$50-70   **MTS**

A small square plate, by Surrey Ceramics, with abstract floral design, impressed marks.

4in (10cm) wide

$22-28   **TCM**

A set of four 1960s Staffordshire Potteries stacking mugs, transfer-printed with caricatures of fashionable people.

3.5in (9cm) high

$50-70   **MTS**

An English Ironstone Tableware flower power teacup and saucer, by Washington Potteries, Staffordshire England.

This is typical of many 1960s ceramic designs, which exploded in a riot of colorful flowers.

3.25in (8cm) high

$12-18   **MTS**

Three Hornsea 'Zoodiac' mugs, designed by John Clappison.

The name of the range is a pun on the design, which combines animals and signs of the zodiac. Hornsea are well known for their novelty mugs.

1974   *3.5in (9cm) high*

$25-35 each   **FD**

SIXTIES & SEVENTIES

A Midwinter 'Tango' milk jug, designed by Eve Midwinter.

1969-76   *5.25in (13cm) long*

$10-15   **MTS**

A 1960s Price Bros. coffee pot, printed and impressed marks "Price Made in England".

The cylinder was a commonly used shape for tableware during the 1960s, as it was modern, easy to manufacture and displays a pattern extremely well. Portmeirion are perhaps the best known maker of cylindrical tableware during this period, with designs by Susan Williams-Ellis.

                          9.5in (24cm) high

$40-60   **TCM**

A CLOSER LOOK AT A HORNSEA POTTERY VASE

Hornsea Pottery was one of the most prolific producers of home and table ware from the 1950s through the 1980s, and are probably most famous for their brown and green 'Heirloom' range.

'Rainbow' was designed by John Clappison, Hornsea Pottery's most prolific and talented designer. He designed for the factory from 1955-72 and 1976-84, devising most of its _____ major ranges.

'Rainbow' was produced from 1961-63 in 14 different shapes.

The colored bands were applied by a fine spray gun – earlier examples have blue banding, with gray bands indicating a later example.

A Hornsea Pottery 'Rainbow' molded small plant pot holder, the base with mold number "563".

1961-63   *4.75in (12.5cm) high*

$35-45   **AGR**

A 1970s transfer-printed chintz tea storage jar, marked "Portugal" on the base.

                          5.5in (14cm) high

$22-28   **MTS**

A large unmarked hand-thrown ovoid vase, decorated with a Modernist pattern of sgraffito triangles and hand-painted yellow circles.

$70-100   **PSI**

A 1960s Arthur Wood & Sons 'flower power' molded and hand-painted floral string holder.

These string holders are more commonly seen with pigs as decoration. Arthur Wood & Son acquired Carlton Ware in 1967, and continued to produce under that tradename.

                          5.75in (14.5cm) diam

$30-50   **MTS**

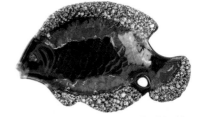

A French 'Vallauris' orange and brown glazed fish dish, with "VALLAURIS" stamp to base.

$25-35   **GAZE**

A CLOSER LOOK AT A CARLTON WARE MONEY BOX

This is part of a series of six money boxes, including a pirate, a clown, a Beefeater and a Scotsman.

This is one of the rarest from the series, probably as it did not have as much appeal to the children of the day as more exciting characters, such as a pirate.

The series was designed by Vivienne Brennan, who is also known for her bug-eyed frog and snail money box designs.

Money boxes are frequently damaged, particularly from use. This example is in excellent condition with no damage.

A Carlton Ware pirate money bank.

6in (15cm) high

$70-90   **MTS**

A 1960s Carlton Ware 'gentleman' ceramic money box.

6.5in (16cm) high

$70-100   **MTS**

A pair of 1960s/70s Carlton Ware salt and pepper shakers, with transfer-printed design of cooks in aprons.

4in (10cm) high

$50-70   **MTS**

A pair of 1960s/70s Carlton Ware salt and pepper shakers, of an Arabian king and queen.

each 3.5in (8.5cm) high

$70-100   **MTS**

A 1970s Italian ceramic money box, in the form of a stylised owl, with painted mark and serial number.

6.75in (17cm) high

$70-100   **TCM**

A 1970s orange ceramic elephant money bank, marked "Italian".

7.5in (19cm) high

$30-40   **MTS**

A 1960s Arthur Wood & Sons hand-painted piggy bank.

These are more commonly found with floral patterns.

6in (15cm) long

$30-50   **MTS**

SIXTIES & SEVENTIES

A pair of 1960s 'I was Lord Kitchener's Valet ' salt and pepper shakers, with 'I was In Carnaby Street' wording to reverse.

5.75in (14.5cm) high

$70-90 MTS

A 1960s 'I was Lord Kitchener's Valet' mug, titled 'I Was In Carnaby Street'.

Ceramics bearing the Union Jack and Carnaby Street slogans were popular souvenirs for foreign tourists during the 1960s when Swinging London was at its peak. 'I Was Lord Kitchener's Valet' was a shop specialising in selling vintage clothes and regimental uniforms, which had become part of 'street fashion'. Owned by Ian Fisk, it also sold new souvenirs bearing the Union Jack and Lord Kitchener and enjoyed patronage from celebrities such as Jimi Hendrix.

3.5in (8.5cm) high

$70-90 MTS

A 1960s 'I was Lord Kitchener's Valet' printed tin tray, titled 'I was In Carnaby Street', with a little rust.

12.5in (31cm) wide

$70-100 MTS

A 'Lady Jane of Carnaby Street Production Cheers' ashtray.

Lady Jane, owned by Harry Fox, was a fashionable women's clothing shop on Carnaby St. Objects marked with the shop's name are far rarer than clothes. 'Lady Jane' was also the title of a Rolling Stones song released in 1966.

5.75in (14.5cm) diam

$70-100 MTS

A 1960s 'I was Lord Kitchener's Valet ashtray, titled 'I was In Carnaby Street'.

c1969 4.5in (11.5cm) high

$70-90 MTS

A 1960s Bilton's Ironstone 'I was Lord Kitchener's Valet' plate, titled 'British Dish'.

6.75in (17cm) high

$50-70 MTS

A 1960s 'Gear of Carnaby Street London' ceramic piggy bank.

The Union Jack was the global symbol of 'Swinging London' during the 1960s.

4.75in (12cm) long

$70-90 MTS

A 1960s Crown Ducal London 'Carnaby St. W1' road sign ashtray, for 'I was Lord Kitchener's Valet'.

4.5in (11cm) diam

$30-50 MTS

An Associated Biscuits Ltd 'Swinging London' biscuit tin, with images of tourist destinations and popular Carnaby Street shops such as 'I Was Lord Kitchener's Valet' and 'Lord John'.

c1966 8.75in (22cm) wide

$50-70 MTS

A rare 'Cool Britannia' tin tray, with a psychedelic Britannia holding a knitting needle with an arc of thread behind her.

14in (35cm) wide

$220-280   **MTS**

A Polypops printed tray showing Queen Victoria.

The style of the design recalls Pop artist Peter Blake, whose images were very popular during the 1960s. In line with the fashion for vintage, military and dandy-like clothing, many historic icons such as Lord Kitchener and Queen Victoria were given a camp '60s makeover.

20.25in (50.5cm) high

$180-220   **MTS**

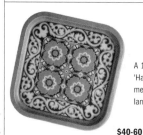

A 1960s JRM Design 'Harriet' pattern printed metal tray, designed by Ian Logan.

14in (35cm) wide

$40-60   **MTS**

A 1960s JRM Design 'Lollipop' pattern printed metal tray, designed by Ian Logan.

Ian Logan is a notable British designer who manages to capture the zeitgeist of an age appealingly. He has worked with a number of high profile clients and continues to design today, with a shop near the Barbican, London.

22.5in (56cm) wide

$80-120   **MTS**

An American psychedelic printed tin tray.

14.25in (35.5cm) diam

$50-70   **MTS**

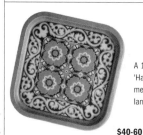

A set of six laminated plastic and cork drinks coasters, designed by Ian Logan.

3.5in (9cm) diam

$30-50   **MTS**

A set of six 1960s Baret Ware 'Mauve Flower Time' printed metal drinks coasters.

3.25in (8cm) diam

$22-28   **MTS**

A Marks & Spencer St Michael flower power biscuit tin.

5.5in (14cm) high

$15-20   **MTS**

A 1960s American Ohio Art psychedelic printed tin recipe card box.

3.75in (9.5cm) high

$30-50   **MTS**

A 1970s yellow plastic desk tidy, probably Italian, with white plastic drawers.

4.5in (11.5cm) high

$15-20   **DTC**

A 1970s Pentagram plastic interlocking 'clam' trinket box, designed by Alan Fletcher.

6.25in (15.5cm) diam

$50-70   **MTS**

A group of six early 1970s Pentagram stacking and interlocking molded plastic ashtrays, with registered number 954.589 for 1971.

Plastic was a popular material during the 1960s, with space age connotations. New advances in plastics and injection molding allowed it to be used durably for furniture and small, inexpensive pieces in ultra-modern forms and fashionably bright colors. Designers such as Finland's Eero Aarnio and Denmark's Verner Panton revelled in the freedom it gave them. The oil and energy crisis of the early 1970s slowed development temporarily, but it soon recovered.

each 1.75in (4.5cm) high

$20-30 (each)   **MTS**

An early 1970s white molded plastic interlocking 'clam' table lighter.

3.5in (9cm) diam

$30-50   **MTS**

A 1970s black plastic table lighter.

4.75in (12cm) high

$12-18   **DTC**

A 1970s Ronson black plastic table lighter.

3.75in (9.5cm) high

$15-20   **DTC**

A 1960s lamp, with a flexible plastic neck, ceramic base and sheet metal hood.

7in (18cm) high

$70-100   **FD**

A Danish ceiling light, by Hoyrup, with sheets of plastic fitted into perspex frame.

These self-assembly plastic lamp shades were popular during the 1960s, with many being designed and made in Denmark. They would arrive in flatpacks to be assembled at home.

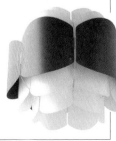

$70-90   **GAZE**

A CLOSER LOOK AT AN 8-TRACK PLAYER

The 8-track cartridge format, released in September 1965, was designed by William Lear who was also responsible for designing the Lear Executive jet. It was initially designed for Ford cars.

This was one of the most popular 8-track portables made, summing up the format for many people. It continues to be sought-after today.

Contemporary advertising read 'Dynamite 8', playing on the fact that this set looked like an explosives detonator, whereas pushing the plunger actually changed the track.

It was available in five different colors – tomato red is the most typical of the 1970s.

A Panasonic red plastic cased 'Dynamite 8' 8-track player, model RQ-830S.

c1972   9in (23cm) high

$50-70   **NOR**

A 1960s American printed vinyl musical photo album, by Annabel, in mint condition, boxed.

13.5in (33.5cm) high

$120-180   **MTS**

A 1960s American General Electrics plastic clock radio, model C3300A.

7.5in (18.5cm) wide

$180-220   **MTS**

A 1960s American plastic Ray-O-Vac flower printed 'New Boutique Lite' torch, boxed.

10in (25.5cm) high

$22-28   **MTS**

A 1970s plastic '7Up' padded cushion, designed for use at an outdoor pop concert.

13.75in (35cm) wide

$50-70   **MTS**

An American printed plastic double flask-holder, with zip lock and handle.

8in (20cm) high

$50-70   **MTS**

A box of molded plastic 'Style Sexy Drinking Straws', in the form of canoodling naked couples, made in Hong Kong, boxed.

box 16in (40cm) high

$40-60   **MTS**

A 1960s/70s American for the German market 'Harlekin Multi-set', made by Phoenix Glass, with nine glass beakers in multi-colored plastic holders, with original box.

Without the box, the value of the full set is more than halved.

Box 14.5in (37cm) diam

$80-120   **MA**

A CLOSER LOOK AT A 1960S CANDLEHOLDER

This sculptural form is comprised of a number of modular sections, each holding three candles, that fit together into many differently shaped structures.

The design is similar to leading British metal designer Robert Welch's three-stemmed candelabrum, released in 1958 and inspired by a visit to a Jackson Pollock art exhibition.

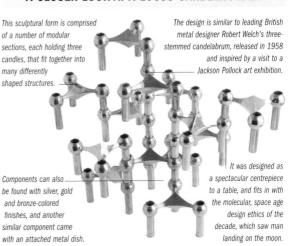

Components can also be found with silver, gold and bronze-colored finishes, and another similar component came with an attached metal dish.

It was designed as a spectacular centrepiece to a table, and fits in with the molecular, space age design ethics of the decade, which saw man landing on the moon.

A 1960s German modular candleholder combination, by Nagel.

Each module 4in (10cm) wide

$250-350 (set)   **FD**

An early 1960s home-made cushion, with hand-woven designs of people dancing and musical notes.

c1964   13.5in (34cm) wide

$70-90   **MTS**

A 1960s wire, felt and plastic children's coat hook, in the form of a cheery elf or Little Red Riding Hood.

11.5in (29cm) high

$22-28   **MTS**

A 1960s miniature home houseplant plastic gardening set, on a flower shaped stand.

Houseplants had come into fashion with the new, young home makers of the 1950s.

9in (23cm) high

$20-30   **MTS**

A 1960s/70s 'flower power' vinyl sewing kit and holder.

5.25in (13cm) wide

$12-14   **MTS**

A 1960s orange and pink 'string art' picture of a butterfly, on a black felt background.

14.75in (37.5cm) wide

$25-35   **NOR**

A 1960s French printed card 'Papiers' card folding rubbish bin.

The use of music hall imagery is typically 1960s.

12.75in (32cm) high

$50-70   **MTS**

An American Russ Berrie & Co. Inc cast hard plastic figurine, with 'I Know What You Want For Your Birthday But I Don't Know How To Wrap It' imprinted wording and manufacturer's stamp to back.

Of such plastic figurines, ones like this with erotic messages are the most sought-after and valuable.

1976   5.75in (14.5cm) high

$10-15   **NOR**

A 1970s American Russ Berrie & Co. Inc sand-filled cast hard resin bust, with 'I Miss Your Touch' imprinted wording and manufacturer's stamp to back.

1971   6in (15.5cm) high

$7-10   **NOR**

A 1960s home-made and hand-painted molded plaster-of-Paris 'Hippie', with 'Rock & Roll' and ' Vote for Love' messages, signed on the base "Anna Love Melanie".

8.75in (22cm) high

$20-25   **NOR**

A 1960s German vinyl nodding head witch troll, the base marked "HEICO".

Heico are known for their highly collectable trolls, but Thomas Dam is the name to look out for.

7in (18cm) high

$40-60   **NOR**

A 1960s plastic 'Peace on Barrel' urinating toy, lacks spectacles, but with original box.

To use this rather anti-establishment Hippie-inspired amusement, fill the barrel with water, push the button at the back and the man 'urinates'.

6.25in (16cm) high

$20-30   **NOR**

A 1960s painted composition money box, in the form of a telephone box, with teenagers and Scottie dog.

7in (17.5cm) high

$20-30   **NOR**

A 1960s/70s small ceramic cat, with hand-painted detailing, possibly Japanese.

2.25in (6cm) high

$12-18   **TCM**

A 1960s molded papiér mâche model of lion, hand-painted in bright psychedelic colors and wearing a crown.

6.75in (17cm) high

$30-40   **MTS**

A 1960s cast resin sculpture, with inset thermometer and deep sea themed internal decoration, including a real seahorse.

4.75in (12cm) high

$12-18   **MTS**

A 1960s/70s psychedelic printed orange and pink 'Gay Day' giraffe, made in South Africa.

18.5in (46.5cm) high

$35-45   **MTS**

A 1960s/70s psychedelic printed fabric dog.

20.5in (51cm) long

$22-28   **MTS**

A Wupper Design (UK) Ltd plastic 'Mr Wupper' ceiling mounted molded plastic spring mobile, mint and boxed.

6.5in (16cm) high

$80-120   **MTS**

An American Springbok Editions 'Psychedelic Mother Goose Puzzle', designed by Larry Bowser, complete and boxed.

c1970

4.25in (10.5cm) diam

$25-35   **MTS**

An American Springbok Editions 'Zany Zodian Puzzle', designed by Donni Giambone, complete and boxed.

Springbok Editions were founded in Missouri in the early 1960s by Katie & Robert Lewin. They were so successful that Hallmark acquired the company in 1967. Today their colorful, often circular, puzzles are sought-after by both puzzle collectors and enthusiasts.

c1970

4.25in (10.5cm) diam

$25-35   **MTS**

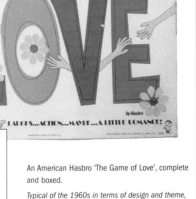

An American Hasbro 'The Game of Love', complete and boxed.

Typical of the 1960s in terms of design and theme, this game is very similar to MB's popular 'Twister' released in 1966.

1969

box 19.5in (48.5cm) wide

$70-100   **MTS**

A Cliff Richards 'Slottizoo' printed card cat, complete and unused, with card envelope.

This does not appear to be related to the pop and musical singer Cliff Richard.

14.25in (35.5cm) high

$40-60   **MTS**

A 1960s printed card balloon pump, with image of band player.

7.5in (18.5cm) high

$7-9   **MTS**

COLLECTORS' NOTES

■ Peter Max was born in Berlin, Germany in 1937, and spent his formative years in Shanghai. He and his family settled in the US in 1953. He went on to study at the Arts Student League in Manhattan.

■ By combining stylized comic strip graphics with undulating lines and psychedelic colors, underpinned by his formal training, Max produced some of the most striking and influential art of the era. His 'cosmic' style, typified by chunky line drawings filled with blocks of color, was a huge commercial success, appearing on everything from pencil cases to movie posters and telephone directories.

■ The imagery of skyscapes, sunbursts and clouds, inspired by his childhood in China, trips to India, Africa and Israel, and his love of astronomy appealed to a generation that was open to experimenting with mystical cultures and mind-altering drugs.

■ Peter Max has subsequently designed postage stamps for the United Nations and painted commissioned work for five US Presidents.

An American Peter Max printed paper school book cover.

13.25in (33cm) high

$50-70　　　　　　　　　**MTS**

An American Peter Max printed paper school book cover.

13.25in (33cm) high

$50-70　　　　　　　　　**MTS**

An American Peter Max Paper Airplane Book, A Pyramid Book, New York, complete.

1971　　　　　　*7in (17.5cm) high*

$50-70　　　　　　　　　**MTS**

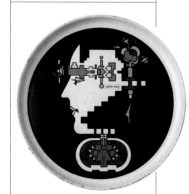

An American Peter Max 'Hello' inflatable plastic cushion.

11.5in (29cm) high

$80-120　　　　　　　　　**MTS**

A Peter Max screen printed tin tray.

13.25in (33cm) diam

$70-90　　　　　　　　　**MTS**

A 1960s American plastic printed coathanger, with mirror lenses.

13.5in (34cm) high

$180-220 **MTS**

A 1960s American plastic printed coathanger, with mirror lenses.

13.5in (34cm) high

$180-220 **MTS**

An Italian 'CIR' printed fabric sticker, printed "CIR TORINO MADE IN ITALY", depicting a man in a hat.

5in (12.5cm) high

$30-50 **MTS**

An Italian 'CIR' printed fabric sticker, printed "CIR TORINO MADE IN ITALY".

5.75in (14.5cm) high

$30-50 **MTS**

A 1960s Disco Light pair of sunglasses, with wipers and lights, mint and carded.

card 8.75in (22cm) high

$40-60 **MTS**

A 1960s printed vinyl handbag/travel bag.

13.5in (34.5cm) wide

$35-45 **MTS**

A 1970s flower power vinyl purse.

8in (20cm) wide

$22-28 **MTS**

A flower power vinyl travelling wash bag.

7in (18cm) wide

$12-18 **MTS**

A 1970s flower power sun hat.

15in (38cm) wide

$22-28 **MTS**

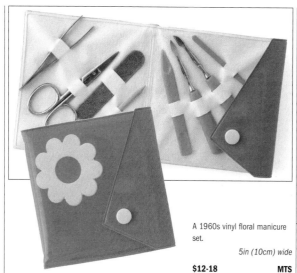

A 1960s molded plastic flower dressing table mirror, molded "MADE IN ENGLAND".

7.75in (19.5cm) diam

$25-35 MTS

A 1960s vinyl floral manicure set.

5in (10cm) wide

$12-18 MTS

A 1960s Daisy plastic bead child's purse, with lining and label reading "Designed by Miss Ellen Made in British Hong Kong".

6in (15.5cm) wide

$22-28 NOR

A Mushroom mirror, made in Japan by Seymour Mann Inc., the dome shaped mirror swivelling on its base, with original box.

9in (23cm) high

$35-45 MTS

A 1960s Mary Quant vinyl travelling toiletry set, missing some contents.

8in (20cm) wide

$30-50 MTS

A 1970s necklace made out of cutlery.

Jewellery made out of cutlery was very popular during the 1970s.

10.25in (26cm) high

$35-45 NOR

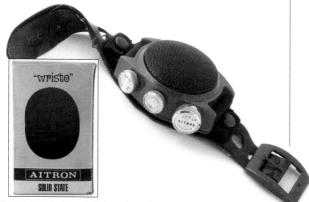

A 1960s Wristo by Aitron Solid State wristwatch radio.

10.5in (26cm) high

$60-80 MTS

COLLECTORS' NOTES

■ Of the many British companies that designed and produced items celebrating 'Swinging' London during the 1960s, and '70s, DODO Designs Ltd was one of the most prolific and best remembered.

■ It specialised in metal wares printed with brightly colored designs that usually poked gentle fun at the Establishment, British history and the British character. Quality was very fine and the variety was vast, particularly as regards enameled plaques.

■ Following the Pop Art movement of the period it also took artwork or logos for well-known British brands, and used them decoratively. The Union Jack and Lord Kitchener were regularly used and items were sold in popular tourist destinations as well as Carnaby Street.

■ Enameled plaques tend to be the most collectible items today, along with printed tins. Pieces with no address or a Westbourne Grove address, printed on the reverse are earlier in date. Look for bright colors and designs typical of the period. Damage such as chipping to the enamel reduces value considerably as pieces are still largely readily available.

A Dodo Designs 'Buckingham Palace Tradesman's Entrance' enameled plaque, with two line Westbourne Grove printed mark.

4.5in (11.5cm) high

$22-28   **MTS**

An early Dodo Designs 'Throne Room, enameled plaque, the reverse stamped 'MADE IN ENGLAND DODO DESIGNS' on two lines.

4.5in (11.5cm) high

$22-28   **MTS**

A Dodo Designs 'No Camping Piccadilly Circus' enameled plaque, with Westbourne Grove printed mark.

4.5in (11.5cm) high

$18-22   **MTS**

A Dodo Designs 'Bed & Breakfast French Lessons Given' enameled plaque, with Westbourne Grove printed mark.

4.5in (11.5cm) high

$18-22   **MTS**

A later Dodo Designs 'Bank of England', enameled plaque, the reverse with circular Tunbridge Wells printed logo.

4.5in (11.5cm) high

$22-28   **MTS**

A Dodo Designs 'No.10 Downing St' enameled plaque, the reverse printed 'DODO DESIGNED 185 WESTBOURNE GROVE LONDON W11 ENGLAND FINEST PORCELAIN ENAMEL MADE IN ENGLAND'.

4.5in (11.5cm) high

$18-22   **MTS**

A Dodo Designs 'UK RULES OK' Union Jack enamel plaque, with later circular Tunbridge Wells logo printed on reverse.

4.5in (11.5cm) wide

$25-35   **MTS**

A Dodo Designs 'Players are requested...', enameled plaque, with Tunbridge Wells address printed on reverse.

4.5in (11.5cm) high

$18-22 **MTS**

A Dodo Designs 'The Royal Mint' enameled plaque, with circular Tunbridge Wells printing. to reverse.

4.5in (11.5cm) high

$18-22 **MTS**

A Dodo Designs 'Camp Coffee' Tunbridge Wells enameled plaque, with circular Tunbridge Wells printing. to reverse.

14.5in (36cm) high

$30-50 **MTS**

A Dodo Designs 'Colman's Mustard' enameled sign.

Like other such signs, this was not official company advertising.

11in (27.5cm) high

$70-90 **MTS**

A Dodo Designs 'Sunlight Soap' enameled metal sign, by permission of Lever Bros, with Tunbridge Wells printing.

8.5in (21.5cm) high

$40-60 **MTS**

A 1960s Dodo Designs 'Lord Kitchener' printed tin, with a hinged lid and a Union Jack background.

6in (15cm) wide

$50-70 **MTS**

A Dodo Designs plastic-coated printed cotton Golden Shred tote bag.

Advertising related pieces tend to be most desirable and valuable.

23.5in (59cm) high

$40-60 **MTS**

An extremely rare 1960s Dodo Designs painted fiberglass shop display mannequin, with hole for a mouth that used to 'smoke' cigarettes, from the original Dodo Designs shop.

20.75in (52cm) high

$400-600 **MTS**

SMOKING ACCESSORIES

COLLECTORS' NOTES

■ As smoking becomes increasingly less accepted and less fashionable, so the market for vintage smoking accessories grows. Collectors appreciate the fine quality workmanship of pieces produced from around 1900 to the 1950s. During the 1920s and '30s smoking was highly fashionable, with wealthy people demanding fine accessories and it is these items that are particularly sought-after today.

■ As well as the fine materials and decoration, practicality plays a part in value. Many late 19thC pieces are finely made and appealing but are impractical as they were aimed at pipe smokers who are far less numerous than cigar or cigarette smokers today. Many older humidors are no longer airtight, meaning they cannot be used without conversion. As such, practical items related to cigar or cigarette smoking tend to be more desirable.

■ Lighters are one of the most collectible examples of smoking memorabilia and names such as Dunhill, Thorens and Ronson are amongst the most popular. Dunhill in particular is noted for its fine lighters and smoking accessories, which are only a small part of its range of gentlemen's accoutrements. Look out for unusual features, such as built-in compacts or watches.

■ Eye-appeal, subject matter and humour are three further features that are worth considering as they can add value. This is particularly true for pieces produced from the 1950s onwards, which can be of lower intrinsic quality. Links to a famous personality or brand, or a sought-after theme such as erotic imagery, can make a later piece desirable and an earlier piece yet more desirable.

A Dunhill 'Miniature' Aquarium petrol table lighter, with intaglio underwater scene of a tropical fish among waterweeds, the reverse with two tropical fish against a bright blue/green background, cast marks.

The complexity, coloring and 'eye appeal' of the design affects value, with this being a good example.

c1950   2.75in (7cm) high

$2,500-3,500   **WW**

A Dunhill 'Miniature' Aquarium petrol table lighter, with intaglio underwater scene of fish among plants against a vivid blue/green ground, the reverse with a single fish, stamped marks.

This lighter is worth more, not only as it is a slightly scarcer 'Miniature', but also because it is in such fine condition with its vivid colors and lack of scratches, wear to the gold plating, or flaking to the internal paint.

c1950   2.75in (7cm) high

$3,500-4,500   **WW**

A Dunhill 'Miniature' Aquarium petrol table lighter, with intaglio underwater scene of two Angel fish among waterweeds, the reverse with two tropical fish, on a silvery blue background, cast marks.

c1950   2.75in (7cm) high

$1,500-2,000   **WW**

A Dunhill 'Miniature' Aquarium petrol table lighter, with intaglio underwater scene of a tropical fish among waterweeds, the reverse with two tropical fish, on a silver blue and yellow background, cast marks.

c1950   2.75in (7cm) high

$1,800-2,200   **WW**

A Dunhill 'Half Giant' Aquarium petrol table lighter, with intaglio underwater scene of a tropical fish, the reverse with an angel fish, on a bright blue ground, cast marks.

The bright blue background is unusual as backgrounds are usually predominately green or green with beige.

c1950   3.5in (8.5cm) high

$3,200-3,800   **WW**

A CLOSER LOOK AT A DUNHILL AVIARY LIGHTER

Dunhill introduced the 'Aquarium' lighter in 1949 and they were sold from the 1950s into the 1960s in 'Standard', 'Half Giant' and 'Miniature' sizes.

The gold-plated body was covered with six rounded Lucite (Perspex) panels, which were reverse-carved by hand and then hand-painted and decorated. Flakes to the paint or foil and surface scratches reduce value.

This is the 'Miniature', which is slightly scarcer than the horizontal format 'Half Giant' size, but not as rare as the taller 'Standard'.

Aquarium lighters with fish are more common – bird designs, known as 'Aviary' lighters, are rare; with horses, ships and other scenes being scarcer still.

A Dunhill 'Miniature' Aviary petrol table lighter, with river scene of a duck wading, the reverse with a swimming duck on a bright blue ground, cast marks to base.

c1950   2.75in (cm) high

$3,500-4,500   **WW**

A Dunhill 'Half Giant' Aquarium petrol table lighter, with intaglio underwater scene of a tropical fish among waterweeds, the reverse with three tropical fish, on a pale green background, cast marks.

c1950   3.5in (8.5cm) high

$2,200-2,800   **WW**

A Dunhill 'Half Giant' Aquarium petrol table lighter, with intaglio underwater scene of two swordtail fish, the reverse with a tropical fish, on a silver-blue background, cast marks.

c1950   3.5in (8.5cm) high

$2,800-3,200   **WW**

A Dunhill 'Half Giant' Aquarium petrol table lighter, with cast marks to base.

4in (10cm) wide

$1,800-2,200   **FRE**

SMOKING ACCESSORIES

A 1950s Dunhill 'Joseph Lucas' perspex and chrome table lighter, with lion decorated side panels and ribbed surround, inscribed on the base "Plastic and Styling by Joseph Lucas Ltd, Birmingham, England".

This lighter was produced by Dunhill for Joseph Lucas, a leading manufacturer of plastics, lighting and car accessories. Despite its shape, it is different from other Aquarium lighters as it has molded, not carved, decoration. Lucas may also have supplied Dunhill with the perspex used on Aquarium lighters.

4in (10cm) wide

$650-750　　　　　　　　**BIG**

A 1950s Dunhill 'Giant' silver-plated table lighter, stamped marks.

An oversize, table variation of the 'Unique' pocket lighter, this was first offered in 1929. Earlier examples have an external bent piece of metal acting as a snuffer arm 'spring'.

4.25in (10.5cm) high

$220-280　　　　　　　　**WW**

A CLOSER LOOK AT A DUNHILL WATCH LIGHTER

First made by Swiss company 'La Nationale', Dunhill watch lighters were introduced in 1926 at the request of a wealthy South American client, Santiago Soulas.

Examples in solid gold are extremely rare, particularly in this condition, as they were a highly expensive, luxury item in their day.

It is marked with Wise & Greenwood's original 1920 Unique lighter patent and "264" on all separately made parts, showing that they are original.

The octagonal interior watch compartment behind the flip-down front, the lack of a secondary striking wheel and shape of the dial, as well as the import mark, show this to be a very early design.

A Swiss Dunhill 'Unique A' 18ct gold pocket watch lighter, with Art Deco flip-down watch panel around an inset watch with Arabic numeral dial and jeweled lever movement signed "Dunhill", the case with Swiss control marks, London import mark for 1926 and signed "Dunhill Switzerland".

1926　　　　　　　　　　　　　　1.75in (4.5cm) high

$5,500-6,500　　　　　　　　　　　　**HAMG**

A very rare Japanese Dunhill-Namiki Savory maki-e lacquer and silver-plated lighter, decorated with gold and silver hira maki-e showing a bird in flight over grass, signed "Shobi" with red seal kao and "Namiki-kan" on one edge, wear from use including rubbed grass and signature.

Shobi Makizawa was born in 1880 and studied under Shosai Shiroyama before joining the staff of Iwate Prefectural Technical High School in 1905. He became an independent artist in 1907, and was recruited to Namiki by the maki-e master Gonroku Matsuda becoming one of the six founding committee members of the Kokkokai artist group in August 1931. His signature is sometimes translated as Shoei and Shohmi. Maki-e lacquer decoration can take many weeks to complete, depending on its complexity.

c1937

$700-900　　　　　　　　　　　　　　　**BLO**

A 1980s French Cartier gold and enamel pocket lighter, with foliate engraved arabesque decoration and blue and turquoise enamel designs, in excellent condition.

$700-1,000　　　　　**BLO**

An American 'Koopman's Magic Pocket Lamp' chrome-plated brass gasoline pocket lighter, by Magic Introduction Co. of New York, with exploding cap dies and striker.

The patent for this very early mechanical pocket lighter was granted in 1889.

c1890

$150-200　　　　　　**ATK**

An American Art Metal Wares Inc of Newark, NJ cast-iron dog-shaped table lighter.

Art Metal Wares was owned by Louis V. Aronson and later became the famous Ronson company.

c1916   4in (10cm) high

$180-220   **ATK**

A rare Austrian 'Bully' standing bulldog cast metal semi-automatic table lighter.

When the dog's tail is pushed down, the head pops open lighting the wick.

1914   8in (20cm) long

$320-380   **ATK**

A German 'Sophisticated Monkey' cast metal petrol table lighter.

c1914   6.25in (16cm) high

$150-200   **ATK**

A 1950s Belgian 'Le Mannequin Pis' cast iron petrol table lighter, a striking wheel on the boy's rear shoots a spark forward lighting a wick covered by his hand.

3.25in (8cm) high

$60-80   **ATK**

An English Art Deco brass nude dancer table petrol striker lighter.

8.25in (22cm) high

$350-450   **ATK**

A 1950s chromed metal 'jet plane' table lighter, on an adjustable base with bakelite platform.

$120-180   **ROS**

A late 1950s Japanese Evanus 'cat and lamp' ceramic, chrome-plated brass and enamel novelty table lighter.

This lighter was patented by Hikojiro Sugimoto in 1956.

5.5in (14cm) high

$220-280   **CVS**

A reproduction German 'Döbereiner' clear glass table lighter, the lid with igniting mechanism.

This was one of the first lighters in the world and was invented by Johann Wolfgang Döbereiner in 1822, under the name 'Gasopyrion'. The principle is similar to a 'Molotov Cocktail' where hydrogen is mixed with oxygen on a platinum sponge to produce the flame. However, like 'Molotov Cocktails' themselves, the results were sometimes highly explosive.

c1970

$320-380   **ATK**

A late 19thC or early 20thC Continental ceramic tobacco jar, in the form of a Scotsman's head, the base inscribed "8959 59".

5.75in (14.5cm) high

$100-150   **PWE**

A late 19thC or early 20thC Continental ceramic tobacco jar, in the form of a caricatured Irishman with a cheroot, green hat and feather, the base stamped "9675 09" and painted "77".

6.25in (16cm) high

$80-120   **PWE**

A late 19thC or early 20thC Continental large ceramic tobacco jar, of a man in a purple bobble hat, possibly a jockey, the base inscribed "3606 20".

9in (23cm) high

$100-150   **PWE**

A late 19thC or early 20thC Continental ceramic tobacco jar, of a smart, moustachioed man smoking a cheroot and wearing a brown hat with a green feather.

6.75in (17cm) high

$80-120   **PWE**

A late 19thC or early 20thC Continental ceramic tobacco jar, of an exotic lady in a head dress, the base stamped "3578 24".

The hand-painted detailing and molding is much finer on this example, leading to its higher price. The exotic female subject matter is also more appealing.

6in (15cm) high

$120-180   **PWE**

A late 19thC or early 20thC Continental ceramic tobacco jar, in the form of an unripened nut or bean, smoking a cigarette, base stamped "JM5 3528".

Tobacco jars were made on the Continent around the turn of the 20thC, before pre-rolled cigarettes had become widely popular. Most are made in ceramic, although wood or metal examples are known. Bernard Bloch at Bohemia's Eichwald factory was a prolific maker, as was Germany's notable Conte & Boehme factory. Most are in the form of heads, which allowed for characters and expressions – amusing or animal forms and famous personalities are among the most popular. Value is determined by the subject matter, the quality of the moulding, painting and the overall condition. Examine rims carefully for cracks or chips.

c1900   *6.25in (16cm) high*

$600-800   **PWE**

A 1920s English printed tin humidor, designed by George W. Horner & Co.

6.75in (17cm) high

$60-80   **PKA**

A turned dark wood tobacco jar, with lid, the base engraved "CJD Petzer AC Petzer St Helena 1900".

St Helena is famous as being the island to which Napoleon was exiled in 1815 until his death in 1821. In 1900, it was again used to hold Boer War prisoners.

6in (15cm) diam

$60-80   **W&W**

A German 'Dog with Basket' cast brass match stand.

c1890   2in (5cm) high

$40-60   **ATK**

A German porcelain match holder, in the form of a seated Chinese man, sticking out his articulated tongue.

c1850   3.25in (8cm) high

$70-100   **ATK**

A Dunhill briar wood 'nutbird' striker and ashtray, with match holder.

3in (8cm) high

$70-100   **MG**

A French Art Deco molded amethyst glass spherical ashtray, inlaid with sterling silver.

3.5in (9cm) high

$80-120   **NOR**

A CLOSER LOOK AT AN ASHTRAY

These novelty bird smoker's companions were retailed by Dunhill but made under the YZ trademark by Henry Howell & Co. of London during the 1920s-30s.

This is unusual as all parts are in cast phenolic plastic. Most are made from hardwoods also used in cane production, with only the beak being cast phenolic.

There are many different forms, with shagreen (sharkskin) match striking panels, holes in the body to store matches, and even attached dinner gongs.

Howell was founded in 1832 and manufactured walking canes and umbrellas. A change in fashion and a series of dry winters lead to the company closing in 1936.

An English YZ for Dunhill burgundy and black cast phenolic ashtray, the base stamped "YZ Trademark Made in England".

These novelty pieces are also known as 'nutbirds' by collectors.

3.5in (9cm) high

$500-700   **MG**

A souvenir ceramic ashtray, of a man's head with a bee on his nose and an open mouth, with transfer for Conneaut Lake Amusement Park, PA to base.

It's the amusing expression, the characterful molding and the survival of the bee that makes this desirable.

3.5in (9cm) high

$40-80   **TOA**

A Japanese ceramic novelty dog ashtray, with gaping mouth.

3.5in (8.5cm) high

$50-70   **RH**

A 1930s wooden cigarette box, topped with a chrome-plated figure of Bonzo and ashtray.

8.75in (22cm) wide

$35-45   **GAZE**

A late 19thC walnut table top smoker's companion, the central two-handled jar with domed cover, apertures for 10 pipes with match holder, striker and ashtray, on a circular base.

9.5in (24cm) high

$220-280   **CLV**

A 1950s Italian clockwork cigarette dispenser, with transfer-printed exotic bird pattern, metal devil's head-shaped feet and an angel finial, with Swiss clockwork mechanism rotating the central panels to reveal cigarettes stored inside.

13.5in (34cm) high

$400-500   **V**

A late 19thC German silver cigarette box, with enamel decoration of a naked lady on a bed, stamped "935A".

The style and lady are typical of the 'Naughty Nineties' of late 19thC Belle Epoque Europe. Erotic subjects are highly sought-after, particularly in as good condition and as finely painted as this example.

3.5in (9cm) high

$700-1,000   **MG**

A 1950s Cartier 18ct gold cigarette case, engraved "AEG", the button with five square-cut inset sapphires, marked "Cartier", in original Cartier red leatherette case, good condition.

$1,800-2,200   **BLO**

Two 19thC Asian 'Chuck Muck' lighters, in leather, brass, copper and iron, one ornamentation missing, the second one with coral.

Often mistaken for small purses, the pocket stored a piece of flint and some wool or dry flammable material. The flint would be struck against the iron base near the wool to create sparks, which would set the wool on fire. Later examples are often found.

5.25in (13cm) high

$180-220   **ATK**

FIND OUT MORE...

The Dunhill Petrol Lighter – A Unique Story, by Luciano Bottoni & Davide Blei, published by Unique Srl, 2004
ISBN: 88-901596-0-X.

Lighters – Accendini, by Stefano Bisconcini, published by Edizioni San Gottardo, 1984.

A Victorian silver-mounted crocodile cigar case, Birmingham 1899.

$150-200   **GORW**

A Swiss Thorens chrome-plated brass gasoline counter or bar refill can, with pump, both side engraved.

c1940   *5.5in (14cm) high*

$150-200   **ATK**

COLLECTORS' NOTES

■ Smurfs first appeared under the name 'stroumpf' in the 1950s and were supporting characters in a Belgian comic strip starring two boy adventurers called Johan & Peewit. The artist was the Belgian cartoonist Pierre Culliford (b.1928) who is also known as Peyo. They became instantly popular and soon had a cartoon devoted solely to them.

■ The first figurines were introduced in 1965, and the increasing popularity of the comic strip was backed up by Father Abraham's 1977 'Smurf Song' and a series of TV cartoons by Hanna Barbera. In addition to a vast range of collectibles, over 400 different Smurf figurines have been designed and millions of examples produced, covering all manner of activities from music to emotions to sports.

■ Look on the base of a Smurf to find out more. A number related to the mold used is stamped on the base and is used by Smurf collectors to correctly identify their figure. The maker's mark, which can vary from 'Schleich' to 'Bully' to 'W.Berrie & Co.', can help to give a clue as to the period when that Smurf was made. The presence of a 'CE' marking indicates a more modern, or even contemporary, model.

■ The date is not the date that a particular model was made, but is either the date that the shape was released, or the date that a worn out mold was replaced with a new one. Shapes can be made for many years, and even reintroduced later. Dates given here indicate the production period for that shape. Colored dots indicate where the Smurf was painted, for example yellow for Portugal and red for Sri Lanka.

■ As millions of Smurfs have been made, most are of a low value, but highly accessible to the budget collector looking for a fun and relevant character collectible. Look out for variations, as these can be worth more. Consider size, form, color and the material used. Shapes produced for short periods of time, such as a Cheerleader Smurfette can also fetch higher prices.

■ Avoid buying examples that are overly dirty or scuffed and look for truly mint examples with their original surface 'sheen'. Where an item is boxed, it is best that the box is in similarly mint condition. Memorabilia connected to the Smurfs can be more varied than the figures themselves and offers great (often useable) variety to a collection.

A 'Gift and Flower' Smurf figure, no.20040, licensed by Schleich Peyo.

Intro. 1978 *2.25in (5.5cm) high*

$3-5 **NOR**

A 'Jester' Smurf figure, with gold painted stars on his hat, licensed by Schleich Peyo.

Look out for hats with green stars as these can be worth up to double the value of the example with gold stars.

1976-91 *2in (5cm) high*

$4-6 **NOR**

A 'Beer' Smurf figure, no.20078, licensed by Schleich Peyo, with Bully stamp.

1974-92 *2in (5cm) high*

$3-5 **NOR**

A 'Soccer' Smurf figure, no. 20035, licensed by Schleich Peyo.

The variation with a yellow top is said to be rarer than this example with a red top.

1978-90 *2.25in (5.5cm) high*

$3-5 **NOR**

A 'Fiddler' Smurf figure, with a brown hat, no.20159, licensed by Schleich Peyo.

1983-89 *2in (5cm) high*

$3-5 **NOR**

A 'CB Operator' Smurf figure, no.20143, with short antenna, licensed by Schleich Peyo.

Look out for a rarer variation with a longer aerial which can be twice as much as this example.

1982-96 *2.25in (5.5cm) h.*

$7-10 **NOR**

An 'Astro Smurf' figure, no.20003, with finger up and no red stripe.

This is one of the most popular Smurfs, and was incorrectly rumored to be worth large sums of money some years ago.

1969-86 *2in (5cm) high*

$4-6 **F**

A 'Brainy' Smurf figure, with black glasses, no.20006, licensed by Schleich Peyo.

Variations with yellow or red glasses exist and can be worth slightly more.

1969-84   1980 2in (5cm) high

$2-3   **NOR**

A 'Valentine Smurfette' Smurf figure, no. 20156, licensed by Schleich Peyo.

The arrow is missing on this example. Variations with longer arrows over 3cm long can be worth up to double the value of those with shorter arrows.

2.25in (5.5cm) high

$1-2   **NOR**

A CLOSER LOOK AT A SMURF

Some claim that this model is much rarer than most think, as it had to be withdrawn shortly after it was introduced, as the use of the 'S' motif on his chest was not licensed from DC Comics.

Interestingly, 'Superman' Smurf was also released in 1981, just after the release of the first two Superman films starring Christopher Reeve.

This is often confused with 'Superman' Smurf, no.20127, which shows a Smurf with a black eye mask and no 'S' chest motif flying over a comet or rocky moonscape.

There is a color variation of this figurine with a white base and red shoes, but this does not affect the value considerably. However, be aware that prices in general for this figurine vary dramatically.

A 'Smurferman' figure, no.20119, with "Bully, W.Germany" mark.

1981 to 2000 (?)   2.5in (6cm) high

$100-150   **NOR**

A 'Graduate Smurfette' Smurf figure, no. 20151, licensed by Schleich Peyo.

Some collectors deem these to be rare, as they were only issued in 1989.

1989   2.25in (5.5cm) high

$6-8   **NOR**

A 'Santa Smurfette' Smurf figure, no.20153, licensed by Schleich Peyo.

Although different shades of green can be found on the gift, values are roughly the same.

1983-90   2in (5cm) high

$8-12   **NOR**

An 'Aero Smurf' metal diecast plane, by Ertl, licensed by Schleich Peyo.

1982   3.25in (8cm) long

$3-5   **NOR**

An Irwin 'Mushroom Umbrella' Smurf figure, no.20118, licensed by Schleich Peyo, in mint condition and carded.

This model was first released in 1981, but this example is a later version.

1995 -2002   7.75in
(19.5cm) high

$10-15   **NOR**

A Galoob Smurf wind-up walker figure, licensed by Schleich Peyo.

3.25in (8cm) high

$20-25 **NOR**

A Wallace Berrie Christmas Smurf ceramic figurine, licensed by Schleich Peyo.

Ceramic Smurf figurines are sought-after by many collectors.

1982 3.25in (8cm) high

$30-40 **NOR**

A Helm collapsible Smurf toy, licensed by Schleich Peyo.

Push the bottom of the base in and he 'collapses' before springing upright again when released.

3.75in (9.5cm) high

$20-25 **NOR**

A Wallace Berrie 'Papa Smurf' Smurf pencil sharpener, licensed by Schleich Peyo.

1983 6in (15.5cm) high

$20-25 **NOR**

A 'Papa Smurf' Smurf pencil top, licensed by Schleich Peyo.

2in (5cm) high

$10-15 **NOR**

A 'Golf' Smurf keyring, licensed by Schleich Peyo.

1980-93 2.25in (5.5cm) high

$5-7 **NOR**

A Smurf 'Is It Break Time Yet? mug, licensed by Schleich Peyo.

3.5in (9cm) high

$7-10 **NOR**

A 'Small Green' Smurf house, no. 40012, with removeable lid, licensed by Schleich Peyo.

Houses tend to be desirable, particularly large playsets, as less were sold. This house can also be found with a red or blue roof. In violet, it is Smurfette's house.

1978 4in (10cm) high

$20-25 **NOR**

A Smurf plastic bathroom or bedroom dressing gown hook, licensed by Schleich Peyo.

5in (13cm) high

$7-10 **NOR**

FIND OUT MORE...

Der Schlumpf Katalog 4, *by Frank Oswald, published by Oswald Gaschers, 2003.*

Unauthorised Guide To Smurfs Around The World, *by Terry & Joyce Losonsky, published by Schiffer Publishing, 1999.*

COLLECTORS' NOTES

■ Soft toys are as loved by collectors today as they were by their original owners. The manufacture of soft toys also pre-dates teddy bears, with Marguerite Steiff making animal pin-cushions during the 1890s. Major manufacturers include Steiff in Germany and Merrythought, Farnell and Chad Valley in the UK.

■ Most collectors collect specific animals, and cats and dogs are popular. Steiff made a range of insects and creatures and, although they are an acquired taste, these and similar examples by other companies also have their devoted fans. Look out for comic book or cartoon characters as these can often be worth more due to increased demand and nostalgic longing.

■ Like teddy bears, many were dearly loved by their original and subsequent owners, so are often found dirty, damaged, faded or repaired. This reduces value considerably as they can be hard to clean. Like teddy bears, never put a soft toy in a washing machine as this can cause damage to the stuffing at the very least.

■ In addition to makers, sizes and characters, also look out for quirky or cute appearances as 'eye appeal' is a considerable factor to desirability and thus to value. As soft toys are not yet as popular as teddy bears, they usually make comparatively less expensive purchases and will form a satisfying and fun collection.

A early Steiff velvet pull-along dachshund soft toy, on a metal frame with wheels.

This is an extremely early and rare Steiff animal, dating from before the ear button was introduced in 1904. The wheel bar going through the feet, rather than the feet resting on top of the bar indicates an early example as well.

c1900   *8in (20cm) long*

$1,800-2,200   **LHT**

A 1920s-30s Steiff 'Molly' seated white mohair dog soft toy, with ear button and metal framed tag.

c1928-30   *5.5in (14cm) high*

$400-600   **SOTT**

A 1950s-60s Steiff 'Molly' mohair dog soft toy, with card tag, bell and ribbon.

4.25in (11cm) high

$120-180   **HGS**

A 1960s Steiff recumbent 'Collie' mohair dog soft toy, number 4250/25, with card tag, ear button and fabric tag.

12.5in (32cm) long

$180-220   **TCT**

A 1950s-60s Steiff 'Arco' mohair German Shepherd dog soft toy, with card tag, button and collar.

4.25in (11cm) high

$180-220   **HGS**

A 1920s/30s Steiff mohair and felt Pomeranian dog soft toy, with ribbon and bells, lacks button.

5.25in (13cm) high

$600-800 SOTT

A CLOSER LOOK AT A SOFT TOY

Steiff pull-along animals are early and popular toys, and included bears, a lion and an elephant.

The saddlecloth is often missing, and the back worn through use - this example is in excellent, complete condition.

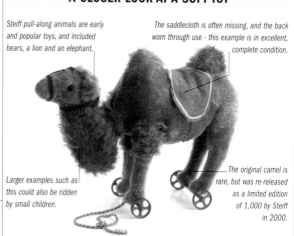

Larger examples such as this could also be ridden by small children.

The original camel is rare, but was re-released as a limited edition of 1,000 by Steiff in 2000.

A Steiff mohair pull-along camel on wheels, with button in ear and original fabric saddlecloth.

c1908 19.75in (50cm) high

$1,000-1,500 HGS

A 1950s/60s Steiff fabric 'Tom Cat' soft toy, with tags and ribbon.

Black cats were often intended for the export to the UK and the US, where they were considered symbols of luck. This is an unusual form, and is hard to find today, possibly as he was largely unappealing.

6in (15cm) high

$200-300 HGS

A 1950s Steiff 'Snurry' mohair snoozing cat soft toy, in original condition.

This shape is also quite hard to find.

6in (15cm) wide

$150-200 SOTT

A Steiff 'Liege' mohair goat soft toy.

1934-43 7.75in (19.5cm) high

$300-500 SOTT

A 1930s Steiff fox soft toy, with button in ear.

11in (28cm) long

$400-600 LHT

A 1950s/60s Steiff mohair ladybird child's stool, with metal legs.

The seat pad is often worn through use and affects value considerably. The ladybird was also made as a stuffed toy.

20in (51cm) long

$300-400 LHT

A Steiff velvet and felt 'Kalle Stropp' grasshopper soft toy, with bendable limbs, in excellent condition.

With his friend Grodan Boll the toad, Kalle Stropp was a character from a Danish fairy tale by Thomas Funck. He was only made in 1956 and is very rare.

8.5in (21.5cm) high

$1,200-1,800 LHT

A 1930s Steiff wool 'pompom' chick, with metal legs and red tag and button on leg.

2.75in (7cm) high

$450-550   **LHT**

A Steiff wool 'pompom' chick, with wire feet and felt beak.

c1930-59   *1.5in (4cm) high*

$50-80   **HGS**

A 1930s Steiff wool 'pompom' owl, with metal feet and felt beak.

Steiff's 'pompom' animals, also known as 'Woolies', were made from the 1930s-50s and were intended to be affordable with an allowance. Post war examples generally have less detailing, such as felt or wire beaks, and often have plastic legs. Birds tend to be the most common animal found, although this owl is rarer. Small accompanying aviaries and trees were also sold, but these are rare.

2.75in (7cm) high

$400-600   **LHT**

A 1930s Steiff wool 'pompom' raven, with red padded felt beak, glass eyes, and button and tag on metal legs.

2.5in (7cm) high

$50-80   **HGS**

A 1950s Steiff wool 'pompom' sparrow, with straw in felt mouth and button and tag on plastic legs.

It is rare to find the straw still present.

2.5in (6.5cm) high

$70-100   **HGS**

A 1920s/30s Steiff wool 'pompom' cat, with glass eyes and original fabric bow.

2.5in (7cm) high

$450-550   **LHT**

A 1950s Steiff wool 'pompom' cat, stock no. 3505, with button and tag in ear.

1954-58   *2.25in (6cm) high*

$50-80   **HGS**

A 1970s Steiff wool 'pompom' mouse, stock no. 7354-04, with glass eyes, whiskers and rubber tail, in mint condition.

1968-84   *1.5in (4cm) high*

$50-80   **HGS**

A 1930s Steiff wool 'pompom' squirrel, with bushy tail and whiskers and button in ear.

2.75in (7cm) high

$250-350   **LHT**

A 1950s American Agnes Brush 'Peter Rabbit' brushed cotton soft toy, in original condition.

Note the obvious whiskers. This was to differentiate him from the similar Piglet toy, that the company also made as part of their Winnie The Pooh series.

9in (23cm) high

$300-400   **HGS**

A CLOSER LOOK AT A SOFT TOY

Eugene Jeep is a friendly dog-like character from Popeye, and was introduced to the cartoon by E.C. Segar in 1936.

Dean's Rag Book, founded in 1903 is a notable English company who also made teddy bears, other soft toys and printed fabric children's books.

He is in very good and bright condition with his original paw printing, the velveteen usually becomes worn and dirty with play.

He was produced in small numbers only as a licensed product, making him very rare today.

A 1930s Dean's Rag Book 'Lucky Jeep' velveteen soft toy.

Jeep, ruler of Jeep Island, can only say 'Jeep', eats only orchids and can foretell the future.

12in (30.5cm) high

$1,000-1,500   **LHT**

A 1930s French Blanchette golden mohair soft toy, with original stitched nose and glass eyes.

3.5in (9cm) high

$100-150   **LHT**

A 1930s Chad Valley velvet 'Bonzo' soft toy, with printed face.

Condition is critical to value as the fabric is dirtied easily. The face can also rub off and the red tongue lost though play.

5.25in (13.5cm) high

$450-650   **TCT**

A 1930s Chad Valley velvet happy bull soft toy, with glass eyes and button in tail.

8in (20cm) long

$150-200   **LHT**

A 1950s Chiltern Toys pink bunny soft toy, in near mint condition, with original card sample and retail tags.

8.5in (21.5cm) high

$220-280   **LHT**

A Dean's Rag Books mohair chimpanzee soft toy, with molded rubber face and hands, with original tag.

c1960   *17in (43cm) high*

$60-80   **RBC**

A 1930s Farnell 'Alpha Toys' mohair girl elephant soft toy, in original condition with original tag and clothing.

A boy version was also sold. Alpha Toys was Farnell's premium brand.

12in (30.5cm) high

$450-550 LHT

A 1920s Farnell 'Pip' mohair dog soft toy, from the Mascot range.

Pip, Squeak (a penguin) and Wilfred (a rabbit) appeared in a popular British 1920s cartoon in the Daily Mirror by Bertram Lamb and Austin Payne, which was introduced in 1919. They are also the names given to a series of three British and Empire commemorative medals from WWI that were issued in 1919.

4in (10cm) high

$220-280 LHT

A Schuco felt and fabric rooster soft toy, with poseable limbs.

c1957   12in (30.5cm) high

$380-420 TCT

A 1920s Schuco felt, flocked and printed metal and mohair tumbling monkey, with rigid revolving arms.

Although the dressed monkey is a recognisable and iconic animal for Schuco, tumbling teddies are worth much more.

8.5in (21.5cm) high

$550-650 LHT

A Schuco black mohair 'YesNo' 'Felix' toy, in excellent condition.

Moving his tail makes him nod or shake his head. This mechanism is typical of Schuco. He will be popular to both Felix and Schuco, and soft toy collectors, hence his high value. Felix is also rarer than the more common monkey or bear.

c1930

5in (12.5cm) high

$1,200-1,800 LHT

A 1930s British William J. Terry blond and brown mohair and pink felt stuffed teddy dog, slightly worn.

This is very rare and unusually large. W.J. Terry was founded around WWI, when German imports were banned.

19in (48.5cm) high

$700-1,000 LHT

A 1960s Native American warrior and horse felt soft toy, unmarked.

9.5in (24cm) long

$20-30 RBC

A late 19thC American Arnold Print Works 'Tabby's Kitten' printed fabric cat soft toy, printed "PAT.JULY 5.92 AND OCT 4.92".

These were supplied on fabric squares to be cut out, sewn together and stuffed at home.

6.5in (16.5cm) high

$25-35 HGS

COLLECTORS' NOTES

■ Baseball is a favorite national pastime. Its popularity, coupled with its long heritage, makes it a favorite with sports collectors.

■ Baseball cards are a popular collecting area. They are easy to display and store and are available at a wide range of values. Some of the first cards were issued by tobacco companies in the late 19thC, with Topps and Bowman supplying cards with bubblegum from the 1950s onwards. Factors affecting value include the date, condition, position of the image on the card, the player and the level of distribution. Pins are another diverse and affordable collecting area, with rare press pins at the top end of the market.

■ Game-used equipment and uniforms tend to fetch the highest values. Items used by popular players such as Babe Ruth, Mickey Mantle and Joe DiMaggio are always sought-after, as are those that featured in important games. Provenance is key to value. Signed bats and balls are always a big hit, though make sure you know what you are buying – many players endorsed retail equipment and these often bear printed signatures.

■ Due to the high value of some baseball memorabilia, fakes and reproductions are found, so ensure you are buying from a reputable source.

A CLOSER LOOK AT A BASEBALL PHOTOGRAPH

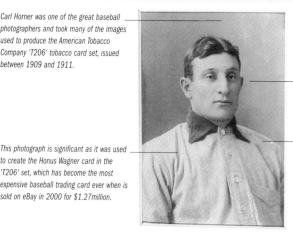

Carl Horner was one of the great baseball photographers and took many of the images used to produce the American Tobacco Company 'T206' tobacco card set, issued between 1909 and 1911.

Only a handful of these prints have come to light. The card based on this image is also very rare as Wagner asked the card to be withdrawn, perhaps because he disapproved of smoking. Approximately 50 cards are thought to have been produced.

This photograph is significant as it was used to create the Honus Wagner card in the 'T206' set, which has become the most expensive baseball trading card ever when is sold on eBay in 2000 for $1.27million.

Honus Wagner (1874-1955) spent the majority of his career with the Pittsburgh Pirates and became their manager and later their coach. Many consider him to be major league baseball's greatest shortstop.

A John 'Honus' Wagner mounted cabinet photograph, by Carl Horner, featuring the young Wagner in Pittsburgh uniform, mount cut to image but image intact, thin line of toning/staining on left edge not visible in matting and frame.
c1903

5.5in (14cm)

$15,000-20,000　　　　　　　　　　　　　　　　　　**HA**

A rare Babe Ruth photographic postcard, advertising a Tour of Ruth and Carl Mays, laminated.

c1922

$250-350　　　**HA**

A Joe DiMaggio large format photograph, signed in blue felt-tip pen, matted and framed, together with a letter of authenticity from PSA/DNA .

20in (51cm) high

$350-450　　　**HA**

A Ted Williams large format photograph, signed in blue felt-tip pen, matted and framed, together with a letter of authenticity from PSA/DNA .

20in (51cm) high

$350-450　　　**HA**

SPORTING MEMORABILIA

A Topps Mickey Mantle #10 card.

1959

$500-600   **HA**

MICKEY MANTLE

A Ty Cobb T-205 card, some creasing.

The 'gold borders' series is probably one of the most popular baseball tobacco-era card series issued and was perhaps also the first to be produced with the players' biographies on the reverse.

1911

$500-600   **HA**

A Bowman Mickey Mantle #253 card.

This card was issued in Mantle's rookie year with the Yankees. In recent years Bowman has become known for its Rookie cards.

1951

$2,800-3,200   **HA**

A limited edition set of 20 'Living Legends' autographed lithographic cards, by Ron Lewis, from an edition of 5,000, each signed by the player and the artist Ron Lewis, including Nolan Ryan, Mickey Mantle, and Sandy Koufax, with the original envelope and a letter of authenticity from PSA/DNA.

1989   *10in (25.5cm) wide*

$700-1,000   **HA**

Two Topps baseball card wax boxes, one pack unopened but remains with its wrapper fairly intact.

1979

$500-600   **HA**

A rare Ted Williams baseball card empty display box, by Fleer, complete with die-cut lid, typical light wear including a few creases and some general wear to the joints.

1959

$450-550   **HA**

A Cleveland Indians official 1951 sketch book.

The team's name and "Chief Wahoo" mascot and logo are controversial and have provoked criticism from Native American activists.

10.75in (27.5cm) high

$70-100   **LDE**

A Colorado Aggies Utah University program, Thanksgiving Day 1933.

10.75in (27.5cm) high

$15-20   **LDE**

A Bowman Color Mickey Mantle #59 card.

1953

$500-700   **HA**

A 'Babe Ruth Baseball Club Member' pin.

1in (2.5cm) diam

$70-100 LDE

A rare 'Never Forgotten Babe Ruth' baseball pin.

This is one of a few mourning pins produced for this hugely popular player. This particular design can also be found with an orange background.

1.5in (4cm) diam

$250-300 LDE

A 'Mike Higgins' Boston Red Sox baseball pin.

1.75in (4.5cm) diam

$30-40 LDE

A New York Yankees printed felt badge.

4.5in (11.5cm) diam

$40-50 LDE

A Baltimore Elite Giants series baseball pin.

1.25in (3cm) diam

$70-100 LDE

A New York Yankees American League baseball pin.

1.25in (3cm) diam

$100-150 LDE

A 'Little Pinkies The Ball Player' advertising pin, by Whitehead and Hoag.

c1890 1in (2.5cm) diam

$35-45 LDE

An Al Lopez store model #246 RHT catcher's mitt, by Hutch, signed on interior thumb, owner's name lightly written on back of thumb, together with a letter of authenticity from PSA/DNA.

$180-220 HA

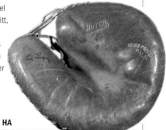

A CLOSER LOOK AT A TED WILLIAMS UNIFORM

Ted Williams (1918-2002) played for the Boston Red Sox for 19 seasons and is arguably the greatest hitter in the history of the game.

This uniform was worn in William's penultimate year in the game. After retirement he became manager of the Washington Senators.

The previous vendor obtained the uniform in 1959 and kept it in a drawer until the late 1980s when he had it authenticated and then displayed at the Sports Museum of New England. This provenance adds to the value as uniforms are often faked.

Despite it's high price, this isn't the most valuable uniform ever sold. Lou Gehrig's uniform, believed to have been worn during his famous farewell speech, sold for $451,000 in 1999.

A rare Ted Williams team issue two-part wool no.9 uniform, with attached uniform maker's tab of Tim McAuliffe, Inc., 24 Lincoln Street, Boston, Mass., shortened sleeves, excellent condition overall.

1959

$80,000-120,000   SK

A Ted Williams Camp baseball grey flannel shirt, youth-size, signed on the front by Williams in black felt-tip pen, together with a letter of authenticity from PSA/DNA .

c1960s

$220-280   HA

A rare 'DiMaggio's Restaurant' vintage grey flannel shirt, signed by DiMaggio in black felt-tip pen on front, retains original Stroh's/San Francisco tag inside collar and includes letter of authenticity from PSA/DNA.

$450-550   HA

A New York Mets printed cloth doll.

12in (30.5cm) high

$20-30   BH

A Philadelphia 'Big 5' printed plastic megaphone.

8.5in (21.5cm) high

$7-10   BH

A hand-painted plate, signed 'Auntie to Wallie Howard', the front decorated with a baseball bat and ball, three bi-planes and a elk representing the Benevolent and Protective Order of Elks, also marked "2/21".

8.75in (22cm) diam

$150-200   LDE

A small Cincinnati Red Legs pennant.

8.25in (21cm) wide

$60-80   LDE

COLLECTORS' NOTES

- Golfing's long heritage and continued popularity as a sport helps to make related memorabilia one of the most popular sport collecting areas.

- While very early pieces, from the birth of the game in the 15thC until the 19thC are rare and expensive, the late 19thC and early 20thC can offer more affordable pieces. Early clubs and balls tend to occupy the high-end of the market, but just about anything with a golfing theme can be of interest.

- The Victorians' passion for the game spilled over into ceramics, glass, silverware and books. Well-known manufacturers such as Royal Doulton and Spode produced themed wares, collected by both golfing enthusiasts and aficionados of the pottery, making them doubly desirable.

- Prints, paintings and photographs of old courses and famous players through the ages form an important historical record and are always sought-after. Depictions of women golfers are much scarcer and will usually fetch a premium

- As golfing equipment was generally play-used, condition has a great effect on value. Specialist auctions are now fairly commonplace, often taking place around the time of the Open Championship in July and offer a great opportunity to view a wide range of items.

An R. Forgan, St Andrews transitional brassie, the scared head stamped with "R. Forgan" and Prince of Wales feathers, the sole with horn insert above the brass plate, leather insert to face, lead counterweight, hickory shaft, with wrapped soft leather grip.

$700-1,000　　　　**L&T**

A W. Park, Musselburgh transitional brassie, the scared head with horn insert above the brass plate, leather insert to face, lead counterweight, hickory shaft, wrapped soft leather grip.

$400-600　　　　**L&T**

A CLOSER LOOK AT A GOLF CLUB

John Henry is a known club maker of center-shafted clubs.

He received British patent no. 15597 on July 13th, 1904 for center-shafted clubs and covered woods, irons and putters.

This type of club rarely comes up for sale.

The center-shaft was intended to reduce the torque on miss-hit shots as well as hit straighter shots and be able to handle tough lies.

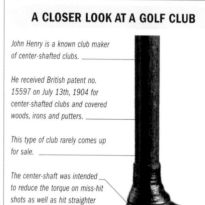

A James Hutchison, North Berwick transitional play club, the scared head stamped "Hutchison", ebony insert to sole, leather insert to face, lead counterweight, fruitwood shaft, wrapped soft leather grip, defective.

$600-800　　　　**L&T**

An R. Simpson of Carnoustie longnose playclub, the scared beech head with horn insert to sole, lead counterweight, later hickory shaft.

$1,000-1,500　　　　**L&T**

A rare John Henry 'Centro' center-shafted driver, horn insert to face, lead counterweight, hickory shaft.
c1890

$7,000-10,000　　　　　　　　　　　　**L&T**

A D.M. Patrick Special longnose spoon, hickory-shafted, the beech head with ebony sole and lead counterweight.

$1,000-1,500　　　　**L&T**

A Reginald Brougham metalwood, the alloy head with wooden insert to the face, stamped trademark incorporating clubs design, hickory shaft, wrapped leather grip.

$500-900　　　　**L&T**

An R. Forgan, St Andrews smooth-faced mid-iron, with maker's shaft stamp and original full-length hide grip and underlisting.

c1895   41in (104cm) high

$70-100   **WW**

A W. Park, Musselburgh, smooth-faced lofting iron, long hosel, hickory shaft, wrapped soft leather grip.

$400-700   **L&T**

A W. Park of Musselburgh smooth-faced general iron, with a 4.5in (11.5cm) hosel complete with period grip and underlisting, stamp mark faded.

c1895

$100-200   **WW**

An R. Simpson 'Premier' putter, the iron head with mesh patterned face, the hickory shaft stamped maker's name, wrapped leather grip.

$700-1,000   **L&T**

A rare Simpson Carnoustie Pat lump back iron, stamped "The Perfect Balance", with hand-cut diamond pattern face markings and full-length leather grip.

$150-200   **WW**

An R.L. Urquhart Patent adjustable head iron, almost smooth face, the adjuster release button unusually set at the front of the hosel, the hickory shaft stamped, "R. Sayers, selected", wrapped leather grip.

Club design was not regulated until 1909 and prior to then a number of ingenious designs, such as this example were patented. This adjustable club, patented c1895 meant that the angle of the head could be altered to suit the shot meaning less clubs needed to be carried.

$700-1,000   **L&T**

A smooth-faced rut niblick, by Gibson, with a 4.5in (11.5cm) hosel and fitted with a full-length hide grip.

$100-200   **WW**

A 'Baxpin' concave face mashie niblick, by Gibson and Gadd.

$50-90   **WW**

A Tom Stewart, St. Andrews left-handed smooth-faced rut niblick, stamped cleek mark, long hosel, hickory shaft, wrapped leather grip.

$400-700   **L&T**

A F. H. Ayres Harry Vardon Autograph niblick, stamped "Harry Vardon Totteridge by F.H. Ayres", with the Maltese cross mark, shaft stamped below rubberized grip.

37in (94cm) high

$30-60   **WW**

A J.&A. Simpson, Edinburgh smooth-faced cleek, hickory shaft, wrapped smooth leather grip.

$150-200   **L&T**

A Standard Mill Co. smooth-faced cleek, early "S.M." and crescent stamped mark, hickory shaft, part wrapped leather grip.

$300-600   **L&T**

A Robert White, St. Andrews smooth-faced cleek, long crimped hosel, hickory shaft, wrapped smooth leather grip.

$200-300   **L&T**

A smooth-faced cleek, with long crimped hosel, hickory shaft, wrapped leather grip.

$100-200   **L&T**

A Ben Sayers smooth-faced driving mashie, showing the maker's North Berwick oval stamp mark and an early Stewart pipe mark, with full length hide grip and underlisting. *c1898*

$50-70   **WW**

A heavy ribbed-face mashie, stamped "Accurate" with a superb full-length original hide grip with underlisting.

$80-120   **WW**

A Jack Nickolas Ping Anser putter, made by Karston Co. for Slazenger, patent no. D2C7227, brass head, steel-shafted.

$600-800   **L&T**

A Tom Stewart, St. Andrews 'Tom Morris' wry necked putter, stamped cleek and Tom Morris portrait marks, hickory shaft, wrapped leather grip.

$250-450   **L&T**

A Fred Saunders, Highgaten 'Straight Line' aluminium putter, hickory shaft stamped.

$600-800   **L&T**

A Winkworth Scott patent putter, with square section, steel shaft, wrapped leather over wood, square section grip.

$500-900   **L&T**

A ebonized fruitwood putter, scared head, indistinctly stamped, horn insert to sole, hickory shaft.

$200-300   **L&T**

A un-named cone-shaped wooden head putter, with hatched face, hickory shaft stamped "A.L. Johnston".

$3,500-4,500   **L&T**

An Ernest Jones swing trainer practice club, with weighted square mesh pattern ball head, spring hosel and hickory shaft.

$700-1,000   **L&T**

A CLOSER LOOK AT A GOLF CLUB

This double-faced, hence Duplex, is a rare hammer-headed club.

The Scottish Dalrymple family have a long association with golf, David Dalrymple, Lord Hailes (1726-92) was captain of the Honourable Company of Edinburgh Golfers at Leith Links.

The shaped design is intended to give the wooden head greater strength and durability.

Sir Walter laid out a nine-hole golf course near Berwick in 1894, and also supported the formation of the Ladies Golf Club in 1888.

A rare Sir Walter Hamilton-Dalrymple 'Duplex' club, with brass sole plate, with hickory center shaft.

$5,000-9,000   **L&T**

A Sunday club, with ivory insert to the face, ebony and lead insert to the sole, lead counterweight, the head stamped I.S., pine shaft mounted with a plated band, inscribed, "A Relic of the Tay Bridge Disaster, 28th December 1879, I. Simpson".

On the evening of December 28th, 1879, during a violent storm, the Tay Rail Bridge collapsed with a train on it killing over 70 people including the son-in-law of the designer Sir Thomas Bouch.

$600-800   **L&T**

A CLOSER LOOK AT A GUTTY BALL

The gutty ball was invented by the Rev. Dr. Robert Adams in 1848 and utilized gutta percha and natural inelastic latex.

The condition of this example, which retains most of its original paint and may never have been used, adds greatly to its value.

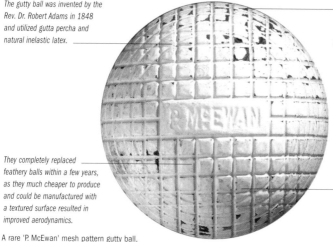

They completely replaced feathery balls within a few years, as they much cheaper to produce and could be manufactured with a textured surface resulted in improved aerodynamics.

The McEwan family began its association with golf in c1770, when James McEwan setup business in Leith, Edinburgh.

A rare 'P. McEwan' mesh pattern gutty ball.

$5,000-9,000　　　　　　　　　　　　　　　　**L&T**

A Capon Heaton & Co. Ltd 'Green Ring' dimple golf ball, with green ring to both poles, stamped.
c1912

$350-550　　　　**L&T**

An 'Eclipse' patent mesh gutty golf ball.
c1905

$600-800　　　　　　　　　　**L&T**

A rare 'Joyce Indented' gutty ball, with impressed shamrocks all over the ball, retaining most of the original paint, looks unused.

The impressed shamrock design is unusual, as is the unused condition, both adding to the value.

$8,000-12,000　　　　**L&T**

An autographed Maxfli golf ball, signed in felt pen by Arnold Palmer.

$200-300　　　**WW**

The 'Victor' bramble pattern rubber core ball, painted red for winter usage.

$500-600　　　**L&T**

A No. 5 Dunlop 'Lattice' wrapper rubber core ball.

$250-350   L&T

A No. 2 Warwick Dunlop wrapped rubber core ball.

$250-350   L&T

A No. 3 Penfold wrapper rubber core ball.

$250-350   L&T

A No. 1 Silver King HV wrapped rubber core ball.

$250-350   L&T

A Slazenger Silver King wrapped rubber core ball.

An unused Silver King Red Dot square mesh ball, in original box.

$400-500   L&T $300-400   L&T

A Spalding 'Needled' Top-Flite wrapped dimple ball.

$250-350   L&T

A 'The Colonel' wrapped rubber core ball, No. 31, by the St. Mungo Mfg. Co., of America.

$250-350   L&T

A 'Cadet' wrapped rubber core ball, by the St. Mungo Mtg. Co. of America, in original wrappers.

$300-400   L&T

A.B., " Told at the 19th Hole: Humorous St. Andrews Golf Stories", published by J. & G. Innes, St. Andrews, pictorial wrappers.

c1930s

$450-650   **L&T**

W. & R. Chambers, "Golfing: A Handbook...", first edition, published by W. & R. Chambers, Edinburgh, illustrated by Ranald M. Alexander.

1887

$350-550   **L&T**

Glenna Collett, "Ladies in the Rough", first edition, published by Knopf, New York, assisted by James M. Neville, foreword by Bobby Jones.

1928

$250-450   **L&T**

W. Dalrymple, "Handbook to Golf", first edition, with diagrams and positions and instructions from Amateur and Professional Champions, engraved illustrations, advertisements, original red pictorial cloth boards, Edinburgh.

1895

$450-650   **L&T**

Robert Hunter, "The Links", first edition, published by Scribner's, New York, illustrated from photographs; plus golf course drawings; decorative endpapers with Dr. MacKenzie's St. Andrews golf course illustration present.

1926

$600-800   **L&T**

Bobby Jones, "Rights and Wrongs of Golf", first edition, published by A.G. Spalding & Bros., New York, photograph frontispiece of Jones, rebound in green leather flexible cover, gilt lettering to cover, original wrappers missing.

1935

$400-500   **L&T**

William Charles Maughan, "Picturesque Musselburgh and its Golf Links", first edition, published by Alexander Gardner, Paisley, illustrated by R. Gemmel Hutchison.

1906

$700-1,000   **L&T**

H.B. Martin, "St. Andrew's Golf Club, 1888-1963", first edition, published by St. Andrew's Golf Club, New York, limited to 500 copies privately printed, illus., portrait frontispiece of John Reid, foreword by Alexander B. Halliday.

1938

$450-650   **L&T**

Gene Sarazen, Denny Shute, Ralph Guldahl, & Johnny Revolta, "From Tee to Cup by the Four Masters", first edition, published by Wilson Sporting Goods, signed on title page by Ralph Guldahl.

1937

$150-200   **L&T**

John Smartt, "A Round of the Links: Views of the Golf Greens of Scotland", facsimile edition of the original of 1893, published by Heritage Press, Aberdeenshire, illustrated from etchings by George Aikman from watercolors by Smart.

1980

$200-300 L&T

J. H. Taylor, "Taylor on Golf: Impressions, Comments and Hints", second edition, published by Hutchinson & Co., London, illustrated with 48 illustrations.

1902

$450-650 L&T

"The Funny side of Golf - From the Pages of Punch', in original pictorial boards, new leather green and gilt spine, foxing.

c1909 11.25in (28.5cm) high

$150-200 WW

Anonymous, "The Seeding and Care of Golf Courses", first edition, published by O.M. Scott & Sons, Marysville, Ohio, illustrated with vignette drawings.
1922

$700-900 L&T

An Open Golf Championship at Muirfield Official programme, for Wednesday, 8th May 1929, cream paper wrappers.

$500-700 L&T

A Open Golf Championship Official programme, Friday 2nd July 1948, autographed in pencil on the back cover by James Braid, R.A. Whitcombe and two others.

$600-800 L&T

An official souvenir programme from the 16th Ryder Cup Golf Matches, Royal Birkdale Golf Club, 7th, 8th & 9th October.

1965

$200-300 L&T

A Ryder Cup dinner menu, dated 20th September 1969, signed by the United States and Great Britain teams.
1969

$500-600 SWO

A George IV One Pound bank note, issued by Andover Old Bank in Andover on 5th October 1825 for Joseph Wakeford, William Wakeford and Robert Wakeford, serial number 12174.

8in (20.5cm) wide

A 1975 Ryder Cup Victory Dinner menu card, signed by numerous players and officials.

$800-1,200 L&T

$300-400 WW

A Foley china puzzle jug, printed and painted with a scene of two golfers and caddie; and with another golfer and caddie to the reverse, gilt rim.

See other puzzle jugs on page 180.

5.25in (15cm) high

$450-650   **L&T**

An Arthur Wood 'Golf' mug, with golf bag handle and printed in colors with golfing figures.

c1950   5.25in (13cm) high

$30-40   **SAS**

A 19thC Copeland late Spode golfing jug, relief decorated with golfers and caddies, surmounted by an ornamental border on a two-tone blue ground, printed and impressed marks to the underside.

7in (17.5cm) high

$600-800   **L&T**

A white jasperware cream jug, decorated in relief with golfers.

4in (10cm) high

$200-300   **WW**

An early 20thC Weller 'Dickensware' pottery vase, or tall tapering cylindrical form, with bulbous base, decorated with a lady golfer amongst trees, printed marks to the underside.

Depictions of female golfers are much scarcer than male players as they only started actively playing in the early 20thC.

9.75in (24.5cm) high

$1,000-1,500   **L&T**

A Foley China ribbed beaker, with printed scene of golfers and caddy, and crossed club motif to reverse with motto reading "Far and Sure".

3.75in (9.5cm) high

$280-320   **MSA**

A Royal Doulton transfer printed seriesware cereal bowl, depicting Crombie golfing figures and the caption "Every dog has his day and every man his hour", marked.

c1911   7.75in (19.5cm) diam

$250-350   **WW**

A Taylor-Tunnicliffe pottery match holder, hand-painted with a scene of Old Tom Morris and caddie.

c1890   2.25in (6cm) high

$350-550   **L&T**

A Rudolstadt porcelain golfing plate, transfer-printed and painted with a scene of lady golfers and caddy, the border with a continuous landscape design, printed mark to the reverse.

9.75in (24.5cm) diam

$550-750   **L&T**

CENTER: A silver-plated golfing comport stand, formed as three upright, longnose clubs, conjoined by a naturalistic circular platform surmounted by a figure of a golfer, the whole supporting an etched glass circular dish.

11in (27.5cm) high overall

$1,000-1,500 L&T

LEFT & RIGHT: A pair of silver-plated golfing candlesticks, each formed as three upright, longnose clubs supporting a mesh pattern ball nozzle, and on a circular base surmounted by a mesh pattern ball.

10in (25.5cm) high

$700-1,000 L&T

A Lytham & St Annes silver golfing trophy, of two-handled circular form, applied in relief with the club badge and inscribed "Aggregate Prize, Spring Meeting 1931, Won by...", on an ebonized circular plinth, Birmingham hallmark for 1926.

$250-450 L&T

A silver golfing trophy, the plain shaped bowl supported by four golfing irons on a circular ebonized base, hallmarked for Birmingham 1918.

$100-150 MAI

A North Manchester Golf Club silver medal, the obverse decorated in relief, with a golfer at the top of his swing and a caddie behind, the reverse inscribed, 'Monthly competition, won by H.B. Wood, 23rd November, 1895' apparently unmarked.

The North Manchester golf course was designed by the famous designer and player James Braid. It was first opened in 1894 making it one of the oldest courses in the region.

1.25in (3cm) diam

$2,000-3,000 L&T

An Oxford University Golf Club silver medal, the obverse decorated in relief with the college emblem and motto and "Oxford University Golf Club" to the outer rim, reverse relief cast with a laurel wreath, engraved "Inter Collegiate Cup, 1914, Trinity, W.F.C. McClure", apparently unmarked.

2in (5cm) diam

$200-300 L&T

A Reg Horne's Ryder Cup British Players sterling silver badge, relief decorated centrally to the obverse with the Ryder Cup, 1947, and inscribed in the border Reg Horne, British Player, clasp to the reverse, Robert A. Hudson, Portland, Oregon.

1947   1.5in (4cm) diam

$700-1,000 L&T

An 'Aircraft Depot Golf Club, B.F.I.' silver medal, relief decorated in the round with a laurel wreath, inscribed centrally "Winner, 1st Div. Handicap, Easter 1935".

1.5in (4cm) diam

$70-100 L&T

A silver-plated golfing ink well set, featuring a Victorian golfer mounted on a circular naturalistic base complete with matching glass ink wells with plated tops, together with a plated quill pen and another pen.

12in (30.5cm) wide

$600-800 MM

A pewter cigarette box mounted with a golf ball and club, inscribed "Dak Ladies International Golf Tournament Wentworth 1958" and "Foursomes Winner".

4.75in (12cm) wide

$150-200 SWO

An Art Deco silver golfing trophy, of two-handled, tapering circular form, inscribed "Purfleet and Erith Golf Challenge Trophy", on ebonite circular plinth, Birmingham hallmark for 1961; and a small Oldham & District Silver two-handled golf trophy, on ebonite circular plinth, Sheffield hallmark for 1960.

$250-450 L&T

A pair of bronze golfing bookends, by the Bradley & Hubbard Mfg. Co., relief-cast respectively with a gentleman and lady golfer in a landscape.

5in (13cm) high

$500-600   L&T

A pair of patinated bronze golfing bookends, by Frankhart Inc., each as a golfer in the follow-through, on a shaped base.

9in (23cm) high

$350-550   L&T

A 'Dunlop-Man' nickel-plated car mascot, the caricature golfing figure standing on a Dunlop 31 golf ball with later ebonized plinth.

5in (13cm) high

$120-180   L&T

A 'Dunlop-Man' brass table bell, the caricature golfing figure standing on a Dunlop 31 golf ball.

$100-150   L&T

A Douglass sand tee gun, marked "patent applied for".

$600-800   L&T

A collection of Peter Oosterhuis medals, badges and memorabilia, including a 1977 Ryder Cup cloth badge; a 1975 Ryder Cup cloth badge; a Walker Cup cloth badge and two lapel pins; a 1968 World Amateur Golf Council badge; a 1982 US Open Golf Championship badge; and a 1992 PGA Tour money clip.

English golfer Oosterhuis (b.1948) represented England in the 1967 Walker Cup and 1968 Eisenhower Trophy. He then turned professional, winning the 1981 British PGA Championship. Since retiring from playing he has been a commentator for CBS Sports and the Golf Channel among others.

$700-1,000   L&T

A Swiss Dom Watch & Cie 'Domatic Score' golf scorer, in the form of a wristwatch, with original strap, instruction pamphlet and box.

$50-90   MSA

An American golfing fan, with wooden handle and unusual image of a lady golfer, copyrighted 1904.

13.75in (35cm) high

$150-200   VSC

An un-named Automaton-type caddie, badly damaged.

$200-300   L&T

SPORTING MEMORABILIA

COLLECTORS' NOTES

■ The first official piece of Olympic memorabilia released was a set of stamps for the 1896 games, issued by the organising committee to balance the event's budget. Olympic coins followed much later in 1951.

■ Lapel badges have been produced since the games restarted. They are an affordable way to start a collection and are usually easy to obtain, with participation medals forming the next step up the ladder. These medals were given to all the participants, officials and members of the International Olympic Committee, so numbers produced can be quite large.

■ Memorabilia from the earliest games tends to be scarce, and so the most valuable, making more recent games a good place to start for collectors on a budget.

■ Look for pieces connected to countries that no longer 'exist', such as the German Democratic Republic or the Soviet Union, as historical interest can add to their value and desirability.

A rare 1920s Olympic Trials Amateur Athletics Union of Canada bronze badge, by Stock & Bickle.

$150-200   **BLO**

A 1932 Los Angeles Olympics cycling event ticket.

1932   *3.25in (8cm) diam*

$40-50   **LDE**

A 1932 Los Angeles Olympics Closing Ceremony ticket.

1932   *4.25in (11cm) long*

$80-120   **LDE**

A 1932 Los Angeles Olympics swimming event ticket.

1932   *4.25in (11cm) wide*

$70-100   **LDE**

A 1932 Los Angeles Olympics participant's pin.

1932   *0.5in (1cm) high*

$40-50   **LDE**

A 1936 German Summer and Winter Olympics programme and tickets of admission schedule, printed in English and German text.

1936   *8.25in (21cm) high*

$80-120   **MM**

A 1936 Berlin Olympics white porcelain bell, with molded decoration and inscription, small chip.

1936   *5in (12.5cm) high*

$70-100   **SAS**

A 1936 German Olympics woven ribbon.

1936   *4.25in (10.5cm) high*

$120-180   **LDE**

A 1936 German Winter Olympics enameled metal badge, with names of the host towns.

1936   *2in (5cm) high*

$120-180   **LDE**

An extremely rare 1954 Badminton Olympics Horse Trials silvered Judge or Official's plaque, with crowned portcullis, motto around horseshoe, suspension bar at rear, slight wear to plating.

1954   *5.25in (13cm) high*

$320-380   **BLO**

A 1960 Rome Olympics blue enamel on brass pin.

1960   *0.75in (2cm) wide*

$50-70   **LDE**

A 1964 Tokyo Olympics commemorative gilt metal tray, hammered with Olympic rings above the title and inscribed with the winners of the individual and team fencing events to each side, decorated with a foliate border, in original fitted case.

This tray was produced after the games, but its exact provenance is unknown.

18.5in (47cm) wide

$220-280   **MM**

A 1964 Innsbruck Winter Olympics enamel-on-brass pin.

1964   *2in (5cm) wide*

$60-80   **LDE**

A 1980 Moscow Olympics commemorative teapot, marked "Made in Russia".

1980   *5.5in (14cm) high*

$70-100   **RCC**

A 1984 Los Angeles Olympics baseball cap, by Adidas, with 'Sam' the Eagle mascot on the front.

$7-9   **BR**

A set of ten 1988 Calgary Winter Olympics silver coins, each depicting a different sport in the Olympic games, issued by the Canadian mint, in a fitted presentation case.

1988   *14.75in (37.5cm) wide*

$220-280   **MM**

A US Postal Service Olympics pin.

0.75in (2cm) high

$4-5   **BH**

FIND OUT MORE...

www.collectors.olympics.org, The Olympics Collectors Commission, official collectors' website.

A rare American flat-top tennis racket, with string detailing at the top, and hand-etched and dated 1876.

Flat-top rackets were popular during the 1880s. By the 1890s the top of the racket began to curve, gradually becoming more oval and more in line with today's equipment.

27.25in (69cm) high

$450-650 VSC

A very rare pair of small 19thC wooden tennis rackets, with green velvet-covered handles.

9in (23cm) high

$350-550 MSA

A tennis player oak and brass hanging paper clip.

c1900 8.25in (15cm) long

$400-500 MSA

A Wm. Sykes Ltd. "Lawn Tennis Racket Gut Preservative" card box, containing a bottle of preservative and brushes.

Box 4.25in (11cm) wide

$100-150 MSA

A brass-cased lawn tennis measure, with label to surface including the measurements for the court.

$35-55 MAI

A spelter figure of a tennis player, mounted on a pink marble base.

10.75in (27cm) high

$600-900 MSA

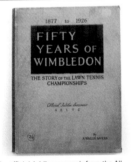

An official Jubilee souvenir from the All England Lawn Tennis Club by A. Wallis Myers, entitled 'Fifty Years of Wimbledon - The Story of the Lawn Tennis Championships 1877-1926'.

10.75in (27.5cm) high

$100-200 MM

A Muller of 147 Strand, London, England, racket catalog, complete with prices, also covering tennis access and cricket bats, cover price 23p.

c1934 7.75in (19.5cm) high

$25-45 MM

A humourous French color sketch, signed by Chenet, depicting a tennis match with a dog in the foreground and the caption "This time she will not call it out".

15.75in (40cm) wide

$60-80 MM

A Miami Redskins 'Home Coming' football banner, stencil on glazed linen depicting a charging ball carrier.

c1910-30   35.5in (90cm) high

$400-500   ISA

A bisque porcelain football player figurine, preparing to hike a ball, with blue quilted jersey.

An original watercolor and graphite drawing, by Charles Addams, rejected TV Guide Super Bowl cover commission, signed by Addams.

9in (23cm) high

$700-1,000   FRE

c1900   6in (15cm) high

$250-350   HA

A Cincinnati Bengals helmet, by Riddell, shows usage wear and surface patina, "56" written in black marker on interior, together with a letter of authenticity from SCD Authentic.

c1971

$300-400   HA

Three felt sports pennents, comprising Washington Redskins, 1970 Baltimore Orioles "World Champions" and New York Jets, some with pin holes and creases.

$20-30   SL

An Ice Capades of 1945 official souvenir pin, designed by George Petty, with original card.

1945   4.25in (11cm) high

$70-100   LDE

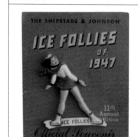

An Ice Follies of 1947 official souvenir painted plastic pin and card.

1947   4in (10.5cm) high

$60-80   LDE

A Skating Vanities official souvenir plastic pin on card, designed by Alberto Varga.

1947   4.25in (11cm) high

$70-80   LDE

A Sonja Henie Hollywood Ice Revue blue felt pennant.

29.25in (74cm) long

$70-90   LDE

A Baltimore Clippers hockey nodder, a few minor surface scratches.

$250-350 HA

A signed 'Stone Cold' Steve Austin publicity photograph.

10in (25.5cm) high

$70-90 LCA

A signed Dwayne 'The Rock' Johnson publicity photograph.

10in (25.5cm) high

$60-80 LCA

A Jack Dempsey signature, laid down to card, reading "World Heavyweight Champion April 20th 1927", ink stain to top and bottom and central fold.

5in (12.5cm) high

$120-180 MM

A B-B Bats candy box by Fairplay Caramels, grey display box decorated with numerous generic sports drawings, some wear.

10in (25.5cm) long

$25-35 HA

A soccer World Cup 1966 scrap book, unused, printed for the Football Association by Collins & World Cup Collectors Club.

1966 *15.25in (38cm) high*

$20-30 MTS

An official World Cup Final programme Sweden vs Brazil, played at the Solna Stadium, 29th June 1958.

$500-600 HA

A large French Niagara No.2 wooden roulette wheel, with chrome metal and painted spinning wheel.

c1900 *19.25in (49cm) diam*

$1,500-2,000 MSA

COLLECTORS' NOTES

▪ For the last 50 or more years taxidermy has been seen by many as extremely unfashionable, slightly distasteful and probably cruel. However, the past few years have seen a resurgence of interest in vintage examples from collectors, interior decorators and people looking for unusual examples to add to eclectic interiors or collections.

▪ Stuffed animals were popular decorative effects during the mid-to late Victorian, and Edwardian eras. They began to go out of fashion during the 1930s, and most commercial outlets closed by the 1970s. Many major towns had at least one practitioner, cities more. Animals were usually mounted in naturalistic settings in glazed cases or contained under glass domes to protect them from dust and other damage.

▪ Birds are one of the most commonly found animals, along with various head 'masks' mounted on shields or plaques. Fish have retained more consistent popularity, mainly due to interest from anglers, and prices can be high. Other popular animals are those that are genetic or biological anomalies, such as albinos or those with clear physical abnormalities. Exotic animals such as giraffes and tiger are also highly valued, mainly as they are rarer.

▪ The type of animal, size, quality of mounting, condition and eye appeal of the whole piece are important factors to consider. The maker is also important with names such as Britain's Rowland Ward, Peter Spicer, James Gardner and John Cooper being among those who are sought-after. Some maker's labels survive, but the quality can be seen from the setting and the way the animal is preserved.

▪ Always consider condition, as it is very hard to repair damaged or faded examples, although cases can be repaired more easily. It is important to note that it is only vintage pieces that are increasing in interest. We do not condone or wish to promote the creation of modern examples. The sale and movement of stuffed animals is closely controlled by state and national laws, which collectors should acquaint themselves with.

A stuffed and mounted green woodpecker, in naturalistic setting and three-sided glazed display case.

This example is more appealing than the example on the right, due to the finer condition and coloring, the better case with glazed sides and blue background, and a better arranged setting.

14in (35.5cm) high

$80-120   **MAI**

A stuffed and mounted green woodpecker, in naturalistic setting and simple glazed display case.

14in (35.5cm) high

$50-70   **MAI**

A stuffed and mounted jay sitting on a branch in a naturalistic setting, contained in a glazed wooden display case.

15in (38cm) high

$30-50   **MAI**

A stuffed and mounted French partridge in a naturalistic setting contained in a glazed wooden case, bearing a label for "G.White Salisbury".

15in (38cm) high

$30-50   **MAI**

A stuffed and mounted English gray partridge and snipe, in a glazed display case, bearing maker's label verso, reading "Wm Drew Ornithologist, – begs leave to inform the curious that he has on sale a number of rare and valuable British birds stuffed with or without cases – rare foreign and domestic birds bought dead or alive – birds stuffed after the most approved method and on reasonable terms".

15in (38cm) wide

$100-150   **MAI**

A stuffed and mounted kestrel with starling prey, in naturalistic setting and glazed display case.

13in (33cm) high

$100-150　　　　　　　　**MAI**

A stuffed and mounted long-eared owl, in naturalistic setting and three-sided glazed display case, bears label verso inscribed "B White, 10 Norwood Terrace, Bath Road, Cheltenham" and dated "August 8 1908".

1908

$180-220　　　　　　　　**MAI**

A collection of stuffed and mounted exotic birds, including a lance-tailed manakin, a broad bill, finches, a bee eater and a Baltimore oriole, mounted on a naturalistic branch setting under a glass dome.

This is a large and complex display with great visual impact. The type of bird also affects the value, with rarely seen examples identified by experienced ornithologists often fetching high prices.

25.5in (65cm) high

$400-500　　　　　　　　**MAI**

A stuffed and mounted parakeet sitting on a branch in a naturalistic setting, contained in a three-sided glazed wooden display case

12.5in (31cm) high

$50-70　　　　　　　　**MAI**

A stuffed and mounted canary, in naturalistic setting and glass fronted display case.

8in (20cm) high

$40-60　　　　　　　　**MAI**

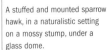

A pair of stuffed and mounted bramble finches in a naturalistic setting, one in flight, one grounded, under a glass dome.

It is worth considering that glass domes themselves are expensive to replace, so always aim to buy undamaged examples.

14in (35.5cm) high

$80-120　　　　　　　　**MAI**

A stuffed and mounted sparrow hawk, in a naturalistic setting on a mossy stump, under a glass dome.

20.5in (52cm) high

$280-320　　　　　　　　**MAI**

A CLOSER LOOK AT A STUFFED FISH

Cased fish by renowned maker John Cooper & Sons of Radnor Street, London (founded c1830), are amongst the most sought-after on the market.

Changes to the design of cases allow rough dating. This is an example of an earlier design with a blue background and many reeds and ground details, mid-20thC examples are green and sparsely furnished.

The use of a bow-fronted case with a gold linear trim and gilt lettering is typical of the company.

Age is not usually a major indicator of value - eye appeal, condition, the complexity of the mounting and the size of the fish for its species are more important.

A stuffed and mounted Chubb in naturalistic setting and and three-sided bow fronted glazed display case, inscribed "Chubb – taken by B J Woodhall, River Severn above Bewdley, Dec. 1927 Wgt 3lbs 7 ozs and label inscribed "Preserved by J Cooper & Sons...".

Malloch of Perth and Homer in London are two other popular British makers to look for.

1927

$800-1,200

MAI

A stuffed and mounted brown trout in naturalistic setting and three-sided bow fronted glazed display case, bears label inscribed "River Severn Holt Fleet, 20th July 1949" and "Preserved and mounted by John Betteridge & Son...".

Betteridge & Son was founded in 1872 in Birmingham, England and was active until 1958, specialising in display work for museums.

1949

$400-600

MAI

A stuffed and mounted brown trout in naturalistic setting and three-sided bow fronted glazed display case, inscribed "Caught at Holden Wood Reservoir with rod and line, Sept 3rd 1901" and bears label inscribed "Preserved by J Cooper & Sons, 28 Radnor Street, St Luke, London EC..."

1901

$600-700

MAI

A stuffed and mounted brown trout in naturalistic setting and glazed display case, bears label inscribed "E.C. Saunders, Naturalist and Taxidermist, Church Plain, Great Yarmouth.....".

$200-250

MAI

A stuffed and mounted pike in naturalistic setting and and three-sided bow fronted glazed display case, bears labels inscribed "Caught by M. Ross, River Trent, 26th October 1949 on a Devon Minnow, 18lbs 7 ozs", and "From Schumach & Son".

1949

$500-700

MAI

A pair of stuffed and mounted graylings in naturalistic setting and three-sided glazed display case, bears label inscribed "Two Grayling caught by T H W Price at the River Lug, 14 Mar. 1958....".

1958

$400-500

MAI

A stuffed and mounted eel in a naturalistic setting, contained in a three-sided bow fronted glazed display case bearing a label inscribed "Eel, Edgbaston Res. 22nd Aug 1949 6lbs 1oz" and "Specimen fish preserved and mounted John Betteridge & Sons ....".

1949

$500-600

MAI

TAXIDERMY

A stuffed gray squirrel, in an inquisitive pose, and mounted on an oak plinth.

6in (15cm) high

$30-50 MAI

A stuffed and mounted gray squirrel playing a piano.

This whimsical style is popular with many collectors and was typical of the notable Potter Collection. However, this is a comparatively simple example, hence its lower value.

12in (30.5cm) wide

$100-150 MAI

A CLOSER LOOK AT TWO FOX HEADS

Peter Spicer & Sons of Royal Leamington Spa, England, operated from c1798-1960 and are considered one of the best taxidermists, being known for their realistic, high quality work.

Spicer's produced a great many fox head 'masks' and became famous for them, and these are in very fine, bright condition, with no damage to the ears or snout as is commonly seen.

The heads are heavy as they are mounted on specially cast plaster manikins.

After the recent ban on fox hunting in Britain, these have become even more sought-after as representing part of British countryside social history, particularly in lively styles and fine condition.

Two stuffed, mounted and posed fox heads, on wooden shield-shaped plaques, the reverses stamped "P. Spicer & Sons Taxidermists Leamington".

11in (28cm) high

$280-320 MSA

A red squirrel posed on its hind legs in a naturalistic setting, under a glass dome.

A license is required to import or export this piece as the red squirrel is an endangered species.

13in (33cm) high

$50-70 MAI

A Rowland Ward mounted long-horned goat head, on an ebonised shield and label "Astor 1922".

Rowland Ward (1835-1912) was said to be the best taxidermist in the world. His company was founded in London c1872 and ran until 1977. His father Henry worked under, and provided taxidermy for, John James Audubon, naturalist and creator of the famous 'The Birds of America'.

41.75in (106cm) high

$1,000-1,500 SWO

A stuffed and mounted mole, posed as emerging from a burrow, under a glass dome.

8in (20cm) high

$80-120 MAI

A small stuffed terrapin.

Small pieces like this have become popular again as quirky desk accessories. However, buyers should be aware that many unmounted pieces were originally components of larger assemblages.

6.75in (17cm) long

$35-45 PC

FIND OUT MORE...

A Record of Spicer's: 1798-1960, by Robert Chinnery, privately published, 2001.

A Guide to Restoring Old Cases of Taxidermy, by Christopher Frost, privately published, 1997.

COLLECTORS' NOTES

- Technology is updated and changed on an almost daily basis and has become vital to the way we live our lives. This revolution began in the 1970s with less expensive electronic pocket calculators, digital watches, and computers that did more than play games.

- Most collectors choose to focus on one area, with calculators, cellular phones and pocket TVs being among the most popular. Although early computers are gaining ground, their size makes storing a collection hard.

- There are a number of factors to consider as regards value. Look for landmark models or those that were considered the first of their type, or forerunners of key movements. Models that captured the public eye are

also important, particularly to nostalgics who hark back to items that were long desired and maybe once owned.

- Design is a further important feature. Many, such as the early Sinclair calculators and the first Apple iMac, have gone on to become design classics. Manufacturer's names and models are also important as a 'look-alike' design by a less well-regarded name will generally be worth less, while popular ranges such as 'Game & Watch' will usually fetch higher sums.

- Always aim to buy in the best condition possible, and preferably in working condition. Check for battery compartment covers, damage to screens, cracked cases and wear to finishes. Original boxes and instructions will add value as most were thrown away.

A Casio TV-21 black and white liquid crystal pocket television.

This example could have a backlight fitted, which resulted in a thicker lid. An earphone was needed for audio and as an antenna.

1985   4.75in (12cm) wide

$20-30   **PTC**

A Casio TV-21 black and white liquid crystal pocket television, with red case and original box.

Red is a scarcer color than black and the value is further bolstered by the box.

1985   4.75in (12cm) wide

$30-50   **PTC**

A Casio TV-300 color liquid crystal pocket television.

This was one of the first and smallest color TVs ever made.

c1988   4.5in (11.5cm) wide

$30-50   **PTC**

A Realistic 'Pocket Vision 3' black and white liquid crystal portable pocket television.

$20-30   **PTC**

A Citizen O6TA LCD pocket television.

This was the first pocket television with an LCD screen, and is commonly found today. A backlight could be purchased for night-time viewing and low power consumption meant battery life was better than other models.

1986   4.5in (11.5cm) wide

$20-30   **PTC**

A Sony FD-210 'Watchman' black and white pocket television.

This was the first Watchman model and used a pre-LCD, CTR screen.

1982   6in (15cm) high

$60-90   **PTC**

A German Adler 80C calculator.

1975   *3in (7.5cm) high*

$15-20   PTC

A Casio JL-810 LCD electronic calculator.

c1982

$10-15   PTC

A Casio fx-31 scientific calculator.

1978   *5.75in (14.5cm) high*

$12-18   PTC

A Commodore Business Machines model 786D electronic calculator.

1975   *5.25in (13.5cm) high*

$20-30   PTC

A Commodore Business Machines model 899A LED electronic calculator.

c1975   *5.75in (14.5cm) high*

$20-30   PTC

A Japanese Decimo 'VatMan Extra M' electronic calculator.

This calculator comes from an enormous range of models, some of which included a key which dealt with tax with one key press.

1975   *5.25in (13cm) high*

$15-20   PTC

A Prinztronic C44 mains-powered calculator.

Prinztronic was the trade name used by UK electronics retailer Dixons.

c1972   *9.5in (24cm) high*

$15-20   PTC

A Sharp EL-120 electronic calculator.

Although can it calculate up to nine digits at a time, only three digits were shown on the tiny screen in a power-saving measure.

6.75in (17cm) wide

$30-50   PTC

An American Texas Instruments TI-30 LCD electronic calculator.

An earlier model had a red LED screen.

6in (15cm) high

$10-15   PTC

A Mattel Electronics Model 9879 'Auto Race' hand-held game.

This was the earliest, entirely electronic, hand-held game sold to the public and had no moving parts.

1976   3in (7.5cm) wide

$70-100   HLJ

A CLOSER LOOK AT A COMPUTER GAME

The company was founded by Masaya Nakamura in 1955 and became known as Namco in 1971. It was sold to Bandai in 1993.

PacLand had a side-scrolling landscape environment, rather than the typical flat maze structure of Pac-Man, and is considered the first of its kind as it arrived before Super Mario Bros.

Namco released its first video game 'Gee Bee' in 1978 and released its best-selling game 'PacMan' two years later. Both, like PacLand, were designed by Toru Iwatani.

This example is in full working condition and retains its battery cover and box.

A Namco Systema 'PacLand' hand-held arcade-style computer game, with original box.

PacLand was also released for other computer formats including Commodore and Atari.

1984

$20-30   PTC

A Grandstand Astro Wars tabletop game.

This 'shoot'em up' game was extremely popular at the time and can be found comparatively easily in varying conditions.

1981   5.75in (14.5cm) wide

$40-60   PTC

A TomyTronic Model 7621 'Shark Attack' 3D hand-held game.

Note the shape of the case, which mimics the head of a shark, even to the point of having eyes on the side. This was released to capitalize on the popular film 'Jaws' released in 1975.

1983

$20-40   PTC

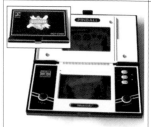

A Nintendo Model PB-59 'Pinball' multi-screen LCD Game & Watch hand-held computer game.

Nintendo's numerous 'Game & Watch' consoles have become increasingly collectible over the past few years, particularly if they retain their boxes. A Panorama Donkey Kong can fetch over $500.

1983   4.25in (11cm) wide

$40-70   PTC

A Nintendo Model BJ-60 'Black Jack' multi-screen LCD Game & Watch hand-held computer game.

1985   4.25in (11cm) wide

$30-50   PTC

A Sega Game Gear hand-held console.

Sega's Game Gear was effectively a portable version of the earlier Master System and was a competitor to the smaller Game Boy. However, its poor battery life and larger size meant it was not as successful. Check that the sound works on vintage models.

1992

$40-70   PTC

TECHNOLOGY

An Amstrad 'PenPad' PDA 600, with writing stylus, box and manuals.

Along with the more expensive, contemporaneous Apple Newton, the PenPad was one of the first PDAs to offer handwriting recognition.

1993 6.25in (16cm) high

$12-18 PTC

A CLOSER LOOK AT A RABBIT TELEPHONE

The Rabbit marks an important crossing point between the home phone and the development of the cellular phone.

The service allowed subscribers to take their home phone handset out and about with them and use it to make calls and pick up messages near a Rabbit basestation, very much like wireless internet HotSpots today.

The service was launched in 1992 and gained 10,000 subscribers, however cheaper cell phone call costs and the ability of cell phones to also receive calls wherever the owner was, led to its closure in December 1993.

Most Rabbit handsets and accessories were discarded in favour of cell phones, particularly when the system was switched off, making examples rare today.

A Rabbit CT2 telephone handset and base station.

Rabbit was founded in 1989 by Hutchison Whampoa, the leading telecommunications and industrial conglomerate behind the UK's Orange network, and now '3'. The company is said to have lost around $240 million in the failed venture.

1992-93

$12-18 PTC

A Psion Series 3a personal organizer, with 2MB of RAM memory.

The clamshell Series 3 followed the popular CM and LZ models, which had sliding covers. It was based on the very rare MC series of laptops, but proved more successful. Although not fetching large sums now, mint and boxed examples are probably worth hanging on to.

1991-93 6.5in (16.5cm) wide

$30-40 PTC

A Cybiko combined hand-held electronic organizer, email composer/reader, games machine, and walkie-talkie.

This is the original model of the Cybiko, released in 2000. It was aimed at teenagers and had over 400 games and could act as a walkie talkie within 300 metres of another unit. After releasing the Cybiko Xtreme a few years later, the company discontinued hardware to focus on games. Is this a collectible of the future?

c2001 5.75in (14.cm) high

$20-30 PTC

A Voice Organizer pocket recording device and manual, by Voice Powered Technology.

c1993

$25-35 PTC

A Grundig Stenorette 2070 portable dictation machine.

1989 6in (15cm) high

$12-18 PTC

An Acorn A3010 professional computer and monitor.

There is a rare German version of this computer, which lacks the green colored keys and has a German language keyboard.

c1992 18.5in (47cm) wide

$25-35 PC

FIND OUT MORE...

Collectable Technology, by Pepe Tozzo, published by Carlton Books, 2005.

COLLECTORS' NOTES

■ Teddy bears derived from US President Theodore Roosevelt's refusal to shoot a bear on a hunting trip in 1902. Entrepreneur Morris Michtom produced a toy bear to commemorate the event to sell in his Brooklyn store and started a craze that is still with us today. Although the US produced the first bears, it was Germany that produced the most and, arguably, the best.

■ Germany's Steiff (founded 1886) is considered the finest maker, and bears made from 1902 to the 1930s are highly desirable, often fetching large sums. Bing, Hermann and Schuco (1921-1970s) are other notable German names. In the UK, Farnell (1908-1960s), Chad Valley (1915-1978), Merrythought (1920-today) and Chiltern (1915-1970s) are amongst the most collectible names. Date ranges given refer only to bear production.

■ Early American bears are scarce and can be hard to identify. For all bears, learn how to recognise forms as this often gives the best indication to the maker and the period, particularly if a bear is not marked.

For those looking to seek out bargains in a crowded market, learn how to recognise bears by smaller makers that others may not know.

■ Earlier, pre-WWII bears tend to have humped backs, long arms with upturned paws and pronounced snouts. Filling tends to be harder than modern bears and mohair is commonly used. Bears from the 1950s onwards tend to be plumper, with rounder faces and bodies and shorter limbs. As sources for desirable early bears dry up and they become more expensive, later bears from the 1950s onwards, and those by less famous makers, are becoming more desirable.

■ As well as the maker, date and form, the size, color and condition are important. Large bears or those in unusual colors will usually fetch more, as will those in better condition with intact fur. Beware of official replica bears, which look like older bears, and also the increasing number of fakes. If in doubt, smell a bear, as the smell of age cannot yet be replicated. Another factor is eye appeal – the cute look of a bear can lead collectors to pay a higher price.

A Steiff cinnamon mohair teddy bear, with blank metal button in his ear.

The blank ear button was used on early bears from c1905 only. This bear is very light in weight, another indication of an early bear, in addition to the form.

c1905   16in (40.5cm) high

$3,000-5,000   **TCT**

A Steiff small brown mohair teddy bear, lacks button in his ear.

c1907   10in (25.5cm) high

$800-1,200   **TCT**

A Steiff blonde mohair teddy bear, with brown woven nose and boot button eyes.

This bear comes with his original gift certificate, dated 1908, which adds to the desirability and value.

c1908   14in (35.5cm) high

$3,800-4,200   **HGS**

A Steiff blonde mohair teddy bear, lacks button in his ear.

c1907-10 9.75in (25cm) high

$2,000-3,000   **HGS**

A Steiff blonde mohair teddy bear, with typical early form, felt pads, woven nose and black boot button eyes.

c1910   17in (43cm) high

$4,500-5,500   **LHT**

A rare Steiff white mohair teddy bear, with original felt pads, boot button eyes and light brown woven nose.

This fine teddy is rare on two counts – he has a very early blank button and he is white, which is an uncommon color. He is also in excellent condition with his original light brown stitched nose.

c1905   12.5in (32cm) high

$3,000-4,000   **HGS**

A CLOSER LOOK AT A STEIFF BEAR

'Centre seam' teddies are so-called due to the sewn seam running down the centre of their heads, which gives them appealing faces.

He displays many characteristics of desirable early bears such as long, curved limbs, a humped back, a pronounced muzzle, and large out-turned paws with original felt pads.

This seam only appeared on every seventh bear and allowed for economical use of fabric – centre seams are thus six times rarer than other bears of the period.

As well as being comparatively large, this teddy is in excellent condition with long plush – on more worn bears, the seam is more visible.

A Steiff brown mohair 'centre seam' teddy bear, with original felt pads, black boot button eyes and woven nose.

c1907   20in (51cm) high

$8,000-12,000   **TCT**

A Steiff blonde mohair teddy bear, with original pads, black boot button eyes and woven nose, in overall extremely clean condition.

c1908   13in (33cm) high

$2,000-2,500   **HGS**

A Steiff blonde mohair teddy bear, with original pads, boot button eyes and woven nose, dressed in a sailor's uniform.

Dressing bears in uniform was popular during the 1920s, the period this suit dates from. This color and style of button was used from c1920 to the 1950s.

c1919   12in (30.5cm) high

$1,200-1,800   **TCT**

A Steiff blonde mohair teddy bear, with original clothing, felt pads, woven nose and boot button eyes, lacks button in ear.

This bear is not in as fine condition as others, and some of his stuffing has degraded, but he is comparatively early.

c1910   13in (33cm) high

$1,200-1,800   **TCT**

A 1920s Steiff blonde mohair teddy bear, with early face, original pads, woven nose and black boot button eyes.

17in (43cm) high

$2,800-3,200   **LHT**

A 1950s Steiff blonde mohair teddy bear, with original pads, woven nose and black boot button eyes.

Note the rounder, plumper and 'stumpier' limbed form of later bears, compared to the earlier examples shown here.

20in (51cm) high

$700-900   **LHT**

A 1950s Steiff brown 'Teddy Baby', with red collar and bell.

Teddy Babies typically have flat feet so they can stand, and open mouths.

9in (23cm) high

$300-500 HGS

A 1950s Steiff white mohair miniature 'Teddy Baby', with velour face and feet, in excellent condition.

The 'Teddy Baby' was introduced in 1930 and was modeled on a bear cub. White is the most desirable color.

3.5in (9cm) high

$750-850 TCT

A 1950s Steiff 'TeddyLi' with poseable plastic arms, legs and feet, and original clothes and tag.

He is hard to find complete and in excellent condition.

4.75in (12cm) high

$500-700 TCT

A 1950s Steiff small 'Zotty' bear, with original tag and ribbon.

The name 'Zotty' derives from the German word 'zottig' for 'shaggy', which is descriptive of the mohair.

6in (15cm) high

$150-200 HGS

A Steiff white mohair and velour 'Zooby' teddy bear.

'Zooby' is based on a Russian circus bear, and like Zotties, it typically has an open mouth.

1954-60   10.5in (26.5cm) high

$350-450 LHT

A 1950s-60s Steiff small blonde mohair teddy bear, with original woven nose and black eyes.

6in (15cm) high

$60-90 TCT

A Steiff small white mohair 'Strong Museum' replica bear, with original ear tag and button.

These bears were made for the famous Margaret Woodbury Strong Museum of juvenalia and toys in Rochester, New York.

c1983   15in (38cm) high

$320-380 TCT

A Steiff large brown mohair 'Margaret Woodbury Strong Museum' teddy bear, with original tags.

The secondary market for replica bears is not yet strong, so keep them in mint condition with all paperwork and boxes.

c1983   23.25in (59cm) high

$550-650 TCT

A 1920s Farnell white mohair teddy bear, with original pads, brown woven nose and glass eyes.

White is a rare color. Early Farnell bears typically have long plump arms, long snouts, woven claws and feet pads inset with cardboard.

19in (48.5cm) high

$3,000-3,500 LHT

A CLOSER LOOK AT A FARNELL BEAR

Founded in 1908, Farnell is known as the 'English Steiff' for its fine quality, highly desirable and valuable teddies.

Only limited numbers were made, making this example rare. Black was neither a standard nor a popular color for teddies.

Black bears were made as mourning bears to commemorate the tragedy of the Titanic – as such they appeal to many collectors today.

Steiff also made black Titanic mourning bears. One, from only 500 made, sold for over $100,000 in 2000.

A very rare Farnell black mohair mourning bear, with original eyes, nose stitching and pads.

1912-14

14in (35.5cm) high

$4,500-5,500 LHT

A Farnell blonde mohair 'Alpha' teddy bear, with original paw pads, stitched nose and glass eyes.

c1914

14in (35.5cm) high

$1,800-2,200 LHT

A Farnell blonde mohair 'Alpha' bear with original paw pads, black boot button eyes and stitched nose, slightly worn.

This is an unusual size. The Alpha bears are typical of Farnell and it is their best known range. Farnell's factory was known as the Alpha Works and the Alpha trademark itself was registered in 1925. The character of Winnie the Pooh was based on the Alpha bear bought for the real-life Christopher Robin in 1921.

9in (23cm) high

$1,000-1,500 LHT

A Farnell red mohair 'Mascot' range miniature bear, in a knitted wool dress.

These patriotically red, white or blue colored bears were made to be sold and given to soldiers going to fight in WWI. Colors such as this are more valuable than blonde or golden mohair.

c1914

5in (12.5cm) high

$450-550 LHT

A 1920s Farnell golden mohair teddy bear, with black boot button eyes, re-stitched black nose and mouth and replaced felt foot pads, worn.

18.5in (47cm) high

$280-320 SAS

A Farnell blue mohair 'Mascot' range miniature bear, in a knitted wool dress.

c1914

5in (12.5cm) high

$450-550 LHT

A 1920s Farnell blonde mohair teddy bear hand puppet, with original glass eyes and stitched nose.

9in (23cm) high

$450-550 LHT

A 1930s/40s Chiltern golden mohair 'Hugmee' teddy bear, with original foot pads, woven nose, glass eyes and original tag.

Original tags are rarely found, without one, he would be worth $300-400.

13in (33cm) high

$700-900   **LHT**

A 1930s/40s Chiltern golden mohair teddy bear, with original foot pads, woven nose, glass eyes.

Note the style of the nose with two extended stitches on top – this is a typical feature of 1930s Chiltern bears.

20in (51cm) high

$500-600   **LHT**

A CLOSER LOOK AT A CHILTERN BEAR

The 'Master Teddy' is Chiltern's earliest bear, and was first produced in 1915.

He retains his rare collar and bow tie and original, early 'googly' eyes and red felt tongue.

He is typically dressed and only the visible mohair parts are made from mohair, the rest is made from cloth.

All examples of the 'Master' bear are rare, particularly very early examples like this.

A Chiltern blonde mohair 'Master Teddy' with original clothing, stitched nose and tongue, in good condition.

1915   12.5in (32cm) high

$1,800-2,200   **LHT**

A 1940s Chiltern golden mohair 'Hugmee' teddy bear, with orange and black glass eyes, original brown painted cloth pads and label on right foot, worn.

14.5in (37cm) high

$180-220   **SAS**

A Chiltern powder blue mohair teddy bear, with feltpads, woven nose and replaced glass eyes.

Powder blue is extremely rare.

c1930   14.5in (37cm) high

$500-600   **LHT**

A 1950s Chiltern golden mohair 'Hugmee' teddy bear, with internal musical bellows and original tag.

Without the tag and in less than immaculate condition, his value would fall to less than $700.

16in (40.5cm) high

$1,000-1,500   **LHT**

A 1950s Chiltern blonde mohair 'Ting-a-Ling' teddy bear, with original glass eyes, black stitched nose, mouth and claws, rexine paw pads pads and internal bell in body, worn.

11.75in (30cm) high

$180-220   **SAS**

A 1950s Chiltern golden mohair 'Ting A Ling Bruin' teddy bear, in original condition with card inset feet allowing him to stand.

11in (28cm) high

$300-500   **LHT**

An early Chad Valley blonde mohair teddy bear.

Chad Valley produced its first bears in 1915 and continued to produce them until the 1970s when they suffered a decline in sales. The company was sold to Palitoy in 1978.

c1919   10in (25.5cm) high

$700-1,000   LHT

A Chad Valley golden mohair teddy bear, in original condition with cork-filled limbs and celluloid covered button.

The cork-filled limbs, general form and style of button denote an early date.

1918   13in (33cm) high

$800-1,200   LHT

A Chad Valley golden mohair 'Aerolite' teddy bear, with glass eye, black stitched nose, mouth and claws and Aerolite metal rimmed button in ear, worn with losses, some repair.

c1925   20.5in (52cm) high

$180-220   SAS

A 1930s Chad Valley golden mohair 'Magna' teddy bear, with glass eyes, typical black stitched horizontal nose, mouth and claws and cloth label on left foot, general wear.

14.5in (37cm) high

$180-220   SAS

A late 1940s Chad Valley art silk musical teddy bear, with internal wind-up Thorens musical mechanism.

Swiss company Thorens are well-known for their excellent musical boxes.

14in (35.5cm) high

$700-900   LHT

A 1950s Chad Valley golden mohair teddy bear, with glass eyes, black stitched muzzle and claws and brown velvet pads.

14.25in (36cm) high

$150-200   SAS

A late 1950s Chad Valley dark brown wool-mix teddy bear, with felt pads, stitched nose, glass eyes and post-1953 label to right foot.

16in (40.5cm) high

$220-280   LHT

A late 1960s Chad Valley Chiltern golden mohair teddy bear, with card tag, lacks foot label.

Chiltern was taken over by Chad Valley in 1967 and for a few years labels bore both names.

11in (28cm) high

$280-320   LHT

A CLOSER LOOK AT A SCHUCO MINIATURE

German company Schreyer & Co (Schuco) is well-known for its 'gadget' bears and soft toys produced between 1920 and 1970.

The bear's head pulls off to reveal a perfume bottle. Other examples contain concealed compacts or lipsticks.

The clip shows that he was also meant to be worn.

The peachy orange is a rarer color than golden or blonde, and adds value and desirability.

A 1930s Schuco peach-colored mohair perfume bottle bear, with pin back.

3.5in (9cm) high

$1,000-1,500   **LHT**

A 1950s Schuco blonde mohair 'Tricky' 'YesNo' teddy bear, with plastic tag.

A 1950s Schuco blonde mohair 'Tricky' musical 'YesNo' teddy bear, with plastic tag.

A Schuco blonde mohair 'YesNo' teddy bear, with brown and black glass eyes, black stitched nose and mouth, some wear.

The soft filled body and limbs indicate this rare example was made for a baby or a very small child. The Schuco Tricky was introduced in 1953.

Introduced in 1921, the 'YesNo' movement made teddy nod or shake his head, depending on how the tail was moved.

3.5in (9cm) high

21in (53.5cm) high

5in (12.5cm) high

$300-500   **HGS** | **$1,000-1,500**   **LHT** | **$120-180**   **SAS**

A 1950s Schuco brown mohair 'Berlin' miniature teddy bear, with crown, sash and original pin.

An early Schuco blonde mohair clockwork tumbling miniature bear, with key.

A 1950s Schuco gold plush miniature bear, in excellent condition.

It is hard to find these bears, first produced in the 1950s and based on the city's logo, with the crown and sash intact.

Schuco are also very well-known for their tinplate toys with wind-up mechanisms. These were also employed in their famous tumbling bears.

3.5in (9cm) high

2.5in (6.5cm) high

4.75in (12cm) high

$120-180   **HGS** | **$80-120**   **SAS** | **$400-600**   **SF**

A Steiff black and white mohair panda, with open mouth and card inset feet allowing him to stand, with tag reading "made in the US Zone Germany".

Pandas became popular alternatives to teddy bears after the first real-life panda was introduced into Chicago Zoo in 1937 and into London Zoo in 1938.

1947-53   11in (28cm) high

$500-700   **LHT**

A 1950s Steiff black and white mohair panda, with open mouth and card inset feet allowing him to stand.

8.5in (21.5cm) high

$300-500   **HGS**

A 1940s British black and white wool plush panda nightdress or pyjama case, with clear and black glass eyes and zip-up back.

17.25in (44cm) high

$100-150   **SAS**

A 1940s British black and white mohair panda, possibly by Tara Toys, with clear and black glass eyes and rexine pads, some general wear.

22in (56cm) high

$150-200   **SAS**

A Farnell 'Mascot' range panda, in excellent, original condition.

c1939-40   4.5in (11.5cm) high

$220-280   **LHT**

A Steiff black and white mohair panda, on all fours, with original tag and bell.

5.5in (14cm) long

$200-250   **SOTT**

A Steiff white mohair polar bear, with original paw pads, stitched nose and mouth and collar.

17.5in (44.5cm) high

$2,200-2,800   **LHT**

A Chad Valley white mohair polar bear, in excellent original condition.

Polar bears became popular after the celebrated birth of Brumas to Ivy. Brumas was the first polar bear born in captivity.

c1950   15in (38cm) high

$1,000-1,500   **LHT**

A 1950s Steiff small white mohair polar bear, on all fours, with original paw pads, stitched nose and mouth and boot button eyes, with tag and bell.

6.25in (16cm) long

$150-200   **HGS**

A CLOSER LOOK AT A HECLA BEAR

Hecla was active for only a short period of time from around 1905, making its bears rarer than others, as less were produced.

The company imported German materials and used immigrant German toy makers to make its high quality bears – as such they can look very much like Steiff or other German bears.

Typical features that distinguish Hecla from Steiff include wide-set ears and a rounder shaped head, set back into the body.

The closely set eyes and light red/brown nose and claw stitching are also other typical Hecla features.

An American Hecla blonde mohair teddy bear, with original glass eyes, stitched nose and mouth and paw pads.

c1907-10   12in (30.5cm) high

$1,500-2,000   **TCT**

An American Hecla blonde mohair teddy bear, with original pads, eyes and stitched nose and mouth.

c1907   15in (38cm) high

$1,500-2,000   **TCT**

An early American blonde mohair teddy bear, by an unknown maker, with original paw pads, glass eyes and stitched nose.

c1908   11.5in (29cm) high

$400-600   **TCT**

A 1940s Knickerbocker cinnamon bear, with original glass eyes, stitched nose and velveteen paw pads.

Knickerbocker was founded in 1869 and produced bears from c1920 to the 1980s. The one-piece rounded face with a thin, short snout indicates an early bear, and the round, low set ears are a hallmark of Knickerbocker designs.

c1935   16.25in (41cm) high

$300-400   **SOTT**

An American Woolnough golden mohair 'Winne The Pooh' teddy bear, in original condition, with foot stamp.

c1930   14in (35.5cm) high

$3,500-4,500   **TCT**

An early American blonde mohair teddy bear, with original paw pads, black stitched nose and mouth, boot button eyes.

When teddy bears became fashionable after 1902, a great number of American factories sprang up to produce them, many in New York. The majority of these bears bore no markings or tags and companies came and went. Typical American features include short, pointed feet and round ears set low on the head.

c1908   10in (25.5cm) high

$700-900   **HGS**

A 1920s American light golden mohair teddy bear, with triangular-shaped head, rounded low set ears, orange and black glass eyes, black stitched nose, mouth and claws, worn and pads replaced.

19in (48cm) high

$280-320   **SAS**

TEDDY BEARS

A 1950s-60s German Anker Drolly plush teddy bear, with velveteen pads and original tag.

7.25in (18.5cm) high

$150-200   LHT

A 1960s British Blue Ribbon Playthings gold mohair teddy bear, with tag, in excellent condition.

Without the tag he could be worth $80-120

14in (35.5cm) high

$250-350   LHT

A 1950s German Diem gray mohair teddy bear, with internal growler.

This teddy is very similar to Steiff's Zotty bear and is unusual in gray.

16.5in (42cm) high

$220-280   LHT

A very rare German Rudolf Haas brown-tipped beige mohair 'Nickle Nackle' teddy bear, in excellent condition.

'Nickle Nackle' bears turn their heads from left to right when the right arm is moved and nod when the left arm is moved. This mechanism was patented by Rudolf Haas in 1928.

A 1950s German Diem gold mohair teddy bear, in excellent condition.

15.5in (39.5cm) high

$150-200   LHT

c1930   21in (53.5cm) high

$1,800-2,200   LHT

A German Jopi blonde mohair teddy bear, the body with internal musical bellows.

Jopi was registered as a trademark in 1922 and the name is formed from the first two letters of the founder's name, Josef Pitrmann.

c1922   13.5in (34cm) high

$700-1,000   HGS

A Merrythought golden mohair 'Cheeky' bear, with orange plastic eyes, orange velvet muzzle, brown felt and cotton pads, black stitched nose, mouth and claws and bell inside.

12.5in (32cm) high

$150-200   SAS

A 1930s-40s Merrythought golden mohair teddy bear, with original paw pads, label, ear button, black boot button eyes and stitched nose and mouth.

These bears are often mistaken for Chiltern Hugmee's due to their shape and nose stitching.

23in (58.5cm) high

$500-700   LHT

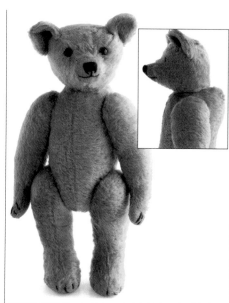

A 1920s British Omega blonde mohair teddy bear, with original paw pads, the feet with inset card, nose stitching and eyes.

Note the similarity to Farnell's Alpha bears.

c1920   14.5in (367cm) high

$1,000-1,500   **LHT**

A 1950s German Petz cinnamon mohair teddy bear, with original glass eyes, black stitched nose, mouth and claws, felt pads and white plastic button on chest.

21.25in (54cm) high

$220-280   **SAS**

A 1920s British Omega golden mohair teddy bear, in original condition.

This is a very rare, large size for Omega. Note the early form, which takes in so many typical features.

24in (61cm) high

$2,200-2,800   **LHT**

A 1940s British Pixie Toys blonde mohair small teddy bear, in original condition with ear tag.

Pixie Toys was founded in 1930 by the wives of two glassmakers in Stourbridge. Many of its bears, produced until its closure in 1962, are similar to Merrythought bears due to the employment of an ex-Merrythought designer.

8.5in (21.5cm) high

$250-350   **LHT**

A late 1950s Irish Tara Toys brown mohair teddy bear, in original but worn condition.

Tara Toys was founded by the Irish government under the name Erris Toys in 1938. It became Tara Toys in 1953 and Soltoys in 1969, before closing in 1979.

36in (91.5cm) high

$300-400   **LHT**

A German Strünz blonde mohair tumbling teddy bear, with metal framed arms, in original condition.

Strünz made bears from 1904 and was in direct competition to Steiff. Strünz even used a similar ear button until 1908. In excellent, working condition, this bear could be worth up to $3,000.

c1912   10in (25.5cm) high

$700-900   **LHT**

A 1940s-50s Belgian Unica pink art silk teddy bear, in original condition.

10in (25.5cm) high

$300-500   **LHT**

A 1930s/40s German Weiersmüller blonde mohair teddy bear, with card inset foot pads allowing him to stand.

7.75in (19.75cm) high

$300-500   **LHT**

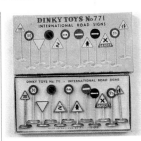

A set of 12 Dinky No. 771 International Road Signs, near mint condition, in good condition box.

1953-65

$100-150 VEC

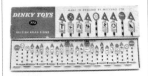

A set of 24 Dinky no. 772 British Road Signs, near mint condition, one road sign broken at base, in good condition box.

1959-63

$250-350 VEC

A Dinky no. 4 boxed set of O-gauge model railway Engineering Staff figures.

1954-56 5.5in (14cm) wide

$150-250 F

A Dinky no. 6 Shepherd Gift Set, box good, near mint.

1954-56

$250-350 CHEF

A CLOSER LOOK AT A DINKY TOYS BOX

Empty boxes appeal to collectors who buy them to fill them, increasing the value of a loose set.

Export-market boxes with their different designs are rarer still.

The design shows that this example was produced for the US market – sometimes red labels are found bearing the name of the US distributor H. Hudson Dobson.

Their survival is comparatively rare as many were thrown away.

An empty Dinky green and blue speckled pattern no. 6 Commercial Vehicles Set box for the US export market, fair condition with some taping.

1948

$250-350 SAS

A Dinky no. 47 road signs set, with closed triangles, box repaired.

1935-41 Box 7in (18cm) wide

$150-250 GAZE

A Dinky no. 964 Elevator Loader, in very good condition, with fair condition box.

1954-68

$45-65 GAZE

A Dinky pre-war no.45 Garage with gloss doors, very good to excellent condition.

$350-450 SAS

COLLECTORS' NOTES

■ Mattel's Hot Wheels range was released in 1968 to balance its mainly girl-orientated catalog and to provide boys with more American, exciting 'muscle' type cars to combat the UK's Dinky and Corgi toy cars. Look out for 'Red Line' wheels or the specially developed bright metallic 'Spectraflame' finishes, especially in pink and purple, which can be rare today.

■ As with many toys, condition is important, with dents, scratches and wear to the paintwork reducing value. Vintage vehicles in their original blister packs are particularly rare, as in order to open the packaging it had to be destroyed. Also look out for smaller production runs and unusual variations in color or accessories, which can fetch higher sums than usual.

A Mattel Hot Wheels 'red line' green Silhouette, no.6209.

Note the wheels with red lines, which were produced from 1968-77 and are hotly sought-after by many collectors.

1968   2.5in (6.5cm) long

$30-40   **SOTT**

A Mattel Hot Wheels 'red line' bronze Twinmill, no.6258, with painted baseplate.

1969   *3in (7.5cm) long*

$40-50   **NOR**

A Mattel Hot Wheels blue Python, no.6219.

1969   *2.25in (5.5cm) long*

$35-45   **SOTT**

A Mattel Hot Wheels silver Race Bait 308, no.2021.

c1982   *2.75in (7cm) long*

$22-28   **SOTT**

A Mattel Hot Wheels 'red line' Power Pad, no.6459.

1970   *2.25in (5.5cm) long*

$15-25   **SOTT**

A Mattel Hot Wheels 'red line' green Custom Fleetside, no.6213.

1968   *3in (7.5cm) long*

$80-120   **SOTT**

A Mattel Hot Wheels orange and silver Peterbilt Tank Truck, no.1689.

1981   *3.25in (8.5cm) long*

$10-15   **SOTT**

A Mattel Hot Wheels 'red line' Heavyweights Funny Money, no. 6005.

This model was produced with a silver finish in Hong Kong in 1972 only, so will be harder to find than many other models as fewer were produced.

1972   *2.5in (6.5cm) long*

$150-200   **SOTT**

An American Aurora 'Model Motoring' AMX slot car, model no. 1414-3.300, mint and boxed.

Based on Britain's Playcraft range, Aurora's 'Model Motoring' range of HO (1:87) size slot cars was released in 1960. As the range grew, more American bodies were added to the line-up, including Mack trucks and a Corvette. As buyers became more interested in model car racing than model railroading, a small range of racing cars introduced in 1964. By 1965, Aurora had sold over 25 million slot cars.

$50-100   **PWE**

An American Aurora 'Model Motoring' black GTO Convertible slot car, model no.1411-3.00, mint and boxed.

$50-100   **PWE**

An American Aurora 'Model Motoring' Mack Dump truck, mint and boxed.

The price shows this model cost $2.50 at the time.

Box 3.75in (9.5cm) long

$50-100   **PWE**

An American Aurora 'Model Motoring' Mack Stake Truck, model no.1363-3.50, mint and boxed.

3.75in (9.5cm) long

$50-100   **PWE**

A Hubley 'Kiddie Toy' diecast red MG open roadster sports car, with silver embossed seating and grill, spare on truck, rubber tires, box missing one inner flap, toy, in near mint condition.

8.75in (22cm) long

$250-350   **BER**

A Hubley 'Kiddie Toy' diecast metal blue painted car, with rubber wheels.

5.5in (14cm) long

$60-80   **BH**

A Hubley diecast red model tractor, with nickel driver, rubber tires, the hood with a partial label reading, "Indiana State Fair", wear to box edges, in pristine condition.

6.75in (17cm) long

$120-180   **BER**

A Hubley diecast red painted hook and ladder fire truck, with nickel-plated ladder supports and three cast iron ladders, nickel windshield and seated driver, black rubber tires, in pristine condition.

9.5in (24cm) long

$400-500   **BER**

8A Metal Masters Co. diecast red painted fire ladder truck, with original metal ladders, seated driver, decals on doors, rubber tires, and tattered box, toy in near mint condition.

10in (25.5cm) long

$300-400   **BER**

A Midgetoys of Rockford, Illinois, diecast metal Roadster toy car, with rubber wheels.

3in (23cm) wide

$4-5   **BH**

A National Products, Inc. diecast metal metallic blue 1934 Studebaker Land Cruiser money bank, embossed 'Replica of Giant World's Fair Studebaker', with 1934 World Fair decal "A Century of Progress", white rubber tires with wood hubs, partial box, in excellent condition.

1934   *6in (15cm) long*

$300-400   **BER**

An early 20thC German Plank diecast metal red and black two-seater fire engine, with louvered bonnet with bell to rear right, brass effect boiler mounted to rear, cast spoked wheels in red and white, two holes on seat for missing firemen, some damage.

2.5in (6.5cm) long

$120-180   **W&W**

A pre-war Tootsietoy silver Ford Tri-Motor airplane, with three propellers and white rubber tyres to undercarriage.

$220-280   **VEC**

A Tootsietoys blue and silver diecast metal Greyhound bus.

6in (15cm) wide

$60-70   **BH**

A Tootsie Toy diecast metal red long low lorry, marked "Made in the United-States of America".

6in (15cm) long

$40-50   **MEM**

A Tootsie Toy diecast red fire truck, with hose but lacks other accessories, marked "Made in the U.S.A.".

6.25in (16cm) long

$40-50   **MEM**

A Topper 'Johnny Lightning' Custom El Camino, with two surf boards on the back.

3.25in (8.5cm) long

$20-30   **NOR**

TOYS & GAMES

COLLECTORS' NOTES

- Cast iron toys saw their golden age during the 1920s and '30s, with production beginning to tail-off during WWII due to restrictions on the usage of metal. By the 1950s, less costly plastics had taken over. A number of companies produced cast iron toys, including the notable Hubley factory that was founded in 1898 and sold to CBS in 1978. Other important companies include Kilgore (c1922-40), and Kenton, Dent and Arcade (founded 1885).

- Values are based on the maker, size and type of model, the complexity of the molding, the color and the condition. Racing cars and stylish cars of the 1920s and '30s that caught the imaginations of little boys at the time tend to be the most desirable today. Rare models, some produced by smaller companies, can also be valuable, as can fire engines and farm vehicles.

- Most toys measured around 6-8in (15-20cm) in length. Larger examples were more expensive at the time, so are rarer today as less were sold. Larger toys also tend to be more complexly molded, with finer detailing such as drivers, wording and nickel grilles. Smaller examples with less detailed molding are the most affordable.

- Bright colors were popular, particularly red. Condition of the paint is vital, especially for more common smaller toys. Most exhibit some wear through play, but look out for degraded paint, which takes on fragmented 'islands' of color and excessive wear as this devalues a model. Do not attempt to repaint a toy, or 'touch up' worn areas as this will devalue it further. A toy in truly mint condition can often fetch many times the value of one in 'good' condition.

A Hubley silver-painted cast iron racer, embossed "7" on hood, with red seated driver, white rubber tires, red wooden hubs, in excellent condition.

5.25in (13.5cm) long

$180-220   **BER**

A rare A.C. Williams silver-painted cast iron racer, with red trim on cast side pipes, rubber tires, in very good condition.

Metal foundry and casters A.C. Williams of Ravenna, Ohio, only made toys during the 1920s and '30s.

c1936   *8.5in (21.5cm) long*

$400-500   **BER**

A Champion red-painted cast iron racer, with a green hood and blue driver, embossed "Champion" behind seating, tires worn, in excellent condition.

The grille design is unusual and appealing.

c1932   *7.25in (18.5cm) long*

$500-600   **BER**

An early 1900s Kenton silver-painted cast iron Peerless racer, embossed 'Peerless' on sides of hood, with disc wheels and original driver, in good condition.

5.75in (14.5cm) long

$300-400   **BER**

An early Hubley red-painted cast iron racer, with gold trim on hood and yellow-painted driver and spoked wheels, chipping to paint, in good condition.

This can also be found in blue and was made from the 1910s into the '20s.

8in (20cm) long

$400-500   **BER**

A 1920s Freidag orange and black-painted cast iron taxi cab, with cast driver at window and license plate embossed, "453", painted disc wheels, in very good condition.

This rare model has a cast-iron spare tire on the back.

5.25in (13.5cm) long

$800-1,000   **BER**

An Arcade red-painted cast iron fire chief car, with cast hood bell trimmed in gold, decal on body, doors embossed "Chief", white rubber tires, in very good condition.

This is the same form as Arcade's Ford Coupé, but the fire chief variation can be hard to find.

c1932   *5in (13cm) long*

$500-600   **BER**

A CLOSER LOOK AT A CAST IRON TOY

Amos and Andy are popular characters who also appeared in a tinplate toy made by Louis Marx & Co. of New York from 1930 onwards.

This model is particularly sought-after by collectors, with the consistent demand leading to generally high prices.

This is one of only two models Dent made based on popular cartoons of the period – the other is the Toonerville Trolley.

It is in very good overall condition, complete with all three figures, and has not been over-painted.

A Dent orange-painted cast iron 'Fresh Air' open taxi, with Amos and Andy and dog seated in front, spoke wheels trimmed in black and extensive embossed lettering overall.

6.25in (16cm) long

$1,800-2,200 **BER**

A Kenton red-painted cast iron fire chief coupé, with bell cast in middle of hood, embossed door, driver cast into window and nickel disc wheels, in very good condition.

Look at the different styles of wheels, different molded details and colors to tell the difference between makers.

5.75in (14.5cm) long

$700-800 **BER**

A Dent red-painted cast iron fire chief coupé, with gold trimmed cast bell on hood, embossed door, driver cast into window and nickel disc wheels, in very good condition.

5.25in (13.5cm) long

$600-700 **BER**

An A.C. Williams black-painted cast iron Ford Model T coupé, with silver-painted spoked wheels, in very good condition.

5.25in (13.5cm) long

$120-180 **BER**

A Freidag black-painted cast iron 1924 coupé, with nickeled spoked wheels and cast driver in window, in very good condition.

c1924   5.75in (14.5cm) long

$500-600 **BER**

A Hubley blue-painted cast iron coupé, with cast driver in window, red and silver painted disc wheels and spare wheel mounted on trunk.

6.75in (17cm) long

$750-850 **BER**

A Dent blue-painted cast iron sport roadster, with two silver-painted passengers seated in open rumble seat, nickel disc wheels, in good, original condition.

The two passengers in a rumble seat was a unique feature to this model and company.

5.75in (14.5cm) long

$180-220 **BER**

TOYS & GAMES

A CLOSER LOOK AT A WARREN CAST IRON STAFF CAR

Warren was based in New York and produced cast metal soldiers and other toys for a short period from 1936-40.

The staff car was made in comparatively small quantities and is very hard to find today.

The shape of the car was based on Kenton's popular Roadster, and the patriotic wartime subject matter makes it appeal to more collectors.

It is complete with soldiers and flags and is in excellent condition, which adds greatly to its value.

A late 1930s Warren Company olive green-painted cast iron staff car, with nickel grille, four soldiers and two flags on poles, in excellent condition.

7.25in (18.5cm) long

$1,500-2,000   **BER**

A Kenton green-painted cast iron Pontiac wrecker, with Type I nickel grille, tow hook, black frame and white rubber tires, in excellent condition.

This example was from the Kenton Sample Room.

4in (10cm) long

$350-450   **BER**

An A.C. Williams Deluxe red-painted cast iron 1936 Ford coupé, with nickel grille and paint wear to roof, otherwise in excellent condition.

This model has a desirable nickel grille, which can be detached. This was one of four models offered in the 'take apart' interchangeable body Deluxe range and is an appealing shape.

c1937   4.5in (11.5cm) long

$700-800   **BER**

A Kilgore red-painted cast iron fire pumper, with nickel grille, two riders, boiler and white rubber tires, in excellent condition.

5in (13cm) long

$350-450   **BER**

A Hubley red-painted cast iron small ladder truck, with cast driver, both original tin ladders and rubber tires, in excellent condition.

This is small and comparatively simply cast model, hence its lower value.

3.5in (9cm) long

$100-150   **BER**

A Dent black-painted cast iron express wagon, with red spoked wheels, single horse and driver seated in removable bench seat, in very good condition.

12in (30.5cm) long

$180-220   **BER**

A rare Harris green-painted cast iron 'Mama Katzen' jammer open cart, with a standing figure and kicking mule cast with legs on cart, wear to spokes, in good condition.

8.25in (21cm) long

$450-550   **BER**

An Arcade red-painted cast iron International Farmall Model M tractor, with decals on sides, nickel driver with drawbar and rubber tires with painted centers, in excellent condition.

c1940   *7in (18cm) long*

$350-450   **BER**

An Arcade red-painted cast iron Ford 9N tractor salesman's sample, with cast driver and wooden black wheels, in pristine condition.

c1941   *3.5in (9cm) long*

$250-350   **BER**

A Hubley green-painted cast iron Oliver 'Orchard' farm tractor, with separately cast driver and seat frame, and wheel cover design and rubber tires.

Not only is this model probably unique, it is also in mint condition.

c1940   *5.25in (13.5cm) long*

$850-950   **BER**

An Arcade black-painted cast iron Avery tractor, with red spoked wheels, in very good condition.

c1925   *4.5in (11.5cm) long*

$150-200   **BER**

A Hubley red-painted cast iron Monarch bulldozer, with black traction treads, in good condition.

An interior cam allows an articulated action when the model is pulled along.

c1932   *5.5in (14cm) long*

$350-450   **BER**

A rare Dent green-painted cast iron road grader, with driver holding two wheel controls, red painted spoke wheels, repair to frame, in good condition.

Construction toys tended to be less popular than more stylish cars at the time, so are often rarer today. However, this example is worn and repaired, hence its lower value.

5.25in (13.5cm) long

$70-100   **BER**

An early Arcade cast iron flatcar wrecking toy, with separate boom on slotted base, levers, nickel trucks and crane holding a cast iron locomotive toy, in very good condition.

13.5in (34.5cm) long

$350-450   **BER**

An Arcade red-painted cast iron McCormick Deering Spreader open bed trailer, with yellow hitch, rubber tires with painted centers, replaced center screw, otherwise in excellent condition.

This model works like a real spreader, with three rotating nickel shafts. It was sold from the mid-1920s onwards with attached horses. From 1932-41 it was sold separately.

1932-41   *15in (38cm) long*

$350-450   **BER**

A Kenton Toys cast iron 'National' wagon, painted in red overall, embossed sides, features pull handle, rubber tires, wear to rim, in very good condition.

7.25in (18.5cm) long

$250-300   **BER**

FIND OUT MORE...

Cast Iron Automotive Toys, *by Myral Yellin and Eric B. Outwater, published by Schiffer Publishing, 2000.*

A CLOSER LOOK AT A TRAIN

Jerome Secor founded Secor in 1872 in Connecticut and became known for his clockwork and mechanical toys.

The form, decoration and material indicates an early date - early American toys of this period are scarce and desirable .

This example is made from cast iron, not tinplate, which is relatively unusual.

Secor was later sold to Ives, one of the most noted American model train manufacturers.

An American hand-painted cast iron Secor clockwork train.

c1882 9in (23cm) long

$1,500-2,500   **AMJ**

A German lithographed tinplate 'penny toy' locomotive '345', with one carriage, possibly by Distler, marked "Made in Germany".

8.5in (21cm) long

$80-100   **WDL**

A scarce and large early tinplate clockwork steam twin dome Continental locomotive.

7in (18cm) wide

$100-150   **W&W**

A Chad Valley LMS lithographed tinplate clockwork locomotive.

10in (25.5cm) long

$40-70   **GAZE**

An 'O' gauge 4-4-0 clockwork locomotive.

11in (28cm) long

$500-750   **GAZE**

A late 1920s Hornby O-gauge No. 2 tender clockwork locomotive, 4-4-0 and six wheel tender in black, RN 2711, two fixed front buffer beam lights.

$250-400   **W&W**

A Bassett Lowke 0-6-0 clockwork locomotive.

9.75in (25cm) long

$450-650   **GAZE**

A CLOSER LOOK AT A TRAIN

Grey is rarer than black, which is a much more common color.

Pre-war trains are harder to find as less examples were made and survive today.

It has a large six-wheel tender, which is unusual as most are around half the size and have four wheels.

This example is in very good condition for a pre-war toy, with only light scratches to the paintwork – this makes it desirable to a collector.

A late 1930s American Lionel Standard gauge locomotive and tender, the tender stamped "392W".
c1937

Locomotive 15.5in (39.5cm) long

$1,000-1,500 **BOM**

A Bassett Lowke LMS electric compound 4-4-0 locomotive and tender.

15.5in (39.5cm) long

$150-250 **GAZE**

A Bassett Lowke O-gauge 4-4-0 A3 Pacific locomotive, with 12-volt center scape pick-up and tender.

20in (51cm) long

$1,000-1,500 **GAZE**

A 4-6-2 12-volt electric locomotive and tender, restored.

22in (56cm) long

$300-400 **GAZE**

A Hornby Dublo 'Caledonian' passenger train set, boxed. Box

20.5in (51.5cm) wide

$150-250 **GAZE**

A Tri-ang R3.A electric model railway, with assorted accessories.

Box 19in (48.5cm) wide

$100-150 **GAZE**

A German Trix 1200 'Der Adler' Set, in excellent condition, in very good condition lidded box.

$100-200 **SAS**

COLLECTORS' NOTES

■ The 'golden age' of the tin sand pail was from the 1930s until around 1960, when the less expensive and more resilient plastic began to take over. Reminiscent of sunny days on sandy beaches, they are popular with nostalgic adults who collect to recall their childhood.

■ All tin pails have lithographed rather than hand-painted designs, colors are typically bright and cheerful and interiors are often plainly decorated in contrasting colors. Prolific makers included the 'Ohio Art Metal', 'US Metal Toys' and T. Cohn as well as notable tinplate toy maker J. Chein.

■ The design and condition are two major indicators for value. Most designs contain children or animals,

often in a beach setting. Look out for patriotic themes or characters, which can add cross-market appeal, leading values to rise. Disney characters and Rosie O'Neil's 'Kewpie' are particularly popular. Other themes such as outer space and circus scenes are also sought-after.

■ As they were made to be used, and most often were, it is very hard to find pails in truly mint condition. Most have dents, dings, or designs that were scratched through contact with sand and days of play. Avoid those that have rusted areas or too much damage, especially if it obscures the design. Mint condition boxed sets including sifters, spades and molds can fetch high sums, sometimes up to $1,000.

A 1950s American lithographed tin sand pail, by US Metal Toys.

A 1950s American lithographed tin sand pail, by Ohio Art Co., artwork by Dan Dean.

5in (12.5cm) high

$30-50   **SOTT**

A 1950s American lithographed tin sand pail, by Ohio Art Company.

7.75in (19.5cm) high

$40-60   **SOTT**

7.5in (19cm) high

$120-180   **SOTT**

A 1950s American lithographed tin sand pail, by T. Cohn.

3.75in (9.5cm) high

$30-50   **SOTT**

An Acme Toys lithographed tin sand pail.

c1960   *5in (12.5cm) high*

$30-50   **DH**

A 1950s American lithographed tin sand pail, by US Metal Toys.

4.75in (12cm) high

$60-80   **SOTT**

A Lilo Product lithographed tin pail.

c1960   *4in (10cm) high*

$30-60   **DH**

TOYS & GAMES

A 1950s American lithographed tin sand pail, by US Metal Toys.

7.5in (19cm) high

$70-100 SOTT

A 1950s American lithographed tin sand pail, by J. Chein.

5.5in (14cm) high

$60-90 SOTT

A 1950s American lithographed tin sand pail, by J. Chein.

Chein, of New York and New Jersey, produced toys from c1903 to 1979. Their tinplate toys are always lithographed and are generally of good quality.

7.25in (18.5cm) high

$70-100 SOTT

A 1940s Happynak Series sand pail.

3.5in (9cm) high

$30-60 DH

A 1950s lithographed tin sand pail, decorated with a flying saucer over a beach.

The theme of space was immensely popular during the 1950s and sand pails with such motifs have cross market appeal and are sought-after, despite the rather incongruous combination of subjects seen here.

5.75in (14.5cm) high

$100-150 DH

A 1950s American lithographed tin sand pail, by US Metal Toys.

4.25in (11cm) high

$80-120 SOTT

An American miniature tin sand pail, with striped decoration.

This pail can be dated to the early 20thC by the plain decoration and the simple metal handle. If the pattern were more complex and appealing and it were larger, it would attract a higher value.

c1900-15   2.75in (7cm) high

$20-30 SOTT

A French embossed lithographed tin sand pail, showing two children on a country road.

This is both an early pail and extremely well decorated. It is also in excellent condition for its age, hence its rarity and corresponding high value.

c1900   5.75in (14.5cm) high

$250-450 DH

FIND OUT MORE...

Sand Pail Encyclopedia: A Complete Value Guide for Tin-litho Sand Toys, by Karen Horman, Polly Minic, published by Hobby House Press, 2002.

COLLECTORS' NOTES

- Being less costly, more versatile and enabling the inclusion of finer details, tinplate had overtaken wood and other materials as material for toys by the mid-19thC. Germany grew to be the center of production, spawning notable names such as Marklin (founded 1856), Gerbruder Bing (1863-1933), Schreyer & Co, known as 'Schuco', (1912-78) and Lehmann (founded 1881). The US also grew to be important with prolific makers including Louis Marx (1896-1912).

- Tinplate made in the 19thC tends to be hand-painted, before the introduction of more cost effective color transfer-printed 'lithography'. This tends to be the most desirable, particularly large models of cars and boats by notable makers. The surface tends to be slightly uneven and brush marks can often be seen. Lithographed surfaces tend to be uniformly flat and shinier.

- After WWII, the center of production moved to the Far East, particularly Japan. Toys became more novelty in format and often included interesting multiple 'mystery actions', including sound. With the introduction of battery power, lights could also be included. Robots are particularly collectible. In the West, developments in injection-molded plastic had taken over in the post war period.

- In all instances, aim to buy examples in as fine condition as possible, particularly post war items which are more numerous and generally less expensive. Additional boxes add value. With items like 'penny toys', small toys sold on late 19thC and early 20thC street corners for one penny, condition is extremely important and a truly mint example will command a considerable premium. Transport toys, particularly elegant cars, planes and zeppelins, tend to be the most desirable forms although novelty figures have an appealing charm that makes them similarly desirable.

An early German tinplate penny toy, in the style of a chauffer driven limousine.

4.5in (11.5cm) wide

$120-180   **W&W**

An early German Georg Fischer tinplate penny toy, in the style of a two draw town sedan, picture of driver to window.

$100-150   **W&W**

An early German tinplate penny toy, in the style of a truck, with driver.

$100-150   **W&W**

An early German tinplate penny toy, in the style of an open limousine, lacks driver.

4.5in (11.5cm) wide

$80-120   **W&W**

A scarce tinplate clockwork military lorry, with driver, canvas rear tilt and simple steering system.

The form and style is very similar to Wells Mettoy.

9.75in (25cm) wide

$250-350   **W&W**

A 1930s German Schuco Examino 4001 clockwork tinplate car.

These forms were also produced after the war.

5.5in (14cm) long

$100-150   **GAZE**

A British GTP lithographed tinplate automatic garage, with three cars and poor condition box.

6in (15cm) wide

$40-70   **GAZE**

A German Schuco lithographed silver tinplate and plastic BMW racing car, signed "BMW Formel 2 260 PS 280 km/h" and model number "1072".

c1969   10in (25cm) long

$100-150   **KAU**

A 1960s Japanese Bandai Cadillac lithographed red tinplate gear shift car, with forward, reverse and neutral gears and 'hi' and 'low' speed action, simple steering mechanism and working front lights, boxed.

10.5in (26.5cm) long

$150-250   **W&W**

A Japanese Masudaya TM Modern Toys tinplate and plastic Boeing 727 aircraft, with battery-operated mechanism.

19in (48.5cm) long

$70-100   **GAZE**

A painted tinplate twin-engine transport aircraft, restored.

20in (51cm) wide

$50-70   **GAZE**

A Lehmann EPL 651 silver-gold and red Airship EPL-1, lacks both stabilizing flaps, in fair to good condition.

$150-250   SAS

A Japanese Haji lithographed tinplate Pan Am Boeing Vertol 707 battery-operated helicopter, with plastic propellers.

Japanese makers often invented or combined elements of design and logos. Surprisingly however, Pan Am did operate shuttle Vertol helicopters.

13in (33cm) long

$120-180   **RBC**

A German tinplate penny toy of a boat, in the style of an early 20th century battleship with naval guns and twin funnels, mounted on three wheels.

3.25in (8.5cm) long

$70-100   **W&W**

An early German tinplate penny toy, in the style of an ocean liner, mounted on three wheels.

4.5in (11.5cm) wide

$120-180   **W&W**

A Sutcliffe Nautilus clockwork lithographed tinplate submarine, marked "Nautilus Copyright Walt Disney Productions", complete with key.

This was produced after Walt Disney's '20,000 Leagues Under the Sea' starring James Mason and Kirk Douglas, and was sold into the 1970s. The body was very similar to Sutcliffe's 'Unda Wunda' submarine toy, but was a different color.

c1954

$50-90   **GAZE**

An American Marx lithographed tinplate clockwork 'Main St', in superb, bright and shiny condition.

Winding up the toy makes the buses and cars go up and down the street, in and out of the garages. Japanese companies produced similar toys, but they are usually smaller and much less detailed.

1927   24in (61cm) long

$1,200-1,800   **TRA**

A late 1920s American Marx 'Busy Bridge' lithographed tinplate clockwork toy.

24in (61cm) long

$500-700   **TRA**

A German Arnold clockwork lithographed tinplate car game 549/1, with a rocket car and looping course, slight damage to original box.

$200-300   **LAN**

An early American Fallows wind-up hand-painted tinplate toy, of two horses, cart and cart rider, lacks string reins.

Fallows was founded in Philadelphia the 1880s and took on the Fallow name in 1894. Their toys were hand-painted and of very fine quality - as such they are much sought-after today. The company closed when lithographed tin toys were introduced during the late 1880s.

c1885   6.25in (16cm) long

$1,500-2,500   **AMJ**

A German Günthermann clock-work handpainted tinplate woman, with an umbrella and basket, partly overpainted and umbrella replaced.

Gunthermann are known for their high quality tinplate toys, often in whimsical forms.

7.25in (18cm) high

$500-900   **LAN**

A German Schuco clockwork police man, marked "Flic 4520, Made in US-Zone Germany'.

c1947   5in (12.5cm) high

$120-180   **GAZE**

A German tinplate clockwork rifleman, in prone position with sparking gun.

4.25in (11cm) long

$150-250   **GAZE**

A 1950s/60s West German Dux Astroman battery-operated plastic robot, lacks antenna and booklet, box with graphics by Arlat.

14in (35.5cm) high

$600-800   **GAZE**

A 1950s Japanese Nomura 'Charley Weaver' lithographed tinplate and rubber bartender.

Nomura, otherwise known as TN, were one of the biggest and most prolific post war Japanese tinplate and plastic toy producers.

12in (30.5cm) high

$30-50 **GAZE**

A West German lithographed tinplate ice cream vendor and tricycle, with composition and tinplate vendor, marked "Made in US-Zone Germany".

c1950 4.25in (11cm) high

$40-60 **GAZE**

A 1920s German Lehmann lithographed tinplate 'Climbing Monkey', with original box.

The box has a US patent date of 1903. The monkey moves up and down the string. Note that reproductions exist, but generally have brighter colors and checked trousers.

$250-450 **GAZE**

A CLOSER LOOK AT A TINPLATE TOY

This is the hardest to find of the 'telephone' series' of tinplate toys.

The lithography is unique and is not found on any other toy from the series.

It is in excellent, working condition and has its even rarer original card box.

It is an appealing subject with good multiple actions - the telephone rings and lights up and the teddy speaks.

A scarce 1950s-60s 'Teddy the Manager' battery powered tinplate toy, retailed by Cragston (S&E), boxed.

$350-550 **W&W**

A 1950s Japanese TPS lithographed tinplate clockwork dog, marked "NGS Made in Japan".

When wound up, this cute puppy's tail spins and his head rocks and ears flap.

5in (12.5cm) high

$90-130 **TRA**

A 1960s Japanese Masudaya TM Modern Toys battery-operated 'Walking Bear' toy, with original box.

11in (28cm) high

$20-30 **GAZE**

A 1950s American Wolverine embossed and lithographed tin watering can, with a merry-go-round scene.

10in (25.5cm) high

$30-40 **SOTT**

COLLECTORS' NOTES

- The first metal soldiers were flat Zinnfiguren manufactured in Germany in the 18thC. One of the first companies to make three-dimensional figures was Paris-based Lucotte.

- William Britain Junior revolutionised the industry in 1893 when he patented his hollow casting process, allowing for the economic manufacture of large numbers of figures.

- Figures with good detail are generally more desirable. Britains soldiers in particular are popular for the authenticity of their uniforms.

- The horrors of WWII meant manufacturer's found that lead soldiers had fallen out of favor with the buying public. Instead, they began to make civilian models, such as fame and zoo sets

- Oxidation is a common problem with lead figures, and, if left unchecked, can destroy fine details and ruin painted finishes, decimating the value of a figure.

- Check figures for lumps and small areas of repainting. This could be a sign of customisation, whereby a figure is amended by replacing its head or making other changes.

- In 1966 the use of lead in children's toys was banned due to its toxicity. Some manufacturers switched to producing plastic figures, and the market for these is growing steadily.

A Britains Hunt in Full Cry set, including three huntsman and four ladies riding side-saddle, 10 chasing hounds and a fox, in good condition.

$600-800   **CHEF**

A Britains Hunt Series The Meet set 1446, mounted huntsman, foot huntsman and huntswoman, together with six hounds, all very good condition.

$150-200   **VEC**

A Britains North American Indians set 208, comprising four mounted and seven foot Indians in various poses, one tomahawk broken, the box with illustrated label, one lid corner repaired.

$550-650   **VEC**

A Britains Prairie Schooner set 2034, comprising green wagon, red wheels, white tin tilt, four-horse team, driver with wife, excellent condition, the box with illustrated label, four lid corners torn.

$800-1,000   **VEC**

Five Britains Knights of Agincourt Foot Knights, various poses, one shield missing, minor paint loss.

$220-280   **VEC**

A Britains Miss Dorothy Paget Racing Colours, excellent condition, in very good condition box.

$550-650   **VEC**

Four Britains American Girl Scouts figures from set 238, in brown uniforms and hats, black stockings, excellent condition.

$400-500   **VEC**

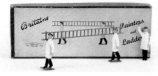

A Britains Painters and Ladder set 1495, comprising two painters with ladder, and a painter with brush, excellent condition, in very good condition box with illustrated label, no insert card.

$700-900   **VEC**

A Britains Royal Artillery Gunners set 313, in original damaged yellow front Whisstock box.

c1928

$180-220 W&W

A Britains African Warriors Zulus Running set 147, comprising eight figures on square beige top bases, with knobkerries or spears to moving right arm, in original box with tie card.

c1948

$180-220 W&W

A CLOSER LOOK AT A BRITAINS SET

This is one of only five or six examples of this set to have come on to the market.

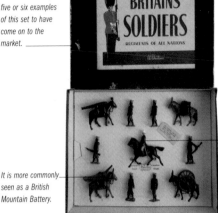

The completeness of the set, the excellent condition of the pieces and the original box help increase the value.

It is more commonly seen as a British Mountain Battery.

Many collectors focus entirely on Britains figures, due to their high quality, accuracy and attention to detail.

A rare Britains Indian Mountain Battery, review order, No 2013, with soldiers and mules, boxed.

$3,200-3,800 W&W

A Britains Argentine Horse Grenadiers set 217, comprising four men with lances, post war painting, in original box.

$100-150 W&W

A Royal Corps of Signals dispatch riders set 1791, comprising four riders on motorcycles, the motorcycles with silver exhaust pipes, on original card in original box.

$320-380 W&W

A scarce Hugar for Britains wooden guard hut, in embossed plywood, wire glazed window, a "Join a Yorkshire Regiment" poster to front, some woodworm holes.

5in (12.5cm) wide

$280-320 W&W

A Britains RAMC 4 horse wagon set 145, with a matt wagon, canvas tilt, collar harness and twisted wire traces, also two stretcher bearers, stretcher, two lying wounded and a nurse in field gray dress with a red cape.

Wagon 11in (28cm) long

$120-180 W&W

A scarce Britains Army Staff car set 1448, with plastic tyred wheels, removable officer passenger and driver casting, with original box with picture lid.

4.25in (10.75cm) long

$320-380 W&W

A Taylor & Barrett Llama Ride, comprising of two wheeled cart, four children, llama and keeper, all very good condition, in original box with illustrated label.

$320-380 VEC

A Taylor & Barrett Wild West Wagon, yellow, red wheels, canvas tilt, driver and two seated women passengers, together with a cowgirl on horseback.

$220-280 VEC

A Taylor & Barrett Brewers Dray, comprising four wheeled dray, gray horse, seat, driver with whip, end broken, Watney's sign replaced, loading ladder and five barrels, some repainting.

$220-280 VEC

A Taylor & Barrett window cleaner, with cart, ladder and bucket, and a bread cart, yellow, red wheels, cream roof, delivery man and basket, both in very good condition.

$280-320 VEC

A Taylor & Barrett donkey ride, two donkeys, two donkeys colts, tethering post with sign, child rider and keeper, together with two parrots on gray stand, all very good condition.

$220-280 VEC

A Taylor & Barrett A.F.S. pump, with hose and two frogmen, blue suits, green helmets, together with chimps tea party, white table, three chairs, three chimpanzees, all good to very good condition.

$280-320 VEC

A Taylor & Barrett donkey ride, comprising donkey hut, two donkey stands with '2d all the way' signs, two donkeys, three donkeys colts, one child rider, keeper, mainly good to very good condition.

$320-380 VEC

Three Taylor & Barrett Air Raid Precautions figures, man carrying two buckets, woman with bucket and stirrup pump, and woman holding hose, all very good condition.

$180-220 VEC

An F.G. Taylor & Sons costermonger's donkey cart set, complete with walking costermonger holding a cauliflower and a basket, two bunches of bananas, two turnips, two carrots and a marrow, good condition, unboxed.

$150-200 DN

A rare 1930s Crescent deep sea diver, part of set NN692, with a gray dive suit, gold-painted removable helmet, elastic airline and air distribution set finished in red, tools missing.

Although part of a larger set, this figure is hard to find with the helmet and air distribution set as they were often lost.

$80-120   W&W

A Crescent Cowboys and Indians display set, comprising of 11 figures, all very good in poor illustrated box, old repairs and tears to lid.

$120-180   VEC

A Crescent Farm Animals set, nine animals, feeding trough, farm girl with bucket, farmer with pitchfork, in illustrated box, corners torn, one lid edge partially missing.

$50-80   VEC

A collection of Crescent Civilian issue figures, including seat with grandma and grandad, milkmaid, nurse, woman customer, man with oilcan, farm girl with bucket, kneeling nurse, porter, woman shopper, farmer with broken pitchfork, milkmaid with stool and gorilla, all in mainly good condition.

$80-120   VEC

A John Hill four-wheeled cattle float, gray with red wheels, includes seated drover and brown horse, in very good condition.

$150-200   VEC

Five John Hill wedding figures, comprising vicar, bride, groom, bridesmaid, further bride figure in blue, no detail painted, some paint loss to bride in white.

$180-220   VEC

A John Hill miniature hunting series, comprising huntsman standing beside horse, mounted huntsman, mounted huntswoman, huntswoman standing with hound, three hounds, in illustrated box.

$320-380   VEC

Six John Hill racehorses with jockeys, in various colors, one head broken, one horse's leg broken.

$80-120   VEC

A Star Wars - The Power of the Force 'Anakin Skywalker' action figure, by Palitoy.

The older version figure of Anakin Skywalker was only produced for a short period of time. In the US it was only available as a loose figure via a mail-in offer. All carded figures were released outside of the US on either a Power of the Force or tri-logo card.

1985   4in (10cm) high

$35-45   KNK

A rare Star Wars - Power of the Force 'Amanaman' action figure, lacks skull staff.

First released on a Power of the Force card and then on a tri-logo card, this figure is desirable in any condition, particularly in the US where it is harder to find.

A rare Star Wars - Return of the Jedi 'Lumat' action figure, with bow and unpainted face.

On this rare variation, the face is unpainted. Standard complete figures are worth around $20.

A Star Wars - The Empire Strikes Back 'Bossk' action figure.

This rare variation has an unpainted arm, a standard loose example would be worth under $20.

c1980   4in (10cm) high

$220-280   KNK

c1984   2.75in (7cm) high

$220-280   KNK

c1985   4.25in (10.5cm) high

$60-90   KNK

A Micromachines Star Wars 'Rebel Blockade Runner', by Galoob.

These were only sold in boxed sets and were not available individually.

c1995   2.25in (6cm) long

$3-4   KNK

A Micromachines Star Wars - Return of the Jedi 'Speeder Bike with Rebel Pilot'.

c1996   1.75in (4.5cm) long

$3-4   KNK

A Star Wars 'Heroes' Super Sonic Power van, gyro-powered with 'Blazin' Action'.

A similarly incongruous Darth Vadar themed van, worth the same, was also produced.

1978   7.25in (18.5cm) long

$50-80   NOR

A Star Wars - The Power Of The Force (II) 'Greedo' carded action figure.

This is the first version released under the Power of the Force (II) banner, and the most desirable.

9in (22.5cm) high

$10-15   KNK

A Star Wars - The Power of The Force (II) 'TIE Fighter Pilot' carded action figure.

This figure was first issued with the 'small parts' warning on a sticker. Later versions have the warning printed directly onto the card. The first version, shown above, is worth about twice as much as the second version.

1995   9in (22.5cm) high

$10-15   KNK

A 19thC English small bone playing chess set, one side stained red, the other side left natural, in a wooden box with a sliding lid.

the king 2.25in (5.5cm) high

$120-180   **BLO**

A unusual 19thC boxwood and ebony old English pattern chess set, the kings with interesting finials, in a mahogany box with a sliding lid.

the king 3in (7.5cm) high

$280-320   **BLO**

A unusual 19thC Jaques Staunton 'colored' ivory chess set, one side stained yellow, the other side stained green, the yellow king stamped "Jaques London" on the underside of the base, in a mahogany box with a green label.

This is an extremely unusual color for an ivory set by Jaques. There appears to be no trace of any previous staining, so it can be assumed that the set was dyed at its time of manufacture. One possibility is that this set was used as a prototype to discover the effect of other dye colors apart from the more usual cochineal red then in use.

the king 2.75in (7cm) high

$2,200-2,800   **BLO**

An Irish boxwood and ebony chess set, possibly Dublin, kings with baluster knops and elongated tops with concave finials, queens with large ball finials, bishops with tulip shaped tops, knights as carved horse's heads, rooks as castles with ramparts and reeded decoration, pawns with baluster knops and ball finials, in a mahogany box with a sliding lid.

c1850   *the king 3in (7.5cm) high*

$500-700   **BLO**

A cast pewter chess set, one side in polished pewter, the other side with an oxidised finish, king topped with crowns and crosses and with multi-knopped columns, queens similar, but of smaller size, bishops with ball finials, knights as horses' heads, rooks as turrets, pawns with baluster knops and ball finials, in a wooden box.

c1930   *the king 4in (10cm) high*

$500-700   **BLO**

A cast lead 'Rose' chess set, painted red and black, some flaking to paintwork, the design based on the popular Staunton set and patented by Mildred Rose.

1942   *the king 2in (5cm) high*

$60-80   **BLO**

An English ceramic chess set, one side with a brown glaze, the other side a creamy brown color, the pieces signed "JU", together with a mahogany and satin-birch chess board.

c1970   *the king 3.5in (9cm) high*

$280-320   **BLO**

A late 19thC German 'Régence' style boxwood and ebonised chess set, in a wooden box with a sliding lid, the pieces wrapped in original light pink waxed paper.

the king 3in (7.5cm) high

$320-380   **BLO**

A late 19thC unusual hardwood chess set, possibly German, one side a chesnut brown, the other side dark brown or black, the set of an unusual pattern and design.

Note the Germanic picklehaube 'helmeted' knights and the almost Islamic type pawns.

the king 3.75in (9.5cm) high

$1,000-1,500   **BLO**

A CLOSER LOOK AT A CHESS SET

Max Esser (1885-1943) was born in Pomerania, and studied at the Berlin Academy under August Gaul, before joining Meissen as a designer.

Despite being in delicate porcelain, it is undamaged. Each piece is skilfully hand-painted and gilded, with fine details typical of Meissen.

This famous set was designed in 1923, and would have been expensive to buy.

This set appeals to collectors of Meissen figures as well as chess sets.

A 20thC Meissen porcelain 'Sea Life' chess set, designed by Max Esser, one side a coral color, the other side grey and white, kings and queens as sea anemones, bishops as lobsters, knights as sea horses, rooks as octopi, pawns as starfish, with Meissen underglaze crossed swords mark in blue.

the king 3.25in (8cm) high

$15,000-20,000   **BLO**

A 19thC Swiss pearwood 'Bear of Berne' chess set with a nice patination, contained in a 19thC wooden box.

The many different and charming poses, finely carved fruit wood and small details such as crowns make this set sought after.

the king 3.25in (8.5cm) high

$3,200-3,800   **BLO**

A 20thC Portuguese Vista Alegre handpainted porcelain figural chess set, modeled as Medieval Christians versus Moors.

Such religious or political historical themes are typical during the 20thC

the king 4.25in (11cm) high

$2,800-3,200   **BLO**

A scarce Czech Republic silver and silver-gilt 'Selenus' pattern chess set, marks for Prague, duty mark for 1810-1824.

This pattern was first seen in "Chess or the King's game" published in 1616 under the assumed name of 'Gustavus Selenus'.

c1815   *the king 2.25in (6cm) high*

$5,000-7,000   **BLO**

A 20thC Italian silver metal heraldic bust chess set, one side with darker, oxidised bases, each piece decorated with coats of arms and stamped '900' and with 'S P' maker's mark.

the king 3in (7cm) high

$1,800-2,200   **BLO**

A mid-20thC Italian olive wood chess set, probably from Sorrento, one side lacquered black, together with a Sorrento inlaid wooden chess board of a later date.

king 2.25in (5.5cm) high

$500-700   **BLO**

A early/mid-19thC Cantonese Chinese export ivory 'puzzleball' chess set, modeled as the Chinese versus the Mongols, all raised on puzzleball bases.

the king 5in (13cm) high

$400-600 BLO

A fine Cantonese Chinese export ivory figural 'King George' chess set, modeled as the Chinese versus the Europeans, white king and queen as George III and Queen Charlotte, bishops as Christian bishops, knights as archer horsemen, rooks as elephants, pawns as footsoldiers, all raised on oval gadrooned bases.

c1810 *the king 5.5in (14cm) high*

$3,000-4,000 BLO

A fine Cantonese Chinese export ivory 'King George' chess set, the kings as King George III, queens as Queen Charlotte, bishops as clergy, knights as rearing horses, rooks as elephants bearing towers, pawns as footsoldiers with shields and raised spears.

Green staining on Cantonese chess sets is unusual, the more common color usually being red. Another rare feature of this set is that there are two European monarch kings and two consort queens. The style of carving on both sides is identical, so we can be sure that this is a complete set from one workshop. This is thus a desirable and valuable example.

c1800 *the king 5in (12.5cm) high*

$3,000-5,000 BLO

A Cantonese Chinese export 'Burmese' style chess set, the kings and queens with with foliate carved, pierced finials.

Although this set shows some similarities to Indian sets and the so-called 'Burmese' patterns, it is more likely to have been produced in Canton.

c1820 *the king 3.25in (8.5cm) high*

$400-600 BLO

A early 19thC Chinese export painted ivory 'King George' chess set, modeled as the Europeans versus the Chinese, the European king and queen as George III and Queen Charlotte and the bishops as mandarins.

the king 4.5in (11.5cm) high

$1,200-1,800 BLO

An early 19thC Cantonese 'Burmese' pattern chess set of large size with extensive finely carved foliate decoration, one red pawn replaced, loss to white queen's filigree top, in a mahogany box.

the king 5.5in (14cm) high

$1,800-2,200 BLO

A 20thC Chinese hardwood 'puzzleball' chess set, from Hong Kong, one side in boxwood, the other side in coromandel, all the chessmen with puzzleball knops, in a chip-carved wooden box with a hinged lid.

the king 6in (15.5cm) high

$120-180 BLO

A 19thC Cantonese export Staunton-pattern ivory chess set.

the king 4in (10cm) high

$1,200-1,800 BLO

A 20thC Japanese rock crystal and obsidian chess set, with bishops as mitres, knights as horses' heads and rooks as turrets.

king 2.25in (6cm) high

$200-300 BLO

A 19thC Anglo-Indian Staunton-pattern ivory chess set, one side stained red, the other side left natural, in a mahogany box with a sliding lid.

the king 2.75in (7cm) high

$600-800   **BLO**

An Indian-export ivory chess set, from Vizagapatnam, each piece with extensive carved foliate and floral decoration, the brown king missing the upper half.

c1810   *the king 5.25in (13.5cm) high*

$1,200-1,800   **BLO**

An Indian ivory chess set, from Vizagapatnam, the pieces with elaborate and extensive carved decoration, kings with ruff collars and elongated spires, queens similar, but with shorter finials, bishops as mitres with crosses, knights as horses' heads over elaborately decorated circular bases, rooks as raised turrets with flags, pawns with spires, in a mahogany box with a sliding lid.

the king 5.5in (14cm) high

$1,500-2,000   **BLO**

A 19thC Indian export ivory chess set, the kings with pierced tops and spray finials over nautical crown collars, queens with bud finials, bishops with feathered mitres, knights as horses' heads, rooks as rusticated turrets with spire finials, pawns with baluster knops, in a mahogany, ivory and boxwood inlaid box.

the king 3in (7.5cm) high

$500-700   **BLO**

An Indian ivory 'Elephant' chess set, from Rajhasthan, one side with black stained bases, the other side left natural, kings as elephants with covered howdahs, queens as elephants with a prince in the howdah, bishops as camels, knights as horse, rooks as elephants, pawns as footsoldiers, in a blue presentation case.

c1950   *the king 2.75in (7cm) high*

$300-400   **BLO**

An Anglo-Indian monobloc ivory chess set, the kings with baluster knops and reeded urn-shaped finials, queens with baluster knops and ball finials, bishops with elegant split mitres, knights as horses' heads, rooks as turrets with battlements, pawns with ball finials.

c1820   *the king 3.25in (8.5cm) high*

$1,200-1,800   **BLO**

A 20thC Indian carved stone chess set, the kings with pierced crowns, queens similar, bishops with further pierced decoration and elongated finials, knights as horses' heads, rooks as turrets, pawns with domes, together with a wooden box .

the king 2.75in (7cm) high

$70-100   **BLO**

A Northern Indian so called 'Muslim' ivory chess set, one side with green stained rings to the base, the other red.

Research suggests strongly that these 'Muslim' sets were in fact, as much an ancient Hindu pattern used in North India.

c1930   *the king 2.25in (5.5cm) high*

$250-350   **BLO**

An American Native American Indian girl 'roly poly' papier-mâché figure.

4.25in (11cm) high

$180-220   **TRA**

An American policeman 'roly poly' papier-mâché figure.

4.5in (11.5cm) high

$250-350   **TRA**

An American black gentleman 'roly poly' papier-mâché figure.

This example would also be desirable to collectors of black Americana and memorabilia and is rarer than many other characters.

6in (15cm) high

$600-800   **TRA**

A Hasbro G.I. Joe 'Air Adventurer' action figure, in mint condition complete with clothes and accessories and with his original box.

'Action Team' Adventurer or Explorer characters were introduced c1970 with the intention of taking G.I. Joe away from the unpopular themes of war and soldiers following the Vietnam war. This example is especially valuable because he is in mint condition and complete with his original box.

c1971

12in (30.5cm) high

$250-350   **NOR**

A 1970s Hasbro G.I. Joe action figure, with flock hair and original orange suit.

11.5in (29cm) high

$25-35   **KNK**

A late 1970s Hasbro G.I. Joe 'Action Team' action figure, with 'Kung Fu' grip, flock hair and speaking mechanism operated by pulling a tag.

The 'Kung Fu' grip was introduced in 1974.

11.5in (29cm) high

$80-120   **MEM**

A late 1960s Hasbro G.I. Joe action figure, with molded plastic hair.

G.I. Joe was introduced in 1964. Molded plastic hair is early, dating from before the introduction of 'life-like' flock hair in 1970.

11.5in (29.5cm) high

$80-120   **MEM**

An American Banthrico die-cast metal 'Futurmatic' concept promotional automobile money bank, painted in red with silver details, in near mint condition.

This is a visually stunning model money bank, with superb period styling.

8in (20cm) long

$120-180   **BER**

An American Thomas Toys red plastic convertible toy car.

$12-18   **BH**

An American F&F blue plastic Mercury toy car.

3in (7.5cm) long

$40-50   **BH**

An American Auburn Rubber Corp. red painted hard rubber streamlined car, the underside marked "Made in Auburn" in a round circle logo.

5in (12.5cm) long

$40-50   **MEM**

An American Auburn Rubber Corp blue hard rubber lorry.

5.25in (13.5cm) long

$40-50   **MEM**

A View-Master picture disc of 'Death Valley', by GAF Corp., packet no. A203.

4.5in (11.5cm) wide

$6-10   **BH**

A View-Master picture disc of 'Scenic USA', by GAF Corp., packet no. A996.

4.5in (11.5cm) wide

$7-10   **BH**

A CLOSER LOOK AT A BOARD GAME

Freedomland was a theme park in Baychester, The Bronx, New York, that was founded by ex-Disney employee Cornelius Wood. It opened in 1960 and promised to be the 'Disneyland of the East'.

Costing $65million to build, it was based on the history of the US, and was even shaped like the US, with visitors entering through Washington, DC.

After a number of unfortunate events, a lack of public support and a misguided change in direction to attract more young people, the park closed amidst much controversy in 1964. As such, memorabilia is comparatively scarce.

Dating from the early part of the park's opening and covering the original historical theme, this example is complete with all its parts and in mint condition, which makes this historic piece of theme park memorabilia even more desirable.

An American Pressman Toy Corp. 'Freedomland' board game, complete with original box and in mint condition.

Since 1969, the Freedomland site has been occupied by a residential housing project, which is also the largest single residential development in the US.

1960

18in (44.5cm) wide

$150-200   **MEM**

COLLECTORS' NOTES

- Kachina dolls are made by the Hopi tribe of north-easten Arizona in south-west America. With a rich artistic heritage and a commitment to traditional ways, the tribe is known for its skill in hand-crafting pottery, basketry and jewelry.

- Although referred to as 'dolls', Kachina dolls were originally intended as spiritual icons. The wooden figures represented Kachina helper deities and were used to teach children religious beliefs and spiritual ancestry. Represented deities include Hututu – a spirit of nature who takes his name from the cry he makes – as well as hundreds of others.

- Dolls are typically made from cottonwood and could be adorned with fur, feathers, leather and cloth. Carvers continue to make the figures today.

- The Zuni people made similar dolls, but these can be distinguished by their slender, elongated form and articulated arms.

A rare early 1900s Iroquois stuffed cornhusk mother and child kachina doll, with bead trimmed dress and leggings, black wrap shawl, and buckskin moccasins.

17in (43cm) high

$800-1,000   **ALL**

A very rare Canadian Cree hand-made hide kachina doll, with beaded face, gloves, and moccasins.

c1930   *13in (33cm) high*

$350-450   **ALL**

A traditional hand-carved and painted kachina doll, of cottonwood, labeled "Mudhead Clown Kachina".

c1930s/50s 7.5in (19cm) high

$180-220   **ALL**

A hand-carved and painted cottonwood root kachina doll, marked "Koyemsi, Mudhead Clown".

c1970s/80s 14in (35cm) high

$180-220   **ALL**

A late 1900s hand-carved and painted cottonwood root kachina doll, marked "Owl Kachina".

12.5in (31.5cm) high

$120-180   **ALL**

A hand-carved and painted cottonwood root kachina doll, marked "Puchkof-Moktaqa (Scorpion)".

c1970s/80s   *12in (30cm) high*

$180-220   **ALL**

A hand-carved and painted cottonwood root kachina doll, marked "Left Handed Kachina".

c1970s/80s 14in (35cm) high

$80-120   **ALL**

A large 'Clown' hand-carved and painted kachina doll, by B. Largo.

c1976   *14in (35cm) high*

$450-550   **ALL**

A Hopi one-piece 'White Wolf' kachina doll, with excellent detail.

c1980   13in (33cm) high

$150-200   ALL

A traditional hand-carved and painted kachina doll, of cottonwood, labeled "Gambler Kachina".

c1930s/50s   11in (27cm) h

$400-500   ALL

A traditional hand-carved and painted kachina doll, of cottonwood, labeled "Soyal Solstice Kachina".

c1930s/50s 9.5in (24cm) high

$350-450   ALL

A hand-carved and painted cottonwood root kachina doll, marked "Lung-Hair, Ang-Ak-China".

c1970s/80s 12in (30cm) high

$70-100   ALL

A hand-carved and painted cottonwood root kachina doll, marked "Solstice Kachina, Ahulani".

c1970s/80s 14in (35cm) high

$60-90   ALL

A Hopi 'Cow' kachina doll, with horns, headdress, and longbow.

c1960   12in (30cm) high

$120-180   ALL

A hand-carved and painted cottonwood root kachina doll, marked "Tawa (Sun Kachina)".

c1970s/80s 18in (45cm) high

$200-250   ALL

A late 1900s hand-carved cottonwood root 'Revival' kachina doll, decorated with pigment paints.

13in (33cm) high

$120-180   ALL

A late 1900s hand-carved cottonwood root 'Revival' kachina doll, decorated with pigment paints.

17.5in (44.5cm) high

$150-200   ALL

COLLECTORS' NOTES

■ Tribal art is the term used to describe the cultural, ritual and functional production of the indigenous peoples of Africa, Oceania, South East Asia and the Americas. As such, it was primarily made for actual use, rather than for purely aesthetic appreciation.

■ Pieces are collected not only for their deep historical and ethnographic significance, but also for their immense visual impact when displayed in today's eclectic interiors. Many items deal with core human themes such as life and death, fertility and spiritual beliefs. Not all tribes made the same items, and many collectors choose to focus on one notable subject, such as West African masks, Navajo weavings or Southwestern American pottery.

■ Key indicators to value are age and provenance. Older pieces with a verifiable history are generally the most valuable, particularly if they were collected from the

area they originated in before the early 20thC. Wear and use adds patination, which is another good sign to look for, but handle as many original pieces from reputable dealers or auction houses as possible, as this patina can be faked.

■ Most pieces found on the market today date from the late 19thC or 20thC onwards. The fact that pieces were used regularly, combined with the extreme climates of many countries, mean that many older pieces have decayed or been destroyed.

■ Interest in the market has risen greatly in the past decade with the upper end of the market being highly priced and the preserve of experienced and wealthy collectors. However, as so many pieces were produced, particularly in the 20thC, and for the tourist market rather than for use, a great many more people can gain access to this exciting and developing field.

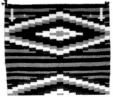

A Navajo rug from the Ganado area, in diamond step pattern with crosses.

Geometric patterns are typical of most Navajo weavings and were one of the earliest designs used. Early blankets were made to be worn.

A Navajo 'Teec Nos Pos' woven tapestry, in 14 different colors.

c1980   *27in (68.5cm) high*

$280-320   **ALL**

c1980   *33in (84cm) wide*

$150-200   **ALL**

A Navajo natural colored hand-spun wool weaving, from the Two Gray Hills area.

c1970   *32in (34.5cm) wide*

$220-280   **ALL**

A 20thC Southwest Navajo pictorial weaving, in natural and commercially dyed homespun wool, with central cornstalk with various colored birds and feathers, bordered on length with serrated triangles.

A 20thC Southwest Navajo pictorial weaving, with natural and commercially dyed homespun yarns, depicting seven multicolored Yei figures on a white ground with two-color border.

A Yei is a Navajo spiritual or holy figure.

                    59in (147.5cm) wide

$1,500-2,000   **SK**

A Navajo tapestry, by Gladys Tsosie from Kayenta, Arizona.

Navajo pictorial rugs tend to date from the 20thC, and were designed to appeal to tourists and the commercial market. Motifs include elements important to the Navajo lifestyle such as corn, livestock and birds.

                    53in (132.5cm) long

$2,200-2,800   **SK**

c1980   *27in (68.5cm) wide*

$70-100   **ALL**

A Southwest coiled basketry bowl, the flared form with braided rim, a bold eight-point star at the base, and radiating stepped devices.

c1900   15.5in (37.5cm) diam

$1,800-2,200   **SK**

A CLOSER LOOK AT A BASKET

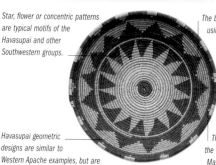

Star, flower or concentric patterns are typical motifs of the Havasupai and other Southwestern groups.

The black areas are created using cane made from the long seed pods of the 'Black Devil's Claw'. The seeds from this annual flowering plant are highly nutritious.

Havasupai geometric designs are similar to Western Apache examples, but are generally less complex.

This example came from the Wistariahurst Museum, Massachusetts, so has an identified provenance.

An early 20thC Southwest Havasupai coiled basketry shallow bowl, with bold black geometric designs.

The Havasupai tribe are based in the Havasupai Reservation, Arizona.

11.5in (29cm) diam

$1,200-1,800   **SK**

A Native American river cane square-section double trinket basket, from the Chitimacha tribe.

Both the form and patterns of this example are typical of the tribe's work.

c1910   5in (12.5cm) wide

$800-1,200   **D&G**

A Southwest pottery olla, with concave base and black and red geometric and abstract floral devices, cream-colored background.

This olla is from the San Ildefonso village, birthplace of renowned Southwest potter Maria Martinez.

c1900   11in (27.5cm) diam

$2,200-2,800   **SK**

A Southwest pottery olla, from San Ildefonso, with concave base with black and red geometric and abstract floral devices on a cream-colored ground.

c1900   12in (30cm) diam

$2,500-3,000   **SK**

A Native American Pueblo pottery bowl, depicting 'Thunderbird', from the Jeddito tribe.

'Thunderbird' is a powerful bird spirit associated with natural forces such as wind, thunder and lightning. The 'spirit line' on the interior of this bowl is broken so as to allow the spirit of the bird to escape.

8.25in (21cm) diam

$1,200-1,800   **D&G**

A late 19thC Central Plains Lakota tribe quilled pictorial cloth and hide vest, partially quilled with multicolored floral and American flag devices on the front, the back with two horses, flags, and abstract floral devices, further decorated with multicolored ribbons and metallic sequins.

22in (55cm) long

$2,000-3,000   **SK**

A late 19thC Central Plains Lakota tribe beaded boy's vest, of buffalo hide with some cloth trim, fully beaded with multicolored geometric devices on a white ground.

From the Wistariahurst Museum, MS.

19in (47.5cm) long

$2,200-2,800 SK

A mid-19thC Great Lakes crescent-shaped feathered cape, with two long tabs down the front, feather tufts on the inside, the outside with various domesticated bird feathers sewn on in a bold geometric pattern.

Feathered clothing is fragile and highly susceptible to discoloration, damage and wear.

26in (65cm) wide

$2,200-2,800 SK

An early 20thC Plains painted wood and hide drum, both sides painted with red 'sunburst' variations, together with a drum beater.

18in (45cm) diam

$800-1,000 SK

An Inuit carved wood mask, with high cheekbones and pierced at the mouth, nostrils, and eyes.

Inuit is the generally accepted modern description for the Alaska, Canada, Greenland, and Eastern Russia-based peoples formerly known as Eskimoes. However, not all groups refer to themselves as 'Inuit' and pieces produced up to the mid-20thC, before the term Inuit was in general use, are often still referred to as 'Eskimo'. The term Inuit will be used here throughout for consistency.

10.5in (26cm) high

$1,500-2,000 SK

A 20thC Inuit carved wood mask, the hollow stylized form with pierced mouth and protruding upper lip, large cheeks, and brow with small pierced eyes and large pierced nostrils.

As there were few or no trees, wooden masks, often representing influential ancestral figures or spirits, were often made from driftwood.

10in (25cm) high

$1,500-2,000 SK

An early 20thC Inuit polychrome carved wood mask, pierced at the mouth, nostrils, and eyes, with traces of red pigment at the mouth, overall white pigment, label on the back reads "Eskimo, St. Michaels, Kuskokwim Alaska."

The terrifying or malevolent appearance of many Inuit masks is due to the fact that Inuit saw many spirits as a constant menace in their perilous world.

8in (20cm) high

$3,500-4,500 SK

An early 20thC Inuit polychrome carved wood mask, in the form of a walrus, with pierced mouth, nostrils, and eyes, wood whisker inserts, painted with brick red pigment, black and white kaolin details, collection label on the back reads "Nonivagmiut Eskimo, Nunivak Island, Alaska".

9in (22.5cm) high

$2,000-2,500 SK

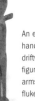

A late 20thC North West Coast hand-carved Tlingit-style revival carving of a fighting figure, with dagger.

18in (46cm) high

$70-100 ALL

An early 20thC Inuit hand-carved driftwood fetish, of a figure with flipper arms and whale fluke nose.

8in (20cm) high

$250-350 ALL

An unusual 20thC African hand-carved hardwood figure of a shaman, with an effigy staff and other adornments.

20in (51cm) high

$150-200   ALL

An African Songye carved wood house charm, holding a figure in its arms, embellished with strips of metal, shells and nails and wearing a lizard skin loin cloth, the hollow antelope horn on its head containing 'magical' substances and with a separate figure tied to each shoulder.

Such fetishistic magical materials are known as 'Bishimba'. This figure would have been used to protect a village from death and disease.

67in (170cm) high

$1,500-2,000   RTC

Five African Yoruba carved wood Ibeji dolls, comprising three male and two female images, three with trade bead attachments.

Ibeji dolls are the best known Yoruba figures and represent deceased twins. They are treated almost like living children and are honored with prayers and libations.

11in (28cm) high

$300-400   SK

A mid-20thC African Yoruba Ifa tapper instrument.

Ifa is the divination system used by the Yoruba tribe. The tapper is used at the start of the riutal where a bowl is tapped rhythmically to invoke the presence of past diviners and of Ifa, the god of divination, to help with the subsequent predictions.

8in (20cm) high

$100-150   OHA

Two African carved wood staffs, one with small breasts, brass tacked eyes, and elaborate coiffure, the other with stylized facial features and elongated head, dark patinas, both with stands.

30in (75cm) high

$350-450   SK

An unusual African Zulu War-period knobkerry, with flared hardwood shaft, egg-shaped head and a good patina.

27in (68.5cm) long

$500-600   W&W

An African Yoruba carved wood helmet mask, the hollow form with pronounced facial features, pierced eyes and elaborate coiffure.

14in (35cm) high

$1,000-1,500   SK

An African Dan carved wood 'Gaegon' mask, with large protruding beak, the articulated lower jaw with animal hair covering, pierced slit eyes, with dark patina from use.

Gaegon masks are used for singing and dancing during village festivals which, today, are performed for tourists.

9in (22.5cm) high

$1,200-1,800   SK

A 19thC African carved gourd container.

Although it looks like a dropper bottle, this is actually used for inserting laxative enemas made from berries!

5in (12.5cm) high

$400-800   WJT

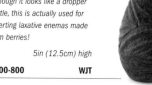

An early 20thC headhunter's rattan hat, with bird's beak and additional embellishments, from the Bontoc/Igorot people of the North Phillipines.

10in (25.5cm) high

$2,000-3,000 **WJT**

An early 20thC headhunter's rattan hat, decorated with a bird's beak and head, from the Highlands of Burma, India.

9in (23cm) long

$600-900 **WJT**

A 19thC human tooth trophy necklace, from the Kiribati (previously known as Gilbert Islands), South Pacific.

31in (78.5cm) long

$2,000-3,000 **WJT**

A mid-20thC New Guinea polychrome carved wood headdress, the conical form in the shape of a face with stylized painted features, the rattan headband with feather remnants.

16in (40cm) high

$180-220 **SK**

A late 19thC Maori carved hardwood 'Taiaha', one end in the form of a stylized effigy head with protruding tongue and abalone inlaid eyes.

The Taiaha club, with its paddle-shaped, tapering blade, was one of the main Maori weapons. Due to its shape it is often mistaken for a spear, with an ornately carved end.

38in (95cm) long

$1,500-2,000 **SK**

An early/mid-20thC wooden spear with metal tip, decorated with animal skin, from the Naga Tribe, in the Highlands of Burma and India.

65in (165cm) long

$400-600 **WJT**

A pair of Vietnamese tribal beaded woven-fibre trousers and a bag, with elaborated beaded and embroidered cuffs, the bag with elaborate finger-woven multicolored geometric beadwork and brass bell attachments.

Pants 20in (50cm) long

$1,200-1,800 **SK**

An Indonesian Pua woven textile.

Pua textiles are woven primarily by the Iban tribe of Sarawak, Boreo. There are a number of different types including the pua sungit, pua kumbo and pua karab.

$250-350 **SK**

An early 20thC Asian hand-carved and painted monkey mask, of ironwood or similar hard wood.

8.5in (21.5cm) high

$45-55 **ALL**

COLLECTORS' NOTES

■ The past two years has seen a popular revival in wristwatches, partly led by fashion magazines and TV programs promoting a smarter look for men. This has prompted many to invest in a fine quality vintage watch. As well as being inherited or received as gifts, vintage watches are also found at dealers' shops, auctions, shows and flea markets.

■ The style of a watch can help you to date it, although vintage styles are popular with today's makers. Small, round 'pocket watch' like shapes with wire lugs are usually early 20thC. Rectangular watches, or simple circular watches with clean-lined designs are usually from the 1930s. From the late 1940s onwards, watches became highly stylized and more innovative in shape, often taking on the styles of contemporary jewelry.

■ Simple, classic styles, particularly from the 1930s and '50s are popular today. Fine quality watches by names such as Rolex or Longines can often be found at lower prices than contemporary examples, sometimes even in precious metals. 1960s and '70s watches are particularly in vogue with many of today's watchmakers copying these styles. Cases tend to be large and heavy, with futuristic designs and use of stainless steel, color and plastic.

■ The brand, movement, materials and functions of a watch will help indicate its value. Leading brands, such as Patek Philippe, are highly sought-after and within a brand certain 'iconic' models will be more desirable, such as Cartier's 'Tank'. The quality of the movement is important and should be correct for that particular watch. The more complex the watch is, the more valuable it is likely to be. Most prices given here are taken from the 'World Wide Traders Mark Room Floor'.

A WWI Rolex military silver wristwatch, with 15-jewel movement.

The shape of this watch clearly shows how early wristwatches were derived from pocket watches. Watches of this period often have narrow straps.

1.5n (3.5cm) diam

$600-700   **GHOU**

An early 1920s Rolex gold-plated ladies' wristwatch, the white porcelain dial with painted red "12".

Although neither the movement nor the dial are signed, the case is usual for Rolex watches of this time.

$850-950   **ML**

A 1930s Art Deco Rolex elongated rectangular gent's wristwatch, with 17-jewel movement, seconds dial and platinum curved case.

1.75in (4.5cm) long

$7,500-10,000   **ML**

A 1930s Rolex Precision 14ct rose gold-cased wristwatch, with 17-jewel movement, in mint condition.

$900-1,200   **ML**

A Rolex 'Oyster Perpetual Explorer' gentleman's stainless steel bracelet watch.

1.25in (3.5cm) diam

$2,800-3,200   **GHOU**

A 1950s Tudor Oyster shockproof wristwatch, with dated presentation engraving to back

Tudor has been a sub-brand of Rolex since 1945. Although Tudor movements have fewer jewels than Rolex watches, the same Oyster case is used.

1959

$400-600   **BLO**

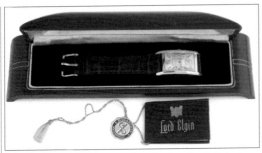

A 1930s Lord Elgin 14ct white gold gentleman's wristwatch, with 23-jewel movement, diamond-set dial, complete with original Art Deco Bakelite box and swingtags.

Lord Elgin denotes higher end watches by Elgin, with 23-jewel movements. This is indicated by the precious metal case and diamond-set dial on this watch.

$800-1,200   **ML**

A 1930s Elgin wristwatch, with 17-jewel movement, 14ct solid green gold cambered case and radium hands and numbers.

It is more unusual for watches to be made of gold in colors other than yellow, such as green or pink.

An early transitional Elgin wristwatch, with stainless steel case, the dial set at 90 degrees.

This watch is unusual due to the unusually set dial. It is also transitional, meaning both pendant wound and key wound.

c1920

A 1950s Lady Elgin cocktail wristwatch, with 14ct white gold case and unusual conical top winding knob.

A 1950s Lord Elgin 'Dunbar' asymmetric gold-filled cased wristwatch, with 23-jewel movement.

$300-500   **ML**   **$250-350**   **ML**   **$100-170**   **ML**   **$220-350**   **ML**

A 1950s Elgin 19 wristwatch, with 19-jewel movement, gold-filled case, angled lugs and second dial.

The case style with angled lugs here is known as 'horned'

A Lord Elgin gold-filled wristwatch, with block lugs.

The 'sword' shaped hour and minutes hands are typically 1950s in style.

A 1950s Lord Elgin Shockmaster 14ct gold-filled wristwatch, with 23-jewel movement, seconds dial, arrow head and dot markers and shaped case.

1.5in (3.5cm) high

$220-280   **ML**   **$250-350**   **ML**   **$220-280**   **ML**

A 1950s Swiss Longines 'Admiral' gold-filled automatic gentleman's wristwatch, with textured and plain gold 'mystery' face, and case.

A 'mystery' dial has hands or indicators that appear to float with no visible means of movement, but actually move with the central dial.

A 1930s Longines 14ct yellow gold 'Diamond Dial' wristwatch, with diamond-set gold markers at '12', '3' and '9' and hooded lugs, the 17-jewel movement signed Longines, in original box.

Hooded lug were popular during 1930s, but disappeared afterwards.

$380-480 ML

$300-400 RSS

A mid-1930s Swiss Longines wristwatch, with 'exploding' number dial sterling silver case and raised, curved crystal.

A 1950s Longines stainless steel wristwatch.

A 1970s Longines 'Ultronic' stainless steel diver's watch.

$350-550 ML

$200-250 RSS

$250-350 RSS

A 1930s Hamilton 14ct white gold-cased rectangular wristwatch, with Hamilton 980 17-jewel movement, and sterling silver, diamond-set dial.

A very rare 1930s Hamilton 'Brock' 14ct white gold wristwatch.

These watches are much more common in yellow gold. A similar yellow gold version of this watch would be worth up to $250.

A 1970s Longines 'Record' automatic sports watch.

$250-350 RSS

$900-1,200 ML

$800-1,200 ML

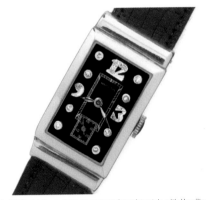

A 1930s Art Deco platinum rectangular wristwatch, with Hamilton 982 19-jewel movement, black diamond-set dial and hooded lugs.

$1,800-2,200   **ML**

A Hamilton 'Tonnneau Plain' square white gold-filled wristwatch, with 17-jewel movement and oversize numbers.

$200-300   **ML**

A 1970s Hamilton gold-plated LED multi-function digital watch.

As with many early digital watches, push the side button to turn the red LEDs on momentarily.

$300-500   **PC**

A rare 1950s Christmas packaged Bulova pink gold-filled wristwatch, with 17-jewel Bulova movement.

It is rare to find the complete original packaging. The watch on its own can be worth up to $180.

7in (18cm) high

$250-350   **ML**

A CLOSER LOOK AT
A PAIR OF BULOVA WATCHES

The watches are sometimes known as drivers watches and are designed to fit the wrist, with the case also tapering from top to bottom.

The Art Deco stepped sides are an appealing and period stylistic feature that adds to the value.

These examples are in excellent condition. Due to the many protruding edges the gold-plating can wear off easily over time.

It is very rare to find a matching set of a ladies' and a gentleman's watch of this type.

A matching pair of 1930s Bulova 'Right Angle' 10ct rolled gold-cased wristwatches.

Left: $160-280 Right: $250-380   **ML**

A 1960s Bulova stainless steel wristwatch, with two-tone blue enamelled face.

1.75in (4.5cm) high

$120-160   **ML**

A 1930s Bulova Art Deco ladies' cocktail wristwatch, with 14ct gold case and strap, set with diamonds and rubies.

$300-380   **ML**

WATCHES

A 1970s Baume & Mercier 18ct gold gentleman's wristwatch, with 17-jewel movement.

$500-700   **BLO**

A 1970s Longines 'Record' automatic sports watch.

$250-350   **RSS**

A 1970s French Pierre Cardin asymmetric 'fashion' stainless wristwatch.

Cardin produced unisex watches, many of which have large, shaped cases in a futuristic style that matched his clothing designs.

1.5in (4cm) widest

$220-380   **ML**

A 1970s French Pierre Cardin stainless steel circular 'fashion' wristwatch, with silvered dial and simple markers and hands.

Early Cardin watches like this used high quality Jaeger Le Coultre watch movements.

$220-350   **ML**

A 1950s Le Coultre gentleman's wristwatch, with 14ct gold case, 17-jewel movement and unusual scalloped lugs.

$400-600   **ML**

A CLOSER LOOK AT A JAEGER LE COULTRE WATCH

These early Jaeger Le Coultre alarm watches are becoming increasingly collectable. The alarm was one of Le Coultre's best features of the period, along with the Powermatic model.

The alarm, developed by 1952, is operated by turning the winder to move the central dial so that the arrow points to the time for the alarm.

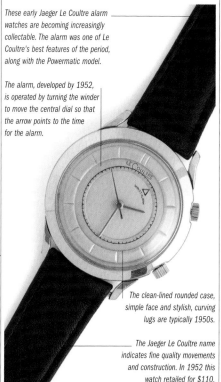

The clean-lined rounded case, simple face and stylish, curving lugs are typically 1950s.

The Jaeger Le Coultre name indicates fine quality movements and construction. In 1952 this watch retailed for $110.

A 1950s Jaeger Le Coultre 'Wrist Alarm' gold-filled gentleman's wristwatch, with 17-jewel movement and internal bell alarm.

$350-550   **ML**

A 1960s Dunhill gentleman's silver wristwatch.

Vintage Dunhill pieces are highly sought-after for their high quality and comparative rarity.

$1,500-2,000   **BLO**

A 1930s Gruen Curvex 'Precision' wristwatch, with 14ct white gold strap and case, faceted magnifying crystal, and inset diamonds at '12', '3' and '9'.

Gruen's Precision range was guaranteed to meet US railroad standards for accuracy.

$750-1,000　　　　　**ML**

A CLOSER LOOK AT A GRUEN WATCH

Curved, rectangular watches were highly fashionable during the mid-1930s. Gruen developed a special standard-sized curved 'Curvex' movement in 1935 that allowed cases to become truly curved.

Despite being launched with great fanfare, and being aimed at young people through selected advertising, they were not commercially successful and had disappeared by 1940, only reappearing briefly in 1950 and in the 1990s.

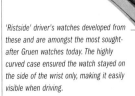

'Ristside' driver's watches developed from these and are amongst the most sought-after Gruen watches today. The highly curved case ensured the watch stayed on the side of the wrist only, making it easily visible when driving.

The case style with parallel lines identify this model as the 'Lord', one of the first Ristside driver's watches, available from 1937.

A Gruen Precision Curvex Ristside 'Lord' driving wristwatch, with 17-jewel Curvex '330' movement, gold-filled case, silver dial with second dial and gold hands and numbers.
c1937　　　　　　　　　　　　　　　　　*1.5in (4cm) high*

$750-1,250　　　　　**ML**

A 1930s American Illinois white gold-filled wristwatch, with 19-jewel movement and fancy 'Marquis' engraved case.

$300-400　　　　**ML**

An American Illinois wristwatch, with 17-jewel movement, and 'Special' nickel-plated case.
1929

$250-450　　　**ML**

A Swiss Louvic gold-filled 'coin' watch, with 17-jewel movement, the sprung hinge lid embossed with the reverse of a coin.
1.5in (3.5cm) diam

ML

A 1930s Movado 'Non Magnetic' 14ct pink gold wristwatch, with Zenith 17-jewel movement.

To prevent watches stopping when they became magnetised, Tissot developed a non-magnetic hair spring in 1930. It was soon adopted by other manufacturers.

$200-300　　　**ML**

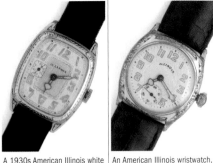

$280-320　　　**ML**

A late 1960s Swiss Nileg chrome-plated wristwatch, with 17-jewel movement, the black dial marked "17 RUBIS Incabloc".

Incabloc relates to a branded shock absorber for a watch's movement.

1.5in (4cm) high

$120-180 **ML**

A 1930s Omega wristwatch, with 15-jewel movement, and unusual hands.

$200-300 **ML**

An Omega 18ct white gold ladies' cocktail bracelet wristwatch, with diamond-set lugs, cal. 484 17-jewel movement, triple signed.

0.75in (1.5cm) diam

$800-1,000 **GHOU**

An Omega military issue wristwatch, once belonging to Lieut. E.G. Maund, D.F.M, R.N.V.R, pattern H.S.8, in original box with provenance.

Provenance can add to the value of a watch, particularly if the owner was notable or famous.

$300-400 **ROS**

An American Pierce gold-filled dress wristwatch, with 17-jewel movement, inset diamanté and curving curled applications, steel back.

$120-180 **ML**

A French Alain Silberstein quartz wristwatch.

Silberstein is a French architect who owns his own watch company producing 'designer' watches that became popular in the 1990s.

$500-600 **RSS**

A Swiss Tressa Lux 'Space Man' chrome-plated steel wristwatch, with original Corfam plastic strap.

This watch was designed by Andre Le Marquand in 1972 and was based on the helmets worn during the 1969 moon landing. He was also responsible for the famous Spaceman Audacieuse.

$600-700 **RSS**

A 1960s Waltham Self Winding wristwatch, with 17-jewel Incablock movement.

1.5in (4cm) high

$180-280 **ML**

A 1960s/70s Swiss Wittnauer dual timezone wristwatch, with oval gold-filled case.

1.5in (3.5cm) diam

$150-200 **ML**

FIND OUT MORE...

Wristwatch Annual 2006: The Catalog of Producers, Models & Specifications, *published by Abbeville Press, 2006.*

Wristwatches: A Connoisseur's Guide, *by Frank Edwards, published by Firefly, 1997.*

COLLECTORS' NOTES

■ Launched in 1983, the first Swatch range of twelve watches was plain in comparison to today's brightly colored, heavily designed models. Since then, the company has released two new collections every year.

■ Conceived as fun, disposable 'second watches', hence the contraction 'Swatch', they were inexpensively produced, consisting of only 51 components in a plastic case. They were marketed at an affordable price, and proved extremely popular. By 1984 over one million units had been produced.

■ Many well-known designers and artists worked with Swatch including Keith Haring, Kiki Picasso, Vivienne Westwood and Christian Lacroix. Today their models are some of the most sought-after by collectors.

■ Swatch collecting reached a peak in the early 1990s. While the market is not as strong as it once was, there is a smaller but stable marketplace for discontinued and limited edition models and a number of dedicated websites and internet auctions. Some models can fetch high prices: an original 1984 'Jelly Fish' can be worth several hundred dollars.

■ Look for watches in mint, unworn condition, with the original packaging and paperwork. These are the most desirable and will hold their value better.

■ Check that the strap is original and correct for the model – a replaced strap can reduce the value of a Swatch by half. Buckle marks also reduce the value, but there are methods for flattening bent straps.

A Swatch '12 Flags' wristwatch, GS 101, from the Skipper series, with black strap.

A '4 Flag' variation was also available.

1984

$280-320   **ML**

A Swatch 'Yamaha Racer' wristwatch, GJ 700, from the Coral Reef series, with black strap.

1985

$200-250   **ML**

A Swatch first series wristwatch, GB 701, with black plastic strap, stamped "C84".

1983

$300-350   **ML**

A Swatch 'Nicholson' wristwatch, GA 705, from the Plaza series, with date function and black strap.

1985

$150-200   **ML**

A Swatch 'Black Magic' ladies' wristwatch, LB 106, from the Carlton series, with shiny gold hands and black strap.

The 1988 version of this watch (LB 119) has matte gold hands and is usually worth half the value of this.

1985

$120-180   **ML**

A Swatch 'Sir Swatch' wristwatch, GB111, from the Coat of Arms series, with replaced black strap.

This model was available as a Maxi at approximately half the value. Look for the rare special gift set, which can have a value of around $250.

1986

$50-70   **ML**

A Swatch 'Ping Pong White' wristwatch, GW105, from the Calypso Beach series, with white strap.

1986

$70-100   **ML**

A Swatch 'Ruffled Feathers' wristwatch, GF 100, from the Kiva series, with brown strap.

1986

$40-60   **ML**

A Swatch 'Newport Two' ladies' wristwatch, LW108, from the Indigo Blues series, with blue strap.

1987

$80-120   ML

A Swatch 'Pulsometer' wristwatch, GA 106, from the Connaught series, with black ribbed strap.

1987

$30-40   ML

A Swatch 'Commander' wristwatch, GB 115, from the Nakiska series, with black ridged strap.

1987

$80-120   ML

A Swatch 'X-Rated' wristwatch, GB 406, from the Neo Geo series, with black ribbed strap.

1987

$200-250   ML

A Swatch 'Calafatti' wristwatch, GK 105, from the Vienna Deco series, with clear and black striped strap.

As with other clear plastic straps, this one has faded to yellow over time.

1987

$70-100   ML

A Swatch 'Blue Bay' ladies' wristwatch, LK 106, from the Color Tech series, with ribbed grey band.

1987

$35-45   ML

A Swatch 'Hearstone' wristwatch, GX 100, from the Heavy Metal series, with brushed chrome-plated case and ribbed black strap.

1988

$70-100   ML

A Swatch 'Rosehip' wristwatch, GP 100, from the Alfresco series, with textured clear strap.

The strap and the case tend to discolor over time to green.

1989

$100-150   ML

A Swatch 'Glowing Arrow' wristwatch, GX 109, from the M.O.C.A series, with metallic grey strap.

This model was also made with a 'twist-o-flex' band, GX 110/111, which can be worth double.

1989

$60-80   ML

A Swatch 'Gilda's Love' wristwatch, GB 133, from the Desert Flowers series, with stamped burgundy leather strap.

1990

$40-60   ML

A Swatch 'Hice-Speed' ladies' wristwatch, LL 110, from the Cold Fever series, with decorated white strap.

1991

$18-22   ML

A Swatch 'Greenroom' wristwatch, GN 103, from the Bondi Beach series, with transparent fuchsia strap.

1989

$70-100   ML

A Swatch 'Rave' wristwatch, GK 134, from the D.J. Ten-Strikes series, with decorated clear strap.

1991

$18-22   ML

A Swatch 'In Our Hands' automatic wristwatch, released for the first Earth Summit, in Rio de Janeiro, boxed and with original receipt for £47.50 ($87.50) from Croydon's department store in England.

1991   *Box 9.75in (25cm) long*

$30-40   GAZE

A late 1980s Swatch Guard Too watch guard, mint and boxed.

$3-5   ML

A Swatch red replacement watch strap.

The packaging helps date the strap.

1985-6   *6.75in (17.5cm high)*

$10-15   ML

A Swatch 'Time & Stripes' Automatic wristwatch, SAN 105, with skeleton back, window face and striped strap, with original packaging.

1993

$30-40   ML

A Swatch 'Tisane' wristwatch, GK 162, from the Tranquille series, with patterned blue strap.

1993

$20-30   ML

FIND OUT MORE...

www.swatch.com - *Official company website.*

www.etswatch.com - *Collectors' website with a comprehensive list of models.*

W. B. S. Collector's Guide for Swatch Watches, *by Wolfgang Schneider, published by W B S Marketing, October 1992.*

Almost Everything You Need to Know About Dealing & Collecting Swatch Watches, *by Roy Ehrhardt, Larry Ehrhardt, published by Heart of America Press, October 1996.*

COLLECTORS' NOTES

- The Wild West and the cowboy are bound inextricably with the history and identity of the US and its population. The 1950s saw the start of an associated popular culture based around the cowboy as an icon of victorious American individualism, with many comic strips, radio and TV shows and Hollywood films arising – all of which spawned an enormous variety of memorabilia. Countrywide, boys and girls were captivated by the adventures of these new all-American heroes and heroines.

- Davy Crockett (1986-1836) is a key figure, whose career spanned army service, politics and frontier activity, which led to his death at the hands of the Mexicans at the Alamo in 1836. During the mid-1950s, his legend was popularised by three Disney films starring Fess Parker, which made him a frontier hero and symbol of patriotism. As such he is usually depicted riding galloping horses, firing guns or piloting canoes.

- Other important names include Gene Autry, 'The Singing Cowboy' and Roy Rogers, called 'The King of the Cowboys'. Rogers (1911-98) was born as Leonard Franklin Slye. His first film was made in 1935, but his first hit came in 1938 when Autry walked out of 'Under Western Stars' and Slye was given the name Roy Rogers and cast as the lead. He gained popularity with The Roy Rogers Show, which aired on radio from 1942 until 1951 when it moved to TV where it lasted until 1964.

- Most memorabilia was aimed at children and was often played with heavily. Quality also varied greatly, and many mass-produced, poor quality items were made. This means that items can be very worn or damaged. Look out for items that exemplify the character, such as Crockett's fox fur hat, and that are in as close to mint condition as possible, unless very rare. The character's face, logos or sayings closely connected to the character will usually add appeal.

A Davy Crockett screenprinted souvenir glass.

5.25in (13.5cm) high

$12-18   **BH**

A scarce Davey Crockett 'Holiday Freeze' printed glass.

7in (17.5cm) high

$15-25   **BH**

A Davy Crocket green screenprinted glass.

6in (15cm) high

$15-25   **NOR**

A Fire King Oven Ware Davy Crocket screenprinted mug.

3.25in (8.5cm) high

$20-30   **NOR**

An American Steerhide Davy Crocket child's leather belt, with metal gun-shaped buckle.

12.25in (31cm) wide

$15-25   **NOR**

A late 1950s Bradley Davy Crocket watch, with original strap.

It is can be hard to find these watches in working condition as the movements were inexpensive and prone to breaking. This example is also in excellent, bright and unscratched condition and retains its original strap.

$100-150   **NOR**

A 1950s-60s Roy Rogers 'The King of The Cowboys' plastic mug, by Fiedler & Fiedler Mold & Die Works.

4.25in (10.5cm) high

$25-35   **NOR**

A scarce Roy Rogers & Trigger money bank, the base molded "Roy Rogers" and "Trigger".

7.25in (18.5cm) high

$150-200   **BEL**

A 1950s Roy Rogers 'Happy Trails' unused note pad.

4.5in (11.5cm) high

$15-25   **BH**

A late 1950s or '60s Japanese Roy Rogers, Trigger and Bullet printed rayon scarf.

30in (67.5cm) diam

$150-200   **NOR**

An American Ohio Art Co. Roy Rogers battery-powered printed tinplate lamp.

Surprisingly for what must have been a popular boy's toy, this example is in mint condition, which makes it very rare today. The horseshoe design and bright colors make it particularly charming.

11.75in (30cm) high

$150-200   **NOR**

A 'Maverick' necktie on original card, featuring a photographic portrait of James Garner as Bret Maverick, marked "(c) 1959 Warner Bros".

James Garner starred as gambler Brett Maverick from 1957-1960. The original card, with its characterful artwork, makes it valuable.

1959   11.25in (28.5cm) high

$60-80   **NOR**

A 1950s Gene Autry 'The Singing Cowboy' boy's watch, with original brown mock crocodile strap, the back stamped with a facsimile "Gene Autry" signature.

Film star, baseball team owner and original singing cowboy Autrey was discovered in 1934. He retired from showbusiness in 1964, having made over 600 records and nearly 100 films.

8in (20cm) long

$100-150   **PWE**

An early 1950s cowboy on a horse celluloid clockwork toy, with lasso and rubber tail, marked "Made in Occupied Japan".

5.5in (14cm) high

$40-60   **GAZE**

A pair of early 20thC Western leather chaps, with tooled latigo belt and trim, and German silver conchos, with "Marshall Wells, Portland" stamp.

36in (91.5cm) long

$200-300   **ALL**

COLLECTORS' NOTES

■ Perhaps the most collectable item in this area is the corkscrew, with many collectors choosing this focus due to the enormous range in types and prices. The first recorded mention of a screw being used to draw a cork was in 1681, but it was the 19thC, the 'age of invention', that saw many thousands of patents being issued for different designs.

■ Corkscrews can be classified into two types; 'straight pull', where the strength of the user is used to draw the cork out, and 'mechanical', where a mechanism helps to draw out the cork. It is usually the latter category that is the most interesting, desirable and valuable. The former category can, however, provide key examples of vintage pieces at more affordable prices.

■ Look for examples with ingenious mechanisms, or those made from precious materials or with maker's names. Such names can often help to identify the date of the patent, although many corkscrew designs were copied by other makers at a later date. Damage to the end of the screw (or worm) and missing or replaced parts will also devalue a corkscrew.

■ Cocktail shakers have risen in value immensely over the past decade and are a collecting area of their own. Some are very rare, particularly those that would have been expensive in their day, often being made from precious materials, or those that display fine Art Deco design features of the period.

■ Names such as Revere and Asprey are highly valuable and desirable, as are those in novelty shapes from the 1930s. Items from the 1950s are becoming increasingly sought-after, although many tend to be less well-made. In general, always look for good design, fine quality or else for a sense of fun and novelty!

A straight-pull corkscrew, with naturally formed and colored Scottish stag antler handle, turned steel stem and plain helical worm.

c1890   4.75in (12cm) long

$20-30   CSA

A late19thC/early 20thC nickel-cased pocket corkscrew.

The handles of these corskscrews unscrew and detach from the middle, with the worm folding in, to be stored within the tube for easy portability.

c1900   2.5in (6.5cm) long

$70-100   BS

An early 20thC American Clough-type advertising corkscrew, the wooden handle with wire fitting for hanging.

Clough-types were made from one piece of wire formed into a corkscrew by machine. The process was invented by W. Rockwell Clough in 1875 and most examples are inexpensive advertising corkscrews such as this.

3.5in (9cm) wide

$30-60   CA

An early 19thC Henshall-type straight-pull corkscrew, with wooden handle with brush and 'button'.

The metal disc, or 'button', gripped the top of the cork, helping to unstick it from the sides of the bottle. The wooden handle was used for brushing cork or dust remains from the lip.

$80-120   MUR

An early 20thC French folding corkscrew, the handles with colored Ivorine panels modeled as a pair of stockinged legs, with steel helix.

These bring to mind dancers at the Folies Bergères and 'fin de siecle' Europe.

2.25in (6cm)

$450-650   ROS

A cast brass two-finger figural ship corkscrew.

c1930   7in (17.5cm) long

$20-30   CSA

WINE & DRINKING

An early 1930s American Demley chrome-plated novelty folding corkscrew, of a gentleman in a top hat, inscribed "Old Snifter".

This was based on Senator Volstead, the Prohibitionist, and the reactions of noted US cartoonist Rollin Kirby's cartoons about Prohibition.

6.5in (16.5cm) high

$60-90 **GORL**

An early 19thC German or French brass mechanical corkscrew, with button and wire helix.

$80-120 **MUR**

A German sprung stem miniature open frame corkscrew, with Archimedean screw and turned ivory grip.

c1890 3.5in (9cm) long

$80-120 **CSA**

A 1950s English 'Valenzina' butterfly double-action metal corkscrew, with registered design number 857383 for 1949.

c1950 9.5in (24cm) long

$20-40 **CSA**

A CLOSER LOOK AT A CORKSCREW

An early to mid-19thC Dowler Patent corkscrew, with turned wooden handle and brass barrel with applied 'Ne Ultra Plus' heraldic shield.

This is a variation of the Thomason-type, where the second (larger) handle is turned to move the screw worm upwards into the barrel on two vertical tracks inside the barrel. The smaller, upper handle twists the screw worm into the cork.

7.75in (20cm) long

$1,000-1,500 **SWO**

A Lund-patent two-piece corkscrew, in good condition.

This 'scissor' design was first registered by Edmund Burke in 1854, with London retailer Lund's version, with its separate worm, being registered in 1855. It can be hard to find the two separate parts together.

c1880 8in (20cm) wide

$120-180 **MUR**

The 'Thomason' type uses a specially designed internal double helix enabling the screw worm to be forced into the cork and the cork extracted with continuous turning.

The mechanism and design were patented in 1802 by Sir Edward Thomason, but were made during the 19thC by other companies including Dowler, Wilmot and Roberts after the patent had expired 14 years later.

This example is particularly notable due to its decorated barrel, most have plain barrels with turned bands and an applied heraldic shield and usually are worth around $350-750.

This example lacks its handle brush for removing detritus from the bottle lip - surprisingly, this does not affect the value considerably, but if the handle was replaced or damaged, the value would be affected.

A James Heeley and Sons, 'A1 Patent Double Lever' steel corkscrew.

c1890

6.75in (17cm) high

$80-120 **ROS**

A mid-19thC Thomason type double-action corkscrew, with turned ivory handle and steel helix within a brass barrel with low relief fruiting vine decoration.

7.5in (19cm) high

$1,000-1,500 **ROS**

WINE & DRINKING

A 1920s French double-pronged Mumford-type cork extractor, with case.

This was designed by Lucian Mumford of San Francisco in 1879, and uses the two 'blades' to grip the cork inside the bottle neck and then gently pull it out as it is twisted. The cork can also be re-inserted using the same device after a half drunk bottle has been topped up, leading this to become a sneaky drinker's favourite!

3.75in (9.5cm) long

$20-30 CSA

A good 1920s champagne tap, with turned wooden handle.

Champagne taps are screwed into the cork, which is not removed. The bottle is tipped up, the valve opened and small amounts of champagne can be poured through the hollow screw and tube at will without losing the fizz.

6in (15cm) long

$150-200 BS

A Victorian champagne tap, with detachable spike.

4.5in (11.5cm) long

$20-30 CSA

A champagne tap, marked "A.N. & Co.", with case.

c1890   5.25in (13.5cm) long

$50-90 CSA

A CLOSER LOOK AT A COCKTAIL SHAKER

The Revere Copper & Brass Co. are known for their fine quality metalwares, usually in Art Deco styles.

This shaker was designed in 1938 by their Director of Design, William Archibald Welden, who was also responsible for the less glamorous, but very popular, copper bottomed stainless steel cookware.

Its curving handle, clean-lined design and architectural appearance, that bring skyscrapers to mind, are essentially Art Deco.

The use of undecorated polished chrome surfaces, that are undented and unscratched on this example, and bright plastic elements are again typical of the period.

An American Revere 'Empire' chrome-plated brass cocktail shaker, with yellow Catalin trim on the spout lid and spire finial.

12.5in (32cm) high

$2,500-3,500 MI

An American Art Deco Manning Bowman chrome-plated metal 'Connoisseur' cocktail shaker, with stepped chrome and yellow bakelite lid.

12in (30.5cm) high

$280-320 MI

A 1970s plastic cocktail shaker, with metal lid and printed design of period advertisements.

9.75in (24.5cm) high

$20-30 MTS

A Swedish Art Deco Guldsmeds Aktie Bolaget of Stockholm silver-plated nickel cocktail shaker, with black Bakelite lid, engraved with lines enhancing the curvilinear form, designed by Folke Arstrom.

1935   8.5in (20cm) high

$1,800-2,800 MI

A 1950s Canadian chrome-plated cocktail set, marked "GH", with red cast phenolic plastic handles.

The superb condition, appealing Art Deco-style design and usefulness of this piece make it desirable and valuable.

$250-350   **GROB**

A 1950s Canadian chrome-plated cocktail set on a revolving stand, with red cast phenolic handles.

It is hard to find sets such as this together in complete, undamaged condition.

13.75in (35cm) high

$300-400   **GROB**

A 1950s enameled metal 'Rolls Royce' decanter and glass set, with molded glass decanters and shot glasses.

These novelty pieces are becoming more sought-after, particularly in complete condition and if they attract buyers from other markets, such as automobilia.

16.5in (42cm) wide

$150-250   **DETC**

A pair of amusing glass decanters, painted to represent the Kaiser Wilhelm II and his wife, Augusta.

c1914   *8in (20.5cm) high*

$70-100   **CA**

A 1930s 'Penguin' chrome-plated ice bucket, by the West Bend Aluminum Co. of West Bend, Wisconsin, USA, with mottled brown Bakelite handles and finial.

10.25in (26cm) wide.

$30-40   **ANAA**

An Japanese battery-powered cocktail shaker, in the form of a vinyl doll, with clip holder to hold a drinking glass fitted to her waist, distributed by Poynter Products Inc. of Cincinnati Ohio.

Turn her on and her vibrating hips mix your drink!

c1969   *15.5in (38.5cm) high*

$150-250   **MTS**

A 1950s unmarked ceramic 'cowboy' decanter and shot glasses set, with slots in his chaps to hold the barrel-shaped glasses, his head the stopper.

Cowboys were a particularly popular character in the 1950s.

10.5in (26cm) high

$40-70   **PSI**

Four 1940s American Art Deco Revere Copper & Brass Co. chrome and green Bakelite 'Empire' cocktail cups, designed by William A. Weldon.

1938   *3.25in (8.5cm) high*

$400-500   **MI**

A wooden folk-art model of a monkey bartender, in front of a mirrored bar with various labeled bottles of liquor.

c1935   *9in (23cm) wide*

$150-250   **DETC**

FIND OUT MORE...

Corkscrews for Collectors, by Bernard Watney & Homer Babbidge, published by Sotheby's Parke Bernet, 1983.

The Ultimate Corkscrew Book, by Donald Bull, published by Schiffer Publishing, 1999.

A 1930s French wooden 'dumb waiter', carved and painted with a red tailcoat and blue trousers.

Despite their politically incorrect nature, these items have been rising in value steadily over the past ten years. They were made to stand next to a chair or at the side of a room and act as drink stands or ashtrays. They were popular from the late 19thC until the late 1930s, although reproductions are often seen today. The more complex and and realistic the carving and painting, or the more unusual the subject, the higher the value.

35.5in (88.5cm) high

$200-250　　　　**KAU**

A late 19thC cast iron horse's head, from a fairground carousel, in good condition but with wear to the paint.

$280-320　　　　**MUR**

A large late 19thC lobster claw, painted to emulate the head of Mr Punch.

18.75in (30cm) high

$800-1,200　　　　**DN**

A late 19thC French painted canvas and carved wood ventriloquist dummy's head, with glass eyes, a lever at the nape of the neck moves the bottom lip up and down.

9in (23cm) high

$500-800　　　　**ANAA**

A mid-19thC silver plated and leather dog collar, with applied silver plaque engraved 'Won by Dick at Birmingham, in a sweepstakes, 12 rats each, dogs of all weigh, Nov.10', with hallmarks for Birmingham, 1852.

1852　　　　*3.75in (9.5cm) diam*

$1,000-1,500　　　　**LFA**

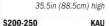

An unusual late 19thC iron animal trap.

$70-100　　　　**MUR**

A CLOSER LOOK AT A VAMPIRE PROTECTION KIT

Vampire hysteria spread through 17thC & 18thC Eastern Europe, based on legends of Russian 'Upir' demons, but there are no records of specialised anti-vampire kits from this period.

Stories of this hysteria combined with the factual historic tale of Romanian ruler 'Vlad the Impaler' influenced Bram Stoker who published novel 'Dracula' in 1897.

The publication of 'Dracula' caused a widespread sensation which led to the creation of anti-vampire items, which were meant as whimsical 'talking points' rather than practical items.

Beware of 'Vampire Killing Kits' by Professor Ernst Blomberg and bearing a gun by Nicholas Plomdeur - a British vintage firearms dealer claims to have made this kit in 1972. Copies were subsequently made by others.

A late 19thC 'Vampire Protection Kit' made by the 'Lord's Protection Company' in London, including everything mythically and culturally associated with the killing of and protection from vampires.

Such complex, well made and complete period 19thC kits are scarce. Many of the ways of killing vampires were devised by Stoker. Beware of examples made for amateur theatrical productions.

Box 22in (56cm) wide

$10,000-15,000　　　　**WJT**

GLOSSARY

A

Acid etching A technique using acid to decorate glass to produce a matt or frosted appearance.

Albumen print Photographic paper is treated with egg white (albumen) to enable it to hold more light-sensitive chemicals. After being exposed to a negative, the resulting image is richer with more tonal variation.

Applied Refers to a separate part that has been attached to an object, such as a handle.

B

Baluster A curved form with a bulbous base and a slender neck.

Base metal A term describing common metals such as copper, tin and lead, or metal alloys, that were usually plated in gold or silver to imitate more expensive and luxurious metals. In the US, the term 'pot metal' is more commonly used.

Bisque A type of unglazed porcelain used for making dolls from c1860 to c1925.

Boards The hard covers of a book.

Brassing On plated items, where the plating has worn off to reveal the underlying base metal.

C

Cabochon A large, protruding, polished, but not faceted, stone.

Cameo Hardstone, coral or shell that has been carved in relief to show a design in a contrasting color.

Cameo glass Decorative glass made from two or more layers of differently colored glass, which are then carved or etched to reveal the color beneath.

Cartouche A framed panel, often in the shape of a shield or paper scroll, which can be inscribed.

Cased Where a piece of glass is covered with a further layer of glass, often of a contrasting color, or else clear and colorless. In some cases the casing will be further worked with cutting or etching to reveal the layer beneath.

Charger A large plate or platter, often for display, but also for serving.

Chromolithography A later development of 'lithography', where a number of printing stones are used in succession, each with a different color, to build up a multi-colored image.

Composition A mixture including wood pulp, plaster and glue used as a cheap alternative to bisque in the production of dolls' heads and bodies.

Compote A dish, usually on a stem or foot, to hold fruit for the dessert course.

Craze/Crazed/Crazing A network of fine cracks in the glaze caused by uneven shrinking during firing. It also describes plastic that is slowly degrading and has the same surface patterning.

Cuenca A technique used for decorating tiles where molded ridges separate the colored glazes, like the 'cloisonné' enameling technique.

Cultured pearl A pearl formed when an irritant is artificially introduced to the mollusc.

D

Damascened Metal ornamented with inlaid gold or silver, often in wavy lines. Commonly found on weapons or armor.

Dichroic Glass treated with chemicals or metals that cause it to appear differently colored depending on how it is viewed in the light.

Diecast Objects made by pouring molten metal into a closed metal die or mold.

Ding A very small dent in metal.

E

Earthenware A type of porous pottery that requires a glaze to make it waterproof.

Ebonized Wood that has been blackened with dye to resemble ebony.

E.P.N.S. Found on metal objects and standing for 'electroplated nickel silver', meaning the object is made from nickel which is then electroplated with silver.

F

Faïence Earthenware that is treated with an impervious tin glaze. Popular in France from the 16th century and reaching its peak during the 18th century.

Faceted A form of decoration where a number of flat surfaces are cut into the surface of an object such as a gem or glass.

Faux A French word for 'false'. The intention is not to deceive fraudulently but to imitate a more costly material.

Finial A decorative knob at the end of a terminal, or on a lid.

Foliate Leaf and vine motifs.

G

Guilloché An engraved pattern of interlaced lines or other decorative motifs, sometimes enameled over with translucent enamels.

H

Hallmark The series of small stamps found on gold or silver that can identify the maker, the standard of the metal and the city and year of manufacture. Hallmarks differ for each country and can consist only of a maker's or a city mark. All English silver made after 1544 was required to be fully marked.

IJKL

Incised Applied to surface decoration or a maker's mark that has been scratched into the surface of an object with a sharp instrument.

Inclusions Used to describe all types of small particles of decorative materials embedded in glass.

Iridescent A lustrous finish that subtly changes color depending on how light hits it. Often used to describe the finish on ceramics and glass.

Lithography A printing technique developed in 1798 and employing the use of a stone upon which a pattern or picture has been drawn with a grease crayon. The ink adheres to the grease and is transfered to the paper when pressed against it.

MNO

Millefiori An Italian term meaning 'thousand flowers' and used to describe cut, multi-colored glass canes which are arranged and cased in clear glass. When arranged with the cut side facing the exterior, each circular disc (or short cane) resembles a small flower.

Mint A term used to describe an object in unused condition with no signs of wear and derived from coinage. Truly 'mint' objects will command a premium.

Mount A metal part applied to an object made of ceramic, glass or another material, with a decorative or functional use.

Nappy A shallow dish or bowl with a handle used for drinking.

Opalescent An opal-like, milky glass with subtle gradations of color between thinner more translucent areas and thicker, more opaque areas.

P

Paisley A stylized design based on pinecones and foliage, often with added intricate decoration. It originated in India and is most often found on fabrics, such as shawls.

Paste (jewelry) A hard, bright glass cut the same way as a diamond and made and set to resemble them.

Patera An oval or circular decorative motif often with a fluted or floral centre. The plural is 'paterae'.

Piqué A decorative technique where small strips or studs of gold are inlaid onto ivory or tortoiseshell on a pattern and secured in place by heating.

Pontil A metal rod to which a glass vessel is attached when it is being worked. When it is removed it leaves a raised disc-shaped 'pontil mark'.

Pot metal Please see 'Base metal'.

Pounce pot A small pot made of wood (treen), silver or ceramic. Found on inkwells or designed to stand alone. It held a gum dust that was sprinkled over parchment to prevent ink from spreading. Used until the late 18th century.

Pressed (Press molded) Ceramics formed by pressing clay into a mold. Pressed glass is made by pouring molten glass into a mold and pressing it with a plunger.

R

Reeded A type of decoration with thin raised, convex vertical lines. Derived from the decoration of classical columns.

Relief A form of molded, pressed or carved decoration that protrudes above the surface of an object. Usually in the form of figures of foliate and foliage designs, it ranges in height from 'low' to 'high'.

Repoussé A French term for the raised, 'embossed' decoration on metals such as silver. The metal is forced into a form from one side causing it to bulge.

S

Sgraffito An Italian word for 'little scratch' and used to describe a decorative technique where the outer surface of an object, usually in glazed or colored ceramic, is scratched away in a pattern to reveal the contrasting colored underlying surface.

Sommerso Technique developed in Murano in the 1930s. Translates as 'submerged' and involves casing one or more layers of transparent colored glass within a layer of thick, clear, colorless glass.

Stoneware A type of ceramic similar to earthenware and made of high-fired clay mixed with stone, such as feldspar, which makes it non-porous.

T

Tazza A shallow cup with a wide bowl, which is raised up on a single pedestal foot.

Tooled Collective description for a number of decorative techniques applied to a surface. Includes engraving, stamping, punching and incising.

V

Vermeil Gold-plated silver.

Vesta case A small case or box, usually made from silver, for carrying matches.

W

White metal Precious metal that is possibly silver, but not officially marked as such.

Y

Yellow metal Precious metal that is possibly gold, but not officially marked as such.

INDEX TO ADVERTISERS

KEY TO ILLUSTRATIONS

Every collectible illustrated in the DK Collectibles Price Guide 2005 by Judith Miller has a letter code identifying the dealer or auction house that sold it. The list below is a key to these codes. In the list, auction houses are shown by the letter A and dealers by the letter D. Some items may have come from a private collection, in which case the code is accompanied by the letter P. Inclusion in this book in no way constitutes or implies a contract or a binding offer on the part of any of our contributors to supply or sell the goods illustrated, or similar items, at the prices stated.

AAB (D)
Ashmore & Burgess
Mob: +44(0)7702 355122
info@ashmoreandburgess.com
www.ashmoreandburgess.com

AAC (A)
Alderfer Auction Company
501 Fairground Road,
Hatfield, PA 19440
Tel: 215 393 3000
info@alderferauction.com
www.alderferauction.com

AB (A) (D)
Auction Blocks
The Auction Blocks, P.O. Box
2321, Shelton, CT 06484
Tel: 203 924 2802
auctionblocks@aol.com
www.auctionblocks.com

ABIJ (D)
Aurora Bijoux
Tel: 215 872 7808
aurora@aurorabijoux.com
www.aurorabijoux.com

AG (D)
Antique Glass at Frank Dux
Antiques
33 Belvedere, Bath BA1 5HR UK
Tel: +44(0)1225 312 367
m.hopkins@antique-glass.co.uk
www.antique-glass.co.uk

AGO (D)
Anona Gabriel
Otford Antiques Centre,
26-28 High Steet, Otford,
Sevenoaks, Kent TN15 9DF UK
Tel: +44(0)1959 522 025
info@otfordantiques.co.uk

AGR (D)
Adrian Grater
25-26 Admiral Vernon Antiques
Arcade, 141-149 Portobello
Road, London W11 2DY UK
Tel: +44(0)20 8579 0357
adriangrater@tiscali.co.uk

AGW (D)
American Art Glass Works
No longer trading

ALL (A)
Allard Auctions
P.O. Box 1030, 419 Flathead
Street, 4, St Ignatius MT 59865
Tel: 460 745 0500
info@allardauctions.com
www.allardauctions.com

AMJ (D)
American Jazz
Box 302, Ossining NY 10562
Tel: 914 762 5519
amjazz@optonline.net

ANAA (D)
Anastacia's Antiques
617 Bainbridge Street,
Philadelphia, PA 19147
Tel: 215 928 0256

AOY (D)
All Our Yesterdays
6 Park Road, Kelvinbridge,
Glasgow G4 9JG UK
Tel: +44(0)141 334 7788

ART (D)
Artius Glass
Street, Somerset BA16 0AN UK
Tel: +44(0)1458 443694
wheeler.ron@ic24.net
www.artiusglass.co.uk

ASG (D)
Anthony Stern Glass
Unit 205, Avro House, Havelock
Terrace, London SW8 4AL UK
Tel: +44(0)20 7622 9463
anthony@anthonysternglass.com
www.anthonysternglass.com

ATK (A)
Auction Team Köln
Postfach 50 11 19,
Bonner Str. 528-530,
D-50971 Köln, Germany
Tel: 00 49 221 38 70 49
www.breker.com

B&H (A)
Burstow & Hewett
Lower Lake, Battle,
East Sussex, TN33 0AT UK
Tel: +44(0)1424 772374
auctions@burstowandhewett.co.uk
www.burstowandhewett.co.uk

B (A)
Dreweatt Neate, Tunbridge Wells
Auction Hall, The Pantiles,
Tunbridge Wells,
Kent TN2 5QL UK
Tel: +44(0)1892 544 500
tunbridgewells@dnfa.com
www.dnfa.com

BAD (D)
Beth Adams
Unit GO43/4, Alfies Antique
Market, 13 Church Street,
London NW8 8DT UK
www.alfiesantiques.com

BAR (A)
Dreweatt Neate (Bristol)
Baynton Road, Ashton
Bristol BS3 2EB UK
Tel: +44(0)117 953 0803
bristol@dnfa.com
www.dnfa.com

BB (D)
Barbara Blau
South Street Antiques Market
615 South 6th Street,
Philadelphia, PA 19147-2128
Tel: 215 739 4995
Tel: 215 592 0256
bbjools@msn.com

BEJ (D)
Bébés et Jouets
c/o Lochend Post Office,
165 Restalrig Road,
Edinburgh EH7 6HW UK
Tel: +44(0)131 332 5650
bebesjouets@tiscali.co.uk

BEL (A)
Belhorn Auction Services
PO Box 20211,
Columbus, OH 43220
Tel: 614 921 9441
auctions@belhorn.com
www.belhorn.com

BER (A)
Bertoia Auctions
2141 Demarco Drive
Vineland, NJ 08360
Tel: 856 692 1881
toys@bertoiaauctions.com
www.bertoiaauctions.com

BEV (D)
Beverley
30 Church Street,
London NW8 8EP UK
Tel: +44(0)20 7262 1576
www.alfiesantiques.com

BGL (D)
Block Glass Ltd
blockglss@aol.com
www.blockglass.com

BH (D)
Black Horse Antiques
Showcases
2180 North Reading Road
Denver PA 17517
Tel: 717 335 3300
info@antiques-showcase.com
www.antiques-showcase.com

BIB (D)
Biblion
1-7 Davies Mews,
London W1K 5AB UK
Tel: +44(0)20 7629 1374
info@biblion.com
www.biblion.com

BLO (A)
Bloomsbury Auctions
Bloomsbury House, 24 Maddox
St, London W1 S1PP UK
Tel: +44(0)20 7495 9494
info@bloomsburyauctions.com
www.bloomsburyauctions.com

BOM (D)
Bob Mauriello
toystrains@comcast.net

BONR (A)
Bonhams
101 New Bond Street,
London W1S 1SR UK
Tel: +44(0)20 7629 6602
info@bonhams.com
www.bonhams.com

BPAL (A) (D)
The Book Palace
Jubilee House, Bedwardine Rd,
Crystal Palace
London SE19 3AP UK
Tel: +44(0)20 8768 0022
orders@bookpalace.com
www.bookpalace.com

BR (D)
Beyond Retro
110-112 Cheshire Street,
London E2 6EJ UK
Tel: +44(0)20 7613 3636
sales@beyondretro.com
www.beyondretro.com

BRB (D)
Bauman Rare Books
535 Madison Avenue,
New York, NY 10022
Tel: 212 751 1011
brb@baumanrarebooks.com
www.baumanrarebooks.com

BS (D)
Below Stairs
103 High Street, Hungerford,
Berkshire RG17 0NB UK
Tel: +44(0)1488 682 317
www.belowstairs.co.uk

BWH (P)
The Big White House
www.thebigwhitehouse.com

C (A)
Cottees
The Market, East Street,
Wareham, Dorset BH20 4NR UK
Tel: +44(0)1929 552 826
auctions@cottees.fsnet.co.uk
www.auctionsatcottees.co.uk

CA (A)
Chiswick Auctions
1 Colville Road,
London W3 8BL UK
Tel: +44(0)20 8992 4442
sales@chiswickauctions.co.uk
www.chiswickauctions.co.uk

CAT (D)
CatalinRadio.com
Tel: 419 824 2469
steve@catalinradio.com
www.catalinradio.com

CG (D)
Cowdy Gallery
31 Culver Street, Newent
Gloucestershire GL18 1DB UK
Tel: +44(0)1531 821 173
info@cowdygallery.co.uk
www.cowdygalleryc.o.uk

CHEF (A)
Cheffins
Clifton House, 1 & 2 Clifton
Road, Cambridge CB1 7EA UK
Tel: +44(0)1223 213 343
fine.art@cheffins.co.uk
www.cheffins.co.uk

CHS (D)
China Search
P.O. Box 1202, Kenilworth,
Warwickshire CV8 2WW UK
Tel: +44(0)1926 512 402
helen@chinasearch.co.uk
www.chinasearch.co.uk

CL/CLG (D)
Chisholm Larsson
45 8th Avenue,
New York NY 10011
Tel: 212 741 1703
info@chisholm-poster.com
www.chisholm-poster.com

CLV (A)
Clevedon Salerooms
The Auction Centre,
Kenn Road, Kenn, Clevedon,
Bristol BS21 6TT UK
Tel: +44(0)1934 830 111
Fax: +44(0)1934 832 538
info@clevedonsalerooms.co.uk
www.clevedon-salerooms.com

COB (D)
Cobwebs
78 Old Northam Road,
Southampton SO14 0PB UK
Tel: +44(0)2380 227 458
www.cobwebs.uk.com

COLC (D)
Collectors Cameras
P.O. Box 16, Pinner,
Middlesex HA5 4HN UK
Tel: +44(0)20 8421 3537

CRIS (D)
Cristobal
26 Church Street,
London NW8 8EP UK
Tel: +44(0)20 7724 7230
steven@cristobal.co.uk
www.cristobal.co.uk

CSA (D)
Christopher Sykes Antiques
The Old Parsonage, Woburn,
Milton Keynes MK17 9QL UK
Tel: +44(0)1525 290 259
www.sykes-corkscrews.co.uk

CSO (D)
Charlie Solomon
Otford Antiques & Collectables
Centre, 28-28 High Street,
Otford, Kent TN15 9DF UK
Tel: +44(0)1959 522 025
info@otfordantiques.co.uk
www.otfordantiques.co.uk

CVS (D)
**Cad Van Swankster at The Girl
Can't Help It**
Alfies Antiques Market,
Stand G100 & G90 & G80,
13-25 Church Street,
London NW8 8DT UK
Tel: +44(0)20 7724 8984
cad@sparklemoore.com

D (A)
Dickens Auctioneers
The Claydon Saleroom, Calvert
Rd, Middle Claydon Buckingham,
Bucks MK18 2EZ UK
Tel: +44(0)1296 714434
info@dickinsauctioneers.com
www.dickinsauctioneers.com

D&G (D)
Domas & Gray Gallery
Tel: 228 467 5294
info@domasandgraygallery.com
www.domasandgraygallery.com

DAC (D)
**Dynamite Antiques &
Collectibles**
eb625@verizon.net

DC/DCOL (P)
Dust Collectors

DD (D)
Decodame.com
Tel: 239 514 6797
info@decodame.com
www.decodame.com

DETC (D)
Deco Etc
122 West 25th Street
New York, NY 10001
Tel: 212 675 3326
deco_etc@msn.com
www.decoetc.net

DF (D)
Dad's Follies
moreinfo@dadsfollies.com
www.dadsfollies.com

DH (D)
Huxtins
david@huxtins.com
www.huxtins.com

DIM (D)
Dimech
Stand F46-49, Alfies Antiques
Market, 13-25 Church Street,
London NW8 8DT UK
Mob: +44(0)7787 130 955

DJI (D)
Deco Jewels Inc
Tel: 212 253 1222
decojewels@earthlink.net

DMI (P)
David Midgley
dgmidgley@yahoo.co.uk

DN (A)
Dreweatt Neate
Donnington Priory Salerooms,
Donnington, Newbury,
Berkshire RG14 2JE UK
Tel: +44(0)1635 553 553
donnington@dnfa.com
www.dnfa.com/donnington

DRA (A)
David Rago Auctions
333 North Main Street,
Lambertville, NJ 08530
Tel: 609 397 9374
info@ragoarts.com
www.ragoarts.com

DSC (P)
British Doll Showcase
squibbit@ukonline.co.uk
www.britishdollshowcase.co.uk

DTC (D)
Design20c
Tel: +44(0)7946 092 138
enquiry@design20c.co.uk
www.design20c.co.uk

DWG (D)
Griffin & Cooper
South Street Antiques Market
615 South 6th Street,
Philadelphia, PA 19147-2128
Tel: 215 592 0256

EAB (D)
Anne Barrett
Otford Antiques & Collectables
Centre, 28-28 High Street,
Otford, Kent TN15 9DF UK
Tel: +44(0)1959 522 025
info@otfordantiques.co.uk
www.otfordantiques.co.uk

ECLEC (D)
Eclectica
2 Charlton Place,
Islington, London N1 UK
Tel: +44(0)20 7226 5625
liz@eclectica.biz
www.eclectica.biz

EG (A)
Edison Gallery
Tel: 617 359 4678
glastris@edisongallery.com
www.edisongallery.com

ELI (D)
Eve Lickver
P.O. Box 1778
San Marcos CA 92079
Tel: 760 761 0868

F (A)
Fellows & Sons
Augusta House, 19 Augusta
Street, Hockley,
Birmingham B18 6JA UK
Tel: +44(0)121 212 2131
info@fellows.co.uk
www.fellows.co.uk

FAN (D)
Fantiques
Tel: +44(0)20 8840 4761
paula.raven@ntlworld.com

FBS (D)
Flo Blue Shoppe
Beverley Hill, Michigan
Tel: 248 433 1933
floblueshoppe@hotmail.com

FD (D)
Fragile Design
14-15 The Custard Factory,
Digbeth, Birmingham B9 4AA UK
Tel: +44(0)121 224 7378
www.fragiledesign.com

FFM (D)
Festival
No longer trading

FM (D)
Francesca Martire
Stand F131-137, Alfie's
Antiques Market, 13-25 Church
Street, London NW8 0RH UK
Tel: +44(0)20 7724 4802
info@francescamartire.com
www.francescamartire.com

FRE (A)
Freeman's
1808 Chestnut Street,
Philadelphia, PA 19103
Tel: 215 563 9275
info@freemansauction.com
www.freemansauction.com

GAZE (A)
Thos. Wm. Gaze & Son
Diss Auction Rooms, Roydon Rd,
Diss, Norfolk IP22 4LN UK
Tel: +44(0)1379 650 306
sales@dissauctionrooms.co.uk
www.twgaze.com

GBA (A)
Graham Budd Auctions
P.O. Box 47519,
London N14 6XD UK
Tel: +44(0)20 8366 2525
gb@grahambuddauctions.co.uk
www.grahambuddauctions.co.uk

GC (P)
Graham Cooley Collection
Mob: +44(0)7968 722 269
graham.cooley@metalysis.com

GGRT (D)
Gary Grant Choice Pieces
18 Arlington Way,
London EC1R 1UY UK
Tel: +44(0)20 7713 1122

GHOU (D)
Gardiner Houlgate
9 Leafield Way, Corsham,
Nr Bath SN13 9SW UK
Tel: +44(0)1225 812 912
auctions@gardinerhoulgate.co.uk
www.gardinerhoulgate.co.uk

GORL (A)
Gorringes, Lewes
15 North Street, Lewes, East
Sussex, BN7 2PD UK
Tel: +44(0)1273 472 503
clientservices@gorringes.co.uk
www.gorringes.co.uk

GORW/GOR (A)
Gorringes, Worthing
44-46 High Street, Worthing,
West Sussex BN11 1LL UK
Tel: +44(0)1903 238 999
clientservices@gorringes.co.uk
www.gorringes.co.uk

APPENDICES

GM (D)
Galerie Maurer
Kurfürstenstrasse 17
D-80799 Munich, Germany
Tel: 0049 89 271 13 45
info@galeriemaurer.de
www.galerie-objekte-maurer.de

GROB (D)
Geoffrey Robinson
Stand GO77-78 & GO91-92,
Alfies Antiques Market,
13-25 Church Street,
London NW8 8DT UK
Tel: +44(0)20 7723 0449
www.alfiesantiques.com

GWRA (A)
Gloucestershire Worcestershire
Railway Auctions
Tel: +44(0)1684 773 487 /
+44(0)1386 760 109
www.gwra.co.uk

H&G (D)
Hope and Glory
131A Kensington Church St,
London W8 7LP UK
Tel: +44(0)20 7727 8424

HA (A)
Hunt Auctions
73 East Ulwchlan Avenue, Suite
130, Exton PA 19341
Tel: 610 524 0822
info@huntauctions.com
www.huntauctions.com

HAMG (A)
Dreweatt Neate (Godalming)
Baverstock House, 93 High St,
Godalming, Surrey GU7 1AL UK
Tel: +44(0)1483 423 567
godalming@dnfa.com
www.dnfa.com

HERR (A)
Auktionshaus W.G. Herr
Friesenwall 35.
D-50672 Köln, Germany
Tel: 0049 221 25 45 48
kunst@herr-auktionen.de
www.herr-auktionen.de

HGS (D)
Harper General Store
Tel: 717 964 3453
lauver5@comcast.net
www.harpergeneralstore.com

HH (P)
Holiday Happenings

HLJ (D)
Hugo Lee-Jones
Tel: +44(0)1227 375 375
electroniccollectables@hotmail.com

HLM (D)
Hi & Lo Modern
161 Montclair Avenue
Montclair NJ 07042
sales@hiandlomodern.com
www.hiandlomodern.com

HP (D)
Hilary Proctor
Advintage, Shop E20,
Grays Antiques Market,
1-7 Davies Mews,
London W1Y 2PL UK
Tel: +44(0)20 7499 7001

ING (D)
Ingram Antiques
669 Mount Pleasant Road
Toronto, Canada M4S 2N2
Tel: 416 484 4601
ingramantiques@bellnet.ca
www.ingramgallery.com

ISA (D)
Ivey Selkirk Auctioneers
7447 Forsyth Boulevard,
St Louis MI 63105
Tel: 314 726 5515
www.iveyselkirk.com

JBC (P)
James Bridges Collection
james@jdbridges.fsnet.co.uk

JDJ (A)
James D Julia Inc
P.O. Box 830,
Fairfield, Maine 04937
Tel: 207 453 7125
jjulia@juliaauctions.com
www.juliaauctions.com

JEG (D)
John English Gifts
6 Princes Arcade,
London SW1Y 6DS UK
Tel: +44(0)20 7437 2082
brian@johnenglishgifts.com
www.johnenglishgifts.com

JES (D)
John Jesse Antiques
By appointment
jj@johnjesse.com

JF (D)
Jill Fenichell
305 East 61st Street,
New York, NY 10021
Tel: 212 980 9346
jfenichell@yahoo.com

JH (D)
Jeanette Hayhurst Fine Glass
32A Kensington Church Street,
London W8 4HA UK
Tel: +44(0)20 7938 1539

JJ (D)
Junkyard Jeweler
sales@junkyardjeweler.com
www.junkyardjeweler.com

JL (D)
Eastgate Antiques
Tel: +44(0)1206 822 712

JN (A)
John Nicholson Auctioneers
The Auction Rooms, 'Longfield',
Midhurst Road, Fernhurst,
Haslemere, Surrey GU27 3HA UK
Tel: +44(0)1428 653727
sales@johnnicholsons.com
www.johnnicholsons.com

KAU (A)
Auktionshaus Kaupp
Schloss Sulzburg, Hauptstrasse
62, 79295 Sulzburg, Germany
Fax: 00 49 7634 5038 50
auktionen@kaupp.de
www.kaupp.de

KCS (D)
KCS Ceramics
Tel: +44(0)20 8384 8981
karen@kcsceramics.co.uk
www.kcsceramics.co.uk

KNK (D)
Kitsch-N-Kaboodle
South Street Antiques Market,
615 South 6th Street,
Philadelphia, PA 19147-2128
Tel: 215 382 1354
kitschnkaboodle@yahoo.com

L (D)
Luna
23 George Street,
Nottingham NG1 3BH UK
Tel: +44(0)115 924 3267
info@luna-online.co.uk
www.luna-online.co.uk

L&T (A)
Lyon and Turnbull Ltd.
33 Broughton Place,
Edinburgh EH1 3RR UK
Tel: +44(0)131 557 8844
info@lyonandturnbull.com
www.lyonandturnbull.com

LAN (A)
Lankes
Triftfeldstrasse 1, 95182,
Döhlau Germany
Tel: +49 (0)928 69 50 50
info@lankes-auktionen.de
www.lankes-auktionen.de

LAW (A)
Lawrences Auctioneers
Norfolk House, High Street,
Bletchingley, Surrey RH1 4PA UK
Tel: +44(0)1883 743 323
www.lawrencesbletchingley.co.uk

LB (D)
Linda Bee
Stand L18-21, Grays Antique
Market, 58 Davies Street,
London W1Y 2LP UK
Tel: +44(0)20 7629 5921
lindabee@grays.clara.net
www.graysantiques.com

LCA (D)
Lights, Camera, Action
6 Western Gardens, Western
Boulevard, Aspley,
Nottingham HG8 5GP UK
Tel: +44(0) 115 913 1116
www.lca-autographs.co.uk

LDE (D)
Larry & Diana Elman
P.O. Box 415, Woodland Hills
California CA 91365

LFA (A)
Law Fine Art
The Long Gallery,
Littlecote House, Hungerford
Berkshire RG17 0SS UK
Tel: +44(0)1635 860 033
info@lawfineart.co.uk
www.lawfineart.co.uk

LHT (D)
Leanda Harwood
Tel: +44(0)1529 300 737
leanda.harwood@virgin.net
www.leandaharwood.co.uk

LOB (D)
Louis O'Brien
Tel: +44(0)1276 32907

LYNH (D)
Lynn & Brian Holmes
By appointment
Tel: +44(0)20 7368 6412

MA (D)
Manic Attic
Alfies Antiques Market, Stand
S48/49, 13 Church Street,
London NW8 8DT UK
Tel: +44(0)20 7723 6105
ianbroughton@hotmail.com

MAC (D)
Mary Ann's Collectibles
South Street Antiques Center
615 South 6th Street,
Philadelphia, PA 19147-2128
Tel: 215 592 0256
Tel: 215 923 3247

MAI (A)
Moore, Allen & Innocent
The Norcote Salerooms,
Burford Road, Norcote, Nr
Cirencester, Glos GL7 5RH UK
Tel: +44(0)1285 646 050
fineart@mooreallen.co.uk
www.mooreallen.co.uk

MAX (A)
Maxwells Auctioneers
133a Woodford Road Woodford,
Cheshire SK7 1QD UK
Tel: +44(0)161 439 5182
info@maxwells-auctioneers.co.uk
www.maxwells-auctioneers.co.uk

MBO (D)
Mori Books
Amherst Book Center,
141 Route 101A,
Amherst NH 03031
Tel: 603 882 2665
moribook@bit-net.com
www.moribooks.com

MEM (D)
Memory Lane
45-40 Bell Blvd, Suite 109,
Bayside, NY 11361
Tel: 718 428 8181
memlnny@aol.com
www.tias.com/stores/memlnny

MC (D)
Metropolis Collectibles, Inc.
873 Broadway, Suite 201,
New York, NY 10003
Tel: 212 260 4147
orders@metropoliscomics.com
www.metropoliscomics.com

MG (D)
Mod Girl
South Street Antiques Market
615 South 6th Street,
Philadelphia, PA 19147-2128
Tel: 215 592 0256

MGL (D)
Mix Gallery
17 South Main Street,
Lambertville NJ 08530
Tel: 609 773 0777
mixgallery1@aol.com
www.mixgallery.com

MGT (D)
Mary & Geoff Turvil
Tel: +44(0)1730 260 730
mary.turvil@virgin.net

MHC (P)
Mark Hill Collection
Mob: +44(0)7798 915 474
books@markhillpublishing.com
www.markhillpublishing.com

MHT (D)
Mum Had That
info@mumhadthat.com
www.mumhadthat.com

MI (D)
Mood Indigo
181 Prince Street,
New York, NY 10012
Tel: 212 254 1176
info@moodindigonewyork.com
www.moodindigonewyork.com

MILLB (D)
Million Dollar Babies
Tel: 518 885 7397

ML (D)
Mark Laino
Mark of Time, 132 South 8th
Street, Philadelphia, PA 19107
Tel: 215 922 1551
lecoultre@verizon.net

MM (A)
Mullock Madeley
The Old Shippon, Wall-under-
Heywood, Church Stretton,
Shropshire SY6 7DS UK
Tel: +44(0)169 477 1771
www.mullockmadeley.co.uk

MSA (D)
Manfred Schotten Antiques
109 Burford High Street,
Burford, Oxon OX18 4RH UK
Tel: +44(0)1993 822 302
enquiries@schotten.com
www.schotten.com

MTS (D)
The Multicoloured Time Slip
eBay Store: multicoloured
timeslip, eBay ID: dave65330
dave_a_cameron@hotmail.com

MUR (A)
Tony Murland Auctions
78 High Street, Needham
Market, Suffolk IP6 8AW UK
Tel: +44(0)1449 722 992
tony@antiquetools.co.uk
www.antiquetools.co.uk

NAI (D)
Nick Ainge
Tel: +44(0)1832 731 063
nick@ainge1930.fsnet.co.uk

NOR (D)
Neet-O-Rama
14 Division Street,
Somerville, NJ 08876
Tel: 908 722 4600
www.neetstuff.com

NPC (D)
No Pink Carpet
Tel: +44(0)1785 249 802
www.nopinkcarpet.com

OG (D)
Ormonde Gallery
No longer trading

OHA (D)
Owen Hargreaves &
Jasmine Dahl
By appointment:
9 Corsham St,
London N1 6DP UK
Tel: +44(0)20 7253 2669
owen@owenhargreaves.com
www.owenhargreaves.com

ON (A)
Onslows
The Coach House, Manor Road,
Stourpaine, Dorset DT11 8TQ UK
Tel: +44(0)1258 488 838
enquiries@onslows.co.uk
www.onslows.co.uk

P&I (D)
Paola & Iaia
Unit S057-58, Alfies Antiques
Market, 13-25 Church Street,
London NW8 8DT UK
Tel: +44(0)7751 084 135
paolaeiaialondon@hotmail.com

PA (D)
Senator Phil Arthurhulz
P.O. Box 12336
Lansing, MI 48901
Tel: 517 334 5000
Mob: 517 930 3000

PAC (D)
Port Antiques Center
289 Main Street
Port Washington NY 11050
Tel: 516 767 3313

PB (D)
Petersham Books
C/O Biblion
1-7 Davies Mews,
London W1K 5AB UK
Tel: +44(0)20 7629 1374
info@biblion.com
www.biblion.com

PC (P)
Private Collection

PCC (P)
Peter Chapman Collection
pgcbal1@supanet.com

PCOM (D)
Phil's Comics
P.O. Box 3433, Brighton
Sussex BN50 9JA UK
Tel: +44(0)1273 673 462
phil@phil-comics.com
www.phil-comics.com

PKA (D)
Phil & Karol Atkinson
May-Oct: 713 Sarsi Tr,
Mercer PA 16137
Tel: 724 475 2490
Nov-Apr: 7188 Drewry's Bluff
Road, Bradenton FL 34203
Tel: 941 755 1733

PL (D)
Peter Layton
London Glassblowing
7 The Leather Market
Weston Street,
London SE1 3ER UK
Tel: +44(0)20 7403 2800
info@londonglassblowing.co.uk
www.londonglassblowing.co.uk

PSA (A)
Potteries Specialist Auctions
271 Waterloo Road, Cobridge,
Stoke-on-Trent ST6 3HR UK
Tel: +44(0)1782 286 622
enquiries@potteriesauctions.com
www.potteriesauctions.com

PSI (D)
Paul Simons
Mob: +44(0)7733 326 574
pauliobanton@hotmail.com

PTC (P)
Pepe Tozzo Collection
info@hampshirepictures.co.uk
www.hampshirepictures.co.uk

PWE (A)
Philip Weiss Auction Galleries
1 Neil Court,
Oceanside, NY 11572
Tel: 516 594 073
info@philipweissauctions.com
ww.philipweissauctions.com

QU (A)
Quittenbaum Kunstauktionen
Hohenstaufenstrasse 1,
D-80801 Munich, Germany
Tel: 0049 89 33 00 756
info@quittenbaum.de
www.quittenbaum.de

RA (D)
Roding Arts
Tel: +44(0)1371 859 359
rodingarts@hotmail.com
http://uk.geocities.com/rodingarts/

RAON (D)
R.A. O'Neil
Ontario, Canada

RBC (D)
Reasons To Be Cheerful
Mob: +44(0)7708 025 579

RCC (D)
Royal Commemorative China
Paul Wynton & Joe Spiteri
Tel: +44(0)20 8863 0625
royalcommemoratives
@hotmail.com

RDL (A)
David Rago/Nicholas Dawes
Lalique Auctions
333 North Main Street,
Lambertville, NJ 08530
Tel: 609 397 9374
Fax: 609 397 9377
info@ragoarts.com
www.ragoarts.com

REL (D)
Relick
8 Golborne Road,
London W10 5NW UK
Tel: +44(0)20 8962 0089

RH (D)
Rick Hubbard Art Deco
Tel: +44(0)7767 267 607
www.rickhubbard-artdeco.co.uk

RITZ (D)
Ritzy
7 The Mall Antiques Arcade,
359 Upper Street,
London N1 0PD UK
Tel: +44(0)20 7704 0127

ROS (A)
Rosebery's
74-76 Knight's Hill, West
Norwood, London SE27 0JD UK
Tel: +44(0)20 8761 2522
www.roseberys.co.uk

RR (D)
Red Roses
Vintage Modes, Grays Antiques
Market, 1-7 Davies Mews,
London W1Y 2PL UK
Tel: +44(0)20 7629 7034
www.vintagemodes.co.uk

RSS (A)
Rossini SA
7 Rue Drouot
75009 Paris, France
Tel: 00 33 1 53 34 55 00
www.rossini.fr

RTC (A)
Ritchies
288 King Street East,
Toronto, Canada M5A 1KA
Tel: 416 364 1864
auction@ritchies.com
www.ritchies.com

RWA (D)
Richard Wallis Antiks
Tel: +44(0)20 8529 1749
info@richardwallisantiks.co.uk
www.richardwallisantiks.com

S&T (D)
Steinberg & Tolkien
193 King's Road
London SW3 5ED UK
Tel: +44(0)20 7376 3660

SAS (A)
Special Auction Services
Kennetholme, Midgham, Nr.
Reading, Berkshire RG7 5UX UK
Tel: +44(0)118 971 2949
mail@specialauctionservices.com
www.specialauctionservices.com

SCG (D)
Gallery 1930 Susie Cooper
18 Church Street, Marylebone,
London NW8 8EP UK
Tel: +44(0)20 7723 1555
gallery1930@aol.com
www.susiecooperceramics.com

SD (P)
Simon Dunlavey Collection
pennyblack@despammed.com

SDR (A)
Sollo:Rago Modern Auctions
333 North Main Street,
Lambertville, NJ 08530
Tel: 609 397 9374
Fax: 609 397 9377
info@ragoarts.com
www.ragoarts.com

SH (D)
Sara Hughes Vintage Compacts,
Antiques & Collectables
Mob: +44(0)775 9697 108
sara@sneak.freeserve.co.uk
http://mysite.wanadoo-
members.co.uk/sara_compacts/

SF (D)
The Silver Fund
1 Duke of York Street,
London SW1Y 6JP UK
Tel: +44(0)20 7839 7664
www.thesilverfund.com

SK (A)
Skinner, Inc.
The Heritage on the Garden
63 Park Plaza,
Boston MA 02116
Tel: 617 350 5400
also at
357 Main Street,
Bolton MA 01740
Tel: 978 7796 241
www.skinnerinc.com

SL (A)
Sloans & Kenyon
7034 Wisconsin Avenue
Chevy Chase MD 20815
Tel: 301 634 2330
www.sloansandkenyon.com

SM (D)
**Sparkle Moore at The Girl
Can't Help It**
Alfies Antiques Market, Stand
G100 & G90 & G80, 13-25
Church Street, Marylebone,
London NW8 8DT UK
Tel: +44(0)20 7724 8984
sparkle@sparklemoore.com
www.sparklemoore.com

SOTT (D)
Sign of the Tymes
Mill Antiques Center,
12 Morris Farm Road,
Lafayette, NJ 07848
Tel: 973 383 6028
jhap@nac.net
www.millantiques.com

STE (D)
Cloud Glass
info@cloudglass.com
www.cloudglass.com

SUM (D)
Sue Mautner Costume Jewellery
No longer trading.

SWA (A)
Swann Galleries Image Library
104 East 25th Street,
New York, NY 10010
Tel: 212 254 4710
swann@swanngalleries.com
www.swanngalleries.com

SWO (A)
Sworders
14 Cambridge Rd, Stansted
Mountfitchet CM24 8BZ UK
Tel: +44(0)1279 817 778
auctions@sworder.co.uk
www.sworder.co.uk

TCA (A)
Transport Car Auctions
14 The Green, Richmond,
Surrey TW9 1PX UK
Tel: +44(0)20 8940 2022
www.tc-auctions.com

TCF (D)
Cynthia Findlay
Toronto Antiques Center
276 King Street West, Toronto,
Ontario Canada M5V 1J2
Tel: 416 260 9057
www.cynthiafindlay.com

TCM (D)
Twentieth Century Marks
Whitegates, Rectory Road,
Little Burstead, Nr Billericay,
Essex CM12 9TR UK
Tel: +44(0)1268 411 000
info@20thcenturymarks.co.uk
www.20thcenturymarks.co.uk

TCS (D)
The Country Seat
Huntercombe Manor Barn,
Nr Henley on Thames,
Oxon RG9 5RY UK
Tel: +44(0)1491 641349
info@whitefriarsglass.com
www.whitefriarsglass.com

TCT (D)
The Calico Teddy
Tel: 410 433 9202
calicteddy@aol.com
www.calicoteddy.com

TD (D)
Two Dots
South Street Antiques Market,
615 South 6th Street,
Philadelphia, PA 19147-2128
Tel: 001 215 592 0256

TDG (D)
The Design Gallery
5 The Green, Westerham,
Kent TN16 1AS UK
Tel: +44(0)1959 561 234
sales@designgallery.co.uk
www.designgallery.co.uk

TEN (A)
Tennants
The Auction Centre, Leyburn,
North Yorkshire DL8 5SG UK
Tel: +44(0)1969 623 780
enquiry@tennants-ltd.co.uk
www.tennants.co.uk

TFR (D)
**Floyd & Rita's Antiques &
Collectibles**
Toronto Antiques Center
276 King Street West, Toronto,
Ontario Canada M5V 1J2
Tel: 416 260 9066
antiques@floydrita.com
www.floydrita.com

TGM (D)
The Glass Merchant
Tel: +44(0)7775 683 961
as@titan.freeserve.co.uk

TM (D)
Tony Moran
South Street Antiques Market,
615 South 6th Street,
Philadelphia, PA 19147-2128
Tel: 215 592 0256

TOA (D)
The Occupied Attic
Tel: 518 899 5030
occupied@nycup.rr.com
seguin12@aol.com

TOJ (D)
These Old Jugs
Susan L. Tillipman
Tel: 410 626 0770
susan@theseoldjugs.com
www.theseoldjugs.com

TP (D)
Tenth Planet
Unit 37a, Vicarage Field
Shopping Centre, Ripple Road,
Barking, Essex IG11 8DQ UK
Tel: +44(0)20 8591 5357
sales@tenthplanet.co.uk
www.tenthplanet.co.uk

TRA (D)
Toy Road Antiques
200 Highland Street, Canal,
Winchester, OH 4310
Tel: 614 834 1786
toyroadantiques@aol.com
www.goantiques.com/
members/toyroadantiques

TRIO (D)
Trio
Showcase V0010
Grays Antiques Market,
1-7 Davies Mews,
London W1K 5AB UK
Tel: +44(0)20 7493 2736
www.graysantiques.com

TSIS (D)
Three Sisters
South Street Antiques Market,
615 South 6th Street,
Philadelphia, PA 19147-2128
Tel: 215 592 0256

TYA (D)
Yank Azman
Toronto Antiques Center
276 King Street West, Toronto,
Ontario Canada M5V 1J2
Tel: 416 260 5662
yank@yank.ca
www.antiquesformen.com

V (D)
Ventisemo – Paolo Bonino
Stand G047/48/50/51
Alfie's Antiques Market,
13-25 Church Street
London NW8 8DT UK
Tel: +44(0)20 7723 1513
boninouk@yahoo.co.uk

VC (D)
Victor Caplin
Stand G075-76
Alfie's Antiques Market
13-25 Church Street
London NW8 8DT UK
victorcaplin@aol.com
http://www.maroc-n-roll.com

VE (D)
Vintage Eyeware of New York
Tel: 646 319 9222
www.vintage-eyeware.com

VEC (A)
Vectis Auctions Ltd
Fleck Way, Thornaby,
Stockton on Tees TS17 9JZ UK
Tel: +44(0)1642 750 616
admin@vectis.co.uk
www.vectis.co.uk

VM (D)
VinMag Co.
39/43 Brewer Street,
London W1R 9UD UK
Tel: +44(0)20 7439 8525
sales@vinmag.com
www.vinmag.com

VSC (D)
Vintage Sports Collector
3920 Via Solano, Palos Verdes
Estates, CA 90274
Tel: 310 375 1723

VZ (A)
Von Zezschwitz
Friedrichstrasse 1a,
80801 Munich, Germany
Tel: 00 49 89 38 98 930
www.von-zezschwitz.de

W&W (A)
Wallis & Wallis
West Steet Auction Galleries,
Lewes, East Sussex BN7 2NJ UK
Tel: +44(0)1273 480 208
auctions@wallisandwallis.co.uk
www.wallisandwallis.co.uk

WAD (D)
Waddington's Auctioneers
111 Bathurst Street, Toronto
Ontario Canada M5V 2R1
Tel: 416 504 9100
www.waddingtons.ca

WDL (A)
**Kunst-Auktionshaus Martin
Wendl**
August-Bebel-Straße 4, 07407
Rudolstadt, Germany
Tel: 011 49 3672 424 350
www.auktionshaus-wendl.de

WJT (D)
William Jamieson Tribal Art
Golden Chariot Productions
468 Wellington Street West,
Suite 201, Toronto,
Ontario Canada M5V 1E3
Tel: 416 596 1396
wrj@jamiesontribalart.com
www.jamiesontribalart.com

WW (A)
Woolley & Wallis
51-61 Castle Street, Salisbury,
Wiltshire SP1 3SU UK
Tel: +44(0)1722 424 500
www.woolleyandwallis.co.uk

ZDB (D)
Zardoz Books
20 Whitecroft,
Dilton Marsh, Westbury,
Somerset BA13 4DJ UK
Tel: +44(0)1373 865 371
www.zardozbooks.co.uk

DIRECTORY OF SPECIALISTS

If you wish to have any item valued, it is advisable to contact the dealer or specialist in advance to check that they will carry out this service and whether there is a charge. While most dealers will be happy to help you with an enquiry, do remember that they are busy people. Telephone valuations are not possible. Please mention the DK Collectibles Price Guide 2005 by Judith Miller when making an enquiry.

ADVERTISING

Senator Phil Arthurhultz
P.O. Box 12336,
Lansing, MI 48901
Tel: 517 334 5000
Mob: 517 930 3000

Phil & Karol Atkinson
May-Oct:
713 Sarsi Tr, Mercer, PA 16137
Tel: 724 475 2490
Nov-Apr:
7188 Drewry's Bluff Road,
Bradenton, FL 34203
Tel: 941 755 1733

The Nostalgia Factory
Original Movie Posters &
Related Ephemera, Charlestown
Commerce Center, 50 Terminal
St., Bldg. 2, Boston MA 02129
Tel: 617-241-8300 / 800-
479-8754
Fax: 617-241-0710
posters@nostalgia.com
www.nostalgia.com

Toy Road Antiques
200 Highland Street, Canal,
Winchester OH 43110
Tel: 614 834 1786
toyroadantiques@aol.com
www.goantiques.com/members
/toyroadantiques

AMERICANA

Richard Axtell Antiques
1 River St, Deposit, NY 13754
Tel: 607 467 2353
Fax: 607 467 4316
raxtell@msn.com
www.axtellantiques.com

Buck County Antique Center
Route 202, Lahaksa, PA 18931
Tel: 215 794 9180

Fields of Glory
55 York St, Gettysburg,
PA 17325
Tel: 717 337 2837
foglory@cvn.net
www.fieldsofglory.com

Larry and Dianna Elman
PO Box 415, Woodland Hills,
CA 91365

Olde Hope Antiques
P.O. Box 718, New Hope,
PA 18938
Tel: 215 297 0200
info@oldehope.com
www.oldehope.com

The Splendid Peasant
Route 23 & Sheffield Rd,
P.O. Box 536,
South Egremont, MA 01258
Tel: 413 528 5755
folkart@splendindpeasant.com
www.splendidpeasant.com

Patricia Stauble Antiques
180 Main Street, P.O. Box 265,
Wiscasset, ME 04578
Tel: 207 882 6341
pstauble@midcoast.com

AUTOGRAPHS

Autographs of America
P.O. Box 461, Provo,
UT 84603-0461
tanders3@autographsofamerica
.com
www.autographsofamerica.com

Platt Autographs
PO Box 135007, Clermont, FL
34711
Tel: 352 241 9164
ctplatt@ctplatt.com
www.ctplatt.com

AUTOMOBILIA

Dunbar's Gallery
54 Haven St. Milford, MA
01757
Tel: 508 634 8697
Fax: 508 634 8697
dunbarsgallery@comcast.net
http://dunbarsgallery.com

BOOKS

Abebooks
www.abebooks.com

Aleph-Bet Books
85 Old Mill River Rd., Pound
Ridge, NY 10576, US Postal
Service
Tel: 914 764-7410
Fax: 914 764-1356
helen@alephbet.com
www.alephbet.com

Bauman Rare Books
535 Madison Ave, between
54th & 55th Streets,
New York, NY 10022
Tel: 212 751 0011
brb@baumanrarebooks.com
www.baumanrarebooks.com

Deer Park Books
Abebooks Inc., #4 - 410
Garbally Road, Victoria, BC V8T
2K1, Canada
Tel/Fax: 860 350 4140
deerparkbk@aol.com
www.deerparkbooks.com

CANADIANA

Yank Azman
Toronto Antiques Centre, 276
King Street West, Toronto,
Ontario, M5V 1J2 Canada
Tel: 416 345 9941
yank@yank.ca
www.antiquesformen.com

The Blue Pump
178 Davenport Road,
Toronto, Canada M5R 1J2
Tel: 416 944 1673
www.thebluepump.com

CERAMICS

The Perrault-Rago Gallery
333 North Main Street,
Lambertville, NJ 08530
Tel: 609 397 1802
www.ragoarts.com

Pair Antiques
12707 Hillcrest Dr, Longmont,
CO 80501-1162
Tel: 303 772 2760

Greg Walsh
P.O. Box 747, Potsdam, NY
13676-0747
Tel: 315 265 9111
gwalsh@northnet.org
www.walshauction.com

Happy Pastime
P.O. Box 1225, Ellicott City,
MD 21041-1225
Tel: 410 203 1101
hpastime@bellatlantic.net
www.happypastime.com

Keller & Ross
47 Prospect Street, Melrose,
MA 02176
Tel: 781 662 7257
kellerross@aol.com
http://members.aol.com/kellerross

Ken Forster
5501 Seminary Road,
Ste 1311, South Falls Church,
VA 22041
Tel: 703 379 1142
(Art Pottery)

Mellin's Antiques
P.O. Box 1115,
Redding CT 06875
Tel: 203 938 9538
remellin@aol.com

Mark & Marjorie Allen
300 Bedford St. Suite 421,
Manchester, NH 03101
Tel: 603 644 8989
mandmallen@adelphia.net
www.antiquedelft.com

Charles & Barbara Adams
By appointment only
289 Old Main St, South
Yarmouth, MA 02664
Tel: 508 760 3290
adams_2430@msn.com

These Old Jugs
Susan L. Tillipman
Tel: 410 626 0770
susan@theseoldjugs.com
www.theseoldjugs.com

CHARACTER COLLECTIBLES

What A Character!
hugh@whatacharacter.com
bazuin32@aol.com
www.whatacharacter.com

COMICS

Carl Bonasera
A1-American Comic Shops,
3514 W. 95th St,
Evergreen Park, IL 60642
Tel: 708 425 7555

Metropolis Collectibles Inc.
873 Broadway, Suite 201,
New York, NY 10003
Tel: 212 260 4147
Fax: 212 260 4304
orders@metropoliscomics.com
www.metropoliscomics.com

The Comic Gallery
4224 Balboa Ave, San Diego,
CA 92117
Tel: 619 483 4853

COSTUME & ACCESSORIES

Andrea Hall Levy
P.O. Box 1243, Riverdale, NY
10471
Tel: 646 441 1726
barangrill@aol.com

Fayne Landes Antiques
593 Hansell Road,
Wynnewood, PA 19096
Tel: 610 658 0566
fayne@comcast.net

Yesterday's Threads
206 Meadow St, Branford,
CT 06405-3634
Tel: 203 481 6452

Lucy's Hats
1118 Pine Street,
Philadelphia, PA

Vintage Eyeware
Tel: 646 319 9222

COSTUME JEWELRY

Aurora Bijoux
Tel: 215 872 7808
aurora@aurorabijoux.com
www.aurorabijoux.com

Barbara Blau
South Street Antiques Market,
c/o South Street Antiques
Market 615 South 6th Street,
Philadelphia, PA 19147-2128
Tel: 215 739 4995/ 592 0256
bbjools@msn.com

The Junkyard Jeweler
www.junkyardjeweler.com

Mod-Girl
South Street Antiques Center,
615 South 6th Street,
Philadelphia, PA 19147
Tel: 215 592 0256

Roxanne Stuart
Langhorne PA
Tel: 215 750 8868
gemfairy@aol.com

Terry Rodgers & Melody LLC
30 & 31 Manhattan Art &
Antique Center, 1050 2nd
Avenue, New York, NY 10022
Tel: 212 758 3164
melodyjewelnyc@aol.com

Bonny Yankauer
Tel: 201 825 7697
bonnyy@aol.com

DISNEYANA

MuseumWorks
525 East Cooper Avenue,
Aspen CO 81611
Tel: 970-544-6113
Fax: 970-544-6044
www.mwhgalleries.com

Sign of the Tymes
Mill Antiques Center, 12 Morris
Farm Road, Lafayette, NJ
07848
Tel: 973 383 6028
jhap@nac.net
www.millantiques.com

DOLLS

Memory Lane
45-40 Bell Blvd, Suite 109,
Bayside, NY 11361
Tel: 718 428 8181
memlnny@aol.com
www.tias.com/stores/memlnny

Treasure & Dolls
518 Indian Rocks Rd, N.
Belleair Bluffs, FL 33770
Tel: 727 584 7277
dolls@treasuresanddolls.com
www.treasuresanddolls.com

FIFTIES & SIXTIES

Deco Etc
122 West 25th Street (btw 6th &
7th Aves), New York, NY 10001
Tel: 212 675 3326
deco_etc@msn.com
www.decoetc.net

Kathy's Korner
Tel: 516 624 9494

Lois' Collectibles
Market III, 413 W Main St,
Saint Charles, IL 60174-1815
Tel: 630 377 5599

Nifty Fifties
Tel: 734 782 3974

Neet-O-Rama
14 Division Street,
Somerville, NJ 08876
Tel: 908 722 4600
www.neetstuff.com

Steve Colby
Off The Deep End, 712 East St,
Frederick, MD 21701-5239
Tel:800 248 0645
Fax: 301-766-0215
contact@offthedeepend.com
www.offthedeepend.com

FILM MEMORABILIA

STARticles
58 Stewart St, Studio 301,
Toronto, Ontario,
M5V 1H6 Canada
Tel/fax: 416 504 8286
info@starticles.com

Norma's Jeans
3511 Turner Lane, Chevy
Chase, MD 20815-2313
Tel: 301 652 4644
Fax: 301 907 0216

George Baker
CollectorsMart, P.O. Box
580466, Modesto, CA 95358
Tel; 290 537 5221
Fax: 209 531 0233
georgeb1@thevision.net
www.collectorsmart.com

GENERAL

Adamstown Antiques Market
Route 272, Adamstown, PA
19501
Tel: 215-484-4385

Anastacia's Antiques
617 Bainbridge Street,
Philadelphia, PA 19147

Antiques of Cape May
Tel: 800 224 1687

**Black Horse Antique
Showcases**
2180 North Reading Road,
Denver PA, 17517
Tel: 717 335 3300

Bucks County Antique Center
Route 202, Lahaska, PA 18931
Tel: 215 794 9180

Burlwood Antique Center
Route 3, Meredith, NH 03523
Tel: 603 279 6387
www.burlwood-antiques.com

Camelot Antiques
7871 Ocean Gateway,
Easton, MD 21601
Tel: 410 820 4396
camelot@goeaston.net
www.about-
antiques.com/CamelotAntiques

Manhattan Art & Antiques Center
1050 Second Avenue (between
55th & 56th Street) New York,
NY, 10022
Tel: 212-355-4400
Fax: 212-355-4403
info@the-maac.com
www.the-maac.com

The Lafayette Mill Antiques
12 Morris Farm Road (Just off
Rte 15), Lafayette NJ 07848
Tel: 973 383 0065
millpartners@inpro.net
www.millantiques.com

South Street Antiques Market
615 South 6th Street,
Philadelphia, PA 19147
Tel: 215 592 0256.

The Showplace
40 W. 25th St., New York City,
New York, United States
Tel: 212 741 8520

Toronto Antiques Centre
276 King Street West, Toronto,
Ontario M5V 1J2 Canada
Tel: 416 345 9941

GLASS

The End of History
548 1/2 Hudson Street,
New York, NY 10014
Tel: 212 647 7598
Fax: 212 647 7634

Past-Tyme Antiques
Tel: 703 777 8555
pasttymeantiques@aol.com

Jeff F. Purtell
31 Pleasant Point Drive,
Portsmouth, NH 03801
Tel: 800-973-4331
jfpurtell@steubenpurtell.com
www.steubenpurtell.com
(Steuben)

Paul Reichwein
2321 Hershey Ave, East
Petersburg, PA 17520
Tel: 717 569 7637
paulrdg@aol.com

Paul Stamati Gallery
1050 2nd Ave, New York,
NY 10022
Tel: 212 754 4533
Fax: 212 754-4552
www.stamati.com

Suzman's Antiques
P.O. Box 301, Rehoboth, MA
02769
Tel: 508 252 5729

HOLIDAY MEMORABILIA

Chris & Eddie's Collectibles
c/o South Street Antiques
Market, 615 South 6th Street,
Philadelphia, PA 19147
Tel: 215 592 0256

Sign of the Tymes
Mill Antiques Center, 12 Morris
Farm Road, Lafayette, NJ
07848
Tel: 973 383 6028
jhap@nac.net
www.millantiques.com

KITCHENALIA

**Dynamite Antiques &
Collectibles**
eb625@verizon.net

Village Green Antiques
Port Antiques Center, 289 Main
Street, Port Washington, NY
11050
Tel: 516 625 2946
amysdish@optonline.net

LUNCH BOXES

Seaside Toy Center
Joseph Soucy
179 Main St,
Westerly, RI 02891
Tel: 401 596 0962

MARBLES

Auction Blocks
P.O. Box 2321, Shelton, CT
06484
Tel: 203 924 2802
auctionblocks@aol.com
www.auctionblocks.com

MECHANICAL MUSIC

The Music Box Shop
6102 North 16th Street,
Phoenix, AZ 85016
Tel: 602 277-9615
musicboxshop@home.com
www.themusicboxshop.com

Mechantiques
The Crescent Hotel,
75 Prospect St,
Eureka Springs, AR 72632
Tel: 479-253-0405
mroenigk@aol.com
www.mechantiques.com

MILITARIA

Articles of War
358 Boulevard,
Middletown, RI 02842
Tel: 401 846 8503
dutch5@ids.net

PENS & WRITING EQUIPMENT

Fountain Pen Hospital
10 Warren Street,
New York, NY 10007
Tel: 212 964 0580
info@fountainpenhospital.com
www.fountainpenhospital.com

Gary & Myrna Lehrer
16 Mulberry Rd, Woodbridge,
CT 06525-1717
Tel: 203 389 5295
Fax: 203 389 4515
garylehrer@aol.com
www.gopens.com

David Nishimura
Vintage Pens, P.O. Box 41452
Providence, RI 02940-1452
Tel: 401 351 7607
www.vintagepens.com

Sandra & L. 'Buck' van Tine
Lora's Memory Lane, 13133
North Caroline St, Chillicothe, IL
61523-9115
Tel: 309 579 3040
Fax: 309 579 2696
lorasink@aol.com

Pendemonium
619 Avenue G, Fort Madison, IA
52627
Tel: 319 372 0881
Fax: 319 372 0882
www.pendemonium.com

PLASTICS

Dee Battle
9 Orange Blossom Trail,
Yalaha, FL 34797
Tel: 352 324 3023

Malabar Enterprises
172 Bush Lane, Ithaca,
NY 14850
Tel: 607 255 2905
Fax: 607 255 4179
asn6@cornell.edu

POSTERS

Posteritati
239 Center St, New York,
NY 10013
Tel: 212 226 2207
Fax: 212 226 2102
mail@posteritati.com
www.posteritati.com

Chisholm Larsson
145 8th Avenue,
New York, NY 10011
Tel: 212 741 1703
www.chisholm-poster.com

Vintage Poster Works
P.O. Box 88, Pittford, NY 14534
Tel: 585 381 9355
debra@vintageposterworks.com
www.vintageposterworks.com

La Belle Epoque
11661 San Vincente, 3304 Los
Angeles, CA 90049-5110
Tel: 310 442 0054
Fax: 310 826 6934
ktscicon@ix.netcom.com

RADIOS

Catalin Radios
5443 Schultz Drive, Sylvania,
OH 43560
Tel: 419 824 2469
Mob: 419 283 8203
steve@catalinradio.com
www.catalinradio.com

ROCK & POP

Heinz's Rare Collectibles
P.O. Box 179, Little Silver,
NJ 07739-0179
Tel: 732 219 1988
Fax: 732 219 5940
(The Beatles)

Tod Hutchinson
P.O. Box 915, Griffith,
IN 46319-0915
Tel: 219 923 8334
toddtcb@aol.com
(Elvis Presley)

SCENT BOTTLES

Oldies But Goldies
860 NW Sorrento Ln. Port St.
Lucie, FL 34986
Tel. 772 873 0968
email@oldgood.com
www.oldgood.com

Monsen & Baer Inc
P.O. Box 529, Vienna, VA
22183-0529
Tel: 703 938 2129
monsenbaer@erols.com

SCIENTIFIC & TECHNICAL, INCLUDING OFFICE & OPTICAL

George Glazer Gallery
28 East 2nd St,
New York, NY 10021
Tel: 212-535-5706
Fax 212-658-9512
worldglobe@georgeglazer.com
www.georgeglazer.com

Tesseract
coffeen@aol.com
www.etesseract.com

The Olde Office
68-845 Perez Rd, Ste 30,
Cathedral City, CA 92234
Tel: 760 346 8653
Fax: 760 346 6479
info@thisoldeoffice.com
www.thisoldeoffice.com

Jane Hertz
Fax: 941 925-0487
auction01122@aol.com
auction@breker.com
www.breker.com
(Cameras, Office & Technical
Equipment)

SMOKING

Richard Weinstein
International Vintage Lighter
Exchange, 30 W. 57th St,
New York, NY 10019
Tel: 212 586 0947
info@vintagelighters.com
www.vintagelighters.com

Ira Pilossof
Vintage Lighters Inc., P.O. Box
1325, Fairlawn,
NJ 07410-8325
Tel: 201 797 6595
vintageltr@aol.com

Mike Cassidy
1070 Bannock #400,
Denver, CO 80204
Tel: 303 446 2726

Chuck Haley
Sherlock's, 13926 Double Girth
Ct., Matthews, NC 28105-4068
Tel: 704 847 5480

SPORTING MEMORABILIA

Classic Rods & Tackle
P.O. Box 288, Ashley Falls, MA
01222
Tel: 413 229 7988

Larry Fritsch Cards Inc
735 Old Wassau Rd, P.O. Box
863, Stevens Point, WI 54481
Tel: 715 344 8687
Fax: 715 344 1778
larry@fritschcards.com
www.fritschcards.com
(Baseball Cards)

George Lewis
Golfiana, P.O. Box 291,
Mamaroneck, NY 10543
Tel: 914 698 4579
findit@golfiana.com
www.golfiana.com

Golf Collectibles
P.O. Box 165892,
Irving, TX 75016
Tel: 800 882 4825
furjanic@directlink.net
www.golfforallages.com

The Hager Group
P.O. Box 952974, Lake Mary,
FL 32795
Tel: 407 788 3865
(Trading Cards)

Hall's Nostalgia
21-25 Mystic St, P.O. Box 408,
Arlington, MA 02174
Tel: 781 646 7757

Tom & Jill Kaczor
1550 Franklin Rd, Langhorne,
PA 19047
Tel: 215 968 5776
Fax: 215 946 6056

Vintage Sports Collector
3920 Via Solano, Palos Verdes
Estates, CA 90274
Tel: 310 375 1723

TEDDY BEARS & SOFT TOYS

Harper General Store
10482 Jonestown Rd, Annville,
PA 17003
Tel: 717 865 3456
Fax: 717 865 3813
lauver5@comcast.net
www.harpergeneralstore.com

Marion Weis
Division St Antiques, P.O. Box
374, Buffalo, MN 55313-0374
Tel: 612 682 6453

TOYS & GAMES

Atomic Age
318 East Virginia Road,
Fullerton, CA 92831
Tel: 714 446 0736
Fax: 714 446 0436
atomage100@aol.com

Barry Carter
Knightstown Antiques Mall, 136
W. Carey St, Knightstown,
IN 46148-1111
Tel: 765 345 5665
bcarter@spitfire.net

France Antique Toys
Tel: 631 754 1399

Roger & Susan Johnson
6264 Valley Creek, Pilot Point,
TX 76258
Tel: 940 686 5686
czarmann@aol.com

Kitsch-N-Kaboodle
c/o South Street Antiques
Market, 615 South 6th Street,
Philadelphia, PA 19147-2128
Tel: 215 382 1354
kitschnkaboodle@yahoo.com

Litwin Antiques
P.O. Box 5865, Trenton,
NJ 08638-0865
Tel/Fax: 609 275 1427
(Chess)

Harry R. McKeon, Jr.
18 Rose Lane, Flourtown,
PA 19031-1910
Tel: 215 233 4094
toyspost@aol.com
(Tin Toys)

Jessica Pack Antiques
Chapel Hill, NC
Tel: 919 408 0406
jpants1@aol.com

The Old Toy Soldier Home
977 S. Santa Fe, Ste 11
Vista, CA 92083
Tel: 760 758 5481
oldtoysoldierhome@earthlink.net
www.oldtoysoldierhome.com

Trains & Things
210 East Front Street, Traverse
City, Michigan 49684
Tel: 231 947 1353
www.tctrains.com

WATCHES

Mark Laino
c/o South Street Antiques
Center, 615 South 6th Street,
Philadelphia, PA 19147
Tel: 215 592 0256

Texas Time
3076 Waunuta St, Newbury
Park, CA 1320
Tel: 805 498 5644
paul@dock.net

WINE & DRINKING

Derek White
The Corkscrew Pages, 769
Sumter Dr, Morrisville,
PA 19067
Tel: 215 493 4143
Fax: 609 860 5380
dswhite@marketsource.com
www.taponline.com

Donald A. Bull
P.O. Box 596, Wirtz, VA 24184
Tel: 540 721 1128
Fax: 540 721 5468
corkscrew@bullworks.net

Steve Visakay Cocktail Shakers
P.O. Box 1517 West Caldwell,
NJ 07007-1517
svisakay@aol.com

DIRECTORY OF AUCTIONEERS

This is a list of auctioneers that conduct regular sales. Auctioneers who wish to be listed in this directory for our next edition, space permitting, are requested to email info@thepriceguidecompany.com by February 2005.

ALABAMA

Flomaton Antique Auctions
P.O. Box 1017, 320 Palafox
Street, Flomaton, AL 36441
Tel: 251 296-3059
Fax: 251 296-1974
www.flomatonantiqueauction.com

ARIZONA

Dan May & Associates
4110 N. Scottsdale Road,
Scottsdale, AZ 85251
Tel: 602 941 4200

ARKANSAS

Ponders Auctions
1504 South Leslie, Stuttgart,
AR 72160
Tel: 501 673 6551

CALIFORNIA

Aurora Galleries International
30 Hackamore Lane, Ste 2,
Bell Canyon, CA 91307
Tel: 818 884 6468
Fax: 818 227 2941
vcampbell@auroraauctions.com
www.auroragalleriesonline.com

Butterfield & Butterfield
7601 Sunset Blvd, Los Angeles,
CA 90046
Tel: 323 850 7500
Fax: 323 850 5843
info@butterfields.com
www.butterfields.com

Butterfield & Butterfield
220 San Bruno Ave, San
Francisco, CA 94103
Tel: 415 861 7500
Fax: 415 861 8951
info@butterfields.com
www.butterfields.com

Clark Cierlak Fine Arts
14452 Ventura Blvd, Sherman
Oaks, CA 91423
Tel: 818 783 3052
Fax: 818 783 3162
gallery@pacbell.net
www.estateauctionservice.com

I.M. Chait Gallery
9330 Civic Center Dr, Beverly
Hills, CA 90210
Tel: 310 285 0182
Fax: 310 285 9740
chait@chait.com
www.chait.com

**Cuschieri's Auctioneers
& Appraisers**
863 Main Street, Redwood City,
CA 94063
Tel: 650 556 1793
Fax: 650 556 9805
www.cuschieris.com

eBay, Inc
2005 Hamilton Ave, Ste 350,
San Jose, CA 95125
Tel: 408 369 4839
www.ebay.com

L.H. Selman
123 Locust St, Santa Cruz,
CA 95060
Tel: 800 538 0766
Fax: 408 427 0111
leselman@got.net

Malter Galleries
17003 Ventura Blvd, Encino,
CA 91316
Tel: 818 784 7772
Fax: 818 784 4726
www.maltergalleries.com

Poster Connection Inc
43 Regency Dr, Clayton,
CA 94517
Tel: 925 673 3343
Fax: 925 673 3355
sales@posterconnection.com
www.posterconnection.com

Profiles in History
110 North Doheny Dr, Beverly
Hills, CA 90211
Tel: 310 859 7701
Fax: 310 859 3842
www.profilesinhistory.com

San Rafael Auction Gallery
634 Fifth Avenue,
San Rafael, CA 9490
Tel: 415 457 4488
Fax: 415 457 4899
www.sanrafael-auction.com

Slawinski Auction Co.
The Scotts Valley Sports Center,
251 Kings Village Road, Scotts
Valley, CA 95066
Tel: 831 335 9000
www.slawinski.com

CONNECTICUT

Alexander Autographs
100 Melrose Ave,
Greenwich, CT 06830
Tel: 203 622 8444
Fax: 203 622 8765
info@alexautographs.com
www.alexautographs.com

Norman C. Heckler & Co.
79 Bradford Corner Road,
Woodstock Valley, CT 0682
Tel: 860 974 1634
Fax: 860 974 2003
www.hecklerauction.com

Lloyd Ralston Gallery
350 Long Beach Blvd,
Stratford, CT 016615
Tel: 203 386 9399
Fax: 203 386 9519
lrgallery@sbcglobal.net
www.lloydralstontoys.com

DELAWARE

Remember When Auctions Inc.
Tel: 302 436 4979
Fax: 302 436 4626
sales@history-attic.com
www.history-attic.com

FLORIDA

Auctions Neapolitan
995 Central Avenue, Naples,
FL 34102
Tel: 941 262 7333
kathleen@auctionsneapolitan.com
www.auctionsneapolitan.com

Burchard Galleries
2528 30th Ave N, St
Petersburg, FL 33713
Tel: 727 821 1167
www.burchardgalleries.com

**Dawson's, now trading as
Dawson's & Nye**
P.O. Box 646, Palm Beach,
FL 33480
Tel: 561 835 6930
Fax: 561 835 8464
info@dawsons.org
www.dawsons.org

Arthur James Galleries
615 E. Atlantic Ave, Delray
Beach, FL 33483
Tel: 561 278 2373
Fax: 561 278 7633
www.arthurjames.com

Kincaid Auction Company
3809 East CR 542, Lakeland,
FL 33801
Tel: 800 970 1977
www.kincaid.com

Sloan's Auction Galleries
8861 NW 19th Terace, Ste
100, Miami, FL 33172
Tel: 305 751 4770
sloans@sloansauction.com
www.sloansandkenyon.com

GEORGIA

Great Gatsby's
5070 Peachtree Industrial Blvd,
Atlanta, GA
Tel: 770 457 1903
Fax: 770-457-7250
www.gatsbys.com

My Hart Auctions Inc
P.O. Box 2511, Cumming,
GA 30028
Tel: 770 888 9006
www.myhart.net

IDAHO

The Coeur D'Alene Art Auction
P.O. Box 310, Hayden, ID
83835
Tel: 208 772 9009
Fax: 208 772 8294
cdaartauction@cdaartauction.com
www.cdaartauction.com

ILLINOIS

Leslie Hindman Inc.
122 North Aberdeen Street,
Chicago, IL 60607
Tel: 312 280 1212
Fax: 312 280 1211
www.lesliehindman.com

Joy Luke
300 East Grove Street,
Bloomington, IL 61701
Tel: 309 828 5533
Fax: 309 829 2266
robert@joyluke.com
www.joyluke.com

Mastronet Inc
10S 660 Kingery Highway,
Willobrook, IL 60527
Tel: 630 471 1200
info@mastronet.com
www.mastronet.com

INDIANA

**Curran Miller Auction &
Realty Inc**
4424 Vogel Rd, Ste 400,
Evansville, IN 47715
Tel: 812 474 6100
Fax: (812) 474-6110
cmar@curranmiller.com
www.curranmiller.com

Kruse International
5540 County Rd 11A,
Auburn, IN 46706
Tel: 800 968 4444
info@kruseinternational.com
www.kruseinternational.com

Lawson Auction Service
P.O. Box 885, North Vernon, IN
47265
Tel: 812 372 2571
www.lawsonauction.com

Stout Auctions
529 State Road 28 East,
Willamsport, IN 47993
Tel: 765 764 6901
Fax: 765-764-1516
info@stoutauctions.com
www.stoutauctions.com

IOWA

**Jackson's Auctioneers &
Appraisers**
2229 Lincoln St, Cedar Falls,
IA 50613
Tel: 319 277 2256
Fax: 319-2771252
www.jacksonsauction.com

Tom Harris auctions
2035 18th Ave, Marshalltown,
IA 50158
Tel: 641 754 4890
Fax: 641 753 0226
tomharris@tomharrisauctions.com
www.tomharrisauctions.com

Tubaugh Auctions
1702 8th Ave, Belle Plaine,
IA 52208
Tel: 319 444 2413 /
319.444.0169
www.tubaughauctions.com

KANSAS

Manions International Auction House
P.O. Box 12214, Kansas City,
KS, 66112
Tel: 913 299 9692
Fax: 913 299 6792
collecting@manions.com
www.manions.com

CC Auctions
416 Court St, Clay Center, KS
67432
Tel: 785 632 6021
dhamilton@cc-auctions.com
www.cc-auctions.com

Brian Spielman Auctions
PO Box 884, Emporia, KS
66801
Tel: 620-341-0637 or 620-
437-2424
spielman@madtel.net
www.kansasauctions.net/spiel
man

KENTUCKY

Hays & Associates Inc
120 South Spring Street,
Louisville, KY 40206
Tel: 502 584 4297
kenhays@haysauction.com
www.haysauction.com

Steffens Historical Militaria
P.O. Box 280, Newport,
KY 41072
Tel: 859 431 4499
Fax: 859 431 3113
www.steffensmilitaria.com

LOUSIANA

New Orleans Auction Galleries
801 Magazine Street, New
Orleans, LA 70130
Tel: 504 566 1849
Fax: 504 566 1851
info@neworleansauction.com
www.neworleansauction.com

MAINE

James D. Julia Auctioneers Inc.
P.O. Box 830, Fairfield, Maine
04937
Tel: 207 453 7125
jjulia@juliaauctions.com
www.juliaauctions.com

Thomaston Place Auction Galleries
P.O. Box 300, 51 Atlantic
Highway, US Rt 1 Thomaston
ME 04861
Tel: 207 354 8141
Fax: 207 354 9523
barbara@kajav.com
www.thomastonauction.com

MARYLAND

Guyette & Schmidt
PO Box 1170, St. Michaels, MD
21663.
Tel: 410-745-0485
Fax: 410-745-0457
decoys@guyetteandschmidt.com
www.guyetteandschmidt.com

Hantman's Auctioneers & Appraisers
P.O. Box 59366, Potomac,
MD 20859
Tel: 301 770 3720
Fax: 301 770 4135
hantman@hantmans.com
www.hantmans.com

Isennock Auctions & Appraisals
4106B Norrisville Road, White
Hall, MD 21161
Tel: 410-557-8052
Fax 410-692-6449
isennock@isennockauction.com
www.isennockauction.com

Sloans & Kenyon
7034 Wisconsin Avenue, Chevy
Chase, Maryland 20815
Tel: 301 634-2330
Fax: 301 656-7074
info@sloansandkenyon.com
www.sloansandkenyon.com

MASSACHUSETTS

Eldred's
P.O. Box 796, 1483 Route 6A
East Dennis, MA 02641
Tel: 508 385 3116
Fax: 508 385 7201
info@eldreds.com
www.eldreds.com

Grogan & Company
22 Harris St, Dedham,
MA 02026
Tel: 800-823 1020
Fax: 781 461 9625
grogans@groganco.com
www.groganco.com

Simon D. Hill & Associates
420 Boston Turnpike,
Shrewsbury, MA 01545
Tel: 508 845 2400
Fax: 978 928 4129
www.simondhillauctions.com

Skinner Inc
The Heritage on the Garden, 63
Park Plaza, Boston, MA 02116
Tel: 617-350-5400
Fax: 617-350-5429
info@skinnerinc.com
www.skinnerinc.com

Willis Henry Auctions
22 Main St, Marshfield,
MA 02050
Tel: 781 834 7774
Fax: 781 826 3520
wha@willishenry.com
www.willishenry.com

MICHIGAN

DuMouchelles
409 East Jefferson Ave,
Detroit, MI 48226
Tel: 313 963 6255
Fax: 313 963 8199
info@dumouchelles.com
www.dumouchelles.com

MINNESOTA

Buffalo Bay Auction Co
825 Fox Run Trail, Edmond, OK
73034
Tel: 405 285 8990
buffalobayauction@hotmail.com
www.buffalobayauction.com

Rose Auction Galleries
3180 Country Drive, Little
Canada, MN 55117
Tel: 651 484 1415 / 888-484-
1415
Fax: 651 636 3431
auctions@rosegalleries.com
www.rosegalleries.com

MISSOURI

Ivey-Selkirk
7447 Forsyth Blvd, Saint Louis,
MO 63105
Tel: 314 726 5515
Fax: 314 726 9908
www.iveyselkirk.com

MONTANA

Allard Auctions Inc
P.O. Box 1030 St Ignatius,
MT 59865
Tel: 406 745 0500
Fax: 406 745 0502
www.allardauctions.com

NEW HAMPSHIRE

Northeast Auctions
93 Pleasant St, Portmouth,
NH 03801-4504
Tel: 603 433 8400
Fax: 603 433 0415
contact@northeastauctions.com
www.northeastauctions.com

NEW JERSEY

Bertoia Auctions
2141 Demarco Dr, Vineland,
NJ 08360
Tel: 856 692 1881
Fax: 856 692 8697
www.bertoiaauctions.com

David Rago Auctions
333 North Main St,
Lambertville, NJ 08530
Tel: 609 397 9374
Fax: 609 397 9377
info@ragoarts.com
www.ragoarts.com

David Rago: Nicholas Dawes Lalique Auctions
333 North Main St,
Lambertville, NJ 08530
Tel: 609 397 9374
Fax: 609 397 9377
info@ragoarts.com
www.ragoarts.com

Dawson & Nye
128 American Road, Morris
Plains, NJ 07950
Tel: 973 984 6900
Fax: 973 984 6956
info@dawsonandnye.com
www.dawsonandnye.com

Greg Manning Auctions Inc
775 Passaic Ave,
West Caldwell, NJ 07006
Tel: 973 883 0004
Fax: 973 882 3499
info@gregmanning.com
www.gregmanning.com

Sollo: Rago Modern Auctions
333 North Main St,
Lambertville, NJ 08530
Tel: 609 397 9374
Fax: 609 397 9377
info@ragoarts.com
www.ragoarts.com

NEW MEXICO

Manitou Gallery
123 West Palace Ave., Santa
Fe, NM 87501
Tel: 800-986-0440
info@manitougalleries.com
www.manitougalleries.com

Parker-Braden Auctions
P.O. Box 1897, 4303 National
Parks Highway, Carlsbad,
NM 88220
Tel: 505 885 4874
Fax: 505 885 4622
www.parkerbraden.com

NEW YORK

Christie's
20 Rockefeller Plaza,
New York, NY 10020
Tel: 212 636 2000
Fax: 212 636 2399
info@christies.com
www.christies.com

TW Conroy
36 Oswego St, Baldwinsville,
NY 13027
Tel: 315 638 6434
Fax: 315 638 7039
info@twconroy.com
www.twconroy.com

Samuel Cottone Auctions
15 Genesee St, Mount Morris,
NY 14510
Tel: 585 658 3119
Fax: 585 658 3152
scottone@rochester.rr.com
www.cottoneauctions.com

William Doyle Galleries
175 E. 87th St, New York,
NY 10128
Tel: 212 427 2730
Fax: 212 369 0892
info@doylenewyork.com
www.doylenewyork.com

Guernsey's Auctions
108 East 73rd St, New York,
NY 10021
Tel: 212 794 2280
Fax: 212 744 3638
auctions@guernseys.com
www.guernseys.com

Phillips, De Pury & Luxembourg
450 West 15 Street, New York
NY 10011
Tel: 212 940 1200
Fax: 212 924 3306
info@phillipsdepury.com
www.phillips-dpl.com

Sotheby's
1334 York Ave at 72nd St,
New York, NY 10021
Tel: 212 606 7000
Fax: 212 606 7107
info@sothebys.com
www.sothebys.com

Swann Galleries Inc
104 E. 25th St, New York,
NY 10010
Tel: 212 254 4710
Fax: 212 979 1017
swann@swanngalleries.com
www.swanngalleries.com

NORTH CAROLINA
Robert S. Brunk
P.O. Box 2135, Asheville,
NC 28802
Tel: 828 254 6846
Fax: 828 254 6545
auction@brunkauctions.com
www.brunkauctions.com

Historical Collectible Auctions
24 NW Court, SquareSuite
201, Graham, NC 27253
Tel: 336 570 2803
Fax: 336 570 2748
auctions@hcaauctions.com
www.hcaauctions.com

NORTH DAKOTA
Curt D Johnson Auction Co.
4216 Gateway Dr., Grand
Forks, ND 58203
Tel: 701 746 1378
figleo@hotmail.com
www.curtdjohnson.com

OHIO
Cowans Historic Americana
673 Wilmer Avenue, Cincinnati,
OH 45226
Tel: 513 871 1670
Fax: 513 871 8670
www.historicamericana.com

DeFina Auctions
1591 State Route 45 Sth,
Austinburg, OH 44010
Tel: 440 275 6674
Fax: 440.275.2028
info@definaauctions.com
www.definaauctions.com

Garth's Auctions
2690 Stratford Rd, Box 369,
Delaware, OH 43015
Tel: 740 362 4771
Fax: 740 363 0164
info@garths.com
www.garths.com

Metropolitan Galleries
3910 Lorain Ave,
Cleveland, OH 44113
Tel: 216 631 2222
Fax: 216 529 9021
www.metropolitangalleries.com

OREGON
Dale Johnson Auction Service
P.O. Box 933,
Prineville OR 97754-0933
Tel: 541 416 8315
d2john@earthlink.net
www.dalejohnauctionsvc.com

PENNSYLVANIA
Alderfer Auction Gallery
501 Fairgrounds Rd,
Hatfield PA 19440
Tel: 215 393 3000
Fax: 215 368-9055
info@alderferauction.com
www.alderferauction.com

Noel Barrett
P.O. Box 300,
Carversville PA 18913
Tel: 215 297 5109
www.noelbarrett.com

Dargate Auction Galleries
214 North Lexington,
Pittsburgh, PA 15208
Tel: 412 362 3558
info@dargate.com
www.dargate.com

Freeman's
1808 Chestnut Ave,
Philadelphia, PA 19103
Tel: 610 563 9275
info@freemansauction.com
www.freemansauction.com

Hunt Auctions
75 E. Uwchlan Ave, Ste 1, 30
Exton, PA 19341
Tel: 610 524 0822
Fax: 610 524 0826
info@huntauctions.com
www.huntauctions.com

Pook & Pook Inc
463 East Lancaster Ave,
Downington PA 19335
Tel: 610 269 4040
Fax: 610 269 9274
info@pookandpook.com
www.pookandpook.com

Skinner's Auction Co.
170 Northampton St,
Easton PA 18042
Tel: 610 330 6933
skinnauct@aol.com
www.skinnersauction.com

Stephenson's Auctions
1005 Industrial Blvd,
Southampton PA 18966
Tel: 215 322 618
info@stephensonsauction.com
www.stephensonsauction.com

RHODE ISLAND
WebWilson
P.O. Box 506,
Portsmouth RI 02871
Tel: 800 508 0022
hww@webwilson.com
www.webwilson.com

SOUTH CAROLINA
Charlton Hall Galleries Inc.
912 Gervais St Columbia,
SC 29201
Tel: 803 799 5678
Fax: 803 733 1701
www.charltonhallauctions.com

TENNESSEE
Berenice Denton Estate Sales and Appraisals
2209 Bandywood Drive, Suite C
Nashville, TN 37215
Tel: 615 292 5765
info@berenicedenton.com
www.berenicedenton.com

Kimball M. Sterling Inc
125 W. Market St, Johnson City,
TN 37604
Tel: 423 928 1471
www.sterlingsold.com

TEXAS
Austin Auctions
8414 Anderson Mill Rd,
Austin, TX 78729-4702
Tel: 512 258 5479
Fax: 512 219 7372
www.austinauction.com

Dallas Auction Gallery
1518 Socum St, Dallas,
TX 75207
Tel: 213 653 3900
Fax: 213 653 3912
info@dallasauctiongallery.com
www.dallasauctiongallery.com

Heritage-Slater Americana
3500 Maple Avenue
Dallas, Texas 75219
Tel: 214 528 3500
www.heritagegalleries.com

Heritage Galleries
3500 Maple Avenue
Dallas, Texas 75219
Tel: 214 528 3500
www.heritagegalleries.com

UTAH
America West Archives
P.O. Box 100, Cedar City,
UT 84721
Tel: 435 586 9497
Fax: 435 586 9497
info@americawestarchives.com
www.americawestarchives.com

VERMONT
Eaton Auction Service
Chuck Eaton, 3428
Middlebrook Road, Fairlee, VT
05045
Tel: 802 333 9717
eas@sover.net
www.eatonauctionservice.com

VIRGINIA
Ken Farmer Auctions & Estates
105A Harrison St, Radford,
VA 24141
Tel: 540 639 0939
Fax: 540 639 1759
info@kfauctions.com
www.kfauctions.com

Phoebus Auction Gallery
14-16 E. Mellen St, Hampton,
VA 23663
Tel: 757 722 9210
Fax: 757 723 2280
bwelch@phoebusauction.com
www.phoebusauction.com

Signature House
407 Liberty Ave, Bridgeport,
WV 25330
Tel: 304 842 3386
Fax: 304 842 3001
editor@signaturehouse.net
www.signaturehouse.net

WASHINGTON DC
Weschlers
909 E St, NW Washington,
DC 20004
Tel: 202 628 1281
Fax: 202 628 2366
fineart@weschlers.com
www.weschlers.com

WISCONSIN
Krueger Auctions
P.O. Box 275, Iola,
WI 54945-0275
Tel: 715 445 3845

Schrager Auction Galleries
2915 North Sherman Blvd,
P.O. Box 100043,
Milwaukee, WI 53210
Tel: 414 873 3738
Fax: 414 873 5229
askus@schragerauction.com
www.schragerauction.com

WYOMING
Cody Old West Show & Auction
P.O. Box 2038, 37555 Hum Rd,
Ste 101, Carefree, AZ 85377
Tel: 307-587-9014
brian@codyoldwest.com
www.codyoldwest.com

CANADA
Pinneys Auctions Les Encans
2435 Duncan Road, Montreal,
Canada H4P 2A2
Tel: 514 345 0571
Fax: 514 731 4081
pinneys@ca.inter.net
www.pinneys.ca

Ritchies
288 King Street East, Toronto,
Ontario Canada M5A 1K4
Tel: 416 364 1864
ritchies.com

Waddington's Auctioneers & Appraisers
111 Bathurst St., Toronto,
Ontario Canada M5V 2R1
Tel: 416 504 9100
www.waddingtons.ca

Walkers
81 Auriga Drive, Suite 18,
Ottawa, Ontario
Canada K2E 7Y5
Tel: 613 224 5814
www.walkersauctions.com

CLUBS, SOCIETIES & ORGANISATIONS

ADVERTISING

Antique Advertising Association of America
P.O. Box 1121, Morton Grove, IL 60053
Tel: 708 446 0904
www.pastimes.org

Coca Cola Collectors' Club International
P.O. Box 49166, Atlanta, GA 30359-1166

Tin Container Collectors' Association
P.O. Box 440101 Aurora, CO 80044

AMERICANA

Folk Art Society of America
P.O. Box 17041, Richmond, VA 23226-70

American Political Items Collectors
P.O. Box 340339 San Antonio, TX 8234-0339
www.collectors.org/apic

AUTOGRAPHS

International Autograph Collectors' Club & Dealers' Alliance
4575 Sheridan St, Ste 111, Hollywood, FL 33021-3515
Tel: 561 736 8409
www.iacc-da.com

Universal Autograph Collectors' Club
P.O. Box 6181, Washington, DC 20044
Tel: 202 332-7388
www.uacc.com

AUTOMOBILIA

Automobile Objets d'Art Club
252 N. 7th St. Allentown, PA 18102-4204
Tel: 610 432 3355
oldtoy@aol.com

BOOKS

Antiquarian Bookseller's Association of America
20 West 44th St, 4th Floor, New York, NY 10036
Tel: 212 944 8291

CERAMICS

American Art Pottery Association
P.O. Box 834, Westport, MA 02790-0697
www.amartpot.com

American Ceramics Circle
520 16th St, Brooklyn, NY 11215
Tel: 718 832 5446
nlester@earthlink.net

American Cookie Jar Association
1600 Navajo Rd, Norman, OK 73026
davismj@ionet.net

Style 1900
David Rago, 9 Main St, Lambertville, NJ 08530

U.S. Chintz Collectors' Club
P.O. Box 50888, Pasadena, CA 91115
Tel: 626 441-4708
Fax: 626 441-4122
www.chintznet.com

Goebel Networkers
P.O. Box 396, Lemoyne, PA 17043

Homer Laughlin China Collectors' Association
P.O. Box 1093
Corbin KY 40702-1093
www.hlcca.org
(Fiesta ware)

Hummel Collectors Club
1261 University Dr, Yardley, PA 19067-2857
Tel: 888 548 6635
Fax: 215 321 7367
www.hummels.com

Roseville of The Past Pottery Club
P.O. Box 656 Clarcona, FL 32710-0656
Tel: 407 294 3980
Fax: 407 294 7836
rosepast@bellsouth.net

Royal Doulton International Collectors' Club
700 Cottontail Lane, Somerset, NJ 08873
Tel: 800 682-4462
Fax: 732 764-4974

Stangl & Fulper Club
P.O. Box 538, Flemington, NJ 08822
Tel: 908 995 2696
kenlove508@aol.com

American Stoneware Collectors' Society
P.O. Box 281, Bay Head, NJ 08742
Tel: 732 899 8707

COSTUME JEWELRY

Leaping Frog Antique Jewelry & Collectible Club
4841 Martin Luther King Blvd, Sacramento, CA 95820-4932
Tel: 916 452 6728
pandora@cwia.com

Vintage Fashion & Costume Jewelry Club
P.O. Box 265, Glen Oaks, NY 11004-0265
Tel: 718 939 3095
vfcj@aol.com

DISNEYANA

National Fantasy Club For Disneyana Collectors
P.O. Box 106, Irvine, CA 92713-9212
Tel: 714 731 4705
info@nffc.org
www.nffc.org

Walt Disney Collectors' Society
500 South Buena Vista St, Burbank, CA 91521-8028
Tel: 800 932 5749

FIFTIES & SIXTIES

Head Hunters Newsletters
P.O. Box 83H, Scarsdale, NY 10583.
Tel: 914 472 0200

FILM & TV MEMORABILIA

The Animation Art Guild
330 W. 45th St, Ste 9D, New York, NY 10036-3864
Tel: 212 765 3030
theaagltd@aol.com

Lone Ranger Fan Club
19205 Seneca Ridge Court, Gaithersburg, MD 20879-3135

GLASS

American Carnival Glass Association
9621 Springwater Lane, Miamisburg, OH 45342

Land of Sunshine Depression Glass Club
P.O. Box 560275, Orlando, FL 32856-0275
Tel: 407 298 3355

HATPINS

American Hatpin Society
20 Montecillo Dr, Rolling Hills Estates, CA 90274-4249
Tel: 310 326 2196
hatpnginia@aol.com
www.collectorsonline.com/AHS

KITCHENALIA

Kitchen Antiques & Collectibles News
4645 Laurel Ridge Dr, Harrisburg, PA 17119

MARBLES

Marble Collectors Unlimited
P.O. Box 206, Northborough, MA 01532-0206
marblesbev@aol.com

MECHANICAL MUSIC

Musical Box Society International
700 Walnut Hill Rd, Hockessin DE 19707
Tel: 302 239 5658
www.mbsi.org

MILITARIA

Civil War Collectors & The American Militaria Exchange
5970 Taylor Ridge Dr, West Chester, OH 45069
Tel: 513 874 0483
rwmorgan@aol.com
www.civiwar-collectors.com

OPTICAL, MEDICAL, SCIENTIFIC & TECHNICAL

International Association of Calculator Collectors
P.O. Box 345, Tustin, CA 92781-0345
Tel: 714 730 6140
Fax: 714 730 6140
mrcalc@usa.net
www.geocities.com/siliconvalley/park/7227/

PENS & WRITING

The Society of Inkwell Collectors
P.O. Box 324, Mossville, IL 61552
Tel: 309 579 3040
director@soic.com
www.soic.com

Pen Collectors of America
P.O. Box 80, Redding Ridge, CT 06876
www.pencollectors.com

PEZ

Pez Collectors News
P.O. Box 14956, Surfside Beach, SC 29587
info@pezcollectorsnews.com
www.pezcollectorsnews.com

ROCK N ROLL

Elvis Forever TCB Fan Club
P.O. Box 1066, Miami, FL 33780-1066

Working Class Hero Beatles Club
3311 Niagara St, Pittsburgh, PA 1213-4223

SCENT BOTTLES

International Perfume Bottle Association
396 Croton Rd, Wayne, PA 19087
Tel: 610-995-9051
jcabbott@bellatlantic.net
www.perfumebottles.org

SMOKING

Cigarette Lighter Collectors' Club
SPARK International
intSpark@aol.com
http://members.aol.com/intspark

APPENDICES

Pocket Lighter Preservation Guild & Historical Society, Inc.
P.O. Box 1054, Addison,
IL 60101-8054
Tel: 708 543 9120

SNOWDOMES

Snowdome Collectors' Club
P.O. Box 53262, Washington,
DC 20009-9262

SPORTING MEMORABILIA

Boxing & Pugilistica Collectors International
P.O. Box 83135, Portland,
OR 97283-0135
Tel: 502 286 3597

Golf Collectors' Society
P.O. Box 24102, Cleveland,
OH 44124
Tel: 216 861 1615
www.golfcollectors.com

National Fishing Lure Collectors' Club
H.C. 33, Box 4012, Reeds
Spring, MO 65737
spurr@kingfisher.com

Society for American Baseball Research
812 Huron Rd, E. 719,
Cleveland, OH 441155
info@sabr.org
www.sabr.org

TEXTILES & COSTUME

The Costume Society of America
55 Edgwater Dr, P.O. Box 73,
Earleville, MD 21919-0073
Tel: 410 275 1619
www.costumesocietyamerica.com

American Fan Collectors' Association
P.O. Box 5473, Sarasota, FL
34277-5473
Tel: 817 267 9851
Fax: 817 267 0387

International Old Lacers
P.O. Box 554, Flanders,
NJ 07836
iolinc@aol.com

TOYS & GAMES

Annalee Doll Society
P.O.Box 1137, Meredith,
NH 03253
Tel: 800 433-6557
Fax: 603 279-6659

The Antique Toy Collectors' of America, Inc
C/o Carter, Ledyard & Milburn,
Two Wall St (13th Floor),
New York, NY 10005

Chess Collectors' International
P.O. Box 166, Commack,
NY 11725-0166
Tel: 516 543 1330
lichness@aol.com

National Model Railroad Association
4121 Cromwell Rd,
Chattanooga, TN 37421
Tel: 423 892 2846
nmra@ttttrains.com

Toy Soldier Collectors of America
5340 40th Ave N, Saint
Petersburg, FL 33709
Tel: 727 527 1430

United Federation of Doll Clubs
10920 N. Ambassador Dr,
Kansas City, MO 64153
Tel: 816-891-7040
ufdc@aol.com

WATCHES

Early American Watch Club
P.O. Box 81555, Wellesley Hills,
MA 02481-1333

National Association of Watch & Clock Collectors
514 Poplar St, Columbia,
PA 17512-2130
Tel: 717 684 8261
www.nawacc.org

WINE & DRINKING

International Correspondence of Corkscrew Addicts
670 Meadow Wood Road
Mississauga Ontario,
L5J 2S6 Canada
dugohuzo@aol.com
www.corkscrewnet.com/icca

COLLECTING ON THE INTERNET

- The internet has revolutionised the trading of collectibles. Compared to a piece of furniture, most collectibles are easily defined, described and photographed. Shipping is also comparatively easy, due to average size and weight. Prices are also generally more affordable and accessible than for antiques and the Internet has provided a cost effective way of buying and selling, away from the overheads of shops and auction rooms. Many millions of collectibles are offered for sale and traded daily, with sites varying from global online marketplaces, such as eBay, to specialist dealers' websites.

- When searching online, remember that some people may not know how to accurately describe their item. General category searches, even though more time consuming, and even purposefully misspelling a name, can yield results. Also, if something looks too good to be true, it probably is. Using this book to get to know your market visually, so that you can tell the difference between a real bargain and something that sounds like one, is a good start.

- As you will understand from buying this book, color photography is vital – look for online listings that include as many images as possible and check them carefully. Beware that colors can appear differently, even between computer screens.

- Always ask the vendor questions about the object, particularly regarding condition. If there is no image, or you want to see another aspect of the object – ask. Most sellers (private or trade) will want to realise the best price for their items so will be more than happy to help – if approached politely and sensibly.

- As well as the 'e-hammer' price, you will probably have to pay additional transactional fees such as packing, shipping and possibly regional or national taxes. It is always best to ask for an estimate for these additional costs before leaving a bid. This will also help you tailor your bid as you will have an idea of the maximum price the item will cost if you are successful.

- As well as the well-known online auction sites, such as eBay, there is a host of other online resources for buying and selling, for example fair and auction date listings.

INTERNET RESOURCES

Live Auctioneers
www.liveauctioneers.com
info@liveauctioneers.com
A free service which allows users to search catalogs from selected auction houses in Europe, the USA and the United Kingdom. Through its connection with eBay, users can bid live via the Internet into salerooms as auctions happen. Registered users can also search through an archive of past catalogs and receive a free newsletter by email.

invaluable.com
www.invaluable.com
sales@invaluable.com
A subscription service which allows users to search selected auction house catalogs from the United Kingdom and Europe. Also offers an extensive archive for appraisal uses.

The Antiques Trade Gazette
www.atg-online.com
The online version of the UK trade newspaper, comprising British auction and fair listings, news and events.

Maine Antique Digest
www.maineantiquedigest.com
The online version of America's trade newspaper including news, articles, fair and auction listings and more.

La Gazette du Drouot
www.drouot.com
The online home of the magazine listing all auctions to be held in France at the Hotel de Drouot in Paris and beyond. An online subscription enables you to download the magazine online.

Auctionnet.com
www.auctionnet.com
Simple online resource listing over 500 websites related to auctions online.

AuctionBytes
www.auctionbytes.com
Auction resource with community forum, news, events, tips and a weekly newsletter.

Auctiontalk
www.internetauctionlist.com.com
Auction news, online and offline auction search engines and live chat forums.

Go Antiques/Antiqnet
www.goantiques.com
www.antiqnet.com
An online global aggregator for art, antiques and collectibles dealers who showcase their stock online, allowing users to browse and buy.

eBay
www.ebay.com
Undoubtedly the largest and most diverse of the online auction sites, allowing users to buy and sell in an online marketplace with over 52 million registered users. Collectors should also view eBay Live Auctions (www.ebayliveauctions.com) where traditional auctions are combined with realtime, online bidding allowing users to interact with the saleroom as the auction takes place.

Tias
www.tias.com
An online global aggregator for art, antiques and collectibles dealers who showcase their stock online, allowing users to browse and buy.

Collectors Online
www.collectorsonline.com
An online global aggregator for art, antiques and collectibles dealers who showcase their stock online, allowing users to browse and buy.

INDEX